Volume Four

X Toolkit Intrinsics Programming Manual

OSF/Motif 1.1 Edition for X11, Release 4

by Adrian Nye and Tim O'Reilly

O'Reilly & Associates, Inc.

Revision and Printing History

First Printing   January 1990.

Second Edition   September 1990. Revised for R4.

Motif Edition   December 1990. Customized for Motif 1.1.

Small Print

[10/91]

Table of Contents

3 More Techniques for Using Widgets 63

9 More Input Techniques 267

10 Resource Management and Type Conversion 293

11 Interclient Communications

Figures

Examples

Tables

Preface

Note that while Motif is used for the examples in this book, the techniques described are equally applicable to and provide a good introduction to programming with any other widget set based on Xt. It is not difficult to convert an application between any of the widget sets listed above, since all of them use the same Xt Intrinsics programming interface.

In This Chapter:

Preface

This book describes how to write X Window System programs using the Xt Intrinsics library (or simply Xt). Xt is a standard established by the X Consortium that provides an object-oriented programming style in the C language.

OSF's Motif library provides user-interface objects to be used with Xt. Motif is not an X Consortium standard, though it may nevertheless become a de-facto industry standard. This book primarily describes the Xt Intrinsics, but it also provides an introduction to Motif and uses Motif for many of the examples.

The Xt Intrinsics together with a second library such as Motif are collectively called the X Toolkit.

Summary of Contents

The discussion of the X Toolkit is divided into two volumes, Volumes Four and Five of the X Window System Series available from O'Reilly & Associates, Inc.

This is Volume Four, *X Toolkit Intrinsics Programming Manual, Motif Edition*. It provides an explanation of the X Toolkit, including tutorial material and numerous programming examples. Arranged by task or topic, each chapter brings together a group of Xt functions, describes the conceptual foundation on which they are based, and illustrates how they are most often used in writing applications. This volume is structured to be useful as a tutorial and also as a task-oriented reference.

Volume Five, *X Toolkit Intrinsics Reference Manual*, includes reference pages for each of the Xt functions, as well as for the widget classes defined by Xt, organized alphabetically for ease of reference; a permuted index; and numerous appendices and quick reference aids.

The two volumes are designed to be used together. To get the most out of the examples in Volume Four, you will need the exact calling sequences of each function from Volume Five. To understand fully how to use each of the functions described in Volume Five, all but the most experienced Toolkit "hacker" will need the explanation and examples in Volume Four.

Both volumes include material from the original Toolkit documentation provided by MIT, though in Volume Four this material is mostly limited to the appendices. We have done our best to incorporate all the useful information from the MIT documentation, to reorganize and present it in a more useful form, and to supplement it with conceptual material, tutorials, reference aids, and examples. In other words, this manual is not only a replacement but is a superset of the MIT documentation.

Those of you familiar with the MIT documentation will recognize that each reference page in Volume Five includes the detailed description of the routine found in *X Toolkit Intrinsics—C Language Interface*, plus in many cases additional text that clarifies ambiguities and describes the context in which the routine would be used. We have also added the definitions of structures and symbolic constants used as arguments or returned values by the function, as well as cross-references to related reference pages and to where additional information can be found in Volume Four.

Assumptions

This book makes no assumptions about the reader's knowledge of object-oriented programming or the X Window System. Readers should be proficient in the C programming language, although examples are provided for infrequently used features of the language that are necessary or useful when programming with the X Toolkit. In addition, general familiarity with the principles of raster graphics will be helpful.

However, even though the Toolkit is intended to hide the low-level X interface provided by Xlib, there are times in writing applications or widgets when Xlib functions will be necessary because no Xt feature exists to do the same thing. This book describes the most common occasions for using Xlib, but does not provide a reference to the particular functions involved. Additional documentation on Xlib, such as that provided by Volume One, *Xlib Programming Manual*, and Volume Two, *Xlib Reference Manual*, will be indispensable.

Related Documents

Eight other books on the X Window System are available from O'Reilly & Associates, Inc.:

Volume Zero	*X Protocol Reference Manual*
Volume One	*Xlib Programming Manual*
Volume Two	*Xlib Reference Manual*
Volume Three	*X Window System User's Guide, Motif Edition*
Volume Five	*X Toolkit Intrinsics Reference Manual*
Volume Six	*Motif Programming Manual (Spring '91)*
Volume Seven	*XView Programming Manual*
Quick Reference	*The X Window System in a Nutshell*

The following book published by Prentice Hall will be necessary to obtain details of the Motif widgets:

OSF/Motif Programmer's Reference

The following documents are included on the X11 source tape (the X distribution from MIT):

> *X Toolkit Intrinsics — C Language Interface*, by Joel McCormack, Paul Asente, and Ralph Swick
> *X Toolkit Athena Widgets — C Language Interface*, by Ralph Swick and Terry Weissman
> *Xlib — C Language X Interface*, by Jim Gettys, Ron Newman, and Robert Scheifler

The following Nutshell Handbooks published by O'Reilly and Associates, Inc. are useful when programming in C:

> *Checking C Programs with lint*, by Ian Darwin
> *Managing Projects with make*, by Steve Talbott
> *Using C on the UNIX System*, by Dave Curry

The following is the classic introduction to C programming:

> *The C Programming Language*, by B. W. Kernighan and D. M. Ritchie

How to Use This Manual

Volume Four explains both application programming with widgets and widget programming (the design and coding of new widgets).

The first five chapters treat widgets largely as "black boxes," which is appropriate considering the object-oriented philosophy of the Toolkit. These chapters also provide an overview of many elements of the X Toolkit, and so are appropriate for all readers.

Chapter 1   *Introduction to the X Window System*, provides a discussion of the context in which X programs operate. Programmers who are comfortable programming with Xlib can skip Chapter 1.

Chapter 2   *Introduction to the X Toolkit and Motif*, describes the conceptual foundations underlying Toolkit programming, and shows how to write simple programs that use widgets from existing widget sets. It introduces such fundamental Toolkit programming concepts as resources, the Translation Manager, callbacks, and actions.

Chapter 3   *More Techniques for Using Widgets*, describes how to use some of the more complex widgets found in applications, including composite widgets, constraint widgets, and popups. It also describes how to define application resources and command-line options, and how to hardcode the value of widget resources when you create a widget. Finally, it describes how to create multiple top-level windows, and how to use application contexts to create applications that are more portable.

Chapter 4   *An Example Application*, describes a complete application, in several iterations. First, it shows a simple version of the program, a bitmap editor, as it would be written assuming the existence of a BitmapEdit widget (which is actually developed in Chapter 6). Then, two refined versions are developed, each demonstrating additional Toolkit programming techniques. Finally, the same application is shown as it would be written if the bitmap editor were implemented in an application window rather than with the BitmapEdit widget, as it would be written if no BitmapEdit widget existed.

Chapter 5   *More About Motif*, describes and illustrates the widgets available in the Motif 1.1 widget set, and introduces the features and functions provided by Motif that add to the programming model defined by Xt. As mentioned earlier, this volume does not contain detailed reference information on each widget, and it gives examples using only a few of the widgets in the Motif widget set. Additional information on each Motif widget is presented in Volume Six, *X Motif Programming Manual* (available Spring '91).

The next two chapters describe widget internals, and the process of creating new widgets. While this information is not essential for all application programmers, many applications require a custom widget to implement their special graphics capabilities.

Chapter 6   *Inside a Widget*, describes the code inside a widget. Much of this code is common to all widgets. You can think of it as a framework that Xt uses to implement a widget's features. After reading this chapter, you should understand the procedure for creating your own widget around this framework.

Chapter 7   *Basic Widget Methods*, describes a widget's `initialize`, `expose`, `set_values`, `destroy`, `resize`, and `query_geometry` methods. (A widget's methods are internal routines called automatically by Xt to give the widget a degree of independence from the application.) The chapter explains when Xt calls each method, and describes in detail what should be in each of these methods. Among other things, these methods prepare for and do the drawing of graphics that appear in a widget. This chapter describes what the Toolkit adds to the graphics model provided by Xlib but does not describe in detail how to draw using Xlib; this topic is described in Chapters 5, 6, and 7 of Volume One, *Xlib Programming Manual*.

Later chapters treat various topics of interest to either application or widget programmers, or both. Some of these topics have been introduced in the earlier chapters and are explored more completely in the following ones.

Chapter 8   *Events, Translations, and Accelerators*, describes the complete syntax of translation tables, which allow the user to configure the mapping of event sequences into widget actions. It also describes accelerators, a mechanism for mapping events in one widget to actions in another.

Chapter 9   *More Input Techniques*, describes how to handle events with event handlers and how to use information from the event structure inside an event handler or action routine. It also describes how to get file, pipe, or socket input, how to use timeouts to call a function after a delay or at particular intervals, and how to use work procedures to do background processing. Finally, it discusses some low-level features of Xt for directly interacting with the event queue.

Chapter 10   *Resource Management and Type Conversion*, is a more thorough discussion of how resources work and how they should be used. This chapter describes in detail the resource file format and the rules that govern the precedence of resource settings. It also describes how to add your own type converter so that you can set application- or widget-specific data through resources. Finally, it describes subresources and how to use them.

Chapter 11   *Interclient Communications*, discusses communication through the X server between an application and the window manager, and between two applications. The application-window manager communication is performed by code in the Shell widget. The application sets shell resources to control this communication with the window manager. Application-application communication is usually done with a process called selections. This form of communication is already implemented in most widgets that display text, but you may want to implement it in your own custom widgets. Selections can also pass other kinds of data such as graphics.

Chapter 12   *Geometry Management*, discusses how composite and constraint widgets manage the layout of widgets, and how to write your own simple composite and constraint widgets.

Chapter 13   *Menus, Gadgets, and Cascaded Popups*, describes how menus work and describes several ways to create menu widgets. One of these ways involves the use of windowless widgets, or gadgets. This chapter also describes how to use more advanced features of the Xt popup mechanism, including modal cascades, to implement cascading popup menus.

Chapter 14   *Miscellaneous Toolkit Programming Techniques*, describes various Xt functions that have not been treated elsewhere in the book. These include functions for error and warning handling, case conversion, and so on.

Appendix A   *Athena, OPEN LOOK, and Motif*, provides a comparison of the widgets available in AT&T's OPEN LOOK widget set and OSF's Motif. These widgets are contrasted with those in the Athena widget set.

Appendix B   *Specifying Fonts and Colors*, gives information on the values that can be used when specifying fonts and colors as resources.

Appendix C   *Naming Conventions*, describes a suggested set of conventions for naming widgets and elements within widget code.

Appendix D   *Release Notes*, describes the changes between Release 3 and Release 4. This manual describes Release 4, but notes the most important changes since Release 3 for those familiar with that release.

Appendix E   *The xbitmap Application*, shows the complete code for an advanced version of the *xbitmap* application and the BitmapEdit widget, which are described in Chapters 5 and 6.

Appendix F   *Sources of Additional Information*, lists where to get the X software, lists companies that offer training in X programming, and describes additional books on the subject that have been or soon will be published.

Glossary   gives you somewhere to turn should you run across an unfamiliar term. Some care has been taken to see that all terms are defined where they are first used in the text, but not everyone will read the manual in sequential order.

Master Index provides a thorough, combined index to Volume Four (Motif Edition) and Volume Five, making it easy to look up all appropriate references to a topic in either volume. Note, however, that Volume Five's master index is based on the Athena version of Volume Four (the generic edition) instead of the Motif edition of Volume Four (this book). As a result, you should use the master index *in this volume* when you want to look up Motif-specific information.

Volume Five consists of a permuted index, reference pages to each library function, and appendices that cover macros, structures, and defined symbols.

Font Conventions Used in This Manual

Italics are used for:

- UNIX pathnames, filenames, program names, user command names, and options for user commands

- New terms where they are defined

`Typewriter Font` is used for:

- Anything that would be typed verbatim into code, such as examples of source code and text on the screen

- The contents of include files, such as structure types, structure members, symbols (defined constants and bit flags), and macros

- Xt, Xaw, and Xlib functions

- Names of subroutines in the example programs

`Italic Typewriter Font` is used for:

- Arguments to functions, since they could be typed in code as shown but are arbitrary

Helvetica Italics are used for:

- Titles of examples, figures, and tables

Boldface is used for:

- Chapter and section headings

Request for Comments

To help us provide you with the best documentation possible, please write to tell us about any flaws you find in this manual or how you think it could be improved.

Our U.S. mail address, e-mail address, and phone numbers are as follows:

O'Reilly & Associates, Inc.
632 Petaluma Avenue
Sebastopol, CA 95472
800-338-6887
international +1 707-829-0515

UUCP: uunet!ora!adrian Internet: adrian@ora.com

Bulk Sales Information

This manual is being resold by many workstation manufacturers as their official X Window System documentation. For information on volume discounts for bulk purchase, call O'Reilly and Associates, Inc., at 800-338-6887 or send e-mail to linda@ora.com (uunet!ora!linda).

For companies requiring extensive customization of the book, source licensing terms are also available.

Obtaining the X Window System Software

The X Window system is copyrighted but freely distributed. The only restriction this places on its use is that the copyright notice identifying the author and the terms of use must accompany all copies of the software or documentation. Thanks to this policy, the software is available for a nominal cost from a variety of sources. See Appendix F, *Sources of Additional Information*, for a listing of these sources.

Obtaining Motif

If your hardware vendor is an OSF member, they may be able to provide Motif binaries for your machine. Various independent vendors also provide binaries for some machines: see Appendix F, *Sources of Additional Information*, for a listing of a few of these. Source licenses must be obtained directly from OSF. Call OSF at 617-621-7300 for ordering information.

Obtaining the Example Programs

The example programs in this book are available free from UUNET (that is, free except for UUNET's usual connect-time charges). If you have access to UUNET, you can retrieve the source code using *uucp* or *ftp*. For *uucp*, find a machine with direct access to UUNET, and type the following command:

```
uucp uunet\!~/nutshell/xt/motifpgs.tar.Z yourhos\!~/yourname/
```

The backslashes can be omitted if you use the Bourne shell (*sh*) instead of *csh*. The file should appear some time later (up to a day or more) in the directory */usr/spool/uucppublic/yourname*.

You don't need to have opened an account to UUNET to be able to access their archives via UUCP from within the United States of America. By calling 1-900-468-7727 and using the login "uucp" with no password, anyone may uucp any of UUNET's online source collection. (Start by copying *uunet!/usr/spool/ftp/ls-lR.Z*, which is a compressed index of every file in the archives.) As of this writing, the cost is 40 cents per minute. The charges will appear on your next telephone bill.

To use *ftp*, *ftp* to *uunet.uu.net* and use *anonymous* as your user name and *guest* as your password. Then type the following:

```
cd nutshell/xt
binary (you must specify binary transfer for compressed files)
get motifpgs.tar.Z
bye
```

The file is a compressed tar archive. To extract files once you have retrieved the archive, type:

```
uncompress motifpgs.tar
tar xf motifpgs.tar
```

The examples will be installed in subdirectories under the current directory, one for each chapter in the book. Imakefiles are included. (Imakefiles are used with *imake*, a program supplied with the X11 distribution that generates proper Makefiles on a wide variety of systems.)

All the app-defaults files are in the main examples directory. The app-defaults files are not automatically installed in the system app-defaults directory (*/usr/lib/X11/app-defaults* on most UNIX systems). (See Chapter 10, *Resource Management and Type Conversion*, for details.) If you have permission to write to that directory, you can copy them there yourself. Otherwise, you can set the XAPPLRESDIR environment variable to the complete path of the directory where you installed the examples. The value of XAPPLRESDIR must end with a / (slash). (Most of the examples will not function properly without the app-defaults files.)

Acknowledgments

As mentioned above, this manual includes some material from the *X Toolkit Intrinsics—C Language Interface*, by Joel McCormack, Paul Asente, and Ralph Swick. This is the document that defines the X Consortium standard for Xt, known as the Xt specification. Overt borrowings from the Xt specification are rare in this volume. However, the Xt specification document, as well as the sample code of Xt distributed with releases of X, provides the intellectual basis for most of what appears here.

We'd like to thank Sony Microsystems for the loan of a Sony NEWS workstation running their implementation of the X Window System. The speed and power of the Sony workstation, and the support of Sony's staff, were a great help in developing these books. Additional development was done on a Sun-3 workstation running MIT's sample server, a Visual 640 X Display Station, and an NCD16 Network Display Station.

We would also like to thank the reviewers of the Alpha draft of this book, even though we almost had to start over because of their comments. They were David Lewis of Integrated Computer Solutions (ICS), Wendy Eisner of Sunquest Information Systems, Dan Heller of Island Graphics, Inc. (now working with O'Reilly and Associates), Miles O'Neal of Systems and Software Solutions, Inc., and Chris Peterson of MIT Project Athena (now of the X Consortium). Ian Darwin of SoftQuad and Bradley Ross of Cambridge Computer Associates reviewed the Beta draft. Extra thanks are due to Ralph Swick, Chris Peterson, and Robert Scheifler, who answered many questions during the development of this book.

Of course, we alone take responsibility for any errors or omissions that remain.

Special thanks go to Mark Langley, who wrote an early draft of this book. He helped to educate us about the Toolkit, and his efforts to make the book a success did not go unnoticed.

Special thanks also go to Integrated Computer Solutions, for their assistance in preparing this Motif edition.

Of course, the authors would like to thank the entire staff of O'Reilly and Associates for producing the book, and the staff of Cambridge Computer Associates, Inc., for lending their support.

Perhaps most of all, we would like to thank our readers and customers for their patience, which we tested by promising that this book would be finished next month—every month for the last eight months. These days, with word processors, it is easy to generate a book-length manuscript, but no easier than it ever was to carve that text into something worth reading. We have had that book-length manuscript for a year, but have not been satisfied until now that it presented the material in a clear, friendly, and authoritative manner. We hope that the extra time we have spent boiling down the facts about this very new and continuously advancing subject will prove worthwhile to you, the reader.

—Adrian Nye and Tim O'Reilly

1

Introduction to the X Window System

This chapter introduces many of the most important concepts on which the X Window System is based, and describes the environment in which the X Toolkit operates. This chapter assumes that you are new to programming the X Window System. If you already have some experience programming the X Window System, you may wish to skim this chapter for a brief review or even begin with Chapter 2.

In This Chapter:

1
Introduction to the X Window System

The X Window System (or simply X)* is a hardware- and operating system-independent windowing system. It was developed jointly by MIT and Digital Equipment Corporation, and has been adopted by the computer industry as a standard for graphics applications.

X controls a "bit-mapped" display in which each pixel on the screen is individually controllable. This allows applications to draw pictures as well as text. Until recently, individual control of screen pixels was widely available only on personal computers (PCs) and high-priced technical workstations. Most general-purpose machines were limited to output on text-only terminals. X brings a consistent world of graphic output to both PCs and more powerful machines. Figure 1-1 compares an X application to an application running on a traditional text terminal.

---

*The name "X Windows" is frowned upon by the developers of X.

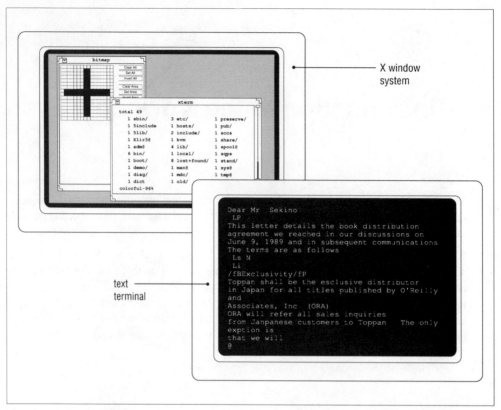

Figure 1-1. An X application, and an application on a traditional text terminal

Like other windowing systems, X divides the screen into multiple input and output areas called *windows*. Using a terminal emulator, windows can act as "virtual terminals," running ordinary text-based applications. However, as shown in Figure 1-1, windows can also run applications designed to take advantage of the graphic power of the bitmapped display.

X takes user input from a *pointer*. The pointer is usually a mouse but could just as well be a track-ball or a tablet. The pointer allows the user to control a program without using the keyboard, by pointing at objects drawn on the screen such as menus and command buttons. This method of using programs is often easier to learn than traditional keyboard control because it is more intuitive. Figure 1-2 shows an application with a typical three-button pointer being used to select a menu item.

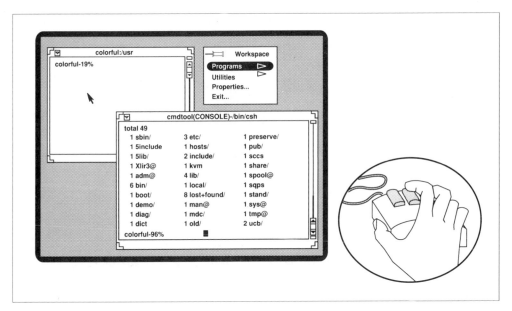

Figure 1-2. A three-button mouse directing the pointer to select a menu item

Of course, X also handles keyboard input. The pointer directs keyboard input from window to window. Only one window at a time can receive keyboard input.

In X, as in many other window systems, each application need not (and usually does not) consist of a single window. Any part of an application can have its own separate subwindow, which simplifies the management of input and output within the application code. Such *child windows* are visible only within the confines of their parent window.

Windows are rectangular and oriented along the same axes as the edges of the display. Each window has its own coordinate system, with the origin in the upper-left corner of the window inside its border. The application or the user can change the dimensions of windows. Figure 1-3 shows a typical screen with several virtual terminals running. The screen also shows some applications, such as *xmh*, *xclock*, and *xload*, that run in their own windows.

Figure 1-3. Screen layout of a typical user's X Window System

X supports both color and black-and-white displays.

Many of the above characteristics are also true of several other window systems. What is unusual about X is that it is based on a network protocol instead of on system-specific procedure and system calls. This network protocol enables X to be ported to different computer architectures and operating systems; it also allows programs to run on one architecture or operating system while displaying on another. Because of its unique design, X can make a network of different computers cooperate. For example, a computationally intensive application might run on a supercomputer, but take input from and display output on a workstation connected across a local area network. To the user, the application would simply appear to be running on the workstation.

1.1 The Server and Client

To allow programs to be run on one machine and display on another, X was designed as a network protocol—a predefined set of requests and replies—between two processes. One of these processes is an application program called a *client*, and the other, the *server*, controls the display hardware, keyboard, and pointer.

The user sits at the machine running the server. At first, this use of the word "server" may seem a little odd, since file and print servers normally are remote machines, but the usage is consistent. The local display is accessible to other systems across the network, and for those systems the X server does act like other types of server.

The X server acts as an intermediary between user programs and the resources of the local system such as the keyboard and screen. It contains all device-specific code, and insulates applications from differences among display hardware. It performs the following tasks:

- Allows access to the display by multiple clients. The server may deny access from clients running on certain machines.

- Interprets network messages from clients and acts on them. These messages are known as *requests*. Some requests command the server to move windows and do two-dimensional drawing, while others ask the server for information. Protocol requests are generated by client calls to Xlib, either directly or through Xt and other function libraries.

- Passes user input to clients by sending network messages known as *events*, which represent key or button presses, pointer motion, and so forth. Events are generated asynchronously, and events from different devices may be intermingled. The server must pass the appropriate events to each client.

- Maintains complex data structures, including windows and fonts, so that the server can perform its tasks efficiently. Clients refer to these abstractions by ID numbers. Server-maintained abstractions reduce the amount of data that has to be maintained by each client and the amount of data that has to be transferred over the network.

In X, the term *display* is often used as a synonym for server, as is the combined term *display server*. However, the terms display and screen are not synonymous. A *screen* is the actual hardware on which the graphics are drawn. A server may control more than one screen. For example, a single server might control both a color screen and a monochrome screen, allowing users to debug an application on both types of screen without leaving their seat.

The user programs displaying on screens managed by a server are called its clients. There may be several clients connected to a single server. Clients may run on the same machine as the server if that machine supports multitasking, or clients may run on other machines in the network. In either case, the *X Protocol* is used by the client to send requests to draw graphics or to query the server for information, and is used by the server to send user input and replies to information requests back to the client.* All communication between client and server

---

*The X Protocol runs on top of any lower-level network protocol that provides bidirectional communication, and delivers bytes unduplicated and in sequence. TCP/IP and DECnet are the most common low-level network protocols currently supported by X servers.

uses the X Protocol. The communication path between a client and the server is called a *connection*.

It is common for a user to have programs running on several different hosts in the network, all invoked from and displaying their windows on a single screen (see Figure 1-4). Clients running remotely can be started from the remote machine or from the local machine using the network utilities *rlogin* or *rsh*.

Figure 1-4. Applications can run on any system across the network

This use of the network is known as *distributed processing*. It allows graphic output for powerful systems that don't have their own built-in graphics facilities. Distributed processing can also help solve the problem of unbalanced system loads. When one host machine is overloaded, users running clients on that machine can arrange for some of their clients to run on other hosts. Eventually there may be automatic load-balancing applications, but currently such remote execution is performed manually. It is not unusual to see users in the X environment having several *xload* load monitor applications running on various systems throughout the network but displaying on their screen, so that they can see the balance of loads throughout the network.

Before leaving the subject of servers and clients, we should mention PC servers and X terminals. Software is available that allows various types of PCs to operate as X servers.* X terminals are special-purpose devices designed to run just an X server, and to connect to remote systems over a local area network. PC servers and X terminals are the least expensive way to provide an X screen for a user. Since most PCs use single-tasking operating systems, they can't run any clients at the same time as the server. Therefore, they too require a network adapter to connect to another system where clients are run.

X terminals and PC servers both demonstrate the strength of X's client-server model. Even though PCs and X terminals aren't able to do multitasking on their own, they give the user the effect of multitasking workstations, because they can interact simultaneously with several clients running on remote multitasking systems.

1.2 The Software Hierarchy

This book is about writing client applications for the X Window System, in C, using the Xt Intrinsics library and a set of widgets. This is only one of the many ways to write X applications, since X is not restricted to a single language or operating system. The only requirement of an X application is that it generate and receive X protocol messages according to the X Consortium Protocol specification.† However, using the Xt Intrinsics and a widget set is, and is expected to be, the most common way of writing applications for several reasons:

- It is quite powerful.

- It results in applications that cooperate well with other X applications.

- It supports several popular user-interface conventions.

- The C Language is widely available.

Figure 1-5 shows the layering of software in an application that uses the Xt Intrinsics and a widget set. Notice that the Intrinsics are based upon Xlib, the lowest-level C-Language interface to X. Xlib provides full access to the capabilities of the X Protocol, but does little to make programming easier. It handles the interface between an application and the network, and includes some optimizations that encourage efficient network usage.

---

*Companies such as Graphics Software Systems, Interactive Systems, and Locus Computing offer server implementations for IBM-compatible PCs. White Pine Software offers an X server that runs under Multifinder on the Macintosh. An Amiga server is available from GfxBase/Boing. X terminals are available from Visual Technology, NCR, Network Computing Devices (NCD), Tektronix, Graphon Corp, and other companies. The number of X products on the market is growing rapidly.

†Volume Zero, *X Protocol Reference Manual*, provides a conceptual discussion of the X Protocol and its detailed specification.

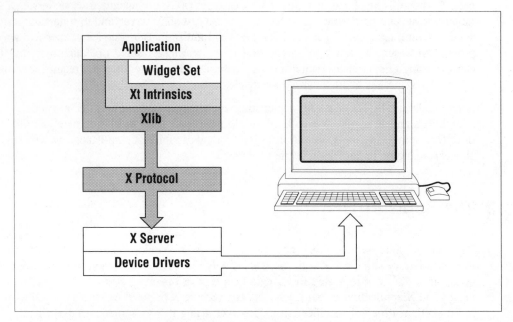

Figure 1-5. The software architecture of Xt Intrinsics-based applications

Xt is built upon Xlib. The purpose of Xt is to provide an object-oriented layer that supports the user-interface abstraction called a widget. A *widget* is a reusable, configurable piece of code that operates independently of the application except through prearranged interactions. A *widget set* is a collection of widgets that provide commonly used user-interface components tied together with a consistent appearance and user interface (also called *look and feel*). Several different widget sets are available from various vendors that are designed to work with Xt. The use of widgets separates application code from user-interface code and provides ready-to-use user-interface components such as buttons and scrollbars. Xt, widgets, and widget sets are described in much more detail in Chapter 2, *Introduction to the X Toolkit and Motif*.

In this book, we'll refer to the combination of the Xt Intrinsics and one widget set as the *X Toolkit* or just the *Toolkit*. When referring to the Xt Intrinsics layer alone, we'll use *Xt*, or *the Intrinsics*.

Applications often need to call Xlib directly to accomplish certain tasks such as drawing. Xt does not provide its own graphics calls, nor does it provide access to every X protocol feature. This book describes the features of Xlib that you may need from an Xt application, but it will not repeat the detailed description of Xlib programming found in Volume One, *Xlib Programming Manual*. You will find Volume One and Volume Two, *Xlib Reference Manual*, invaluable when you need to make Xlib calls.

Xlib, Xt, and several widget sets are available on MIT's public software distribution. The Motif and OPEN LOOK widget sets are not on the Release 3 or Release 4 distributions from MIT, but they are available for minimal cost from the vendors themselves (OSF, AT&T, or

Sun, respectively.) The darkly shaded areas of Figure 1-5 indicate interfaces that are exclusive standards of the X Consortium. That Xlib is an exclusive standard means that computer manufacturers wishing to comply with the X Consortium standard must offer Xlib and cannot offer any other low-level X interface in C. The lightly shaded areas (such as the Xt Intrinsics) are nonexclusive standards—vendors are required to provide Xt but are also allowed to provide other toolkit-level layers for the C Language. For example, Sun and AT&T offer Xt, but they also offer XView as an alternate C-Language toolkit-level layer. XView was originally designed for porting existing SunView™ applications to X, but it can also be used for writing new applications. Volume Seven, *XView Programming Manual*, describes programming with XView.

X software is unlike that of many other window systems in that it was designed to provide mechanism without mandating any certain style of user interface. In the words of its designers, X provides "mechanism without policy." The Xlib and Xt layers are standard because they can support any kind of interface. It is the widget set that actually imposes user-interface conventions, and it is this layer for which no standard has yet been considered by the X Consortium. However, because there is a strong need in the market for one or two standard widget sets that provide consistent appearance and user-interface conventions, it is likely that one or two widget sets will emerge as de-facto standards in the near future.

It is important to note that the X Consortium standards for Xlib and Xt define the programming interface to each library (often referred to as the Application Programmer's Interface, or API), not the underlying code. This means that vendors are allowed to modify or rewrite the code to gain the best performance from their particular system, as long as they keep the programming interface the same. To you, the application writer and user of the Intrinsics, this means that you must always rely on documented behavior if you want your application to run on different systems. You must avoid accessing private structures, because they may be different in another vendor's release of the library, or they may be changed in a future release of X.

1.3 Event-driven Programming

Programming a graphically-based window system is fundamentally different from standard procedural programming. In traditional character-based interfaces, once the application starts, it is always in control. It knows only what kind of input it will allow, and may define exclusive modes to limit that input. For example, the application might ask the user for input with a menu, and use the reply to go down a level to a new menu, where the actions that were possible at the previous level are no longer available. Or a text editor may operate in one mode in which keyboard input is interpreted as editor commands, and another in which it is interpreted as data to be stored in an editor buffer. In any case, only keyboard input is expected.

In a window system, by contrast, multiple graphic applications may be running simultaneously. In addition to the keyboard, the user can use the pointer to select data, click on buttons or scrollbars, or change the keyboard focus from one application to another. Except in special cases (for example, where a "dialog box" will not relinquish control until the user provides some necessary information), applications are modeless—the user can suddenly switch from the keyboard to the mouse, or from one application area to another. Furthermore, as the user moves and resizes windows on the screen, application windows may be obscured or redisplayed. The application must be prepared to respond to any one of many different events at any time.

An X event is a data structure sent by the server that describes something that just happened that may be of interest to the application. There are two major categories of events: user input and window system side effects. For example, the user pressing a keyboard key or clicking a mouse button generates an event; a window being moved on the screen also generates events—possibly in other applications as well if the movement changes the visible portions of their windows. It is the server's job to distribute events to the various windows on the screen.

Event-driven window programming reduces modes to a minimum, so that the user does not need to navigate a deep menu structure and can perform any action at any time. The user, not the application, is in control. The application simply performs some setup and then goes into a loop from which application functions may be invoked in any order as events arrive.

1.4 The Window Manager

Because multiple client applications can be running simultaneously, rules must exist for arbitrating conflicting demands for input. For example, does keyboard input automatically go to whichever window the pointer is in, or must the user explicitly select a window? How does the user move or resize windows?

Unlike most window systems, X itself makes no rules about this kind of thing. Instead, there is a special client called the *window manager* that manages the positions and sizes of the main windows of applications on a server's display. The window manager is just another client, but by convention it is given special responsibility to mediate competing demands for the physical resources of a display, including screen space, color resources, and the keyboard. The window manager allows the user to move windows around on the screen, resize them, and usually start new applications. The window manager also defines much of the visible behavior of the window system, such as whether windows are allowed to overlap or are forced to tile (side by side), and whether the keyboard focus simply follows the pointer from one window to the next window, or whether the user must click a pointer button in a window to change the keyboard focus.

Applications are required to give the window manager certain information to help it mediate competing demands for screen space or other resources. For example, an application specifies its preferred size and size increments. These are known as *window manager hints* because the window manager is not required to honor them. The Toolkit provides an easy way for applications to set window manager hints.

The conventions for interaction with the window manager and with other clients have been standardized by the X Consortium as of July 1989 in a manual called the *Inter-Client Communication Conventions Manual* (ICCCM for short). The ICCCM defines basic policy intentionally omitted from X itself, such as the rules for transferring *selections* of data between applications, for transferring keyboard focus, for installing colormaps, and so on.

As long as applications and window managers follow the conventions set out in the ICCCM, applications created with different toolkits will be able to coexist and work together on the same server. Toolkit applications should be immune to the effects of changes from earlier conventions because the conventions are implemented by code hidden in a standard widget called Shell. However, you should be aware that some older applications and window managers do not play by the current rules.

1.5 Extensions to X

X is also *extensible*. The code includes a defined mechanism for incorporating extensions, so that vendors aren't forced to modify the existing system in incompatible ways when adding features. An extension requires an additional piece of software on the server side and an additional library at the same level as Xlib on the client side. After an initial query to see whether the server portion of the extension software is installed, these extensions are used just as Xlib routines and perform at the same level.

As time goes on, some extensions will become a basic part of what is called "X," and perhaps will become X Consortium standards themselves. For example, MIT has developed a package of extensions that includes support for non-rectangular windows, which has become widely available. The C programming library used to access these features is –lXext.

Among the extensions currently being developed are support for 2-D spline curves, 3-D graphics, and display PostScript™. These extensions can be used in Toolkit applications just as Xlib can.

2

Introduction to the
X Toolkit and Motif

This chapter provides a conceptual introduction to the X Toolkit (including the Motif widget set), followed by a practical tutorial that starts with the most fundamental toolkit program, a "hello world" type application consisting of only a single widget. This application is successively refined until the major elements of any X Toolkit program have been introduced.

In This Chapter:

2
Introduction to the X Toolkit and Motif

It is difficult to build applications that have a graphical user interface using a low-level programming library such as Xlib. To simplify development, each of the user-interface elements of a graphical application—scrollbars, command buttons, dialog boxes, popup or pulldown menus (everything but the main application window)—should ideally be available ready-made, so the programmer need only integrate them with the application code.

The purpose of the X Toolkit is to provide such a simplified approach to graphical user-interface programming. However, in keeping with the X philosophy of "mechanism, not policy," the designers of the X Toolkit didn't develop a fixed set of components with a predefined look and feel. Instead, they created a general mechanism for producing reusable user-interface components so that these components can be built either by the application programmer himself, or by lower-level "object programmers" and then collected in libraries for use by the application. Motif is such a library of ready-to-use user-interface elements.

The heart of the Toolkit is a C library called Xt, also known as the X Toolkit Intrinsics. Xt provides routines for creating and using user-interface components called widgets. A typical application uses Xt along with a library of pre-built widgets (a widget set) such as Motif. This widget set includes menus, dialog boxes, scrollbars, command buttons, and so forth, which all work together to provide a consistent "look and feel" for an application.

2.1 Programming with Widgets

The simplest way to understand the role of widgets in an application is to look at a hypothetical application, as shown in Figure 2-1.

If you are at all familiar with graphical applications, you will recognize many of the widgets called out in the figure as standard user-interface elements:

- *Push buttons*, which initiate an action when clicked on with the mouse. (Pushbuttons are sometimes called command buttons in other widget sets, but in Motif a Command widget is used for typing in commands.)

- A *scrollbar*, which allows the user to scroll data visible in a display window. (The position of a "thumb" within the scrollbar indicates the position of the visible data within a

Figure 2-1. A widget-based application

larger data buffer, and lets the user change the current position in the buffer by dragging the thumb with the mouse. Widget sets have various names for the scrollbar thumb.)

- A *data entry area*, in which the user can type information requested by the application.

Other widgets in the application may not be as obvious:

- *Composite widgets*, which are used to contain other widgets. In all widget sets, special classes of widgets manage the position (and possibly the size) of the *child* widgets they contain.

  Composite widgets are an important part of any widget set, since they insulate the application programmer from having to place each widget individually, or from having to reposition or resize various widgets when the application is resized by the user. Composite widgets automatically adjust the layout of their children when child widgets are added or removed.

- *Shell widgets.* In any X Toolkit application, a special widget called a Shell widget is created by the call to initialize the Toolkit. This widget is used as the parent of all other application widgets (with the exception of popups, which receive their own transient Shell widget as a parent), and includes special functionality that allows it to interact with the window manager. The Shell widget is invisible, since it is overlaid by the main widget of the application (typically a composite widget), which is exactly the same size.*

- *A special-purpose application window.* Most applications have at least one window that has unusual characteristics not supported by an existing widget. For example, in our hypothetical application, the main application window is used to graph the performance of a stock portfolio.

  There are several ways to implement such windows. Which to use depends on the complexity of what you plan to draw, the types of input you want it to accept, and whether you know how to write a widget. You can add graphics to a DrawingArea widget. You can add functionality to an existing widget (usually called a Primitive widget) by adding actions as described in Chapter 4, *An Example Application*, or you can write your own widget, as described in Chapter 6, *Inside a Widget*. As you will see, no matter how you write application code to operate the special-purpose window, making a widget that does the same thing is mostly a matter of rearranging the code and changing variable names. Placing code into a widget gives you easier access to the configurability features of Xt, and neatly packages up the code to operate the special window.

- *A popup dialog box.* A *popup* is a widget that appears temporarily on the screen, until the user provides a certain kind of input. Popups are usually invisible when the application starts up. Using Xt, applications create popups very much like permanent widgets. The only difference is that a special kind of Shell widget called a *popup shell* needs to be created as the parent of the widget to be popped up. Many types of menus and dialog boxes (also referred to as "notices") are intended to be used as popups.

There is one other element in the figure that is not strictly part of the application, and is not provided by the widget set. This is the titlebar, which is added to the application by the window manager. Typically, the titlebar displays the window or application name, and also provides control areas for moving, resizing and iconifying the application.

While the titlebar isn't a widget, it is a window. The window manager adds the titlebar by "reparenting" the application. That is, it inserts another window between the application's toplevel window and the root window. The visible portion of this window is the titlebar.

The titlebar in the figure has been added by the *twm* window manager, which is standard in X11 R4 from MIT. Clicking on the small X logo in the left corner of the titlebar iconifies the application; dragging the pointer in the nested box symbol in the right corner resizes the window. The window can be moved by holding down the pointer anywhere else in the titlebar and dragging the window to a new location.

---

*The Shell widget is actually a type of composite widget, which is designed to have only one child widget. Its layout policy is extremely simple. It just makes its child widget exactly the same size as itself.

2.1.1 About Widget Sets

Shell widgets, and a few other base widget classes (Core, Composite, and Constraint) that are used to build more complex widgets, are defined by Xt. The special-purpose application window is written by the application programmer. All of the other widgets shown in Figure 2-1 come from a *widget set*—a library of pre-built user-interface components. Specifically, they are from the Athena widget set, developed at MIT.

The Athena widget set is distributed free along with the MIT X Window System distribution, and as a result, is the basis for many of the demonstration applications shipped by MIT and a great deal of public-domain X software. However, the Athena widget set was not intended to be complete—it was built mainly for testing and demonstrating the Intrinsics. Furthermore, the Athena widgets do not have a particularly attractive appearance nor user-interface conventions. For these reasons, we suggest that serious application development efforts should begin with a commercial widget set.

Two commercial widget sets that are easily available and quite complete are OSF's Motif and AT&T's OPEN LOOK widgets. Both Motif and OPEN LOOK contain menus, scrollbars, command buttons, dialog boxes, and a wide variety of composite widgets. Both have an attractive appearance and consistent, well defined user-interface conventions. Each comes with a style guide that contains suggestions for designing applications to blend in well with other applications using that widget set.

In order to highlight some of the added value provided by a commercial widget set such as Motif, Figure 2-2 shows the same hypothetical application constructed with Motif widgets, and with a titlebar provided by the *mwm* window manager.

As you can see, Motif has a distinctive appearance, using shadowed outlines to simulate a 3-D appearance (buttons appear to be pushed in when you click on them, and so forth). What is more important, Motif has conventions about the use of its widgets that lead to a consistent look among all applications using Motif. The *OSF/Motif Style Guide* contains recommendations for application design and layout, and whenever possible, these recommendations are actually embodied in the design of the widget set. For example, the Motif MainWindow widget provides a menubar at the top of the application, which can contain titles for standard "pulldown" menus for file manipulation and on-line help, as well as for various application functions.

Motif also provides many more widgets than Athena, making it easy to create control areas such as radio boxes (groups of buttons, of which only one can be chosen at a time) or check boxes (groups of buttons that may be set independently of each other, say for making application configuration choices.) There are also convenience functions for creating many common combinations of widgets.

The *mwm* window manager provides similar functions to *twm*, but also always provides support for a help feature (invoked by clicking on the box in the upper right corner of the titlebar).

---

*The Athena widgets are described on reference pages in Volume Five, *X Toolkit Intrinsics Reference Manual*.

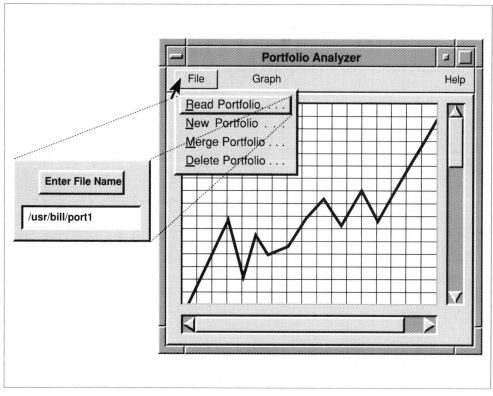

Figure 2-2. A Motif widget-based application

The Motif widgets also support some advanced features for internationalization such as language-independent "compound strings," keyboard traversal (moving around widgets with keyboard keys rather than a mouse—this is very helpful for the design of data-entry applications) and mnemonic key equivalents for invoking menu commands.

This book provides examples that use the Motif 1.1 widget set. However, the techniques described in this book for using, modifying, and creating widgets are defined by Xt, and therefore are the same regardless of which widget set you use. You can use the same techniques to create applications using AT&T's OPEN LOOK widget set, or using the Athena widgets.

Note, however, that Motif provides many Xt-level functions (such as support for keyboard traversal and compound strings) that go beyond those provided by Xt. These features, are not portable to other widget sets. If you plan to write an application that will be portable between widget sets, you may wish to stay away from these Motif-specific features.

An important reminder here is that this is a book on the Xt Intrinsics, not primarily on Motif. Motif-specific features are introduced, but not described in minute detail. Moreover, Motif-specific features are carefully distinguished from the basic Xt features, to make it is easier to know what features are portable between widget sets. (Motif-specific features are described primarily in Chapter 5, *More About Motif*.) Volume Six, *X Motif Programming Manual*, provides a more complete description of how to use each Motif widget, how to properly design an application according to the Motif style guide, and how to use the Motif-specific features and functions.

2.1.2 Widget Classes and Instances

A widget set defines *classes* of widgets. DrawingArea is a class of widget, as are Arrow-Button, PushButton, ScrollBar, and the various widgets shown in our hypothetical application.* Each time you create a widget, you create an *instance* of one of these predefined classes. For example, you might create several PushButton widgets, each with a unique name, containing a unique text label, and each invoking different application code when it is clicked on. All these widgets would be of class PushButton. They would have similar characteristics, but they would not necessarily look or act exactly the same since each could have been configured differently.

A widget class has certain fixed features which are common to all instances of that class, and certain characteristics which can be changed from one instance to the next.

How you view a class depends on whether you are using existing widget classes or are also writing new ones. Eventually you will thoroughly understand both these views of a class, since you will be competent in both using and writing widgets. For the first four chapters of this book, we will concentrate on the widget user's point of view. Both views are introduced here because we don't want to mislead you by telling you only the widget user's view, half the story of what a class is.

For a user of existing widget classes (a widget set), a widget class is a black box that has certain fixed features and certain configurable features, both of which are documented on the widget class's reference page. You need not know anything about how a class is implemented in Xt. You know that when you create an instance of that widget class, the instance will have the documented fixed features and that you can set the configurable features. A user of existing widget classes is most interested in the configurable features, since setting these is a big part of programming an Xt application. Each configurable feature is called a *resource*. Resources are more fully introduced in the next section.

If you are writing a widget class, or if you have written one and see things from that perspective, a class seems slightly different. To you, a widget class is a set of files in which the widget class is implemented. The widget class is no longer a black box—it is an open box. Knowing what widget class code looks like, you know that its fixed features and its configurable features are implemented in distinct sections of the code. You know that each resource is actually represented by a field in a structure. You know that each class has a structure (the class structure) that contains all the fixed features (both code and data) of that class. Even though you don't necessarily have access to the source code for a widget class, your definition of a class is based on how that class is implemented.

---

*The names of all Motif widget classes actually begin with Xm. However, to make the text more readable, we have omitted the Xm prefix when referring to these widgets, except in examples and discussions of code where the prefix must actually be used.

Figure 2-3 illustrates these two ways of viewing what a class is.

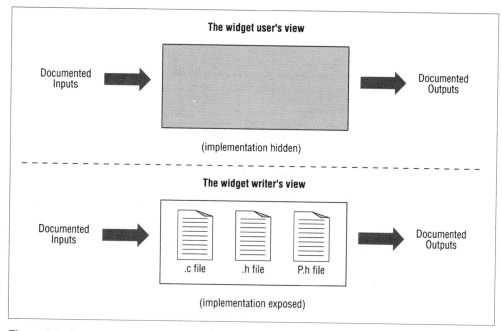

The widget user's view

Documented Inputs

Documented Outputs

(implementation hidden)

The widget writer's view

Documented Inputs

.c file   .h file   P.h file

Documented Outputs

(implementation exposed)

Figure 2-3. Two ways to think about a class

These two views of a class take on special relevance when looking at a characteristic of the Toolkit called class inheritance. Widget features and characteristics can be *inherited* from other, more basic classes of widgets. To a widget user, class inheritance is important only because it means that the resources (configurable features) of a widget class are defined not only by the class itself but also by the classes from which the class inherits features, called its *superclasses*. When you look up a widget class's features on its reference page, either all its superclass's resources will be described, or you will have to look up its superclass and look on that page also, and continue up the class inheritance hierarchy to the most basic widget, in order to get a complete list of its capabilities. This sounds difficult, but in reality you get to know the features of the most basic classes by heart, and the classes are not deeply nested.

From the widget writer's point of view, inheritance means that a new class of widget needs to define only its own unique features, and need not re-implement features common to all widgets, or already implemented by an existing superclass. All classes exist in a single-inheritance hierarchy that defines which other classes each class inherits features. (Note that the class hierarchy is completely different from the parent-child relationship of widget instances you create in an application. The class hierarchy of a particular widget set is fixed by the creators of the widget set, while the instance hierarchy is different in every application, and is determined solely by the writer of the application. The instance hierarchy specifies which widgets contain which other widgets on the screen.)

Figure 2-4 shows the class inheritance hierarchy for the Motif widget set. Classes defined by Xt (which are the same for all widget sets) are shaded gray.* This section describes the Xt classes, as well as the most basic Motif classes, in order to clarify the concept of classing as implemented in the Toolkit. A description and illustration of each of the Motif widgets is given later in the book.

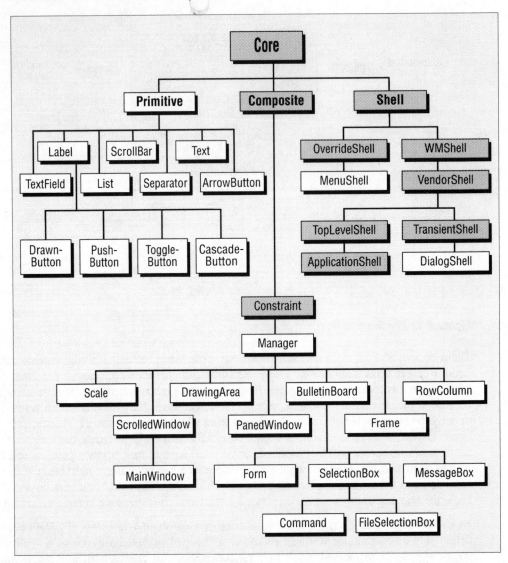

Figure 2-4. Class hierarchy of the Motif widget set

The Core widget class, defined by the Intrinsics, is the root of the hierarchy, from which all other classes descend. The Core class defines characteristics common to all widgets, such as size and position.

---

*Note that the X Toolkit supports only *single inheritance*. That is, characteristics can be inherited directly from only one superclass (though that superclass may itself have inherited characteristics from prior superclasses. A widget class can inherit only from the classes on a direct path upward from the class to Core.

The Motif Primitive widget class inherits basic widget features from Core and adds a few minor features of its own (for example, control of Motif style 3-D shadows) that are common to many Motif widgets. The Label widget in turn adds the ability to display a string or a pixmap, and adds mechanisms for changing the font and placement of the string. PushButton then inherits features from Label (including those already inherited from Core and Primitive) and adds more features, such as the ability to accept user input and highlight the button. PushButton is known as a *subclass* of Label, and Label is the *superclass* of PushButton. In general, lower classes in the hierarchy have more features.

The Composite class adds geometry-management capabilities to the basic characteristics defined by Core. Constraint is a further refinement of Composite that allows the application or the user to supply instructions on how the size and position of each child should be managed. All Motif geometry-managing widgets are subclasses of Manager, which is itself a subclass of Constraint. Manager is Motif's equivalent of Primitive for geometry-managing widgets—it adds features such as 3-D shadows so that they are available in virtually all Motif widgets.

Shell is a special class of Composite widget designed for interaction with the window manager.

New widgets can be subclassed by the widget programmer directly from Core, Composite, or Constraint, or can be subclassed from an existing widget in any widget set that has some of the desired behavior. For example, it is easy to imagine creating a subclass of Primitive in order to develop a custom graphics window.

As long as appropriate widget classes are available, the application programmer needs to know little or nothing about widget internals. In fact, even if widget internals are known, it is unwise to depend on them. Widgets should be treated as black boxes with documented inputs and outputs. If only these documented interfaces are used, the widget internals can be modified without affecting the application, and the application can be modified without affecting the widget.

2.1.3 Widget Configurability with Resources

To serve their purpose as reusable user-interface components, widgets must be highly configurable. For example, an application programmer must be able to define not only a separate label for each PushButton widget, but also the application function that is invoked when the button is clicked. The programmer will also want to let the user define additional attributes such as font and color.

To support this degree of configurability, widget classes can declare variables as named *resources* of the widget. The application can pass the value of widget resources as arguments to the call to create a widget instance, or can set them after creation using the Intrinsics call XtSetValues. Even before that, though, as an application starts up, a part of Xlib called the *resource manager* reads configuration settings placed in a series of ASCII files by the user and/or the application developer, and Xt automatically uses this information to configure the widgets in the application. The collection of resource name/value pairs contained in the various resource files and set directly by the application is collectively referred to as the *resource database*.

Figure 2-5 shows several Label widgets configured with different resource settings, to show you how radically the appearance of even such a simple widget can be altered. Note that a widget's input characteristics can also be configured (although the Label class has no input characteristics to configure).

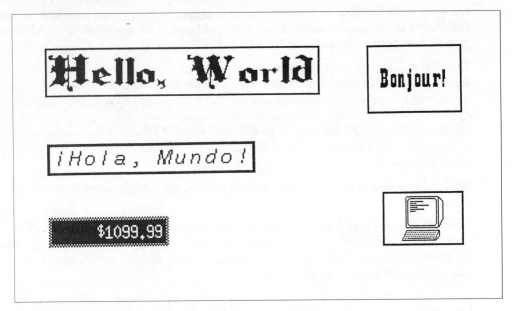

Figure 2-5. Several Label widgets configured using resources

The resource manager provides a flexible mechanism for generalizing the behavior of widgets. The application developer can "hardcode" the value of those resources that must not be changed because they could cripple the application (as when changing the label of the Quit widget to Save), and can establish reasonable defaults for other resources, so that the user can configure all nonessential aspects of an application's look and feel.

Note that the term "resource" is used somewhat ambiguously in X. First, in the original documentation for Xlib and the X Protocol, various data structures that are maintained by the server and identified to clients only by an integer ID are referred to as resources. These data structures include windows, colormaps, fonts, and so forth. In this series, these are normally called *server resources* where there is possible confusion.

Second, the term is commonly used to refer both to a widget variable publicly declared as a widget resource, and to the name/value pairs in the resource database. In this book, we will use the term *resource* to refer to the actual variable and its current value in a widget instance, and the term *resource setting* to refer to a name/value pair in the database. The two are closely related, but may not be identical. For example, separate settings for the same resource may be requested in an app-defaults file and in an individual's user-preference file.* Furthermore, the value of a resource may be set on the fly by a call to XtSetValues, but

---

*There are several possible sources of resource settings. If two or more contain resource settings for the same resource of the same widget, which will actually take effect is determined by rules of precedence that are described

this value is never saved in the resource database. (This value can be retrieved from within a widget or application by a call to XtGetValues.)

2.1.4 Widget Independence

Each widget operates, to a large degree, independently of the application. Xt dispatches events to a widget, which performs the appropriate actions according to the design of its class, without application help. For example, widgets redraw themselves automatically when they become exposed after being covered by another window.* Widgets also handle the consequences when the values of their resources are changed. An instance of Label, for example, does not depend on the application that created it to determine its size. By default, Label will choose a size large enough to accommodate the current string in the current font. If the application changes the text or font in the Label widget with a call to XtSetValues, the Label widget itself will attempt to keep its own window large enough to accommodate the current string. (Of course, if necessary, the application can also explicitly choose the Label widget's size.) When the application tells a Label widget what font to display its string in, the widget knows how to load a new font, recalculate its own size, and redraw its string—the application doesn't have to micro-manage any of this. The application simply sets the font resource of the widget, and the widget does the rest.

Figure 2-6 and Figure 2-7 illustrate how a widget operates independently of the application and how XtSetValues lets the application set how a widget operates itself.

(along with the various sources of resource settings) in Chapter 10, *Resource Management and Type Conversion*.
*Redrawing is necessary because the contents of X windows are maintained by the X server only while they are visible. When one window is obscured by another, the contents of the obscured area of one of the windows is lost and must be redrawn when it later becomes exposed. X clients are responsible for redrawing the contents of their windows when this happens. Fortunately, Xt automatically redraws correctly written widgets at the appropriate times so that your application doesn't have to worry about this.

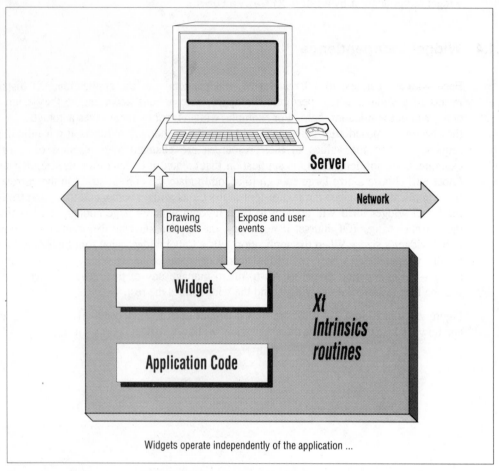

Server

Network

Drawing
requests

Expose and user
events

Widget

*Xt
Intrinsics
routines*

Application Code

Widgets operate independently of the application ...

Figure 2-6. Widgets operate independently of the application

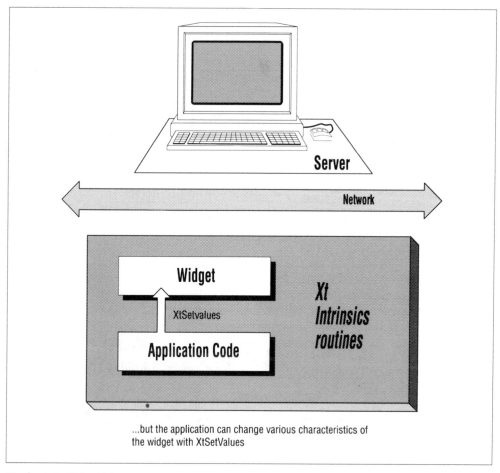

...but the application can change various characteristics of
the widget with XtSetValues

Figure 2-7. XtSetValues lets the application set how a widget will operate itself

2.1.5 Widget-Application Interaction

In the other direction, widgets are designed to let the user control the application. Therefore, widgets have the ability to invoke certain sections of application code—sections of the application's own choosing. Again, widgets will operate fine without invoking any application code, but if they don't invoke any, they won't do anything for the user.

One way that the application arranges for widgets to invoke application code is by registering application functions with Xt. Once the application is running, Xt will call these functions in response to some occurrence in the widget. For example, a PushButton widget usually invokes an application function when the user clicks on the widget. (Thus, the widget labeled "Quit" might invoke the code that checks whether data has been saved, and if so, exits the application.) Or the ScrollBar widget notifies the application when the user has moved the thumb, by calling a function that the application has registered with the widget for that purpose. Figure 2-8 and Figure 2-9 illustrate how an application registers a function during the startup phase, and how Xt then calls the function during the event-loop phase in response to a particular occurrence in the widget.

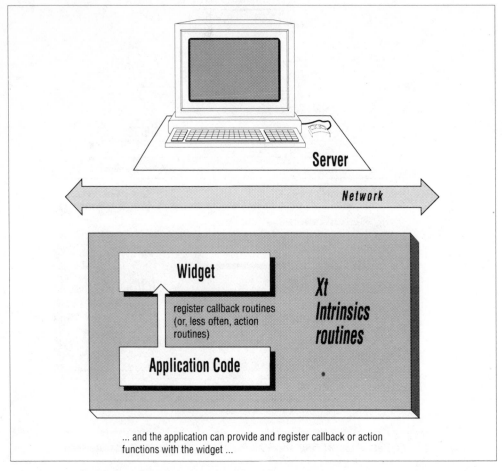

... and the application can provide and register callback or action functions with the widget ...

Figure 2-8. Application registers a function with Xt during startup phase

There are three separate mechanisms that can be used to link widgets and application functions: callbacks, actions, and event handlers.

Generally speaking, a widget expecting to interact with an application will declare one or more *callback lists* as resources; the application adds functions to these callback lists, which will be invoked whenever the predefined callback conditions are met. Callback lists are resources, so that the application can set or change the function that will be invoked.

Callbacks are not necessarily invoked in response to any event; a widget can call the specified routines at any arbitrary point in its code, whenever it wants to provide a "hook" for application interaction. For example, all widgets provide a destroyCallback resource to allow applications to provide a routine to be executed when the widget is destroyed. All callbacks have what Motif calls a *reason*—a well-defined occurrence of some kind that causes the callback to be triggered.

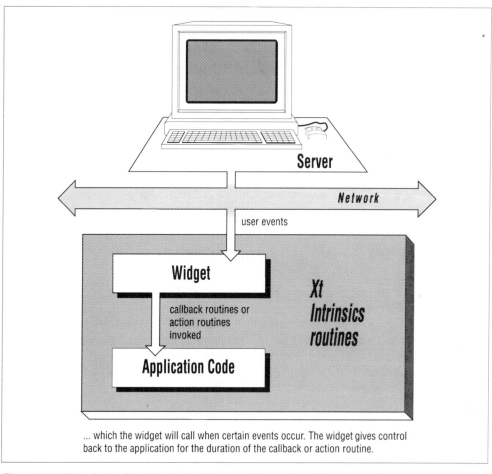

... which the widget will call when certain events occur. The widget gives control back to the application for the duration of the callback or action routine.

Figure 2-9. Xt calls the function during the event-loop phase in response to an occurrence

Although a callback reason need not be an event, callbacks are often invoked by widgets from within *actions*, which are event-driven. Action routines are called directly by Xt in response to events specified in a *translation table*. Xt supports a high-level event-specification syntax, which allows easy specification of complicated event sequences (such as double- or triple-clicks, or key- and button-press combinations) as the trigger for actions. Furthermore, the translation table is a resource, allowing the application developer or the user to configure the events that will invoke a given widget action.

Actions are usually internal to the widget and require no interaction with the application. (For example, in the Text widget, all editing operations are carried out entirely by the widget, using functions defined as actions. The only role required of the application is to read and write files.) However, an application can also add actions to a widget, which can function in much the same way as callbacks, but without the widget class having made provision for them.

The purpose of a well-designed widget set is to implement a particular user interface, which provides conventions designed to make all applications operate in the same way. A widget's callbacks are often designed to support the intended use of the widget, while adding actions to a widget can make it behave in ways the designer did not foresee and that the user might not expect. Nonetheless, there are cases in which the best way to implement the desired behavior is to add actions to an existing widget.

In addition to callbacks and actions, it is also possible for an application (or a widget) to implement *event handlers*, which use an event-selection mechanism similar to that used in Xlib. Event handlers are rarely used by application programmers, since actions are simpler and configurable without recompiling.

Some widgets also declare public routines, which can be used by an application to control aspects of the widget's behavior or to get widget data. Usually, the purpose of public routines is to provide a more convenient means for setting or getting widget data that would otherwise have to be accessed through resources.

2.1.6 Xt and Object-oriented Programming (OOP)

Xt provides an object-oriented programming (OOP) style, where the objects are widgets. However, since Xt is written in C, a language that provides no special support for OOP, Xt depends on programming conventions and programmer discipline to maintain the semblance of objects. It is very important that the programmer understand the goals and rules of OOP, because the language and the system won't enforce these rules. If you are familiar with another object-oriented system, you will need to understand Xt's particular implementation of OOP. On the other hand, if Xt is your first exposure to OOP, an explanation of its goals and concepts should make the whole system make a lot more sense.

Traditionally, object-oriented programming is defined in terms of the five words *object*, *method*, *message*, *class*, and *instance*, and the concept of *encapsulation*. We've already talked about classes and instances. This section describes the remainder of these terms.

2.1.6.1 The Object

In OOP, an object contains two elements: the data that represents a state, and code that reads or writes that data (called methods) and performs some action based on it. For example, the string displayed by a Label widget is part of its state data, and the code that actually draws the string on the window is a method that reads the state data and draws based on it. Inside widget code, the state data is represented as structure members, and the methods are represented as pointers to functions. Some state data members are public; they are resources that can be set or retrieved from outside the object. Other state data members are private; they cannot be read or written from outside, but they help the widget keep its own house in order.

2.1.6.2 Methods

What is called a method in traditional OOP is either a method or an action in Xt. In Xt, methods are a set of functions that are fixed for a particular class, triggered in fixed ways usually in response to Xt function calls made by the application (with one special case, the `expose` method, triggered directly by the `Expose` event). A widget's methods supply its most basic functions, such as the code needed to create a window, or to redraw itself. Actions, on the other hand, are called in response to the events specified in a translation table, and thus the events that trigger actions are user configurable. Actions supply most of the features of widgets, and these features can be added to or replaced by the application, as demonstrated in Sections 4.3 and 4.4.

From the widget writer's point of view, each method is just a function whose pointer has a place in the class structure. Each method has particular responsibilities in managing the basic functions necessary for a widget to be a widget. For example, every widget class must have a method that responds to calls to `XtSetValues`. What each of the vital methods must do is described in Chapter 7, *Basic Widget Methods*. Each method has different arguments and returned values.

Every action, on the other hand, has the same set of arguments. Actions generally perform the features of the widget that are triggered by events. You could say that actions are the widget's occupation: it needs them to do anything useful but not to exist.

2.1.6.3 Messages

In pure OOP, input to objects and communication between them are called *messages*. In Xt, however, the forms of communication are function calls, events, actions, and callbacks. As you have seen, applications can communicate with widgets using function calls, such as to set or get widget resources using `XtSetValues` and `XtGetValues`. Widgets also respond directly to events from the user. Widgets contact the application when certain things occur using callbacks or actions. Widgets pass data back and forth using special kinds of events. All these types of communication can be thought of as forms of messages.

2.1.6.4 Encapsulation

Objects are intended to be black boxes with documented inputs and outputs. In other words, a program that uses an object must not depend on the internal implementation of the object, but instead only on the known inputs and outputs. This is called code *encapsulation*. The advantages of code encapsulation are that programmers can use the object without needing to understand its internal implementation (hiding details), and that the internal implementation of the object can be changed at any time because no other code depends on it. This can be stated in another way: it minimizes interdependencies. In large software projects, this one feature makes OOP worthwhile.

This encapsulation is very effective in Xt. You should be able to get a long way toward completing an application without even needing to know what the code inside a widget looks like, let alone the details that implement a particular widget. For that reason, in this book we don't show you what is inside a widget until Chapter 6, *Inside a Widget*. Even when you do know how widgets are implemented, it is a good idea to "forget" while writing application code, so that you are not tempted to depend on implementation details.

Each widget class has a public include file and a private include file. The application includes just the public include file, while the actual widget code includes the private (which happens also to include the public). The names of both include files are based on the class name of the widget, but the private include file adds the letter P to the end. For example, the Label widget's public include file is *Label.h*, while its private include file is *LabelP.h*. Application code should include only the public include file, to maintain the desired encapsulation. It is tempting for beginning Xt programmers to include the private include file, because it allows you to take shortcuts, but you should resist the temptation.*

2.2 Structure of Motif Applications

All Motif applications have the same basic structure, as follows:

1. Include *<Xm/Xm.h>*, the standard header file for Motif. (Note that *<X11/Intrinsic.h>* and *<X11/StringDefs.h>* replace *<Xm/Xm.h>* when using other widget sets.)

2. Include the public header file for each widget class used in the application. (Each widget class also has a private header file, which is used in the widget code. Do not include this file.)

3. Initialize the Toolkit with XtAppInitialize or XtVaAppInitialize. (These two functions do exactly the same thing but have slightly different argument styles. The difference is described in Section 2.5.1. Many other Xt functions also have two versions with and without "Va" in their names. In the future, unless specifically stated otherwise, you can assume that when a sentence mentions one version it also applies to the other.)

4. Create widgets and tell their composite parent widget about them. This requires one call to XtVaCreateManagedWidget for each widget. (Separate XtVaCreate-Widget and XtManageChildren calls can also be used to speed startup of applications with many widgets.) In Motif, there are also individual functions for creating many individual widgets and combinations of widgets. We use these "convenience functions" only for combinations of widgets, since XtVaCreateManagedWidget is more general, more concise, and no more difficult to use.

5. Register callbacks, actions, and event handlers, if any, with Xt.

6. Realize the widgets by calling XtRealizeWidget. This function has to be called only once in the entire application, passing it the shell widget returned by XtVaApp-Initialize. This step actually creates the windows for widgets and maps them on the screen. This step is separate from creating the widgets themselves, because it allows all interdependent widgets to work out their relative size and position before any windows are created. (For more on *geometry management*, see Chapter 12, *Geometry Management*.)

---

*In a language designed for OOP, such as C++, these shortcuts are generally prevented by the compiler or by the language itself.

7. Begin the loop processing events by calling `XtAppMainLoop`. At this point, Xt takes control of your application and operates the widgets. If any widgets are to call functions in your application, you must have registered these functions with Xt before calling `Xt-AppMainLoop`.

The four steps (3 through 6 above) of initializing the Toolkit, creating widgets, registering application functions with Xt, and realizing widgets, comprise the setup phase of the application. Your application should do as much of its work as possible in this phase, before calling `XtAppMainLoop`, in order to speed up the second phase of the application (which is the event loop). This policy improves the response time to user events.* As we will see in Chapter 6, *Inside a Widget*, this policy also applies to the code inside a widget. It is basic to X, and indeed to any event-driven system.

2.3 A Simple X Toolkit Application

Some application code that uses the X Toolkit will go a long way to illustrate the basic concepts introduced above.

Figure 2-10 shows the actual window created by a minimal "hello, world" Toolkit application *xhello*, and Example 2-1 shows the code for it. *xhello* simply displays the string "hello" in a window.

Figure 2-10. xhello: appearance on screen

Most window managers add a decorated border above or surrounding the window; this is not part of the application. Likewise, the placement of the widget on the screen depends on the window manager. Since no coordinates are specified as resources for the widget, most window managers will require the user to place it interactively. Some window managers can be configured to place new windows at an arbitrary default location.

---

*In X Protocol terms, the setup phase consists of requests to the server that are generally long, and often require immediate replies, which tends to slow performance. The event loop phase, on the other hand, generally consists of short requests and very few "round-trip" requests. For a full description of this concept, see the introductory chapter to Volume Zero, *X Protocol Reference Manual*.

2.3.1 The Code

Example 2-1 shows the code for *xhello.c*.

Example 2-1. xhello.c: a minimal "hello, world" application

```
/*
 * xhello.c - simple program to put up a banner on the display
 */

/*
 * Header file required for all Motif programs is <Xm/Xm.h>.
 * In other Xt-based widget sets:
 * #include <X11/Intrinsic.h>
 * #include <X11/StringDefs.h>
 */
#include <Xm/Xm.h>      /* Standard Motif definitions */

/*
 * Public header file for widgets actually used in this file.
 */
#include <Xm/Label.h>      /* Motif Label Widget */

main(argc, argv)
int argc;
char **argv;
{
    XtAppContext app_context;
    Widget topLevel, hello;

    topLevel = XtVaAppInitialize(
            &app_context,           /* Application context */
            "XHello",               /* Application class */
            NULL, 0,                /* command line option list */
            &argc, argv,            /* command line args */
            NULL,                   /* for missing app-defaults file */
            NULL);                  /* terminate varargs list */

    hello = XtVaCreateManagedWidget(
            "hello",                /* arbitrary widget name */
            xmLabelWidgetClass,     /* widget class from Label.h */
            topLevel,               /* parent widget */
            NULL);                  /* terminate varargs list */

    /*
     *  Create windows for widgets and map them.
     */
    XtRealizeWidget(topLevel);

    /*
     *  Loop for events.
     */
    XtAppMainLoop(app_context);
}
```

Each of the four Xt Intrinsics calls in *xhello* do more than meets the eye:

* `XtVaAppInitialize` performs several important tasks. It reads the resource data-bases and merges in any command-line arguments so that Xt can use this information to configure widgets as they are created. It also opens a connection to the server, and

creates a Shell widget that is designed to interact with the window manager and to be the parent for other widgets created in the application.

The first argument to `XtVaAppInitialize` passes the *address* of an `XtApp-Context`. An `XtAppContext` is an opaque pointer to a large structure in which Xt will manage all the data associated with the application. The only use of the `XtApp-Context` returned from `XtVaAppInitialize` in a typical application is to pass it to `XtAppMainLoop` and possibly a few other functions. The true purpose for the `Xt-AppContext` being a public variable is complicated and is discussed later.

The second argument (a string) is the class name of the application. It is the string that can be used in resource files to set resources for this application, and it is also the name of the app-defaults file, in which the application writer establishes default resource settings for the application. By convention, the class name is the same name as the application name (the string typed to invoke the application), except with the first letter capitalized, or if the application name begins with X, the first two letters capitalized. For the current application, the class name is `XHello` since the application name is *xhello*.

The remaining arguments have special purposes that are not used in this application. We will introduce them briefly here but reserve complete treatment of them for Chapter 3, *More Techniques for Using Widgets*. The third and fourth arguments are a pointer to and length of an array of application-specific command-line arguments that you can define. The fifth and sixth arguments are the common *argc* and *argv*—which `XtVaAppInitialize` parses for a variety of standard X Toolkit options and the ones you defined in the previous arguments. The seventh argument is where you specify fallback resource settings in case the app-defaults file is not installed properly. The final argument terminates a variable-length argument list which can be used to customize the Shell widget with resources: this application uses the default Shell widget and therefore provides no resource settings in the list.

The Shell widget returned by the call to `XtVaAppInitialize` is used as the parent of the first widget created in the application.

- The `XtVaCreateManagedWidget` call both creates the Label widget and tells the parent (the Shell widget) that the Label widget's geometry is to be managed. It is also possible to call `XtVaCreateWidget` and either `XtManageChild` or `XtManage-Children` separately, but this is usually done only if you want to create many children of a single widget, then put them all under parental management at once.

`XtVaCreateManagedWidget` is used for creating any class of widget. The first argument is the instance name, which Xt uses to look up settings in the resource database. The second argument specifies the class of widget to create—this variable comes from the header file for that widget, and should always be found on the reference page for a widget. The third argument is the parent, which in this case is the Shell widget returned by `XtVaAppInitialize`, but in a more complex example could be a composite widget deeper in a hierarchy of nested widgets. The fourth argument terminates a varargs list, unused in this example, that is for hardcoding widget resources. (More on varargs lists later.)

Notice that `XtVaCreateManagedWidget` and `XtVaAppInitialize` each return a value of type `Widget`. This type is an opaque pointer that is used to refer to a widget instance. It is used anywhere in the application that you need to refer to a particular widget. We sometimes refer to this as a *widget ID*, since even though it is a pointer to a structure, the individual fields in that structure should never be accessed from the application, so it can be treated just as a unique number.

- The steps of initializing the Toolkit and creating widgets seem logical. However, what does it mean to realize a widget? `XtRealizeWidget` actually makes windows for the widgets, whereas creating the widgets simply creates and initializes various internal widget data structures.* Creation and realization of widgets are separate because some window geometries cannot be known until all the widgets are created and the composite widgets have determined their geometries. The realization step says "OK, all the widgets are created now; calculate their sizes and positions and make windows for them." However, note that it is acceptable to create additional widgets after calling `XtRealize-Widget` as long as there is a good reason to do so (for example, when it cannot be known whether the widget would be needed until a certain user event arrives).

  The realization step also maps all the widget windows. Mapping is an X concept, not something added by Xt. Mapping a window makes it eligible for display. For a window to actually become visible, all its ancestors must be mapped. Since `XtRealize-Widget` is called for the widget created by `XtVaAppInitialize`, which is the ancestor of all widgets in the application, the end result is that the entire application is displayed.†

- `XtAppMainLoop` transfers control of the application to Xt. From this point on, Xt drives all the widgets in response to events, and it interacts with the application only at times the application has arranged ahead of time. *xhello* did not arrange any interaction with the widget, so Xt operates the Label widget without returning to *xhello*'s code. Example 2-3 demonstrates how to make such arrangements.

  Xt programming is event-driven. `XtAppMainLoop` dispatches events to widgets and functions in the order in which they occur. These events can be caused by user actions such as pressing a key or by window system actions such as displaying a new window. This is fundamentally different from procedural programming, where the application is in charge and polls for user input at certain points.

---

*A widget is a client-side object. It has no presence on the server other than as a normal X window. The Xt and widget set libraries running on the client side maintain the data that allow programs to work with the abstraction perceived as a widget.

†There are several other conditions that can prevent or delay a window from becoming visible, described in Section 2.2.5 of Volume One, *Xlib Programming Manual* (Section 2.2.4 in the 2nd edition of Volume One). These will not affect your Toolkit application as long as you draw into windows at the right times, using one of the techniques described in Section 4.3 and Section 6.3.

2.3.2 Compiling the Application

You can get the code for *xhello.c* and all the rest of the examples in this book via *uucp* or anonymous *ftp*, as described in the Preface. It is a good idea to compile and run each example as it is presented.

The example programs come with Imakefiles that should make building them easy if you have the *imake* program (which should already be in */usr/bin/X11* on UNIX-based systems that have X11 Release 4 installed), and you need the configuration files, in */usr/lib/X11/config* on most UNIX-based systems. The source for *imake* and the configuration files are also in the X11R4 distribution from MIT (see Appendix F, *Sources of Additional Information*, for how to get this distribution).

An Imakefile is a system-independent makefile that is used by *imake* to generate a Makefile. This is necessary because it is impossible to write a Makefile that will work on all systems. You invoke *imake* using the *xmkmf* program (also in */usr/bin/X11* and on the R4 distribution). Complete instructions for compiling the examples using *imake* are provided in a *README* file in the example source. Note that the examples are designed to work with Motif 1.1, and probably will not work with Motif 1.0.

To compile any of the examples on a UNIX system without using *imake*, use the following command line:

```
cc -O -o filename filename.c -1Xm -1Xt -1X11
```

If you want to do debugging, replace –O with –g in this command line. The order of the libraries is important. Xm relies on Xt, and both Xm and Xt rely on Xlib (the *–lX11* link flag specifies Xlib).

Note that unlike the Athena widget set, Motif does not use the Xmu miscellaneous utilities library, or the Xext extension library, both provided by MIT.

2.3.3 The App-defaults File

As mentioned above, the resource mechanism allows widgets to be customized. Widget resources can be set from any one of several sources, including a user's resource file, the command line, or an application-specific defaults file.

Each resource of a widget has a default value determined by the widget class that declared the resource. However, in many cases, the application wants a different default value, but still wants the user to be able to change the value of that resource.

The Label widget is a case in point. Example 2-1 (*xhello*) sets the default string displayed in the Label widget, "hello," by naming the widget `hello` in the call to `XtVaCreate-ManagedWidget`. It just so happens that the Label widget uses its widget name as the string to be displayed if no other string has been specified in the resource database. However, this trick doesn't exist for the other resources of Label or of other widgets.

Is the X Toolkit Too Complex?
An editorial aside

Window systems may be simple to use, but they are very complex to program. The first thing that strikes the novice X programmer is how complicated everything is. Learning to program the X Window System, even with the help of the X Toolkit, is a far cry from learning say, the C programming language, where the very first page of the tutorial presents a complete running program. The program itself is trivial, but this, the "hello world" program, has become a tacit benchmark of programmability. The assumption is "if you can't write 'hello world' simply, things are badly designed."

In fact, "hello, world" is a pathological example for X; it is a case where the stylized scaffolding outweighs the functional code. You've just seen an X Toolkit equivalent to "hello world," and it is nearly thirty lines long. But it is node-independent, does device-independent graphics, and can be customized by the user to control what font to use, and what color to use for the border, background, and text.

The "hello world" example is indeed a good benchmark of language complexity, but it is not necessarily a good general benchmark for overall programming complexity. It is an especially poor measure for a system that encompasses a generalized distributed software environment, network communication, and device-independent graphics. Most people write complicated applications, not trivial programs like "hello, world," and it is the ease with which a complicated program can be written that is the true test of a language.

For example, consider the difference in the number of lines of code between "hello world" and a text editor. Kernighan & Ritchie's C Programming Language, *where "hello world" was first introduced, doesn't present an editor. However, Kernighan and Plaugher's* Software Tools, *an equally sacred reference from the same era, presents a text editor that contains well over one thousand lines. Furthermore, the editor is line-oriented, not screen-oriented. By comparison, because of the modular design of the Toolkit, and the development of widgets as reusable user-interface components, a programmer can construct a simple screen editor using the Motif Text widget in about 170 lines of code. This editor is user-configurable, device-independent, and based on a ready-made component that can easily be incorporated into any program needing to provide text-editing capabilities.*

This is not to invite absurd comparisons of incommensurate programming tools, but to emphasize that the complexity of X is the outgrowth of added functionality, not unnecessary convolutions of straightforward algorithms. What really matters is what features are provided, how difficult is it to write the kind of application you want to write, and what performance can be achieved.

—Mark Langley

The application can provide a default value for resources by hardcoding them in the application source file using the fallback resources argument of XtAppInitialize. However, changing these settings would require recompiling the source. Xt provides a better way.

To provide defaults, applications should always create an "app-defaults" resource file, which on UNIX systems is usually stored in the directory */usr/lib/X11/app-defaults*.* For any application, the name of this file should be the same as the `classname` argument to XtVaApp-Initialize. By convention, this string is the same as the name of the application, with the first letter capitalized. If the application name begins with X, the first two letters should be capitalized. For *xhello* this is *XHello*.†

Example 2-2 shows the contents of the app-defaults file necessary to make *xhello* display the string "Hello, World!" instead of the default "hello."

Example 2-2. XHello: the app-defaults file

```
*hello.labelString:      Hello, World!
```

The name of the widget instance whose string we are setting is `hello`, and the Label widget's resource that sets the string is `labelString`. After the colon is the string we want the widget to display. The string should not be quoted. White space after the colon is ignored.

The app-defaults file has the same format as all other resource database files. In brief, there are two types of resources: application resources and widget resources. (You already know about widget resources. Application resources are the same except that they apply to the application code instead of to individual widgets. Application resources are defined by the application writer—how to do this is described in Chapter 3, *More Techniques for Using Widgets*.)

The syntax for specifying application resources in a resource file is simple:

application_name.resource_name: *value*

Widget resources are more complicated since there may be multiple instances of the same widget class in an application. As a result, you must specify the name not only of the widget, but a pathname starting with the application name and containing the name of each widget in the widget hierarchy leading to the desired widget. For example, in the application *xhello*, the complete resource specification for the resource called *label* for the Label widget called *hello* would be:

```
xhello.hello.labelString:   Hello, World!
```

The xhello refers to the widget created by XtVaAppInitialize, and hello is its child created by XtVaCreateManagedWidget. One possible source of confusion is that the shell widget instance returned by XtVaAppInitialize is not named xhello by the arguments of that call (no instance name string is specified there at all—only its class

---

*New in Release 4 of Xt is a mechanism that allows you to provide a different app-defaults file for each language. This will be described in Chapter 10, *Resource Management and Type Conversion*.

†Note that existing applications do not always follow this latter convention. For example, the app-defaults file for *xmh* is called *Xmh*, not *XMh*.

name string XHello). Its instance name is the same as the name of the application (specified on the command line): xhello.

To simplify resource specifications, a wildcard syntax may be used, specifying an asterisk instead of a dot, and omitting one or more terms of the fully qualified name. For example, as we've shown above:

```
*hello.labelString:   Hello, World!
```

or since there is no other Label widget in the application, even:

```
*labelString:   Hello, World!
```

If you specify a widget correctly and the resource name correctly, but provide an illegal value, the widget should display an error message: the Motif widget set is fairly thorough about this. But the resource manager (the part of Xlib that processes resource specifications) silently ignores resource specification errors of any kind, so they can be difficult to track down. The kinds of errors that are not reported include:

- Misspelling any widget name or resource name.

- Leaving out a level in the hierarchy when using the . (period) binding.

- Setting a resource on a widget that doesn't exist.

- Setting a resource that doesn't exist for the widget.

You should also be aware that widget classes can be used in resource specifications. For example, instead of setting the foreground resource of each PushButton widget one at a time using their widget instance names, they can all be set with one line using the widget class name in place of the instance name:

```
*XmPushButton.foreground:   blue
```

Because widget instance names take precedence over class names, however, one can override a class setting with a specific resource setting, by using a name for an individual widget instance. Therefore, you can set the foreground of all PushButtons to blue with one line, but then override that for one widget with one other line by setting the foreground using the widget's instance name.

Note that all resource specifications in files are given as strings, even though the data required for the resource may be of a different type. Xt automatically converts the string found in the resource database files into the appropriate destination type. For example, colors are specified as color names, which are automatically converted to the pixel values that are required for drawing. These converters are normally defined by Xt or the widget class.

Note also that in resource files, you and users specify the resource name as shown above. But in any Xt calls from source code, you always use symbolic constants of the form Xm-*NresourceName* (e.g., XmNforeground). (Standard Xt, as used for example with the Athena widget set, uses symbolic constants that begin with XtN instead.) Resource names are actually strings, and it improves compile-time checking to use symbolic constants instead of typing the string in directly.

The complete list of sources for resource database settings, the precedence rules used for establishing the actual resource value when there are conflicting settings in different database sources, and the mechanics of type conversion, are all described in detail in Chapter 10, *Resource Management and Type Conversion.* (See also Chapter 10, *Setting Resources,* in Volume Three, *X Window System User's Guide, Motif Edition.*) We'll also be returning to the topic of resources with each new example.

2.3.4 To Hardcode or Not to Hardcode

The resource settings you place in the app-defaults file for your application are, as the name suggests, only defaults. The user can place similar settings in a separate resource file, and these user settings override your app-defaults settings. This allows the user to customize the application.

There are pros and cons to applications that can be radically customized by the user through resources. The pros are quite clear:

- A flexible application will meet the needs of a wider audience.

- Users will have a wide variety of systems on which different colors and fonts will look best.

- Users may have a special job in mind for which the application can be customized.

Some of the cons are that:

- A user may make a mistake in the configuration that makes the application inoperable in some way.

- Documentation and technical support become more difficult.

A partial solution is to document the default resource specifications and require that users reinstall those default specifications before a technical support person tries to solve their problems. In some cases, dialog boxes can be added that require the user to confirm any irreversible actions.

In any case, you may eventually want to hardcode certain resources in the application so that they are not user-configurable. This would be done for resources that, if set incorrectly, would make your application operate in an unsafe fashion. Hardcoding a widget resource is done by placing the resource name and the desired value in the final arguments to `Xt-VaCreateManagedWidget` or `XtCreateManagedWidget`.

This technique is demonstrated later, because you won't need it until the later stages of developing your application. While an application is under development, it is better to leave as many resources as possible configurable from resource files, because this allows you to change them in the app-defaults file without recompiling the source.* When the code is sta-

---

*There are a few resources in Motif that currently cannot be set from resource files. OSF may correct this in later releases.

ble and almost ready for release, then it's time to determine which resources need to be hard-coded, and then to hardcode them.

2.4 Connecting Widgets to Application Code

The Toolkit is designed so that the code that implements the user interface and the code that implements application features can be kept separate. This is an advantage, because it allows either part to be modified without affecting the other. However, these two pieces of code need to be intimately connected, because the user interface must drive the application code.

This section describes the two basic ways of making this connection using callbacks and actions. As mentioned earlier, the general idea of both techniques is that the application registers functions to be called by Xt in response to occurrences within certain widgets.

The two techniques differ in the way that the registered function is invoked. For callbacks, the trigger is an abstract occurrence defined by the widget, which may or may not be event related. When this happens, the routines on one of a widget's callback lists are invoked by the widget code, using a call to `XtCallCallbacks` or `XtCallCallbackList`. Actions, on the other hand, are invoked directly by Xt's translation mechanism, as the result of an event combination.

An *action* is a function that performs one widget feature. A *callback* is a function that performs one application feature. This distinction should be kept in mind, but is not quite as clear as it sounds, since one widget feature is often the ability to call a function that implements an application feature. In this case a callback is invoked by a widget from within an action routine. For example, the PushButton widget defines a callback resource called `Xm-NactivateCallback` and several action routines, one of which, `Activate`, simply calls the functions registered with the `XmNactivateCallback` resource. This combination of the two mechanisms allows one to customize the abstract occurrence that triggers a callback. In other words, when these mechanisms are combined you can configure what user behavior will trigger the callback by using the translation manager which maps events into actions.

The two mechanisms also differ in the way they are added to a widget. The application can add a callback routine to a widget using `XtAddCallback` or `XtAddCallbacks` only if the widget has declared a callback list as a resource. When a widget has a callback resource, it means that the widget writer foresaw that users of the widget would want to have application code called in response to a particular user behavior in that widget. Actions, on the other hand, can be added to a widget using `XtAppAddActions` without the widget's knowledge or consent. Usually actions are added when the feature to be added was not foreseen by the widget writer.

A widget class may have more than one callback resource. The Motif ScrollBar widget, for example, has eight, in addition to those defined by its superclasses Primitive and Core! Each callback resource represents a very specific occurrence in the widget. This allows you to specify a different function to handle each of these different occurrences. One of these resources, `XmNpageIncrementCallback`, is called when the user indicates that the information displayed should be paged down. `XmNincrementCallback` is similar but it indicates that the data should be moved a smaller amount. The purpose of the XmNpage-DecrementCallback, XmNtoTopCallback, and XmNtoBottomCallback should now be obvious. Each of these callbacks indicates a different kind of user behavior, and requires a different kind of movement of the data in the associated window. The callback function registered with each of these callback resources would actually move the data in the various ways. All widgets also have the callback XmNdestroyCallback, which is called when the widget is destroyed.

Note that a callback function is registered for a specific callback resource and on a specific widget instance. Therefore, two widgets can have different functions registered for the same callback resource.

Widgets define actions in order to implement their basic features in a modular way that allows the event sequences that trigger the actions to be customizable. Motif widgets allow customization of the events that trigger the actions that call callbacks, but this is not advisable since the user interface could become inconsistent—identical looking widgets would no longer operate identically.

Action functions are more global than callbacks. When a widget class has a certain action function, all instances of that class have that action. Action functions cannot be different between one instance and another of the same class.

Applications can also add actions to add features that a widget does not already provide. When working with a widget set such as Motif or OPEN LOOK that has clearly-defined user-interface conventions, adding new behavior to a widget is usually not an appropriate thing to do. In addition, using actions is somewhat more complex than using callbacks, and actions have no advantages over callbacks when an appropriate callback is available.

The next section describes how to use callbacks, since they are by far the more often used of the two techniques to link the user interface with application code. The use of actions is demonstrated in Chapter 4, *An Example Application*.

2.4.1 Callbacks

To illustrate the use of callbacks from the application, we will write an application that uses the PushButton widget. Some analogue of this widget is present in every widget set. It contains a string or picture, and executes a command when a pointer button is clicked on it.

A PushButton widget calls an application function when you press and release the first pointer button (by default) in its window. When you press and hold the pointer button in the PushButton widget's window, the PushButton widget redraws the window in a slightly darker color, and swaps the colors of the two portions of the 3-D shadow surrounding the window. This gives the illusion that the button is actually being pressed into the screen. Moving the held button out of the window resets the widget without executing the command.

The *xgoodbye* program creates a single PushButton widget. It is very similar to *xhello*, but takes advantage of the callback provided by the PushButton widget. Clicking on the "Goodbye, Cruel World" button exits the program.

Figure 2-11 shows the window that *xgoodbye* creates if you have installed the suggested app-defaults file (otherwise, it will display "goodbye"). It is suggested that you compile and run *xgoodbye.c*, testing its response to moving the pointer in and out of its window, and clicking the various pointer buttons on its window.

Figure 2-11. The appearance of xgoodbye when the pointer is in the window

This example is not as frivolous as it seems. Many applications use code identical to this to implement their "Quit" button.

The code for *xgoodbye.c* is shown in Example 2-3.

Example 2-3. xgoodbye.c: complete code

```
/*
 * xgoodbye.c - simple program to put up a banner on the display
 *        and callback an application function.
 */

#include <stdio.h>
/*
 * Include file required for all Motif programs
 */
#include <Xm/Xm.h>  /* Standard Motif definitions */

/*
 * Public include file for widgets we actually use in this file.
 */
#include <Xm/PushB.h>    /* Motif PushButton Widget */

/*
 * Quit button callback function
 */
/* ARGSUSED */
void Quit(w, client_data, call_data)
Widget w;
XtPointer client_data, call_data;
{
    fprintf(stderr, "It was nice knowing you.\n");
    exit(0);
}

main(argc, argv)
int argc;
char **argv;
{
```

Example 2-3. xgoodbye.c: complete code (continued)

```
XtAppContext app_context;
Widget topLevel, goodbye;

topLevel = XtVaAppInitialize(
        &app_context,          /* Application context */
        "XGoodbye",            /* Application class */
        NULL, 0,               /* command line option list */
        &argc, argv,           /* command line args */
        NULL,                  /* for missing app-defaults file */
        NULL);                 /* terminate varargs list */

goodbye = XtVaCreateManagedWidget(
        "goodbye",             /* arbitrary widget name */
        xmPushButtonWidgetClass, /* widget class from PushB.h */
        topLevel,              /* parent widget*/
        NULL);                 /* terminate varargs list */

XtAddCallback(goodbye, XmNactivateCallback, Quit,
        0 /* client_data */);

/*
 *   Create windows for widgets and map them.
 */
XtRealizeWidget(topLevel);

/*
 *   Loop for events.
 */
XtAppMainLoop(app_context);
}
```

And here is *xgoodbye*'s app-defaults file:

Example 2-4. XGoodbye: the app-defaults file

```
!
! Core resources
!
*goodbye.width: 200
*goodbye.height: 100
*goodbye.alignment: XmALIGNMENT_END
!
! Label resources
!
*goodbye.foreground: mediumblue
*goodbye.fontList: *courier-bold*180*iso8859-1
*goodbye.labelString:  Click on me.
```

The differences between *xgoodbye* and *xhello* all apply to adding a callback function. In this example we have some application code (the Quit function) that we register with Xt as a callback function for the widget called goodbye using the XtAddCallback call.

The Quit function is defined before main, so that we can use the function pointer Quit in the XtAddCallback call. It is also legal in C to declare Quit as a function pointer early in the application, but actually to define it further down in the source code.

The XtAddCallback call used to register Quit as the PushButton widget's callback is as follows:

```
XtAddCallback(goodbye, XmNactivateCallback, Quit, 0);
```

The first argument, goodbye, is the widget that is to trigger the callback. The second argument, XmNactivateCallback, is a symbolic constant that identifies which of the widget's callback resources is being set. (This constant, like almost all resource names in Motif, is defined in the file *<Xm/Xm.h>*. Other widget sets define resource name constants in the public header files of individual widgets.)

The third argument of XtAddCallback is the function the widget is to call, and the last argument is any data to be passed to the callback function. No data is to be passed to Quit. Later on we'll show many examples where this argument is used to pass data.

The Quit function itself, like all callback functions, takes three arguments:

```
void Quit(w, client_data, call_data)
```

- The first argument is the widget that triggered the callback, as specified as the first argument in XtAddCallback. You would use the value of this argument in your callback function if you registered the same function as a callback for two different widgets, and if you wanted to distinguish in the callback which widget the user clicked on.

- The second argument, *client_data*, is the value passed as the last argument of Xt-AddCallback. This can be any data that you need in the callback function.

- The third argument, *call_data*, is a piece of data passed from the widget. Some classes of widget set this argument, but others do not. The documentation for the widget will specify the contents of this data if it is used. The PushButton widget doesn't provide any *call_data*, but the ScrollBar widget, for example, passes back the current position of the thumb.

If you are intentionally not going to use one or more of these arguments, you should place the comment /* ARGSUSED */ on the line before the function. This prevents the C program checker *lint* from complaining about the unused arguments. The *lint* program can help you catch problems in your code that the C compiler can't detect. See the Nutshell Handbook *Checking C Programs with lint* for more details.

By convention, callback function names (and as you will see, action function names as well) are capitalized. This lessens the chance of collision with other variables names because callback functions are global in the source file. If this convention is not used, the most common collision is between callback functions and widget IDs of type Widget. It is tempting to call the quit callback function quit, and also to call the quit widget quit, but this will result in mysterious errors or a core dump. If you follow the convention that callback functions are given a capitalized name such as Quit, you avoid this potential problem.

2.5 More About Resources

You now have read about enough techniques to construct an application that uses widgets for its user interface and connects the widgets to application code. However, in order to really take advantage of any widget class, you have to learn about its resources, so that you can set the desired resources in the app-defaults file.

A class defines its own resources and also inherits the resources of all its superclasses. For example, PushButton supports not only its own resources but also the resources of its superclasses, Label, Primitive, and Core. The documentation for a widget class may describe only the resources for that class and list the name of the immediate superclass (which you can then look up), or it may list all the resources of that class and all superclasses.

2.5.1 Setting and Getting Resources from the Application

Resources are not just for customization of widgets at application startup. The application can change resources of widgets that have already been created, before or while the application is displayed. The application can also query the value of most resources. This section describes first how to set resources and then how to get them.

Setting resources is perhaps most often used for resetting strings in Label widgets. This can be very useful, but you should be aware that setting a resource from the application wipes out the app-defaults or user-specified value for that same resource (if any), unless you first query the resource, and then set it based on its earlier value. It is especially important not to hard-code strings if you want to be able to change the language used by the application simply by changing app-default files.

There are two parallel sets of functions that set or get resources. The two versions of each function have the same name except that one begins with XtVa and the other with Xt only. The arguments of both functions pass in or pass out resource name/value pairs, but they do it using a slightly different format of arguments. The XtVa style uses an ANSI C varargs list, which is a NULL-terminated list of resource name/value pairs. The Xt version takes an array of Arg structures (called an ArgList) and an array length. Each Arg structure contains a resource name/value pair. We will call these two styles the *varargs* style and the *ArgList* style.

The ArgList routines were the only interface until R4, and they can still be used. Using the ArgList form of call is slightly more efficient than the varargs form, since internally the varargs routines simply massage their arguments into the ArgList forms. However, the ArgList form is more verbose, hard to read, and error-prone, and lacks some of the features supported by the varargs form. The loss of efficiency of the varargs form is probably insignificant unless you depend on maximum speed in setting or getting resources many times in a loop. We use the varargs interface in most of this book, but will also show you how to use the ArgList form in the following sections so that you can understand existing applications written using them. Also, Motif provides only ArgList forms for some of its functions.

The following sections demonstrate how to set and get resources of an existing widget using the ArgList and varargs interfaces. The same form of arguments are used in many other functions that set resources, often while creating various types of widgets. Table 2-1 presents the parallel lists of Xt functions. The final arguments of all of these (many of which have not yet been described) are used in exactly the same manner as in the examples shown in Sections 2.5.1.1 and 2.5.1.2.

Table 2-1. Functions that Set Resources: ArgList and varargs Counterparts

ArgList	Varargs
`XtSetValues`	`XtVaSetValues`
`XtGetValues`	`XtVaGetValues`
`XtCreateWidget`	`XtVaCreateWidget`
`XtCreateManagedWidget`	`XtVaCreateManagedWidget`
`XtAppCreateShell`	`XtVaAppCreateShell`
`XtGetSubresources`	`XtVaGetSubresources.`
`XtGetApplicationResources`	`XtVaGetApplicationResources`
`XtCreatePopupShell`	`XtVaCreatePopupShell`
`XtSetSubvalues`	`XtVaSetSubvalues`
`XtGetSubvalues`	`XtVaGetSubvalues`
`XtAppInitialize`	`XtVaAppInitialize`

2.5.1.1 Setting Resources with the Varargs Interfaces

The easiest way to set and get resources is to use the Xt functions `XtVaSetValues` and `XtVaGetValues`. Each of these functions takes a widget argument and a variable length list of resource name/value pairs, terminated by `NULL`. These interfaces are new to R4.

Note that the resource to set is called `XmNlabelString`, and its value must be a special type called a *compound string*, represented by a structure of type `XmString`. A single compound string can be multi-lingual, multiline, and multifont. A compound string contains a string, a character set, and a draw direction (left to right or right to left). The strings we specified in the app-defaults files for *xhello* and *xgoodbye* were automatically converted into compound strings by Xt. However, to set a string in the application code, we must do this conversion ourselves. This is done easily with the Motif function `XmStringCreate-Simple`. (Motif provides numerous functions for manipulating compound strings.)

Example 2-5 shows the code needed to change the string of a Label widget—this will work any time after the widget has been created, either before or after the widget is realized.

Example 2-5. Using XtVaSetValues to set a widget resource

```
static String new_label = "Hi there."
XmString text;
      .
      .
      .
text = XmStringCreateSimple(new_label);

XtVaSetValues(w,                            /* widget being modified */
        XmNlabelString, text,               /* resource setting */
        XmNalignment, XmALIGNMENT_END,      /* resource setting */
        NULL);                              /* terminate varargs list */

XmStringFree(text);
```

Note that a single `XtVaSetValues` call can set any number of resources of a single widget instance. This example also changes the justification of the string (which by default is centered). (In order for justification to appear, the widget must be wider than the string being displayed. This can be arranged with the resource setting `*hello.width: 400`.)

The resource names used in the above example are `XmNalignment` and `XmNlabelString`. The include file *<Xm/Xm.h>* contains these resource name symbolic constants. Resource names are actually strings. These strings are stored in symbolic constants to improve compile-time checking. If you misspell a symbolic constant, the compiler will note the error. If you misspell a string, on the other hand, the error will go unnoticed by the compiler and go unnoticed at run time as well, but the resource setting will do nothing. Therefore, all resource names are specified using constants of the form `XmN`*name*, where *name* is the resource name.

When you use a widget set other than Motif, you include *<X11/StringDefs.h>* instead of *<Xm/Xm.h>*. In *StringDefs.h* the same set of strings are given symbolic constants that begin with `XtN`. Motif has redefined these symbols just so that all its symbols and functions begin with Xm.

Also note that the value specified for each resource setting must be the type expected by the widget for that resource, or an error will occur. In this case, the type is `XmString`. If you were to attempt to pass a normal `char *` as the value, the widget would report the error at run time. In `XtVaSetValues` calls (and `XtSetValues` calls described in the next section), conversion from strings to the appropriate type does not happen automatically as it does for settings in resource files. However, you can arrange for it to happen by placing special arguments in the `XtVaSetValues` call, as described in Section 3.8.1. (Note that this is a feature of the varargs interfaces that is not supported by the ArgList interfaces.)

2.5.1.2 Setting Resources with the ArgList Interfaces

As mentioned above, the use of the ArgList interfaces is less elegant than the varargs interfaces just described, and ArgList interfaces lack the ability to use Xt's value conversion mechanism. However, the ArgList interfaces were the only interfaces until R4, and therefore are used in most existing applications. Example 2-6 shows how to set resources using `Xt-SetValues`.

Example 2-6. Using XtSetValues to set a widget resource

```
Arg arg;
static String new_label = "Hi there."
XmString compound;
    .
    .
    .
compound = XmStringCreateSimple(new_label);

XtSetArg(arg, XmNlabelString, compound);
XtSetValues(w, &arg, 1);

XmStringFree(compound);
```

The `Arg` type is defined as a structure containing the name and value pair that defines a resource:

```
typedef struct {
    String      name;
    XtArgVal    value;
} Arg, *ArgList;
```

The definition of `XtArgVal` differs depending on architecture — its purpose is precisely to make code portable between architectures with different byte sizes. Its use in application code is demonstrated in Section 3.8.1. All resource values (in all varargs and ArgList calls) are limited to the size of `XtArgVal`, which is the largest of `char *`, `caddr_t`, `long`, `int *`, and `proc *`. This means that for larger pieces of data, a pointer must be used. For example, data of type `float` or `double` must be passed as pointers. The documentation for a widget class that declares a resource with a large value should document the fact that a pointer must be passed rather than the value itself.

`XtSetArg` is a macro that makes it more convenient to set the two members of the `Arg` structure. If desired, you can also set the `Arg` structure members like any other C structure by using the `.` or `->` syntax.

Note that the first member of `Arg` is of type `String`, but should be set to one of the `XmN` resource name constants.

`XtSetValues` is the call that actually changes the widget resource. You pass it the widget to be reconfigured, a list of `Arg` structures, and the length of the list. Example 2-6 sets only one resource, so the list length is 1.

`XtSetValues` can set any number of resources of a single widget instance. Example 2-7 shows the code necessary to set two resources. Compare this to Example 2-5 to see how much clearer the varargs interfaces are.

Example 2-7. Code fragment to set multiple resources of a widget

```
static String new_label = "Hi there."
XmString compound;
Arg args[3];
int i;
    .
    .
    .
compound = XmStringCreateSimple(new_label);
```

```
i = 0;
XtSetArg(args[i], XmNalignment, XmALIGNMENT_END);   i++;
XtSetArg(args[i], XmNlabelString, compound);   i++;
XtSetValues(w, args, i);

XmStringFree(compound);
```

Note that the counter i cannot be incremented inside the XtSetArg macro, because that macro references its first argument twice. Therefore, the counter is customarily incremented on the end of the same line, so that additional resource settings can easily be added.

2.5.1.3 Getting a Resource Value

It is also useful to be able to get the current value of a widget resource. One use of this is in finding out what value the user has specified for a particular resource, so that it can be modified with application data. Because C-Language arguments are passed by value, and some resource values are not actual values but pointers to them, it is important to thoroughly understand pointers while getting widget values. Example 2-8 shows how to get a pointer to the current string in a Label widget, using the varargs interface. This has to be done in two steps: first query the XmNlabelString resource to get the compound string, and then extract the character array from the compound string. Querying other resources is easier.

Example 2-8. Code fragment to get a widget resource using XtVaGetValues

```
#define MAXLEN 256
        .
        .
        .
    Widget hello;
    String p;            /* NOTE – memory for array not allocated */
    XmString       compound;
        .
        .
        .
    /* XmLabel widget named hello created here. */
    XtVaGetValues(hello,
            XmNlabelString, &compound,
            NULL);

    (void) XmStringGetLtoR(compound, XmSTRING_DEFAULT_CHARSET, &p);
```

The type String is defined by Xt to be char *. In the Athena widgets, a string queried from a resource must not be modified or freed by the application, since it points directly to private widget data. In Motif, the compound string returned from XtVaGetValues (or XtGetValues, of course) should be freed after use with XmStringFree or XtFree (they are equivalent), since Motif widgets pass a pointer to a copy of the resource value stored in the widget, not to a pointer to the widget's internal data. However, because of a bug in Motif 1.1, there are some exceptions. The resources listed in Table 2-2 must not be freed after querying them, because Motif does not copy them.

Table 2-2. Compound String Resources That Must Not be Freed After Querying

Widget Class	Resource
BulletinBoard	XmNdialogTitle
FileSelectionBox	XmNdirectory
	XmNnoMatchString
RowColumn	XmNlabelString
Scale	XmNtitleString
List	XmNitems
	XmNselectedItems

Example 2-9 shows how to query a widget resource using the ArgList interface, `XtGet-Values`.

Example 2-9. Code fragment to get a widget resource using XtGetValues

```
#define MAXLEN 256
        .
        .
        .
    Widget hello;
    Arg arg;
    String p;      /* NOTE - memory for array not allocated */
    XmString compound;

        NULL);

        .
        .
        .
    /* Label widget named hello created here. */
    XtSetArg(arg, XmNlabelString, &compound);
    XtGetValues(hello, &arg, 1);

    (void) XmStringGetLtoR(compound, XmSTRING_DEFAULT_CHARSET, &p);
```

Note, however, that some resources are not designed to be queried. For example, translation tables and callbacks are compiled into an internal representation, so it is pointless to try to read them.

2.5.2 Core Resources

The most basic widget class defined by Xt is Core. All widgets are subclasses of Core. Therefore, the resources of the Core class are available for all widgets. Table 2-3 shows the Core resources. Note that the resource name constants all begin with *Xm*. These constants are defined in the file *<Xm/Xm.h>*. In standard Xt, the resource name constants begin with *Xt*, and are defined in *<Xt/StringDefs.h>*.

Table 2-3. Core Resources

Name	Type	Default
XmNx	Position	0
XmNy	Position	0
XmNwidth	Dimension	0
XmNheight	Dimension	0
XmNscreen	Pointer	from Display
XmNcolormap	Pointer	from parent
XmNdepth	int	from parent
XmNbackground	Pixel	White
XmNbackgroundPixmap	Pixmap	NULL
XmNborderWidth	Dimension	1
XmNborderColor	Pixel	Black
XmNborderPixmap	Pixmap	NULL
XmNtranslations	XtTranslations	NULL
XmNaccelerators	XtTranslations	NULL
XmNmappedWhenManaged	Boolean	True
XmNdestroyCallback	Pointer	NULL
XmNsensitive	Boolean	True
XmNancestorSensitive	Boolean	True

The fact that size and position are resources of all widgets means that your app-defaults file can control the layout of the application. You should always resize widgets by setting these resources—never resize or move a widget's window using Xlib calls since this would make Xt's knowledge of window geometries inaccurate. Nor should you use the Xt functions Xt-ConfigureWidget, XtMoveWidget, or XtResizeWidget from the application. These routines are intended to be used only by geometry-managing composite widgets.

The XmNscreen, XmNcolormap, and XmNdepth resources hold the default screen, colormap, and depth (the number of bits per pixel used for indexing colors in the colormap). The top-level shell widget gets the screen from the DISPLAY environment variable or *-display* command-line option; other widgets inherit that value and cannot change it. The top-level shell widget gets the root window's depth, visual, and default colormap; other widgets inherit these attributes from their parent, so unless an intervening widget has set these attributes differently, a widget will inherit the root window's attributes by default. Normally you will set the depth, visual, and colormap resources only on Shell widgets and only when your application has special color requirements.

The XmNbackground, XmNbackgroundPixmap, XmNborderWidth, Xm-NborderColor, and XmNborderPixmap widget resources control the background and border of the window created by a widget. The background and border of a window are maintained by the X server, and setting these resources causes an immediate change in the window on the screen. You can set either a background color or a background pixmap, but not both. Whichever is set later takes priority. The same applies to the border. Details on the possible values to which these may be set are in Chapter 4 of Volume One, *Xlib Programming Manual*.

A *pixmap* is similar to a window but is off-screen. It is an array of pixels. When used as a background or border, a pixmap is *tiled* by laying out multiple copies of it side by side, for the purpose of patterning. Pixmaps are also used for icon patterns, in drawing, and as a temporary drawing surface later copied to a window.

The XmNbackground and XmNborderColor resources can be set using either a color name string or a hexadecimal color specification. (See Appendix B, *Specifying Fonts and Colors*, for more information on acceptable forms of color specification.)

The value of the XmNbackgroundPixmap and XmNborderPixmap resources should be a pathname to a file containing the bitmap, or to a bitmap created in your program. On UNIX systems, standard X bitmaps are stored in the directory */usr/include/X11/bitmaps*. See Appendix C in Volume Three, *X Window System User's Guide, Motif Edition*, for information on these standard bitmaps.

XmNtranslations is the resource that contains the translation table that maps events into actions. As is described exhaustively in Chapter 8, *Events, Translations, and Accelerators*, by setting this resource you can change the events that trigger a widget's actions or the actions your application has registered. XmNaccelerators contains an accelerator table. (Accelerators are an extended form of translations that allow events in one widget to be bound to actions in another.)

XmNmappedWhenManaged is a resource used by geometry-managing widgets to specify whether a widget should be eligible for display (i.e., mapped to the screen) as soon as it is placed under parental geometry management, or whether this should not happen until some later time. We'll talk more about this concept in Chapter 12, *Geometry Management*.

The XmNdestroyCallback resource, as mentioned in Section 2.4.1 above, lets you provide an application function to be called when a widget is destroyed. This is infrequently used, since the Toolkit normally handles the job of freeing widget data structures and any server resources.

The XmNsensitive resource controls whether a widget responds to user input. This allows you to turn on or off user input in a certain widget at will. For example, if you have a PushButton widget whose command is not allowed at certain times, you would set Xm-Nsensitive to False during the period the command is not allowed. The PushButton widget changes its own look to indicate that it is invalid.

The XmNancestorSensitive resource specifies whether the widget's parent (or earlier ancestor) is sensitive. Sensitivity is automatically propagated downward, such that if any ancestor is insensitive, a widget is insensitive. This resource rarely needs to be set, but is sometimes useful to query.

2.5.3 Other Inherited Resources

Besides the resources inherited from Core, a widget inherits resources from each of its superclasses. For example, the PushButton widget used in *xgoodbye* inherits resources from its superclass, the Label widget class, and from Label's superclass, Primitive. As shown in Table 2-4, these include, in addition to the label itself, a font list, a foreground color, spacing above and below the string, and a value specifying how the string should be placed in the widget. (Note that there are many other resources not listed.)

Table 2-4. Label Resources

Name	Type	Default
XmNfontList	XmFontList*	the default font
XmNforeground	Pixel	XmForegroundColorDefault
XmNhighlightOnEnter	Boolean	False
XmNmarginHeight	Dimension	2 (pixels)
XmNmarginWidth	Dimension	2 (pixels)
XmNalignment	unsigned char	XmALIGNMENT_CENTER
XmNlabelString	XmString (compound)	NULL

It is a worthwhile exercise to experiment with the resources available to an application through its widgets, even with such a simple example as *xgoodbye*. For example, consider the resource settings for *goodbye* shown in Example 2-10.*

Example 2-10. Alternate resource settings for xgoodbye

```
! Core resources
!
! The following two lines don't work, but demonstrate a point
*goodbye.x: 100
*goodbye.y: 100
!
! Even though the following specification syntactically applies to
! all widgets in the application, and all windows have borders, the
! borderWidth resource value is only used by certain widgets.
! PushButton is not one of them, so this instruction is ignored.
!
*borderWidth: 10
!
*goodbye.width: 250
*goodbye.height: 100
*goodbye.alignment: XmALIGNMENT_END
!
! Label resources
!
*goodbye.foreground: red
*goodbye.fontList: *courier-bold*180*iso8859-1
*goodbye.labelString:  Click on me.
```

---

*See Appendix B, *Specifying Fonts and Colors*, for more information on the font resource specification shown in the example.

Note that an exclamation point (!) in column zero begins a comment line in a resource file. The number sign (#), the standard UNIX comment symbol, should not be used.

These settings can either be placed in an *Xdefaults* file in your home directory, or you can save them in any file you like and load them into the server using the *xrdb* client, as follows:

```
xrdb -merge resource_file
```

(If you want to repeat the experiment with different values, you should be aware that once resources are set with *xrdb*, they remain in effect. Subsequent invocations of *xrdb -merge* will replace settings for the same resources, but won't remove any others that were set before. To start with a clean slate, use *xrdb -load* instead. Note, however, that this will replace *all* of your resource settings, including those for other applications. See Chapter 10, *Setting Resources*, of Volume Three, *X Window System User's Guide, Motif Edition*, for more information on using *xrdb*. See Chapter 10 of this book for more information on other possible sources of resource settings.)

The window that results when you run *xgoodbye* with these resource settings is shown in Figure 2-12.

Figure 2-12. xgoodbye run with new resource settings

If you spend some time playing with different resource settings, you will find some unexpected behavior. For instance, setting the value of the x and y resources has no effect. Regardless of their value, the *xgoodbye* application is simply placed at the current pointer position.

The reason for this is that these resources set the widget position relative to its parent, and since the goodbye widget is a child of an identically sized Shell widget, they are meaningless. In its geometry-management policy, the shell widget ignores the value of these resources.

If instead you use the x and y resources to try to set the position of the application:

```
xgoodbye.x:    100
xgoodbye.y:    100
```

they are ignored also, for a similar reason. It is customary for the window manager to assert control over the position of the main application window (in this case the Shell widget goodbye), and take the value of these resources, whether set by the application or by the user, simply as "hints" to the desired behavior. There is no guarantee that the window manager will honor these hints. The application is generally free to move widgets within its own window, but not to move itself. The basic X philosophy is that the user (through the window manager), not the application, should be in control. (Kill the window manager, or run a window manager that honors application position hints, and the resource specifications shown just above will work.)

Likewise, you will find that specifying:

```
*goodbye.borderWidth:   10
```

has no effect, while:

```
*borderWidth: 10
```

works. The reason for this behavior is that while the PushButton widget inherits the borderWidth resource from Core, it does nothing with its value. Only certain widget classes (Shells) use the borderWidth resource to set the border width of their window. Just because a resource is inherited by a widget does not mean that the widget's methods do anything to use its value.

Another surprising fact appears if you set the foreground resource to the same color as the background. No text appears in the window, and it does not highlight itself when you move the mouse inside. However, if you click a button, you will find that the widget is still working. What is happening is that the background and foreground colors are now both white, and therefore there is no contrast with which to see the widget's drawing. The widget is not sophisticated enough to check that its two colors are not the same. (Adding this simple check would be easy, but it is much more difficult to tell whether two colors that are not the same contrast enough.)

The cautionary point is that there may be unexpected interactions between resources in widget code. Like programs in general, widgets tend to do what you say, not what you mean. A well-designed widget will minimize ill effects, but given the amount of customization that is possible, it may take some time to uncover all the possible pitfalls. Unfortunately, the documentation for most existing widgets doesn't always do a good job of explaining how resources are used inside the widget.

2.6 Advice on X Programming

The X Window System is a very complex collection of software, not to try your patience, but to do things that no programming tools have done before. Not only does X provide tools to build a nice user interface, but it does so with network transparency, so that programs can run on any hardware and operating system and display on any other.

Probably the best feature of all from the application developer's point of view is the portability of the source between hardware and operating systems. It is worth a lot of aggravation to be able to write just one version of a piece of software, and have it able to compile and run on anything from a PC-compatible to a Cray.

The price you pay for these features is additional complexity. The key to programming X successfully is to keep things as simple as possible by keeping this complexity hidden.

By choosing to use Xt and Motif, you have taken a first step to isolate your application from the details of the lower levels of X software. In general, use the highest-level tools available. Use Motif functions instead of Xt functions when equivalents are available, and Xt functions instead of Xlib functions.

Also beware of configuring widgets too extensively. Every widget has many resources, and the number of possible permutations in even one widget makes it impossible fo OSF to test them exhaustively. At the same time, programmers tend to abuse this flexibility by overly configuring widgets. Often developers try to make Motif applications work in a particular way that Motif's developers didn't intend or foresee. One way to avoid this problem is to make sure your intended interface conforms to the conventions specified in the *OSF/Motif Style Guide*.

Although Motif will undoubtedly be improved to support even more varied interfaces, this will take time, and there will always be features that Motif will not support without contortions. If you can compromise a little on the details of how your interface should work, you will be better off. With Motif, you can get 90 percent of what you want in a very short time. Think twice before spending lots of time trying to get the last 10 percent. First think if there is some other user interface design that can fulfill your needs while being more consistent with Motif style. If you still insist on having that functionality, think carefully about the best way to implement it (and consult with someone who knows X intimately, because such a decision may require an understanding of Motif, Xt, and the lower levels of X).

To be advised to compromise in this fashion may rub some programmers the wrong way. Most programmers program systems where they have total control over their environment. Many have the whole screen to play with, and worry about only one target system. In these environments, it is more practical to learn everything there is to know about the system, so that you can implement exactly what you want. Since X is a much larger piece of software than the operating system or toolbox of any one computer, it is less practical to obtain a complete understanding of every level of it. That's why it is better to use your creativity to design a good interface that can be implemented easily, using existing components in the ways they were designed to be used.

3

More Techniques for Using Widgets

This chapter describes how to use some of the more complex widgets found in applications, including composite widgets, constraint widgets, and popups. It also describes how to define application resources and command-line options, and how to hardcode the value of widget resources when you create a widget.

In This Chapter:

3

More Techniques for Using Widgets

The techniques described in Chapter 2, *Introduction to the X Toolkit and Motif*, will get you started writing applications. But there are more tools at your disposal. This chapter describes the following techniques:

- How to use composite and constraint widgets to create a hierarchy of widgets in an application. This section describes how to use these different kinds of geometry-managing widgets so that the application can be resized and still look good. It also shows how to set resources for a widget hierarchy in the app-defaults file.

- How to build one style of application that conforms to the Motif style guide conventions.

- How to use popup widgets such as dialog boxes and menus.

- How to use callback lists (instead of single callback functions), and how to pass data to callback functions.

- How to make your applications easier for the user to customize by defining application-specific resources and command-line arguments.

- How to hardcode the value of resources when you create a widget.

- How and why you should use application contexts.

3.1 Using Composite Widgets

The examples in Chapter 2, *Introduction to the X Toolkit and Motif*, were atypical because they contained only one widget. Because any real application has several widgets, some way of laying them out is needed. This is tedious to do manually. Therefore, the first widget you create after calling `XtAppInitialize` is usually a composite widget, whose job it is to manage the layout of a group of child widgets. The parent of this composite widget is the Shell widget created by `XtAppInitialize`, usually called `topLevel`.

This chapter's first example is a small application, *xrowcolumn*, that creates two PushButton widgets contained in a RowColumn widget. Figure 3-1 shows how the application looks on the screen.

Figure 3-1. xrowcolumn: appearance on the screen

Example 3-1 shows the code that implements *xrowcolumn*.

Example 3-1. xrowcolumn.c: complete code

```
/*
 *   xbox1.c - simple button box
 */

/*
 *   So that we can use fprintf:
 */
#include <stdio.h>

/*
 * Standard Motif include file:
 */
#include <Xm/Xm.h>

/*
 * Public include files for widgets used in this file.
 */
#include <Xm/RowColumn.h>
#include <Xm/PushB.h>

/*
 * quit button callback function
 */
/*ARGSUSED*/
void Quit(w, client_data, call_data)
Widget w;
XtPointer client_data, call_data;
{
    exit(0);
}

/*
 * "Press me!" button callback function
 */
/*ARGSUSED*/
void PressMe(w, client_data, call_data)
Widget w;
XtPointer client_data, call_data;
{
    fprintf(stderr, "Thankyou!\n");
```

Example 3-1. xrowcolumn.c: complete code (continued)

```
}
main(argc, argv)
int argc;
char **argv;
{
    XtAppContext app_context;
    Widget rowColumn, quit, pressme, topLevel;

    topLevel = XtVaAppInitialize(
            &app_context,          /* Application context */
            "XRowColumn1",         /* Application class */
            NULL, 0,               /* command line option list */
            &argc, argv,           /* command line args */
            NULL,                  /* for missing app-defaults file */
            NULL);                 /* terminate varargs list */

    rowColumn = XtVaCreateManagedWidget(
            "rowColumn",            /* widget name */
            xmRowColumnWidgetClass, /* widget class */
            topLevel,               /* parent widget*/
            NULL);                  /* terminate varargs list */

    quit = XtVaCreateManagedWidget(
            "quit",                   /* widget name */
            xmPushButtonWidgetClass,  /* widget class */
            rowColumn,                /* parent widget*/
            NULL);                    /* terminate varargs list */

    pressme = XtVaCreateManagedWidget(
            "pressme",                /* widget name */
            xmPushButtonWidgetClass,  /* widget class */
            rowColumn,                /* parent widget*/
            NULL);                    /* terminate varargs list */

    XtAddCallback(quit, XmNactivateCallback, Quit, 0);
    XtAddCallback(pressme, XmNactivateCallback, PressMe, 0);

    XtRealizeWidget(topLevel);

    XtAppMainLoop(app_context);
}
```

Example 3-1 creates a RowColumn widget called rowColumn as a child of topLevel, and then creates each PushButton widget as a child of rowColumn. Notice how the parent argument of each generation of widgets is used. Also notice that the Shell widget topLevel is exactly the same size as rowColumn and therefore is not visible.

Example 3-1 creates only two children of its RowColumn widget. If your application creates many children for a single widget, it may be preferable to create the children with XtVa-CreateWidget, and then manage all the children of that parent with a single call to XtManageChildren (instead of calling XtVaCreateManagedWidget for each child).*

---

*Just a reminder that all statements about functions such as XtVaCreateWidget also apply to the other version of these same functions, such as XtCreateWidget, unless specifically stated otherwise.

At the same time, if you are creating a lot of widgets, it pays to consider using gadgets instead of widgets. A *gadget* is a windowless widget, with somewhat reduced features. Motif provides gadget versions of many of its smaller, simpler widgets, such as PushButton. The gadget version of PushButton is PushButtonGadget. For the most part, gadgets are created and used just like widgets. Since a gadget has no window, it loads the server and the network less and can attain better performance. For example, one of the Motif demos, *xmfonts*, creates over 100 PushButtonGadgets as children of a single RowColumn widget. In that case, it definitely makes sense to use gadgets. Probably the most common use of gadgets in applications, though, is for the panes in menus. Therefore, we will reserve our major discussion of gadgets until Chapter 13, *Menus, Gadgets, and Cascaded Popups*.

3.1.1 Setting Resources for an Instance Hierarchy

You have already seen how an app-defaults file can set the string for a PushButton widget. However, *xrowcolumn* has an instance hierarchy that contains a RowColumn widget with two PushButton widgets as children. It is worth seeing how to set the PushButton widget labels in this new situation. (We will be returning often to the subject of setting resources, because it is so important to Toolkit programming. Each time, new ideas will be presented.)

Example 3-2 shows an app-defaults file for *xrowcolumn*.

Example 3-2. XRowColumn: app-defaults file

```
*pressme.labelString:      Press Me
*quit.labelString:         Quit
*XmPushButton.fontList:    variable
*XmRowColumn.background:    green4
```

When an application contains multiple widgets of the same class, resource specifications can either identify individual widget instances by name or can use wildcards or widget class names to reference more than one widget. The first two specifications in the example identify the `pressme` and `quit` widgets by instance name. The third specification uses the class name `PushButton` to set the font of both PushButton widgets in the application. This line shows that resources of groups of widgets can be set with a single line. The fourth specification uses the class name `RowColumn` to set the background of the RowColumn widget (but not the PushButton widgets) to the color green. Whenever you use a class name, it will match all widgets of that class in the application, even ones we add later in a later revision of the application.

By changing the period in the fourth specification to an asterisk, the specification will change the background color of not only all RowColumn widgets in the application, but also all their children, and their children, recursively. Remember from Chapter 2 that an asterisk matches zero or any number of intervening widget instance names or class names. In *xrowcolumn*, this setting will make the background of the RowColumn and PushButton widgets green. Try not to get careless with asterisks, though. They lead you to think you don't have to remember the instance hierarchy in your application, but this can backfire, because it is easy to set resources on more widgets than you realize.

Note that you need to know the instance name for each widget in the application in order to set its resources individually. This is true for all resource files, including the ones customized by the user. Therefore, in the documentation for your application, be sure to include the name and class of each widget in your instance hierarchy. To be thorough, also include a description of the resources of each class, and specify which resources the user can customize.

The first argument of each `XtVaCreateManagedWidget` call is the widget instance name. This is the name used to set resources for this widget in the resource databases. Most programmers make the widget instance name the same as the variable name of type `Widget` that holds the widget ID. This lexical connection is not mandatory, but it is highly recommended because it reduces confusion by helping you to remember the connection between entries in the app-defaults file and the widget instances in the application.

3.1.2 Geometry Management in Practice

The purpose of geometry managing widgets is two-fold:

1. They take most of the tedium out of determining the initial positions of widgets.

2. They recalculate the positions of all the widgets when the user resizes the application, so that the application still looks good.

Build and run *xrowcolumn*, and then try resizing it to see how the RowColumn widget deals with various geometries. This is the default behavior of RowColumn—it can be customized with resources to use many different layout rules. Try adding the following resource settings to its app-defaults file, run it again, and try out its resizing characteristics.

```
*rowColumn.packing: XmPACK_TIGHT
*rowColumn.orientation: XmHORIZONTAL
```

Two of the resulting geometries are shown in Figure 3-2.

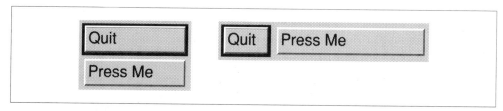

Figure 3-2. *Two configurations of xrowcolumn*

What happens if you use resource settings in the app-defaults file to directly set the size or position of a widget that is being managed by a geometry managing widget? Depending on the specific geometry managing widget, you may not get the desired effect. For example, trying to set the size of the PushButton widgets managed by RowColumn may not work. For example, if you added the resource setting `*pressme.height: 400`, it would have no effect on the height of the `pressme` widget unless `allowShellResize` is also set to *True* (if you are using mwm). This is because the RowColumn widget needs to ask its parent, the shell widget, to be resized, and this will be denied unless *mwm* allows the shell to resize itself. However, it is possible to set things like geometries in the application code, as will be demonstrated later in this chapter.

Every widget's size and position is ultimately under the control of the window manager.* A RowColumn widget attempts to make itself just big enough to hold its children, using the resources provided by the application as a guide, but the window manager can override anything the widget or the application does.

What happens when the user resizes an application is only part of the picture. The application itself may need to resize one of its widgets in order to display more widgets. Or the application may tell a widget to display more data and the widget will have to ask its parent to be resized. For example, what happens when the application changes the string in one of the PushButton widgets while the application is displayed? The PushButton widget attempts to resize itself to display the current string, by asking its parent for permission.

Whether this request is granted depends on the position of the widget in the instance hierarchy, the resizing policy imposed by each composite widget in the hierarchy, and the window manager. This is because each widget, from the PushButton widget on up, negotiates with its parent when the PushButton widget requests a new size. The PushButton widget tries to change size to accommodate the new string (larger or smaller), and the RowColumn widget must approve this change. Since the RowColumn widget is already the same size as the Shell widget, RowColumn can't get any larger without asking Shell. The Shell widget is responsible for negotiating with the window manager.

The *mwm* window managers will allow applications to resize themselves only if the user has set the `allowShellResize` resource to `True`. (Some other window managers, such as *twm*, never allow it.) Otherwise, the RowColumn widget will reject the resize request unless the original change made the PushButton widget smaller. If the new size is rejected, the PushButton widget will still display the new string, but it may not show all of the string (if the new string is longer than the old one) or there may be extra space left over (if the old string was longer).

Fortunately, all this negotiation is done by the widgets themselves. The application doesn't need to do anything. However, you should be aware that any widget resource change that results in a widget size change may not work unless there is enough room in the application for the change to be granted without resizing the top-level window.

The RowColumn widget is Motif's most comprehensive and powerful geometry managing widget. It is widely used for managing groups of small widgets in many settings. (Some of these uses of RowColumn are under other names, such as CheckBox, PullDownMenu, and MenuBar.) However, it treats all its children the same, and therefore isn't appropriate for widgets of radically different geometries. RowColumn's decisions about where to place the widgets can be inappropriate. Figure 3-3 shows the results upon resizing of a RowColumn widget that is attempting to manage two ScrollBar widgets and a BitmapEdit widget.†

---

*BulletinBoard creates an exception to this rule. Since BulletinBoard never resizes its children, the window manager controls which of these children are visible, but does not resize them.

†The BitmapEdit widget is not part of the Motif widget set. It is used to build an application in Chapter 4, *An Example Application*, and written from scratch in Chapter 6, *Inside a Widget*, and Chapter 7, *Basic Widget Methods*.

Figure 3-3. Results upon resize of ScrollBar widgets inside a RowColumn widget

Those two large triangles are actually ArrowButtons on the ends of a very wide but short ScrollBar! It might be possible to use the RowColumn resources to make this application look better, but it would be difficult to keep it good looking after resizing.

Because no single geometry managing widget can satisfy all needs, there are several different types of composite widgets in most widget sets, each with different rules about how it places children. Many widget sets, including Motif, have a widget specifically designed to place scrollbars next to a main window. In Motif, this widget is called ScrolledWindow.

Of course, applications are not limited to using only one composite widget. It is quite common for the application's main window to be a large composite widget which contains several smaller composite widgets, each of which in turn contains certain groups of related widgets. You'll need to design the layout of widgets in your application, decide where in the instance hierarchy to place composite widgets, and experiment to find out which composite widgets provide the best appearance when the application is resized. The following application shows how several kinds of geometry managing widgets can be used together in an application.

Figure 3-4 shows the *xmh* application and the instance hierarchy used to create it. This application is built using the Athena widgets. However, analogues of all these widgets are available in Motif, and the application could easily be ported. The top composite widget in *xmh* is of the Athena Paned class (equivalent to PanedWindow). The Paned widget creates several horizontal panels, or panes, one for each child, with a sash positioned on the line between each pane. Each pane contains a different functional area of the application.

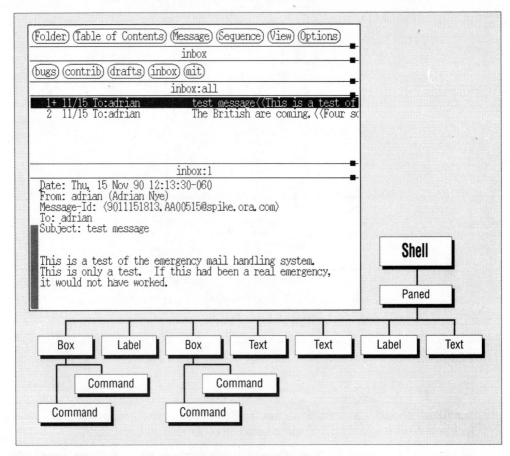

Figure 3-4. The xmh application and its instance hierarchy

- The top pane is a menubar (implemented with a Box widget, a simpler version of RowColumn) containing oval Athena MenuButton widgets (equivalent to CascadeButton).

- The next pane is a Label widget (equivalent to Label).

- The third pane is another Box widget containing Command widgets (equivalent to PushButton). The fourth pane is another Label widget.

- The fifth pane is a geometry managing widget called a Viewport (equivalent to Scrolled Window) containing a Text widget (equivalent to Text).

So, you see, there are three different kinds of geometry managing widgets in this application: Paned, Box, and Viewport. In a Motif port of this application, they would be PanedWindow, RowColumn, and ScrolledWindow.

The *xmh* application does not use geometry managing widgets, called constraint widgets.

3.2 Using Constraint Widgets

Constraint widgets, like composite widgets, manage the layout of children. The difference is that constraint widgets let the application provide layout information for each child. This is a more powerful way to arrange children because it allows you to provide different rules for how each child will be laid out.

In an application, you create a constraint widget just as you would any other widget. But you don't just set resources of the constraint widget to specify how each child is laid out. You also set resources of each *child* of the constraint widget. Once any child widget is placed under the management of a constraint widget, the child suddenly has a special set of resources defined by the constraint widget, which controls its layout. As usual, these resources can be set from the app-defaults file, from any other resource database file, or in the application code.

We'll demonstrate how constraint widgets work by replacing the RowColumn widget in *xrowcolumn* (Example 3-1) with a Motif Form widget (a constraint widget). This example is called *xform* in the example source code. We won't show this entire code, because the differences from *xrowcolumn1* are slight. The basic change is that all occurrences of `rowColumn` and `RowColumn` are changed to `form` and `Form`, respectively. The real difference between *xrowcolumn* and *xform* lies in the setting of resources.

The Form widget defines a number of constraint resources, which to the user appear to be resources of the child widgets managed by the Form. Looking at these resources gives you a good idea of the kinds of things that can be done with constraints.* Each edge of each child can be positioned in one of four ways. Different children can use different rules at the same time, and in fact different edges of the same child can be positioned using different rules. The following is a summary of what you can do with Form constraints. For details, see the Motif Reference Manual, because the complete behavior of Form is quite complicated.

For brevity, the following lists the various ways the left edge of a child can be positioned. You can substitute right, top, and bottom in any of the following.

1. Relative to one edge of the Form widget. To do this, you set the `XmNleftAttachment` to `XmATTACH_FORM`. This child edge will then be positioned the default distance from the same edge of the Form. You can specify a different distance from the

---

*Note that even though the Motif Form widget and the Athena Form widget are both constraint widgets and have similar names, they have radically different constraint resources.

edge of Form with the `XmNleftPosition` or `XmNleftOffset` resources. The latter is a fixed distance that won't change after resizing.

2. Relative to an edge of one of the other children. To do this, you set the `XmNleftAttachment` to `XmATTACH_WIDGET`, and set `XmNleftWidget` to the Widget ID of the other child you want this child to be next to. `XmNleftWidget` can only be set in the application code, not in resource files.

3. To a percentage position within the Form widget (i.e., 50% would place the edge in the center of the Form widget, and upon resizing the edge would always be centered.) Set `XmNleftAttachment` to `XmATTACH_POSITION`, then set `XmNleftPosition` and `XmNfractionBase` so that `XmNleftPosition` / `XmNfractionBase` is the fraction of the width of the Form where the edge should be located.

4. To a percentage position established by the child's initial position within the Form widget. For example, if the application code initially positioned the child edge 20 pixels horizontally from the Form origin, and `XmNfractionBase` is set to 100 to represent the initial width of the Form, then the child edge will always be kept at 20% of the width of the Form. Set `XmNleftAttachment` to `XmATTACH_SELF`, then set `XmNfractionBase` so that the current `XmNx` position divided by `XmNfractionBase` is the fraction of the width of the Form where the edge should be located. The difference between XmATTACH_POSITION and XmATTACH_SELF is only that the former requires the setting of `XmNleftPosition`, while the latter takes the initial position directly from the child.

Note that the `XmNresizable` resource is a constraint that controls whether a child is allowed to resize itself, or be resized by the application. It does not affect whether the Form widget will resize that widget—Form is always allowed to resize any of its children.

The Form also has a number of normal resources (that are set on the Form, as opposed to constraint resources that are set on its children) that control default distances and so on. One of these is `XmNrubberPositioning`, which governs how unattached edges of children behave.

OSF has chosen to make some Form constraints not settable from the app-defaults file, so they must be set in the application code. Although this is where they should be set in a final commercial product, it makes debugging more difficult, since the code must be changed and recompiled every time a new combination of Form constraints is to be tried. Example 3-3 shows the resource settings in *xform.c* that position the two PushButton widgets within the Form. This technique for setting resources in code is described in Section 2.5.1.1.

Example 3-3. xform: constraint resource settings added

```
}
    Widget quit, pressme;
        .
        .
        .
    quit = XtVaCreateManagedWidget("quit",  /* widget name */
            xmPushButtonWidgetClass,       /* widget class */
            form,                          /* parent widget*/
            XmNleftAttachment, XmATTACH_WIDGET,  /* resource setting */
```

Example 3-3. xform: constraint resource settings added (continued)

```
        XmNleftWidget, pressme,                 /* resource setting */
        NULL);  /* terminate varargs list  of resource settings */
   .
   .
   .
}
```

Notice that since these are constraints, these resources are being set on the `quit` child of Form, but the Form will actually use this information. It is actually an instruction for the Form widget about where to place the `quit` widget relative to the `pressme` widget. The effect of this resource setting is shown in Figure 3-5. Note that both widgets referenced in a constraint must be child widgets of the same constraint widget, in this case the Form widget. If they are not, Form will print a message at run time.

If you run this program, you can compare its behavior on resize with the behavior of *xrowcolumn*, and you can experiment with different resource settings for the Form widget.

Figure 3-5. Effect of the Form XmATTACH_WIDGET constraint resource

Both the Form and RowColumn widgets are able to resize the PushButton widgets in addition to or instead of moving them. In the Athena widget set there is a composite widget, Box, that moves but never resizes its children. Note that the difference between composite and constraint widgets is not their ability to resize children; it is that constraint widgets allow different layout rules for each child.

Without constraint settings, Form widgets pile up their children. This can also happen if you make an error in setting the constraints. Sometimes this can make it appear that one of the widgets has completely disappeared!

3.3 The Standard Motif Instance Hierarchy

Most Motif applications have a standard screen layout, which leads to a certain amount of boilerplate code in every application. This section describes that code. Figure 3-6 shows an example application, *xmainwindow*, which has this standard layout. Of course, in a real application the lower area would be more than an empty box.

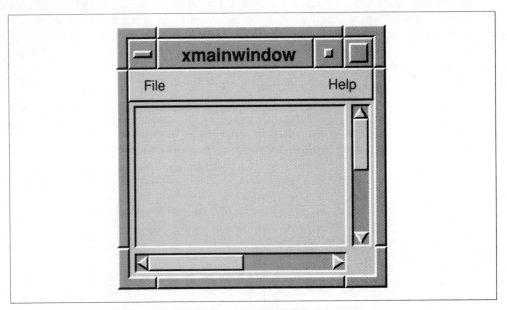

Figure 3-6. xmainwindow: an application with standard Motif screen layout

Customarily, the first widget created in a Motif application (after the one created by `XtApp-pInitialize`) is a MainWindow widget. A MainWindow is a geometry managing widget designed to manage a work area (often a custom window) with scrollbars, and optional menubar and Command widgets. In a drawing application, the drawing area would be the custom window, and MainWindow would automatically manage scrollbars that would allow the user to draw in an area larger than the application's total screen area. In our first example that includes a MainWindow, the work area will be simulated with a Frame widget, which is an empty box with a 3-D appearance.

Most Motif applications also have a menubar across the top of the main window. Visually, the menubar contains labels which indicate the titles of the menus available. In widget terms, each of these labels is a CascadeButton, which is similar to a PushButton except that CascadeButton is specifically designed to invoke a pulldown menu or dialog box instead of an application function. Two of the most common labels visible in a menubar are File and Help. The File button brings up a menu that includes the commands for reading and writing files, if any, and also the command to quit the application. According to the Motif style guide, the

File button has the position at the far left in the menubar, and the Help button has the far right.* The Help button brings up a dialog box which contains help text appropriate for the current situation.

A Command widget is another horizontal band across the application, just below the work area. A Command widget contains two windows, one that allows you to type in commands, and the other that shows you the history of prior commands. The Command widget is optional in a MainWindow and is less common than the menubar.

3.3.1 Motif Widget Creation Routines

All the previous examples have used `XtVaCreateManagedWidget` to create widgets. As you may recall, you specify which type of widget you want by supplying an argument such as `xmPushButtonWidgetClass`. But Motif also provides its own functions for creating widgets. To create a PushButton, Motif's function is `XmCreatePushButton`. Note, however, that Motif's function does not manage the widget, so you need to call `XtManageChild` separately. (If you forget, the widget won't be visible.) Also, as you will see later, it is harder to set widget resources with the Motif widget creation functions. In the cases where the two techniques are identical, our examples stick with the basic Xt routine.†

In some cases, however, the Motif widget creation routines have code beyond just calling the Xt widget creation routine. Some set resources in particular ways. For example, `XmCreateMenuBar` actually creates a RowColumn widget, but with some special resource settings. It is a lot more convenient to use `XmCreateMenuBar` than to use the Xt widget creation routine and set the resources yourself.

As in the case of `XmCreateMenuBar`, the Motif widget creation routines often have names that are different from the widgets they create. There is no such thing as a MenuBar widget. Remember this when you look up a widget's resources in the Motif reference manual. If you are unsure of the widget class, look on the page for the Motif widget creation function first.

Other Motif widget-creation functions actually create a combination of widgets. More will be said about this later.

3.3.2 Building a Main Window

With that introduction, we are ready to show you the code needed to implement a standard Motif MainWindow and its usual children. Example 3-4 shows a portion of *xmainwindow.c*, the code for implementing the application shown in Figure 3-6.

---

*The menubar and the File menu are common features of window-based graphical applications using other widget sets and other window systems, including the Macintosh.

†This is less verbose, less prone to error, and saves one function call.

```
/*
 *  xmainwindow.c - main window with help and quit
 */

/* Standard Motif include files: */
#include <Xm/Xm.h>

/*
 * Public header files for widgets used in this file.
 */
#include <Xm/MainW.h>          /* MainWindow */
#include <Xm/RowColumn.h>      /* for MenuBar (actually a RowColumn) */
#include <Xm/Frame.h>          /* Frame (simulated custom widget) */
#include <Xm/PushB.h>          /* PushButton (for menu buttons) */
#include <Xm/CascadeB.h>       /* CascadeButton (for menubar labels) */
#include <Xm/MessageB.h>       /* MessageBox dialog (for help) */

 /* callback functions defined here */

main(argc, argv)
int argc;
char **argv;
{
    XtAppContext app_context;
    Widget topLevel, mainWindow, menuBar, frame;
    Widget fileButton, fileMenu, quit, getHelp, helpBox;

    topLevel = XtVaAppInitialize(
            &app_context,       /* Application context */
            "XMainWindow",      /* application class name */
            NULL, 0,            /* command line option list */
            &argc, argv,        /* command line args */
            NULL,               /* for missing app-defaults file */
            NULL);              /* terminate varargs list */

    /* create main window */
    mainWindow = XtVaCreateManagedWidget(
            "mainWindow",       /* widget name */
            xmMainWindowWidgetClass, /* widget class */
            topLevel,           /* parent widget*/
            NULL);              /* terminate varargs list */

    /* create menubar along top inside of main window */
    menuBar = XmCreateMenuBar(
            mainWindow, /* parent widget*/
            "menuBar",  /* widget name */
            NULL,       /* no arguments needed */
            0);         /* no arguments needed */
    XtManageChild(menuBar);

    frame = XtVaCreateManagedWidget(
            "frame",            /* widget name */
            xmFrameWidgetClass, /* widget class */
            mainWindow,         /* parent widget*/
            NULL);              /* terminate varargs list */
```

```
/* Set MainWindow areas */
XmMainWindowSetAreas (mainWindow, menuBar, NULL, NULL, NULL,
        frame);
        .
        .
        .
}
```

This code creates a MainWindow that contains two widgets: a menubar (which is actually a kind of RowColumn configured as a menubar via resources automatically set by the convenience function used to create the widget) and a Frame. Note that the `parent` arguments of functions that create the menubar and the Frame are both `mainWindow`.

We use `XtVaCreateManagedWidget` to create the main window, but `XmCreateMenuBar` to create the menubar, for the reasons described above. Notice that widget name and widget parent arguments are in a different order in the two functions.

The menubar must be managed with a separate call to `XtManageChild`, because `XmCreateMenuBar` does not manage it.

`XmMainWindowSetAreas` tells the main window which of its children should be treated as the menubar (placed across the top of the application), and which as the work area (at the bottom, with scrollbars if needed). The work area in this case is the Frame widget. The three unused arguments, here set to `NULL`, allow you to tell MainWindow which widget is the Command window, and which widgets are the scrollbars that will control the work area.

You might ask, why does MainWindow need to be told which widget is which, since it has access to its list of child widgets? This is done mainly for added flexibility, so that you can switch work areas or other children.

The purpose of the scrollbar arguments in `XmMainWindowSetAreas` is a common point of confusion. MainWindow is a subclass of ScrolledWindow. That means that MainWindow has all the features of ScrolledWindow, plus more. Therefore, MainWindow automatically creates its own scrollbars and uses these scrollbars to control the work area. Why, then, should `XmMainWindowSetAreas` allow you to tell MainWindow which scrollbars to use, when MainWindow already has its own scrollbars and knows how to use them? The answer is that in some cases an application wants to provide its own code to handle the callbacks that connect its scrollbars with its work region. In practically all cases, however, an application can use the scrollbars created automatically by MainWindow or ScrolledWindow, even if it wishes to manually connect those widgets with the work area.*

---

*The Motif code and reference documentation differ on the definition of MainWindow and ScrolledWindow. The documentation states that you have to create the scrollbars managed by these widgets, and then pass them to `XmMainWindowSetAreas` or `XmScrolledWindowSetAreas`. But in reality, the widgets automatically create the scrollbars, which makes more sense. We have described the behavior of the code, rather than that described by the documentation. There is no way of knowing, however, whether in later releases OSF will change the documentation to match the code, or vice-versa.

Chapter 3 of the *OSF/Motif Programmer's Guide* also provides an incorrect example of the use of scrollbars in MainWindow. It unnecessarily creates a ScrolledWindow as a child of MainWindow, since MainWindow already provides all the features of ScrolledWindow.

A resource setting is necessary in order to make MainWindow display scrollbars and use them to control the custom window. Here is the portion of the *XMainWindow* app-defaults file that applies to the code shown so far:

```
! Set initial size of application
*XmMainWindow.width:  200
! Frame will be bigger that application, thus requiring scrollbars
*XmFrame.width:  300
*XmFrame.height:  300
! Make MainWindow display scrollbars and use them to
! pan around in the frame.
*XmMainWindow.scrollingPolicy:  XmAUTOMATIC
```

The remaining part of the boilerplate code in a standard Motif application is to build the File menu and Help button in the menubar, that you see in *xmainwindow*. This is described in the next section.

3.4 Using Popups

A *popup* is a widget that is displayed on the screen for short periods, instead of being permanently visible.

The two most common kinds of popup widgets are menus and dialog boxes. Menus are familiar to most people, but dialog boxes are less so. A dialog box is a box on the screen that contains a message, or asks for user input, or both. Sometimes a dialog box provides a way to get input that is needed only occasionally and therefore doesn't deserve a place in the permanently visible user interface. Fitting into this category is the Motif file selection box, which is commonly used as a dialog box. At other times, a dialog box requires immediate response by the user before the application can continue. For example, many applications that write files are capable of displaying a dialog box that says "Warning: file exists. Do you wish to overwrite?"

A menu becomes visible when the user presses a mouse button while the pointer is in one of the CascadeButtons in the menubar. It becomes invisible again once the user has selected an item from the menu, released the button outside the menu, or moved into another Cascade-Button in the menubar. Dialog boxes usually become visible either because a button such as Help was clicked on by the user, or because the program needs occasional user input that is best supplied through a temporary window instead of as a permanently visible part of the application user interface. Dialog boxes become invisible when the user clicks on the OK or Confirm button in the dialog box, or provides the input that the dialog box is requesting.

Popups are not a kind of widget, but rather a way of using widgets. Any widget can be used as a popup. However, some classes of widgets are more commonly used as popups, and Motif has simplified the interface by providing routines that not only create these widgets, but also prepare them for use as popups. For example, Motif provides `XmCreatePopup-Menu` for creating an empty popup menu. Internally, this routine creates a special parent widget called an OverrideShell, and then creates a RowColumn widget inside it, with special resource settings. It is then your job to create widgets (or gadgets) to appear in the menu.

A Motif menubar, as described in Section 3.3, usually contains a File menu and a Help button that brings up a dialog box. We'll discuss creating the File menu first, and then the Help dialog box.

3.4.1 Creating a Basic Menu

Motif provides three different types of menus: popup, pulldown, and option. Popup menus and pulldown menus are popups as we have defined them, but option menus are always visible. RadioBox and CheckBox can also be thought of as kinds of menus. The menus that are invoked from the menubar are pulldown menus. Figure 3-7 shows *xmainwindow* with the File pulldown menu displayed. The techniques for creating all three types of menus are very similar, but we'll reserve discussion of the other types until Chapter 13, *Menus, Gadgets, and Cascaded Popups.*

Figure 3-7. xmainwindow with the File pulldown menu displayed

Creating a pulldown menu is a four-step process:

1. Create a CascadeButton as a child of the menubar. This will be the button in which the user will click in order to pull down the menu.

2. Create an empty menu with XmCreatePulldownMenu as a child of the menubar. This actually creates a RowColumn with certain resource settings.

3. Create PushButtons or PushButtonGadgets for each menu item, as children of the pulldown menu.

4. Tell the CascadeButton that just created the ID of the menu, it should pop up. This can't be done until step 2 is done.

In Motif, the RowColumn widget created by XmCreatePulldownMenu is called a menu *pane*, and the buttons contained by that menu are called menu *items*.

This process sets up the popup widget, but does not put it on the screen. Somewhere in your code you need to call XtManageChild to pop up the widget. This is typically done in the XmNactivateCallback callback routine of the CascadeButton. Motif takes care of popping down the menu at the appropriate times according to its conventions.

Example 3-5 shows the code needed to add a File menu containing only a quit button to an existing menubar.

Example 3-5. Adding a File menu to an existing menubar

```
/*
 * quit button callback function
 */
/*ARGSUSED*/
void Quit(w, client_data, call_data)
Widget w;
XtPointer client_data, call_data;
{
    exit(0);
}

main(argc, argv)
int argc;
char **argv;
{
    Widget fileMenu, fileButton, quit;
      .
      .
      .
    /*
     *   CREATE FILE MENU AND CHILDREN
     */

    /* create the File button in the menubar */
    fileButton = XtVaCreateManagedWidget(
            "fileButton",/* widget name */
            xmCascadeButtonWidgetClass, /* widget class */
            menuBar,      /* parent widget*/
            NULL);        /* terminate varargs list */

    /* create menu (really a Shell widget
     * and RowColumn widget combo) */
    fileMenu = XmCreatePulldownMenu(
            menuBar,      /* parent widget*/
            "fileMenu",   /* widget name */
            NULL,         /* no argument list needed */
            0);           /* no argument list needed */

    /* Notice that fileMenu is intentionally NOT managed here */

    /* create button in menu that exits application */
    quit = XtVaCreateManagedWidget(
            "quit",       /* widget name */
            xmPushButtonWidgetClass,    /* widget class */
            fileMenu,     /* parent widget*/
            NULL);        /* terminate varargs list */
```

Example 3-5. Adding a File menu to an existing menubar (continued)

```
/*
 * Specify which menu the fileButton will pop up.
 */
XtVaSetValues(fileButton,
        XmNsubMenuId, fileMenu,
        NULL);

/* arrange for quit button to call function that exits. */
XtAddCallback(quit, XmNactivateCallback, Quit, 0);
        .
        .
        .
}
```

This code sample exactly matches the four steps listed above for creating a menu. First it creates the button that pops up the menu, followed by the menu pane itself, followed by a button that will appear in the menu. Finally, it tells `fileButton` that it should pop up `fileMenu` whenever activated.

There are several important things to remember about this example. Note that `fileMenu` is not managed after it is created, unlike the widgets in all previous examples. Motif itself will manage the widget when it comes time to pop it up. Also note how, by setting the `XmNsubMenuId` resource, we connect the `fileButton` widget with `fileMenu`. Finally, note that both `fileButton` and `fileMenu` are children of the menubar, while `quit` is a child of `fileMenu`. This instance hierarchy is important.

3.4.2 Creating a Basic Dialog Box

Motif has even more different types of dialog boxes than it has menus. Luckily, they are also more uniform in the way they are created! This section will demonstrate creating a dialog box to provide help. Chapter 13, *Menus, Gadgets, and Cascaded Popups*, describes the variations in how to use other types of Motif dialog boxes. Figure 3-8 shows *xmainwindow* with the Help dialog box displayed.

This dialog box is a MessageBox widget. Motif doesn't provide a dialog widget that is ideal for providing help, since MessageBox provides Help buttons and Cancel buttons that are normally not needed in Help dialog boxes.

A Help button is created just like the `fileButton` in the previous example. It is a CascadeButton created as a child of the menubar. The dialog box that will contain the text is created with `XmCreateMessageDialog`.

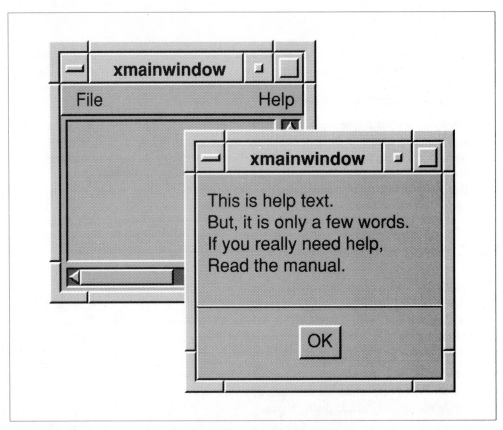

Figure 3-8. xmainwindow with the Help dialog box displayed

Example 3-6 shows the code required to add a Help button and dialog box to *xmainwindow*.

Example 3-6. xmainwindow: creating a Help button and Help dialog box

```
        .
        .
        .
/*
 * callback to pop up help dialog widget (or any other dialog)
 */
/*ARGSUSED*/
void ShowHelp(w, client_data, call_data)
Widget w;
XtPointer client_data;
XtPointer call_data;
{
    Widget dialog = (Widget) client_data;
    XtManageChild(dialog);
}
        .
        .
        .

main(argc, argv)
int argc;
char **argv;
{
    XtAppContext app_context;
    Widget topLevel, mainWindow, menuBar, frame;
    Widget fileButton, fileMenu, quit, getHelp, helpBox;
    Widget temp;
        .
        .
        .

    /*
     *   CREATE HELP BUTTON AND BOX
     */

    /* create button that will bring up help popup */
    getHelp = XtVaCreateManagedWidget(
            "getHelp",  /* widget name */
            xmCascadeButtonWidgetClass, /* widget class */
            menuBar,    /* parent widget*/
            NULL);      /* terminate varargs list */

    /* tell menuBar which is the Help button
     * (will be specially positioned. */
    XtVaSetValues(menuBar,
            XmNmenuHelpWidget, getHelp,
            NULL);

    /* create popup that will contain help */
    helpBox = XmCreateMessageDialog(
            getHelp,    /* parent widget*/
            "helpBox",  /* widget name */
            NULL,       /* no arguments needed */
            0);         /* no arguments needed */

    temp = XmMessageBoxGetChild (helpBox, XmDIALOG_CANCEL_BUTTON);
    XtUnmanageChild (temp);
    temp = XmMessageBoxGetChild (helpBox, XmDIALOG_HELP_BUTTON);
    XtUnmanageChild (temp);
```

```
    /* arrange for getHelp button to pop up helpBox */
    XtAddCallback(getHelp,        /* widget that takes user input */
        XmNactivateCallback,    /* callback resource */
        ShowHelp,    /* callback function */
        helpBox);    /* data passed as client_data
                      * to callback function */
    .
    .
    .
}
```

As shown in Example 3-6, the first step in creating a Help feature is to create a CascadeButton widget as a child of the menubar. Then, you set the XmNmenuHelpWidget resource of the menubar to tell the menubar that this particular CascadeButton is the Help button. This is necessary because the menubar treats the Help button specially; it is a Motif convention that the Help button appears at the extreme right of the menubar. Third, you create the dialog box with XmCreateMessageDialog. Finally, you register a callback function, here called ShowHelp, with the CascadeButton widget. ShowHelp simply calls XtManageChild to put the dialog widget on the screen. (If you have several dialog widgets, they can all share this callback function because it doesn't have any code that depends on any particular type of dialog widget.)

If you get a run-time error that says "Error: Attempt to manage a child when parent is not Composite," it may mean that you have used XmCreateMessageBox instead of XmCreateMessageDialog. XmCreateMessageBox creates a widget with the same appearance, but it does not create the Shell widget parent that allows the message box to be used as a popup. This can also happen with file selection boxes, radio boxes, selection boxes, and check boxes.

The parent of the dialog box can be any widget in the application, since it is only used to determine on which screen to create the dialog. However, it is useful to use some consistent system of parenting, to make it easier to keep track of the purpose of each dialog. In this case, the parent is the CascadeButton widget that pops up the dialog, getHelp.

XmCreateMessageDialog actually creates two widgets for you, an OverrideShell and a MessageBox as its child. The OverrideShell handles communication with the window manager, and the MessageBox displays the help text and creates the OK button that pops down the dialog. By default, a MessageBox (and most Motif dialogs) contains three buttons, that read by default OK, Cancel, and Help. Since we are providing help, we have no need for the Cancel and Help buttons. Unfortunately, Motif does not provide a dialog widget with just the OK button. But it is easy enough to take the Cancel and Help widgets off the dialog by unmanaging them. We get their IDs with the Motif function XmMessageBoxGetChild, and then unmanage them with XtUnmanageChild. The MessageBox widget then automatically centers the OK button.

Note that the help text is not specified anywhere in the application code. At least until the application is final, it can be specified in the app-defaults file. Example 3-7 shows this portion of the app-defaults file for *xmainwindow*.

```
*helpBox.messageString:  This is help text.\n\
But it is only a few words.\n\
If you really need help,\n\
I'm afraid you'll have to read the manual.
! The following used if the window manager titles the dialog.
*helpBox.dialogTitle:  Help
```

By ending lines with \n\, you can use a multi-line string as a resource value.

3.4.3 Popup Window Hierarchy

You may notice that dialog boxes can extend outside the application. This is because their Shell widgets are child windows of the root window, not the top-level window of the application, no matter which widget you supply as parent. By default in Xt, a child of the root is positioned at the top-left corner of the screen. However, Motif automatically positions most menus and dialog boxes in a suitable location in or over the application before popping them up. Dialog boxes or menus that are not triggered by a mouse button press, though, need to be positioned by the application. How to do this will be described in Chapter 13, *Menus, Gadgets, and Cascaded Popups*.

Figure 3-9 shows the widget instance hierarchy of *xmainwindow*, and its X window hierarchy. Note that the only difference between the two is the parentage of the dialog and menu widgets.

Note that when you create a PulldownMenu, you are actually creating a Shell widget with the menu as its child. The same is true of MessageDialog. Each separate window hierarchy has a shell widget at the top.

If you have a popup widget that might never be used, or whose characteristics are not known until just before it is popped up, you can create the popup shell and widget just before popping it up, in the callback function or action that pops up the widget. This technique makes the startup time of the application marginally faster, but slows the pop up time the first time the popup is used.

Popups, and menus in particular, will be described in much more detail in Chapter 13, *Menus, Gadgets, and Cascaded Popups*.

Using Widgets

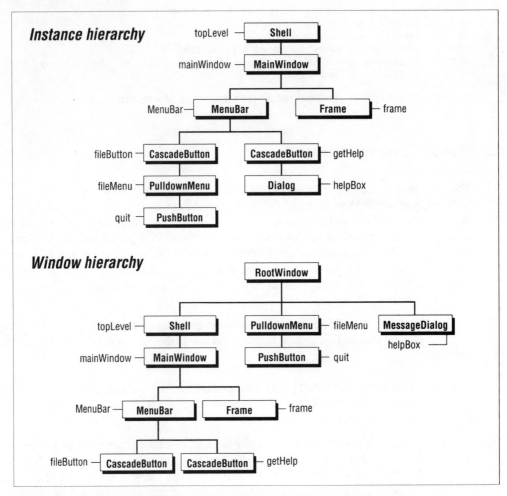

Figure 3-9. The widget instance and X window hierarchies are different only for popups

3.5 More About Callbacks

As you may recall, a callback is a function that your application wants called in response to a certain occurrence in a certain widget. The application simply declares the callback function and then calls XtAddCallback. While Chapter 2, *Introduction to the X Toolkit and Motif*, discussed the concept of callbacks and demonstrated the most common use, it did not completely describe all the useful tricks. You can pass application data to callback functions. You can arrange for more than one callback function to be called (in a particular order) when the callback is triggered, and add and remove functions from this list at will. You can declare callbacks statically using a callback list instead of calling XtAddCallback or XtAdd-Callbacks.

3.5.1 Passing Data to Callback Functions

A callback function is called with three arguments: `widget`, `client_data`, and `call_data`.

The `widget` argument is necessary if you have registered the same callback function for two widgets, and you need to know which widget called the function. It also may be used in routine ways, such as for the argument of macros. The application determines the use of `client_data`, whereas the widget determines the use of `call_data`.

3.5.1.1 The client_data Argument

You may pass a single piece of data as the `client_data` argument, or pass a pointer to a structure containing several pieces of data. You may ask, "Why bother with passing data to a callback when I can just declare a global variable?" For one thing, it is a general principle of good C coding to use a global variable only where the variable is needed in several functions and the arguments would otherwise prove unwieldy. Secondly, using the `client_data` argument makes clear the purpose of your variable, whereas it is difficult to trace where a global variable is set or referenced. However, if you find it necessary to change the `client_data` argument in a number of functions in the application, you will need a global variable anyway, and there is nothing that says you must use `client_data` (but be sure to document what you are doing!).

Example 3-8 demonstrates how to pass a single piece of data into a callback function.

Example 3-8. Passing a single value to a callback function

```
/*ARGSUSED*/
void PressMe(w, client_data, call_data)
Widget w;
XtPointer client_data, call_data;
{
    fprintf(stderr, "%s\n", client_data);
}

main(argc, argv)
int argc;
char **argv;
{
    Widget pressme;
    .
    .

    /* XtAppInitialize, create pressme widget */
    .
    .

    /* last argument is client_data */
    XtAddCallback(pressme, XmNactivateCallback, PressMe, "Thanks");
    .
    .
}
```

Using Widgets

Example 3-9 demonstrates passing a pointer to a structure into a callback function. `XtPointer` is a generic pointer type with an implementation-dependent definition. It is used just like the standard C-type `caddr_t`.

Example 3-9. Passing a pointer to a structure to a callback function

```
typedef struct {
    String name;
    String street;
    String city;
} app_stuff;

/*ARGSUSED*/
void PressMe(w, client_data, call_data)
Widget w;
XtPointer client_data;    /* to be cast to app_stuff */
XtPointer call_data;
{
    /* cast required in ANSI C */
    app_stuff *address = (app_stuff) client_data;

    fprintf(stderr, "%s\n%s\n%s\n", address->name, address->street,
            address->city);
}

main(argc, argv)
int argc;
char **argv;
{
    XtAppContext app_context;
    Widget box, quit, pressme, topLevel;

    static app_stuff stuff = {
        "John Doe",
        "1776 Constitution Way",
        "Philadelphia, PA 01029"
    };
        .
        .
        .

    /* XtVaAppInitialize, create pressme widget */
        .
        .

    XtAddCallback(pressme, XmNactivateCallback, PressMe, &stuff);
        .
        .
        .
}
```

Note that two coding conventions are required by ANSI C and should be followed, even though many compilers will not complain if they are not used. The first is that all three arguments of the callback must be declared, even if the trailing ones are not used. Many compilers will work fine if unused trailing arguments are omitted from the definition of the callback function. The second is that many compilers will automatically cast `XtPointer` to the type you want if you declare the callback function arguments using that type. The cast on the first line of the `PressMe` callback is required by ANSI C. Example 3-10 shows a definition of the above callback function that works on many compilers but is not ANSI C conformant. Compare Example 3-10 with Example 3-9.

Example 3-10. ANSI non-conformant callback function definition

```
/*ARGSUSED*/
void PressMe(w, address /* call_data omitted */)
Widget w;
app_stuff *address;        /* ANSI non-conformant cast */
/* third arg omitted - ANSI non-conformant */
{
    fprintf(stderr, "%s\n%s\n%s\n", address->name, address->street,
}
```

3.5.1.2 The call_data Argument

The *call_data* argument is passed in to the callback function from the widget itself. This argument's value is described in the documentation for the widget class unless it is not used. In the Motif widgets, this argument is usually a structure named after the widget that is performing the callback. For example, the structure passed by the PushButton widget is XmPushButtonCallbackStruct. Example 3-11 shows this structure.

Example 3-11. The XmPushButtonCallbackStruct structure

```
typedef struct {
    int     reason;
    XEvent  *event;
    int     click_count;
} XmPushButtonCallbackStruct;
```

Every Motif callback structure contains reason and event fields. Remember that widgets often have several callback resources. The reason field tells you which callback resource was triggered. For example, the PushButton widget has three callback resources, each of which has a different reason value:

- XmNactivateCallback, a commonly used resource, triggered when the user presses and releases the first mouse button on the PushButton. The callback function invoked is passed a call_data structure with the reason field set to XmCR_ACTIVATE.

- XmNarmCallback resource, which is triggered when the first mouse button is pressed and held on the PushButton. The callback function invoked is passed a call_data structure with the reason field set to XmCR_ARM.

- XmNdisarmCallback resource, which is triggered when the first mouse button is released outside the PushButton. The callback function invoked is passed a call_data structure with the reason field set to XmCR_DISARM.

Application callback functions rarely have to read the reason field since separate functions are usually registered for the different callback resources. In other words, an application that registers callback functions for all three of PushButton's callback resources would not need to use the reason field in any of the callback functions unless it registered the same function for two or more of the callbacks.

Using Widgets

Most callback functions don't use the `event` field passed to the callback function either, but it is potentially useful, since it contains a lot of data about the user event that triggered the callback. If a button press or release triggered the callback, this event structure will be an `XButtonEvent` structure. This structure can be passed to `XmMenuPosition` to position a menu created with `XmCreatePopupMenu`, as will be described in Chapter 13, *Menus, Gadgets, and Cascaded Popups*. If the triggering event was a key press or release, an `XKeyEvent` would be passed. In some cases it may be useful to process this event to determine which key was pressed. Remember that due to Motif's keyboard interface, most callback functions can be invoked by either a keyboard or a mouse command. When this is the case, your callback function must be written so that it can handle either type of event.

Other widget sets do not use the `call_data` argument as heavily as Motif. For example, the Athena Widgets rarely use it at all.

3.5.2 Callback Lists

You may register any number of callback functions for a single widget callback resource. In other words, when a callback is triggered by a user event, all the functions in the current callback list for that callback for that widget instance will be called, one at a time, in the specified order. Multiple callback functions are not needed in many applications, but can be useful if applied creatively.

Remember that most widgets also have more than one callback list, each triggered by a different occurrence. What we are talking about here is that you can register a series of functions to be called in response to one occurrence.

Let's take an example of how a callback list might be used. Perhaps you have the functions *A*, *B*, and *C*, and you need to be able to call them separately in response to events in three different PushButton widgets, or to call all of them in order in response to events in a fourth PushButton widget. This fourth PushButton widget might have a callback list including the functions *A*, *B*, and *C*. While the fourth PushButton widget's code can also be implemented by creating a function *D* that calls *A*, *B*, and *C* and then registering *D* as the callback of the fourth PushButton widget, you can't pass a different piece of data into each routine, and you can't change the order of the functions called by *D*. You can do both easily if *A*, *B*, and *C* are specified in a callback list. The order in which the callback functions are called can be changed by removing them from the list (using `XtRemoveCallback` or `XtRemove-Callbacks`), and then adding them in a different order. You can also call the same function more than once in a callback list.

NOTE

Never use `XtRemoveAllCallbacks` when using the Motif widget set. Motif adds its own callback functions to many of the widgets, and it depends on these functions to operate properly.

One way to add more than one callback function is to call XtAddCallback more than once. Another way is to call XtAddCallbacks, which takes an XtCallbackRec array as an argument. This array is usually initialized at compile time, as shown in Example 3-12. The final NULL, NULL entry terminates the list. (This particular list registers the functions do_A and then_B, and passes them both 0 as *client_data*.)

Example 3-12. Initializing a callback list

```
XtCallbackRec quit_callback_list[]={
    {do_A, 0},
    {then_B, 0},
    {(XtCallbackProc) NULL, (XtPointer) NULL}
};
```

This form of XtCallbackRec list can also be used to replace a callback list with XtSet-Values (but not to *get* a callback list, because Xt compiles the list into an internal form). An XtCallbackRec list can also be used to register one or more callbacks when creating a widget.

3.6 Application Resources

You already know that widgets declare resources that can be configured through the resource mechanism. In addition, the application itself may have variables that it wants the user to be able to configure from the resource databases, even though these variables have nothing to do with widgets. These are called *application resources.*

Application resources are just like widget resources except that they apply to application code, not to the widgets it creates.

There are three steps for adding application resources. You must:

1. Create an application data structure containing the variables to be set via the resource mechanism.

2. Create a resource table defining the type and default value for each variable.

3. Call XtGetApplicationResources with pointers to the application data structure and resource table as arguments. When this function returns, the application data structure will contain the current settings from the resource databases.

To demonstrate how to get application resources, we will jump ahead and describe a portion of the code for the *xbitmap4* bitmap editor example described in Chapter 4, *An Example Application*. Because this application draws into a widget using Xlib, it needs two colors with which to draw. The bitmap editor also allows the user to specify the dimensions of the bitmap in cells, and the size of each cell in pixels. And, for general utility, it includes a debug flag that can be set in a resource file to invoke or ignore debugging code without recompiling.

3.6.1 The Application Data Structure

The structure type that contains all the application variables to be set through resources is commonly called `AppData`. Once this structure type is declared, memory can be allocated for a structure called `app_data`. Example 3-13 shows the code that defines the structure type and then allocates memory for the actual structure.

Example 3-13. xbitmap: getting application resources

```
typedef struct {
    Pixel copy_fg;
    Pixel copy_bg;
    int pixmap_width_in_cells;
    int pixmap_height_in_cells;
    int cell_size_in_pixels;
    Boolean debug;
} AppData;

AppData app_data;
```

As usual in C, the members of the `app_data` structure will be referenced throughout the application code using the dot format. For example, the value of the `debug` field of `app_data` will be referenced with `app_data.debug`.

3.6.2 The Resource List

The resource list looks complicated, but it is easy to understand and even easier to write because it conforms to a consistent pattern. Each field in the application data structure has an entry in the resource list. Each resource entry in turn has seven fields, which describe the name of the resource, its type and default value, and various other information.

The resource list controls Xt's value conversion facilities. Since user resources are always strings, and application data structure fields can be any type, a conversion may have to take place. Xt has built-in converters to convert from string to most common types needed by applications. These types are called *representation types* by Xt, and they are indicated by constants starting with `XmR` in Motif, or `XtR` in standard Xt. The representation type of a string (`char *`) is `XmRString`. A Motif compound string is `XmRXmString`. You control the conversion simply by specifying a resource as a certain representation type in the resource list.

It is possible to represent the same value in several different representation types. For example, a color may be represented as an ASCII color name such as "blue," as a structure containing Red, Green, and Blue values, or as a pixel value (an index into a colormap). Also note that a representation type is different from a C-Language type. It is also possible for two different representations of something to both use the same C-Language type. For example, two hypothetical representation types might be `XtRInch` and `XtRMeter`. Both represent distances and both would probably be integers or floating point numbers, but each would have a different value for the same distance.

See Chapter 10, *Resource Management and Type Conversion*, for a description of the standard representation types, as well as information on how to write your own converter routine.

Example 3-14 shows the resource list for *xbitmap4*, followed by a description of each of the fields in each entry.

Example 3-14. The resource list for xbitmap4

```
/*
 * The following could be placed in a "xbitmap.h" file.
 */
#define XtNdebug "debug"
#define XtCDebug "Debug"
#define XtNpixmapWidthInCells "pixmapWidthInCells"
#define XtCPixmapWidthInCells "PixmapWidthInCells"
#define XtNpixmapHeightInCells "pixmapHeightInCells"
#define XtCPixmapHeightInCells "PixmapHeightInCells"
#define XtNcellSizeInPixels "cellSizeInPixels"
#define XtCCellSizeInPixels "CellSizeInPixels"

static XtResource resources[] = {
    {
        XtNforeground,
        XtCForeground,
        XtRPixel,
        sizeof(Pixel),
        XtOffsetOf(AppData, copy_fg),
        XtRString,
        XtDefaultForeground
    },
    {
        XtNbackground,
        XtCBackground,
        XtRPixel,
        sizeof(Pixel),
        XtOffsetOf(AppData, copy_bg),
        XtRString,
        XtDefaultBackground
    },
    {
        XtNpixmapWidthInCells,
        XtCPixmapWidthInCells,
        XtRInt,
        sizeof(int),
        XtOffsetOf(AppData, pixmap_width_in_cells),
        XtRImmediate,
        (XtPointer) 32,
    },
    {
        XtNpixmapHeightInCells,
        XtCPixmapHeightInCells,
        XtRInt,
        sizeof(int),
        XtOffsetOf(AppData, pixmap_height_in_cells),
        XtRImmediate,
        (XtPointer) 32,
    },
```

Example 3-14. The resource list for xbitmap4 (continued)

```
    {
        XtNcellSizeInPixels,
        XtCCellSizeInPixels,
        XtRInt,
        sizeof(int),
        XtOffsetOf(AppData, cell_size_in_pixels),
        XtRImmediate,
        (XtPointer) 30,
    },
    {

        XtNdebug,
        XtCDebug,
        XtRBoolean,
        sizeof(Boolean),
        XtOffsetOf(AppData, debug),
        XtRImmediate,
        (XtPointer) False,
    },
};
```

A resource list entry has the following fields:

- The first two fields of each entry are the name and class of the resource; both strings. These are specified as symbolic constants to improve compile-time checking, and should be selected from *<Xm/Xm.h>* if any there have an appropriate name, or they can be defined in your application's own include file. For the debug resource entry, the resource name and class strings would be "debug" and "Debug", respectively defined in the application's include file as XtNdebug and XtCDebug. Note that in this case we have chosen to spell the symbols XtN instead of XmN. This is just to highlight the fact that these are not built-in Motif symbols. You can use XtN, XmN, or your own prefix.

- The third field is the representation type. A representation type is a symbolic constant, beginning with XtR or XmR, that defines the data type of a resource. Because user resource specifications are always in the form of strings while the actual resources may be of any type, Xt uses resource converters to convert the string representation to the actual target type. If necessary, you can define your own representation type in your application include file, but you will also have to provide Xt with a way to convert from string to this type with a type converter function, as described in Chapter 10, *Resource Management and Type Conversion*. Table 3-1 lists the correspondence between some of the representation types defined in *<Xm/Xm.h>* and actual C data types and structures.

- The fourth field, the size of the representation, is specified using the C macro sizeof with the actual C type as an argument. For example, when the representation type is XmRBoolean, the size field is sizeof(Boolean).

- The fifth field identifies the place in your application's data structure where Xt is to place the converted value. In Example 3-15, the structure is called AppData. This field for the debug resource entry is specified using the XtOffsetOf macro as XtOffsetOf(AppData, debug). Note that the field name in the application data structure is often the same as the resource name, except with all word transitions marked with an underscore instead of a capital letter.

- The sixth field specifies the representation type of the default value (the seventh field). Xt has routines for converting data between types. They are used to translate strings from the resource databases into certain representation types. Therefore, you can specify the default value as a string (among other things) and if the default value is needed Xt will convert it to the representation type you specified in field three. If the representation type in field three is not standard in Xt or Motif, you will have to write the conversion routine that converts from `XmRString` to that representation, as described in Chapter 10, *Resource Management and Type Conversion*. You can also use the special constant `XmRImmediate` here, which indicates that the value in field seven can be used without conversion. Using `XmRImmediate` should lead to faster startup.

- The seventh field is the default value, using the representation type specified in field six. This default value will be set into the application data structure field if there is no setting for this resource in the resource database.

Table 3-1 lists Motif and standard Xt resource types and the C data types they represent.

Table 3-1. Motif Resource Type Strings

Motif Resource Type	Standard Xt Resource Type	Data Type
XmRAcceleratorTable	XtRAcceleratorTable	XtAccelerators
XmRBoolean	XtRBoolean	Boolean
XmRBool	XtRBool	Bool
XmRCallback	XtRCallback	XtCallbackList
XmRColor	XtRColor	XColor
XmRCursor	XtRCursor	Cursor
XmRDimension	XtRDimension	Dimension
XmRDisplay	XtRDisplay	Display*
XmRFile	XtRFile	FILE*
XmRFloat	XtRFloat	float
XmRFont	XtRFont	Font
XmRFontStruct	XtRFontStruct	XFontStruct*
XmRFunction	XtRFunction	(*) ()
XmRInt	XtRInt	int
XmRPixel	XtRPixel	Pixel
XmRPixmap	XtRPixmap	Pixmap
XmRPointer	XtRPointer	XtPointer
XmRPosition	XtRPosition	Position
XmRShort	XtRShort	short
XmRString	XtRString	char*
XmRTranslationTable	XtRTranslationTable	XtTranslations
XmRUnsignedChar	XtRUnsignedChar	unsigned char
XmRWidget	XtRWidget	Widget
XmRWindow	XtRWindow	Window
XmRXmString		XmString

Using Widgets

3.6.3 Getting the Resources

Once the application data structure and resource list are set up, you pass pointers to them to `XtGetApplicationResources`, just after calling `XtAppInitialize`. `XtGet-ApplicationResources` will search the databases for any matching resource settings and set the fields in the application data structure.

The last requirement is that you check the values specified by the user to make sure they are acceptable. Example 3-15 shows these two steps from *xbitmap4*.

Example 3-15. Calling XtGetApplicationResources and checking values

```
    .
    .
    .
AppData app_data;
    .
    .
    .

main(argc, argv)
int argc;
char *argv[];
{
    XtAppContext app_context;
    Widget toplevel, vpane, buttonbox, quit, output;
        .
        .
        .

    /* call XtAppInitialize here */

    XtVaGetApplicationResources(toplevel,
            &app_data,
            resources,
            XtNumber(resources),
            /* varargs list here for making
             * application resources
             * non-user-configurable */
            NULL);          /* terminate varargs list */

    /*
     * We must check the application resource values here.
     * Otherwise, user could supply out of range values.
     * Conversion routines do this automatically, so
     * colors are already checked.
     */
    if ((app_data.pixmap_width_in_cells > MAXBITMAPWIDTH) ||
            (app_data.pixmap_width_in_cells < MINBITMAPWIDTH) ||
            (app_data.pixmap_height_in_cells > MAXBITMAPWIDTH) ||
            (app_data.pixmap_height_in_cells < MINBITMAPWIDTH)) {
        fprintf(stderr, "xbitmap: error in resource settings:",
                "bitmap dimension must be between %d and %d cells\n",
                MINBITMAPWIDTH, MAXBITMAPWIDTH);
        exit(1);
    }

    if ((app_data.cell_size_in_pixels < MINCELLSIZE) ||
```

```
            (app_data.cell_size_in_pixels > MAXCELLSIZE)) {
        fprintf(stderr, "xbitmap: error in resource settings:",
                "cell size must be between %d and %d pixels\n",
                MINCELLSIZE, MAXCELLSIZE);
        exit(1);
    }
    .
    .
    .
}
```

Because Xt automatically converts the user's color specifications (such as "blue") into the form required by X, it warns the user when an unknown color is specified.* Therefore, your code doesn't need to check this kind of validity for values that Xt or Motif converts. However, you may need to check for other kinds of validity of the same values. For example, you may wish to check that two colors are not the same by comparing values after conversion. In this case, only the bitmap dimensions and cell size are checked, since they are critical to the application's operation.

3.7 Command-line Options

You already know that Xt automatically customizes widgets according to the resource database, but this is not the whole story. Users often expect command-line arguments for the most important aspects of an application. By default, XtAppInitialize understands only a minimal set of command-line arguments; more need to be added so that application resources and certain widget resources can be set from the command line.

There is no point, however, in trying to make every widget resource settable from the command line, because that's the purpose of the resource database. You should concentrate on the resources that the user is most likely to want to have different between two simultaneous instances of the application (since it is difficult to arrange this with the resource database).

Before describing how to define your own command-line arguments, we need to describe what command-line arguments XtAppInitialize already handles.

*That is, if the resource in a database file is specified properly, but the value is not, Xt will warn the user. However, if the resource is not specified properly, Xt has no way of knowing that the resource was intended to specify a color, and therefore, no message will be issued. For example, "*background: grein" will elicit a warning message because grein is an unknown color, but "*background: green" will not, because the resource identifier is unknown. Unknown resource identifiers are simply ignored, because they could apply to some other widget or even some other application.

3.7.1 Standard Command-line Options

First of all, `XtAppInitialize` recognizes the *-xrm* option for setting any widget or application resource. For example:

```
spike% xhello -xrm '*background: blue'
```

This command-line argument sets all widget resources and application resources that are named background to blue. This option style is awkward. Not only is it long, but *csh* users must quote the string with right-handed single quotes so that the asterisk (*) is not interpreted by the shell.

`XtAppInitialize` also understands some command-line options that were considered so basic that they should be the same for all applications. The above *-xrm* command line can be replaced by:

```
spike% xhello -background blue
```

or:

```
spike% xhello -bg blue
```

`XtAppInitialize` also understands any unique abbreviation of an option name, such as:

```
spike% xhello -backg blue
```

These resources will work with any application written using the X Toolkit—with any widget set. Try the command line above if you have a color screen. If not, try specifying a different font, using the *-fn* or *-font* option.

Table 3-2 lists the complete set of standard options.* Resources starting with a dot rather than an asterisk indicate that that option affects only the application's top-level Shell.

Table 3-2. Standard Command-line Parameters

Option	Resource	Value	Sets
-bg	`*background`	Next argument	Background color
-background	`*background`	Next argument	Background color
-bd	`*borderColor`	Next argument	Border color
-bw	`.borderWidth`	Next argument	Width of border in pixels
-borderwidth	`.borderWidth`	Next argument	Width of border in pixels
-bordercolor	`*borderColor`	Next argument	Color of border
-display	`.display`	Next argument	Server to use
-fg	`*foreground`	Next argument	Foreground color
-fn	`*font`	Next argument	Font name
-font	`*font`	Next argument	Font name

---

*There is no legitimate way for the application to access this parse table, which is necessary to show the user an error in a parameter. Furthermore, this table is in the source for Xt and therefore not available online to some Toolkit users. However, this parse table is not expected to change radically in new releases. Therefore it can probably be safely copied from this document into application code to provide a synopsis of valid options, if desired. Most current applications simply say "This application understands all standard X Toolkit command-line options."

Table 3-2. Standard Command-line Parameters (continued)

Option	Resource	Value	Sets
`-foreground`	`*foreground`	Next argument	Foreground color
`-geometry`	`.geometry`	Next argument	Size and position
`-iconic`	`.iconic`	"on"	Start as an icon
`-name`	`.name`	Next argument	Name of application
`-reverse`	`*reverseVideo`	"on"	Reverse video
`-rv`	`*reverseVideo`	"on"	Reverse video
`+rv`	`*reverseVideo`	"off"	No Reverse Video
`-selectionTimeout`	`.selectionTimeout`	Null	Selection timeout
`-synchronous`	`*synchronous`	"on"	Synchronous debug mode
`+synchronous`	`*synchronous`	"off"	Synchronous debug mode
`-title`	`.title`	Next argument	Title of application
`-xrm`	value of argument	Next argument	Depends on argument

Note that many of these command-line options set the resource of every widget in the application to the same value. A few of them set the resources only of the application's top-level Shell widget.

3.7.2 Defining Your Own Command-line Options

Supplying your own command-line options allows you to simplify the customization of your application. It also allows the user to customize things that are difficult with the resource database (such as setting different values for the same resource in two instances of the application).

You make `XtAppInitialize` understand additional command-line options by initializing a `XrmOptionDescRec` structure (called the *options table*) and passing it as an argument to `XtAppInitialize`. Example 3-16 shows the code that implements command-line options for the application resources added in Example 3-14.

Example 3-16. xbitmap: specifying command-line options

```
/* include files, etc. */
        .
        .
        .
#define MINBITMAPWIDTH   2
#define MAXBITMAPWIDTH   1000
#define MINBITMAPHEIGHT  2
#define MAXBITMAPHEIGHT  1000
#define MINCELLSIZE   4
#define MAXCELLSIZE   100

static XrmOptionDescRec options[] = {
    {"-pw",          "*pixmapWidthInCells",  XrmoptionSepArg, NULL},
    {"-pixmapwidth", "*pixmapWidthInCells",  XrmoptionSepArg, NULL},
    {"-ph",          "*pixmapHeightInCells", XrmoptionSepArg, NULL},
```

Using Widgets

Example 3-16. xbitmap: specifying command-line options (continued)

```
    {"-pixmapheight",  "*pixmapHeightInCells", XrmoptionSepArg, NULL},
    {"-cellsize",      "*cellSizeInPixels",    XrmoptionSepArg, NULL},
    {"-fg",            "*foreground",          XrmoptionSepArg, NULL},
    {"-foreground",    "*foreground",          XrmoptionSepArg, NULL},
    {"-debug",         "*debug",               XrmoptionNoArg, "True"},
};
static void Syntax(argc, argv)
int argc;
char * argv[];
{
    int i;
    static int errs = False;

    /* first argument is program name - skip that */
    for (i = 1; i < argc; i++) {
        if (!errs++) /* do first time through */
            fprintf(stderr, "xbitmap4: command line option unknown:\n");

        fprintf(stderr, "option: %s\n", argv[i]);
    }
    fprintf(stderr, "xbitmap understands all standard Xt\
            command-line options.\n");

    fprintf(stderr,"Additional options are as follows:\n");
    fprintf(stderr,"Option        Valid Range\n");
    fprintf(stderr,"-pw           MINBITMAPWIDTH to\
            MAXBITMAPWIDTH\n");
    fprintf(stderr,"-pixmapwidth  MINBITMAPWIDTH to\
            MAXBITMAPWIDTH\n");
    fprintf(stderr,"-ph           MINBITMAPHEIGHT to\
            MAXBITMAPHEIGHT\n");
    fprintf(stderr,"-pixmapheight MINBITMAPHEIGHT to\
            MAXBITMAPHEIGHT\n");
    fprintf(stderr,"-cellsize     MINCELLSIZE to\
            MAXCELLSIZE\n");
    fprintf(stderr,"-fg           color name\n");
    fprintf(stderr,"-foreground   color name\n");
    fprintf(stderr,"-debug        no value necessary\n");
}
main(argc, argv)
int argc;
char *argv[];
{
    XtAppContext app_context;
    Widget toplevel, vpane, buttonbox, quit, output;
        .
        .
        .

    toplevel = XtVaAppInitialize(&app_context;
            "XBitmap4",
            options,                /* command line option table */
            XtNumber(options),
            &argc,
            argv,
```

Example 3-16. xbitmap: specifying command-line options (continued)

```
            NULL,
            NULL);

    /* XtVaAppInitialize always leaves at least prog name in args */
    if (argc > 1)
        Syntax(argc, argv);
            .
            .
            .

}
```

Each options table entry consists of four fields:

- The option to be searched for on the command line. As with standard command-line options, Xt will automatically accept any unique abbreviation of the option specified here. For example, the option *–pixmapWidthInPixels* will be recognized if typed on the command line as *–pixmapW*. However, if you wanted the option *–pw* to set the same resource, then you would need another entry, since `pw` is not the leading string of `pixmapWidthInPixels`.

- The resource specification. This must identify a widget resource or an application resource, but not provide a value. Since it has the same form as allowed in the resource databases, it may apply to a single widget or to many widgets. If it applies to no widgets, no error message will be issued.

- The argument style. This field is one of seven constants describing how the option is to be interpreted. These constants are described below in Table 3-3.

- The value. This field is the value to be used for the resource if the argument style is `XrmOptionNoArg`. This field is not used otherwise. Note that this value must already be converted to the value expected for the resource (often not a string). You may be able to use Xt's type converter routines explicitly to convert this data to the right type (see Section 10.3.5).

The `enum` constants that specify the various command-line argument styles are as shown in Table 3-3.

Table 3-3. XrmOptionKind: Command-line Option Style Constants

Constant	Meaning
XrmoptionNoArg	Take the value in the `value` field of the options table. For example, this is used for Boolean fields, where the option might be *–debug* and the default value `False`.
XrmoptionIsArg	The flag itself is the value without any additional information. For example, if the option were *–on*, the value would be "on." This constant is infrequently used, because the desired value such as "on" is usually not descriptive enough when used as an option (*–on*).

Constant	Meaning
`XrmoptionStickyArg`	The value is the characters immediately following the option with no white space intervening. This is the style of arguments for some UNIX utilities such as *uucico* where *–sventure* means to call system *venture*.
`XrmoptionSepArg`	The next item after the white space after this flag is the value. For example, *–fg blue* would indicate that "blue" is the value for the resource specified by *–fg*.
`XrmoptionResArg`	The resource name and its value are the next argument in `argv` after the white space after this flag. For example, the flag might be: `-res 'basecalc*background:white';` then the resource name/value pair would be used as is. This form is rarely used because it is equivalent to *–xrm*, and because the C shell requires that special characters such as * be quoted.
`XrmoptionSkipNArgs`	Ignore this option and the next N arguments in `argv`, where N is the value in the last field of this option table entry.
`XrmoptionSkipArg`	Ignore this option and the next argument in `argv`.
`XrmoptionSkipLine`	Ignore this option and the rest of `argv`.

The options table is passed to `XtAppInitialize` as its third argument, and the number of options table entries as the fourth. The `XtNumber` macro is a convenient way to count the number of entries (this is only one of many contexts in which you'll see this macro used).

Note that you *cannot* override the standard options by providing options with the same names in your own parsing table. If you try this, your options with the same names will simply not be set to the values specified on the command line. Instead, the standard options will be set to these values. This was a design decision in Xt, one of the few cases where a user-interface policy is enforced. Uniformity in this basic area was deemed more valuable than flexibility.

Also note that there is no way to instruct Xt to interpret more than one argument format for the same option. For example, you cannot arrange for *–size 3* and *–size3* both to work.

`XtAppInitialize` removes all the arguments it recognizes (including those in your options table) from `argv` and `argc`. If all goes well, only the application name will remain in `argv`, and `argc` will equal one. It is important to check whether there is more than one argument left after `XtAppInitialize` has returned. Command-line options that `Xt-`

AppInitialize doesn't recognize will be left in *argv* and *argc*. This is your chance to catch this error and tell the user.* The Syntax function shown in Example 3-16 demonstrates code that informs the user of the proper syntax and the option that was not understood. (In response to incorrect command-line options, UNIX programs traditionally print only the correct calling sequence. However, you can be even nicer to the user by printing the option or options that were in error, by passing *argv* and *argc* into your Syntax function, as is done in Example 3-16.

Experienced UNIX programmers will note that Xt applications can (but usually don't) use the single-letter command-line arguments mandated by POSIX and the System V Interface Definition. As mentioned earlier, Xt automatically matches any unique abbreviation for any command-line option. For example, by default the *–display* option can be specified as *–d*, but only if you haven't included any other option in the options table that also begins with d. You can define the meaning of single-letter options simply by including them verbatim in the options table. In other words, if you specify that *–d* turns on a debugging resource, Xt will no longer try to match any other, longer option that also begins with *d*.

Note that the *argc* and *argv* arguments of XtAppInitialize are in the same order as in the call to main. This is the opposite order of arrays and array lengths throughout other Motif, Xt and Xlib routine calls. Also note that the address of *argc*, not *argc* itself, is passed to XtAppInitialize. This is so that XtAppInitialize can decrement the count to reflect recognized options. Watch out for these snags.

3.8 Preventing User Customization of Widget Resources

Although user customization is good to a certain degree, some resources need to be hardcoded to make sure that an application will run properly regardless of user configuration. This is particularly true of widget geometry resources and constraints. For example, it is easy to make a mistake with Form widget constraints such that some important widget is hidden behind others.

You prevent user customization of particular resources by setting them in the calls to Xt-VaCreateManagedWidget or XtCreateManagedWidget, using a varargs list or an argument list as was shown in XtVaSetValues and XtSetValues calls in Section 2.5. When you use a Motif widget creation function such as XmCreateMenuBar, the easiest way to hardcode that widget's resources is to follow the creation call with a call to Xt-VaSetValues. This section will review those techniques and show a few more tricks.

When resources are set in the calls to create widgets, the application can still modify these resources any time later using XtVaSetValues or XtSetValues. Therefore, this is hardcoding only from the user's perspective. Also note that Xt will not tell the user that you have hardcoded certain resources—your application documentation should do this.

---

*You can, of course, intentionally treat the arguments remaining after XtAppInitialize as filenames or other pieces of data.

The time to hardcode widget resources is when development of an application is almost finished, because until then the resource settings are still in flux and it is quicker to edit the app-defaults file than it is to recompile the application.

Motif itself prevents user customization of certain resources, because it does not allow them to be set from resource files.* These resources must be set in the code if they are to be set at all. This is unfortunate because these resource settings can't be debugged in the usual way, by modifying the app-defaults files. This leads to time-consuming recompilation.

Selecting which resources to hardcode is something we can't help you with, because there isn't enough experience to go on yet. Some application developers will hardcode almost everything, while others will hardcode almost nothing. Only time will tell where the proper balance lies. For example, there is a tradeoff between hardcoding strings such as "Quit" so that the user can't change them, and setting them in the app-defaults file so that they can be easily changed for operation in a different language.

3.8.1 Using the Varargs Interfaces

Setting widget resources in `XtVaCreateManagedWidget` is the cleanest and most powerful way to do it. You have already seen the style of call shown in Example 3-17, but pay particular attention to the `XtVaTypedArg` entry. This example also shows the special technique required to set a Motif compound string in the code.

Example 3-17. The R4 varargs interface to creating a widget

```
main(argc, argv)
int argc;
char **argv;
{
    XtAppContext app_context;
    Widget topLevel, layout, quit;
    XmString text;
        .
        .
        .
    layout = XtVaCreateManagedWidget("layout", formWidgetClass,
            topLevel, NULL);

    text = XmStringCreateLtoR("Quit", XmSTRING_DEFAULT_CHARSET);

    quit = XtVaCreateManagedWidget("quit", xmPushButtonWidgetClass,
            topLevel,
            XmNwidth, 200,
            XtVaTypedArg,       XmNbackground,
            XmRString,          "red", strlen("red")+1,   /* cont'd */
            XmNsensitivity,     True,
```

---

*Unfortunately, exactly which Motif resources can't be set from resource files is poorly documented. One sure sign is when Motif prints an error message telling you that there is no converter for that resource.

Example 3-17. The R4 varargs interface to creating a widget (continued)

```
              XmNlabelString,          text,
              NULL);
     .
     .
     .
}
```

The standard varargs list entry is a resource name/value pair. The value must be already converted into the type required for that resource (documented on the widget's reference page). XtVaTypedArg (not Xm . . .) is a special symbol used just before a resource name, which, when encountered, indicates that the next four arguments specify a resource that needs to be converted.* In Example 3-17, the value "red" needs to be converted into a pixel value, which is the index to the colormap register that contains the correct RGB values to display on the screen. The argument XmNbackground is the resource to be set. XmRString is the type of the value to be converted. The final two arguments are the pointer to the value (or the pointer to the pointer to the value if not a string) and the size of the value pointed to in bytes. XtVaTypedArg can be used to convert any string that is valid in a resource file but is otherwise difficult to set in the source file. But don't use XtVaTypedArg unnecessarily, since it adds overhead.

The varargs interfaces will also accept an arglist as one item in the list, using the symbol XtVaNestedList as the resource name. XtVaNestedList allows you to create one argument list and pass it to a series of widget creation routines, instead of listing all the same resource settings in each widget creation routine. For more details on this, see Chapter 10, *Resource Management and Type Conversion*.

There is some extra overhead involved in using the varargs interfaces because they massage the arguments into an argument list and call XtCreateWidget, XtCreateManagedWidget, XtSetValues, or XtGetValues. However, the added convenience seems worth it. Furthermore, the XtVaTypedArg feature is not supported in the ArgList style of call (described in the next section).

Unless you use the XtVaTypedArg feature, no diagnostic is printed when you specify a resource value incorrectly in the argument list. Therefore, make sure you specify the resource values correctly, and recognize this as a possible place to begin looking for bugs. (This is another reason to hardcode resources only when the application is almost ready for release. If you do it all at once in a methodical fashion, you are less likely to make mistakes than if you are always adding, subtracting, and changing values in the argument lists.)

NOTE

If you use the varargs style of arguments, but forget to type the Va in the function name, you can get various types of errors. If you specify resources in the call, you will get a core dump at run time, but you can detect the problem with *lint*, which will note the function as having a variable number of arguments. If

---

*Note that XtVaTypedArg does not begin with Xm. It is a symbol defined by Xt.

you don't specify resources in the call, the application will work but you will get the message:

```
Warning: argument count > 0 on NULL argument list
```

3.8.2 Using the Argument List Interfaces

Widget resources can also be hardcoded by creating an argument list containing the resources to be set and their values, and passing it to `XtCreateManagedWidget`. This method of setting resources is less convenient that the varargs technique just described, but it was the only way until R4, and therefore many existing applications use it.

An *argument list* is just an array of `Arg` structures, of the same type as you set up to call `XtSetValues` or `XtGetValues`. Once set, this array is used as an argument to `XtCreateManagedWidget`. Each `Arg` structure contains a resource/value pair. Attributes specified here override the same ones specified from the command line or from resource databases.

Example 3-18 shows an argument list that hardcodes the sensitivity of a PushButton widget and its callback list. Sensitivity is a good thing to hardcode for PushButton widgets, because if accidentally set by the user it could disable an application.* The callback list cannot be specified by the user anyway; setting it here is just an alternative to calling `XtAddCallback`.

The `XtArgVal` type used in the callback list aids in porting Toolkit programs to different architectures. It allows the system manufacturer to select the type in the `typedef` for `XtArgVal`, so that the application program need not worry about it. The `value` field of the `Arg` structure may be a number or a pointer.

Example 3-18. An argument list

```
Arg quit_args[] = {
    XmNsensitive,        (XtArgVal) True,
    XmNactivateCallback,        (XtArgVal) quit_callback_list,
};
```

An argument list can be used as an argument in the call to create a widget, as shown in Example 3-19.

---

*Sensitivity is a basic resource of all widgets. When set to `True`, the default, a widget accepts input and operates normally. When `False`, a widget displays itself in gray (or otherwise indicates insensitivity) and does not act on user input. The purpose of sensitivity is to allow the application to disable certain commands when they are not valid. If sensitivity were left configurable, the user could turn it off on some widgets and effectively cripple an application. It is hard to imagine the user doing this by accident, but it is not worth taking a gamble.

X Toolkit Intrinsics Programming Manual, Motif Edition

Example 3-19. Using an argument list in widget creation

```
/* define quit_args */

main(argc, argv)
int argc;
char *argv[];
{
    Widget quit, box;

    /* create box */
        .
        .
        .

    quit = XtCreateManagedWidget(
            "quit",                    /* widget name */
            xmPushButtonWidgetClass,    /* widget class */
            box,                       /* parent widget*/
            quit_args,                 /* argument list*/
            XtNumber(quit_args)        /* arglist size */
            );
        .
        .
        .
}
```

Note the use of the XtNumber macro to calculate how many arguments there are in the statically initialized argument list. This macro eliminates the need to keep track of the number of resources you have set.

Note also that the value field in the argument list must be in the correct representation type for that resource, which is often not a string. You may need to call XtConvertAndStore to arrive at the right representation of the data to be placed in the argument list. For details on calling XtConvertAndStore, see Chapter 10, *Resource Management and Type Conversion*. An easier way to do this is to use the XtVaTypedArg feature supported by the varargs interfaces.

As mentioned earlier, unless you invoke a converter, no diagnostic is printed when you specify a resource value incorrectly in the argument list. Therefore, make sure you specify these correctly.

3.8.2.1 Another Way to Set Arguments

Instead of creating the argument list as a static array, you can allocate storage at run time and use the XtSetArg macro to set values into the storage. This is the coding style favored in Motif 1.0 applications.

XtSetArg sets a single argument to a resource identifying a constant and a value. Example 3-20 shows the code that would create an argument list with the same contents as the one created in Example 3-18 above. Some people prefer this technique because it places the argument list setting closer to the XtCreateWidget call, making the code easier to read. (However, it is still more difficult to read than when using the varargs interfaces.)

Example 3-20. Setting the argument list with XtSetArg

```
int i;
Arg args[10];
/* XtAppInitialize may be called before or after the XtSetArg calls */
i = 0;
XtSetArg(args[i], XmNactivateCallback, (XtArgVal)
        quit_callback_list); i++;
XtSetArg(args[i], XmNsensitive, (XtArgVal) True); i++;

banner = XtCreateManagedWidget(
        banner,                     /* widget name */
        xmPushButtonWidgetClass,    /* widget class from Label.h */
        toplevel,                   /* parent widget */
        args,                       /* argument list */
        i);                         /* arg list size from XtSetArg counter */
```

Notice that i is used as the number of arguments in the XtCreateManagedWidget call, *not* XtNumber. XtNumber would in this case return the value 10, the total length of the Arg array.

Remember that i must be incremented outside the macro, because XtSetArg references its first argument twice. The following code will not work because XtNresource2 will be set into widget_args[2] instead of widget_args[1], as desired. Example 3-21 shows you how *not* to use XtSetArg:

Example 3-21. Incorrectly setting the argument list with XtSetArg

```
Arg arg[10];
int num_args;
/* This example will NOT work correctly! */
num_args = 0;
/* The next two lines are wrong! */
XtSetArg(args[num_args++], XtNresource1, (XtArgVal) 10);
XtSetArg(args[num_args++], XtNresource2, (XtArgVal) 40);
          .
          .
          .
```

The XtSetArg method has three advantages over static initialization:

- It moves the code that sets the argument list closer to where it is really used in the call to create a widget.

- It allows run-time value modification using the same method.

- The same storage can be used for multiple argument lists.

The disadvantages of the XtSetArg method are as follows:

- It performs all assignments at run time, which slows startup slightly.

- It is possible to try to set more arguments than space has been allocated for, leading to a core dump.

- It is possible to misplace the counter increment, leading to improper operation.

- An argument list and a counter variable must be kept until the call to create the widget instance; the static method requires keeping only the argument list.

- It may waste a small amount of storage since the argument list array is usually initialized larger than the required size.

- Lots of XtSetArg calls make for ugly code.

As you can see, these differences are mostly subjective. However, the varargs interfaces have many of the advantages of the XtSetArg method, but none of its disadvantages. The only disadvantage of the varargs interfaces is the slight overhead they add. You may use whichever method you prefer, or some combination.

3.8.2.2 Merging Argument Lists

XtMergeArgLists takes two argument lists and counts all arguments, allocates the storage for a single argument list big enough to hold them, and stores all the entries from both in the returned argument list. It does not remove duplicate entries. The calling application can use XtNumber to determine the resulting argument count (or can add the original counts).

3.9 More About Application Contexts

We have used application contexts in the examples so far, but not discussed what they really are or what they are for.

An application context is a structure maintained by Xt that stores all the data associated with the application, including the functions registered by the application and other information about the application. Primarily, its purpose is to allow Xt applications to run without modification on certain operating systems that do not have a separate address space for each process. These systems include the Xerox Cedar environment, the Symbolics Genera environment, and the TI Explorer system. Although systems like this are not common, the goal of all X software in C is to be portable to any system that supports C.*

Why then is the XtAppContext exposed in the programming interface? It is possible, though difficult, to create more than one application context within a single program. This is rarely done and its implications are complex, so we will reserve discussion of it until Section 14.6.

The important thing to remember is that for maximum portability, you need to use the versions of routines that begin with XtApp instead of those that don't. For instance, use Xt-

`AppInitialize` instead of `XtInitialize` and `XtAppMainLoop`, not `XtMain-Loop`.

Of the routines you have seen so far in this book, only `XtVaAppInitialize`, `XtApp-Initialize`, `XtAppMainLoop`, and `XtAppAddActions` use explicit application contexts. The complete list of routines that have equivalents is presented in Section 14.6.

Throughout this book we will continue to use the routines that use the explicit application context.

4

An Example Application

This chapter describes a complete application, in several iterations. First, it shows a simple version of the program, a bitmap editor, as it would be written assuming the existence of a BitmapEdit widget (which is actually developed in Chapter 6, Inside a Widget). Then, two refined versions are developed, each demonstrating additional Toolkit programming techniques. Finally, the same application is shown as it would be written if the bitmap editor were implemented in an application window rather than with the BitmapEdit widget.

In This Chapter:

4
An Example Application

Enough of these trivial programs! Now for an (almost) real application. This chapter describes the development of a bitmap editor. Although it is simple, it can be easily extended to be quite powerful without any new techniques.

We will show several versions of *xbitmap*, beginning with a simple version that assumes the existence of a BitmapEdit widget (which will actually be developed in Chapter 6, *Inside a Widget*, and Chapter 7, *Basic Widget Methods*). Subsequent versions add two widgets that display the bitmap in small scale (one normal, one reverse video), and finally implement the same application without the use of the specialized BitmapEdit widget.

These examples will demonstrate the techniques described in Chapter 2, *Introduction to the X Toolkit and Motif*, and Chapter 3, *More Techniques for Using Widgets*, as they would appear in a real application, and will bring up a number of new topics:

• The initial version introduces the bitmap editor application, and demonstrates the way the application can access the data within a widget using a public function defined by the widget class.

• The second version demonstrates two ways of adding the small-scale bitmaps, one using a standard widget and one drawing into a Core widget from the application. This allows us to introduce actions and translations, another way to link widgets with application code.

• The third version does not use the BitmapEdit widget, but instead implements its features by drawing into a Primitive widget. This demonstrates one way to prototype features and prepare to write your own widget. It also allows us to describe the code necessary to implement the bitmap editor so that you will already understand this code when you see it in the internal framework of a widget described in Chapter 6 and Chapter 7.

Many applications have at least one custom window for which no existing widget will suffice. This chapter demonstrates that there are several ways to implement such a window, and describes the tradeoffs between the different options. Many features can be added from the application code by building on a DrawingArea widget, creating a Core or Primitive widget to draw into, or by creating a custom widget. By the end of Chapters 6 and 7, you will have seen how to implement this application entirely with existing widgets and application code, how to implement it using custom widgets, and how to implement a mixture of the two.

4.1 xbitmap1: Bitmap Editor Using a BitmapEdit Widget

The screen appearance of *xbitmap1* is shown in Figure 4-1. As usual, it is a good idea to compile and run each example as it is discussed.*

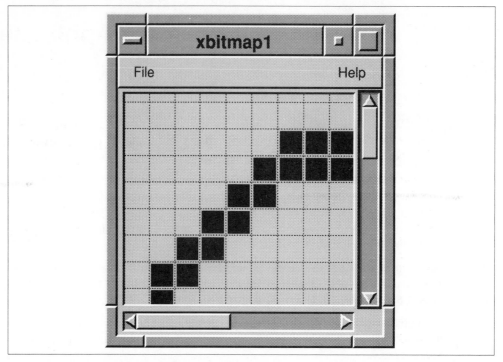

Figure 4-1. xbitmap1: how it looks on the screen

The BitmapEdit widget lets you set bits in the visible bitmap by clicking the first pointer button or dragging the pointer with the first button held down, lets you erase bits using the second button, or lets you toggle bits using the third button. The File menu contains a Print button which simply prints on the standard output an array of ones and zeroes representing the set and unset bits in the bitmap. (Code to read and write standard X11 bitmap files is added in a later version.) The File menu also contains a Quit button.

xbitmap1 is implemented by adding a small amount of code to *xmainwindow*, described in Chapter 3, *More Techniques for Using Widgets*. We replaced the Frame widget with a BitmapEdit widget, and added the Print button to the menu. Of course, a callback for the print button also has to be added.

The code for *xbitmap1* is shown in Example 4-1. The only new technique shown in this example is the use of the public function `BitmapEditGetArray` defined by the Bitmap-Edit widget. `BitmapEditGetArray` gets a character array which represents the contents

---

*How to get and compile the example source code is described in the Preface and Section 2.6.2.2.

of the bitmap being edited, and the dimensions of the bitmap. This information is necessary for the application to print out the bitmap (or write it to a file). Although these values are widget resources that can be queried with XtGetValues, this function makes it more convenient. Several Motif widgets also provide public functions to make it more convenient to set or get resources or manipulate internal widget data. All Motif public functions begin with Xm.

Example 4-1. xbitmap1: complete code

```
/*
 *   xbitmap1.c - bitmap in main window with help and quit
 */

/*  So that we can use fprintf: */
#include <stdio.h>

/* Standard Toolkit include files: */
#include <Xm/Xm.h>

/* Public include files for widgets used in this file.  */
#include <Xm/PushBG.h>    /* push button gadget */
#include <Xm/PushB.h>     /* push button */
#include <Xm/MainW.h>     /* main window */
#include <Xm/MessageB.h>  /* message box */
#include <Xm/CascadeB.h>  /* cascade button */

#include "BitmapEdit.h"          # include <Xm/RowColumn.h>

/*
 * The printout routine prints an array of 1s and 0s representing the
 * contents of the bitmap.  This data can be processed into any
 * desired form, including standard X11 bitmap file format.
 */
/* ARGSUSED */
static void
PrintOut(widget, client_data, call_data)
Widget widget;
XtPointer client_data;   /* cast to bigBitmap */
XtPointer call_data;     /* unused */
{
    Widget bigBitmap = (Widget) client_data;
    int x, y;
    int width_in_cells, height_in_cells;
    char *cell;

    cell = BitmapEditGetArray(bigBitmap, &width_in_cells,
            &height_in_cells);

    (void) putchar('\n');
    for (y = 0; y < height_in_cells; y++) {
        for (x = 0; x < width_in_cells; x++)
            (void) putchar(cell[x + y * width_in_cells] ? '1' : '0');
        (void) putchar('\n');
    }
    (void) putchar('\n');
}
/*
 * callback to pop up help dialog widget
 */
```

Example 4-1. xbitmap1: complete code (continued)

```
/*ARGSUSED*/
void ShowHelp(w, client_data, call_data)
Widget w;
XtPointer client_data;
XtPointer call_data;
{
    Widget dialog = (Widget) client_data;
    XtManageChild(dialog);
}
/*
 * quit button callback function
 */
/*ARGSUSED*/
void Quit(w, client_data, call_data)
Widget w;
XtPointer client_data, call_data;
{
    exit(0);
}

main(argc, argv)
int argc;
char **argv;
{
    XtAppContext app_context;
    Widget topLevel, mainWindow, menuBar;
    Widget fileButton, fileMenu, quit, getHelp, helpBox;
    Widget temp;
    Widget bigBitmap, output;

    /* never call a Widget variable "exit"! */
    extern exit();
    static XrmOptionDescRec table[] = {
        {"-pw",           "*pixmapWidthInCells",   XrmoptionSepArg, NULL},
        {"-pixmapwidth",  "*pixmapWidthInCells",   XrmoptionSepArg, NULL},
        {"-ph",           "*pixmapHeightInCells",  XrmoptionSepArg, NULL},
        {"-pixmapheight", "*pixmapHeightInCells",  XrmoptionSepArg, NULL},
        {"-cellsize",     "*cellSizeInPixels",     XrmoptionSepArg, NULL},
    };

    topLevel = XtVaAppInitialize( &app_context, "XBitmap1",
            table, XtNumber(table), &argc, argv, NULL, NULL);

    /* create main window */
    mainWindow = XtVaCreateManagedWidget( "mainWindow",
            xmMainWindowWidgetClass, topLevel, NULL);

    /* create menu bar along top inside of main window */
    menuBar = XmCreateMenuBar( mainWindow, "menuBar",
            NULL, 0);
    XtManageChild(menuBar);

    bigBitmap = XtVaCreateManagedWidget("bigBitmap",
            bitmapEditWidgetClass, mainWindow,
            NULL);

    /*  Set MainWindow areas and add tab groups */
```

Example 4-1. xbitmap1: complete code (continued)

```
XmMainWindowSetAreas (mainWindow, menuBar, NULL, NULL, NULL,
        bigBitmap);

/*
 *   CREATE FILE MENU AND CHILDREN
 */

/* create button that will pop up the menu */
fileButton = XtVaCreateManagedWidget ("fileButton",
        xmCascadeButtonWidgetClass, menuBar, NULL);

/* create menu (really Shell widget-RowColumn widget combo) */
fileMenu = XmCreatePulldownMenu( menuBar,
        "fileMenu", NULL, 0);

/* create the quit button up in the menu */
quit = XtVaCreateManagedWidget( "quit",
        xmPushButtonWidgetClass, fileMenu, NULL);

/*
 * Specify which menu fileButton will pop up.
 */
XtVaSetValues(fileButton,
        XmNsubMenuId, fileMenu,
        NULL);

/* arrange for quit button to call function that exits. */
XtAddCallback(quit, XmNactivateCallback, Quit, 0);

/*
 *   CREATE BUTTON TO OUTPUT BITMAP
 */

/* create button that will pop up the menu */
output = XtVaCreateManagedWidget( "output",
        xmPushButtonGadgetClass, fileMenu, NULL);

XtAddCallback(output, XmNactivateCallback, PrintOut, bigBitmap);

/*
 *   CREATE HELP BUTTON AND BOX
 */

/* create button that will bring up help popup */
getHelp = XtVaCreateManagedWidget( "getHelp",
        xmCascadeButtonWidgetClass, menuBar, NULL);

/* tell menuBar which is the help button
 * (will be specially positioned. */
XtVaSetValues(menuBar,
        XmNmenuHelpWidget, getHelp,
        NULL);

/* create popup that will contain help */
helpBox = XmCreateMessageDialog( getHelp,
        "helpBox", NULL, 0);

temp = XmMessageBoxGetChild (helpBox, XmDIALOG_CANCEL_BUTTON);
XtUnmanageChild (temp);
temp = XmMessageBoxGetChild (helpBox, XmDIALOG_HELP_BUTTON);
XtUnmanageChild (temp);
```

Example 4-1. xbitmap1: complete code (continued)

```
    /* arrange for getHelp button to pop up helpBox */
    XtAddCallback(getHelp, XmNactivateCallback, ShowHelp, helpBox);

    XtRealizeWidget(topLevel);

    XtAppMainLoop(app_context);
}
```

You should recognize the command-line options table as the one described in Section 3.7.2. If there is anything you don't understand in Example 4-1, review Chapter 3, *More Techniques for Using Widgets*.

Adding a Print button to the menu is a simple matter of creating another PushButton as a child of `fileMenu`. In this case, for purpose of demonstration, we added a PushButton-Gadget instead. When you run the application, you will notice that the PushButton (labeled Quit) and the PushButtonGadget (labeled Print Array) look and operate identically. The main difference between them is that the gadget shares the colors of its parent, and its user response is fixed, not individually customizable. These limitations are acceptable in most menus. The advantage of using a gadget is that performance should be better (though not noticeably so with only one gadget). In general, you should use gadgets unless there is a good reason not to.

The `Printout` callback function gets the array of ones and zeroes from the BitmapEdit widget and prints them to the standard output. Some widget public functions like `Bitmap-EditGetArray` are provided simply because they are more convenient to use than calling `XtSetValues` or `XtGetValues`. Others are supplied by a widget class that wants certain data to be readable or writable by the application, but for some reason does not want the data both readable *and* writable as would be the case if it were a resource. Sometimes a widget class has features that it wants controllable from the application but never user-customizable (because they are meaningless at startup, for example), and therefore it provides a function for setting them.

4.1.1 XBitmap1 App-defaults File

Example 4-2 shows the app-defaults file for *xbitmap1*. This app-defaults file is identical to *XMainWindow* with the addition of resource settings to set an appropriate help message, the label Print Array for the new menu button, the size in cells of the bitmap, and the size in pixels of each cell in the bitmap.

Example 4-2. XBitmap1: app-defaults file

```
! BitmapEdit resources
*cellSizeInPixels:      30
*pixmapWidthInCells:    30
*pixmapHeightInCells:   30
! fonts
*fontList:      variable
! strings
*getHelp.labelString:      Help
*quit.labelString:      Quit
```

Example 4-2. XBitmap1: app-defaults file (continued)

```
*output.labelString:     Print Array
*fileButton.labelString:     File
!
*helpBox.messageString:  To set bits, press or drag\n\
the first mouse button.\n\
To clear bits, use the second mouse button.\n\
To toggle bits, use the third mouse button.
! The following used if the window manager titles the dialog:
! mwm does, twm doesn't
*helpBox.dialogTitle:    Help
! Turn on scrollbars
*XmMainWindow.scrollingPolicy:    XmAUTOMATIC
*XmMainWindow.width:     300
*XmMainWindow.height:    300
```

Note that by default the MainWindow will make itself big enough for only a few bitmap cells to be visible. The resource settings for the width and height of MainWindow make sure that the application has a reasonable initial size.

4.2 xbitmap2: Adding Graphics to Display the Bitmap

In addition to displaying the bitmap in blown-up, editable form, a bitmap editor should display the bitmap in true scale, how the bitmap really looks when displayed on the screen. It is customary to present this bitmap in both normal and reverse video, and update it every time the user toggles a cell in the enlarged bitmap. Figure 4-2 shows the appearance of the application with this feature added.*

There are three ways to implement the small pixmap widgets. (All of them would look the same to the user.) One approach is to use the Label widget, which can display a pixmap instead of a string. However, it is then difficult to make the Label widget redraw the pixmap each time a cell is toggled. This is difficult because we are changing the contents of the pixmap (by drawing into it) without the Label widget's knowledge; therefore the widget does not know to redraw itself. The only obvious way to tell Label to redraw is to clear the widget's window; this generates an Expose event and forces the widget to redraw itself. However, this results in a flashing effect that is unacceptable. You can avoid flashing by synthesizing an Expose event (creating an XExposeEvent structure and filling it with values) and sending it to the Label widget using XSendEvent. This is a bit of a kludge but it works. If Label provided a public function called XmLabelRedrawPixmap, we could more cleanly correct the flashing bug. Although adding this function to the widget code would be easy, we could no longer call the remaining widget class Label; we would be creating a new widget class.

---

*You may notice that we have abandoned the MainWindow used in *xbitmap1*, and instead used PanedWindow as the main window of the application. This is because there is no easy way to fit the two additional small pixmap widgets into the layout scheme of MainWindow. (We originally intended to place the small pixmaps in the menubar, but it can accept only CascadeButton widgets. This restriction is intended to enforce the convention that the menubar is only for menus.)

*Example
Application*

Figure 4-2. xbitmap2: true-scale normal and reverse bitmaps added

Another way to display the small pixmaps is to use a DrawingArea widget, which is an empty widget that provides callbacks in which you can place drawing code. DrawingArea is useful for building simple custom windows that don't have complicated graphics or user input. This technique is implemented in *xbitmap2*.

The third possibility is to draw into a Core or Primitive widget. This would use code very similar to that in *xbitmap2*, but would link the application code with the widget using actions and translations instead of with callbacks. We will be demonstrating this technique in *xbitmap3* as an introduction to translations and actions.

4.2.1 Exposure Strategy

The redrawing technique used in *xbitmap2* works as follows. Two pixmaps (off-screen drawable areas) are created to record the current state of each bitmap. Whenever a cell is toggled, a pixel in each pixmap is changed by drawing into each pixmap. Then each entire pixmap is copied into the corresponding widget. The same routine that copies from pixmap to widget is used whenever the widgets become exposed. Figure 4-3 illustrates this technique.

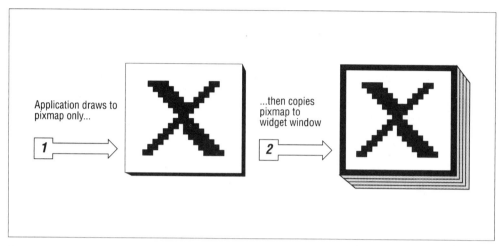

Figure 4-3. Application draws into Pixmap and copies it to widget window

In the actual code, two single-plane pixmaps are created during application startup, the same size as the bitmap displayed in the BitmapEdit widget. Each of the two bitmap display areas is implemented with a DrawingArea widget. DrawingArea provides a callback resource called `XmNexposeCallback`. The application calls `XtAddCallback` to register a function with each of the two widgets for the `XmNexposeCallback` resource. This function, called `RedrawSmallPicture`, copies from the pixmaps into the widget's window. This function takes care of redrawing the widgets whenever exposure occurs, and it also can be called whenever a cell is toggled. The BitmapEdit widget has an `XtNtoggle-Callback` resource. The function registered for this widget and resource draws into the two pixmaps, and then calls `RedrawSmallPicture` to copy the updated pixmap information to the window (alternately, it could draw directly into window instead of copying from the pixmap).

Three new routines are needed: `RedrawSmallPicture`, `SetUpThings`, and `Cell-Toggled`. These three routines are primarily composed of Xlib calls that set up for and perform graphics. The `RedrawSmallPicture` routine copies a pixmap into a widget, `SetUpThings` creates the pixmaps and the GCs (introduced in the next subsection, 4.2.2) needed to draw into these pixmaps, and `CellToggled` is a callback function registered with the BitmapEdit widget that updates the pixmaps whenever a cell is toggled. Code is also added to `main` to create the two DrawingArea widgets and register `RedrawSmall-Picture` with them. We'll show these routines one at a time. Example 4-3 shows the improvements to the `main` routine.

Example 4-3. xbitmap2: implementing small pixmaps with DrawingArea widgets

```
/*
 * Public include files for widgets used in this file.
 */
    .
    .
    .
#include <Xm/DrawingA.h>   /* drawing area */
    .
    .
    .
/* Structure to hold private data (avoids lots of globals). */
struct {
    GC draw_gc, undraw_gc;
    Pixmap normal_bitmap, reverse_bitmap;
    Widget showNormalBitmap, showReverseBitmap;
    String filename;        /* filename to read and write */
    Dimension pixmap_width_in_cells, pixmap_height_in_cells;
} bitmap_stuff;
    .
    .
    .
main(argc, argv)
int argc;
char **argv;
{
    XtAppContext app_context;
    Widget topLevel, mainWindow, menuBar;
    Widget fileButton, fileMenu, quit, getHelp, helpBox;
    Widget temp;
    Widget bigBitmap, output, smallPixmapBox;
    Widget scrolledWin, frame1, frame2;
        .
        .
        .
    /*
     * Size of bitmap must be queried so that small pixmaps
     * of the right size can be created.
     */
    XtVaGetValues(bigBitmap, XtNpixmapWidthInCells,
            &bitmap_stuff.pixmap_width_in_cells,
            XtNpixmapHeightInCells,
            &bitmap_stuff.pixmap_height_in_cells,
            NULL);

    /*
     * Create pixmaps and GCs, draw initial contents into pixmaps */
     */
    SetUpThings(topLevel);
        .
        .
        .
    /* create RowColumn to hold small pixmap widgets */
    smallPixmapBox = XtVaCreateManagedWidget("smallPixmapBox",
            xmRowColumnWidgetClass, mainWindow,
            NULL);

    /* create Frame so small pixmap widget appears in box */
```

```
    frame1 = XtVaCreateManagedWidget("frameNormal",
            xmFrameWidgetClass, smallPixmapBox,
            NULL);

    /* create DrawingArea for small pixmap widget - must set size. */
    bitmap_stuff.showNormalBitmap = XtVaCreateManagedWidget(
            "showNormalBitmap", xmDrawingAreaWidgetClass, frame1,
            XmNwidth, bitmap_stuff.pixmap_width_in_cells,
            XmNheight, bitmap_stuff.pixmap_height_in_cells,
            NULL);

    /* create Frame so small pixmap widget appears in box */
    frame2 = XtVaCreateManagedWidget("frameReverse",
            xmFrameWidgetClass, smallPixmapBox,
            NULL);

    /* create DrawingArea for small pixmap widget - must set size. */
    bitmap_stuff.showReverseBitmap = XtVaCreateManagedWidget(
            "showReverseBitmap", xmDrawingAreaWidgetClass, frame2,
            XmNwidth, bitmap_stuff.pixmap_width_in_cells,
            XmNheight, bitmap_stuff.pixmap_height_in_cells,
            NULL);

    /* register RedrawSmallPicture as the redrawing function */
    XtAddCallback(bitmap_stuff.showNormalBitmap, XmNexposeCallback,
            RedrawSmallPicture, 0);

    XtAddCallback(bitmap_stuff.showReverseBitmap, XmNexposeCallback,
            RedrawSmallPicture, 0);

    /* Register CellToggled to be called whenever a cell is toggled. */
    XtAddCallback(bigBitmap, XtNtoggleCallback, CellToggled, 0);

    XtRealizeWidget(topLevel);

    XtAppMainLoop(app_context);
}
```

The `main` routine registers `RedrawSmallPicture` as the `XmNexposeCallback` function for each DrawingArea widget. It also registers `CellToggled` as the `Xt-NtoggleCallback` for the BitmapEdit widget, to be called whenever a bitmap cell is toggled.

`SetUpThings` uses Xlib calls to create the pixmap that will be used as an off-screen copy of what will be displayed in the DrawingArea widgets. `SetUpThings` also creates GCs that will be used to draw into these pixmaps. `CellToggled` does the drawing, and `RedrawSmallPicture` performs the copying. These routines are shown in the next section, which describes how graphics work in Xt programs.

4.2.2 Graphics from the Application

Drawing in the X Window System is done by creating a *graphics context* (GC) that specifies such things as colors and line widths, and then calling a drawing routine that specifies what shape is to be drawn. These two steps are basic to X and required in programs written in any language with or without a toolkit. For example, the call to draw a line specifies only the start and endpoints of the line. The GC specifies everything else about how the server will actually draw this line.

A GC is a server-side object that must be created by the application. The purpose of the GC is to cache on the server side information about how graphics are to be executed by the server, so that this information doesn't have to be sent over the network with every graphics call. If X did not have GCs, every graphics call would have many arguments and this would waste network time (and be annoying to program). Instead, you create a small number of GCs before drawing (in the startup phase of the application). Each represents a particular color or line style you will need to draw with at some point. You then specify one of these GCs in each call to draw. For example, to draw text and be able to highlight it at will, it is customary to create two GCs, one for drawing in white on black, and one for drawing in black on white (where colors can be substituted for black and white on color screens).

Once created, a GC is referred to by its ID, of type GC. This ID is specified in calls to draw using that GC.

From the application, the Xlib routine XCreateGC is usually used to create GCs. Xt also provides the XtGetGC routine for creating GCs, but it is typically used only inside widget code when there could be many of the same GCs created. XtGetGC is very similar to XCreateGC, except that it arranges for GCs to be shared among widgets (within one application). XtGetGC will be described in Section 7.2.1.

In *xbitmap2*, the SetUpThings routine is responsible for creating two pixmaps that act as off-screen drawing surfaces, and two GCs that will be used to draw and undraw pixels in the pixmaps. Whenever the DrawingArea widgets need to be updated, the pixmaps are copied into the widgets. This is only one possible exposure-handling approach. Another is to draw the required points directly into the DrawingArea widgets each time they need to be updated, keeping a record of the drawn points so that the entire widget can be redrawn in case of exposure.

Example 4-4 shows SetUpThings, which creates pixmap and GCs and then initializes the pixmaps.

Example 4-4. xbitmap2: creating pixmaps and GCs

```
static void
SetUpThings(w)
Widget w;
{
    XGCValues values;

    bitmap_stuff.normal_bitmap = XCreatePixmap(XtDisplay(w),
            RootWindowOfScreen(XtScreen(w)),
            bitmap_stuff.pixmap_width_in_cells,
            bitmap_stuff.pixmap_height_in_cells, 1);
```

Example 4-4. xbitmap2: creating pixmaps and GCs (continued)

```
        bitmap_stuff.reverse_bitmap = XCreatePixmap(XtDisplay(w),
                RootWindowOfScreen(XtScreen(w)),
                bitmap_stuff.pixmap_width_in_cells,
                bitmap_stuff.pixmap_height_in_cells, 1);

        values.foreground = 1;
        values.background = 0;
        /* note that normal_bitmap is used as the drawable because it
         * is one bit deep.  The root window may not be one bit deep */
        bitmap_stuff.draw_gc = XCreateGC(XtDisplay(w),
                bitmap_stuff.normal_bitmap,
                GCForeground | GCBackground, &values);

        values.foreground = 0;
        values.background = 1;
        bitmap_stuff.undraw_gc = XCreateGC(XtDisplay(w),
                bitmap_stuff.normal_bitmap,
                GCForeground | GCBackground, &values);

        /* pixmaps must be cleared - may contain garbage */
        XFillRectangle(XtDisplay(w),
                bitmap_stuff.reverse_bitmap, bitmap_stuff.draw_gc,
                0, 0, bitmap_stuff.pixmap_width_in_cells + 1,
                bitmap_stuff.pixmap_height_in_cells + 1);
        XFillRectangle(XtDisplay(w),
                bitmap_stuff.normal_bitmap, bitmap_stuff.undraw_gc,
                0, 0, bitmap_stuff.pixmap_width_in_cells + 1,
                bitmap_stuff.pixmap_height_in_cells + 1);
}
```

Notice that GCs can only be used on windows or pixmaps with the same depth as the window or pixmap that is passed in the call to create the GC. In this case, the pixmaps created contain only one plane, even when running on a server with a color screen. These pixmaps are passed to XCreateGC to set the depth of the GCs. These GCs can only be used to draw into the single plane pixmaps. As you will see in Example 4-6, a separate GC (the default GC) is used to copy from the pixmaps into the windows, since on color screens the windows have multiple planes. (You know you have done this incorrectly if you get an error only on color screens.)

Xt does not provide drawing calls of its own. You must call Xlib directly to draw. An Xlib drawing routine is known as a *primitive*. Under X, text is drawn by a graphics primitive, just as lines, arcs, and other graphics are drawn.

Colors are normally specified by the user as strings such as "blue," but the X server understands colors only when specified as numbers called pixel values. A pixel value is used as an index to a lookup table called a colormap, which contains values for the RGB (red-green-blue) primaries used to generate colors on the screen. However, a particular pixel value does not necessarily always map to the same color, even when run twice on the same system, because the contents of the colormap are configurable on most color systems. The wide variation of graphics hardware that X supports has required that the design of color handling in X be very flexible and very complex.

Fortunately, as long as your widget or application requires only a small number of colors, and you do not particularly care whether the colors you get are exactly the colors you requested, Xt provides a simplified interface. It hides the actual Xlib calls involved in the Resource Manager's converter routines. As described in Chapter 3, *More Techniques for Using Widgets*, if you specify application resources for colors in a resource list, Xt will automatically convert color names specified as resource settings into pixel values. If you need to do more advanced color handling, then you will need to make Xlib calls yourself. For a description of Xlib's color handling, see Chapter 7, *Color*, in Volume One, *Xlib Programming Manual*.

xbitmap1 works either in color or monochrome, since the widgets it creates can have their color set by resources. All of *xbitmap2* except the small pixmaps we have been implementing also support color. To support color in the small pixmaps takes more work. We would need to add application resources to get the pixel values that will be set into the GCs used when drawing, as described in Section 3.6.

Example 4-5 shows the CellToggled routine. As you may recall, this routine is a callback function registered with the BitmapEdit widget, to be called whenever a cell is toggled.

Example 4-5. xbitmap2: the CellToggled routine

```
/* ARGSUSED */
static void
CellToggled(w, client_data, call_data)
Widget w;
XtPointer client_data;  /* unused */
XtPointer call_data;    /* will be cast to cur_info */
{
    /* cast pointer to needed type: */
    BitmapEditPointInfo *cur_info = (BitmapEditPointInfo *) call_data;
    /*
     * Note, BitmapEditPointInfo is defined in BitmapEdit.h
     */

    XDrawPoint(XtDisplay(w), bitmap_stuff.normal_bitmap,
            ((cur_info->mode == DRAWN) ? bitmap_stuff.draw_gc :
            bitmap_stuff.undraw_gc), cur_info->newx, cur_info->newy);
    XDrawPoint(XtDisplay(w), bitmap_stuff.reverse_bitmap,
            ((cur_info->mode == DRAWN) ? bitmap_stuff.undraw_gc :
            bitmap_stuff.draw_gc), cur_info->newx, cur_info->newy);

    RedrawSmallPicture(bitmap_stuff.showNormalBitmap,
            cur_info->newx, cur_info->newy);
    RedrawSmallPicture(bitmap_stuff.showReverseBitmap,
            cur_info->newx, cur_info->newy);
}
```

Note that BitmapEdit passes a structure called BitmapEditPointInfo into the callback function as an argument. This structure is defined in the public include file, *BitmapEdit.h*, and it provides the information necessary to keep the small bitmaps displaying the same pattern as BitmapEdit. The fields of BitmapEditPointInfo are the mode (whether drawn or undrawn) and the coordinates of the point toggled. The CellToggled routine draws points into the pixmaps according to the information passed in, and then calls Redraw-SmallPicture to copy the pixmaps into each Core widget.

The first line of CellToggled casts the generic pointer info into the structure type defined by BitmapEdit, BitmapEditPointInfo. Under most compilers this can also be done (perhaps more clearly) by declaring the info argument as type BitmapEditPoint-Info in the first place. However, ANSI C compilers require a cast.

The RedrawSmallPicture routine is shown in Example 4-6.

Example 4-6. xbitmap2: the RedrawSmallPicture routine

```
/*ARGSUSED*/
static void
RedrawSmallPicture(w, client_data, call_data)
Widget w;
XtPointer client_data;
XtPointer call_data;
{
    Pixmap pixmap;

    if (w == bitmap_stuff.showNormalBitmap)
        pixmap = bitmap_stuff.normal_bitmap;
    else
        pixmap = bitmap_stuff.reverse_bitmap;

    if (DefaultDepthOfScreen(XtScreen(w)) == 1)
        XCopyArea(XtDisplay(w), pixmap, XtWindow(w),
                DefaultGCOfScreen(XtScreen(w)), 0, 0,
                bitmap_stuff.pixmap_width_in_cells,
                bitmap_stuff.pixmap_height_in_cells,
                0, 0);
    else
        XCopyPlane(XtDisplay(w), pixmap, XtWindow(w),      copies entire
                DefaultGCOfScreen(XtScreen(w)), 0, 0,            pixmap
                bitmap_stuff.pixmap_width_in_cells,
                bitmap_stuff.pixmap_height_in_cells,
                0, 0, 1);
}
```

RedrawSmallPicture is called from CellToggled, and also by Xt in response to Expose events because we registered it as a callback for the DrawingArea widgets. The use of one of two Xlib routines, depending on the depth of the screen, is an optimization. XCopyArea is faster, but can be used for this job only on monochrome displays, because the pixmaps used here are one plane deep on all displays and must be translated into multiple planes with XCopyPlane on color displays.

See Volume One, *Xlib Programming Manual*, for details.

4.2.3 Writing a Bitmap File

Once we have pixmaps in our application that contain the current bitmap, it is a trivial matter to change the printout callback function to write a bitmap file instead of just printing an array of ones and zeroes to the standard output. This is easy because there is an Xlib function, **XWriteBitmapFile**, that writes the contents of a single-plane pixmap into a file. Example 4-7 shows the code that gets a filename from the command line and then writes the bitmap file.

Example 4-7. xbitmap2: writing a bitmap file

```
String filename;                        /* filename to read and write */

/* ARGSUSED */
static void
Printout(widget, client_data, call_data)
Widget widget;
XtPointer client_data, call_data; /* unused */
{
    XWriteBitmapFile(XtDisplay(widget), bitmap_stuff.filename,
            bitmap_stuff.normal_bitmap,
            bitmap_stuff.pixmap_width_in_cells,
            bitmap_stuff.pixmap_height_in_cells, 0, 0);
}

main(argc, argv)
int argc;
char *argv[];
{
    .
    .
    /* XtAppInitialize */
    .
    .

    if (argv[1] != NULL)
        bitmap_stuff.filename = argv[1];
    else {
        fprintf(stderr, "xbitmap: must specify filename\
            on command line.\n");
        exit(1);
    }
    .
    .
    .

}
```

Contrast this version of Printout to the one shown in Example 4-1.

Note that reading a bitmap file requires some more complicated Xlib programming, not Xt programming, so we will not take the space to describe it. If you are curious, the complete code for *xbitmap5*, which both reads and writes bitmap files, is shown in Appendix E, *The xbitmap Application*.

4.3 xbitmap3: Another Way to Create a Custom Window

The small bitmaps added in the last section provided a simple example of making a custom window by creating a DrawingArea widget and drawing into it from the application. DrawingArea also provides a callback for keyboard and pointer (mouse) input, so that you can implement simple user response from the application. However, you will quickly find that to implement a more complicated custom window you need a lot more control than DrawingArea gives you.

The two other ways to implement a custom window are to add features to an empty widget such as Core or Primitive using actions and translations, or to write your own widget. Until you have experience working with widget code, it's easier to prototype the custom window for your application by adding to a Primitive widget from the application code. Once this code is working, and you have read Chapter 6, *Inside a Widget*, and Chapter 7, *Basic Widget Methods*, you can easily move the code into a widget when you want to package it or take advantage of any of the features of Xt that are inaccessible from the application. The code for the BitmapEdit widget was originally written as an application (in *xbitmap3*), and later moved into a widget.

In the next section we describe *xbitmap3*, which works just like *xbitmap1* without using the BitmapEdit widget.

4 *P 138*

4.3.1 Actions

So far in the book we have used callbacks to link widgets with application code. When you are implementing a custom window, callbacks are useless because they are defined by each widget class, and none of the existing widget classes has the callbacks or features that you need.

Therefore, you need to use a different technique for linking application code with widget code: the combination of actions and translations. You can use actions to add features to a Primitive or Core widget. (Actions are also used inside widget code to implement widget features.)

In *xbitmap3* we will make the RedrawSmallPicture function into an action function instead of a callback function (this means just giving it different arguments). Then we need to arrange for Xt to call RedrawSmallPicture whenever one of the Primitive widgets becomes exposed. The general procedure for arranging this is the same as in *xbitmap2*—you register the function during the setup phase of the application, and then Xt will call it in response to Expose events. Registering an action, though, is quite different from registering a callback.

To register the action, you first declare an *actions table*, which maps action name strings to action function pointers. Then you must register the actions table with Xt by calling Xt-AppAddActions. Finally you create a translation table and store it in the app-defaults file or hardcode it in the application. A translation table is a widget resource which contains a mapping between events or event sequences and action names. Figure 4-4 shows a translation table and an action table, and shows how each is used in the process of mapping events to action function calls. (The format of these two tables is described in the following sections and in Chapter 8, *Events, Translations, and Accelerators*.) This two-stage mapping is necessary so that translations can be specified in resource files. Since resource files contain only strings, a translation specified in a resource file can only translate an event into an action name. The action table, which can only be specified in the code, translates the action name into the actual action function pointer.

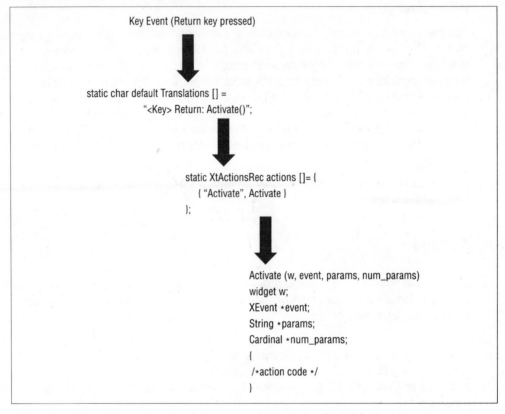

Figure 4-4. Two-stage mapping with translation table and action table

When an event arrives in a particular widget, Xt searches that widget's translation table resource. If that event is not found in the table, Xt does nothing. If the event is found, the matching action name is searched for in the action table. If the action name is found, the corresponding action function is called.

We'll describe the format of the action table and translation table, using *xbitmap3* as an example.

4.3.1.1 The Actions Table

The format of an actions table is defined as follows:

```
typedef struct _XtActionsRec{
    char *string;
    XtActionProc proc;
} XtActionsRec;
```

By convention, the string and the function name are identical, and begin with upper-case letters, as in the following example:

```
static void RedrawSmallPicture();

static XtActionsRec actions[] = {
    {"RedrawSmallPicture", RedrawSmallPicture},
    /* {"Quit", Quit}, */
};
```

The entry that is commented out in the action table shows how additional action functions would be specified in the table if they were needed. *xbitmap3* needs only one action function. In *xbitmap4* you will see a practical example of multiple action functions.

Action names and action functions should not start with Xt or xt: these are reserved for the Intrinsics.

Example 4-8 shows the code from *bitmap3* that creates the action table and registers it with `XtAppAddActions`.

Example 4-8. xbitmap3.c: adding a feature to a Primitive widget

```
main(argc, argv)
int argc;
char **argv;
{
    /* other declarations */
       .
       .
       .
    static XtActionsRec actions[] = {
        {"RedrawSmallPicture", RedrawSmallPicture},
    };
       .
       .
       .
    /* XtAppInitialize */
       .
       .
       .
    XtAppAddActions(app_context, actions, XtNumber(actions));
       .
       .
       .
    /* XtAppMainLoop */
}
```

Actions defined by a widget class are usable only by all instances of that widget class. Actions added with `XtAppAddActions`, on the other hand, are global to the application context, and therefore usable by any widget instance of any class in the application. Which widgets they are actually used with is defined by the translation table, as described below.

The names of widget class actions and application actions do not conflict. For example, if an application were to define an action called Move, and some widget class in Motif already has an action by that name, the two actions would not conflict with each other.

When you map the action to events in a particular widget (using a translation table), the same is true, with a slight caveat. If you write an action called Move, and the widget you install it on already has a Move action, your version will be ignored. This implies that you are trying to replace a widget action with your own, and this is not allowed. You have to write a subclass of the widget to replace a widget action.

4.3.1.2 Format of an Action Function

An action function is just a pointer to a function with four arguments: a widget, an event, a string containing any arguments specified for the action in the translation table (described in Section 4.3.2.3), and the number of arguments contained in the string. Example 4-9 shows the action version of RedrawSmallPicture.

Example 4-9. An XtActionProc with widget and event arguments

```
/* ARGSUSED */
static void
RedrawSmallPicture(w, event, params, num_params)
Widget w;
XExposeEvent *event;
String *params;
Cardinal *num_params;
{
    Pixmap pixmap;

    if (w == bitmap_stuff.showNormalBitmap)
        pixmap = bitmap_stuff.normal_bitmap;
    else
        pixmap = bitmap_stuff.reverse_bitmap;

    if (DefaultDepthOfScreen(XtScreen(w)) == 1)
        XCopyArea(XtDisplay(w), pixmap, XtWindow(w),
                DefaultGCOfScreen(XtScreen(w)), event->x, event->y,
                event->width, event->height, event->x, event->y);
    else
        XCopyPlane(XtDisplay(w), pixmap, XtWindow(w),
                DefaultGCOfScreen(XtScreen(w)), event->x, event->y,
                event->width, event->height, event->x, event->y, 1);
}
```

Compare this version of RedrawSmallPicture to the callback version in Example 4-8. Action functions are directly passed the event structure that describes the event that triggered the action, in this case an XExposeEvent structure. This structure contains the position and dimensions of the area that was exposed. This version of RedrawSmallPicture copies only the necessary parts of the pixmap to refresh the areas that are exposed.

The callback version shown in Example 4-8 copies the entire pixmap to the widget regardless of which part of the widget was exposed. This is slightly inefficient but the difference is not noticeable when the pixmap is small. Under Motif, but not Athena, callback functions are passed the event structure as part of a larger structure, which is passed as the `call_data` argument (for example `XmAnyCallbackStruct`). Therefore, you have access to the event structure from within both callbacks and actions.

However, be aware that if you are allowing user configuration of the translation table (which is discussed below), an action may be called with different kinds of events. You should at least check the event type in the action routine and print an appropriate message if the user has arranged to call the action with the wrong type of event. We'll show how to do this in Chapter 8, *Events, Translations, and Accelerators*.

Note that for true ANSI C portability, all four arguments to the action function must be declared, even though many compilers allow you to leave off trailing arguments that are not referenced in the function. If some of the arguments are not used, you should be sure to include the *lint* comment `/* ARGSUSED */`.

One difference between action functions and callback functions is that, unlike callbacks, there is no argument provided for passing in application data. You can only pass application data into an action function through global variables.

4.3.2 Translations

Once you have an action table registered, those actions are ready to be used by any widget in the application. But which widgets will they be used in, and which will trigger them? Translations determine these things.

You need to set a translation table resource, `XmNtranslations`, on any widget you want to be able to call an application action. In the case of *xbitmap3*, we want `RedrawSmall-Picture` to be called when `Expose` events occur in the widgets that are displaying the small pixmaps. This means that we need to set the `XmNtranslations` resource on those two widgets, and the value of the resource should be a translation that maps an `Expose` event into a `RedrawSmallPicture` call.

4.3.2.1 The Translation Table

Every widget that contains actions also has a default translation table that maps event combinations into those actions. The application can override, augment, or replace this table to make a widget call application-registered actions in addition to the widget's own actions. Registering actions with `XtAppAddActions` makes them eligible for inclusion in translation tables.

Each line of a translation table maps a sequence of events to a sequence of actions. The entire translation table is simply a string consisting of one or more event specifications in angle brackets, with optional modifiers, followed by a colon and a function name string defined in an action table. Multiple translations can be specified as part of the same string.

By convention, the string is continued on several lines, one for each translation, each line except the last terminated with a linefeed (\n) and a backslash (\).

We'll describe the details of event specification and other aspects of translation table syntax in Chapter 8, *Events, Translations, and Accelerators*. For now, an example should get the point across quite clearly.

The translation we need for *xbitmap3*, as it would appear in the application code, is shown in Example 4-10. This example also shows how the translation table must be converted into an internal form with `XtParseTranslationTable` before it can be used to set an `Xm-Ntranslations` resource.

Example 4-10. A simple translation table

```
XtTranslations mytranslations;

static char transTable[] =
    "<Expose>:  RedrawSmallPicture()";
    .
    .
    .

bitmap_stuff.showReverseBitmap =
        XtVaCreateManagedWidget("showReverseBitmap",
        XmPrimitiveWidgetClass, frame2,
        XmNtranslations, XtParseTranslationTable(transTable);
        XmNwidth, bitmap_stuff.pixmap_width_in_cells,
        XmNheight, bitmap_stuff.pixmap_height_in_cells,
        NULL);
    .
    .
    .
```

The default translations for the PushButton widget are as follows:

Example 4-11. A complex translation table

```
static char defaultTranslations[] =
    "<Btn1Down>:          Arm()\n\
    <Btn1Down>,<Btn1Up>: Activate() Disarm()\n\
    <Btn1Down>(2+):      MultiArm()\n\
    <Btn1Up>(2+):        MultiActivate()\n\
    <Btn1Up>:            Activate() Disarm()\n\
    <Key>osfSelect:      ArmAndActivate()\n\
    <Key>osfActivate:    ArmAndActivate()\n\
    <Key>osfHelp:   Help()\n\
    ~Shift ~Meta ~Alt <Key>Return:  ArmAndActivate()\n\
    ~Shift ~Meta ~Alt <Key>space:   ArmAndActivate()\n\
    <EnterWindow>:       Enter()\n\
    <LeaveWindow>:       Leave()";
```

Notice that this entire translation table is a single string. This translation table shows a number of useful techniques, which is described in full detail in Chapter 8, *Events, Translations, and Accelerators*:

- How to detect a button press followed by a release (second line).

- How to invoke two successive actions in response to an event sequence (second line).

- How to detect a double click (lines 3 and 4).

- How to detect the press of a particular key (lines 5, 6, and 7).

- How to detect a key press but only if certain modifier keys are not being held (8 and 9).

Like most other resources, translations can be specified in resource files. While debugging, it is a good idea to specify translation tables in files, to minimize recompiling. Example 4-12 shows the part of the app-defaults file for *xbitmap3* that sets the translation table.

Example 4-12. XBitmap3: specifying translations in the app-defaults file

```
*XmPrimitive.translations:\
    <Expose>:    RedrawSmallPicture()
```

Note that since resource files are strings, no quotation marks are needed. However, for multiple-line translation tables, you still need to escape the ends of each line with \n\.

The resource set here is `translations`. (This resource has the same name for all widgets.) As you know, the contents of the app-default file consist solely of strings, so Xt processes the setting for `translations` into a translation table using what's called a resource converter. The resource converter calls `XtParseTranslationTable` for you when you specify translations in a resource file.

In principle, you can modify the translations of existing widgets to customize their behavior. However, Motif discourages this practice since it tends to break user-interface conventions. In fact, some Motif widgets allow you to modify their translations (no error is generated), but they do not actually modify their behavior.* When modifying the translations of a widget with existing translations, you may specify a directive to control what happens when there are conflicts between your new translations and the existing translations. Xt recognizes one of three directives in a translation table, beginning with # on the first line, which tell how to handle existing translations (either set as widget defaults, or in other resource database files):

- `#replace` (the default if no directive is specified). Replace the old translations with the current table.

- `#augment`. Merge the new translations into the existing translation table, but not to disturb any existing translations. If a translation already exists for a particular event, the conflicting translation specification that appears in a table beginning with `#augment` is ignored.

- `#override`. Merge the new translations into the existing translation table, replacing old values with the current specifications in the event of conflict.

We used `#override` because this allows us to keep the translations for `<EnterWindow>` and `<LeaveWindow>` events in place. In addition, the PushButton widget's `set` and `unset` actions will also remain in effect for `<Btn1Down>` and `<Btn1Up>`. (For more

---

*Which translation you cannot modify, and in which widget classes, is not precisely documented in Motif. In general, you should avoid modifying translation of existing widget classes altogether (with the exception of Primitive).

details on why these aren't overridden by the new translations, see Chapter 8, *Events, Translations, and Accelerators*.)

The translation:

```
<Btn1Down>,<Btn1Up>:  confirm()
```

specifies that the confirm action should be called in response to a pair of events, namely a button press followed by a button release, with no other events intervening.

The translations:

```
<Btn2Down>:          set()\n\
<Btn2Down>,<Btn2Up>: quit()
```

specify that the PushButton widget's internal set action should be invoked by pressing button 2, and that our own quit action should be invoked by clicking button 2. Note that we don't bother to bind the PushButton widget's unset action to <Btn2Up>, since the application will disappear as a result of the quit action. (The unset action is still used when the user presses button 2 and then moves the pointer outside the widget before releasing button 2. This is one of PushButton's default bindings that we have not overridden.) If we were using the widget for any other purpose, we would map <Btn2Up> to unset, so that the widget was restored to its normal appearance when our own action was completed.

4.3.2.2 Hardcoding Translations

There are cases in which an application may want not only to specify translations in an app-defaults file, but also to hardcode them into the application. When you specify translations only in the app-defaults file, the user has unlimited configurability; if the default translations are deleted or changed beyond recognition, the application may no longer work. But you can hardcode a minimum set of translations in the code, and then supplement these with a set of translations in the app-defaults file that you want to be user-customizable. Among resources, translations are unique because the final value can be the result of merging the values in the resource files with the values in the application (with other resources you get one or the other, but not a combination).

Three Xt functions are used for setting translation tables from the application code:

- XtParseTranslationTable is used to compile a string translation table into the opaque internal representation XtTranslations. (For translations specified in re-source files, this conversion is performed automatically by a resource converter.)

- XtAugmentTranslations is used, like the #augment directive in a resource file, to nondestructively merge translations into a widget's existing translations.

- XtOverrideTranslations is used, like the #override directive in a resource file, to destructively merge translations into a widget's existing translations.

Both XtAugmentTranslations and XtOverrideTranslations take as arguments a widget and a compiled translation table returned by XtParseTranslation-Table.

There is no function that completely replaces a widget's translations; however, you can do this by calling XtSetValues, the general routine for setting resources (whose use is demonstrated later in this chapter) that set the value of a widget's XmNtranslations resource to a compiled translation table returned by XtParseTranslationTable.

To set the same translations specified in the app-defaults file from the application itself, we would have used the following code:

Example 4-13. Code fragment: specifying translations in the program

```
static char defaultTranslations[] = "#override\n\
        <Btn1Down>,<Btn1Up>:    confirm()\n\
        <Btn2Down>:             set()\n\
        <Btn2Down>,<Btn2Up>:    quit()";

XtTranslations mytranslations;
        .
        .
        .
mytranslations = XtParseTranslationTable(defaultTranslations);
XtOverrideTranslations(farewell, mytranslations);
```

As mentioned earlier, you will find it more convenient to place the translation table in the app-defaults file until the last minute, because this allows changes without recompiling the source.

4.3.2.3 Action Parameters

The *params* and *num-params* arguments of an action function are passed in from the translation table by Xt. For example, consider an action called *Move*, which can move some data left of right. A translation table that selects events that will invoke *Move* is shown in Example 4-14.

Example 4-14. A translation table with action parameters

```
*tetris.translations:\n\
<Key>Left: Move(l)\n\
<Key>Right: Move(r)
```

With this translation table, *Move* will be passed a params argument "l" when the left arrow key is pressed, and "r" when the right arrow key is pressed.

4.3.3 Adding Actions to Existing Widgets

It is also possible to add actions to widgets other than Core and Primitive, but it takes more care. Usually, when a widget does not provide a certain callback, it also does not provide various other characteristics that you want. For example, to make the Label widget work like PushButton (pretending that the PushButton widget didn't already exist), you would have to make it accept more kinds of input, add the drawing code to highlight the border and draw the window darker to simulate shadow, and add the ability to call an application function. All of this can be done with actions, but it would take a lot of work. What can make it difficult is that your code may interact with the widget's code in unpleasant ways. When the changes are major, it makes more sense to create a new widget subclass that shares some characteristics and code with its superclass. As we will see, that is exactly how PushButton is implemented, as a subclass of Label. The Primitive and DrawingArea widgets, on the other hand, have no input or output semantics at all, and therefore it is simpler to add actions to them without conflict.

4.4 xbitmap4: A Bitmap Editor Without a BitmapEdit Widget

The *xbitmap4* implements an application almost identical to *xbitmap1*, but without using the BitmapEdit widget. The custom bitmap editing window is done in a Primitive widget, with all the code in the application. This is an example of a custom window that could not be easily built using DrawingArea. This application is a culmination of everything you have seen so far. It is also a preview of what you will see in the next chapter. The same code in *xbitmap4* that is used to implement the bitmap editor will be moved into widget code in Chapters 6 and 7.

This example takes advantage of application resources to set the configurable parameters of the bitmap code. The code that sets up the application resources is described in Section 3.6. When moving the code into a widget framework, the same resource list will be used verbatim. The example also provides command-line options to set the important parameters of the bitmap code. The code for processing these options is described in Section 3.7. The code is the same whether used for setting application resources or widget resources, except no call equivalent to XtGetApplicationResources is necessary in a widget.

The exposure strategy used for the bitmap editor is the same as for the small bitmaps in the previous section. The application creates a large pixmap of depth one that stores the current image of the bitmap being edited. Whenever the screen needs updating, the applicable part of the pixmap is copied to the Core widget in the Redraw_picture routine. Because this pixmap is much bigger than the ones in the last section, it is an important optimization that only the required parts of the pixmap are copied. (This is not the only possible exposure strategy. This particular strategy has very low network load, but uses a relatively large amount of server memory. For this reason it is not ideal for PC servers.)

The SetUpThings routine creates the pixmap, draws a grid into it that will persist for the life of the application, and creates three GCs. One GC is for copying from the pixmap to the window, and two are for drawing and undrawing cells in the pixmap. The btn_event routine draws and undraws cells in the pixmap according to pointer clicks and drags, and calls Redraw_picture to update the Core widget display.

Redraw_picture is called both from the application and from Xt. This is a common trick used to reduce the duplication of drawing code. Since Redraw_picture is an action, it has an event argument that is used by Xt to pass in the Expose event describing the area exposed. This application also uses this argument by constructing a fake event to pass in information about which part of the widget to draw.

The application adds actions and sets the XmNtranslations resource of the Core widget so that Xt calls the application routine Redraw_picture whenever Expose events arrive, and calls btn_event when ButtonPress or MotionNotify events arrive.

Example 4-15 shows the complete code for *xbitmap4*. You have seen all the techniques here in various examples before. You should work through the code and make sure you understand the purpose of each section. However, don't worry about the details of the Xlib calls, since they are specific to this application.

Example 4-15. xbitmap4: implementing the bitmap editor from the application

```
/*
 * xbitmap4.c
 */
#include <Xm/Xm.h>

#include <Xm/PanedW.h>
#include <Xm/RowColumn.h>
#include <Xm/PushB.h>
/* we use XmPrimitive, but no header file needed (in Xm.h) */

#include <stdio.h>

/* The following could be placed in an "xbitmap.h" file. */
#define XtNdebug "debug"
#define XtCDebug "Debug"
#define XtNpixmapWidthInCells "pixmapWidthInCells"
#define XtCPixmapWidthInCells "PixmapWidthInCells"
#define XtNpixmapHeightInCells "pixmapHeightInCells"
#define XtCPixmapHeightInCells "PixmapHeightInCells"
#define XtNcellSizeInPixels "cellSizeInPixels"
#define XtCCellSizeInPixels "CellSizeInPixels"

#define DRAWN 1
#define UNDRAWN 0

#define DRAW 1
#define UNDRAW 0

#define MAXLINES  1000

#define MINBITMAPWIDTH  2
#define MAXBITMAPWIDTH  1000
#define MINBITMAPHEIGHT  2
#define MAXBITMAPHEIGHT  1000
#define MINCELLSIZE  4
#define MAXCELLSIZE  100

#define SCROLLBARWIDTH 15
/*
 * Data structure for private data.
 * (This avoids lots of global variables.)
 */
typedef struct {
    Pixmap big_picture;
    GC draw_gc, undraw_gc; /* for drawing into the
                            * big_picture, 1-bit deep */
    GC copy_gc;            /* for copying from pixmap
                            * into window, screen depth */
    Widget bitmap;         /* this is the drawing surface */
```

```
    char *cell;         /* this is the array for printing output
                         * and keeping track of cells drawn */
    int cur_x, cur_y;
    Dimension pixmap_width_in_pixels, pixmap_height_in_pixels;
} PrivateAppData;

/* data structure for application resources */
typedef struct {
    Pixel copy_fg;
    Pixel copy_bg;
    int pixmap_width_in_cells;
    int pixmap_height_in_cells;
    int cell_size_in_pixels;
    Boolean debug;
} AppData;

AppData app_data;
PrivateAppData private_app_data;

/* resource list */
static XtResource resources[] = {
    {
        XmNforeground,
        XmCForeground,
        XmRPixel,
        sizeof(Pixel),
        XtOffsetOf(AppData, copy_fg),
        XmRString,
        XtDefaultForeground
    },
    {
        XmNbackground,
        XmCBackground,
        XmRPixel,
        sizeof(Pixel),
        XtOffsetOf(AppData, copy_bg),
        XmRString,
        XtDefaultBackground
    },
    {
        XtNpixmapWidthInCells,
        XtCPixmapWidthInCells,
        XmRInt,
        sizeof(int),
        XtOffsetOf(AppData, pixmap_width_in_cells),
        XmRImmediate,
        (XtPointer) 32,
    },
    {
        XtNpixmapHeightInCells,
        XtCPixmapHeightInCells,
        XmRInt,
        sizeof(int),
        XtOffsetOf(AppData, pixmap_height_in_cells),
        XmRImmediate,
        (XtPointer) 32,
    },
```

```
        {
            XtNcellSizeInPixels,
            XtCCellSizeInPixels,
            XmRInt,
            sizeof(int),
            XtOffsetOf(AppData, cell_size_in_pixels),
            XmRImmediate,
            (XtPointer) 30,
        },
        {
            XtNdebug,
            XtCDebug,
            XmRBoolean,
            sizeof(Boolean),
            XtOffsetOf(AppData, debug),
            XmRImmediate,
            (XtPointer) False,
        },
};

/* Command-line options table */
static XrmOptionDescRec options[] = {
    {"-pw",              "*pixmapWidthInCells",    XrmoptionSepArg, NULL},
    {"-pixmapwidth",     "*pixmapWidthInCells",    XrmoptionSepArg, NULL},
    {"-ph",              "*pixmapHeightInCells",   XrmoptionSepArg, NULL},
    {"-pixmapheight",    "*pixmapHeightInCells",   XrmoptionSepArg, NULL},
    {"-cellsize",        "*cellSizeInPixels",      XrmoptionSepArg, NULL},
    {"-fg",              "*foreground",            XrmoptionSepArg, NULL},
    {"-foreground",      "*foreground",            XrmoptionSepArg, NULL},
    {"-debug",       "    *debug",                 XrmoptionNoArg,  "True"},
};

/* callback function to print cell array to stdout */
/* ARGSUSED */
static void
PrintOut(w, event, params, num_params)
Widget w;
XEvent *event;
String *params;
Cardinal *num_params;
{
    /*
     * The absense of the small pixmaps in this version makes it
     * more difficult to call XWriteBitmapFile.  Therefore, we will
     * stick with the printed output for this version.
     */
    int x, y;
    putchar('\n');
    for (y = 0; y < app_data.pixmap_height_in_cells; y++) {
        for (x = 0; x < app_data.pixmap_width_in_cells; x++)
            putchar(private_app_data.cell[x + y *
                    app_data.pixmap_width_in_cells] ? '1' : '0');
        putchar('\n');
    }
    putchar('\n');
}
```

```
static void RedrawPicture(), DrawCell(), UndrawCell(), ToggleCell(),
       DrawPixmaps();

static void Syntax(argc, argv)
int argc;
char * argv[];
{
    int i;
    static int errs = False;

    /* first argument is program name - skip that */
    for (i = 1; i < argc; i++) {
        if (!errs++) /* do first time through */
            fprintf(stderr, "xbitmap4: command line\
                    option not understood:\n");
        fprintf(stderr, "option: %s\n", argv[i]);
    }

    fprintf(stderr, "xbitmap understands all standard Xt\
            command line options.\n");

    fprintf(stderr, "Additional options are as follows:\n");
    fprintf(stderr, "Option              Valid Range\n");
    fprintf(stderr, "-pw                 MINBITMAPWIDTH to\
            MAXBITMAPWIDTH\n");
    fprintf(stderr, "-pixmapwidth        MINBITMAPWIDTH to\
            MAXBITMAPWIDTH\n");
    fprintf(stderr, "-ph                 MINBITMAPHEIGHT to\
            MAXBITMAPHEIGHT\n");
    fprintf(stderr, "-pixmapheight       MINBITMAPHEIGHT to\
            MAXBITMAPHEIGHT\n");
    fprintf(stderr, "-cellsize           MINCELLSIZE to\
            MAXCELLSIZE\n");
    fprintf(stderr, "-fg                 color name\n");
    fprintf(stderr, "-foreground         color name\n");
    fprintf(stderr, "-debug              no value necessary\n");
}

main(argc, argv)
int argc;
char *argv[];
{
    XtAppContext app_context;
    Widget topLevel, vpane, buttonbox, quit, output;
    extern exit();
    /* translation table for bitmap core widget */
    String trans =
    "<Expose>:  RedrawPicture()        \n\
        <Btn1Down>:   DrawCell()                 \n\
        <Btn2Down>:   UndrawCell()               \n\
        <Btn3Down>:   ToggleCell()               \n\
        <Btn1Motion>: DrawCell()                 \n\
        <Btn2Motion>: UndrawCell()               \n\
        <Btn3Motion>: ToggleCell()";

    static XtActionsRec window_actions[] = {
        {"RedrawPicture",   RedrawPicture},
        {"DrawCell",    DrawCell},
```

```
        {"UndrawCell",   UndrawCell},
        {"ToggleCell",   ToggleCell},
    };

    topLevel = XtVaAppInitialize(
            &app_context,        /* Application context */
            "XBitmap4",
            options, XtNumber(options),
            &argc, argv,         /* command line args */
            NULL,                /* for missing app-defaults file */
            NULL);               /* terminate varargs list */

    /* XtInitialize leaves program name in args */
    if (argc > 1)
        Syntax(argc, argv);

    XtGetApplicationResources(topLevel,
            &app_data,
            resources,
            XtNumber(resources),
            NULL,
            0);

    /*
     * We must check the application resource values here.
     * Otherwise, user could supply out of range values and crash
     * program. Conversion routines do this automatically, so
     * colors are already checked.
     */
    if ((app_data.pixmap_width_in_cells > MAXBITMAPWIDTH) ||
            (app_data.pixmap_width_in_cells < MINBITMAPWIDTH) ||
            (app_data.pixmap_height_in_cells > MAXBITMAPWIDTH) ||
            (app_data.pixmap_height_in_cells < MINBITMAPWIDTH)) {
        fprintf(stderr, "xbitmap: error in resource settings:\
                dimension must be between %d and %d cells\n",
                MINBITMAPWIDTH, MAXBITMAPWIDTH);
        exit(1);
    }
    if ((app_data.cell_size_in_pixels < MINCELLSIZE) ||
            (app_data.cell_size_in_pixels > MAXCELLSIZE)) {
        fprintf(stderr, "xbitmap: error in resource settings:\
                cell size must be between %d and %d pixels\n",
                MINCELLSIZE, MAXCELLSIZE);
        exit(1);
    }

    /* begin application code */

    set_up_things(topLevel);

    private_app_data.cell = XtCalloc(app_data.pixmap_width_in_cells *
            app_data.pixmap_height_in_cells, sizeof(char));

    if (app_data.debug)
        fprintf(stderr, "xbitmap: pixmap dimensions are %d by %d\n",
                app_data.pixmap_width_in_cells,
                app_data.pixmap_height_in_cells);

    vpane = XtVaCreateManagedWidget("vpane", xmPanedWindowWidgetClass,
            topLevel, XmNwidth,
```

Example
Application

```
                    private_app_data.pixmap_width_in_pixels, NULL);

        buttonbox = XtVaCreateManagedWidget("buttonbox",
                xmRowColumnWidgetClass, vpane, NULL);

        output = XtVaCreateManagedWidget("output", xmPushButtonWidgetClass,
                buttonbox, NULL);

        XtAddCallback(output, XmNactivateCallback, PrintOut, NULL);

        quit = XtVaCreateManagedWidget("quit", xmPushButtonWidgetClass,
                buttonbox, NULL);

        XtAddCallback(quit, XmNactivateCallback, exit, NULL);

        /* note: no header file needed to create xmPrimitive */
        private_app_data.bitmap = XtVaCreateManagedWidget("bitmap",
                xmPrimitiveWidgetClass, vpane,
                XmNtranslations, XtParseTranslationTable(trans),
                XmNwidth, private_app_data.pixmap_width_in_pixels,
                XmNheight, private_app_data.pixmap_height_in_pixels,
                NULL);

        XtAppAddActions(app_context, window_actions,
                XtNumber(window_actions));

        XtRealizeWidget(topLevel);

        XtAppMainLoop(app_context);
}

set_up_things(w)
Widget w;
{
        XGCValues values;
        int x, y;
        XSegment segment[MAXLINES];
        int n_horiz_segments, n_vert_segments;

        private_app_data.pixmap_width_in_pixels =
                app_data.pixmap_width_in_cells *
                app_data.cell_size_in_pixels;
        private_app_data.pixmap_height_in_pixels =
                app_data.pixmap_height_in_cells *
                app_data.cell_size_in_pixels;

        private_app_data.big_picture = XCreatePixmap(XtDisplay(w),
                RootWindowOfScreen(XtScreen(w)),
                private_app_data.pixmap_width_in_pixels,
                private_app_data.pixmap_height_in_pixels, 1);

        values.foreground = 1;
        values.background = 0;
        values.dashes = 1;
        values.dash_offset = 0;
        values.line_style = LineOnOffDash;

        private_app_data.draw_gc = XCreateGC(XtDisplay(w),
                private_app_data.big_picture, GCForeground | GCBackground
                | GCDashOffset | GCDashList | GCLineStyle, &values);

        values.foreground = 0;
```

```
        values.background = 1;
        private_app_data.undraw_gc = XCreateGC(XtDisplay(w),
                private_app_data.big_picture, GCForeground | GCBackground
                | GCDashOffset | GCDashList | GCLineStyle, &values);

        values.foreground = app_data.copy_fg;
        values.background = app_data.copy_bg;
        private_app_data.copy_gc = XCreateGC(XtDisplay(w),
                RootWindowOfScreen(XtScreen(w)),
                GCForeground | GCBackground, &values);

        XFillRectangle(XtDisplay(w), private_app_data.big_picture,
                private_app_data.undraw_gc, 0, 0,
                private_app_data.pixmap_width_in_pixels,
                private_app_data.pixmap_height_in_pixels);

        /* draw permanent grid into pixmap */
        n_horiz_segments = app_data.pixmap_height_in_cells + 1;
        n_vert_segments = app_data.pixmap_width_in_cells + 1;

        for (x = 0; x < n_horiz_segments; x += 1) {
            segment[x].x1 = 0;
            segment[x].x2 = private_app_data.pixmap_width_in_pixels;
            segment[x].y1 = app_data.cell_size_in_pixels * x;
            segment[x].y2 = app_data.cell_size_in_pixels * x;
        }

        /* drawn only once into pixmap */
        XDrawSegments(XtDisplay(w), private_app_data.big_picture,
                private_app_data.draw_gc, segment, n_horiz_segments);

        for (y = 0; y < n_vert_segments; y += 1) {
            segment[y].x1 = y * app_data.cell_size_in_pixels;
            segment[y].x2 = y * app_data.cell_size_in_pixels;
            segment[y].y1 = 0;
            segment[y].y2 = private_app_data.pixmap_height_in_pixels;
        }

        /* drawn only once into pixmap */
        XDrawSegments(XtDisplay(w), private_app_data.big_picture,
                private_app_data.draw_gc, segment, n_vert_segments);
}
/* ARGSUSED */
static void
RedrawPicture(w, event, params, num_params)
Widget w;
XExposeEvent *event;
String *params;
Cardinal *num_params;
{
    register int x, y;
    unsigned int width, height;

    if (event) {     /* drawing because of expose or button press */
        x = event->x;
        y = event->y;
        width = event->width;
        height = event->height;
    }
```

```
        else {   /* drawing because of scrolling */
            x = 0;
            y = 0;
            width =  10000;   /* always the whole window! */
            height =  10000;
        }

        if (DefaultDepthOfScreen(XtScreen(w)) == 1)
            XCopyArea(XtDisplay(w), private_app_data.big_picture,
                    XtWindow(w), private_app_data.copy_gc, x +
                    private_app_data.cur_x, y + private_app_data.cur_y,
                    width, height, x, y);
        else
            XCopyPlane(XtDisplay(w), private_app_data.big_picture,
                    XtWindow(w), private_app_data.copy_gc, x +
                    private_app_data.cur_x, y + private_app_data.cur_y,
                    width, height, x, y, 1);
}

/* ARGSUSED */
static void
DrawCell(w, event, params, num_params)
Widget w;
XButtonEvent *event;
String *params;
Cardinal *num_params;
{
    DrawPixmaps(private_app_data.draw_gc, DRAW, w, event);
}

/* ARGSUSED */
static void
UndrawCell(w, event, params, num_params)
Widget w;
XButtonEvent *event;
String *params;
Cardinal *num_params;
{
    DrawPixmaps(private_app_data.undraw_gc, UNDRAW, w, event);
}

/* ARGSUSED */
static void
ToggleCell(w, event, params, num_params)
Widget w;
XButtonEvent *event;
String *params;
Cardinal *num_params;
{
    static int oldx = -1, oldy = -1;
    GC gc;
    int mode;
    int newx = (private_app_data.cur_x + event->x) /
            app_data.cell_size_in_pixels;
    int newy = (private_app_data.cur_y + event->y) /
            app_data.cell_size_in_pixels;

    if ((mode = private_app_data.cell[newx + newy *
```

```
                 app_data.pixmap_width_in_cells]) == DRAWN) {
        gc = private_app_data.undraw_gc;
        mode = UNDRAW;
    }
    else {
        gc = private_app_data.draw_gc;
        mode = DRAW;
    }

    if (oldx != newx || oldy != newy) {
        oldx = newx;
        oldy = newy;
        DrawPixmaps(gc, mode, w, event);
    }
}

/* Private Function */
static void
DrawPixmaps(gc, mode, w, event)
GC gc;
int mode;
Widget w;
XButtonEvent *event;
{
    int newx = (private_app_data.cur_x + event->x) /
            app_data.cell_size_in_pixels;
    int newy = (private_app_data.cur_y + event->y) /
            app_data.cell_size_in_pixels;
    XExposeEvent fake_event;

    /* if already done, return */
    if (private_app_data.cell[newx + newy *
            app_data.pixmap_width_in_cells] == mode)
        return;

    XFillRectangle(XtDisplay(w), private_app_data.big_picture, gc,
            app_data.cell_size_in_pixels*newx + 2,
            app_data.cell_size_in_pixels*newy + 2,
            (unsigned int) app_data.cell_size_in_pixels - 3,
            (unsigned int) app_data.cell_size_in_pixels - 3);

    private_app_data.cell[newx + newy *
            app_data.pixmap_width_in_cells] = mode;

    fake_event.x = app_data.cell_size_in_pixels * newx -
            private_app_data.cur_x;
    fake_event.y = app_data.cell_size_in_pixels * newy -
            private_app_data.cur_y;
    fake_event.width = app_data.cell_size_in_pixels;
    fake_event.height = app_data.cell_size_in_pixels;

    RedrawPicture(private_app_data.bitmap, &fake_event);
}
```

Of particular interest in the code for *xbitmap4* is the Syntax function. Notice that it prints out the options that were not understood, in addition to printing out a list of valid options.

Example Application

5

More About Motif

This chapter describes each widget in the Motif set that has not yet been introduced, and describes the features that Motif adds to the model provided by the Xt Intrinsics.

In This Chapter:

5
More About Motif

This book is primarily about how to program with the Xt Intrinsics, and has used the Motif widgets to demonstrate those techniques. It has so far not described many of the Motif widgets, and hasn't touched the surface of the topic of how to combine them to best advantage. Complete coverage of these topics is left to the forthcoming Volume Six, *X Motif Programming Manual*. However, this chapter will acquaint you with the default appearance and general purpose of the Motif widgets we have not yet used. With this information, you should gain a general idea of the range of widgets you have to choose from.

Motif also provides many features that are roughly at the same level as those provided by Xt, but that go beyond those provided by Xt. Part of Motif, therefore, is a kind of extension of Xt. This chapter will provide sufficient introduction so that you know the purpose and capabilities of each of these features. This will enable you to determine whether these features will be useful in your application, and warrant further investigation. Again, more complete coverage of these features, with examples, will be left to Volume Six, *X Motif Programming Manual*.

5.1 The Remaining Motif Widgets and Gadgets

Let's begin with the primitive widgets that you haven't yet seen in examples in this book. These are widgets that do not manage child widgets. Although we have not explicitly created ArrowButton and ScrollBar widgets, you have seen them as part of MainWindow and ScrolledWindow. ArrowButton is the widget used at the ends of ScrollBars. ScrollBars, in turn, are created automatically by MainWindow and ScrolledWindow.

Command widgets are for keeping track of typed commands. The upper window shows the history of past commands typed, and the lower window shows the command currently being typed. Figure 5-1 shows a Command widget.

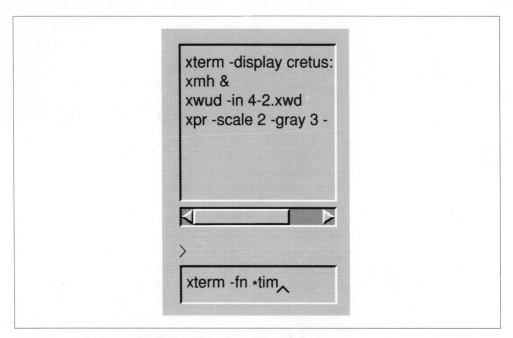

Figure 5-1. A Command widget

The FileSelectionBox is a complex widget which allows the user to move through the file system to select a file. See Volume Three, *X Window System User's Guide, Motif Edition*, for a description of how the user manipulates this widget. A FileSelectionBox can be created by itself (with XmCreateFileSelectionBox), or it can be created as part of a dialog with XmCreateFileSelectionDialog. Figure 5-2 shows a FileSelectionBox widget.

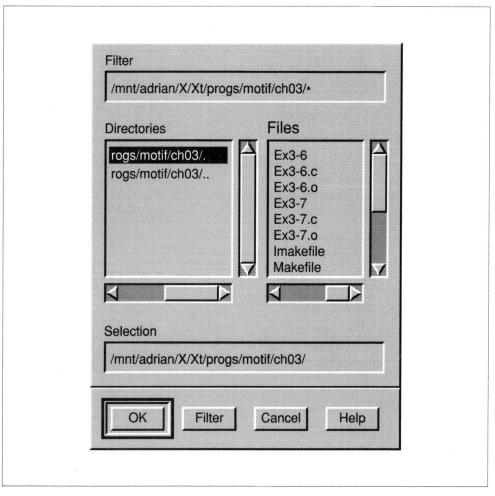

Figure 5-2. A FileSelectionBox widget

A SelectionBox allows the user to choose from a list of alternatives. It provides a scrolled list, and a text area. The user can select from the list using the pointer, or type the name from the list.

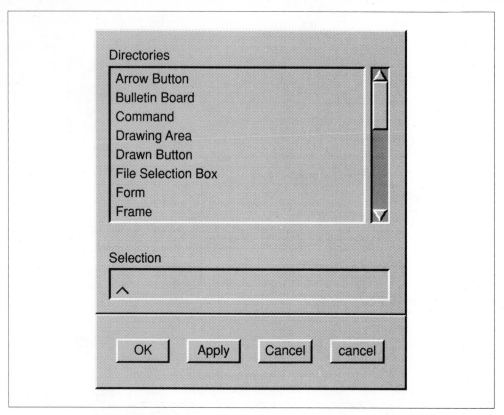

Figure 5-3. A SelectionBox widget

Text is a text editor in a single widget. It can edit single line or multiline text. By default it uses Emacs-style editing commands. TextField is a single line text editor with provision for verification that the user supplied acceptable data. The Text and TextField widgets provide a multitude of functions for accessing and manipulating their contents from the application. The XmCreateScrolledText function is used for creating a Text widget with Scroll-Bars. Figure 5-4 shows a Text and a TextField widget.

Figure 5-4. A Text and TextField widgets

The Separator widget is used to visually separate distinct areas within larger components. It just draws a line between widgets. Separators can be used to separate items in popup menus, action areas within dialog boxes, or simply adjacent geometry managing widgets. Usually you should use a SeparatorGadget instead. Figure 5-5 shows a menu containing elements separated with Separator widgets.

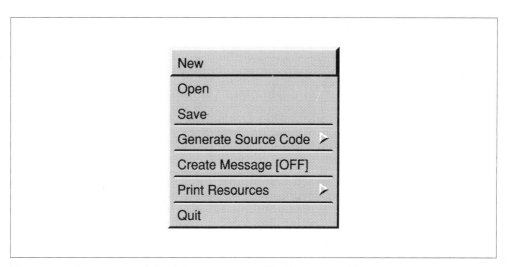

Figure 5-5. A menu containing buttons separated by Separator widgets

A ToggleButton sets a boolean value. ToggleButton is designed to be added in groups to a RadioBox or a CheckBox. See Figure 5-6. Both RadioBox and CheckBox are implemented using a RowColumn widget. The resources that distinguish these two types of user interface elements are automatically set when you use the XmCreateRadioBox or XmCreate-SimpleCheckBox convenience functions. Each ToggleButton in a RadioBox has a diamond-shaped indicator, and only one ToggleButton at a time can be chosen. In a CheckBox, each ToggleButton has a square indicator and any number of the ToggleButtons can be selected at the same time.

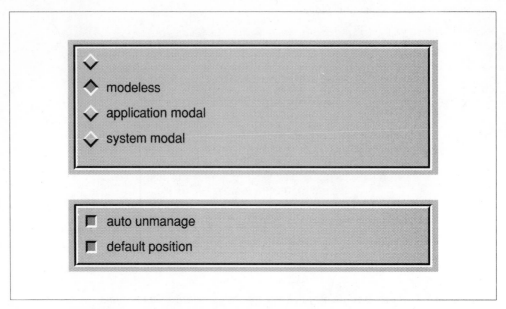

Figure 5-6. ToggleButton widgets used in a RadioBox and a CheckBox

DrawnButton is a widget that works like PushButton but that is empty except for a button shadow. It provides callbacks for exposure and resize, so that you can provide your own drawing code. DrawnButton is not often used, since PushButton allows you to supply either text or a pixmap as its label. DrawnButton can be used to implement an animated button (where the contents change frequently), or to draw text that is beyond the capabilities of PushButton. Since DrawnButton has no distinctive appearance, it is not shown.

Scale is really a slider widget, which can be used for input or output. Scale is shown in Figure 5-7.

Figure 5-7. A Scale widget

Six types of simple widgets are also available as gadgets: PushButtonGadget, LabelGadget, ArrowButtonGadget, CascadeButtonGadget, SeparatorGadget, and ToggleButtonGadget.

5.1.1 Geometry Managing Widgets

All Motif geometry managing widgets are subclasses of the Manager class. Instances of Manager itself are never created. Manager serves the same purpose for geometry managing widgets as Primitive does for graphics widgets. It provides the features common to all Motif widgets, such as 3-D shadows, keyboard traversal, and so on.

Motif uses RowColumn very heavily. All of the following are not separate widget classes; they are RowColumn widgets with certain resource settings:

- WorkArea—the default RowColumn type.

- CheckBox—a box designed to contain ToggleButtons, in which several can be selected at the same time.

- RadioBox—a box designed to contain ToggleButtons, in which only one can be selected.

- OptionMenu—appears as a button and an associated menu. The button shows the current selection from the menu. The menu appears over the button.

- PulldownMenu—a menu that appears just below a button that pops it up.

- PopupMenu—a menu that pops up at the pointer position.

- MenuBar—a horizontal bar across the top of the application's main window, containing CascadeButtons that pop up menus or dialogs.

RowColumns do not have a three dimensional appearance, so they may be placed next to one another without giving the user the impression that their sub-elements are grouped independently. However, they can be placed within Frame to generate a 3-D appearance.

BulletinBoard is a geometry managing widget that has very simple rules. It is used by Motif in most dialog widgets. After resizing, it leaves child widgets where they were originally placed, or it moves them somewhat to avoid overlapping. Motif supplies `XmCreate-BulletinBoard` for general use and `XmCreateBulletinBoardDialog` for building your own dialogs. Some applications use BulletinBoard as their work area, so that they have a static layout which does not change upon resizing (for example, Motif's *periodic* demo). If a BulletinBoard is resized smaller than the current layout of the widgets it contains, the widgets are clipped and may not be completely visible.

The List widget provides an array of string choices. Figure 5-8 shows the *xmfonts* demo, which contains a list widget containing numerous PushButtonGadgets. `XmCreate-ScrolledList` creates a specialized form of List that is for managing large lists.

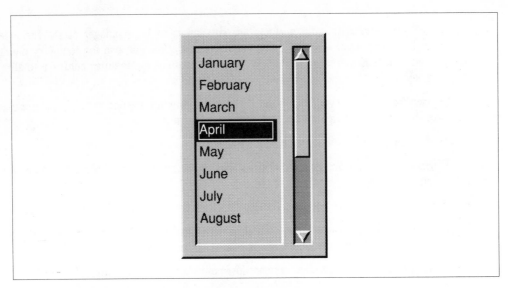

Figure 5-8. A List widget containing PushButtonGadgets

The ScrolledWindow widget is used to implement a "window" into a data object (such as text or graphics). If the data being viewed is larger than the ScrolledWindow, scrollbars are attached to enable the user to view portions of the window interactively. ScrolledWindow is capable of automatically creating and operating its own ScrollBar widget children. You have to provide ScrolledWindow with a work area to manage.

The MainWindow widget acts as the standard layout manager for the main application's window. It is designed specifically to contain a MenuBar, an optional command window, a work region, and scrollbars. This widget is an extension of the ScrolledWindow widget. You have to provide MainWindow with a work area and menu bar to manage.

The Frame widget manages one child within a visible border that the Frame draws. It is most often used to provide a 3-D border for RowColumn and Form widgets, which otherwise have no 3-D look.

The PanedWindow widget manages its children in a vertically tiled format only. Its width fluctuates with the widest widget in its list of managed children. The widget provides a sash to allow the user to adjust the height of each pane.

The Form widget has an elaborate means of linking the edges of its children to itself and to one another. Different layout criteria can be specified for each child. Form widgets are good managers to use as children of DialogShells that you build yourself. Like RowColum widgets, Forms have no border, allowing them to be placed next to other geometry managing widgets without giving the appearance that their items are grouped separately. A Frame widget is used to give Forms visible boundaries.

5.1.2 Dialog Widgets

DialogShell and MenuShell perform the window manager interaction as parent widgets of dialog widgets and menus respectively. DialogShell is created alone only when you are creating a custom dialog box that is not based on BulletinBoard or Form (since `XmCreate-BulletinBoardDialog` and `XmCreateFormDialog` exist). MenuShell is used when you are creating a menu that is not one of the standard types created by `XmCreate-PulldownMenu`, `XmCreatePopupMenu`, `XmCreateOptionMenu`, etc.

A simple Help dialog box was demonstrated in Section 3.4.2. This was a MessageBox created as a dialog using `XmCreateMessageDialog`. A MessageBox widget can be configured to display a symbol that represents the kind of information being displayed. Motif defines six symbols for this purpose, and provides a widget creation function that creates a MessageBox as a dialog for each symbol. They are `XmCreateErrorDialog`, `XmCreateInformationDialog`, `XmCreateMessageDialog`, `XmCreateQuestionDialog`, `XmCreateWorkingDialog`, and `XmCreateWarningDialog`. Figure 5-9 shows these five types of dialogs.

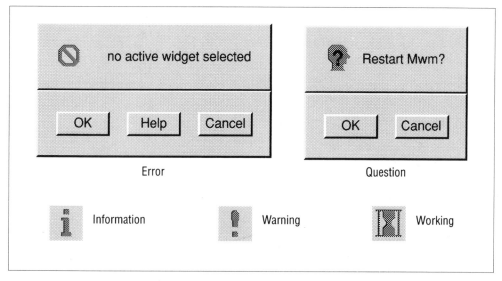

Figure 5-9. Dialog boxes with the five standard symbols

As noted in Chapter 3, *More Techniques for Using Widgets*, there is no standard dialog for help information. However, the InformationDialog seems most appropriate, once its Cancel button and possibly its Help button are unmanaged.

5.2 Widget Creation Functions

You have already seen a few of the functions Motif provides for creating widgets. For example, in Chapter 3 we used `XmCreatePulldownMenu`, `XmCreateMenuBar`, and `XmCreateMessageDialog` in *xmainwindow*. As you may recall, these are very similar to Xt's widget creation functions except that in the Motif routines:

- The widget parent argument comes before the widget instance name argument (the reverse of the Xt functions).

- No widget class pointer is necessary (it is implied by the function name).

- A separate `XtManageChild` call is required to display the widget.

There are many more of these functions. Some of them create single widgets, some create single widgets with certain special resource settings, and some create combinations of widgets.

For users of other widget sets such as Athena, the use of the IDs returned by Motif widget creation functions can be a bit confusing. The functions that create combinations of widgets don't always return the top level widget of the combination. For example, `XmCreate-MessageDialog` returns the ID of the MessageBox widget, not the ID of the DialogShell that `XmCreateMessageDialog` creates as its parent. This allows you to easily set the resources of the MessageBox. When you want to pop up the dialog, you call `XtManage-Child` with the ID of the MessageBox, not its DialogShell parent. (Users of the Athena widget set popup widgets by calling `XtPopup` on the Shell widget.)

Here is a complete list of the `XmCreate*` functions, and a brief description of what the object created is intended for.

Table 5-1. XmCreate Functions

Function	Description
`XmCreateArrowButton`	Create an ArrowButton widget.
`XmCreateArrowButtonGadget`	Create an ArrowButtonGadget.
`XmCreateBulletinBoard`	Create a BulletinBoard widget.
`XmCreateBulletinBoardDialog`	Create BulletinBoard widget with DialogShell parent.
`XmCreateCascadeButton`	Create a CascadeButton widget.
`XmCreateCascadeButtonGadget`	Create a CascadeButtonGadget.
`XmCreateCommand`	Create a Command widget.
`XmCreateDialogShell`	Create a DialogShell widget.
`XmCreateDrawingArea`	Create a DrawingArea widget.
`XmCreateDrawnButton`	Create a DrawnButton widget.
`XmCreateErrorDialog`	Create a MessageBox with error symbol.
`XmCreateFileSelectionBox`	Create a FileSelectionBox widget.
`XmCreateFileSelectionDialog`	Create a FileSelectionBox with a DialogShell parent.
`XmCreateForm`	Create a Form widget.

Table 5-1. XmCreate Functions (continued)

Function	Description
`XmCreateFormDialog`	Create a Form widget with DialogShell parent.
`XmCreateFrame`	Create a Frame widget.
`XmCreateInformationDialog`	Create a MessageBox with information symbol.
`XmCreateLabel`	Create a Label widget.
`XmCreateLabelGadget`	Create a LabelGadget.
`XmCreateList`	Create a List widget.
`XmCreateMainWindow`	Create a MainWindow widget.
`XmCreateMenuBar`	Create a RowColumn widget with resource settings for being a menubar.
`XmCreateMenuShell`	Create a MenuShell widget.
`XmCreateMessageBox`	Create a MessageBox widget.
`XmCreateMessageDialog`	Create a MessageBox with a DialogShell parent.
`XmCreateOptionMenu`	Create a RowColumn widget with resource settings for being an option menu.
`XmCreatePanedWindow`	Create a PanedWindow widget.
`XmCreatePopupMenu`	Create a RowColumn widget with resource settings for being a popup menu.
`XmCreatePromptDialog`	Create a SelectionBox widget with a DialogShell parent.
`XmCreatePulldownMenu`	Create a RowColumn widget with resource settings for being a pulldown menu.
`XmCreatePushButton`	Create a PushButton widget.
`XmCreatePushButtonGadget`	Create a PushButtonGadget.
`XmCreateQuestionDialog`	Create a MessageBox with question symbol.
`XmCreateRadioBox`	Create a RowColumn widget with resource settings to be a radio box.
`XmCreateRowColumn`	Create a RowColumn widget.
`XmCreateScale`	Create a Scale widget.
`XmCreateScrollBar`	Create a ScrollBar widget.
`XmCreateScrolledList`	Create a ScrolledWindow widget containing a List widget.
`XmCreateScrolledText`	Create a Text widget.
`XmCreateScrolledWindow`	Create a ScrolledWindow widget.
`XmCreateSelectionBox`	Create a SelectionBox widget.
`XmCreateSelectionDialog`	Create a SelectionBox widget with a DialogShell parent.
`XmCreateSeparator`	Create a Separator widget.
`XmCreateSeparatorGadget`	Create a SeparatorGadget.
`XmCreateSimpleCheckBox`	Create a RowColumn widget with resource settings to function as a CheckBox, and children.
`XmCreateSimpleMenuBar`	Create a RowColumn widget with resource settings to function as a MenuBar, and children.

Table 5-1. XmCreate Functions (continued)

Function	Description
XmCreateSimpleOptionMenu	Create a RowColumn widget with resource settings to function as a OptionMenu, and children.
XmCreateSimplePopupMenu	Create a RowColumn with resource settings to function as a popupMenu, and children.
XmCreateSimplePulldownMenu	Create a RowColumn widget with resource settings to function as a PulldownMenu, and children.
XmCreateSimpleRadioBox	Create a RowColumn widget with resource settings to function as a RadioBox, and children.
XmCreateText	Create a Text widget.
XmCreateTextField	Create a TextField widget.
XmCreateToggleButton	Create a ToggleButton widget.
XmCreateToggleButtonGadget	Create a ToggleButtonGadget.
XmCreateWarningDialog	Create a MessageBox with warning symbol.
XmCreateWorkArea	Create a RowColumn widget with resources to function as a WorkArea.
XmCreateWorkingDialog	Create a MessageBox with working symbol.

5.3 Compound Strings and Font Lists

Compound strings are designed to address two issues frequently encountered by application designers: the use of foreign character sets to display text in other languages, and the use of multiple fonts when rendering text.

Many character sets used by foreign languages are too large for the characters to be represented by the char type, as English can be. Compound strings solve this problem by representing characters as 16 bit values ("words") rather than the classic 8 bit values ("chars"). Also, since some languages such as Hebrew and Arabic are read from right-to-left, compound strings also store directional information for rendering purposes.

A compound string is made of three elements: a character set, a direction and text. Compound strings that incorporate multiple fonts are achieved by concatenating separate compound strings with different character sets together to produce a single string.

5.3.1 Simple Compound Strings

Almost all of the Motif widgets require a compound string when specifying text. Labels, PushButtons, Lists—all require their text to be given in compound string format, whether or not you require the additional flexibility compound strings provide.* Therefore, the most

---

*Currently, the Text widget does not require compound strings, but it will in future releases of Motif.

common use for compound strings in English-language applications is simply to convert standard C-style null-terminated text strings for use in a widget.

First of all, strings specified in resource files need not be converted, since Motif will automatically do the conversion.

To do the conversion for strings specified directly in the application code, we use the function XmStringCreateSimple().

```
XmString
XmStringCreateSimple(text)
    char *text;
```

The text parameter is a common C char string. The value returned is of type XmString which is an opaque type to the programmer.

As its name implies, XmStringCreateSimple() does nothing special. The function converts a C string into a compound string using the default font and direction. You cannot specify a font, a string direction, or have multiple lines. Common usage might be as follows:

```
XmString str = XmStringCreateSimple("Push Me");

widget = XtVaCreateManagedWidget("widget_name",
    xmPushButtonGadgetClass, parent,
    XmNlabelString,  str,
    NULL);

XmStringFree(str);
```

XmStringCreateSimple(), along with the other functions that create compound strings, allocates memory to store the strings created. Widgets whose resources take compound strings as values always allocate their own space and store copies of the compound string values you give them, so you must free your copy of the string after having set it in the widget resource. Compound strings are freed using XmStringFree().

This three-step process is typical of the type of interaction you will have with compound strings. You create a string, set it in a widget, then free the string (unless you want to use it in another widget). However, this process involves quite a bit of overhead; memory is allocated by the string creation function, then again by the internals of the widget for its own storage, and then your copy of the string must be deallocated (freeing memory is also an expensive operation).

This process can be simplified by using the XtVaTypedArg feature in Xt. This symbol is used in variable argument list specifications for functions like XtVaCreateManaged-Widget or XtVaSetValues. It allows you to specify resources in any type—most likely a more convenient one—and have Xt do the conversion for you. In the case of compound strings, this method can be used convert between C strings and compound strings without having to do it yourself. The following code fragment has the same effect as the example shown above without the overhead of the three-step process.

```
widget = XtVaCreateManagedWidget("widget_name",
    xmPushButtonWidgetClass, parent,
    XtVaTypedArg,
        XmNlabelString, XmRString, "Push Me", sizeof(char *),
    NULL);
```

`XtVaTypedArg` takes four additional parameters: the resource whose value is going to be set, the type of the value we are giving the resource, the value itself, and the size of the value's data type. (Note that this fourth parameter is the size of the type, not the size of the value itself!)

The resource is `XmNlabelString`, and its value is of type `XmString` (a compound string). We want to avoid doing the conversion explicitly, and so we are giving it a `char *` (string) resource. Thus, we specify `XmRString` as the type of the value we are going to provide.* The string `"Push Me"` is that value and it is of type `char *` (otherwise known as `String`), and thus of conversion type `XmRString`. The size of the data type can be returned by `sizeof(char *)`. This is the size of the `String` type, not the length of the string itself.

5.3.2 Character Sets and Font Lists

In order to use any of the Motif compound string creation functions other than `XmString-CreateSimple`, you need to know a bit more about the concept of character sets.

Strictly speaking, the term *character set* in X refers to a particular mapping between byte values and characters.† Character sets are often defined by standards bodies such as the ISO (International Standards Organization). For example, the ISO Latin-1 character set (ISO8859-1) defines encoding for the characters used in all Western languages. The first half of Latin-1 is standard ASCII, and the second half (with the eighth bit set) contains accented characters needed for Western languages other than English. Character 65 in ISO Latin-1 is a capital 'A', while 246 is a lower case 'o' with an umlaut.

The jisx0208.1983 character set, on the other hand, encodes the familiar ASCII characters in the lower seven bits, and Japanese kanji characters in the eight bit values.

There *is* a connection between this use of the term *character set* and its use in Motif compound strings, in that the character set can be used to select different fonts for use with different languages. However, for practical purposes, you can think of the character set simply as an arbitrary identifier that enables Motif widgets to pick their font at runtime from a list of fonts.

---

*This terminology can get extremely confusing. Xt uses the typedef `String` for `char *`. The representation type used by Xt resource converters for this datatype is `XtRString` (`XmRString` in Motif). A compound string, on the other hand, is of type `XmString`, with the representation type used with resource converters specified as `XmRXmString`. Is that clear now? You just have to read the symbols carefully. And it helps if you have a good understanding of the underlying mechanism of resource converters, which are described in detail in Chapter 9, *More Input Techniques*.

†Note that this is different from the definition of a font, which is a collection of glyphs used to represent the characters corresponding to each value encoded in a character set. In fact, each X font name includes a description of its encoding, along with other font information such as the font family, point size, weight, slant, and so on. (For a full description of X font naming conventions, see Chapter 6, *Font Specification*, in Volume Three, *X Window System User's Guide, Motif Edition*.)

Here's how it works:

1. Except for `XmStringCreateSimple`, the Motif compound string creation functions take as one of their arguments an arbitrary character set identifier. For example:

    ```
    XmStringCreate(text, charset)
        char *text;
        XmStringCharSet charset;
    ```

    (`XmStringCharSet` is actually just a typedef for `char *`, so the *charset* parameter is a typical C string.) `XmStringCreateSimple()` creates a compound string with the default character set, which is typically the first character set specified in a widget's font list.

2. Motif widgets have a `fontList` resource (class `FontList`) that specifies a list of fonts for the widget, together with optional, associated character set identifiers. For example, an app-defaults file might specify a font list as follows:

    ```
    *fontList: -*-courier-*-r-*--12-*=charset1, \
               -*-courier-*-r-*--14-*=charset2, \
               -*-courier-*-r-*--18-*=charset3
    ```

3. At runtime, the compound string is rendered in the first font in the widget's fontList that matches the character set identifier specified in the compound string creation function.

This loose binding between the compound string and the font used to render it is useful in a number of ways:

*   It allows the same compound string with the same character set identifier to be rendered in a different font in individual widgets, simply by specifying a different font=charset association in each widget. For example:

    ```
    *widget1.fontList: -*-courier-*-r-*--12-*=charset1
    *widget2.fontList: -*-helvetica-*-r-*--12-*=charset1
    ```

*   Compound strings rendered in different fonts can be concatenated together to create multi-font strings, with the font for each segment selected from the widget's font list by means of its unique charset identifier.

*   Compound strings can be language-independent, with the charset identifier used to select between fonts with different character set encodings. (It is this last use that gives the charset parameter its name, though this is perhaps the least common use, at least in current applications.)

The first character set specified in a widget's font list becomes the default character set for that widget. If the widget has no font list, the widget uses a "universal" character set referred to in applications by the constant `XmSTRING_DEFAULT_CHARSET`. If the user has his `"LANG"` environment variable set*, its value becomes the definition of the universal character set. If this value is invalid or its associated font cannot be used, Motif uses the value of `XmFALLBACK_CHARSET` (which is currently defined to be "ISO8859-1").

---

*See Volume Three, *X Window System User's Guide, Motif Edition*, for specifics on how to set this variable.

If a character set is listed more than once in a font list, then the first matching font is used. If a compound string specifies a character set that is not listed in the widget's XmNfontList, no error message is produced and the default character set for the widget is used.

5.3.3 Strings with Multiple Fonts

The power of compound strings is easily illustrated by an example that shows how to display a string using multiple fonts.

To incorporate more than one font in a single compound string, you must create a fontList that specifies multiple character sets. Then you must either create the compound text in *segments* using the function XmStringSegmentCreate() (a routine that allows you to control both the character set and the direction of a compound string), or you must create separate compound strings using XmStringCreate() and then concatenate them with XmStringConcat(). This concatenated string will have information embedded in it to indicate character set changes (and thus, font changes). Example 5-1 demonstrates how a compound string can be created to contain three fonts.

Example 5-1. multi_font: code to use multiple fonts in a compound string

```
/* multi_font.c --
 * Create three compound strings using 12, 14 and 18 point fonts
 * The user can specify resources so that each of the strings
 * use different fonts by setting resources similar to that shown
 * by the fallback resources.
 */
#include <Xm/Label.h>

String fallbacks[] = {
    "*fontList: -*-courier-*-r-*--12-*=charset1, \
                -*-courier-bold-o-*--14-*=charset2, \
                -*-courier-medium-r-*--18-*=charset3",
    NULL
};

main(argc, argv)
char *argv[];
{
    Widget          toplevel;
    XtAppContext    app;
    XmString        s1, s2, s3, text, tmp;
    String          string1 = "This is a string ",
                    string2 = "that contains three ",
                    string3 = "separate fonts.";

    toplevel = XtVaAppInitialize(&app, argv[0], NULL, 0,
        &argc, argv, fallbacks, NULL);

    s1 = XmStringCreate(string1, "charset1");
    s2 = XmStringCreate(string2, "charset2");
    s3 = XmStringCreate(string3, "charset3");

    /* concatenate the 3 strings on top of each other, but we can only
     * do two at a time.  So do s1 and s2 onto tmp and then do s3.
     */
    tmp = XmStringConcat(s1, s2);
```

Example 5-1. multi_font: code to use multiple fonts in a compound string (continued)

```
    text = XmStringConcat(tmp, s3);

    XtVaCreateManagedWidget("widget_name",
        xmLabelWidgetClass, toplevel,
        XmNlabelString,     text,
        NULL);

    XmStringFree(s1);
    XmStringFree(s2);
    XmStringFree(s3);
    XmStringFree(tmp);
    XmStringFree(text);

    XtRealizeWidget(toplevel);
    XtAppMainLoop(app);
}
```

The output of this code fragment is shown in Figure 5-10.

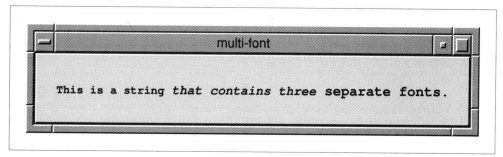

Figure 5-10. multi_font: how it looks on the screen

The XmNfontList resource is initialized to have three character set and font name pairs. Each string is created using XmStringCreate() with the appropriate text and character set specified. Then, the strings are concatenated together using XmStringConcat(), two at a time, until we have a single compound string that contains all the texts and includes all the character set changes.

It is possible to specify compound text strings (such as the XmNlabelString resource of the Label widget) in resource files as normal strings. This is possible because Motif takes care of the conversion to compound strings. However, when you want font changes within a string, you need to create compound strings or segments explicitly within the application as illustrated in Example 5-1.

5.3.4 Manipulating Compound Strings

Most C programmers are used to dealing with functions such as `strcpy()`, `strcmp()`, and `strcat()`, to copy, compare and modify strings. However, these functions are ineffective with compound strings since compound strings are not based on a byte-per-character format and they have other types of information embedded within them (character sets, directions and separators). In order to accomplish some of these common tasks, you can either convert the compound string back into C strings or use the functions Motif provides to manipulate compound strings directly. Your choice depends largely on the complexity of the compound strings you have and the complexity of the manipulations you need to do.

We've already seen how `XmStringConcat()` is used to concatenate compound strings. The following utility functions are also provided:

```
Boolean
XmStringByteCompare(str1, str2)
    XmString str1, str2;

Boolean
XmStringCompare(str1, str2);
    XmString str1, str2;

XmString
XmStringConcat(str1, str2)
    XmString str1, str2;

XmString
XmStringNConcat(str1, str2, n)
    XmString str1, str2;
    int n;

XmString
XmStringCopy(str)
    XmString str;

XmString
XmStringNCopy(str, n)
    XmString str;
    int n;

int
XmStringHasSubstring(string, substring)
    XmString string, substring;

int
XmStringLength(str)
    XmString str;
```

The `XmStringNConcat()` and `XmStringNCopy()` functions differ from their "N-less" brethren in that they concatenate or copy, respectively, only *n* characters from the specified string. Otherwise, the purpose of these functions is readily apparent from their names. Note however that since a compound string includes various tags, direction indicators and segment separators, `XmStringLength()` cannot be used to get the length of the text represented by the compound string (i.e., it's not the same as `strlen()`).

5.3.5 Converting Compound Strings to Text

If the functions provided by the Motif routines in the previous section are inadequate, you can convert compound strings back into C strings. This process can be simple or complicated depending on the complexity of the compound string to be converted. If the compound string has one character set associated with it and it has a left-to-right orientation, the process is quite simple. Fortunately, this is likely to be the case most of the time.

To make the conversion, you can use the function:

```
Boolean
XmStringGetLtoR (string, charset, text)
    XmString            string;
    XmStringCharSet     charset;
    char                **text;
```

The function takes a compound string and a character set and converts it back into a C character string. If successful, the function returns `True` and the `text` parameter will point to a newly allocated pointer to a string.

The function only gets the text from the compound string that is associated with the character set specified in `charset`. If the string contains multiple character sets, only the text associated with those segments with the same character set is copied into the returned text.

As its name implies, this function gets only left-to-right oriented text. In order to convert compound strings that have either a right-to-left orientation or multiple character sets, you will have to scan through the elements of a compound string segment by segment (a process described in Volume Six, *X Motif Programming Manual*).

5.3.6 Rendering Compound Strings

Motif always renders compound strings automatically within its widgets. More precisely, the widgets themselves manage compound string rendering. However, Motif provides convenient functions for doing the rendering which you may find useful if you are writing your own Motif-compatible widgets or extensions to Motif widgets.

For more information on this topic, see Volume Six, *X Motif Programming Manual*.

5.4 Pixmap and Image Caching Functions

As you by now know, a pixmap is an off-screen drawable maintained by the server. It is accessed from the application using an ID. A pixmap can be created using a pattern defined in file, or drawn into, and copied to a window.

Motif's pixmap caching has a simple use and a more complicated use. The simple use is described in this paragraph. Motif provides `XmGetPixmap`, which reads a bitmap file from disk and creates a pixmap of the default depth of the screen. `XmGetPixmap` caches the pixmap so that subsequent requests for the same filename will return the original pixmap.

The only thing slightly confusing about `XmGetPixmap` is that you specify your filename (including path) in the *image-name* argument.

X also defines a client-side representation of a window area, called an *image*. An image is usually generated by grabbing a portion of an existing window or pixmap using `XGetImage`. An image is a structure that contains all the data from a window area, using the server's natural data format. The structure also includes fields that describe the combination of byte-order, bit-order, and image format used by the server. Unlike many other Xlib structures, the image structure is public—its fields are documented—since it is stored on the client side. Because of the many permutations of server formats that are possible, Xlib provides generalized functions for manipulating image data, though they are rather slow because they always convert the data into the client's natural format before processing it. An image can be dumped into a window or pixmap using `XPutImage`.

Motif uses images to allow pixmaps to be specified in resource files, and to allow multiple instances of a widget to share one pixmap stored in the server. For example, you know that the MessageBox widget has several variations, with different symbols for information, warning, error, question, and working. Each of these symbols is created by MessageBox using `XmInstallImage`. (This happens before any instances of the widget class are created, in the `class_initialize` method, which will be described later.) To install each image, first an image structure is created and filled with data in standard X11 bitmap file format. Then this structure is passed to `XmInstallImage`. Also passed is the string name for this image, which will be used to used to refer to the image in resource files. For example, the question symbol is called `default_xm_question`.

When an instance of MessageBox is created using a call such as `XmCreateQuestionDialog`, the `XmNdialogType` resource is automatically set to `XmDIALOG_QUESTION`. In a switch statement, MessageBox maps this symbol into the corresponding image name, "default_xm_question." MessageBox calls `XmGetPixmap` to get the pixmap specified by this image name. If the pixmap already exists because another QuestionDialog has already been created, then this pixmap is set into the `XmNsymbolPixmap` resource. If the pixmap does not yet exist, it is created, cached for later use by widgets of this type, and set into `XmNsymbolPixmap`. (You can also bypass this entire facility from the application by creating your own pixmap and setting `XmNsymbolPixmap` directly.)

Motif keeps reference counts in order to free these cached pixmaps when they are no longer needed. Therefore, MessageBox calls `XmDestroyPixmap` when the `XmNsymbolPixmap` is set directly, when the dialog type is changed, or when the widget itself is destroyed. `XmDestroyPixmap` just decrements the reference count to a pixmap—the pixmap is destroyed only if no other widgets are using it.

Motif defines a group of images that are pre-installed in the image cache. Each of these is converted into pixmaps when they are first used to set a widget resource, using the current foreground and background colors for that first widget. Table 5-2 lists and describes these pixmaps.

Table 5-2. Built-in Motif Pixmaps

Image Name	Description
`background`	Solid background.
`25_foreground`	25% foreground, 75% background.
`50_foreground`	50% foreground, 50% background.
`75_foreground`	75% foreground, 25% background.
`horizontal`	Horizontal lines of foreground and background.
`vertical`	Vertical lines of foreground and background.
`slant_right`	Up to right lines of foreground and background.
`slant_left`	Up to left lines of foreground and background.

Any of these pre-installed images or the images installed by Motif widgets such as Message-Box can be specified in resource files. For example, the following resource setting could appear in an app-defaults file:

```
*XmCascadeButton.backgroundPixmap: 25_foreground
```

This resource setting makes the background of CascadeButtons slightly darker than they usually are, which makes their outline visible over the menubar.

5.5 Dynamic Resource Defaulting

Most resources have a fixed default value determined by the widget class. However, several of the basic appearance resources supported by Primitive have defaults that are set at run time. Namely, the foreground, background, and the two shadow colors used by a widget are set dynamically depending on the type of screen being used and on the settings of each other. The highlight color, used to redraw the background when the user clicks on a PushButton, is also dynamically defaulted.

By default on a color screen, Motif chooses a light blue background, a black foreground, a very light blue-gray top shadow, a dark blue-gray bottom shadow, and a medium blue highlight color. These are carefully chosen to strengthen the 3-D effect of the interface. If the user sets the background color to sea green, Motif adjusts the foreground, background, shadow colors, and highlight color so that they work well with a green background. If the user chooses a dark color for the background, white instead of black is used for the text. However, the user should be informed that light colors work best for the background, since the highlight color must be darker than the background color to make buttons look pressed in.

On a gray-scale screen, Motif selects a black foreground, white background, and uses light gray and dark gray for the shadows. Medium gray is used for the highlight color. On a black and white screen, the same colors are used, but light gray and dark gray are simulated using pixmaps containing different percentages of white and black.

Dynamic resource defaults are implemented using a standard feature of the R4 Xt Intrinsics called `XmRCallProc` (called `XtRCallProc` in standard Xt). In the resource list, which has not yet been introduced, you can either specify a default value or a function to be called to calculate the default value. Motif does the latter for these resources.

5.6 Resolution Independence

As you know, the units for all Xlib and Xt calls are pixels. Motif allows you to set some resources using units such as inches, so that the size and spacing of widgets will appear the same size on any display, regardless of the pixel spacing on that display.

This resolution-independence is built into all position, dimension, spacing, padding, offset, and thickness resources of all Motif widgets. The interpretation of dimensions within each widget is controlled by the XmNunitType resource, which can be set anywhere where resources can be set, including in resource files.

For some applications, such as desktop publishing, resolution independence is important. For others, it is irrelevant, or in fact harmful, because while size of graphics will be the same on all screens, the quality of those graphics will vary. What is clear on a 1280 by 1024 screen may not be clear on a 640 by 480 screen if the graphics are the same size.

XmNunitType can be set to the following values:

- XmPIXELS—all values provided to the widget are treated as normal pixel values.

- Xm100TH_MILLIMETERS—all values provided to the widget are treated as 1/100 millimeter.

- Xm1000TH_INCHES—all values provided to the widget are treated as 1/1000 inch.

- Xm100TH_POINTS—all values provided to the widget are treated as 1/100 point. A point is a unit used in text processing applications and is defined as 1/72 inch.

- Xm100TH_FONT_UNITS—all values provided to the widget are treated as 1/100 of a font unit.

The font unit allows you to specify sizes based on a font that will be chosen at run time according to your specifications. The font used is the one the user specifies with the *–font* command-line option or by setting the XmNfont resource (not XmNfontList) in a resource file. (XmNfont is used only for this in Motif.) The font unit is calculated from the dimensions of the specified font. A font unit can also be set with XmSetFontUnits. Note that once XmNunitType is set to Xm100TH_FONT_UNITS, and the font set, the actual numbers used to set resources are integral and generally large.

Unless XmNunitType is explicitly set, all widgets that are subclasses of Manager inherit the unit type of their parent. All widgets that are subclasses of Primitive have a default unit type of XmPIXELS. (They do not inherit their parent's unit type.)

Once a unit type is set, you can set resources using this unit type, and when you query them with XtVaGetValues, you will get values that use this unit type. A one-time rounding error may occur, though, which could make the value you query slightly different from the value you set. Repeated queries and sets will not make the rounding error worse. (Internally, widgets still store all their values in pixels. This becomes important to you only when you begin to write widgets.)

Motif also provides XmConvertUnits for converting between units. If you need to write your own widget that implements resolution independent custom graphics, you can use Xm-ConvertUnits, or you can use Xlib macros that give you the number of pixels and the size of the screen.

5.7 Keyboard Traversal and Focus

All Motif widgets are able to operate with keyboard input instead of pointer input. This is primarily so that people can use the keyboard to navigate forms conveniently, but it is also so that Motif applications can be run on systems that don't have a mouse.

Xt directs keyboard input to only one window at a time; this window has the keyboard focus. All Motif widgets and gadgets have code that gives them the ability to draw a highlight rectangle around themselves when they have the keyboard focus. (In practice, geometry managing widgets do not draw a highlight rectangle because they do not take user input.) The parent tells a gadget when to highlight, since gadgets can never get the focus themselves since they have no window.

The traversal works in two levels. The first level is movement between tab groups, and the second level is movement within a tab group. A tab group is one or more widgets. As you build the instance hierarchy of an application, Motif automatically links the widgets together into groups. By default, most simple widgets are a tab group by themselves. Most manager widgets are also tab groups, with all their children in the same tab group. For example, a MessageBox widget is really a Form widget containing a Label widget and three PushButton widgets; the Form, the Label, and the three pushbutton widgets are a tab group. However, since the Form and Label widgets set XmNtraversalOn to False since they don't take user input, they are not active in the tab group.

You can move the keyboard focus around in a tab group by using the arrow keys (also called navigation keys, since other keys may be mapped to this function).

Pressing the Tab key moves the focus to the first widget in the next tab group. Pressing Tab while holding the Shift key moves the focus to the first widget in the previous tab group.

Without doing anything, you should be able to negotiate your entire application using the keyboard, since Motif sets up default tab groups. However, you may want to tailor the order in which widgets are traversed within each tab group, and also the order in which tab groups are traversed.

The order of traversal of the widgets within a tab group is the same as the order in which the widgets were created. If a widget is normally included in a tab group, but you don't want it to be, set its XmNtraversalOn resources to False.

You can modify the order of traversal between tab groups using XmAddTabGroup and XmRemoveTabGroup. Each of these functions is passed a widget whose tab group should be added to the end of the traversal list, or removed from it. Both functions just set the specified widget's `XmNnavigationType` resource. There are various other settings for this resource that you can use if you set the resource directly instead of using these functions.

You can also move the focus by clicking the pointer in a widget that can accept the focus (has `XmNtraversalOn` set to `True`). Within Motif applications, you can choose between a click-to-type model, which supports keyboard traversal, and a pointer-following model, which does not support keyboard traversal. The default is the click-to-type model. You can change this by setting the `XmNkeyboardFocusPolicy` resource of a Shell widget, but this is not recommended. Note that this resource sets the keyboard focus model within this one application; this is completely separate from the model you choose for *mwm*, although the two choices available in each case are the same.

List, ScrollBar, multiline Text widgets, and Option menus must be sole members of a tab group, because they use the arrow keys for other purposes.

Because keyboard traversal depends on Motif moving the keyboard focus around, applications should not set the keyboard focus explicitly. In other words, you should never call `Xt-SetKeyboardFocus` or `XSetInputFocus`. Instead you can call `XmProcess-Traversal`.

Even Motif menus can be operated using the keyboard. A menu can be mapped by a mnemonic such as Alt-F typed anywhere in the application. Once mapped, the menu can be traversed with the arrow keys, and an item selected with the Return key. Alternately, if the strings in the menu have mnemonics defined, they will have letters underlined, and the user can type these letters to select the item. Finally, menu items can be selected without the menu being mapped by using accelerator keys, which are described in Chapter 8, *Events, Translations, and Accelerators*.

5.8 Motif Virtual Keyboard Bindings

The main alphabetic area of keyboards on different systems is very uniform, but the modifier keys such as Control, Alt, Meta, Hyper, and Super, and the function keys, are not uniform. The X keyboard model hides many of the differences between the different keyboards that are available on different systems. Each X server contains a mapping between the keycodes for each physical key, and keysyms, which are symbolic constants each of which represents a standardized meaning of a key combination. For example, there are separate keysyms `XK_A` and `XK_a` which represent the "a" key with and without the Shift key pressed. See Volume One, *Xlib Programming Manual*, for an extensive discussion of this model.

Motif adds another level of mapping to this system. Translation tables for Motif widgets reference keysyms not defined by the Xlib standard. For example, a line in the translation table of every Motif widget reads as follows:

```
static char defaultTranslation[] =
    .
    .
    <Key>osfHelp:    Help()";
```

The string `osfHelp` is in the position normally occupied by a keysym, but in this case it is a Motif virtual keysym. Motif then internally maps this string into a real keysym.

Motif maps virtual keysyms into real keysyms using the file *XKeysymDB*, which is usually in */usr/lib/X11* on UNIX-based systems. The contents of this file are different for each system, and installing this file is part of installing Motif. For example, on systems that have a Help key, osfHelp will be mapped to that key. On systems that don't have a Help key, some other key is chosen. The advantage of the Motif virtual binding system is that you can be assured that there actually is a key that performs the Help function, even if it isn't marked, and that all Motif applications on that system will use the same key. Also, on single user systems this gives the user the option of changing which key is used for each function.

5.9 The Motif User Interface Language

Motif is a hybrid of technology developed by DEC, Hewlett Packard, IBM, and Microsoft. DEC's contribution was the Application Programming Interface (API) used in DECWindows. This included a tool called the User Interface Language, or UIL.

UIL is a language for describing a Motif user interface. It looks similar to a programming language except that it has no control flow. Part of it, stored in a separate library, is called the Motif Resource Manager (MRM). You specify your user interface in a file. The *.c* file is compiled in the standard fashion, and linked with the –lMrm library (in addition to –lXt, –l-Xm, and –lX11). The *.uil* file has to be compiled with a program called *uil*, to form a *.uid* file.

The *.c* file is similar to a standard Xt application, but after XtAppInitialize you call MrmOpenHierarchy, which reads the *.uid* to create the hierarchy of widgets. The *.c* file is primarily boilerplate, except for the callback functions for the widgets in your application. Example 5-2 shows the *.c* file for a simple application built with UIL.

Example 5-2. The .c file for a simple UIL application

```
#include <stdio.h>
/*
 * Declare our callback functions.
 */
static void button_selected();

/*
 * Miscellaneous UIL boilerplate: next 8 lines
 */
#include <Mrm/MrmAppl.h>                     /* Motif Toolkit */
static MrmHierarchy      s_MrmHierarchy; /* MRM database hierarchy id */
static char      *vec[]={"hellomotif.uid"}; /* MRM database file list */
static MrmCode          class ;
static MrmCount         regnum = 1 ;
static MrmRegisterArg   regvec[] = {
    {"button_selected",(caddr_t) button_selected }
};
/*
 * Define our callback functions.
 */
static void button_selected(widget, call_data, client_data)
```

Example 5-2. The .c file for a simple UIL application (continued)

```
        Widget    widget;
        XtPointer client_data;
        XtPointer call_data;
{
        XmAnyCallbackStruct *data = (XmAnyCallbackStruct *) call_data;
        char *tag = (char *) client_data;

        printf("button selected\n");
}

int main(argc, argv)
int argc;
char **argv;
{
        XtAppContext        app_context;
        Widget topLevel, appMain;

        /*
         *   Initialize the MRM
         */
        MrmInitialize ();

        topLevel = XtVaAppInitialize(
                &app_context,          /* Application context */
                "XUilDemo",            /* application class name */
                NULL, 0,               /* command line option list */
                &argc, argv,           /* command line args */
                NULL,                  /* for missing app-defaults file */
                NULL);                 /* terminate varargs list */

        /*
         *   Define the Mrm.hierarchy (only 1 file)
         */

        if (MrmOpenHierarchy (1,               /* number of files */
                vec,                                  /* files */
                NULL,
                &s_MrmHierarchy)          /* ptr to returned id */
                != MrmSUCCESS) {
            printf ("Mrm can't open hierarchy\n");
        }

        /*
         *      Register our callback routines so that the resource
         *      manager can resolve them at widget-creation time.
         */

        if (MrmRegisterNames (regvec, regnum)
                != MrmSUCCESS)
            printf("Mrm can't register names\n");

        /*
         *   Call MRM to fetch and create the pushbutton and its container
         */

        if (MrmFetchWidget (s_MrmHierarchy,
                "helloworld_main",
                topLevel,
                &appMain,
                &class) != MrmSUCCESS)
```

Example 5-2. The .c file for a simple UIL application (continued)

```
        printf("Mrm can't fetch interface\n");
    /*  Manage the main window of the hierarchy created by Mrm. */
    XtManageChild(appMain);

    XtRealizeWidget(topLevel);

    XtAppMainLoop(app_context);
}
```

This *.c* file stays essentially the same for a much more complicated application, with the
exception of added callback functions and added event handlers for popping up popup widgets. The description of the hierarchy of widgets lies in one or more *.uil* modules. Example
5-3 shows the *.uil* module for the application whose C code is shown above.

Example 5-3. The .uil file for a simple UIL application

```
module helloworld
    version = 'v1.0'
    names = case_sensitive
procedure
    button_selected();
object
    helloworld_main : XmRowColumn {
    controls {
        XmLabel our_label;
        XmPushButton    our_button;
    };
    };
object
    our_button : XmPushButton {
    arguments {
        XmNlabelString = compound_string('Hello',separate=true)
                & 'World!';
    };
    callbacks {
        XmNactivateCallback = procedure button_selected();
    };
    };
object
    our_label : XmLabel {
    arguments {
        XmNlabelString =
                compound_string('Press button once',separate=true) &
                compound_string('to change label;',separate=true) &
                'twice to exit.';
    };
    };
end module;
```

The question is: Should you develop your application with pure C code or use UIL?

Right away you should know that UIL is cumbersome if your application will contain custom widgets. UIL contains a complete description of the widgets it knows about in a syntax called the Widget Meta Language (WML). Motif's data is stored in *motif.wml*. If you want to add a new widget, you have to make a copy of this file, and edit it to include a description of your widget. Then you have to rebuild UIL to incorporate this data. You will have to update both your widget and the *.wml* file, and then update the UIL compiler, every time you change the resources of your custom widget.

Assuming you will not be creating custom widgets, the following is an attempt to weigh the benefits and disadvantages of each programming method.

UIL's benefits seem to be:

- More complete separation of user interface description from application code. The former is in the *.uil* file, and the latter in the *.c* file. Theoretically, different programmers can be working on each type of file, since they only interact in the names of callback functions.

- Better compile time checking than standard Xt programming. UIL checks your user-interface specification at compile time to make sure you don't try to set resources that don't exist on the widget you are setting them on, and checks that you are using the right type of value. It also issues a warning if you create a child under a parent that doesn't support that type of child.

- Forward references to widgets that have not yet been created are allowed. This can clarify a program, since the children of each widget are listed where the widget is created. In standard C code, you have to find out the variable of type `Widget` for the geometry managing widget, and then search throughout the code for widgets that use that widget as parent.

- Since the source code is boilerplate with the exception of callback functions, the application needs compiling and linking less often. The user interface can be modified by changing the *.uil* file, and compiling it with *uil*, which is fast.

UIL's disadvantages are:

- You have to learn another syntax to use it.

- Large increase in executable file size. While a Motif "hello, world" program using pure C programming is about 720K bytes in size on my system,* the same application is 1250K in size using UIL. This size penalty is serious from the point of view of disk space, loading time, and memory utilization. On systems with shared libraries, however, there will be only one copy of the libraries in memory. This solves two of the above complaints, leaving only a slower linking time at run time.

- When the callbacks in the *.c* module must be changed, you have to recompile and relink, which takes longer (without shared libraries) than linking the same application using pure

---

*A Sony NWS-841 workstation running BSD 4.3. Note that this is already quite big enough!

C programming. In my experiment, using the *time*(1) utility built into *csh* and */bin/time*, the UIL version takes about 50 percent longer. This disadvantage is balanced by the fact that the *.c* module has to be recompiled less often.

- Need to recompile UIL whenever custom widgets change.

- Longer startup time of the finished application.

When deciding whether to use UIL or standard C, it is also relevant to consider the other programming tools available. First of all there are User Interface Management Systems (UIMSs) and Interface Development Tools (IDTs) on the market. These are programs that let you build your user interface interactively, and then output either C code or UIL code that describes the interface. These eliminate the tedium of building the interface in C, and eliminate the need to learn UIL's syntax. UIMSs and IDTs also contain lists of Motif widgets and resources, but since they output C code you can easily add your own custom widgets.

Another tool worth researching is the Widget Creation Library (WCL), written by Martin Brunecky and David Smyth. This library performs a similar job as UIL, but allows you to specify the interface in resource files instead of using UIL syntax. This resource file is read at run time and therefore does not require compiling. The WCL library is much smaller than UIL.*

---

*WCL is available via anonymous ftp from *devvax.jpl.nasa.gov* or *expo.lcs.mit.edu*. As of publication, the *pub* directory on *devvax*, and the *contrib* directory on *expo*, contains the following files:

```
-rw-r--r--  1 0        0        201775 Oct 19 10:00 Wcl_04.tar.Z
-rw-r--r--  1 0        0         90621 Oct 19 10:10 Wcl.ps.Z
-rw-r--r--  1 0        0        186612 Oct 19 10:10 WclSlides.ps.Z
```

expo also has what appears to be an earlier version, *Wcl_03.tar.Z*. The *.ps* files contain documentation in PostScript format. All files must be uncompressed, as described in the Preface.

6

Inside a Widget

This chapter describes the code inside a basic widget. Much of this code is common to all widgets. You can think of it as a framework that Xt uses to implement a widget's features. After reading this chapter, you should understand the procedure for creating your own widget around this framework.

In This Chapter:

6
Inside a Widget

This chapter reveals the framework of code common to all widgets. As an example, it describes the code for the BitmapEdit widget that was used in versions of the *xbitmap* applications early in Chapter 4, *An Example Application*. Later examples in that chapter described how to implement the bitmap editor without a BitmapEdit widget. Therefore, you have already seen the code that is specific to this widget, and can concentrate on the framework and how to place widget-specific code within this framework.

Some applications use only the standard user interface elements defined in the widget set. If you are writing an application like this, you have no need to write your own widgets, and no real need to understand the internals of widgets. However, many applications have at least one custom window which has features not supported by any existing widget. To implement such features, you can add to a Core or Primitive widget from your application code or you can write your own widget.

Placing specialized user-interface code into a widget has several advantages. For one, the widget becomes a self-contained module that can be modified and documented separately and used in other programs. Second, the code will take advantage of Xt's automatic dispatching of events to widgets, and several other features that you can't use from the application. Finally, it is a general premise of Xt that application code should be separated as much as possible from user-interface code.

It is important to remember that widget classes are never written from scratch. People always start from template files that contain the framework for a widget without the specific code, or even better, if possible, from an existing widget that has some similar characteristics. Therefore, you'll never have to type in the framework you're about to see. You'll only have to learn where to insert your code into it. The beauty of the widget framework is that the code within it is very modular—each module has a specific place and purpose. Once you understand the framework, you can locate these modules in existing code and use them as examples. Chapter 7, *Basic Widget Methods*, shows you how to write the most important modules within the framework.

By and large, a widget whose superclass is Core can operate under any widget set without modification. However, both the Motif widget set and the OPEN LOOK widget set have Primitive classes beneath Core that add some basic features common to all widgets in each set. In the case of Motif, by subclassing from Primitive you get support for keyboard traversal with highlighting, resolution independence, shadows, Motif's automatic color selection, and a Help key callback. These features are basic to Motif's user-interface conventions, and therefore a widget that doesn't use them would look out of place in a Motif application. In order to inherit these features, BitmapEdit is a subclass of Primitive; it not compatible with other widget sets. Converting it, however, is a trivial matter, and will be described later in the chapter.

6.1 Widget Source File Organization

A widget is implemented in two header files and an executable code file. Each of these files contains specific elements. The names of these files are derived from the name of the widget class, which in this case is BitmapEdit:

- The private header file, *BitmapEdiP.h*, defines the widget's class and instance structures, including pointers to the widget's methods.

- The implementation file, *BitmapEdit.c*, contains the actual code for the widget, including the widget's methods and actions.

- The public header file, *BitmapEdit.h*, contains declarations needed by the application to use the widget.

The final "P" in the include file name stands for Private. Only *BitmapEdit.c* and any modules that implement subclasses of BitmapEdit should include *BitmapEdiP.h*. If an application includes this file and references any of its contents, it is breaking the rules of encapsulation, and changes to this widget may affect the application.

An application program that uses a widget includes only *BitmapEdit.h*.

The implementation filenames (and all the filenames used by your application, for that matter) should have 12 or fewer characters so that the code can be copied easily to some System V systems.* That's why the "t" in *BitmapEdiP.h* is left out.

The next three major sections describe the contents of the three files that make up a widget. These files are treated in the order shown in the above list because they are generally developed in this order.

---

*These systems have a 14-character filename limit; the 12-character limit allows files to be placed under source control or compressed. The X Consortium keeps all filenames to a maximum of 12 characters. That limits the actual class name to 9 characters, to leave room for the P.h suffix. If the widget class name is longer than 9 characters, it is truncated in the filename. For example, the private include file for the Constraint class is *ConstrainP.h* (without the final t).

6.2 The Private Header File—BitmapEdiP.h

Xt implements classes and instances with two structures, the class structure and the instance structure. By definition of C structures, the fields in both structures are fixed at compile time. Both of these structures are defined in the private include file for the class, in this case *BitmapEdiP.h*.

There is only one copy of the class structure in the running application, which all instances share. But each instance has its own copy of the instance structure, whose fields are set by the resource database as the instance is created. Fields in the instance structure can also be set by `XtVaSetValues` or read by `XtVaGetValues`.

The class structure's fields contain pointers to methods and pieces of data that control how Xt handles instances of this class.

The instance structure carries a complete widget state, including everything that can be different between one instance and the next. For example, the instance structure of the Core class, which every widget inherits, has fields for x, y, $width$, and $height$ values, which correspond to the size of the widget and its location relative to the top-left corner of its parent. These particular fields are public; they can be set from the resource database or with `XtVaSetValues`, and their values can be read with `XtVaGetValues`. Other instance structure fields are private, and are used only for convenience to make data globally available within the widget.

Actually, the instance structure is not global in the normal C sense. When Xt invokes a method, it passes the method a pointer to the widget instance structure. Methods do their work by using the public fields and changing the private fields in this instance structure. For example, a method that draws in the window can get the window's dimensions directly from the widget instance structure. When action functions are called, they also are passed a pointer to the instance structure. Therefore, the fields inside the instance structure are available just about everywhere in the widget code.

6.2.1 Parts and Records

The organization of both class and instance structures is determined by the hierarchy of widget classes from which the current widget class is derived. For example, in the code for the BitmapEdit widget whose class hierarchy is shown in Figure 6-1, the class structure begins with the class fields defined by the Core class, followed by the class fields defined by Primitive, followed by the class fields defined by BitmapEdit.

Xt supplies three basic classes that are used as the basis for custom widgets, Core, Composite, and Constraint.* Figure 6-1 also shows the relationship of these classes to each other. Core is the class upon which all widgets are based. It defines common characteristics of all widgets, such as their methods, and basic resources such as height and width. Even if your widget is unlike any existing widget, it will still inherit features from the Core widget. The

---

*Shell, the fourth Intrinsics-supplied widget class, is not usually subclassed by application or widget programmers.

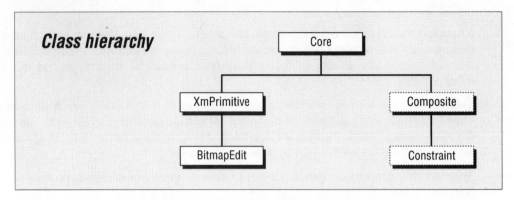

Figure 6-1. The class hierarchy of the BitmapEdit widget (with other classes shown dotted)

class and instance structures of a subclass of Composite such as Box begin with the fields from Core, continue with fields from Composite, and end with the fields defined by Box. Composite and Constraint are subclasses of Core that have additional methods that allow them to manage children; they are described in Chapter 12, *Geometry Management*. This chapter concentrates on the features of the Core widget.

Xt requires that you implement each class's new fields as a separate structure called a `Part`, and then combine this `Part` structure with each superclass's `Part` structure in the complete structure called a `Rec`, or record. In real code, these structures are called *widgetname*`ClassPart` and *widgetname*`ClassRec` for the class structure, and simply *widgetname*`Part` and *widgetname*`Rec` for the instance structure.

The reason for this "structure within a structure" design is primarily to reduce the changes in the code of subclasses that would be required if changes were made to the superclass's structures. As we will see later, only the portion of the *.c* file that initializes the class structure will need changing if a superclass class structure is changed. A second benefit of this design is that it reduces the amount of typing required to implement a new class.

6.2.2 Class Part and Class Record

Let's make these ideas concrete by showing the class structure for BitmapEdit. The complete class structure is called `BitmapEditClassRec`, and the partial structure is called `BitmapEditClassPart`. Their definitions from *BitmapEdiP.h* are shown in Example 6-1.

Example 6-1. BitmapEdiP.h: the class part and class record

```
/*
 * BitmapEditP.h - Private definitions for BitmapEdit widget
 */

/* protect against multiple including of this file */
#ifndef _ORABitmapEditP_h
#define _ORABitmapEditP_h
```

Example 6-1. BitmapEdiP.h: the class part and class record (continued)

```
/*
 * Include private header file of superclass.
 * In this case, however, Primitive's header file is
 * thrown into XmP.h.
 */
#include <Xm/XmP.h>
/*
 * Include public header file for this widget.
 */
#include "BitmapEdit.h"
/* New fields for the BitmapEdit widget class record */
typedef struct {
    int make_compiler_happy;    /* need dummy field */
} BitmapEditClassPart;

/* Full class record declaration */
typedef struct _BitmapEditClassRec {
    CoreClassPart        core_class;
    XmPrimitiveClassPart     primitive_class;
    BitmapEditClassPart      bitmapEdit_class;
} BitmapEditClassRec;
```

Like most widget classes, BitmapEdit provides no new fields in the class part, but it needs one dummy member to make the C compiler happy. A class defines new class part fields to allow a subclass to choose to inherit a function or to replace it. Most classes don't define fields here because they don't plan to have subclasses. This fine point is described in Section 12.4.5.

The `CorePart` and `CoreClassPart` structures are defined in Core's private header file *<X11/CoreP.h>*, which is included by *<Xm/XmP.h>*. `XmPrimitivePart` and `Xm-PrimitiveClassPart` are also defined in *<Xm/XmP.h>*. In general, you need to include the private header file of the superclass at the top of your private header file. The header files begin with an `ifndef` statement that allows the preprocessor to make sure that no header file is included twice.

If the class structure contains a pointer to an extension structure, you can add to the class structure in later releases of your widget and maintain binary compatibility with subclasses. This feature is used in the basic Intrinsics classes Composite and Constraint, but is unlikely to be useful to you. However, when you do define an extension structure, you do so in the private header file. Extension structures are discussed in Section 14.13.

6.2.3 Instance Part and Instance Record

The instance record is built exactly like the class structure: by defining new fields in a part structure, and then by combining the instance parts of all superclasses in the instance record. `BitmapEditPart` defines BitmapEdit's new widget instance fields, and the entire widget instance record is `BitmapEditRec`. These structures are defined in *BitmapEdiP.h* (along with the class structures just shown) and are shown in Example 6-2. We've included several likely instance variables, but none of those shown is an essential part of the widget structure.

Example 6-2. BitmapEdiP.h: the instance part and instance record

```
/* New fields for the BitmapEdit widget record */
typedef struct {
    /* resources */
    Pixel   foreground;
    XtCallbackList  callback;/* application installed callback fns */
    Dimension  pixmap_width_in_cells;
    Dimension  pixmap_height_in_cells;
    int   cell_size_in_pixels;
    int   cur_x, cur_y;       /* pstn of visible corner in big pixmap */
    char  *cell;              /* for keeping track of array of bits */
    Boolean showAll;          /* whether bitmap should display
                                 entire bitmap */

    /* private state */
    Dimension  pixmap_width_in_pixels;
    Dimension  pixmap_height_in_pixels;
    Pixmap  big_picture;
    GC   draw_gc;             /* for drawing into pixmap */
    GC   undraw_gc;           /* for undrawing into pixmap */
    GC   copy_gc;             /* for copying pixmap into window */
} BitmapEditPart;

/*
 * Full instance record declaration
 */
typedef struct _BitmapEditRec {
    CorePart          core;
    XmPrimitivePart     primitive;
    BitmapEditPart     bitmapEdit;
} BitmapEditRec;

#endif                      /* _ORABitmapEditP_h */
```

Unlike the class part, which generally defines no new fields, the instance part of a widget almost always defines new instance variables. These variables control all the configurable elements of the widget, and they hold the widget's state.

Some of these instance variables are resources because they are listed in the resource list in the *BitmapEdit.c* file. (This resource list has exactly the same format as the resource list you saw in the application code in Section 3.6.2). These variables are known as public instance variables (because they are readable and writable from the application). By convention, the public instance variables are placed first in the instance part structure, and comments indicate which fields are public. When the application instantiates the widget, Xt sets the public fields based on the resource databases, the command line (the *-xrm* form), and the argument list passed to `XtVaCreateManagedWidget`. Later on, the application may change these fields using `XtVaSetValues`.

The private instance structure fields (not listed in the widget's resource list) are either derived from resource values or they hold some aspect of the widget's state (such as whether it is highlighted). As in Example 6-2, graphics contexts (GCs) are always found here as private fields if the widget draws any graphics. Graphics contexts are needed for doing drawing, and are derived from public instance structure fields such as colors and fonts, because it is the GC that actually carries color and font information to the X server. GCs were introduced in Section 4.2.

You may notice that the `Part` structures of the superclasses are referenced in the `Bitmap-EditRec` structure. As mentioned earlier, you get these by including the private include file of the immediate superclass, which in turn includes the private include file of its own superclass, and so on.

Both the class and instance structures defined in *BitmapEdiP.h* are `typedef` templates; they do not allocate storage. Xt allocates storage for the instance record when the application calls `XtVaCreateWidget` or `XtVaCreateManagedWidget` to create the widget. The class record, on the other hand, is initialized statically (at compile time) in the *.c* file. The compiler makes sure that the definition of the class record (in *BitmapEdiP.h*) and the initialization of the class record (in *BitmapEdit.c*) use identical structures, since *BitmapEdiP.h* includes *BitmapEdit.c*. If a field is accidentally left out of the class structure in either file, the compiler will catch the problem (but if the same member is left out of both files, the problem won't be caught and Xt will likely dump core).

BitmapEdiP.h contains an `extern` reference to the class structure initialized in *Bitmap-Edit.c*. This reference is shown in Example 6-3.

Example 6-3. BitmapEdiP.h: declaring the external class record

```
extern BitmapEditClassRec bitmapEditClassRec;
```

Because the private header file includes the public header file, there is no obvious reason for this `extern` declaration. But since all widget code seems to have it, we go along with the convention.

The naming conventions for the various structure declarations in the private header file are important, and can be confusing. A table summarizing the conventions for types and variables in the widget implementation files is shown in Section 6.6 (after the contents of the *.c* and *.h* files are shown).

That's all there is in the private header file! If you should need to refer back to the private header file for BitmapEdit, it is listed with the rest of the source for the widget in Appendix E, *The xbitmap Application*.

6.3 The Widget Implementation File—BitmapEdit.c

The central element of the *.c* file is the initialization of the class record. Remember that the `typedef` of the class record was declared in *BitmapEdiP.h*, but the record is allocated and the actual values in each field are set in *BitmapEdit.c*. When Xt takes over control of the widgets after the application calls `XtAppMainLoop`, it is the values in this class record that supply Xt with all the information it uses to manage widget instances.

The organization of the *.c* file is quite simple. First, it defines everything that will be placed into the class record, and then initializes the class record, setting fields using these definitions. The major things that need defining are the functions that implement each method, the resource list, the translation table, and the actions table. It would be logical to define these four things at the beginning of the source file, and then put the class record last. This is almost the case, except that by convention the methods and actions are declared at the top of the source file and then defined at the end *after* the class record initialization. This actually makes the widget code clearer because the method declarations provide a complete list of the methods that will be defined later in the file, and the class record remains near the top of the file where it's easier to find. (Not all the methods have to be defined by a class, because some methods can be inherited or not used, as we will discuss in Section 6.3.8.) Figure 6-2 summarizes the conventional order of code in the *.c* file.*

6.3.1 Obligatory Include Files

The *.c* file begins with the standard includes:

- *<stdio.h>*, since `printf` always comes in handy for debugging purposes.

- *<Xm/XmP.h>*, which includes *<X11/IntrinsicP.h>* (which includes *<X11/Intrinsic.h>*) for the Xt supplied widget classes Core, Composite, and Constraint, declarations of Intrinsics functions, and several useful macros. *XmP.h* also includes *<Xm/Xm.h>* for the standard resource names used in defining the resource list.

- For widget sets other than Motif, include *<X11/IntrinsicP.h>* and *<X11/StringDefs.h>*.

- The private header file for this widget: *"BitmapEdiP.h"*.

Example 6-4. BitmapEdit.c: include files

```
#include <stdio.h>
#include <Xm/XmP.h>
#include "BitmapEdiP.h"
```

Remember that *BitmapEdiP.h* includes the private header file of the immediate superclass (which includes the private header file of its own superclass, and so on), and each private header file includes the public header file for its class, so that all the information in all the public and private header files for all superclasses is available to this *.c* file as a result of this one include statement.

We'll look at *BitmapEdit.c* in seven parts, in an order corresponding to Figure 6-2.

---

*Here we use the terminology defined in Kernighan and Ritchie's *The C Programming Language* (Prentice-Hall 1978). A *declaration* announces the properties of a variable (its type, size, etc.), while a *definition* causes storage to be allocated. This distinction is important in the Toolkit because many things are declared and defined in separate steps.

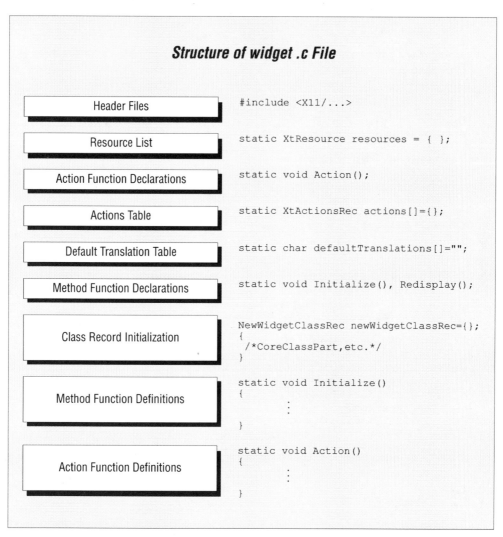

Structure of widget .c File

Header Files	`#include <X11/...>`
Resource List	`static XtResource resources = { };`
Action Function Declarations	`static void Action();`
Actions Table	`static XtActionsRec actions[]={};`
Default Translation Table	`static char defaultTranslations[]="";`
Method Function Declarations	`static void Initialize(), Redisplay();`

Class Record Initialization	`NewWidgetClassRec newWidgetClassRec={};`
	`{`
	`  /*CoreClassPart,etc.*/`
	`}`

Method Function Definitions	`static void Initialize()`
	`{`
	`   :`
	`}`

Action Function Definitions	`static void Action()`
	`{`
	`   :`
	`}`

Figure 6-2. Order of code in widget .c file

6.3.2 Defining the Resource List

A widget inherits the resources defined by its superclasses, and it can also add its own resources by defining a resource list and setting it into the class structure. A widget resource list is identical to an application resource list, which you saw added to *xbitmap* in Chapter 4. The only difference is that a widget need not call `XtGetApplicationResources`.

In creating an application resource list, we created a structure called `app_data` whose fields were to be set through resources. In widget code, the instance part structure is used just like `app_data`, except that the private instance structure fields will not appear in the resource list. Each member of the instance structure that is to be a resource must have an entry in the resource list.

Example 6-5 shows a resource list for the public instance variables defined previously in Example 6-2.

Example 6-5. BitmapEdit's resource list

```
#define offset (field) XtOffsetOf (BitmapEditRec, field)
static XtResource resources[] = {
    {
    XtNtoggleCallback,
    XtCToggleCallback,
    XtRCallback,
    sizeof(XtPointer),
    offset(bitmapEdit.callback),
    XtRCallback,
    NULL
    },
    {
    XtNcellSizeInPixels,
    XtCCellSizeInPixels,
    XtRInt, sizeof(int),
    offset(bitmapEdit.cell_size_in_pixels),
    XtRImmediate,
    (XtPointer)DEFAULT_CELL_SIZE
    },
    {
    XtNpixmapWidthInCells,
    XtCPixmapWidthInCells,
    XtRDimension,
    sizeof(Dimension),
    offset(bitmapEdit.pixmap_width_in_cells),
    XtRImmediate,
    (XtPointer)DEFAULT_PIXMAP_WIDTH
    },
    {
    XtNpixmapHeightInCells,
    XtCPixmapHeightInCells,
    XtRDimension,
    sizeof(Dimension),
    offset(bitmapEdit.pixmap_height_in_cells),
    XtRImmediate,
    (XtPointer)DEFAULT_PIXMAP_HEIGHT
    },
    {
    XtNcurX,
    XtCCurX,
    XtRInt,
    sizeof(int),
    offset(bitmapEdit.cur_x),
    XtRImmediate,
    (XtPointer) 0
    },
    {
    XtNcurY,
```

Example 6-5. BitmapEdit's resource list (continued)

```
    XtCCurY,
    XtRInt,
    sizeof(int),
    offset(bitmapEdit.cur_y),
    XtRString,
    (XtPointer) NULL
      },
      {
    XtNcellArray,
    XtCCellArray,
    XtRString,
    sizeof(String),
    offset(bitmapEdit.cell),
    XtRImmediate,
    (XtPointer) 0
      },
      {
    XtNshowEntireBitmap,
    XtCShowEntireBitmap,
    XtRBoolean,
    sizeof(Boolean),
    offset(bitmapEdit.showAll),
    XtRImmediate,
    (XtPointer) True
      },
};
```

The details of each field in a resource list entry is presented in Chapter 10, *Resource Management and Type Conversion*.

As mentioned earlier, a widget class inherits all the resources defined in the resource lists of its superclasses. If a resource is given the same name as a superclass resource, it overrides the superclass resource. One reason to create a new resource with the same name as a superclass resource is to give it a new, subclass-specific default value. The Primitive widget does this to replace Xt's default value for XmNbackground and XmNbackgroundPixmap. Another reason is to provide further processing on a resource value. For example, Primitive redefines the XmNx and XmNy resources so that it can add code to calculate these values using the current unit type (to implement resolution independence).

When defining a resource list, use constants defined in *<Xm/Xm.h>* whenever possible. However, any constant unique to this widget class can be defined in the public include file, as is described in the next section.

Table 6-1 summarizes the conventions for the constants used in the resource list.

Table 6-1. Resource List Constant Conventions

Prefix	First word capitalization	Description
XmN	Lower	Resource name
XmC	Upper	Resource class
XmR	Upper	Representation type

The representation type of a resource is a string that represents the type in which the widget stores the resource value. Xt constants and functions of all types use upper case letters whenever a word break might otherwise be called for. Two examples of resource names following this convention are `XmNborderColor` and `XmNmappedWhenManaged`.

Example 6-6 shows how the resource list is entered into the class structure. You'll see this again in Section 6.3.5 where we show the entire class record and describe how to initialize it. The names of the fields in the class structure are shown in the comments at right.

Example 6-6. Setting the resource list into the class structure

```
BitmapEditClassRec bitmapEditClassRec = {
    {   /* Core class part */
        .
        .
        resources,              /* resources */
        XtNumber(resources),    /* resource_count */
        .
        .
    },
    {   /* Primitive class part */
        .
        .
        .
    },
    {   /* BitmapEdit class part */
        0,                      /* dummy_field */
    }
};
```

Note that a widget or an application can get the resource list for a class using `XtGet-ResourceList`, which returns a pointer to a resource list of the same form as shown above. This function isn't needed in most applications or widgets.

6.3.3 The Translation Table and Actions Table

You may recall that the translation table maps event sequences into string action names, and the action table then maps string action names into actual action functions. This is done in two steps so that the translation table is a single string that can be specified in the resource databases (since resource databases are always composed entirely of strings). The action table is not configurable through the resource database, but it can be added to the application or with `XtAppAddAction(s)`.

Like the resource list, the default translation table and the actions table have to be defined before the class record can be initialized. They determine which events this widget will respond to, and which functions defined in this source file will be triggered by those events.

The translation table is a resource defined by the Core class. It is a strange resource in several ways. It has no default value in the resource list. Instead, the default translation table is initialized into the class structure. Translations are not inherited like other resources—you do not get the sum of all the translation tables registered by the superclasses. Rather, the translation table you specify in the class structure is the only one (in the code) that matters. However, you can *choose* to use the immediate superclass's translation table instead of defining one, in which case you initialize the translation table field in the class structure to be Xt-InheritTranslations.

Each widget has its own action list, and if the application registers an action list, it is kept as a separate list. When an event combination occurs in a widget, Xt translates the event combination into an action string and searches that widget's action list. If the action string is found in the widget's action list, the search stops and that action function is called. If the action string is not found in the widget's action list, then the application's action list is searched. If neither list contains the appropriate action string, Xt prints a diagnostic warning. If the application and the widget both define the same action string in the actions table, the application's function mapped to that string will never be called. Two widget classes, however, may have the same action function name, and they will not conflict.

Example 6-7 shows a default translation table and an action table. Note that, like methods, the action functions are declared before being used in the actions table, but they will actually be defined later in the source file.

Example 6-7. The default translation table and the actions table

```
static void DrawCell(), UndrawCell(), ToggleCell();

static char defaultTranslations[] =
    "<Btn1Down>:    DrawCell()              \n\
     <Btn2Down>:    UndrawCell()            \n\
     <Btn3Down>:    ToggleCell()            \n\
     <Btn1Motion>:  DrawCell()              \n\
     <Btn2Motion>:  UndrawCell()            \n\
     <Btn3Motion>:  ToggleCell()";

static XtActionsRec actions[] = {
    {"DrawCell", DrawCell},
    {"UndrawCell", UndrawCell},
    {"ToggleCell", ToggleCell},
};
```

The pointers to the actions table and translation table are placed into the class structure just like the resource list (but of course into different fields), as shown in Example 6-8. The names of the fields in the class structure are shown in the comments at right. (You'll see this again shortly in the section on class structure initialization.)

Example 6-8. Translations in the Core class record

```
BitmapEditClassRec bitmapEditClassRec = {
    {  /* core class part */
        .
        .

        actions,                 /* actions */
        XtNumber(actions),       /* num_actions */
        .
        .

        defaultTranslations,     /* tm_table */
    },
    {  /* Primitive class part */
        .
        .
        .

    },
    {                            /* BitmapEdit class part */
      0,                         /* dummy_field */
    }
};
```

Note that the default translation table cannot be compiled with `XtParseTranslation-Table` before being placed in the class structure, since the class structure initialization occurs at compile time. Xt compiles the default translations when the class is initialized.

The translation table and actions table are discussed more fully in Chapter 8, *Events, Translations, and Accelerators*.

6.3.4 Declaring Methods

Xt calls a method when the application calls a certain Xt function. For example, when an application creates a widget with `XtVaCreateManagedWidget` (or any similar call), Xt calls the `initialize` method of that widget class. There are separate methods called when `Expose` events occur, when `XtVaSetValues` is called, and when `XtDestroy-Widget` is called. Methods are distinct from actions in that methods are called in response to application function calls and `Expose` events, while actions are usually called in response to user-selectable events. Methods also each have their own field in the class structure, while actions are listed in a table that is stored in one field of the class structure. Pointers to action functions are placed in an action table which is then entered into the class structure, while a pointer to each method function is entered directly into its field of the class structure.

The widget's methods should be declared near the top of the .c file. This is so that the class structure initialization can appear before the method definitions. As usual in C, they should be declared as the actual type returned, such as `void` or `Bool`.* They should be declared static so that the scope of these variables is limited to this source file, eliminating possible

---

*Note that you cannot declare methods using the prototype procedure symbols Xt defines such as `XtExposeProc` (for the `expose` method), since these are defined to be pointers to functions that return the right type; they are not return types. Their only use is within Xt.

conflicts with other widget classes. Example 6-9 shows the method declarations from BitmapEdit.

Example 6-9. BitmapEdit.c: function type declarations

```
/* Declaration of methods */

static void Initialize();
static void Redisplay();
static void Destroy();
static void Resize();
static Boolean SetValues();
static XtGeometryResult QueryGeometry();

/* these Core methods not needed by BitmapEdit:
 *
 * static void ClassInitialize();
 * static void Realize();
 */

/* the following are functions private to BitmapEdit */
static void DrawPixmaps(), DoCell(), ChangeCellSize();

/* the following are actions of BitmapEdit */
static void DrawCell(), UndrawCell(), ToggleCell();
```

6.3.5 Initializing the Class Record

We've already shown you how to create the resource list, the translation table, and the actions table, and set into the class structure. A major part of the work is done. Now we just need to insert the method names we declared earlier into the class record, and set a few of the miscellaneous data fields.

As we saw in the discussion of the private header file, the BitmapEdit class record includes class parts for BitmapEdit itself and for each superclass of BitmapEdit, in this case Primitive and Core. To initialize the class record, each class part has to be initialized field by field. Fortunately this is easy because the majority of the fields are always initialized to the same values.

6.3.5.1 The Core Class Part

Since all widget classes are subclasses of Core, all need to initialize the Core class part. Example 6-10 shows the core part initialized as needed by the BitmapEdit widget. The actual name of each field is shown in the comment at left. Each field will be discussed after the example.

Example 6-10. BitmapEdit.c: initialization of Core class record

```
BitmapEditClassRec bitmapEditClassRec = {
    {          /* core_class fields */
      /* superclass */               (WidgetClass) &coreClassRec,
      /* class_name */               "BitmapEdit",
      /* widget_size */              sizeof(BitmapEditRec),
```

```
            /* class_initialize */        NULL,
            /* class_part_initialize */   NULL,
            /* class_inited */            False,
            /* initialize */              Initialize,
            /* initialize_hook */         NULL,
            /* realize */                 XtInheritRealize,
            /* actions */                 actions,
            /* num_actions */             XtNumber(actions),
            /* resources */               resources,
            /* num_resources */           XtNumber(resources),
            /* xrm_class */               NULLQUARK,
            /* compress_motion */         True,
            /* compress_exposure */       True,
            /* compress_enterleave */     True,
            /* visible_interest */        False,
            /* destroy */                 Destroy,
            /* resize */                  Resize,
            /* expose */                  Redisplay,
            /* set_values */              SetValues,
            /* set_values_hook */         NULL,
            /* set_values_almost */       XtInheritSetValuesAlmost,
            /* get_values_hook */         NULL,
            /* accept_focus */            NULL,
            /* version */                 XtVersion,
            /* callback_private */        NULL,
            /* tm_table */                defaultTranslations,
            /* query_geometry */          QueryGeometry,
            /* display_accelerator */     XtInheritDisplayAccelerator,
            /* extension */               NULL
    },
    {       /* Primitive class part */
            /* border_highlight */        _XtInherit,
            /* border_unhighlight */      _XtInherit,
            /* translations */            XtInheritTranslations,
            /* arm_and_activate*/         NULL,
            /* syn resources */           NULL,
            /* num_syn_resources */       0,
            /* extension */               NULL,
    },
    {       /* BitmapEdit class part */
            /* extension */     0,
    },
};
```

If you are like most programmers, the core class part structure is the biggest structure you have ever seen! Don't worry, because many of the fields you will never have to worry about, and the rest you will gradually come to know as you need them. We will introduce all the fields here, but you are not expected to absorb all the details in a single sitting. Treat this section both as an introduction and as a summary to which you can turn back when you encounter a field you don't understand. Also, all of the methods and some of the data fields are described in more detail later in the book. These field descriptions reference the section in this book where you will find additional information about the field.

- The superclass field is set to a pointer to the superclass's class structure. This defines which widgets this class can inherit from. For a subclass of Core this would be

&coreClassRec (`widgetClassRec` was used in previous releases); for a subclass of Composite, &compositeClassRec; for a subclass of Constraint, &constraintClassRec, and so on.

- The next field, `class_name`, contains the name that will be used to set resources by class. In other words, this is the string that you want to appear in the resource database when setting resources for all instances of this class.

- The `widget_size` field is the size of the instance record. This should always be specified using `sizeof` with the complete instance record declaration for this class, defined in *BitmapEdiP.h*, as an argument. In this case the field is initialized to `sizeof(BitmapEditRec)`. Xt uses this field to allocate memory for instance records at run time.

- The next field, `class_initialize`, is the first of many pointers to widget methods. There are several issues regarding methods that require separate treatment, so we'll describe these in the next section. The complete list of methods in the Core part structure is as follows: `class_initialize`, `class_part_init`, `initialize`, `realize`, `destroy`, `resize`, `expose`, `set_values`, `set_values_almost`, `query_geometry`, and `accept_focus`.

- The `display_accelerator` field is used in conjunction with accelerators, which are a way of redirecting events to actions in different widgets, and will be discussed in more detail in Chapter 10, *Resource Management and Type Conversion*.

- The `class_inited` field is used internally by Xt to indicate whether this class has been initialized before. Always initialize it to `False`.

- The `initialize_hook`, `set_values_hook`, and `get_values_hook` fields are for use in widgets that have `get_values_hook` fields is for use in widgets that have subparts that are not widgets. Subparts can have their own resources, and can load them from the resource databases as a widget can. This method is called immediately after the `get_values` method, and is for performing the same operations except on subparts. This field is described in Chapter 10, *Resource Management and Type Conversion*. (Most widgets that used subparts have now been converted to use non-widget objects or gadgets instead.)

- The fields relating to resources, the default translation table, and the actions table have already been described. The only one of these fields without an obvious name is the `tm_table` field, in which you place the default translation table.

- The `xrm_class` field is used internally by Xt, and must always be initialized to NULLQUARK. This is a fixed initialization value.

- The `compress_motion`, `compress_exposure`, and `compress_enterleave` fields control the Toolkit's *event filters*. Basically, these filters remove events that some widgets can do without, thus improving performance. Unless a widget performs complicated drawing or tracks the pointer, `compress_exposure` should usually be `Xt-ExposeCompressMultiple` and the other two fields should usually be `True`. These filters are described in Chapter 9, *More Input Techniques*.

- The `visible_interest` field can be set to `True` if your widget wishes to get `VisibilityNotify` events, which signal changes in the visibility of your widget.

Normally this is set to `False`, because `Expose` events cause the widget to be redrawn at the proper times. For some widgets, however, `Expose` events are not enough. If your widget draws continuously, as in a game, it can stop computing output for areas that are no longer visible. There are other cases where `VisibilityNotify` events are useful.

- Xt uses the `version` field to check the compiled widget code against the library the widget is linked against. If you specify the constant `XtVersion` and it is different from the version used by the libraries, then Xt displays a run-time warning message. However, if you have intentionally designed a widget to run under more than one version of Xt, you can specify the constant `XtVersionDontCheck`.

- The `callback_private` field is private to Xt, and you always initialize it to NULL.

- The `extension` field is for later expansion of the widget while maintaining binary compatibility. When used, it is a pointer to an extension structure containing additional class structure fields.

The fields in the Primitive class part are there so that subclasses like BitmapEdit can inherit or replace certain features of Primitive. We are happy to inherit the relevant ones, and disable the rest by setting them to zero or NULL as appropriate. We inherit the `border_highlight`, `border_unhighlight`, and `translations` fields so that BitmapEdit can highlight itself and be a tab group. However, we turned these features off in the application that uses BitmapEdit (by setting `XmNtraversalOn` to `False` in *xbitmap1*) since there is not yet a keyboard interface for navigating within the bitmap.

6.3.5.2 Initializing the Core Methods

As you've just seen, there are several places for pointers to methods stored in the Core class structure. We will describe the purpose of each of these methods in the next section. But first, a word about how to set the method fields.

Fortunately, the Core class already defines some of the methods, and you can choose to inherit them instead of writing your own. In general, when you set out to write a widget, you will pick as your superclass the widget that has the most methods that you can inherit instead of writing from scratch.

Broadly speaking, there are two types of methods, self-contained methods and chained methods.

A *self-contained* method is one that is called alone—the methods of the same name in the widget's superclasses are not called. For example, `expose` is self-contained. When you write the `expose` method, you are writing all the drawing code for the widget. The `expose` method of the superclass will not be called even if it was designed to do drawing. Therefore, by writing an `expose` method you replace the `expose` method of the superclass.

A *chained method* is one that is not called alone—it is called either before or after all the methods of the same name in its superclasses and subclasses. Therefore, you can't replace any of the code in this method in the subclasses or superclasses, you can only add to it by writing your own.

Inheritance works differently for chained and self-contained methods. For self-contained methods, such as `realize` and `expose`, inheritance works almost as it does for default translations. When initializing a field in the class record that represents a self-contained method, you have three choices:

- You can define these methods in your widget code by placing the name of the function in the class record and defining that function somewhere in the source file.

- You can inherit that method from the immediate superclass by placing a special symbol beginning with `XtInherit` in that field in the class record.

- You can use the first technique, but reference the superclass's method in your method. This allows you to add features to the superclass's method without having to completely copy it and modify it.

These techniques are demonstrated in Section 6.3.8. Chained methods, on the other hand, use one of two flavors of inheritance. Some are *downward chained*, which means that the Core method is called first, followed by the same method in each subclass. Other methods are *upward chained*, which means that the Core class method is called last. For both upward and downward chained methods, your choice is whether to specify additional code by defining your own method, or to go with what the other classes have already defined. You cannot prevent the code from the other classes from being executed.

Here is how chaining works for the `initialize` method in BitmapEdit. Remember that BitmapEdit is a subclass of Primitive and then Core. The Core class record contains only the Core part structure. The Primitive class record contains the Core part structure and the Primitive part structure. The BitmapEdit class record contains the Core, Primitive, and BitmapEdit part structures. The `initialize` method is present in the Core part structure of all three classes. When an application creates an instance of the BitmapEdit widget, Xt calls the function specified in the `initialize` field in the Core class record first, followed by the one in the Primitive class record, and finally the one in the BitmapEdit class record. This is an example of downward chaining.

The `destroy` method, on the other hand, is upward chained. That is, the `destroy` method in BitmapEdit would be called first, followed by the `destroy` method for Primitive, and finally the one for Core.

If you specify NULL in your class structure for a method that chains upward or downward, it is equivalent to specifying a function that does nothing. The function for that method of the superclasses and subclasses will still be called normally.

Table 6-2 lists which methods fall into each type of inheritance. It also shows how translations, actions, and resources are chained.

Table 6-2. Inheritance Style of Various Methods

Self-contained	Upward chained	Downward chained
`class_initialize`	`destroy`	`class_part_init`
`realize`		`initialize`
`resize`		`set_values`
`expose`		`get_values_hook`
`accept_focus`		`set_values_hook`
`set_values_almost`		`initialize_hook`
`query_geometry`		
translations	actions	resources

6.3.6 Description of Core Methods

Here is a brief description of the purpose of each Core method, and where in this book the method will be described in detail. All these methods, except `realize`, can be set to NULL in the class record and the widget will still function. However, all widgets that draw into their window will also require the `expose` method, the `initialize` method, and usually the `resize` method. And to be good children, widgets should define a `query_geometry` method. The `realize` method is shown in Section 6.3.8, and the rest of the commonly-used methods immediately after that in Chapter 7, *Basic Widget Methods*.

This list describes *all* the methods, even those that are rarely used. There is a lot of detail here that you should not expect to absorb in a first reading. Like the list of Core class structure fields, treat this as an introduction and come back to it later for reference when you come across a method you don't know how to use, or if you have something you want to do and you don't remember in which method to do it.

- `initialize` sets initial values for all the fields in the instance part structure. This method is responsible for checking that all public fields have been set to reasonable values. This method is downward chained, so each class's `initialize` method sets the initial values for its own instance part structure. This method is described in Chapter 7, *Basic Widget Methods*.

- `initialize_hook` is called immediately after the `initialize` method of the same class. It is obsolete as of R4 (though still called for compatibility); its job has been added to that of `initialize`. It allows the widget to initialize subparts, and is used only in widgets that have subparts. Subparts have their own resources and are described in Section ssubparts. `initialize_hook`, a downward chained method, is also described there.

- `class_initialize` is called once, the first time an instance of a class is created by the application. The widget registers type converters here, if it has defined any nonstandard ones. `class_initialize` is self-sufficient and is described in Chapter 10, *Resource Management and Type Conversion*.

- `class_part_init` is called once the first time an instance of a class is created by the application. It is different from `class_initialize` only in that it is downward chained. This method resolves inheritance of self-sufficient methods from the immediate superclass. It is needed only in classes that define their own methods in their class part (but is not present in Core, Composite, or Constraint, because Xt handles inheritance in these). This method is described in Chapter 14, *Miscellaneous Toolkit Programming Techniques*.

- `realize` is called when the application calls `XtRealizeWidget`. This method is responsible for setting window attributes and for creating the window for the widget. It is self-sufficient, and is described in Section 6.3.8.

- `expose` redraws a widget whenever an `Expose` event arrives from the server (but note that Xt can coalesce consecutive `Expose` events to minimize the number of times it is called). This method is responsible for making Xlib calls to draw in the widget's window. The widget's instance variables are often used in the `expose` method to guide the drawing. This method is self-sufficient. This method is described in Chapter 7, *Basic Widget Methods*.

- `resize` is called when the parent widget resizes the widget. It recalculates the instance variables based on the new position and size of its window, which are passed into the method. This method is self-sufficient and is described in Chapter 7, *Basic Widget Methods*, and in Chapter 12, *Geometry Management*.

- `set_values` is called whenever the application calls `XtSetValues` to set the resources of the widget. This method recalculates private instance variables based on the new public instance variable values. It contains similar code to the `initialize` method, but is called at different, and perhaps multiple, times. The `set_values` method is downward chained. This method is described in Chapter 7, *Basic Widget Methods*.

- `set_values_almost` is used to process application requests to change this widget's size. This field should never be NULL. Unless you've written your own `set_values_almost` method, this field should be set to `XtInheritSetValuesAlmost`. Most classes inherit this procedure from their superclass. This method is self-contained and is described in Chapter 12, *Geometry Management*.

- `set_values_hook` sets resource values in subparts. It is now obsolete (though still called for compatibility); its job has been added to that of `set_values`. This method is used only in widgets that have subparts, as described in Section ssubparts. It is downward chained and is described in Chapter 10, *Resource Management and Type Conversion*.

- `accept_focus` is NULL for most widgets (or, at least, for all the Athena widgets). When it is present, this method should set the keyboard focus to a subwidget of this widget. This would be used, for example, to allow the application to set the input focus to the Text widget within a Dialog widget. This method is invoked when the application calls

`XtCallAcceptFocus`. This method is self-contained and is described in Chapter 14, *Miscellaneous Toolkit Programming Techniques*.

- `get_values_hook` is called just after `get_values` and is used to return the resources of subparts. This method is downward chained and is described in Chapter 10, *Resource Management and Type Conversion*.

- `destroy` deallocates local and server memory allocated by this widget. This is called when an application destroys a widget but remains running. This method is described in Chapter 7, *Basic Widget Methods*.

- `query_geometry` may be called when the parent widget is about to resize the widget. The method is passed the proposed new size, and is allowed to suggest a compromise size, or to agree to the change as specified. This method it self-contained. It is described in Chapter 7, *Basic Widget Methods*.

Initialization of the Composite and Constraint class parts, including the methods in those structures, is described in Chapter 12, *Geometry Management*, since this is necessary only in widgets that manage children.

6.3.7 Packaging the Class Record for Application Use

The final requirement of the *.c* file is a pointer to the class record, called `bitmapEdit-WidgetClass`, that applications use as an argument to `XtCreateManagedWidget` to create instances of this widget class. This is shown in Example 6-11.

Example 6-11. BitmapEdit.c: declaring the class record pointer

```
WidgetClass bitmapEditWidgetClass = (WidgetClass) &bitmapEditClassRec;
```

`bitmapEditWidgetClass` is set to be a pointer to the `bitmapEditClassRec`, the complete class record. Remember that since the actual declaration of the class structure is in the private include file, the application cannot access class structure fields, and therefore this pointer is opaque to the application.

6.3.8 A Sample Method

Each method has a particular job to do, and is described in the chapter that discusses that job. However, we'll describe the `realize` method now, because it is simple and demonstrates the two techniques of inheriting for self-contained fields that were described in Section 6.3.5.2. The `realize` method is responsible for creating the widget's window, and all widgets have a window.* The first technique is to inherit wholesale the method defined by the immediate superclass. The superclass may have its own `realize` method, or it may also inherit the method from its superclass, and so on. The Core widget's `realize` method

---

*Gadgets don't have windows, and therefore don't have a `realize` method. The code to implement a gadget is described in Chapter 13, *Menus, Gadgets, and Cascaded Popups*.

creates a basic window.* In your subclasses of any of these widgets, you can inherit the Core `realize` method without modification by initializing the `realize` member of the Core class record to the symbolic constant `XtInheritRealize`, as shown in Example 6-12.

Example 6-12. BitmapEdit.c: inheriting a self-contained method

```
BitmapEditClassRec bitmapEditClassRec = {
    {                       /* Core class part */
        .
        .
        .
        XtInheritRealize,  /* realize */
        .
        .
        .
    },
    {  /* Primitive class part */
        .
        .
        .
    },
    {  /* BitmapEdit class part */
        0,                  / * dummy_field */
    }
};
```

Xt also defines symbolic constants for inheriting for every other self-contained method. They all begin with `XtInherit`, and in general continue with the capitalized name of the method field.

An important part of the process of creating an X window is the setting of window attributes. Therefore, a brief aside on window attributes is necessary. (You can skim the next page if you are already familiar with them.)

Window attributes are basic features of the way the server makes windows look and act. Window attributes can also be changed later if necessary, but the `realize` method is the place to set them initially. The Core class `realize` method sets some basic window attributes such as the window background and border colors or patterns, and it gets these values from Core resources. Here is a list of the window attributes that you may wish to set:

Background   Can be a solid color, pattern, or transparent.

Border   Can be a solid color or pattern.

Bit Gravity   Determines how partial window contents are preserved when a window is resized. This is an optimization that can save redrawing.

---

*If you have the source code for Xt, you may discover that the Core widget is actually an amalgamation of several other superclasses called WindowObj, RectObj, and so on. (You might also notice the include files for these classes in /usr/include/X11.) The Core widget actually inherits the `realize` procedure from WindowObj. These classes are an implementation detail that will affect you only if you want to look in some of these superclasses to find the code that implements features normally attributed to Core. From application code or widget code, it is always safe to assume that Core is the top of the class tree. For gadgets, you need to know more about these "hidden" classes, so we'll discuss them in Chapter 13, *Menus, Gadgets, and Cascaded Popups*.

Backing Store	Provides hints about when a window's contents should be preserved by the server even when the window is obscured or unmapped. This is useful for widgets that are very time-consuming to redraw. Not all servers are capable of maintaining a backing store. Check the value returned from the Xlib `DoesBackingStore` macro to determine whether this feature is supported on a particular screen on your server.
Saving Under	Provides hints about whether or not the screen area beneath a window should be saved while a window such as a popup menu is in place, to save obscured windows from having to redraw themselves when the popup is removed. Not all servers can save under windows. You can find out whether this feature is supported on a particular screen with the Xlib `DoesSaveUnders` macro.
Colormap	Determines which virtual colormap should be used for this window. If your widget requires a lot of specific colors—for example, to draw a shaded image, it may need to create its own virtual colormap. In that case, it would set this attribute to the ID of the created colormap. For more information, see Chapter 7, *Color*, in Volume One, *Xlib Programming Manual*.
Cursor	Determines which cursor should be displayed when the pointer is in this window. You must create this cursor before setting this attribute. This can be done with a standard type converter, as described in Chapter 14, *Miscellaneous Toolkit Programming Techniques*.

It may clarify the picture to describe the features that window attributes *do not* affect. Setting the window attributes does not determine a window's parent, depth, or visual. These are all set when a window is created, and are permanent. The window attributes are also not used for setting the size, position, or border width of a widget. These are set using `XtSetValues`. Window attributes do not determine how graphics requests are interpreted; this is the job of the graphics context (GC).

Note that some of the window attributes are not listed here because they should not be set directly by widgets, in the `realize` method or anywhere else. These include the `event_mask`, which controls which events are sent to this widget. Xt itself sets this window attribute based on the translation table. Another is `override_redirect`, which is handled by the Shell widget.

You could write a `realize` method that set your desired attributes and then called `XtCreateWindow`. But this is slightly wasteful, since Core already has a `realize` method that creates a window and you can take advantage of it. This is the second inheritance scheme used for self-contained fields. You define your own `realize` method just as if you were going to write it from scratch, but then you call the superclass's `realize` method directly, as shown in Example 6-13.

Example 6-13. Inheriting by invoking the superclass method from a widget method

```
#define superclass      (&coreClassRec)

static void Realize(w, valueMask, attributes)
Widget w;
XtValueMask *valueMask;
```

```
XSetWindowAttributes *attributes;
{
    /* this is already set, but just for example */
    *valueMask |= CWBitGravity;
    attributes->bit_gravity = NorthWestGravity;

    /* use realize method from superclass */
    (*superclass->core_class.realize) (w, valueMask, attributes);
}
```

Xt passes to the `realize` method a set of window attributes based on Core instance structure values. You update these values as necessary, and then call the superclass's `realize` method, as shown.

See the `XtRealizeProc` reference page in Volume Five, *X Toolkit Intrinsics Reference Manual*, to find out the default settings of the window attributes as passed into the `realize` method.

You may wonder what happens if the superclass also inherited its `realize` method—does the code in Example 6-13 crash by assuming the superclass field contains a function pointer when it actually contains the constant `XtInheritRealize`? No. When the class is initialized, Xt reconciles all the inherited methods and resets the class record fields to be pointers to the right methods.

What is happening behind the scenes when you inherit the `realize` method is that the Core `realize` method calls the Toolkit function `XtCreateWindow`, which in turn calls the Xlib function `XCreateWindow`. You may need to call the Xlib routine yourself in the `realize` method if you want to use a visual other than the default. See the reference page for `XCreateWindow` in Volume Two, *Xlib Reference Manual*, and Chapter 7, *Color*, in Volume One, *Xlib Programming Manual*, for details on depth, visual, and the issue of color in general.

6.4 The Public Header File—BitmapEdit.h

The public header file defines the aspects of the widget that can be accessed from the application. Public header files tend to be short. The two obligatory features of the *BitmapEdit.h* file are:

- An external declaration of `bitmapEditWidgetClass`, the class record pointer used by applications in calls to `XtCreateWidget` to create an instance of this widget class.

- A pointer to the widget instance record, in this case `BitmapEditWidget`. Xt calls all methods and actions with an argument of type `Widget`. To access any of the fields in the instance structure, this pointer must be cast to type `BitmapEditWidget`. The easiest way to do this is to declare the argument of the method as type `BitmapEditWidget` (the other way is to cast in an assignment).

If your resource list uses XmN, XmC, or XmR constants not defined in *<Xm/Xm.h>* (*<X11/StringDefs.h>* for standard Xt applications), you must define them in the public include file. The definitions should have only a single space between the definition and the value, with no trailing comment or space. This reduces the possibility of compiler warnings from similar but not identical definitions in multiple classes. If you want, you can use a different convention for the symbol names, to distinguish your constants from those defined by Motif. For example, you could start them all with Xo.

If a widget offers any public functions, they would be declared `extern` here (and actually defined in the *.c* file). Public functions allow the application to read or change certain private data in certain more restricted or more convenient ways than is possible with resources. For example, the BitmapEdit widget provides the public function `BitmapEditGetArray` that applications can call to get the array of bits currently stored as private data in the widget. (This array is an attribute readable with `XtGetValues`, but using this function is more convenient because it also returns the dimensions of the array.)

Example 6-14 shows BitmapEdit's public header file.

Example 6-14. BitmapEdit.h: complete public header file

```
#ifndef _ORABitmapEdit_h
#define _ORABitmapEdit_h

/* BitmapEdit Widget public include file */

/*
 * The public header file for the immediate superclass normally
 * must be included.  However, not in this case because the public
 * header file for Primitive is in Xm.h, which is already included
 * in all Motif applications.
 */

/* #include <Xm/Superclass.h>  */

/*
 * This public structure is used as call_data to the callback.
 * It passes the x, y position of the cell toggled (in units of
 * cells, not pixels) and a mode flag that indicates whether the
 * cell was turned on (1) or off (0).
 */
typedef struct {
    int mode;
    int newx;
    int newy;
} BitmapEditPointInfo;

#define XtNtoggleCallback "toggleCallback"
#define XtNcellSizeInPixels "cellSizeInPixels"
#define XtNpixmapWidthInCells "pixmapWidthInCells"
#define XtNpixmapHeightInCells "pixmapHeightInCells"
#define XtNcurX "curX"
#define XtNcurY "curY"
#define XtNcellArray "cellArray"
#define XtNshowEntireBitmap "showEntireBitmap"

#define XtCToggleCallback "ToggleCallback"
#define XtCCellSizeInPixels "CellSizeInPixels"
```

Example 6-14. BitmapEdit.h: incidental declarations (continued)

```
#define XtCPixmapWidthInCells "PixmapWidthInCells"
#define XtCPixmapHeightInCells "PixmapHeightInCells"
#define XtCCurX "CurX"
#define XtCCurY "CurY"
#define XtCCellArray "CellArray"
#define XtCShowEntireBitmap "ShowEntireBitmap"

extern char *BitmapEditGetArray(); /* w */
    /* Widget w; */

/* Class record constants */
extern WidgetClass bitmapEditWidgetClass;

typedef struct _BitmapEditClassRec *BitmapEditWidgetClass;
typedef struct _BitmapEditRec       *BitmapEditWidget;

#endif /* _ORABitmapEdit_h */
/* DON'T ADD STUFF AFTER THIS #endif */
```

6.5 The Process of Widget Writing

The process of writing a widget always begins with the same steps. They are:

- Copy all three files of the widget most similar to the one you intend to write; pick one that has many methods defined so that you don't need to type them in. (It's easier to delete than to retype.)

- Globally change the widget class name in the files. The fastest way to do this under UNIX is with *sed*, using a script similar to the following:

  ```
  s/BitmapEdit/NewName/g
  s/bitmapEdit/newName/g
  ```

  Place this script in the file *sedscr*, and run the command:

  ```
  spike% sed -f sedscr file > newfile
  ```

  on each file. (Or write a simple `for` loop to run it on multiple files.)

- Start from the top of the *.c* file, and begin by writing the resource list. While writing the resource list, you may need to edit the public header file to define new resource names and classes (XmN and XmC symbols). While writing the resource list (and during the entire widget-writing process), you will also need to edit the private header file in order to add and remove instance part structure fields, as you determine a need for them while writing methods and actions. Later you will probably discover additional parameters that you want to define as resources.

- Design the output you expect your widget to draw. Your instance part structure fields must hold all the information necessary to redraw everything when the window is exposed—add the necessary fields.

- Design the user input you expect your widget to accept. Start with as many separate actions as you can—one for each distinguishable user input idiom. For example, Bitmap-

Edit has three actions for changing one bitmap cell: `DrawCell`, `UndrawCell`, and `ToggleCell`. Even though these invoke almost identical underlying code, it is best to keep them as separate actions.

- Design a default translation table to have these actions called in response to the appropriate events. Help in this area is available in Section 8.1.2.

- Write the `expose` method and actions. Just how to do this is described in the next chapter. But in summary, both the `expose` method and actions often draw into the widget. The `expose` method must always be able to redraw what the actions drew. Therefore, it usually pays to have common elements of code called by both an action and the `expose` method. Neither the action nor the `expose` method pass arguments to this common code. Instead, the actions set instance variables that are read in the `expose` method or common code. The instance variables act as global variables because they are available almost everywhere in the widget code.

- Add parameters that allow your drawing code to work smoothly in any size window, and add a `resize` method that sets these parameters.

- Add the `initialize` method to check resource values that might have been user supplied and to initialize private instance variables.

- Add the `set_values` method to check application-supplied resource values and reset private instance variables based on the new resource values.

- Declare the methods and actions you have defined, near the top of the .c file.

- Enter all these functions and tables you have defined into the class structure initialization.

It is useful to have a simple application available for testing your widget as you develop it. One that simply creates the widget under construction and provides a Quit button is quite adequate. Then you can add code to the widget incrementally, assuring at each step that the program compiles, links, and runs without error.

As this list implies, it is a good idea to start simply by completing all the above steps for a small subset of the features you eventually want. Once you have a working widget that you can test, you can add features one at a time by going through the list again. If instead you attempt to write an ambitious widget in one pass, you will spend much longer debugging it.

Once you have learned how to write methods and actions in the next chapter, *Basic Widget Methods*, you should be ready to write a simple widget.

6.6 Summary of Conventions

The naming conventions for the various structure declarations in the widget source files can be confusing. Table 6-3 summarizes these conventions, using the BitmapEdit widget as an example, and describes where each type is used. This table is just to help you read the code. If you create a new class starting from an existing class, and globally change the names as described above, all of the definitions and references listed here will already be done for you.

Table 6-3. Summary of Xt Structure Name Conventions

Structure Name	Description
`BitmapEditClassPart`	Partial class structure typedef (usually dummy field only) used for defining `BitmapEditClassRec` in *P.h* file.
`BitmapEditClassRec`	Complete class structure typedef, declared `extern` in *P.h* file, used for initializing class structure in *.c* file.
`bitmapEditClassRec`	Name of complete class structure allocated in *.c* file, declared `extern` in *P.h* file, allocated in *.c* file, used as superclass in class record initialization of subclasses of this widget (*.c* file).
`BitmapEditPart`	Partial instance structure typedef, used for defining `BitmapEditRec` in *P.h* file.
`BitmapEditRec`	Complete instance structure typedef, also used to initialize `widget_size` field of class record in *.c* file.
`_BitmapEditRec`	Type of `BitmapEditRec`, used for defining `BitmapEditWidget` pointer in *.h* file.
`_BitmapEditClassRec`	Type of `BitmapEditClassRec`, used for defining `BitmapEditWidgetClass` pointer in *.h* file.
`BitmapEditWidget`	Pointer to `BitmapEditRec` (complete instance structure), used to reference instance structure fields in *.c* file (passed as argument to methods).
`BitmapEditWidgetClass`	Pointer to `_BitmapEditClassRec`, used to cast `bitmapEditClassRec` for superclass in class record initialization of subclasses of this widget (*.c* file).
`bitmapEditWidgetClass`	Of type `WidgetClass`, address of `bitmapEditClassRec`, used in `XCreateWidget` calls to identify class to be created.

7

Basic Widget Methods

This chapter describes the initialize, expose, set_values, resize, query_geometry, and destroy methods. It explains when Xt calls each method, and describes in detail what should be in each of these methods. Among other things, these methods prepare for and do the drawing of graphics that appear in a widget. This chapter describes what the Toolkit adds to the graphics model provided by Xlib, but does not describe in detail how to draw using Xlib; this topic is described in Chapters 5, 6, and 7 of Volume 1, Xlib Programming Manual. This Chapter also describes how to write action routines that work in the widget framework.

In This Chapter:

7
Basic Widget Methods

This chapter describes the `initialize`, `expose`, `set_values`, `resize`, `query_geometry`, and `destroy` methods. These are the methods you need to write to make a functioning widget (although `destroy` is optional). The common thread in most of these methods is that they have a role in drawing graphics, although all but the `expose` method are also responsible for other things. We will describe all the responsibilities of these methods, but focus on the issues involving graphics because they are so important.

Three of these methods are called by Xt in response to application function calls:

- The `initialize` method is called when the application calls `XtVaCreate-ManagedWidget`.

- The `set_values` method is called when the application calls `XtVaSetValues`.

- The `destroy` method is called when the application calls `XtDestroyWidget`.

A fourth method, `expose`, is called in response to `Expose` events, which occur whenever part or all of a widget's window becomes newly visible on the screen.*

When the parent widget, which is usually a geometry-managing Composite or Constraint widget, needs to resize one of its children, it may call the child's `query_geometry` method to find the child's opinion of the proposed change. Once the parent has actually resized the child, Xt calls the child's `resize` method, which is responsible for calculating private instance variables, so that the child is prepared to redraw itself in its new window size.

Applications that use the Toolkit should do all their drawing in widgets. Although it is possible to create normal X windows and draw into them from the application code, you lose the advantage of Xt's event dispatching, event filtering, and other features. It's just as easy to draw in a widget, and it's easier to add processing of user input as described in Chapter 8, *Events, Translations, and Accelerators*.

---

*Note that `Expose` events are also handled through the translation mechanism like any other event. When they are present in the translation table, the action registered for `Expose` events will be called in addition to the `expose` method. Widgets do not normally include the `Expose` event in their translation table, because they already have the `expose` method. Applications might, conceivably, have `Expose` in their translation table to add drawing capability to a widget, although it is difficult to calculate where to do this drawing from the application since the widget's size may change.

7.1 The X Graphics Model Inside Widgets

Section 4.2.2 described the X graphics model and how drawing from the application is accomplished. In summary, the process consisted of creating GCs and then drawing from a function that Xt calls on receipt of `Expose` events. Drawing from inside a widget follows the same general procedure, but the code is organized differently.

Inside a widget, you normally create GCs with the Xt routine `XtGetGC` instead of the Xlib routine `XCreateGC`. `XtGetGC` is similar to the Xlib routine except that it arranges for the sharing of GCs among widgets within an application. This is important because each GC has some overhead and servers can achieve better performance when handling fewer GCs. Because Xt applications often have many instances of the same widget class, each needing the same GC characteristics (unless the user specifies a different color for each one), Xt arranges for them to share GCs when possible.

Xt organizes GC creation and drawing into separate methods. Setting initial values for the GC and creating the GC is done in the `initialize` method, and actual drawing is done in the `expose` method. This makes it very easy to find this code in existing widgets and straightforward to write this code for new widgets.

Since Xt allows resources to be changed during program execution by calling `XtVaSet-Values`, the widget code must be prepared to change the GC at any time if the GC components depend on resource values. The `set_values` method calculates the new values based on resource changes and updates the appropriate GCs.

The next six major sections discuss the code needed to implement the `initialize`, `expose`, `set_values`, `resize`, `query_geometry`, and `destroy` methods.

7.2 The initialize Method

As described in Section 6.3.5.2, the `initialize` method has basically one function: it sets instance structure members (also called instance variables).* This job has two parts: setting the initial values of private instance variables, and checking to make sure that the values of the public instance variables are valid (since they are user configurable). Since the `initialize` method is upward chained (defined in Section 6.3.5.2), the method for this class needs to initialize only the fields present in the instance part structure for this class. The exceptions are `width` and `height`. Even though they are instance variables of Core, they need to be checked by the subclass, because only this class knows its desired initial size.

Example 7-1 shows the `initialize` method from BitmapEdit.

---

*As described in Chapter 12, *Geometry Management*, the `initialize` method can also be used for creating child widgets, to build a compound widget. This is a way of getting around Xt's geometry management scheme, and is not frequently done.

Example 7-1. The initialize method

```
/* ARGSUSED */
static void
Initialize(treq, tnew, args, num_args)
Widget treq, tnew;
ArgList args;
Cardinal *num_args;
{
    BitmapEditWidget new = (BitmapEditWidget) tnew;
    new->bitmapEdit.cur_x = 0;
    new->bitmapEdit.cur_y = 0;
    /*
     * Check instance values set by resources that may be invalid.
     */

    if ((new->bitmapEdit.pixmap_width_in_cells < 1) ||
                (new->bitmapEdit.pixmap_height_in_cells < 1))  {
        XtWarning("BitmapEdit: pixmapWidth and/or pixmapHeight\
                is too small (using 10 x 10).");
        new->bitmapEdit.pixmap_width_in_cells = 10;
        new->bitmapEdit.pixmap_height_in_cells = 10;
    }

    if (new->bitmapEdit.cell_size_in_pixels < 5) {
        XtWarning("BitmapEdit: cellSize is too small (using 5).");
        new->bitmapEdit.cell_size_in_pixels = 5;
    }

    if ((new->bitmapEdit.cur_x < 0) ||
                (new->bitmapEdit.cur_y < 0)) {
        XtWarning("BitmapEdit: cur_x and cur_y must be\
                non-negative (using 0, 0).");
        new->bitmapEdit.cur_x = 0;
        new->bitmapEdit.cur_y = 0;
    }

    /*
     * Allocate memory to store array of cells in bitmap, if not
     * already done by application.
     */
    if (new->bitmapEdit.cell == NULL)
        new->bitmapEdit.cell =
                XtCalloc(new->bitmapEdit.pixmap_width_in_cells
                * new->bitmapEdit.pixmap_height_in_cells,
                sizeof(char));
    else
        new->primitive.user_data = True; /* user supplied cell array */

    /* Calculate useful values */
    new->bitmapEdit.pixmap_width_in_pixels =
            new->bitmapEdit.pixmap_width_in_cells
            * new->bitmapEdit.cell_size_in_pixels;

    new->bitmapEdit.pixmap_height_in_pixels =
            new->bitmapEdit.pixmap_height_in_cells
            * new->bitmapEdit.cell_size_in_pixels;

    /*
     * Motif Primitive sets width and height to provide enough room
     * for the highlight and shadow around a widget.  (This means
```

Example 7-1. The initialize method (continued)

```
    * it does not honor user-specified sizes for widgets.)
    * BitmapEdit doesn't use these features.  A widget that did use
    * these features would *add* its desired dimensions to those set
    * by Primitive.  To use this widget with another widget set,
    * remove the following two lines.
    */
   new->core.width = 0;
   new->core.height = 0;

   /* set initial size of window */
   if (new->core.width == 0) {
       if (new->bitmapEdit.showAll == False)
           new->core.width =
                   (new->bitmapEdit.pixmap_width_in_pixels >
                   DEFAULTWIDTH) ? DEFAULTWIDTH :
                   (new->bitmapEdit.pixmap_width_in_pixels);
       else
           new->core.width =
                   new->bitmapEdit.pixmap_width_in_pixels;
   }

   if (new->core.height == 0) {
       if (new->bitmapEdit.showAll == False)
           new->core.height =
                   (new->bitmapEdit.pixmap_height_in_pixels >
                   DEFAULTWIDTH) ? DEFAULTWIDTH :
                   (new->bitmapEdit.pixmap_height_in_pixels);
       else
           new->core.height =
                   new->bitmapEdit.pixmap_height_in_pixels;
   }

   /* Tell Primitive not to allow tabbing to this widget,
    * since there is no keyboard interface for using it. */
   XtVaSetValues(new,
       XmNtraversalOn, False,
       NULL);

   CreateBigPixmap(new);

   GetDrawGC(new);
   GetUndrawGC(new);
   GetCopyGC(new);

   DrawIntoBigPixmap(new);
}
```

Even though the specific instance variables initialized here are particular to BitmapEdit, the techniques are common to all `initialize` methods. Some private instance variables, such as `cur_x` and `cur_y`, do not depend on resource settings and are simply initialized to a fixed value. Public instance variables are checked; if their values are out of range, `Xt-Warning` is called to print a message on the standard output and they are instead initialized to a fixed value. Some private instance variables are set based on public instance variables. GCs are the most common example.

As you should recall from Chapter 6, *Inside a Widget*, all the variables set in `initialize` are declared in the `BitmapEditPart` instance structure in the private header file.

Note that most of the arguments of `initialize` are rarely used. When `initialize` is called, the *request* argument is an instance structure containing the same values as *new*. But as *new* is changed, *request* provides a sometimes useful record of the resource settings originally made by the user. The *args* and *num_args* arguments contain the resource settings provided in the call to `XtVaCreateManagedWidget`. These are sometimes useful in distinguishing between settings made by the application (*args*) from settings made by the user (which already appear in *new* and *request*). As of R4, the code in the `initialize` hook method, described in Chapter 10, *Resource Management and Type Conversion*, can optionally be placed in the `initialize` method.

7.2.1 Creating GCs

In any widget that does drawing, some of the private instance variables will hold the IDs of GCs created in the `initialize` method. These variables will be read when the GCs are needed in the `expose` method, and will be reset if necessary in the `set_values` method. Example 7-1 called separate routines, `GetDrawGC`, `GetUndrawGC`, and `GetCopyGC` to create the GCs. Example 7-2 shows these routines.

A program prepares for creating a GC by setting the desired characteristics of the GC into members of a large structure called `XGCValues` (defined by Xlib), and specifying which members of `XGCValues` it has provided by setting a bitmask. This bitmask is made by ORing the GC mask symbols defined in *<X11/X.h>*. Each bitmask symbol represents a member of the `XGCValues` structure. Every GC field has a default value, so only those values that differ from the default need to be set. The default GC values are discussed in Volume One, *Xlib Programming Manual*.

Widget code normally creates a GC with the `XtGetGC` call, not the Xlib analogue `XCreateGC`. `XtGetGC` keeps track of requests to get GCs by all the widgets in an application, and creates new server GCs only when a widget requests a GC with different values. In other words, after the first widget creates a GC with `XtGetGC`, any subsequent widget that calls `XtGetGC` to create a GC with the same values will get the same GC, not a new one. Using this client-side caching also reduces the number of requests to the server.

Xlib provides `XChangeGC` to change the values in an existing GC. Xt provides no analogue. Because of the sharing of GCs allocated with `XtGetGC`, you must treat them as read-only. If you don't, you may confuse or break other widgets. In cases where your widget creates a GC that needs changing in such a way that it is impractical to create a new GC each time, it may be appropriate to use the Xlib call `XCreateGC` instead of the Xt call `XtGetGC`.

BitmapEdit must use `XCreateGC` for two of its three GCs because these GCs are for drawing into pixmaps of depth 1, while `XtGetGC` always creates GCs for drawing into windows or pixmaps of the default depth of the screen. In other words, `XtGetGC` would work on a monochrome screen, but not on color. However, this is an unusual situation. Most widgets can use `XtGetGC` exclusively.

Example 7-2. Creating GCs from the initialize method

```
static void
GetDrawGC(w)
Widget w;
{
    BitmapEditWidget cw = (BitmapEditWidget) w;
    XGCValues values;
    XtGCMask mask = GCForeground | GCBackground | GCDashOffset |
            GCDashList | GCLineStyle;

    /*
     * Setting foreground and background to 1 and 0 looks like a
     * kludge but isn't.  This GC is used for drawing
     * into a pixmap of depth one.  Real colors are applied with a
     * separate GC when the pixmap is copied into the window.
     */
    values.foreground = 1;
    values.background = 0;
    values.dashes = 1;
    values.dash_offset = 0;
    values.line_style = LineOnOffDash;

    cw->bitmapEdit.draw_gc = XCreateGC(XtDisplay(cw),
            cw->bitmapEdit.big_picture, mask, &values);
}

static void
GetUndrawGC(w)
Widget w;
{
    BitmapEditWidget cw = (BitmapEditWidget) w;
    XGCValues values;
    XtGCMask mask = GCForeground | GCBackground;

    /* Looks like a kludge but isn't--see comment in GetDrawGC */
    values.foreground = 0;
    values.background = 1;

    cw->bitmapEdit.undraw_gc = XCreateGC(XtDisplay(cw),
            cw->bitmapEdit.big_picture, mask, &values);
}

static void
GetCopyGC(w)
Widget w;
{
    BitmapEditWidget cw = (BitmapEditWidget) w;
    XGCValues values;
    XtGCMask mask = GCForeground | GCBackground;

    values.foreground = cw->primitive.foreground;
    values.background = cw->core.background_pixel;

    /* This GC is the same depth as screen */
    cw->bitmapEdit.copy_gc = XtGetGC(cw, mask, &values);
}
```

As shown in Example 7-2, some GC components are set based on other instance variables, and some are just hardcoded. In this example, the foreground pixel value (color) in the GC is set to be the value of the foreground instance variable, which is derived from a resource of Primitive.* The background pixel value is derived from a resource of the Core widget. (Core defines a background resource but no foreground.) On the other hand, the `line_style` member of `XGCValues` is set to `LineOnOffDash` regardless of resource settings. In general, you hardcode the GC components that you don't want to be user customizable. (All these instance variables are defined in the *yourwidgetP*art structure defined in *yourwidgetP.h*.)

Certain GC parameters are traditionally handled as resources rather than being hardcoded. Colors and fonts are the most basic examples. In the X Window System you can't use a color until you allocate a pixel value for it, and you can't use a font until you load it. The code that processes resources called by `XtAppInitialize` automatically allocates and loads the colors and fonts specified as resources, and sets the instance variables to the right representation type as specified in the resource table. Therefore, it is actually easier to provide user customizability than to convert values to the representation types required to hardcode them.

How the resource conversion process works is described in more detail in Chapter 10, *Resource Management and Type Conversion*. To decide which GC settings you need for your application, see Chapter 5, *The Graphics Context*, in Volume One, *Xlib Programming Manual*.

7.3 The expose Method

The `expose` method is responsible for initially drawing into a widget's window and for redrawing the window every time a part of the window becomes exposed. This redrawing is necessary because the X server does not maintain the contents of windows when they are obscured. When a window becomes visible again, it must be redrawn.

The `expose` method usually needs to modify its drawing based on the geometry of the window and other instance variables set in other methods. For example, the Label widget will left-justify, center, or right-justify its text according to the `XmNalignment` resource, and the actual position to draw the text depends on the widget's current size. The Label widget has an instance structure field called `alignment`, which is set initially in the `initialize` method, and is read in Label's `expose` method.

Another factor to consider when writing the `expose` method is that many widgets also draw from action routines, in response to user events. For example, BitmapEdit toggles bitmap cells in action routines. The `expose` method must be capable of redrawing the current state of the widget at any time. This means that action routines usually set instance variables when they draw so that the `expose` method can read these instance variables and draw the right thing.

Most widgets keep track of what they draw in some form of arrays or display lists. When they need to redraw, they simply replay the saved drawing commands in the original order to redraw the window. For example, BitmapEdit keeps track of the state of each bitmap cell in

---

*To work with the Athena widget set, BitmapEdit would have to define its own `XtNforeground` resource.

a character array. It could easily traverse this array and redraw each cell that is set in the array.

However, BitmapEdit does not use this strategy. In order to improve its scrolling performance, the `expose` method copies an off-screen pixmap into the window whenever redisplay is required. The actions draw into this off-screen pixmap (in addition to updating the character array), and then call the `expose` method directly to have the correct portion of the pixmap copied to the window.

The `expose` method is passed an event that contains the bounding box of the area exposed. To achieve maximum performance it copies only this area from the pixmap to the window. The BitmapEdit actions take advantage of this, too. They manufacture an artificial event containing the bounding box of the cell to be toggled, and pass it when they call `expose`. This causes the `expose` method to copy that one cell that was just updated to the window.

Example 7-3 shows the `expose` method from the BitmapEdit widget.

Example 7-3. The expose method

```
/* ARGSUSED */

static void
Redisplay(w, event)
Widget cw;
XExposeEvent *event;
{
    BitmapEditWidget cw = (BitmapEditWidget) w;
    register int x, y;
    unsigned int width, height;
    if (!XtIsRealized(cw))
        return;

    if (event) {  /* called from btn-event */
        x = event->x;
        y = event->y;
        width = event->width;
        height =  event->height;
    }

    else {/* called because of expose */
        x = 0;
        y = 0;
        width = cw->bitmapEdit.pixmap_width_in_pixels;
        height = cw->bitmapEdit.pixmap_height_in_pixels;
    }

    if (DefaultDepthOfScreen(XtScreen(cw)) == 1)
        XCopyArea(XtDisplay(cw), cw->bitmapEdit.big_picture,
                XtWindow(cw), cw->bitmapEdit.copy_gc, x +
                cw->bitmapEdit.cur_x, y + cw->bitmapEdit.cur_y,
                width, height, x, y);

    else
        XCopyPlane(XtDisplay(cw), cw->bitmapEdit.big_picture,
                XtWindow(cw), cw->bitmapEdit.copy_gc, x +
                cw->bitmapEdit.cur_x, y + cw->bitmapEdit.cur_y,
                width, height, x, y, 1);
}
```

Note that the expose method first checks to see that the widget is realized using Xt-IsRealized. This is a precaution against the unlikely event that an instance of this widget is suddenly destroyed or unrealized by an application while Expose events are still pending. If this did happen, drawing on the nonexistent window would cause an X Protocol error.

Next, BitmapEdit's expose method sets the rectangle it will redraw based on the event passed in by Xt. We also call this method directly from the action that processes button presses. That action routine creates a pseudo-event to pass to expose to describe the area to be drawn.

If the compress_exposure field of the class structure is initialized to XtExpose-CompressMultiple (or one of a few other constants, described in Chapter 9, *More Input Techniques*), as it is in BitmapEdit, Xt automatically merges the multiple Expose events that may occur because of a single user action into one Expose event. In this case, the Expose event contains the bounding box of the areas exposed. BitmapEdit redraws everything in this bounding box. For widgets that are very time-consuming to redraw, you might want to use the third argument of the expose method, which is a region. The Region type is opaquely defined by Xlib (internally a linked list of rectangles). The Region passed into expose describes the union of all the areas exposed by a user action. You can use this region to clip output to the exposed region, and possibly calculate which drawing primitives affect this area. Xlib provides region mathematics routines (such as XRectInRegion) to compare the regions in which your widget needs to draw with the region needing redrawing. If certain areas do not require redrawing, you can skip the code that redraws them, thereby saving valuable time. However, if this calculation is complicated, its cost/benefit ratio should be examined. Consider the arrangement of windows shown in Figure 7-0.

Window 1 and Window 3 are other applications, and Widget 2 is an application consisting solely of our widget.

Initially, Window 3 is on top, Window 1 is behind it, and Widget 2 is hidden completely behind Window 1. When Window 1 is lowered, Widget 2 becomes visible, except where it is still overlapped by Window 3. The newly-exposed area can be described by two rectangles; A and B. If compress_exposure is False, Widget 2's expose method will be called twice and passed an Expose event first describing Rectangle A, then Rectangle B. But if compress_exposure is True, Widget 2's expose method will be called just once, passed an Expose event describing the bounding box of all the original Expose events (which would be the entire widget in this case), and passed a Region which is the union of the rectangles described by all of the Expose events. The region argument of the expose method is unused unless compress_exposure is True. Each of these exposure-handling techniques may be the best for certain widgets. For a widget like BitmapEdit, any of the three methods will work, but the bounding box method is the most efficient and convenient. For a complete description of Expose event handling strategies, see Chapter 8, *Events*, in Volume One, *Xlib Programming Manual*.

The remainder of BitmapEdit's expose method shown in Example 7-3 consists of a single Xlib call to copy from a pixmap into the widget's window. As described in Chapter 4, *An Example Application*, BitmapEdit makes a large pixmap that is one plane deep and draws the

Figure 7-1. compress_exposure: 2 rectangles if XtExposeNoCompress; bounding box and region if XtExposeCompressSeries or XtExposeCompressMultiple

current bitmap into it. When needed in the `expose` method, this pixmap just has to be copied into the window. This approach was chosen for its simplicity. When scrollbars are added, the widget is able to pan around in the large bitmap quickly and efficiently. Note that one of two Xlib routines is called based on the depth of the screen. This is because `XCopy-Area` is slightly more efficient than `XCopyPlane` and should be used when running on a monochrome screen.

Note that instance variables are used for the arguments of the Xlib routines in Example 7-3. Don't worry about exactly what each Xlib routine does or the meaning of each argument. See the reference page for each routine in Volume Two, *Xlib Reference Manual*, when you need to call them in your code.

See Chapters 5, 6, and 7 in Volume One, *Xlib Programming Manual*, for more information on the GC, drawing graphics, and color, respectively.

7.4 The set_values Method

When the application calls `XtVaSetValues` (or `XtVaSetValues`) to change widget resources during run time, Xt calls the `set_values` method. The `set_values` method is where a widget responds to changes in its public instance variables. It should validate the values of the public variables, and recalculate any private variables that depend on public variables that have changed.

Example 7-4 shows the `set_values` method for BitmapEdit.

Example 7-4. The set_values method

```
/* ARGSUSED */
static Boolean
SetValues(current, request, new, args, num_args)
Widget current, request, new;
ArgList args;
Cardinal *num_args;
{
    BitmapEditWidget curcw = (BitmapEditWidget) current;
    BitmapEditWidget newcw = (BitmapEditWidget) new;
    Boolean do_redisplay = False;

    if (curcw->primitive.foreground != newcw->primitive.foreground) {
        XtReleaseGC(curcw, curcw->bitmapEdit.copy_gc);
        GetCopyGC(newcw);
        do_redisplay = True;
    }

    if ((curcw->bitmapEdit.cur_x != newcw->bitmapEdit.cur_x) ||
            (curcw->bitmapEdit.cur_y != newcw->bitmapEdit.cur_y))
        do_redisplay = True;

    if (curcw->bitmapEdit.cell_size_in_pixels !=
            newcw->bitmapEdit.cell_size_in_pixels) {
        ChangeCellSize(curcw, newcw->bitmapEdit.cell_size_in_pixels);
        do_redisplay = True;
    }

    if (curcw->bitmapEdit.pixmap_width_in_cells !=
            newcw->bitmapEdit.pixmap_width_in_cells) {
        newcw->bitmapEdit.pixmap_width_in_cells =
                curcw->bitmapEdit.pixmap_width_in_cells;
        XtWarning("BitmapEdit: pixmap_width_in_cells cannot\
                be set by XtSetValues.\n");
    }

    if (curcw->bitmapEdit.pixmap_height_in_cells !=
            newcw->bitmapEdit.pixmap_height_in_cells) {
        newcw->bitmapEdit.pixmap_height_in_cells =
                curcw->bitmapEdit.pixmap_height_in_cells;
        XtWarning("BitmapEdit: pixmap_height_in_cells cannot\
                be set by XtSetValues.\n");
    }

    return do_redisplay;
}
```

Basic Widget Methods

The set_values method is called with three copies of the widget's instance structure as arguments: *current*, *request*, and *new*. The *current* copy includes the current settings of the instance variables, and *request* includes the settings made through Xt-VaSetValues but not yet changed by the superclasses' set_values methods. The *new* copy is the same as *request* except that it has already been processed by the set_values methods of all superclasses.

For each public variable, set_values compares the current value and the new value, and if they are different, validates the *new* value or changes any private values that depend on it. The *new* copy is the only one that the method changes; *request* and *current* are only for reference. As in the initialize method, you have to deal only with the instance variables for your subclass, and perhaps with width and height, because the set_values method is downward chained. Superclass set_values methods take care of setting all the superclass instance fields. However, if desired, you can change superclass fields in your method since it is called last. For example, this might be useful if your class has different criteria for determining valid values or dependencies.

The *request* copy of the instance variables is used only if your class needs to decide between a superclass setting and your widget's setting; disagreements about this usually occur over the size of the widget. For more information on when to use *request*, see the reference page for XtSetValuesFunc in Volume Five, *X Toolkit Intrinsics Reference Manual*.

It is also important to notice that the set_values method, if it exists at all (that is, if it is not specified as NULL in the class structure), must return True or False to indicate whether the changes made to the state variables require the widget to be redrawn. If it is True for this class or any superclass, Xt calls the Xlib routine XClearArea with the *exposures* argument set to True (to force the background of the widget to be redrawn, which normally occurs only after Expose events), and then Xt calls the expose method. In other words, you should make set_values return True whenever the changes to the instance variables will change what is drawn in the widget.

Note, however, that set_values should *not* return True if width and height change, because the X server automatically generates Expose events for a window when it is resized. If you do return True in this case, your expose method will be called twice.

Since the application may call XtVaSetValues before the widget is realized, it is important not to assume in the set_values method that the widget has a window. In other words, the code must use XtIsRealized to check whether the widget is realized before using the XtWindow macro, such as in a call to set window attributes.

As mentioned earlier, some of the private variables are usually GCs. Whenever the public variable for a color or font is changed through XtVaSetValues, a GC also has to be changed. This is an example of a private variable depending on a public one. GCs allocated with XtGetGC should not be changed since they may be shared by other widgets. Therefore, the normal response to a change in one of the resources on which a GC depends is to release the GC with XtReleaseGC and request a new one with XtGetGC.

If some of your widget's GCs are unlikely to be shared by other widget instances in an application (either because each instance will use different values for the GC components or there will be only one instance), and the widget needs to be able to make changes to them, and the changes are not predictable enough or few enough to reasonably create a GC for each variation, then the `XtGetGC`/`XtReleaseGC` approach is not ideal. What happens in this situation is that `XtGetGC` creates a new GC and `XtReleaseGC` frees the old GC every time a change is made, even if the changes are small. It is more efficient in this situation to change the affected values in the existing GC. But this can be done only with an Xlib routine—there is no Toolkit routine for changing a GC. To implement this approach, you create, modify, and free the unusual GC using Xlib routines only. You call `XCreateGC` in the `initialize` method to create the GC, `XChangeGC` in the `set_values` method to change the GC, and `XFreeGC` in the `destroy` method to free the GC. All of these Xlib routines are described in Chapter 5, *The Graphics Context*, in Volume One, *Xlib Programming Manual*.

`XtGetGC` always creates a GC that can only be used on drawables (windows and pixmaps) of the default depth of the screen. Drawing into a pixmap of depth one using a GC created with `XtGetGC` works on a monochrome display, but usually does not work on a color display. (The depth is the number of bits per pixel used to represent colors on the screen.) This is another situation in which you will need to call `XCreateGC` instead of `XtGetGC`.

Note also that BitmapEdit does not allow two of its resources to be changed by `XtVaSetValues`; they can be set only until the widget is created. To disallow changes to a resource, the `set_values` method must actively set the value in the new widget (newcw) to the value in the current widget (curcw), wiping out the setting made through `XtVaSetValues`. It is also advisable that the widget print a message describing that the resource cannot be set through `XtVaSetValues`.

The `XtWarning` call used in the example is simply an alternative to calling `fprintf`, that helps to make all error messages uniform, and is described in Chapter 14, *Miscellaneous Toolkit Programming Techniques*. As of R4, the code in the `set_values_hook` method, described in Chapter 10, *Resource Management and Type Conversion*, can optionally be placed in the `set_values` method.

7.5 The resize Method

When a widget is used in an application, it is created with a parent that will manage its geometry. Depending on the layout policy of this parent widget in the application, the widget's window may change size when the application is resized.* Most widgets need to recalculate the position and size of their graphics when their window changes size. This is the job of the `resize` method.

---

*Also note that the application may be resized when it is first mapped on the screen, when the user sizes the rubberband outline of the application provided by most window managers. (You may not think of this as resizing, but it is.) When this happens, the application has already created its widgets and the widgets have created windows. Therefore, the `resize` method of a widget will be called if its parent widget is forced to resize it.

The `resize` method is passed only one argument, the widget instance structure pointer (of type `Widget`). This structure contains the new position, size, and border width of the widget's window. The method changes any instance part fields that depend on the size or position of the widget. When the `resize` method returns, Xt calls the `expose` method, regardless of whether or not the contents need redrawing. (It is a basic characteristic of the X server that it generates `Expose` events when a window is resized.)

A Label widget whose text is centered would reset the starting position of its text in the `resize` method.

In some widgets, it takes some thought to determine the correct response to resizing. Take BitmapEdit, for example. BitmapEdit can be configured to show only a portion of the bitmap, so that scrollbars can pan around in the complete bitmap. When the application is resized, should BitmapEdit show more cells or increase the cell size? Up to the point where the entire bitmap is shown, it is easier to increase the number of cells shown. When Bitmap-Edit is resized larger than necessary to show the entire bitmap, it should probably increase the cell size. We will use this strategy in the `resize` method of the BitmapEdit widget, which is shown in Example 7-5.*

Example 7-5. BitmapEdit: the resize method

```
/* ARGSUSED */
static void
Resize(w)
Widget w;
{
    BitmapEditWidget cw = (BitmapEditWidget) w;
            /* resize does nothing unless new
             * size is bigger than entire pixmap */
    if ((cw->core.width > cw->bitmapEdit.pixmap_width_in_pixels) &&
        (cw->core.height >
         cw->bitmapEdit.pixmap_height_in_pixels)) {
      /* Calculate the maximum cell size that will
       * allow the entire bitmap to be displayed. */
      Dimension w_temp_cell_size_in_pixels,
              h_temp_cell_size_in_pixels;
      Dimension new_cell_size_in_pixels;

      w_temp_cell_size_in_pixels = cw->core.width /
              cw->bitmapEdit.pixmap_width_in_cells;
      h_temp_cell_size_in_pixels = cw->core.height /
              cw->bitmapEdit.pixmap_height_in_cells;

      if (w_temp_cell_size_in_pixels < h_temp_cell_size_in_pixels)
          new_cell_size_in_pixels = w_temp_cell_size_in_pixels;
      else
          new_cell_size_in_pixels = h_temp_cell_size_in_pixels;

      /* if size change mandates a new pixmap, make one */
      if (new_cell_size_in_pixels
              != cw->bitmapEdit.cell_size_in_pixels)
```

---

*This resize strategy does have one problem; it never reduces the cell size. This is not a serious problem because BitmapEdit has a resource that controls the cell size. The application that uses this widget could provide a user interface for setting the cell size if the application writer was concerned about this problem.

Example 7-5. BitmapEdit: the resize method (continued)

```
                    ChangeCellSize(cw, new_cell_size_in_pixels);
        }
}

static void
ChangeCellSize(w, new_cell_size)
Widget w;
int new_cell_size;
{
    BitmapEditWidget cw = (BitmapEditWidget) w;
    int x, y;

    cw->bitmapEdit.cell_size_in_pixels = new_cell_size;

    /* recalculate variables based on cell size */
    cw->bitmapEdit.pixmap_width_in_pixels =
            cw->bitmapEdit.pixmap_width_in_cells *
            cw->bitmapEdit.cell_size_in_pixels;

    cw->bitmapEdit.pixmap_height_in_pixels =
            cw->bitmapEdit.pixmap_height_in_cells *
            cw->bitmapEdit.cell_size_in_pixels;

    /* destroy old and create new pixmap of correct size */
    XFreePixmap(XtDisplay(cw), cw->bitmapEdit.big_picture);
    CreateBigPixmap(cw);

    /* draw lines into new pixmap */
    DrawIntoBigPixmap(cw);

    /* draw current cell array into pixmap */
    for (x = 0; x < cw->bitmapEdit.pixmap_width_in_cells; x++) {
        for (y = 0; y < cw->bitmapEdit.pixmap_height_in_cells; y++) {
            if (cw->bitmapEdit.cell[x + (y *
                    cw->bitmapEdit.pixmap_width_in_cells)] == DRAWN)
                DoCell(cw, x, y, cw->bitmapEdit.draw_gc);
            else
                DoCell(cw, x, y, cw->bitmapEdit.undraw_gc);
        }
    }
}

static void
DoCell(w, x, y, gc)
Widget w;
int x, y;
GC gc;
{
    BitmapEditWidget cw = (BitmapEditWidget) w;
    /* otherwise, draw or undraw */
    XFillRectangle(XtDisplay(cw), cw->bitmapEdit.big_picture, gc,
            cw->bitmapEdit.cell_size_in_pixels * x + 2,
            cw->bitmapEdit.cell_size_in_pixels * y + 2,
            (unsigned int)cw->bitmapEdit.cell_size_in_pixels - 3,
            (unsigned int)cw->bitmapEdit.cell_size_in_pixels - 3);
}
```

Basic Widget Methods

Because of the two-phase resize strategy used by BitmapEdit, and because BitmapEdit uses a pixmap in its repaint strategy, this `resize` method is more complicated than most. When the widget is resized larger that necessary to show the entire bitmap in the current `cell_size`, it destroys the current pixmap and creates a new one. Since this should not happen very often and because resizing does not require extremely fast response, the time it takes to recreate the pixmap and draw into it is acceptable.

One difficulty in writing the `resize` method is that you do not have access to the old size or position of the window. The widget instance structure passed in has already been updated with the current size and position. If you need the old information, you can cache the old size in an instance part field, set first in the `initialize` method, and again at the end of the `resize` method.

It is also important to note that the `resize` method is not allowed to request that the parent resize the widget again to get a better size. (How to suggest properly to the parent that your widget be resized is described in Chapter 12, *Geometry Management*.)

7.6 The query_geometry Method

When your widget is used in an application, its parent widget will be a composite or constraint widget that manages its size and position. Parent widgets need to know the preferred size of a widget so they can make good decisions about the size of each child. The `query_geometry` method is called when the parent is about to make a size change to some of its children but is not yet sure which ones and by how much. (How geometry management works is described in Chapter 12, *Geometry Management*. For now, we are concentrating on what you need to do to write a simple widget.)

If your widget specifies NULL in the class structure for the `query_geometry` method, the parent will be told that your widget's current geometry is its preferred geometry. This is often wrong information. For example, if your widget has already been resized to be one-pixel-by-one-pixel because the user has resized an application to be very small, the parent would receive the message that your widget prefers to be that small. When the application is resized to be larger again, the parent will have no information on which to base its resizing decisions. Even if your widget has no particular preference for size, it is a good idea to specify the widget's default size in `query_geometry`. Then, at least, the parent has a ballpark figure for typical sizes for your widget. The parent could at least find out that BitmapEdit is intended to be larger than a Label widget.

The `query_geometry` method is passed pointers to two copies of the XtWidget-Geometry structure, one containing the parent's intended size for your widget, and the other to contain your reply to the parent's suggestion. The XtWidgetGeometry structure is shown in Example 7-6.

Example 7-6. The XtWidgetGeometry structure

```
typedef struct {
    XtGeometryMask request_mode;
    Position x, y;
    Dimension width, height;
    Dimension border_width;
    Widget sibling;
    int stack_mode;
} XtWidgetGeometry;
```

The `request_mode` field is a mask that indicates which other fields in the structure are set. It is a bitwise OR of any or all of the symbolic constants shown in Table 7-1.

Table 7-1. XtWidgetGeometry request_mode Symbols

Symbol	Description
CWX	The *x* coordinate of the widget's top left corner is specified.
CWY	The *y* coordinate of the widget's top left corner is specified.
CWWidth	The widget's width is specified.
CWHeight	The widget's height is specified.
CWBorderWidth	The widget's borderwidth is specified.
CWSibling	A sibling widget is specified, relative to which this widget's stacking order should be determined.
CWStackMode	A `stack_mode` value is present, specifying how this widget should be stacked relative to the widget identified as `sibling`.

The `sibling` and `stack_mode` fields are used together to indicate where in the stacking order of its siblings your widget will be placed. The symbols for `stack_mode` are `Above` `Below`, `TopIf`, `BottomIf`, `Opposite`, and `XtSMDontChange`. (These symbols are used singly, not combined with OR.) Their meanings are summarized in Table 7-2.

Table 7-2. XtWidgetGeometry stack_mode Symbols

Stacking Flag	Position
Above	*w* is placed just above *sibling*. If no *sibling* is specified, *w* is placed at the top of the stack.
Below	*w* is placed just below *sibling*. If no *sibling* is specified, *w* is placed at the bottom of the stack.
TopIf	If *sibling* obscures *w*, then *w* is placed at the top of the stack. If no *sibling* is specified, then if any sibling obscures *w*, *w* is placed at the top of the stack.
BottomIf	If *w* obscures *sibling*, then *w* is placed at the bottom of the stack. If no *sibling* is specified, then if *w* obscures any sibling, *w* is placed at the bottom of the stack.

Table 7-2. XtWidgetGeometry stack_mode Symbols (continued)

Stacking Flag	Position
`Opposite`	If *sibling* occludes *w*, *w* is placed at the top of the stack. If *w* occludes *sibling*, *w* is placed at the bottom of the stack. If no *sibling* is specified, then if any sibling occludes *w*, *w* is placed at the top of the stack, or if *w* occludes any sibling, *w* is placed at the bottom of the stack.
`XtSMDontChange`	Current position in stacking order is maintained.

Note that Xt's handling of stacking order is currently incomplete, and these symbols might not be honored. By default, the most recently created widget appears on the bottom.

One more issue about the `query_geometry` method must be raised before showing an example: the method's return value. The `query_geometry` method must return one of the three enum values `XtGeometryYes`, `XtGeometryAlmost`, or `XtGeometryNo`. `XtGeometryResult` is an enum name, and it is the returned type of `query_geometry`.

- If the proposed geometry is acceptable without modification, `query_geometry` returns `XtGeometryYes`.

- If the proposed geometry is not acceptable, your widget returns `XtGeometryAlmost` and sets its suggested changes to the proposed geometry back in the reply structure.

- If the proposed geometry is the same as the current geometry, `query_geometry` returns `XtGeometryNo`. This symbol is slightly misleading—think of it as `XtGeometryNoChange` (a symbol that is not defined). The symbol is `XtGeometryNo` because all three of these symbols are used in another context within composite and constraint widgets, as is described in Chapter 12, *Geometry Management*.

Note that, in all three cases, `query_geometry` must set any fields in the reply structure that it potentially cares about, even if it is only accepting the proposed geometry.

Example 7-7 shows the `query_geometry` method from BitmapEdit. All widgets should have at least this code in the method, substituting their initial size, or their current preferred size if known. (For example, a Label widget would set its preferred size based on the width and height of the current string.)

Example 7-7. BitmapEdit: the query_geometry method

```
static XtGeometryResult QueryGeometry(w, proposed, answer)
Widget w;
XtWidgetGeometry *proposed, *answer;
{
    BitmapEditWidget cw = (BitmapEditWidget) w;

    /* set fields we care about */
    answer->request_mode = CWWidth | CWHeight;

    /* suggest our default width or full size, whichever smaller */
```

Example 7-7. BitmapEdit: the query_geometry method (continued)

```
    answer->width = (cw->bitmapEdit.pixmap_width_in_pixels >
            DEFAULTWIDTH) ? DEFAULTWIDTH :
            cw->bitmapEdit.pixmap_width_in_pixels;
    answer->height = (cw->bitmapEdit.pixmap_height_in_pixels >
            DEFAULTHEIGHT) ? DEFAULTHEIGHT :
            cw->bitmapEdit.pixmap_height_in_pixels;

    if (   ((proposed->request_mode & (CWWidth | CWHeight))
            == (CWWidth | CWHeight)) &&
            proposed->width == answer->width &&
            proposed->height == answer->height)
        return XtGeometryYes;
    else if (answer->width == cw->core.width &&
            answer->height == cw->core.height)
        return XtGeometryNo;
    else
        return XtGeometryAlmost;
}
```

7.7 The destroy Method

When a widget is destroyed by the application, its `destroy` methods are invoked in sub-class to superclass order. Therefore, the `destroy` method for any given class needs to free only the memory allocated by itself; it need not worry about memory allocated by super-classes.

Any server resources created by Xt (such as GCs requested through `XtGetGC`) should be freed in the `destroy` method. In addition, if you called any Xlib routines, such as `XCreateGC`, that allocate server- or client-side resources, be sure to free them here. BitmapEdit creates pixmaps for use in the drawing process, so it must free them. It must also free the GCs it allocated.

If this is not done, then the server resources allocated for the widget will not be freed until the application exits. This is not a fatal problem. It matters only in applications that destroy widgets and then continue running for a while before they exit, which is unusual. Example 7-8 shows the `destroy` method code from the BitmapEdit widget. It frees the pixmaps created in the `initialize` method shown in Example 7-1.

Example 7-8. The destroy method

```
static void
Destroy(w)
Widget w;
{
    BitmapEditWidget cw = (BitmapEditWidget) w;
    if (cw->bitmapEdit.big_picture)
        XFreePixmap(XtDisplay(cw), cw->bitmapEdit.big_picture);

    if (cw->bitmapEdit.draw_gc)
        XFreeGC(XtDisplay(cw), cw->bitmapEdit.draw_gc);
```

Example 7-8. The destroy method (continued)

```
    if (cw->bitmapEdit.undraw_gc)
        XFreeGC(XtDisplay(cw), cw->bitmapEdit.undraw_gc);

    if (cw->bitmapEdit.copy_gc)
        XtReleaseGC(cw, cw->bitmapEdit.copy_gc);

    /* Free memory allocated with Calloc.  This was done
     * only if application didn't supply cell array.
     */
    if (!cw->primitive.user_data)
        XtFree(cw->bitmapEdit.cell);
}
```

If your widget allocated memory for any of its instance variables (or other global variables)
using the Toolkit routines `XtMalloc` or `XtCalloc` (which operate just like the C library
but add error checking), then it should free that memory here with `XtFree`. Many widgets,
including BitmapEdit, allow the application to supply the working memory, or the widgets
can allocate it themselves. BitmapEdit maintains a flag (`user_allocated`) to indicate
who originally allocated the memory.

If your widget called `XtAddEventHandler` or `XtAddTimeOut`, then you should call
`XtRemoveEventHandler` and `XtRemoveTimeOut`, respectively (these routines are
described in Chapter 9, *More Input Techniques*).

7.8 Actions in the Widget Framework

Although actions, strictly speaking, are not methods, writing them is part of the process of
writing a simple widget. Fortunately, you have already seen action routines added from the
application. Action routines look and work the same in the widget framework as in the application, except that they use instance structure fields as data instead of the application data
structure fields. Example 7-9 shows the actions of BitmapEdit.

Example 7-9. BitmapEdit: action routines

```
/*ARGUSED*/
static void
DrawCell(w, event)
Widget w;
XEvent *event;
String *params;
Cardinal *num_params;
{
    BitmapEditWidget cw = (BitmapEditWidget) w;
    DrawPixmaps(cw->bitmapEdit.draw_gc, DRAW, cw, event);
}
/*ARGUSED*/
static void
UndrawCell(w, event)
Widget w;
XEvent *event;
String *params;
```

Example 7-9. BitmapEdit: action routines (continued)

```
Cardinal *num_params;
{
    BitmapEditWidget cw = (BitmapEditWidget) w;
    DrawPixmaps(cw->bitmapEdit.undraw_gc, UNDRAW, cw, event);
}

/*ARGUSED*/
static void
ToggleCell(w, event)
Widget w;
XEvent *event;
String *params;
Cardinal *num_params;
{
    BitmapEditWidget cw = (BitmapEditWidget) w;
    static int oldx = -1, oldy = -1;
    GC gc;
    int mode;
    int newx, newy;

    /* This is strictly correct, but doesn't
     * seem to be necessary */
    if (event->type == ButtonPress) {
        newx = (cw->bitmapEdit.cur_x + ((XButtonEvent *)event)->x) /
                cw->bitmapEdit.cell_size_in_pixels;
        newy = (cw->bitmapEdit.cur_y + ((XButtonEvent *)event)->y) /
                cw->bitmapEdit.cell_size_in_pixels;
    }
    else {
        newx = (cw->bitmapEdit.cur_x + ((XMotionEvent *)event)->x) /
                cw->bitmapEdit.cell_size_in_pixels;
        newy = (cw->bitmapEdit.cur_y + ((XMotionEvent *)event)->y) /
                cw->bitmapEdit.cell_size_in_pixels;
    }

    if ((mode = cw->bitmapEdit.cell[newx + newy *
            cw->bitmapEdit.pixmap_width_in_cells]) == DRAWN) {
        gc = cw->bitmapEdit.undraw_gc;
        mode = UNDRAW;
    }
    else {
        gc = cw->bitmapEdit.draw_gc;
        mode = DRAW;
    }

    if (oldx != newx || oldy != newy) {
        oldx = newx;
        oldy = newy;
        DrawPixmaps(gc, mode, cw, event);
    }
}
static void
DrawPixmaps(gc, mode, w, event)
GC gc;
int mode;
Widget w;
```

Example 7-9. BitmapEdit: action routines (continued)

```
XButtonEvent *event;
{
    BitmapEditWidget cw = (BitmapEditWidget) w;
    int newx = (cw->bitmapEdit.cur_x + event->x) /
            cw->bitmapEdit.cell_size_in_pixels;
    int newy = (cw->bitmapEdit.cur_y + event->y) /
            cw->bitmapEdit.cell_size_in_pixels;
    XExposeEvent fake_event;

    /* if already done, return */
    if (cw->bitmapEdit.cell[newx + newy *
            cw->bitmapEdit.pixmap_width_in_cells] == mode)
        return;

    /* otherwise, draw or undraw */
    XFillRectangle(XtDisplay(cw), cw->bitmapEdit.big_picture, gc,
            cw->bitmapEdit.cell_size_in_pixels*newx + 2,
            cw->bitmapEdit.cell_size_in_pixels*newy + 2,
            (unsigned int)cw->bitmapEdit.cell_size_in_pixels - 3,
            (unsigned int)cw->bitmapEdit.cell_size_in_pixels - 3);

    cw->bitmapEdit.cell[newx + newy *
            cw->bitmapEdit.pixmap_width_in_cells] = mode;
    info.mode = mode;
    info.newx = newx;
    info.newy = newy;

    fake_event.x = cw->bitmapEdit.cell_size_in_pixels *
            newx - cw->bitmapEdit.cur_x;
    fake_event.y = cw->bitmapEdit.cell_size_in_pixels *
            newy - cw->bitmapEdit.cur_y;
    fake_event.width = cw->bitmapEdit.cell_size_in_pixels;
    fake_event.height = cw->bitmapEdit.cell_size_in_pixels;

    Redisplay(cw, &fake_event);
    XtCallCallbacks(cw, XtNcallback, &info);
}
```

Notice that as in methods, the widget instance pointer passed in is declared as type `Widget`, and then, in the first line of the action, cast to the desired type. This is necessary for ANSI C conformance.

An action routine in widget code can set and read fields in the widget instance structure passed in, while an action added from the application can access its own application data structure but not the widget's internal data structure because of the encapsulation rule (see Section 2.1.6.4). This is one of the advantages of moving this code into a widget.

You should now be ready to go back near the end of Chapter 6, *Inside a Widget*, and follow the directions to write your first widget. You will need to review parts of both Chapter 6 and this chapter as the process of actually writing a widget raises new questions in your mind.

8

Events, Translations, and Accelerators

This chapter describes the complete syntax of translation tables, and describes a mechanism called accelerators for mapping events in one widget to actions in another. Motif mnemonics, which are keyboard shortcuts for invoking menu items in visible menus, are also discussed.

In This Chapter:

Translations and
Accelerators

8
Events, Translations, and Accelerators

Events drive the application. They send a great variety of information from the server to the client and from the user to the application. More knowledge of events is necessary both to use existing widgets successfully in large applications and to write widgets.

Events are sufficiently central to X that we've devoted two chapters in this book to them. This chapter provides a closer look at translations and actions; Chapter 9, *More Input Techniques*, looks at lower-level event handlers, as well as at other sources of input. Appendix C, *Event Reference*, in Volume Five, *X Toolkit Intrinsics Reference Manual*, will also be useful when you need details about any of the event types.

The basic concept and use of translations and actions has already been described. But translation tables have a complicated syntax which can be used to do much more than the simple mappings you have seen up until now. Translation tables can detect user-interface idioms such as double- and triple-button clicks or key combinations such as Shift-Meta-M. This chapter focuses on the more advanced features of translation tables.

Next, we discuss a variation of translations called *accelerators*. Accelerators bind events that occur in one widget to actions in another. This is a flexible feature with many uses. One common use is to supply a keyboard interface to a normally pointer-driven application. By adding accelerators to the top-level window of the application, a keyboard event typed with the pointer anywhere in the application can be translated into an action in the correct widget. The name "accelerator" comes from the fact that many advanced users find it faster to use keyboard shortcuts instead of menus.

As mentioned in Chapter 3, *More Techniques for Using Widgets*, it is a very good idea to specify translation tables (and accelerator tables, too) in the app-defaults file instead of hard-coding them in the application, especially while an application is under development. This lets you develop the translations and accelerators without recompiling the application every time you want to make a change.

8.1 Translation Table Syntax

If you are reading this book in sequence, you've already seen translations used many times. However, we haven't given a formal description of their syntax or a complete listing of the events you can translate.

A translation table consists of an optional directive, which specifies how the table should be merged with any other existing translation tables, followed by a series of production rules, of the form:

[*modifier_list*] <*event*> [, <*event*> ...] [(*count*)] [*detail*] : *action* ([*arguments*]) [*action* ...]

where brackets ([ ]) indicate optional elements, an ellipsis (...) indicates repetition, and italics indicate substitution of an actual modifier, event, detail, or action name.

At a minimum, a translation must specify at least one event, specified by a predefined event name or abbreviation enclosed in angle brackets; a colon separator; and at least one action. However, a sequence of events can be specified; likewise, more than one action can be invoked as a result. The scope of event matching can be limited by one or more optional modifiers, and, in the case of some events, by a "detail" field that specifies additional information about the event. (For example, for key events the detail field specifies which key has been pressed.) Repeated occurrences of the same event (e.g., a double-click) can be specified by a count value in parentheses. A colon and optional white space separates the translation and the action.

The examples below are all valid translations:

```
<Enter>:  doit()                          invoke doit() on an EnterWindow event
<Btn1Down>,<Btn1Up>:  doit()              invoke doit() on a click of Button 1
<Btn1Up>(2):  doit()                      invoke doit() on a double-click of Button 1
Button1<Btn2Down>,<Btn2Up>:  doit()
        invoke doit() on a click of Button 2 while Button 1 is held down
Shift<BtnDown>:  doit()
        invoke doit() on a click of any button while the shift key is held down
<Key>y:  doit()                           invoke doit() when the y key is pressed
```

A translation table is a single string, even when composed of multiple translations. If a translation table consists of more than one translation, the actual newlines are escaped with a backslash (except for the last one), and character newlines are inserted with the \n escape sequence, as you've seen demonstrated in examples throughout this book.

The following sections provide additional detail on each of the elements of an event translation. We'll talk first about the directive, followed by event specifiers, details, modifiers, and counts. We'll also provide some pointers on the proper sequence of translations, and discuss what happens when translations overlap.

8.1.1 The Directive

As we've already seen, the three possible directives are `#replace`, `#override`, or `#augment`.

`#replace` says to completely replace the value of the `translations` resource in the widget. If no directive is specified, `#replace` is the default.

The difference between `#override` and `#augment` is more subtle. They differ in how they treat event combinations in the new translation that also appear in the old. With `#override`, the new translation takes priority, while with `#augment`, the old one does.

For example, say a widget has a default translation table that includes a translation for the Return key, and an application that uses this widget has an app-defaults file consisting of a translation table that applies to this widget. If the translation table in the app-defaults file began with `#override`, any translation for the Return key would take priority over the default translation for the Return key. On the other hand, if the translation table in the app-defaults file began with `#augment`, the default translations would take priority.

Remember that the difference between `#augment` and `#override` is only in the treatment of overlapping translations. Any translations added with either directive for events that do not already appear in the existing translation table will always be added.

Because of potential overlap between translations, when you are debugging your intended translations it is best to use `#replace` at first, then test with `#augment` or `#override` as appropriate once you are sure that the translations themselves have the desired effect.

8.1.2 Selecting the Events to Translate

An X event is a packet of data sent by the server to a client in response to user behavior or to window system changes resulting from interactions between windows. There are 33 different types of events defined by X. Most (though not all*) events can be thought of as occurring in a window: the pointer entering or leaving a window, pointer motion within a window, pointer button presses, key presses, and so on. However, most events are not sent to a window unless the window has explicitly selected that event type; events are selected on a per-window basis. In Xlib programming, events are selected by specifying an event mask as a window attribute. Some events, which are sent to all windows regardless of whether a window has selected them or not, are called non-maskable events. One of the most complex aspects of Xlib programming is designing the event loop, which must take into account all of the possible events that can occur in a window.

Xt's translation manager selects the events that are specified in the current translation table for each widget. In translations, events can be specified either by their actual names, as shown in Column 1 of Table 8-1, or by means of the abbreviations shown in Column 2. A

---

*Others reflect internal changes in the window system not related to any window. For example, a mapping `Notify` event occurs in response to a change in the mappings of keysyms (portable key symbols) to keycodes (actual codes generated by physical keys).

complete reference to each event type is provided in Appendix C, *Event Reference*, in Volume Five, *X Toolkit Intrinsics Reference Manual*.

Table 8-1. Event Type Abbreviations in Translation Tables

Event Type	Abbreviations	Description
ButtonPress	BtnDown	Any pointer button pressed
	Btn1Down	Pointer button 1 pressed
	Btn2Down	Pointer button 2 pressed
	Btn3Down	Pointer button 3 pressed
	Btn4Down	Pointer button 4 pressed
	Btn5Down	Pointer button 5 pressed
ButtonRelease	BtnUp	Any pointer button released
	Btn1Up	Pointer button 1 released
	Btn2Up	Pointer button 2 released
	Btn3Up	Pointer button 3 released
	Btn4Up	Pointer button 4 released
	Btn5Up	Pointer button 5 released
KeyPress	Key	Key pressed
	KeyDown	Key pressed
	Ctrl	KeyPress with Ctrl modifier
	Meta	KeyPress with Meta modifier
	Shift	KeyPress with Shift modifier
KeyRelease	KeyUp	Key released
MotionNotify	Motion	Pointer moved
	PtrMoved	Pointer moved
	MouseMoved	Pointer moved
	BtnMotion	Pointer moved with any button held down
	Btn1Motion	Pointer moved with button 1 held down
	Btn2Motion	Pointer moved with button 2 held down
	Btn3Motion	Pointer moved with button 3 held down
	Btn4Motion	Pointer moved with button 4 held down
	Btn5Motion	Pointer moved with button 5 held down
EnterNotify	Enter	Pointer entered window
	EnterWindow	Pointer entered window
LeaveNotify	Leave	Pointer left window
	LeaveWindow	Pointer left window
FocusIn	FocusIn	This window is now keyboard focus
FocusOut	FocusOut	This window lost keyboard focus
KeymapNotify	Keymap	Keyboard mappings changed
Expose	Expose	Part of window needs redrawing
GraphicsExpose	GrExp	Source of copy unavailable
NoExpose	NoExp	Source of copy available
ColormapNotify	Clrmap	Window's colormap changed
PropertyNotify	Prop	Property value changed
VisibilityNotify	Visible	Window has been obscured
ResizeRequest	ResReq	Redirect resize request to window manager

Table 8-1. Event Type Abbreviations in Translation Tables (continued)

Event Type	Abbreviations	Description
`CirculateNotify`	`Circ`	Stacking order modified
`ConfigureNotify`	`Configure`	Window resized or moved
`DestroyNotify`	`Destroy`	Window destroyed
`GravityNotify`	`Grav`	Window moved due to win gravity attribute
`MapNotify`	`Map`	Window mapped
`CreateNotify`	`Create`	Window created
`ReparentNotify`	`Reparent`	Window reparented
`UnmapNotify`	`Unmap`	Window unmapped
`CirculateRequest`	`CircRec`	Redirect stacking order change to window manager
`ConfigureRequest`	`ConfigureReq`	Redirect move or resize request to window manager
`MapRequest`	`MapReq`	Redirect window map request to window manager
`MappingNotify`	`Mapping`	Keyboard mapping changed
`ClientMessage`	`Message`	Client-dependent
`SelectionClear`	`SelClr`	Current owner is losing selection
`SelectionNotify`	`Select`	Selection is ready for requestor
`SelectionRequest`	`SelReq`	Request for selection to current owner

Many of these events are handled automatically by the Toolkit separately from the translation mechanism. For example, Expose events are automatically sent to the expose method of the appropriate widget. When there is also a translation for Expose events, the action is called in addition to the expose method. The only reason you would need a translation for Expose events is to add drawing to a Core widget. Because the Core widget doesn't have an expose method, there is rarely, if ever, a case where there is both an expose method and a translation for Expose events for the same widget. The point to remember is that any event can be specified in a translation, even when that event is also used in some other way by Xt.

GraphicsExpose and NoExpose events are useful when your application copies from a visible window with XCopyArea or XCopyPlane. They notify the application when part of the source of the copy is obscured. If you want GraphicsExpose and NoExpose events, you must explicitly select them by setting the graphics_exposures GC component in the GC used for the copy. Then you can provide a translation for them, or if you are writing a widget you can have them sent to your expose method by setting the compress_exposure field of the Core structure to a special value, as described in Section 9.6.2. (While *xbitmap* and BitmapEdit use XCopyArea and XCopyPlane, they copy from an off-screen pixmap that cannot be obscured, and therefore GraphicsExpose and NoExpose events are not needed. For a description of these events, see Chapter 5, *The Graphics Context*, in Volume One, *Xlib Programming Manual*.)

Several of the *Notify events are automatically handled by the Toolkit. Xt places this information in internal structures so that it can satisfy queries for widget positions and geometries without querying the server. MappingNotify events are automatically handled; Xt gets the current keyboard mapping from the server. `VisibilityNotify` events are handled automatically if the `visible_interest` field in the Core structure is set to `True` (see Section 9.4.1).

With the exception of `SelectionRequest`, the `*Request` events are intended for use only by window managers. The selection events are described in Chapter 11, *Interclient Communications*.

The keyboard traversal code built into the Motif Primitive class handles `EnterNotify`, `LeaveNotify`, `FocusIn`, and `FocusOut` events.

Whether or not they are already handled by Xt or in translations, events can also be selected explicitly by installing event handlers in a widget (as described in Chapter 9, *More Input Techniques*).

8.1.3 Details in Keyboard Events

As you've seen, Xt provides special event abbreviations to specify which pointer button was pressed or released. With key events, this approach would be a little impractical, since there are so many keys. Instead, the Translation Manager allows you to follow the event specification with an optional detail field. That is:

```
<Key>:  doit()
```

means that you want the `doit()` action to be invoked when any key has been pressed, while:

```
<Key>y:  doit()
```

means that you want the `doit()` action to be invoked only if the *y* key has been pressed.

What you actually specify as the detail field of a Key event is a keysym, as defined in the header file *<X11/keysymdef.h>*.* Keysyms begin with an `XK_` prefix, which is omitted when they are used in translations.

Before we explain any further, we need to review X's keyboard model, which, like many things in X, is complicated by the design goal of allowing applications to run equally well on machines with very different hardware.

The keyboard generates `KeyPress` events, and may or may not also generate `KeyRelease` events. These events contain a server-dependent code that describes the key pressed, called a *keycode*. *Modifier* keys, such as Shift and Control, generate events just like every other key. In addition, all key events also contain information about which modifier keys and pointer buttons were held down at the time the event occurred.

Xt provides a routine that translates keycode and modifier key information from an event into a portable symbolic constant called a *keysym*. A keysym represents the meaning of the key pressed, which is usually the symbol that appears on the cap of the key. For example, when the *a* key is pressed, the keysym is `XK_a`; when the same key is pressed while the Shift key is

---

*Note, however, that this file includes foreign language keysym sets that are not always available. Only the MISCELLANY, LATIN1 through LATIN4, and GREEK sets are always available.

held down, the resulting keysym is XK_A (upper case). Note that even though both the *a* and the *A* events have the same keycode, they generate a different keysym because they occurred with different modifier keys engaged. (The mapping between keycodes and keysyms is discussed further in Section 14.5.)

You may specify either the keysym name, omitting the XK_ prefix, or its hexadecimal value (also shown in *<X11/keysymdef.h>*), prefixed by 0x or 0X (zero followed by *x* or *X*).

This is fairly straightforward, though there are several provisos:

- The keysym for nonalphanumeric keyboard keys may not always be obvious; you will need to look in *<X11/keysymdef.h>*. For example, the keyboard for the Sun workstation has keys labeled "Left" and "Right." Their keysyms are XK_Meta_L and XK_Meta_R, respectively. Fortunately, most common named keys have mnemonic keysym names (XK_Return, XK_Linefeed, XK_BackSpace, XK_Tab, XK_Delete, and so on) so you can often get by without looking them up. Notice, though, the small things that can trip you up: BackSpace, not Backspace, but Linefeed, not LineFeed. You can't count on consistency.

- The definitions in *<X11/keysymdef.h>* spell out keysym names for punctuation and other special characters. For example, you'll see XK_question rather than XK_?, and so on. Nonetheless, you need not use this long keysym name; the Translation Manager will accept the equivalent single character, as long as it is a printing character. This is also true of digits. There are a few exceptions, namely the characters that have special meaning in a translation table. If you ever need a translation for colon, comma, angle brackets, or backslash, you'll have to use the keysym name rather than the single printing character.

- The keycode-to-keysym translator built into the Translation Manager makes case distinctions only if the key event is prefaced with the colon (:) modifier. This means that `<Key>a` and `<Key>A` will be treated identically by default. We'll return to this subject when we discuss modifiers.

In sum, the following are all valid key event translations:

```
<Key>q:    quit()            invoke quit() when q or Q is pressed
:<Key>?:   help()            invoke help() when ? (but not /) is pressed
<Key>Return:  newline()      invoke newline() when the Return key is pressed
<Key>:     insert_char()     invoke insert_char() when any key is pressed
```

8.1.4 Details in Other Event Types

Key events are the most likely to require details, but details are also available for several other event types. They simplify your action function because they instruct Xt to call the action only when the event contains the matching detail. One type of detail, for Motion-Notify, actually affects the selection of events.

Trivially, the detail values `Button1` through `Button5` can be supplied as details for `ButtonPress` or `ButtonRelease` events; because of the available abbreviations, though, these button detail values should not often be necessary. It is easier to say:

```
<Btn1Down>: quit()
```

than:

```
<BtnDown>Button1:  quit()
```

The `EnterNotify`, `LeaveNotify`, `FocusIn`, and `FocusOut` events can take as details any of the notify mode values shown in Table 8-2.

Table 8-2. *Notify Mode Values for Enter, Leave, and Focus Events*

Detail	Description
Normal	Event occurred as a result of a normal window crossing.
Grab	Event occurred as a result of a grab.
Ungrab	Event occurred when a grab was released.

Normally, `EnterNotify` and `LeaveNotify` events are generated when the pointer enters or leaves a window, and `FocusIn` and `FocusOut` events are generated when a click-to-type window manager changes the keyboard focus window—the window that receives all keyboard input regardless of pointer position. In these cases the detail is `Normal`. But these events are also generated when the keyboard or pointer is grabbed by an application with a call to `XtGrabPointer`, `XtGrabButton`, `XtGrabKeyboard`, or `XtGrabKey`. A *grab*, which is usually invoked by a popup window, also causes keyboard and/or pointer input to be constrained to a particular window. When these events are generated because of a grab or the release of a grab, the detail is `Grab` or `Ungrab`.

Details for additional events were added in Release 4. For `MotionNotify` events you can now select normal motion events or motion hints by specifying a detail of `Normal` or `Hint`. Normal motion events are used when you need a complete record of the path of the pointer. The `compress_motion` Core field, described in Chapter 9, is for use with normal motion events. Motion hints are used when you need only periodic pointer position updates. Each time you receive a motion hint you call `XQueryPointer` (an Xlib call) to get the current pointer position. Note that the `MotionNotify` detail is the only one that affects event selection.

For `PropertyNotify`, `SelectionClear`, `SelectionRequest`, `Selection-Notify`, and `ClientMessage` events, the detail is an atom described in Table 8-3.

Table 8-3. Atom Details for Various Events

Event Type	Detail Atom
PropertyNotify	Property that is changing.
SelectionClear	Selection atom (such as PRIMARY).
SelectionRequest	Selection atom (such as PRIMARY).
SelectionNotify	Selection atom (such as PRIMARY).
ClientMessage	Message type.

For MappingNotify, the detail can be Modifier, Keyboard, or Pointer. Xt automatically does what is normally required to handle keyboard (and modifier) mapping changes. However, the *Pointer* detail might be used to make sure that the user has not disabled (by mismapping) any pointer button that is necessary for the safe operation of the application. You would simply write a translations such as <Mapping> Pointer: ButtonMapCheck and then call XGetPointerMapping in the ButtonMapCheck action to make sure the pointer mapping is still acceptable.

The detail values for each event type corresponds to certain members of the associated event structure, as shown in Table 8-4. See Appendix C, *Event Reference*, in Volume Five, *X Toolkit Intrinsics Reference Manual*, for more details.

Table 8-4. Event Structure Fields Used As Translation Table Hints

Event Type	Event Structure Field
ButtonPress, ButtonRelease	button
MotionNotify	is_hint
EnterNotify, LeaveNotify	mode
FocusIn, FocusOut	mode
PropertyNotify	atom
SelectionClear	selection
SelectionRequest	selection
SelectionNotify	selection
ClientMessage	message_type
MappingNotify	request

8.1.5 Modifiers

Certain events include as part of their data the state of the pointer buttons and special keyboard modifier keys at the time the event was generated. The events for which this state is available include ButtonPress, ButtonRelease, MotionNotify, KeyPress, KeyRelease, EnterNotify, and LeaveNotify.

For these events, you can specify a desired modifier state using one or more of the modifier keywords listed in Table 8-5. An error is generated if you specify modifiers with any other types of events.

Table 8-5. Modifiers Used in Translation Tables

Modifier	Abbreviation*	Description
Ctrl	c	Control key is held down.
Shift	s	Shift key is held down.
Lock	l	Caps Lock is in effect.
Meta	m	Meta key is held down.
Hyper	h	Hyper key is held down.
Super	su	Super key is held down.
Alt	a	Alt key is held down.
Mod1		Mod1 key is held down.
Mod2		Mod2 key is held down.
Mod3		Mod3 key is held down.
Mod4		Mod4 key is held down.
Mod5		Mod5 key is held down.
Button1		Pointer Button 1 is held down.
Button2		Pointer Button 2 is held down.
Button3		Pointer Button 3 is held down.
Button4		Pointer Button 4 is held down.
Button5		Pointer Button 5 is held down.

8.1.5.1 Physical Keys Used as Modifiers

The meaning of the Meta, Hyper, Super, Alt, and Mod1 through Mod5 keywords may differ from server to server. Not every keyboard has keys with these names, and even if keysyms are defined for them in *<X11/keysymdef.h>*, they may not be available on the physical keyboard.†

For example, the file *<X11/keysymdef.h>* includes the following definitions:

```
/* Modifiers */

#define XK_Shift_L        0xFFE1  /* Left shift */
#define XK_Shift_R        0xFFE2  /* Right shift */
#define XK_Control_L      0xFFE3  /* Left control */
#define XK_Control_R      0xFFE4  /* Right control */
```

---

*The abbreviations did not work in MIT's R3 sample implementation, but they work in R4.

†The contents of *<X11/keysymdef.h>* are the same on every machine. What is different is the default mapping of keysyms to physical keycodes, which occurs in the server source. The only way to find out the mappings is through documentation (which is usually not available) or experimentation (as described in Chapter 11 of Volume Three, *X Window System User's Guide*, Second or Third Edition).

```
#define XK_Caps_Lock            0xFFE5   /* Caps lock */
#define XK_Shift_Lock           0xFFE6   /* Shift lock */

#define XK_Meta_L               0xFFE7   /* Left meta */
#define XK_Meta_R               0xFFE8   /* Right meta */
#define XK_Alt_L                0xFFE9   /* Left alt */
#define XK_Alt_R                0xFFEA   /* Right alt */
#define XK_Super_L              0xFFEB   /* Left super */
#define XK_Super_R              0xFFEC   /* Right super */
#define XK_Hyper_L              0xFFED   /* Left hyper */
#define XK_Hyper_R              0xFFEE   /* Right hyper */
```

There are two things you must learn before you can use these modifiers:

1. Which physical key generates a given keysym, if it is not obvious from the name.

2. Which modifiers are valid on your server.

The best way to find out what keysym a key generates is with the *xev* client, which prints detailed information about every event happening in its window. To find out a keysym, run *xev*, move the pointer into its window, and then press the key in question.

On the Sun-3, there is only one control key, on the left side of the keyboard. It generates the keysym XK_Control_L. There are two shift keys, one on each side, which generate the keysyms XK_Shift_L and XK_Shift_R. The Meta modifier is mapped to the keys labeled "Left" and "Right." Even though there is an Alternate keyboard key, which generates the keysym XK_Alt_R, this key is not recognized as a modifier. There are no Super and Hyper keys.

The list of valid modifiers can be displayed with the *xmodmap* client, as follows:

```
isla% xmodmap
xmodmap:  up to 2 keys per modifier, (keycodes in parentheses):

shift         Shift_L (0x6a),  Shift_R (0x75)
lock          Caps_Lock (0x7e)
control       Control_L (0x53)
mod1          Meta_L (0x7f),  Meta_R (0x81)
mod2
mod3
mod4
mod5
```

That is, either of the two shift keys will be recognized as the Shift modifier, the Caps Lock key as the Lock modifier, and either the Left or Right keys as the Meta modifier. The Left and Right keys are also mapped to the Mod1 modifier. The Alt key is not recognized as a modifier.

xmodmap also allows you to add keysyms to be recognized as the given modifier. For example, the following command would cause the F1 function key to be recognized as mod2:

```
isla% xmodmap -e 'add mod2 = F1'
```

For more information on *xmodmap* and *xev*, see Chapter 11 of Volume Three, *X Window System User's Guide, Motif Edition* (Second Edition).

8.1.5.2 Default Interpretation of the Modifier List

If no modifiers are specified in a translation, the state of the modifier keys and pointer buttons makes no difference to a translation. For example, the translation:

```
<Key>q:      quit()
```

will cause the `quit` action to be invoked when the *q* key is pressed, regardless of whether the Shift, Ctrl, Meta, or Lock key is also held, and regardless of the state of the pointer buttons.

Likewise, if a modifier is specified, there is nothing to prohibit other modifiers from being present as well. For example, the translation:

```
Shift<Key>q:     quit()
```

will take effect even if the Ctrl key is held down at the same time as the Shift key (and the *q* key).

There are a number of special modifier symbols that can be used to change this forgiving state of affairs. These symbols are shown in Table 8-6.

Table 8-6. Modifier Symbols

Symbol	Description
None	No modifiers may be present.
!	No modifiers except those explicitly specified may be present.
:	Apply shift (and lock) modifier to key event before comparing.
~	The modifier immediately following *cannot* be present.

The syntax of these special modifiers symbols is somewhat inconsistent, and made clearest by example.

8.1.5.3 Prohibiting a Modifier

The tilde (~) is used to negate a modifier. It says that the specified modifier may not be present. For example:

```
Button1<Key>:  doit()
```

says that `doit()` should be invoked by a press of any key when button 1 is being held down, while:

```
~Button1<Key>:  doit()
```

says that `doit()` should be invoked by a press of any key *except* when button 1 is being held down.

A ~ applies only to the modifier that immediately follows it. For example:

```
~Shift Ctrl<Key>:  doit()
```

says that `doit()` should be invoked when Ctrl is held down in conjunction with any key, except if Shift is depressed at the same time.

8.1.5.4 Requiring an Exact Match

An exclamation point at the start of a modifier list states that only the modifiers in that list may be present, and must match the list exactly. For example, if the translation is specified as:

```
!Shift<Key>q:   quit()
```

the translation will take effect only if the Shift key is the only modifier present; if Caps Lock were in effect, or if a pointer button were depressed at the same time, the translation would no longer work.

The modifier `None` is the same as `!` with no modifiers specified. That is:

```
None<Key>q:   quit()
```

or:

```
!<Key>q:   quit()
```

will invoke `quit` only if no modifier keys at all are pressed.

8.1.5.5 Paying Attention to the Case of Keysyms

The `:` modifier, like `!`, goes at the beginning of the modifier list and affects the entire list. This one is really in a category by itself, since it applies only to Key events.

Normally, the translations:

```
<Key>a:   doit()
```

and:

```
<Key>A:   doit()
```

have identical results: both will match either a lowercase or an uppercase *A*. Preceding the translation with a colon makes the case of the keysym significant. For example, to create commands like those in the UNIX *vi* editor, you might specify the following translations:

```
:<Key>a:   append()  \n\
:<Key>A:   appendToEndOfLine()
```

In this case, *a* and *A* are distinct. You could achieve somewhat the same result by specifying:

```
~Shift<Key>a:   append()  \n\
Shift<Key>a:    appendToEndOfLine()
```

However, this second example is both more complex and less effective. While the colon syntax will match an upper-case character generated as a result of either the Shift or Lock modifiers, the example shown immediately above will handle only Shift. You could use the following translation to prohibit both Shift and Lock from being asserted, but there is no way to specify that either Shift or Lock may be present:

```
~Shift ~Lock<Key>a:    append()  \n\
Shift<Key>a:    appendToEndOfLine()
```

Note that you cannot specify both the Shift or Lock modifier and an upper-case keysym. For example:

```
Shift<Key>A:    doit()
```

will have no effect, since you cannot further shift an uppercase character. The sequence !: at the beginning of a translation means that the listed modifiers must be in the correct state and that no other modifiers except the Shift and Lock keys may be asserted. In other words, !: by itself means the translation is triggered only if the specified key is pressed, considering case, and no other modifier is pressed.

For more details on how the Toolkit handles the ins and outs of case conversion, see Chapter 14, *Miscellaneous Toolkit Programming Techniques*. A more rigorous discussion of how the colon modifier works is also given in Appendix F, *Translation Table Syntax*, in Volume Five, *X Toolkit Intrinsics Reference Manual*.

8.1.6 Event Sequences

The left-hand side of a translation may specify a single event or a sequence of events that must occur for the action to be invoked. For example, we might want a certain action to be invoked only if the first button is clicked twice in succession.

Each event specified in the sequence is one of the abbreviations for an event type enclosed in angle brackets, optionally led by any set of modifiers and special characters, as described in Section 8.1.5. Each modifier-list/event pair in the sequence is separated by a comma.

For example, the translation to perform an action in response to a button press followed by a release of the same button (a button click) is the following:

```
<BtnDown>,<BtnUp> : doit()
```

Button press events may be specified in the translation table followed by a count in parentheses to distinguish a multiple click. The translation to detect a double click is:

```
<Btn1Down>(2) : doit()
```

or:

```
<Btn1Up>(2) : doit()
```

Notice that though they have the same effect for the user, these two translations are actually interpreted differently. The first is equivalent to saying:

```
<Btn1Down>,<Btn1Up>,<Btn1Down>:  doit()
```

while the second is equivalent to:

```
<Btn1Down>,<Btn1Up>,<Btn1Down>,<Btn1Up>:  doit()
```

A plus (+) may appear immediately after the count inside the parentheses to indicate that any number of clicks greater than the specified count should trigger the action.

The following translation detects two or more clicks:

```
<Btn1Down>(2+) : doit()
```

The maximum count that can be specified is 9.

In R3, the above click translations would be triggered even if you clicked once, went to lunch, and then clicked again when you returned. Xt uses a timing technique to solve this problem beginning in R4. The time is controlled by the `XmNmultiClickTime` application resource, which defaults to 200 milliseconds. If 200 milliseconds or more of idle time passes between clicks, Xt does not consider that a match. You can set this resource to different values for each display using `XtSetMultiClickTime`.

8.1.6.1 Special Considerations Involving Motion Events

Beware of interaction between pointer motion events and double clicking. If no motion events are specified in a translation table, these events are never selected, so there is no problem if they occur between other events. This allows a double click to be detected even if the user inadvertently jiggled the pointer in the course of the click. However, if motion events are selected for anywhere in the table, they may interfere with the expansion of events specified with the repeat notation. By definition, multiple clicks are detected only if there are no intervening events. Motion events would usually occur between the button presses and releases.

Multiple motion events will match any single motion selected event in the translation. That is:

```
<Motion>: doit()
```

will cause `doit()` to be invoked many times, once for each motion event generated by the pointer movement, unless the `compress_motion` event filter is turned on in the Core class structure. (This filter is described in Section 9.6.2.)

8.1.6.2 Modifiers and Event Sequences

A modifier list at the start of an event sequence applies to all events in the sequence. That is:

```
Shift<BtnDown>,<BtnUp>: doit()
```

is equivalent to:

```
Shift<BtnDown>,Shift<BtnUp>: doit()
```

However, if modifiers and events are interspersed, the modifier applies only to the event immediately following. As an extreme case to demonstrate this behavior, consider the following translation:

```
Ctrl<Btn2Down>, ~Ctrl<Btn2Up>: doit()
```

which requires that the Ctrl key be depressed when pointer button 2 is pressed; however, the key must not be depressed when the button is released.

8.1.6.3 Using Modifiers to Specify Button Event Sequences

Remember that there are modifiers for specifying the state of pointer buttons as well as modifier keys. These modifiers provide another way of expressing some event sequences. For example, the following translation would invoke the action when the F1 key is pressed while button 1 is being held down:

```
Button1<Key>F1:     doit()
```

This is equivalent to:

```
<Btn1Down>,<Key>F1:  doit()
```

The following translations could be used to call an action when both the first and second pointer buttons are down, regardless of the order in which they are pressed.

```
!Button1<Button2>:    doC() \n\
!Button2<Button1>:    doC()
```

8.1.6.4 Key Event Sequences

The Translation Manager specification provides a special syntax for specifying a sequence of Key events—as a string. That is:

```
"yes":  doit()
```

is theoretically equivalent to:

```
<Key>y,<Key>e,<Key>s:  doit()
```

We say "theoretically" because, at least in the R3 and R4 sample implementations from MIT, the "yes" syntax does not work. It may or may not work in other implementations.

Within a sequence of key events expressed as a string (on systems where the "yes" syntax does work, if any), the special character ^ (circumflex) means Ctrl and $ means Meta. These two special characters, as well as double quotes and backslashes, must be escaped with a backslash if they are to appear literally in one of these strings.

8.1.7 Interactions Between Translations

One of the most difficult things to learn about translations is how to predict the interactions between overlapping translations.

8.1.7.1 Translations in Multiple Resource Files

Much more will be said about resource files and resource matching in Chapter 10, *Resource Management and Type Conversion*. However, it is important to make one point here.

If several resource files contain translation tables for the same widget, only the one that takes priority according to file precedence and resource matching will have any effect even if all of them specify `#augment` or `#override`. This is because the translation table is the value of the resource, and only one resource value will override all other values.

In other words, even if all the translation tables specify `#augment` or `#override`, a maximum of two translation tables are merged by Xt: the widget's default translation table and the one translation table that takes priority as determined by the process of reading and merging all the resource files (and the command line) and then the process of resource matching. If you call `XtOverrideTranslations` or `XtAugmentTranslations` in the application, this is a third level of merging, but it is unrelated to the resource files.

8.1.7.2 Order of Translations

The order of translations in a table is important, because the table is searched from the top when each event arrives, and the first match is taken. Therefore, more specific events must appear *before* more general ones. Otherwise, the more specific ones will never be reached.

For example, consider a text entry widget that wants to close itself and dispatch a callback once the user presses the Return key, indicating that entry is complete. The widget's translations might be:

```
<Key>Return:    gotData()     \n\
<Key>:          insertChar()
```

If the translations were specified in the reverse order:

```
<Key>:          insertChar() \n\
<Key>Return:    gotData()
```

`insertChar()` would be called in response to a press of the Return key, and `gotData()` would never be called.

Keeping track of translation order is made more complicated when translations are merged. For example, if one of the above lines is in the default translations of a widget class, and the other is in a translation table in a resource file, in what order are the resulting translations? Though not documented in the Xt specification, it appears that the MIT implementation of Xt places the more specific translation first.

8.1.7.3 Event Sequences Sharing Initial Events

An exception to this rule of more specific translations being placed earlier in the translation table occurs with event sequences. One translation can contain an event or event sequence that appears in another translation. If the leading event or event sequence is in common, both will operate correctly. For example, the translations:

```
<Btn1Down>,<Btn1Up>:    actionB()\n\
<Btn1Down>:             actionA()
```

execute `actionA()` when button 1 is pressed and `actionB()` when it is then released. This is true regardless of which translation appears first in the table.

This is the reason, alluded to in Chapter 2, *Introduction to the X Toolkit and Motif*, why it is not possible to bind two different actions to a single and a double click of the same button in the same widget. Specifying:

```
<Btn1Up>(2):    quit() \n\
<Btn1Down>,<Btn1Up>:  confirm()
```

will invoke the `confirm()` action on a single click and both the `confirm()` and `quit()` actions on a double click.

This behavior was a design decision on the part of the X Consortium. Otherwise, the Intrinsics could never dispatch the single-click action until the double-click interval had passed, since it would have no way of knowing if a second click was coming. Applications needing to have single and double clicks in the same widget must do so by designing the two actions appropriately, rather than relying on the Translation Manager to make the distinction.

8.1.7.4 Event Sequences Sharing Noninitial Events

If a noninitial event sequence is common between two translations, each translation will match only event sequences where the preceding event does not match the other translation. Consider the translation:

```
<Btn1Down>,<Btn1Up>:    actionB()\n\
<Btn1Up>:               actionA()
```

When a `Btn1Up` event occurs, it triggers `actionA()` only if not preceded by `Btn1Down`.

The way this works is that Xt keeps a history of recent events. When each event arrives, Xt compares this event and its immediate history to the event sequences in a translation table. An event in the sequence may have already triggered an action, but that is irrelevant. Any translation whose final event in the event sequence matches the current event and whose earlier event sequence matches the event history is matched. If there are two translations that can match a particular event sequence, then the translations are considered overlapping, the latter will override the former, and Xt will print a run-time warning message at startup (not waiting for the overlapping actions to be invoked). This is an exception to the rule stated earlier that the translation manager executes the first match.

8.2 Accelerators and Mnemonics

As defined by Xt, accelerators are simply translation tables registered to map event sequences in one widget to actions in another. This is a general mechanism, but its name is based on a common use—adding keyboard shortcuts for widgets that are normally triggered by mouse button presses, such as PushButton widgets—because for advanced users a keyboard interface is often faster.

What Motif calls accelerators are implemented using Xt's accelerators, but the two are not at all the same. Motif implements a more convenient interface for providing keyboard shortcuts in menus, which it calls accelerators, but at the same time disables the more general accelerators feature in standard Xt. We will begin with a discussion of accelerators as defined by Xt, using the Athena widget set in the examples since they will not work in Motif. Then we will proceed with how Motif accelerators and mnemonics work. If you are interested only in how to program with Motif, then you can skip to Section 8.2.5.

8.2.1 Xt Accelerators

Every widget has an `XtNaccelerators` resource, inherited from the Core widget class. This resource contains an accelerator table, which is identical in format to a translation table; it maps event sequences to action sequences. Accelerator tables can be set into the `Xt-Naccelerators` resource in all the same ways translation tables can. The widget on which the `XtNaccelerators` resource is set is the widget whose actions are to be invoked from events in other widgets.

Once the `XtNaccelerators` resource of a widget is set, the application must call `Xt-InstallAccelerators` or `XtInstallAllAccelerators` to specify which widget will be the source of the events to invoke the actions specified in the accelerator table.

The MIT Intrinsics documentation refers to these two widgets as the *source* and *destination*. This can be confusing, especially since the arguments are referenced in reverse order in the call to `XtInstallAccelerators`:

```
void XtInstallAccelerators(destination, source)
    Widget destination;
    Widget source;
```

Just remember that the source is the widget whose actions you want executed, and the destination is the widget you want the events to be gathered in. To understand the use of the phrase *install accelerators*, think of the accelerators as the `XtNaccelerators` resource of the *source* widget, together with the actions of that widget, and the *destination* as the widget to which these actions are transplanted (i.e., "installed").

`XtInstallAccelerators` is always called from the application. (Widgets never install accelerators, because by definition they don't know about any other widgets.) In applications, accelerators can be installed any time, before or after the widgets are realized. Just before the `XtAppMainLoop` call is a good place.

As an example, we'll add accelerators to the *xbox1* application from Chapter 3, *More Techniques for Using Widgets*. This application displays two Command widgets in a Box, as shown in Figure 8-1.

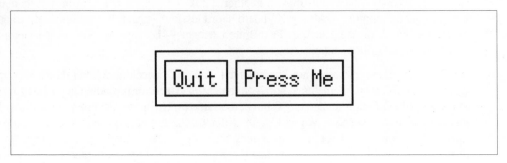

Figure 8-1. xbox1: two Command widgets in a Box

To add accelerators requires a single line of code—a call to XtInstallAccelerators, as shown in Example 8-1.

Example 8-1. Installing accelerators in an application

```
main(argc, argv)
int argc;
char **argv;
{
    XtAppContext app_context;
    Widget topLevel, box, quit;
        .
        .
        .
    /* allow quit widget's actions to be invoked by events in box. */
    XtInstallAccelerators(box, quit);

    XtAppMainLoop(app_context);
}
```

The actual value of the accelerator table is set through the resource mechanism. The Xt-Naccelerators resource is set for the widget whose actions are to be invoked from another widget. Xt stores this accelerator table, in compiled form, in the widget's instance structure when the widget is created. When the application calls XtInstall-Accelerators, the accelerator table stored in the widget is merged with the translation table of the widget that will be capturing the events. (If XtRemoveAccelerators is called, the original translation table, prior to merging with the accelerators from the source widget, is restored.)

Example 8-2 shows a possible app-defaults file.

Example 8-2. Specifying the XtNaccelerators resource from the app-defaults file

```
*quit.label:   Quit
*pressme.label:  Press me
*quit.accelerators:\n\
        <KeyPress>q:    set() notify()
```

This resource setting will allow a *q* typed anywhere in the Box widget that comprises the *xbox1* application window to invoke the quit widget's `notify()` action (which, as you may recall from Section 2.4, in turn invokes the `Quit` callback installed by the application). Notice that the accelerators are specified as a resource of the source widget, even though the events that invoke them will come from the destination widget.

There are some differences in the translation tables that can be used for accelerators.

- Abbreviations for event types are not valid. Only the event names that were shown in Column 1 of Table 8-1 may be used (although `Key` works in place of `KeyPress`).

- The None, Meta, Hyper, Super, Alt, or ANY modifier symbols are not valid.

- The default directive for accelerator tables is `#augment` rather than `#replace`. If specified, the `#replace` directive is ignored. It is important to realize that accelerators are merged with the source widget's translations. `#override` thus says that the accelerators take priority over any matching translations in the source widget, and `#augment` says that the accelerators have lower priority.

- Parameters passed to actions must be quoted with double quotes.

8.2.2 Event Propagation

If you install accelerators in the Box widget as shown in Example 8-2, you will notice that even though the destination widget is Box, keyboard input will also be accepted in the children of `box`, including not only the quit widget but also the `pressme` widget. This is because of a characteristic of X called *event propagation*.

The server sends to the client only the types of events the client selects. Internally, Xt selects events using the Xlib call `XSelectInput`. From a Toolkit application, this is hidden because the translation mechanism automatically selects the appropriate event types specified in the translation table. (As we will see in Chapter 9, *More Input Techniques*, Xt provides a low-level event-handling mechanism that exposes event selection more directly.)

Event selection reduces the amount of network traffic, the number of events the server has to generate, and the number of unneeded events the client must process only to throw away.

Most event types are selected on a per-window basis. Each selected event that arrives at the client contains the window ID of the window it was selected for. (Non-maskable events, the last five event types in Table 8-1, are the exception; they are selected using a different mechanism or are not selected at all.)

Pointer and keyboard events propagate *through* windows that have not selected them, as shown below in Figure 8-2. That is, if the `pressme` widget's window has not selected `KeyPress` events, any key events that occur in that window will be passed on to its parent, the Box widget. If the Box widget's window didn't select them either, they would be passed on to the window created by the top-level Shell widget, and so on. Events propagate through the window hierarchy all the way to the root window, until they reach a window that selected them. (If no window has selected them, they are never sent by the server.) Xt treats an event that originally occurred in some descendent widget just as if it actually happened in the widget that selected the event.

1
q Key pressed with pointer in `pressme` widget ...

2
No translation for keyboard events on `pressme` widget, event propagated to `box` ...

3
`box` widget has accelerator for keyboard events, and processes event propagated from `pressme`. `box` has installed accelerator that maps the q key event into the `notify` and set actions of the `quit` widget

Figure 8-2. Key event propagation in xbox

Propagation is a characteristic of `ButtonPress`, `ButtonRelease`, `KeyPress`, `KeyRelease`, `MotionNotify`, `EnterNotify`, and `LeaveNotify` events only. As mentioned earlier, keyboard events are the events most often used as accelerators.

In the version of *xbox* we just looked at, keyboard events propagate through the Command widgets to the Box widget, because they are not selected by the Command widgets. When they reach the Box widget, they match the events specified in the accelerator table and invoke actions from the `quit` widget.

The Command widgets have a default translation table that includes pointer button events and enter/leave events. Xt, therefore, selects these events for each Command widget. Before accelerators are installed, the Box widget has no translation table and therefore has no events selected for it. When the accelerators are installed, the accelerator table is merged with the (nonexistent) translation table of the Box widget and becomes the Box's translation table. Xt then selects keyboard events for the Box widget.

But consider the resource settings in Example 8-3.

Example 8-3. Conflicting translations and accelerators

```
*quit.label:  Quit
*pressme.label:  Press me
*pressme.translations:  #override\n\
        <KeyPress>p:    set() notify()
*quit.accelerators:\n\
        <KeyPress>q:    set() notify()
```

No key event will propagate through a widget that has a translation for any key event. With the resource settings in Example 8-3, since pressme has a translation for the *p* key, the *q* key will not propagate through the widget. Therefore, it is often better to specify all key events as accelerators and install them on a common ancestor.

Accelerators are just merged into translations—they are not a completely different mechanism. The #augment (default) or #override directives used in accelerator tables specify whether the accelerator should override or augment existing translations for the destination widget. For example, if box had a translation of its own that matched the event sequence in the accelerator installed on the same widget, whether the translation or the accelerator would be invoked depends on whether #augment (the default) or #override had been specified as the accelerator directive. (This example is a little farfetched, since the Box widget defines no actions or translations—but it illustrates the point.)

When using or writing widgets, event propagation is usually important only for accelerators, because widgets are rarely layered in such a way that any of the ones that accept input are obscured.

8.2.3 Installing Accelerators in Multiple Widgets

If you want to install accelerators from more than one widget, you can call XtInstall-Accelerators once for every widget whose actions you want executable from the destination. Alternatively, you can call XtInstallAllAccelerators just once for a whole application, specifying the application's top-level window as both the destination and the source. XtInstallAllAccelerators recursively traverses the widget tree rooted at the source, and installs the accelerators of each widget onto the destination.

For example, to install accelerators from both the quit and pressme widgets onto box, you could replace the call to XtInstallAccelerators shown in Example 8-3 with:*

Example 8-4. Installing accelerators from both command widgets

```
XtInstallAllAccelerators(box, box);
```

---

*In a more complex application, where the Box widget was not the main window but only a subarea containing command buttons, you might instead use the call:

```
    XtInstallAllAccelerators(topLevel, box);
```

which would make the actions from only the widgets contained in box available from anywhere in the application.

You could then define an app-defaults file such as the following:

Example 8-5. Accelerators resource settings for two widgets

```
*quit.label:  Quit
*pressme.label:  Press me
*pressme.accelerators:  \n\
        <KeyPress>p:    set() notify()
*quit.accelerators:  \n\
        <KeyPress>q:    set() notify()
```

Because you would be most likely to specify distinct KeyPress events to invoke the actions in each Command widget, you would normally specify each accelerator resource separately, as shown above. But in the unlikely case that you wanted actions of multiple Command widgets to be invoked by the exact same event, you could do this instead. For example:

```
*Command.accelerators:  \n\
        <KeyPress>:  set() notify()
```

would invoke the set and notify actions of every Command widget, but not of widgets belonging to other classes.

Or assuming that there were multiple Box widgets in an application, one containing options, and the other commands, you might specify something like this:

```
*optionsbox*accelerators:  \n\
        <KeyPress>:  set() notify()
```

to invoke the actions of every Command widget in optionsbox only.

The point is that, like any resource setting, an accelerator table can apply to only one widget, to a group of children of a widget, or to an entire class, depending on how you identify the widgets for which you are setting the XtNaccelerators resource.

8.2.4 Defining the Accelerator Table in the Code

If you want to install a default accelerator table from within a program, you must follow similar steps to those used for translations, but with the following differences:

- You must set the XtNaccelerators resource instead of XtNtranslations.

- Instead of using XtParseTranslationTable to convert the ASCII translation table into Xt's internal form, use XtParseAcceleratorTable.

- There are no accelerator equivalents of XtOverrideTranslations or Xt-AugmentTranslations. Instead you can use XtVaSetValues and use the accelerator directive by specifying #augment or #override.

8.2.5 Motif Accelerators and Mnemonics

Motif accelerators are keyboard shortcuts for menus, but they are used in a way that is completely different from that of the standard Xt accelerators just described.

When a RowColumn widget has been configured to operate as a popup menu or MenuBar, its `XmNmenuAccelerator` resource is activated. This resource can be set to a keysym which, when pressed, will pop up the popup menu or move the focus to the first item in the MenuBar. For example, the effective default value for `XmNmenuAccelerator` for the MenuBar is `<KeyUp>F10`.

RowColumn also has a subpart which has an `XmNbuttonAccelerators` resource. The `XmNbuttonAccelerators` resource is set to an array of keysyms, which when pressed will trigger the respective buttons. The `XmNbuttonAcceleratorText` resource is an array that lets you provide text that will appear in each button, to show the user the accelerator for each button.

All the resources that begin with `XmNbutton` can only be used when a menu is created with a function that begins with `XmCreateSimple` (there is one for each of the six types of Motif menus). These functions create a menu and populate it with children. Here are the other RowColumn subresources that configure the children as they are created:

- `XmNbuttonCount` specifies the total number of menu buttons, separators, and titles to create.

- `XmNbuttons` specifies a list of compound strings to use as labels for the buttons created. The list contains one element for each button, separator, and title created.

- `XmNbuttonType` specifies a list of button types associated with the buttons to be created. The list contains one element for each button, separator, and title created. If this resource is not specified, each button in a MenuBar is a CascadeButtonGadget; each button in any other type of RowColumn widget is a PushButtonGadget. Each entry in the button type array can have several possible values such as `XmPUSHBUTTON`.

These resources work only when set while creating a menu using `XmCreate-Simple*Menu` such as `XmCreateSimplePopupMenu`. Setting them at any later time will have no effect. Some resources that configure the children of menus are not listed here.

8.2.5.1 Mnemonics

A *mnemonic* is a keyboard shortcut as well. However, a mnemonic is available only when a menu is visible, while an accelerator can invoke a menu entry even when the menu is not visible. Therefore, accelerators must be unique application-wide, while mnemonics only need to be unique within a single menu. Consequently, a mnemonic is a particular key regardless of modifiers, while accelerators are usually key combinations such as Ctrl-C.

A mnemonic is indicated in a button by underlining a character in the button label. Motif does this automatically as long as the mnemonic you choose appears in the label. The `Xm-NbuttonMnemonics` subresource of RowColumn specifies a mnemonic for each button created, but can only be used while creating the menu with one of the

`XmCreateSimple*Menu` routines. The list contains one element for each button, separator, and title created. The mnemonic for a particular button can also be set using the `Xm-Nmnemonic` resource of any kind of button widget.

Further discussion of mnemonics is provided in the forthcoming Volume Six, *X Motif Programming Manual*.

8.2.6 The display_accelerators Method

Xt calls the source widget's `display_accelerators` method when the accelerators are installed. The purpose of this method is to display to the user the installed accelerators. The method is passed a string representation of the accelerator table, which the method can theoretically manipulate into a form understandable by the user.

All Motif widgets just set this method to NULL. All of the Athena widgets inherit the Core widget's `display_accelerators` method by initializing the appropriate member of the class structure to `XtInheritDisplayAccelerators`. This default method, as implemented in the MIT distribution, does nothing.

9

More Input Techniques

This chapter describes how to handle events with event handlers, and how to use information from the event structure inside an event handler or action routine. It also describes how to get file, pipe or socket input, how to use timeouts to call a function after a delay or at particular intervals, and how to use work procedures to do background processing. Finally, it discusses some low-level features of Xt for directly interacting with the event queue.

In This Chapter:

9

More Input Techniques

In addition to translations, there is a lower-level mechanism called *event handlers*. Event handlers can be used from application or widget code. An event handler is a function registered with XtAddEventHandler to be called in response to a particular event or group of events (but not an event sequence or detail, as is possible with translations). This is a low-level, non-user-configurable means of getting events. Event handlers provide no additional capabilities over translations and actions. But they allow Xt to skip the step of searching a translation table before dispatching the event to an event handler. This speed advantage is possibly significant for events that come in large numbers, such as pointer motion events, or in applications with large translation tables. (Despite this speed difference, good performance in tracking pointer motion can be achieved with translations.)

Both event handlers and actions are passed as an argument the actual event structure that caused them to be invoked. Many event handlers and actions use data in the event. For example, a routine handling motion events may want to obtain the current pointer position from the event structure. After describing how to add and remove event handlers, we discuss the event structures and show a routine that uses specific event data.

Next, this chapter discusses three ways to register functions Xt will call for input other than events, since some programs do not live by X events alone.

- XtAppAddInput registers a procedure to be called when input is available from a file (or pipe or socket). This procedure can be used to perform code necessary when reads, writes, or exceptions are detected.

- XtAppAddTimeOut registers a function to be called at a particular relative time. This function can be used to implement delays or to execute code repeatedly at known intervals.

- XtAppAddWorkProc registers a work procedure. Work procedures are called when input from other sources is *not* available. They perform background tasks while the application is waiting for user input.

Finally, we provide more background on how the Toolkit dispatches events from XtApp-MainLoop, and describe the low-level routines that can be used to construct your own main loop. We also describe Xt's event filters, which are controlled by flags in the Core class structure. These filters tell Xt whether or not to compress multiple motion, enter, leave, or expose events occurring in the same widget.

9.1 Event Handlers

An event handler is a function you provide to handle a particular type of event or group of event types. You register this function with a call to `XtAddEventHandler` or `Xt-InsertEventHandler`, specifying the widget in which the events are to be monitored. The difference between these two functions is described below.

You can later stop the function from being called with `XtRemoveEventHandler`. On any widget, you can register as many event handlers as you want, each for the same or for different types of events. When more than one routine is registered for an event, the order in which they are invoked is undefined.

Within Motif applications, event handlers have one common use; they are used to pop up Motif popup menus. A popup menu is mapped where the user presses a mouse button in a particular widget, usually the application's main window. Since the application's main window probably doesn't have an `XmNactivateCallback` resource, the function that pops up the menu can't be registered as a callback. It can be registered as an event handler, however, because this requires no prior agreement from the widget. This function could also be added as an action from the application, but the required translations could interfere with the operation of the main window if it already uses ButtonPress events. Event handlers have the advantage that they work in parallel with Xt's other event dispatching mechanisms, and therefore they don't interfere. Example 9-1 shows how a typical application uses an event handler. The meaning of each argument will be described in a moment.

Example 9-1. Using an event hander to pop up a popup menu

```
static void
PostMenu (w, client_data, event)
Widget          w;
XtPointer       client_data;
XEvent          *event;
{
    Widget popup = (Widget) client_data;

    if (event->button != Button3)
        return;

    XmMenuPosition(popup, event);

    XtManageChild(popup);
}

main(argc, argv)
int argc;
char **argv;
{
    Widget mainW, Menu;
        .
        .
        .
    Menu = XmCreatePopupMenu(mainW, "popMenu", NULL, 0);

    XtAddEventHandler(mainW,         /* events sent to this widget */
            ButtonPressMask,         /* events desired */
            False,                   /* non-maskable events */
```

Example 9-1. Using an event hander to pop up a popup menu (continued)

```
        PostMenu,              /* function */
        Menu);                 /* client_data passed to function */
    .
    .
    .
}
```

Within widget code, event handlers are used for various special requirements of individual widgets. For example, RowColumn uses an event handler to implement keyboard mnemonics in menus. Manager uses event handlers to generate synthetic events for its gadget children. (Since gadgets do not have windows, they would normally not get `EnterNotify` and `LeaveNotify` events. So the Manager widget class keeps track of the pointer position, and when the pointer enters one of the gadget children, Manager sends that child a synthetic `EnterNotify` event.)

In general, however, event handlers are infrequently used in application or widget code. None of the Athena widgets use them, and, out of the 40 applications in MIT's core distribution, only *xterm* and *xman* use them. As mentioned earlier, event handlers are useful for handling high-volume events, such as `MotionNotify` events, with maximum speed. An event handler for motion events would probably be the best way to implement a drawing program. However, translation tables provide good speed even for motion events on most systems.

Event handlers would also be useful when the type of events being handled changes frequently, because there is some overhead involved in compiling and merging translation tables. Event handlers can also be used to handle events for which the user-configurability of translations is not needed or wanted, such as `EnterWindow`, `LeaveWindow`, `FocusIn`, and `FocusOut` events.

Another possible use of event handlers is to speed the handling of certain events when there is a very large translation table. For example, editors typically have a large number of translations for various key combinations. If an editor was to accept pointer motion as well (to allow drawing of simple graphics), it might pay to handle motion events in an event handler instead of through translations.

The call to `XtAddEventHandler` specifies which events trigger the event handler function. This is done with an *event mask* argument.* In an event mask, each bit represents one or more event types. Symbolic constants are defined by Xlib for each event mask bit. Multiple types of events can be selected at the same time by ORing together different masks with the bitwise OR operator (|). Note that there is not a one-to-one correspondence between event masks and event types. Some event masks select only one event, but others select multiple events. Furthermore, several of the masks select the same event type, but specify that it be delivered only when it occurs under special conditions. Table 9-1 shows the event masks and the event types they select.

---

*The event mask used in `XtAddEventHandler` is the same as the one used in the Xlib call `XSelectInput`.

Table 9-1. Event Masks and Event Types

Event Mask	Event Type
KeyPressMask	KeyPress
KeyReleaseMask	KeyRelease
ButtonPressMask	ButtonPress
ButtonReleaseMask	ButtonRelease
OwnerGrabButtonMask	n/a
KeymapStateMask	KeymapNotify
PointerMotionMask	MotionNotify
PointerMotionHintMask	
ButtonMotionMask	
Button1MotionMask	
Button2MotionMask	
Button3MotionMask	
Button4MotionMask	
Button5MotionMask	
EnterWindowMask	EnterNotify
LeaveWindowMask	LeaveNotify
FocusChangeMask	FocusIn
	FocusOut
ExposureMask	Expose
selected in GC by	GraphicsExpose
graphics_expose component)	NoExpose
ColormapChangeMask	ColormapNotify
PropertyChangeMask	PropertyNotify
VisibilityChangeMask	VisibilityNotify
ResizeRedirectMask	ResizeRequest
StructureNotifyMask	CirculateNotify
	ConfigureNotify
	DestroyNotify
	GravityNotify
	MapNotify
	ReparentNotify
	UnmapNotify
SubstructureNotifyMask	CirculateNotify
	ConfigureNotify
	CreateNotify
	DestroyNotify
	GravityNotify
	MapNotify
	ReparentNotify
	UnmapNotify
SubstructureRedirectMask	CirculateRequest
	ConfigureRequest
	MapRequest
(always selected)	MappingNotify

Table 9-1. Event Masks and Event Types (continued)

Event Mask	Event Type
(always selected)	ClientMessage
(always selected)	SelectionClear
(always selected)	SelectionNotify
(always selected)	SelectionRequest

The events that are always selected are called *nonmaskable events*. These can also be handled with an event handler, but not by specifying them in the event mask. An argument to the XtAddEventHandler call, `non_maskable`, is a Boolean value that, if True, specifies that the event handler should be called for nonmaskable events. This event handler then must branch according to which of the seven types of nonmaskable events it is passed. A typical nonmaskable event handler is shown in Section 9.1.2.

9.1.1 Adding Event Handlers

Event handlers are added with a call to XtAddEventHandler or XtInsertEvent-Handler. XtAddEventHandler takes five arguments: the widget for which the handler is being added, an event mask, a flag that specifies whether or not this handler is for non-maskable events (see below), the name of the handler, and optional client data. Xt-InsertEventHandler takes these and one additional argument: the position, either XtListTail or XtListHead.

A list of event handlers can be registered for the same event; but the same function will appear only once in the list with the same `client_data`. If the same function/`client_data` pair is registered again with XtAddEventHandler, nothing will happen except that the event mask for that function may change. But if the same function/`client_data` pair is registered again with XtInsertEventHandler, the function will be moved to the beginning or the end of the function list.

XtAddEventHandler or XtInsertEventHandler may be called before or after a widget is realized. In application code, this means the call can appear anywhere before Xt-AppMainLoop. In a widget, XtAddEventHandler or XtInsertEventHandler calls are placed in the `initialize` or `realize` methods.

Example 9-2 shows the code from *xterm* that registers an event handler for FocusIn and FocusOut events, and a gutted version of the event handler itself.

Example 9-2. Registering an event handler, and the handler function itself

```
extern void HandleFocusChange();

static void VTInitialize (request, new)
XtermWidget request, new;
{
    .
    .
    .
```

```
        XtAddEventHandler(topLevel,      /* widget */
                FocusChangeMask,         /* event mask */
                False,                   /* non-maskable events */
                HandleFocusChange,       /* event handler */
                (Opaque)NULL);           /* client_data */

        .
        .
        .

}
/*ARGSUSED*/
void HandleFocusChange(w, unused, event, continue_to_dispatch)
Widget w;
register XFocusChangeEvent *event;
XtPointer unused;                        /* client_data */
Boolean *continue_to_dispatch;
{
    if (event->type == FocusIn) {
                                         /* process FocusIn */
        .
        .
        .
    }
    else {
                                         /* process FocusOut */
        .
        .
        .
    }
    /*
     * If subsequent event handlers registered for this event
     * should not be called, set *continue_to_dispatch = False;
     * This is not recommended.
     */
}
```

In typical usage, either the event mask argument is a mask and the *non_maskable* argument is set to False, or the event mask argument is set to zero and *non_maskable* is set to True. Example 9-1 demonstrated the former case; now we'll look at the latter.

9.1.2 Adding Nonmaskable Event Handlers

The *non_maskable* argument of XtAddEventHandler specifies whether the specified event handler should be called in response to the events that can't be selected as described above. The nonmaskable events are GraphicsExpose, NoExpose, Mapping-Notify, SelectionClear, SelectionRequest, SelectionNotify, and ClientMessage. The first two of these events are selected using the graphics_exposure component of the GC, and the rest are always sent to the client whenever they occur. `MappingNotify` is automatically handled by Xt, so it isn't passed to event handlers and you don't need to worry about it. The selection events are described in Chapter 11, *Interclient Communications*.

Because there are several nonmaskable event types, a nonmaskable event handler must be sure to branch according to the type of event, and throw away any event types not handled. You need not have all the code to handle all the types in a single event handler. Instead, you can handle each type in a separate handler, each registered separately. However, each handler would still need to check the event type because the entire list of them would be called for every nonmaskable event.

Example 9-3 shows the registration of a nonmaskable event handler and the handler itself, from *xman*.

Example 9-3. Adding a nonmaskable event handler

```
static void
Realize(w, valueMask, attributes)
register Widget w;
Mask *valueMask;
XSetWindowAttributes *attributes;
{
    .
    .
    .

    XtAddEventHandler(w, 0, True,
            GExpose, NULL); /* Get Graphics Exposures */
} /* Realize */

/* ARGSUSED */
static void
GExpose(w, client_data, event)
Widget w;
XtPointer client_data;
XEvent *event;
{
    if (event->type == GraphicsExpose)
        Redisplay(w, event, NULL); /*call the expose method directly*/
}
```

This event handler is sometimes used because Xt does not normally call the `expose` method in response to `GraphicsExpose` events. But in R4, another way to accomplish this has been introduced. If the `compress_exposure` field in the Core structure is set to (`Xt-ExposeCompressMultiple | XtExposeGraphicsExpose`), Xt will call the `expose` method with these events.

9.1.3 Removing Event Handlers

`XtRemoveEventHandler` takes the same arguments as `XtAddEventHandler`; if there are parameter mismatches, the call is quietly ignored. For example, the client data argument may be used to distinguish between different event handlers; if the client data argument does not match that which was passed in the `XtAddEventHandler`, then `Xt-`

`RemoveEventHandler` will do nothing. `XtRemoveEventHandler` is also silent about failing to remove a handler that was never added or a handler that was incorrectly specified.

9.1.4 Adding Raw Event Handlers

Xt also allows you to add event handlers without actually selecting events. The main purpose of this feature is for Xt to register functions before widgets are realized (because events can't be selected until windows are created during realization). Event handlers registered without selecting events are called *raw* event handlers, and are added with `XtAddRaw-EventHandler` or `XtInsertRawEventHandler`, which have the same calling sequences as `XtAddEventHandler` and `XtInsertRawEventHandler`. The event mask indicates which events the handler will be called in response to, but only when these events are selected elsewhere. Raw event handlers are supported mostly because they are used inside Xt. They are mentioned here only for completeness—you are unlikely to need them.

A raw event handler might be used to "shadow" another event handler (both added with the same event mask), such that until a primary event handler is added, the shadow handler will never be called. The primary handler will be added with `XtAddEventHandler`, which will select events, and then both handlers will be called when the appropriate events occur.

However, the "shadowing" technique is not necessary to assure that multiple calls to `Xt-AddEventHandler` don't result in wasted `XSelectInput` calls in which the event mask has not changed. Xt keeps a cache of the event masks of each widget, and calls `XSelectInput` only when it is necessary to change the window's event mask attribute in the server.

Raw event handlers are removed with a call to `XtRemoveRawEventHandler`.

9.2 Writing Routines That Use Specific Event Data

An event is a packet of information that the server sends to the client. Xlib takes this packet from the network and places it into an `XEvent` structure and places it on a queue until the client program requests it. Xt requests events from this queue and dispatches the event to the appropriate action routine or event handler for the widget in which the event occurred. The event itself is passed as an argument to the routine.*

Actually, `XEvent` is a C-Language union of many event structures all the same size but with some different field names. The first member of the union, and of any of the individual event structures, is the event `type`. Table 9-2, later in this section, lists the event types and the matching event structure types.

---

*We'll look at the low-level routines Xt provides for directly manipulating the event queue later in this chapter.

Many action routines are intentionally written not to depend on the detailed information inside any particular type of event, so that the user can specify translations to call the action in response to different types of events. For example, it is useful for an action routine normally triggered by a pointer click to work when called in response to a key instead. Such an action should not depend on the event structure fields unique to button events.

However, many other action routines, and most event handlers, do use the detailed information inside event structures. The first member, type, identifies which type of event this structure represents, and hence implies which other fields are present in the structure.

To access event structure fields other than type you need to cast XEvent into the appropriate event structure type. If you are expecting only one type of event to trigger this action, then you can simply declare the argument as the appropriate type, as shown in Example 9-4.

Example 9-4. Casting the event structure by declaring action routine arguments

```
/*ARGSUSED*/
static void
ActionA(w, event, params, num_params)
Widget w;
XEvent *event;
String *params;
Cardinal *num_params;
{
    if ((event->type != ButtonPress) && (event->type != KeyPress)) {
        XtWarning("ActionA invoked by wrong event type.");
        /* possible exit here */
    }
        .
        .
        .
}
```

When an action routine or event handler depends on the fields in a particular event structure, it is a good practice to check the event type in that action unless you are sure that the user can't change the translation (and thus the events used to invoke the action).

If you want the same code called for two event types, then you would do better to create two separate translations and two separate actions that each call a common routine. However, it is sometimes more convenient to have an action called by two different events. Example 9-5 shows the ToggleCell action from the BitmapEdit widget, which is called in response to either MotionNotify or ButtonPress events. This action inverts a pixel in the bitmap either if the pointer is clicked on a cell in the widget, or if it is dragged across the cell with the pointer buttons held down.

Example 9-5. Handling multiple event types in an action routine

```
static void
ToggleCell(w, event)
Widget w;
XEvent *event;
{
    BitmapEditWidget cw = (BitmapEditWidget) w;
    static int oldx = -1, oldy = -1;
    GC gc;
    int mode;
```

More Input Techniques

```
    int newx, newy;

    if (event->type == ButtonPress) {
        newx = (w->bitmapEdit.cur_x + ((XButtonEvent *)event)->x) /
                w->bitmapEdit.cell_size_in_pixels;
        newy = (w->bitmapEdit.cur_y + ((XButtonEvent *)event)->y) /
                w->bitmapEdit.cell_size_in_pixels;
    }
    else if  (event->type == MotionNotify) {
        newx = (w->bitmapEdit.cur_x + ((XMotionEvent *)event)->x) /
                w->bitmapEdit.cell_size_in_pixels;
        newy = (w->bitmapEdit.cur_y + ((XMotionEvent *)event)->y) /
                w->bitmapEdit.cell_size_in_pixels;
    }
    else
        XtWarning("BitmapEdit: ToggleCell called with wrong event\
            type\n");
    .
    .
    .
}
```

Notice that some code is repeated to cast the event structure to the two different event types. With the current MIT implementation of Xlib, the positions of the x and y fields in the XButtonEvent and XMotionEvent structures are the same, and therefore this casting is unnecessary on many compilers. However, for strict ANSI C conformance these casts are necessary, and furthermore it is improper to depend on any particular implementation of Xlib. The order of the fields in one of these events could be different in some vendor's implementation of Xlib.

9.2.1 Event Types and Structure Names

Table 9-2 lists the event types and the matching event structure types. The event descriptions in the table will give you a general idea of what each event is for. Many of these events are not often used in applications, and more of them are automatically handled by Xt. We've already discussed how to use the most common event types and their abbreviations in translation tables in Chapter 8, *Events, Translations, and Accelerators*. Appendix C, *Event Reference*, in Volume Five, *X Toolkit Intrinsics Reference Manual*, provides a complete reference to the circumstances under which each event is generated, what it is for, and the fields in each of the event structures. You will need this information to write action routines that use event-specific data.

Table 9-2. Event Types and Event Structures

Event Type	Structure	Description
KeyPress	XKeyPressedEvent	Key pressed.
KeyRelease	XKeyReleasedEvent	Key released.
ButtonPress	XButtonPressedEvent	Pointer button pressed.
ButtonRelease	XButtonReleasedEvent	Pointer button released.
KeymapNotify	XKeymapEvent	State of all keys when pointer entered.
MotionNotify	XPointerMovedEvent	Pointer motion.
EnterNotify	XEnterWindowEvent	Pointer entered window.
LeaveNotify	XLeaveWindowEvent	Pointer left window.
FocusIn	XFocusInEvent	This window is now keyboard focus.
FocusOut	XFocusOutEvent	This window was keyboard focus.
Expose	XExposeEvent	Part of window needs redrawing.
GraphicsExpose	XGraphicsExposeEvent	Source of copy unavailable.
NoExpose	XNoExposeEvent	Source of copy available.
ColormapNotify	XColormapEvent	Window's colormap changed.
PropertyNotify	XPropertyEvent	Property value changed.
VisibilityNotify	XVisibilityEvent	Window has been obscured.
ResizeRequest	XResizeRequestEvent	Redirect resize request to window manager.
CirculateNotify	XCirculateEvent	Stacking order modified.
ConfigureNotify	XConfigureEvent	Window resized or moved.
DestroyNotify	XDestroyWindowEvent	Window destroyed.
GravityNotify	XGravityEvent	Window moved due to win gravity attribute.
MapNotify	XMapEvent	Window mapped.
ReparentNotify	XReparentEvent	Window reparented.
UnmapNotify	XUnmapEvent	Window unmapped.
CirculateRequest	XCirculateRequestEvent	Redirect stacking order change to window manager.
ConfigureRequest	XConfigureRequestEvent	Redirect move or resize request to window manager.
MapRequest	XMapRequestEvent	Redirect window map request to window manager.
MappingNotify	XMappingEvent	Keyboard mapping changed.
ClientMessage	XClientMessageEvent	Client-dependent.
SelectionClear	XSetSelectClearEvent	Current owner is losing selection.
SelectionNotify	XSelectionEvent	Selection is ready for requestor.
SelectionRequest	XSelectionRequestEvent	Request for selection to current owner.

9.3 File, Pipe, and Socket Input

`XtAppAddInput` allows a program to obtain input from a file. This is not merely reading the file once, but monitoring it for further activity. Under UNIX this can be used to get input from pipes and sockets, since they are variations of files. We will demonstrate getting file and pipe input in this section.

The `XtAppAddInput` routine takes four arguments: a file descriptor, a flag (see below), your function, and `client_data`.

`XtAppAddInput` returns an ID that uniquely identifies the `XtAppAddInput` request. You can use the ID to cancel the request later with `XtRemoveInput`.

One argument of `XtAppAddInput` is a file descriptor (this file must be open before calling `XtAppAddInput`). Since implementation of files varies between operating systems, the actual contents of the parameter passed as the file descriptor argument to these routines is operating system-dependent. Therefore, this code is inherently nonportable.

Possible values for the mask and their meanings are as shown in Table 9-3.

Table 9-3. Other Input Source Masks

Mask	Description
`XtInputReadMask`	File descriptor has data available.
`XtInputWriteMask`	File descriptor available for writing.
`XtInputExceptMask`	I/O errors have occurred (exceptions).
`XtInputNoneMask`	Never call function registered.

Calling these argument values masks is something of a misnomer, since they *cannot* be ORed together. However, you can call `XtAppAddInput` additional times to register a separate function (or the same function) for each of these masks on the same file descriptor.

9.3.1 Getting File Input

In Example 9-6, a program called *xfileinput* reads new characters from a file whenever they appear. In other words, the program will initially print to the standard output the contents of the file specified on the command line, and it will print any characters that are later appended to that file. Try the program *xfileinput* as follows:

```
echo "test string" > testfile
xfileinput testfile &
echo "more text" >> testfile
```

A program such as this functions similarly to the UNIX command *tail –f*. It could be used to monitor system log files, or other similar files that grow.

The code shown in Example 9-6 opens the file and calls `XtAppAddInput` in `main`. The `get_file_input` function registered with `XtAppAddInput` reads and prints characters from the file.*

Example 9-6. Getting file input with XtAppAddInput

```
/* header files */
    .
    .
    .

/* ARGSUSED */
get_file_input(client_data, fid, id)
XtPointer client_data;      /* unused */
int *fid;
XtInputId *id;
{
    char buf[BUFSIZ];
    int nbytes;
    int i;

    if ((nbytes = read(*fid, buf, BUFSIZ)) == -1)
        perror("get_file_input");

    if (nbytes)
        for (i = 0; i < nbytes; i++)
            putchar(buf[i]);
}
main(argc, argv)
int argc;
char **argv;
{
    XtAppContext app_context;
    Widget topLevel, goodbye;
    FILE *fid;
    String filename;

    topLevel = XtVaAppInitialize(&app_context, "XFileInput", NULL,
            0, &argc, argv, NULL, NULL);

    if (argv[1] == NULL) {
        fprintf(stderr, "xfileinput: filename must be specified on\
                command line.\n");
        exit(1);
    }

    filename = argv[1];
        .
        .
        .

    /* open file */
    if ((fid = fopen(filename, "r")) == NULL)
        fprintf(stderr, "xfileinput: couldn't open input file.\n");

    /* register function to handle that input, NULL arg
     * is client_data */
```

---

*Note that the code for opening and reading files is probably not portable to operating systems other than UNIX.

Example 9-6. Getting file input with XtAppAddInput (continued)

```
XtAppAddInput(app_context, fileno(fid), XtInputReadMask,
      get_file_input, NULL);

XtRealizeWidget(topLevel);

XtAppMainLoop(app_context);
}
```

The function registered with `XtAppAddInput` is called with *client_data* (used for passing in any application data), a pointer to the file descriptor, and the ID of the `XtApp-AddInput` request. You can use a call to `XtRemoveInput` in the function registered with `XtAppAddInput` if that function is only to be called once. One argument of the `Xt-RemoveInput` call is the ID of the `XtAppAddInput` request.

Under some operating systems, the function registered with `XtAppAddInput` is called very frequently even when no new input is available. This is because Xt makes a system call to detect whether the file is "ready for reading," and some operating systems say the file is ready even when there is nothing new to read. The example shown above works, but it loads down the system much more than necessary. You may wish to check the file every quarter second instead of continuously, by adding and removing your input handler periodically using timeouts (as described in Section 9.4). The same goes for input from a pipe.

9.3.2 Getting Pipe Input

The code to get pipe input is almost identical to the code just shown that gets file input. The only difference is that we use *popen* instead of *fopen*, and change the various error messages. Now instead of treating the command-line argument as a filename, it is treated as a program run under a shell. This program's output is piped into our application. For example, here is an example of how to invoke this version of *xpipeinput*:

```
spike% xpipeinput "cal 11 1989"
      November 1989
   S   M Tu   W Th   F   S
               1   2   3   4
   5   6   7   8   9 10 11
  12 13 14 15 16 17 18
  19 20 21 22 23 24 25
  26 27 28 29 30
```
(Program continues to monitor pipe for further input until application exits.)

Note that *xpipeinput* is reading the string "cal 11 1989" from the command line, invoking a shell, running the command specified by the string under this shell, reading the output of the shell, and then printing it on the standard output. This is an easy way to use all kinds of shell scripts and utilities from within a program.

If you want your application to accept standard input, this is even easier. Remove the code that reads the filename from the command line and remove the `popen` call to open the pipe, since the pipe from `stdin` is always open. Then use the `XtAppAddInput` function as shown in Example 9-7.

Example 9-7. Reading stdin from an Xt application

```
XtAppAddInput(app_context, fileno(stdin), XtInputReadMask,
        get_file_input, NULL);
```

Once you have done this, you can invoke *xpipeinput* as follows:

```
spike% cal 11 1989 | xpipeinput
      November 1989
   S   M Tu   W Th   F   S
               1   2   3   4
   5   6   7   8   9 10 11
  12 13 14 15 16 17 18
  19 20 21 22 23 24 25
  26 27 28 29 30
```
(Program continues to monitor pipe for further input until application exits.)

Note that in this case, *xpipeinput* is reading directly from stdin, and then printing the output to stdout. With more code, it could display this calendar in a Text widget instead.

Also note that *xpipeinput* loads down the system for the same reasons as *xfileinput*, described at the end of the last section. Solutions to this problem are also described there.

9.4 Timeouts

A program may wish to be notified when a period of time has elapsed, while being able to do other things in the meantime. For example, a clock widget requires a periodic nudge to change the time it is displaying, but must also be able to redisplay itself at any time in case of exposure.

This is done by using `XtAppAddTimeOut`. This routine is passed a time interval in milliseconds, and the address of a function to be invoked when the time interval expires. As usual, a `client_data` argument can also be registered. The `XtAppAddTimeout` routine returns a handle that can be used to cancel the timeout before it triggers, if necessary.

A timeout is automatically removed when the registered function is called. Therefore, to have a function called repeatedly, every *N* milliseconds, the registered function must add the timeout again by calling `XtAppAddTimeOut`.

One of the major applications of timeouts other than clocks is in real-time games. Figure 9-1 shows the appearance of a game called *xtetris* after it has been played for a couple of minutes.

The object of the game is to steer falling blocks and rotate them so that they fit well into the existing fallen blocks.* The game is over when the blocks pile up to the top of the window.

---

*This game is provided with the example source code. It is an X version of a game available on the Macintosh called *Tetris*, trademark of AcademySoft-ELORG, copyright and trademark licensed to Andromeda Software Ltd. The original concept of the game is by Alexi Pazhitnov and Vadim Gerasimov.

More Input Techniques

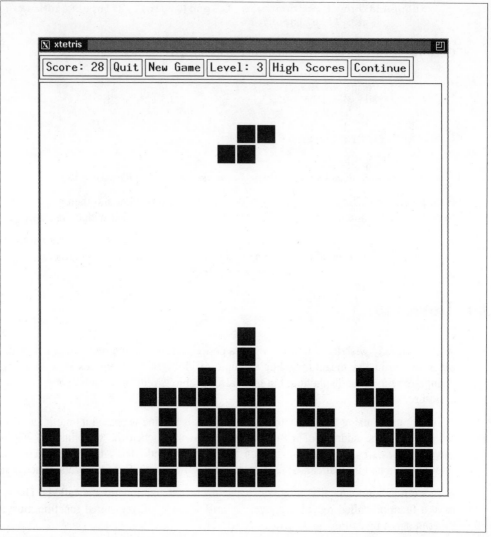

Figure 9-1. xtetris in play

Every time a row is completely filled, it is removed and all the blocks above it move down one row. The window in which the blocks fall is a specialized widget. This game uses timeouts to time the falling of the blocks.

Example 9-8 is an excerpt from a widget used by *xtetris* that adds the timeout. The timeout function itself is also shown.

Example 9-8. xtetris: registering a timeout and the timeout function

```
static XtIntervalId timer;

static void
StartBlock(w)
TetrisWidget w;
{
    w->tetris.cur_x = 9;
    w->tetris.cur_y = 0;

    w->tetris.type = PickType();

    DrawBlock(w, DRAW);

    timer = XtAppAddTimeOut(XtWidgetToApplicationContext(w),
            w->tetris.delay, MoveDown, w);
}

static void
MoveDown(w)
BitmapEditWidget w;          /* client_data */
{
    if (CanMoveDown(w)) {
        drawBlock(w, UNDRAW);
        w->tetris.cur_y++;
        DrawBlock(w, DRAW);
        CopyBlock(w);
        timer = XtAppAddTimeOut(XtWidgetToApplicationContext(w),
                w->tetris.delay, MoveDown, w);
    }
    else { /*block has hit bottom or other stationary blocks*/
        UpdateCellArray(w);
        KillRows(w);
        Score(w);
        w->tetris.delay -= 5;
        StartBlock(w);
    }
}
```

Notice that in widget code, the application context is specified using XtWidget-ToApplicationContext.

Notice also that a timeout function is called with only one argument, `client_data`. Inside a widget, this argument is commonly used to pass in the widget instance pointer. Also notice that every time a block hits the bottom, the instance variable delay is decremented by 5, which reduces the number of milliseconds of delay used when XtAppAddTimeOut is next called. In other words, the blocks fall progressively faster.

xtetris also needs to remove a timeout in one of its routines. The user can "drop" a block to score extra points (if there is enough time). Whenever a block is dropped, the block is immediately moved down as far as it will go, and a new block is started. If the Drop action did not remove the timeout, the new block would be started with a new timeout while an existing timeout was already in force. This would mean that the MoveDown timeout function would be invoked twice in quick succession when each of these timeouts expired. Example 9-9 shows the XtRemoveTimeOut call in the Drop action.

More Input Techniques

Example 9-9. xtetris: calling XtRemoveTimeOut

```
/*ARGSUSED*/
static void
Drop(tw, tevent, params, num_params)
Widget tw;
XEvent *tevent;
String *params;
Cardinal *num_params;
{
    TetrisWidget w = (TetrisWidget) tw;
    XButtonEvent *event = (XButtonEvent *) tevent;
    XtRemoveTimeOut(timer);

    while (CanMoveDown(w)) {
        DrawBlock(w, UNDRAW);
        w->tetris.cur_y++;
        DrawBlock(w, DRAW);
        CopyBlock(w);
    }

    UpdateCellArray(w);
    KillRows(w);
    score++;
    Score(w);
    w->tetris.delay -= 5;
    StartBlock(w);
}
```

Notice that the `timer` ID returned from the calls to `XtAppAddTimeOut` is a global variable. Xt calls the timeout function with only one argument, and that argument passes in the widget instance pointer. We could have created a structure containing the widget instance pointer and the timer ID and passed its pointer to the timeout function. But this wouldn't help, because the action routine in which we remove the timeout is passed with no `client_data` argument. (It has string parameters, but these are hardcoded in the actions table.) Therefore, we are forced to have a global variable for the timer ID.

Note that between the time when the timeout is registered and when it triggers, the application processes events in `XtAppMainLoop`. Therefore, all the widget's actions and `expose` method are in operation between the invocations of the timeout function.

9.4.1 Visibility Interest

Timeouts operate regardless of the visibility of the application. Since it is pointless for most games to continue operating while obscured, it makes sense to remove the game's timeouts when the game is partially or fully obscured (or iconified). To do this, you can set the `visible_interest` field in the Core class structure to `True`, and then check the `visible` field of the Core instance structure periodically. When the application is fully obscured, you add a separate timeout to continue testing the visibility status. When the visibility status is satisfactory once again, the game can add its timeout again. All these changes are in the widget's *.c* file. First we set the `visible_interest` field to `True` in the Core structure:

```
TetrisClassRec tetrisClassRec  = {
    /* core_class fields */
    .
    .
    .
    /* visible_interest          */ True,
    .
    .
    .
}
```

Second we change:

```
timer = XtAppAddTimeOut(XtWidgetToApplicationContext
    (w), w->tetris.delay, MoveDown, w);
```

to:

```
if (w->core.visible == False)
        timer = XtAppAddTimeOut(XtWidgetToApplicationContext
            (w) 250, CheckVisibility, w);
    else
        timer = XtAppAddTimeOut(XtWidgetToApplicationContext
(w)
w->tetris.delay, MoveDown, w);
```

And finally, we add the timeout function that continues to check the visibility status.

```
static void
CheckVisibility(w)
BitmapEditWidget w;     /* client_data */
{
    if (w->core.visible == False)
        timer = XtAppAddTimeOut(250, CheckVisibility, w);
    else
        timer = XtAppAddTimeOut(w->tetris.delay,
            MoveDown, w);
}
```

Unfortunately, the Core `visible` field is `True` even if a tiny sliver of the widget is visible. The only way to get around this is to add an event handler (or translation) for `VisibilityNotify` events and to add an instance variable to maintain the visibility state. The event handler or action would check the `state` field of the event, and put the game into hibernation if the window is only partially obscured. However, this approach has the opposite problem; it disables the game even when only a sliver is obscured.

There is nothing you can do about the game continuing to run while being moved or resized with the window manager. However, using the Core `visible_interest` field does stop the game when it is iconified.

9.5 Work Procedures

A work procedure is an application-supplied function that is executed while an application is idle waiting for an event. Work procedures are registered with XtAppAddWorkProc. They can perform any calculation that is short enough that the routine will return in a small fraction of a second. If the work procedure is too long, the user's response time will suffer.

If a work procedure returns True, then Xt will remove it and it will not be called again. But if one returns False, it will be called repeatedly every time there is idle time, until the application calls XtRemoveWorkProc. A work procedure would return True if it performs a one-time setup such as creating a popup widget. It would return False if it were continuously updating a disk file as security against a system crash or server connection failure.

You can register multiple work procedures, and they will be performed one at a time. The most recent work procedure added has the highest priority. Therefore, for example, if you want to create ten popup widgets during idle time, you should add ten work procedures. The popup that you expect to need first should be added in the last work procedure registered.

The call to register a work procedure is shown in Example 9-10.

Example 9-10. Registering an Xt work procedure

```
static Boolean create_popup();
    .
    .
    .
main(argc, argv)
int argc;
char **argv;
{
    XtAppContext app_context;
    XtWorkProcId popup_work_ID;
    Widget topLevel;
        .
        .
    /* XtAppInitialize, create widgets, etc. */
        .
        .
    popup_work_ID = XtAppAddWorkProc(app_context,
            create_popup, topLevel);
        .
        .
    /*
     * popup_work_ID not actually needed because work proc
     * unregisters itself by returning True.
     */

    XtRealizeWidget(topLevel);
    XtAppMainLoop(app_context);
}
```

Notice that XtAppAddWorkProc returns an ID of type XtWorkProcId, which is used only in any subsequent call to XtRemoveWorkProc. You can cast the returned value to void if you do not intend to explicitly remove the work procedure.

The *client_data* argument passes application data into the work procedure. It is used just like the same argument in callback functions. Example 9-11 shows a work procedure to create a popup widget.

Example 9-11. A work procedure to create a popup widget

```
Widget getHelp;

/* work procedure */
Boolean
create_popup(client_data)
XtPointer client_data;
{
    Widget parent = (Widget) client_data;
    Widget helpBox;
    Widget temp;

    helpBox = XmCreateMessageDialog(parent, "message", NULL, 0);

    temp = XmMessageBoxGetChild (helpBox, XmDIALOG_CANCEL_BUTTON);
    XtUnmanageChild (temp);
    temp = XmMessageBoxGetChild (helpBox, XmDIALOG_HELP_BUTTON);
    XtUnmanageChild (temp);

    /* arrange for getHelp button to pop up helpBox */
    XtAddCallback(getHelp, XmNactivateCallback, PopupDialog, helpBox);

    return(True);    /* makes Xt remove this work proc automatically */
}
```

Remember that Xt cannot interrupt a work procedure while it is running; the procedure must voluntarily give up control by returning, and it must do so quickly to avoid slowing user response.

If your application has any big jobs that it must do, the only way to do them without resulting in long delays is to write the code that does the big job in a way that voluntarily interrupts itself and saves its state so that it can be restarted where it left off. One way to run such a task is as a work procedure, but this is only useful for tasks that need not be done before other application tasks can begin. If you want Expose processing to continue but no other application task to begin until your task is done, you would use the same type of code but place low-level event management routines in it, or make the rest of the application insensitive until the task is done.

9.6 Low-level Management of the Event Queue

As you know, an X Toolkit application simply calls `XtAppMainLoop` to begin processing events. `XtAppMainLoop` itself is quite simple: it consists of an infinite loop calling two lower-level routines, `XtAppNextEvent` and `XtDispatchEvent`. `XtAppNextEvent` extracts the next event from the application's event queue; `XtDispatchEvent` actually uses the event to invoke the appropriate actions or event handlers. (The functions registered by `XtAppAddInput` and `XtAppAddTimeOut` are dispatched directly by `XtAppNextEvent`; if no events are available, `XtAppNextEvent` flushes the X output buffer, and calls any work procedures registered by `XtAppAddWorkProc`.)

An application can provide its own version of this loop, as shown in Example 9-12. For example, it might test some application-dependent global flag or other termination condition before looping back and calling `XtAppNextEvent`. Or for fine-grained debugging, it might be worthwhile to insert a routine that prints out the type of each event dispatched.

Example 9-12. Skeleton of a custom main loop

```
void MyMainLoop(app_con)
XtAppContext app_con;
{
    XEvent event;

    for (;;) {
        XtAppNextEvent(app_con, &event);
        XtDispatchEvent(&event);

    /* Do application-specific processing here */

    }
}
```

9.6.1 XtPending and XtPeekEvent

All event sources depend on idle time in the application to return to `XtAppMainLoop` where Xt can check to see if input is available from any of the various sources. If an application has long calculations to make, the program may not return to `XtAppMainLoop` frequently enough to detect important input in a timely fashion. The application itself should, if possible, suspend lengthy calculations for a moment to check whether input is available. Then it can determine whether to process the input before continuing, or finish the calculation.

To detect whether input from any input source is available, you can call `XtPending`. This function returns a mask composed of a bitwise OR of the symbolic constants `XtIMXEvent`, `XtIMTimer`, and `XtIMAlternateInput`. These constants refer to X events, timer events, and alternate input events, respectively.

To find out what the first event in the queue contains, you can call `XtPeekEvent`. This function returns an event structure without removing the event from Xlib's queue.

X Toolkit Intrinsics Programming Manual, Motif Edition

It is also possible to remove and process a single event. `XtAppProcessEvent` combines some (but not all) of the functions from `XtAppNextEvent` and `XtDispatchEvent`. That is, while `XtAppNextEvent` takes the next event from the queue, whatever it is, `XtAppProcessEvent` allows you to specify as a mask a bitwise OR of the symbolic constants `XtIMXEvent`, `XtIMTimer`, and `XtIMAlternateInput`. This lets you select only some of these event types for processing. In addition, `XtAppProcessEvent` actually calls `XtDispatchEvent` to dispatch X events, so only this one call is necessary.

9.6.2 Event Filters

As you saw in Chapter 6, *Inside a Widget*, the class structure contains three Boolean fields that control Xt's event filters. These are `compress_motion`, `compress_enterleave`, and `compress_exposure`. Widgets set these fields to `True` when repeated events of these types are unwanted. Each would be used in different situations. If turned on, they tell Xt to search Xlib's queue for a certain event sequence and then remove repeated occurrences of those events from the queue.

When the `compress_motion` filter is set to `True`, and there is a series of `MotionNotify` events on the queue (which occurs when the application gets behind in processing them), the filter throws out all but the last one (the most recent position). This is useful for widgets that need the most up-to-date position but do not need a complete history of pointer positions.

The `compress_enterleave` filter throws out all `EnterNotify/LeaveNotify` pairs on the same window in which there are no intervening events. This would be used by a widget that is interested in enter and leave events, but not if the application falls behind. For example, even the Command widget sets `compress_enterleave` to `True`. It highlights its border when the pointer enters, and clears it when the pointer leaves. But if for some reason the widget falls behind and has not highlighted the border by the time the `LeaveNotify` event arrives with no intervening events, the border will not be highlighted. To see this, move the pointer quickly across a large panel of Command widgets such as in *xmh*, and you will see that not all of them draw and then undraw the border.

The symbols used for setting the `compress_exposure` filter have changed in R4. If the field of this name in the Core class structure is set to `False` or `XtExposeNoCompress`, a widget's expose method is called once in response to each `Expose` event in a contiguous series. Each event specifies a different rectangle of the widget that needs redrawing.

With `compress_exposure` set to `True` or `XtExposeCompressSeries`, however, a contiguous series of events resulting from one user action is compressed into a single modified `Expose` event and the expose method is called only once. This modified `Expose` event contains the bounding rectangle of the union of all the rectangles in the individual events. In this case the expose method is also passed an Xlib `Region` that describes in detail the area exposed. Probably the most useful value for `compress_exposure` is `XtExposeCompressMultiple`, which compresses all the contiguous events resulting from multiple contiguous user actions.

When ORed with any of the `XtCompress*` symbols, the `XtExposeGraphicsExpose` symbol causes Xt to call the `expose` method with any `GraphicsExpose` events that occur. Remember that you must set the `graphics_exposures` component to `True` in the GC used in `XCopyArea` or `XCopyPlane` in order to get `GraphicsExpose` events. `XtExposeGraphicsExposeMerged`, when ORed with an `XtCompress*` symbol, merges contiguous `Expose` and `GraphicsExpose` events together before calling the `expose` method.

The `XtExposeNoExpose` symbol causes Xt to dispatch `NoExpose` events to the `expose` method. This doesn't make much sense; if you need `NoExpose` events it is better to add an event handler or translation to handle them.

The remaining symbol is `XtExposeCompressMaximal`. This symbol is dangerous and should not be used: it merges non-continuous `Expose` events into one event before calling the `expose` method. This is unwise because the intervening events could be `ConfigureNotify` events that change the size of the window. When this happens, the application will redraw itself, then receive the `ConfigureNotify`, but then it will not redraw itself in the new size because the `Expose` event that would trigger the drawing has already been removed from the queue.

Almost all widgets except those that display a large amount of text should set this filter to `XtExposeCompressMultiple`. Text widgets can very efficiently redraw only the needed parts of the window because each character is in a fixed location. (Characters are in fixed locations in the Text widget because it uses fixed-width fonts—this is not applicable to widgets that display proportional fonts.) Therefore, it can efficiently process all the `Expose` events one at a time.

9.6.3 Input Sensitivity

There are times when some widgets should be insensitive to events in which they are usually interested. For example, a Command widget should be insensitive when the command that it executes is already in operation.

Widget sensitivity is inherited. For example, if a parent widget is insensitive, then its children are too. In other words, an entire box full of widgets can be set insensitive by simply setting the box widget insensitive. Note, however, that this process can be a little slow because all the widgets in the box that honor sensitivity will redraw themselves dimmed or grayed. A widget is made insensitive from an application by calling `XtSetSensitive` with the `sensitive` argument set to `False`, or using `XtVaSetValues` on the `XmNsensitive` resource (`XtSetSensitive` is slightly faster).

Any widget that may need to be disabled for a time by the application should change its visible appearance when insensitive.

The widget that has one of the `XtCallback*` standard popup callback functions registered on its callback list will automatically be set insensitive when the callback is triggered. If the `XtCallbackPopdown` callback function is registered on this widget it will automatically be set sensitive again when this callback is invoked.

10

Resource Management
and Type Conversion

*This chapter is a more thorough discussion of how resources work and how
they should be used. This chapter describes in detail the resource file format
and the rules that govern the precedence of resource settings. It also
describes how to add your own type converter so that you can have application or widget-specific data set through resources. Finally, it describes
subresources and how to use them.*

In This Chapter:

Resource Management and Type Conversion

This chapter provides a thorough discussion of how resources work and how they should be used. First, we describe how to define resources, the complete syntax of resource files, and the rules that describe the precedence of one resource setting over another. For the sake of completeness, and to make sure that the ideas are presented in context, there is some repetition of material that has been presented earlier.

Next, the chapter describes the resource conversions performed automatically by Xt. As you may recall from the discussion in Chapter 2, *Introduction to the X Toolkit and Motif*, a value converter is invoked by Xt to convert a resource from the string form specified in resource files to the representation type actually used in the application or widget. For the representation types understood by Xt, simply listing the representation symbol (a constant beginning with XmR, or XtR in standard Xt) in the resource list is enough to make Xt automatically perform the conversion. But if you create a representation type unknown to Xt, you need to write a type converter routine and register it with Xt before the automatic conversion can take place. We discuss both the standard converters and how to write a new one.

Finally, the chapter describes a mechanism Xt provides whereby widgets or applications may have subparts with separate sets of resources. Special routines are provided for setting and getting these resources. The R3 Athena Text widget used subparts to implement replaceable units that provide the data storage and display for text data. This allowed the same central code to edit a disk file or a string. But using subparts is now out of favor; the R4 Text widget and the Motif Text widgets now use objects to accomplish the same modularity (see Chapter 14, *Miscellaneous Toolkit Programming Techniques*).

10.1 Review of Resource Fundamentals

As we've previously discussed, widgets and applications can declare some or all of their variables as resources. Not every variable need be a resource—only those for which values need to be supplied by the user (or for a widget, also by the application programmer) through the Resource Manager. Both applications and widgets may use nonresource variables for internal bookkeeping, or for storing values calculated or otherwise derived from resources.

Resources are defined using an `XtResource` structure, which is declared as follows:

```
typedef struct {
    String resource_name;        /* specify using XmN symbol */
    String resource_class;       /* specify using XmC symbol */
    String resource_type;     /* actual data type of variable */
    Cardinal resource_size;      /* specify using sizeof() */
    Cardinal resource_offset;  /* specify using XtOffsetOf() */
    String default_type; /* will be converted to resrce_type */
    XtPointer default_address;   /* address of default value */
} XtResource, *XtResourceList;
```

For example, Example 10-1 shows three of the resources defined by the Primitive widget:

Example 10-1. Three resources defined by the Motif Primitive widget

```
static XtResource resources[] = {
    .
    .
    .

    {
    XmNforeground,    /* Resource name is foreground */
    XmCForeground,    /* Resource class is Foreground */
    XmRPixel,         /* Resource type is Pixel */
    sizeof(Pixel),    /* allocate enough space to hold a Pixel value */
    XtOffsetOf(XmPrimitiveRec,
            primitive.foreground),       /* where in instance strct */
    XmRCallProc,      /* type of default value */
    _XmForegroundColorDefault /* Address of deflt value, or function */
    },
    .
    .
    .

    {
    XmNhighlightColor,
    XmCHighlightColor,
    XmRPixel,
    sizeof (Pixel),
    XtOffsetOf (XmPrimitiveRec, primitive.highlight_color),
    XmRString,
    "Black"
    },
    .
    .
    .

    {
    XmNtraversalOn,
    XmCTraversalOn,
```

```
XmRBoolean,
sizeof (Boolean),
XtOffsetOf (XmPrimitiveRec, primitive.traversal_on),
XmRImmediate, (caddr_t) True
},
      .
      .
      .
}
```

The fields in the `XtResource` structure are used as follows:

- The resource name is usually similar to the name of the variable being set by the resource; by convention, the resource name begins with a lower-case letter, and no underscores are used to separate multiple words. Instead, the initial character of subsequent words is given in upper case. For example, the resource name for a variable named `border_width` would be `borderWidth`, and the defined constant used to refer to this name would be `XmNborderWidth`.

  As previously described, the name, class, and representation type of resources are specified in the resource list (and elsewhere in Xt code, but not in user database files) using symbolic constants defined in *<Xm/Xm.h>* (or *<X11/StringDefs.h>* in standard Xt), and consist of the resource name, class, or type preceded by the characters XmN, XmC, or XmR, respectively. Use of these constants provides compile-time checking of resource names, classes, and types. Without the constants, a misspelling would not be noticed by the compiler, since resource names, classes, and representation types are simply strings. The misspelling would be considered a real resource at run time. Nothing would happen if it were set from the application, because no widget would actually use it. If, on the other hand, the misspelling were in the widget resource list, the application's setting of the intended resource would have no effect.

  Newly-defined resources may use a name, class, or type constant defined in *<Xm/Xm.h>* (or *<X11/StringDefs.h>* if not using Motif), if an appropriate constant exists. Otherwise, the constant is defined in the widget's public header file, or for application resources, in the application itself, or in the application header file, if any.

- For many resources, the class name is simply the same as the resource name, except that the XmC prefix is used, and, the first letter of the name is conventionally capitalized. For example, the class name constant for the `XmNbackgroundPixel` resource is `XmCBackgroundPixel`. However, when appropriate, a single class can be used for a group of related resources. This allows a single setting in the resource database to control the value of multiple resources.

  For example, a widget can have several elements that use pixel values (i.e., colors) as resource settings: background, foreground, border, block cursor, pointer cursor, and so on. Typically, the background defaults to white and everything else to black. If the `background` resource has a class of `Background`, and all the other pixel resources a class of `Foreground`, then a resource file needs only two lines to change all background pixels to offwhite and all foreground pixels to darkblue:

```
*Background:       offwhite
*Foreground:       darkblue
```

- The representation type of the resource is specified by the `resource_type` field of the resource list, using a symbolic constant prefixed by XmR. Table 10-1 lists the correspondence between the XmR symbols defined by Xt, and actual C data types or X data types and structures.

Table 10-1. Resource Type Strings

Resource Type	Data type
XmRAcceleratorTable	XtAccelerators
XmRAtom	Atom
XmRBitmap	Pixmap (of depth one)
XmRBoolean	Boolean
XmRBool	Bool
XmRCallback	XtCallbackList
XmRCallProc	*see final bullet below*
XmRCardinal	Cardinal
XmRColor	XColor
XmRColormap	Colormap
XmRCursor	Cursor
XmRDimension	Dimension
XmRDisplay	Display *
XmREnum	XtEnum
XmRFile	FILE *
XmRFloat	float
XmRFont	Font
XmRFontStruct	XFontStruct *
XmRFunction	(*)()
XmRGeometry	String - format as defined by XParseGeometry
XmRImmediate	*see final bullet below*
XmRInitialState	int
XmRInt	int
XmRLongBoolean	long
XmRObject	Object
XmRPixel	Pixel
XmRPixmap	Pixmap
XmRPointer	XtPointer
XmRPosition	Position
XmRScreen	Screen *
XmRShort	short
XmRString	char *
XmRStringArray	String *
XmRStringTable	char **
XmRTranslationTable	XtTranslations

Table 10-1. Resource Type Strings (continued)

Resource Type	Data type
XmRUnsignedChar	unsigned char
XmRVisual	Visual *
XmRWidget	Widget
XmRWidgetClass	WidgetClass
XmRWidgetList	WidgetList
XmRWindow	Window

As we'll discuss in detail in Section 10.3.5, Xt automatically converts values in the resource database (which always have the type XmRString, since resource files are made up entirely of strings) into the target type defined by resource_type.

- The resource_size field is the size of the resource's actual representation in bytes; it should always be specified as sizeof(*type*) (where *type* is the C-Language type of the resource) so that the compiler fills in the value.

- The resource_offset field is the offset in bytes of the field within the widget instance structure or application data structure. The XtOffsetOf macro is normally used to obtain this value. This macro takes as arguments the data structure type, and the name of the structure field to be set by the resource.

- If no value is found in the resource database, the value pointed to by the default_address field will be used instead. The type of this default value is given by the default_type field. If the default_type is different from the resource_type, a conversion will be performed automatically in this case as well.

There are two special resource types that can be used only as the default_type. XmRImmediate means that the value in the default_address field is to be used as the actual resource value, rather than as a pointer to it (or in the case of a string, the value is a pointer to a string, rather than a pointer to a pointer to a string). The other special resource type, XmRCallProc, is a pointer to a function that will supply the default value at run time. We'll demonstrate the use of these values in Section 10.3.3.

10.2 How the Resource Database Works

Xt's resource handling is based on the resource manager built into Xlib, but Xt adds a great deal. While using the resource manager from Xlib is cumbersome, from Xt it is easy: to use resources in existing widgets, all you have to do is write the app-defaults file.

Xt's handling of resources occurs in two stages:

1. When the application starts up, with a call to XtAppInitialize, Xt reads the app-defaults file, along with several other resource files, command-line options, and the RESOURCE_MANAGER property stored in the server by the user with *xrdb*. (Any, all, or

none of these may contain data.) It merges all these sources of data into one internal database that is used when each widget is created.

2. Whenever you create a widget, the call to `XtVaCreateManagedWidget` reads the resource database and automatically sets widget resources to the values in the database. In order to explain this stage more clearly, we further divide it into two separate steps in the sections that follow. First, Xt compares the settings in the database to the widget's class and instance hierarchy, to find which settings apply to the widget being created. Second, Xt decides which of the (possibly conflicting) settings that apply to that widget should actually be used.

If the value of a resource is hardcoded by passing arguments to `XtVaCreateManaged-Widget` or `XtVaSetValues`, the hardcoded value overrides the value looked up from the resource database.

To retrieve the value of application resources from the database, an application must make an explicit call to `XtGetApplicationResources`, as described in Section 3.6.3.

10.2.1 Form of Resource Specifications

As discussed in Chapter 2, each entry in the merged database (and in the source databases) is a resource specification/value pair. For application resources, the specification is the application name followed by a period and the resource name. The value to which the resource is to be set follows, after a colon and optional white space.* For example:

```
xterm.scrollBar:   on
```

An asterisk can be used as a "wildcard" in place of the application name. For example:

```
*scrollBar:   on
```

would set a resource named `scrollBar` to "on" in any application that recognized a resource of that name.

For widget resources, the specification leading up to the resource name may contain a widget instance or class hierarchy (or a mixed instance/class hierarchy). Some examples are shown below. (Remember that instance names begin with a lower case letter, while class names begin with an upper case letter.)

specification	value	
xbitmap.rowColumn.quit.label:	Quit	*fully-specified instance hierarchy*
XBitmap.RowColumn.PushButton.Foreground:	blue	*fully-specified class hierarchy*
XBitmap.RowColumn.quit.foreground:	blue	*mixed class and instance hierarchy*

---

*Note the distinction between what we are calling the resource *specification* (the fully qualified name of the resource, up to the colon), and the *value* (the actual value to which the resource is to be set). We refer to both the specification and the value together as a *resource setting*.

An instance hierarchy describes the instance names of the widget's ancestors. A class hierarchy describes the class names of the widget's ancestors. This portion of the resource specification may consist of a mixture of instance names and class names (each of which describes one generation in the widget's hierarchy), separated by periods or asterisks.

- A period (.) is referred to as a *tight* binding.

- An asterisk (*) is referred to as a *loose* binding.

A tight binding means the left component must be the parent of the right component in the instance hierarchy. A loose binding means the left component must only be an ancestor of the right component; there can be any number of levels in the hierarchy between the two.

Loose bindings are preferable because they stand a better chance of working when the instance hierarchy changes. Tight bindings are rarely necessary at every position in the resource specification, since widget names are usually unique and single widgets can be identified by name. Furthermore, it takes more text to specify the complete instance hierarchy for every widget to be set.

Using loose bindings, the instance, class, or instance/class hierarchy may be abbreviated to the point where specifying the hierarchy as a single asterisk would indicate that any instance or class hierarchy (any widget in the application) will match. However, care should be taken when using loose bindings. One common mistake is to abbreviate a hierarchy too much, so that resource settings that were supposed to apply to only one widget now apply to several. This can be particularly serious (and hard to trace) when the resources being set are translation tables or constraints.

The resource name must be the string that appears in the resource name or resource class field in a resource list. This is the value of the XmN or XmC symbolic constant used in that field of the resource list.

Any entry that is not a resource specification/value pair or does not match any resource for any widget in the application or any application resource is quietly ignored (no warning message is printed). This means that a slight error in the resource specification of an entry will cause that entry to be quietly and completely ignored. It is often difficult to detect such errors.

Lines beginning with an exclamation point (!) are treated as comments. Some people have been using # instead, since it is currently supported in MIT's sample implementation of Xt. But # is not mandated in the Xt specification and therefore may be eliminated in future sample implementations from MIT or in a vendor's implementation. You are advised to use the exclamation point. (Even in the MIT implementation, # elicits warning messages from *xrdb*.)

10.2.2 Merging of Resource Files

XtAppInitialize constructs the resource database by consulting the following sources of resource settings, in this order:

1. A file usually in the directory */usr/lib/X11/LANG/app-defaults* (implementation dependent) on the machine running the client, where *LANG* is an optional language string (see Section 10.2.3 for details). This file is commonly called the app-defaults file, named after the directory containing it. It is intended to be written by the application developer. The name of this file is the application class (specified in the XtAppInitialize call), usually the same as the application name except with the first letter capitalized. If the application name begins with *x*, then the first two letters are capitalized. (This latter convention is not always followed.) The installation procedure for the application should install this file in the correct directory (or one per language, each in a different directory).

2. A file in the directory named by the shell environment variable XUSERFILE-SEARCHPATH, or XAPPLRESDIR with *LANG* optionally appended (see Section 10.2.3). The filename searched for is the class name of the application. If XAPPLRESDIR is not set, the file is looked for in the user's home directory. This file is intended to be the user's, or possibly the site administrator's, customization for the particular application. The application developer can also set XAPPLRESDIR so that resource files for an application can be in the same directory as the application. (This is particularly useful when debugging the app-defaults file.) Note that the value of this variable must end with a slash (/).*

3. Resources loaded into the RESOURCE_MANAGER property of the root window by *xrdb*. Unlike any of the resource files, these resources are accessible regardless of the machine on which the client is running. Therefore, *xrdb* saves you from having to keep track of resource files on several different systems. Typically, the user arranges to have *xrdb* run automatically from *.xinitrc* or its equivalent under *xdm*, the display manager. This is intended to be the method whereby the user specifies server-wide resources (to apply to all clients no matter which system they are running on).

    If the RESOURCE_MANAGER property is not set, the resource manager looks for an *.Xdefaults* file in the user's home directory. Support for *.Xdefaults* is mostly for compatibility with earlier releases of X. (See Volume Three, *X Window System User's Guide, Motif Edition*, for more information on using *xrdb*.)

4. Next, the contents of any file (on the system running the client) specified by the shell environment variable XENVIRONMENT will be loaded. The difference between this and APPLRESDIR above is that this is a complete path name including the file name.

    If this variable is not defined, the resource manager looks for a file named *.Xdefaults-hostname* (with a hyphen) in the user's home directory, where *hostname* is the name of the host where the client is running. (On systems with a network file system, the home

---

*If you break the conventions by giving your program binary a capitalized name, or by giving your app-defaults file a lower-case name, it is possible to have the binary accidentally interpreted as an app-defaults file. The entire binary will be searched for resource lines! Since the binary is so large, your application will start up *very* slowly. No error will be reported because the resource manager quietly ignores entries it doesn't understand.

directory may be on a system different from the one where the application is running, the one where the server is running, or both.)

5. Any values specified on the command line with the *–xrm* option will be loaded for that instance of the program.

6. If the application has defined any command-line options by passing an options table to `XtAppInitialize`, values from the command line will override those specified by any other resource settings.

The order in which these various sources are loaded, as shown in the list above, is the reverse order of their priority. That is, those that are loaded first will be overridden by those loaded later if an identical specification is found.

If a resource value is hardcoded in the arguments of the call to create a widget, that value takes precedence over any value for that resource in the resource database. If a widget is created and no setting exists in the database for a particular resource, the value pointed to by the `default_address` field of the resource list in the widget is used. This is also true for application resources and subresources.

Figure 10-1 shows where Xt looks for resource files and in what order, on most UNIX-based systems. The exact directories are operating system and implementation dependent. Remember that the app-defaults file is written by the application writer, and all the rest of the resource sources are for the user. In practice, few users use more than one or two of these sources of resource settings.

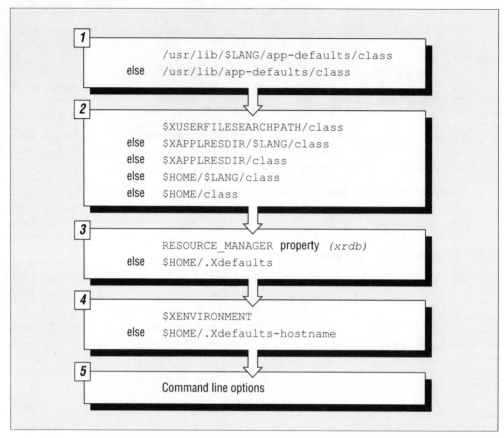

```
1
                   /usr/lib/$LANG/app-defaults/class
           else    /usr/lib/app-defaults/class

2
                   $XUSERFILESEARCHPATH/class
           else    $XAPPLRESDIR/$LANG/class
           else    $XAPPLRESDIR/class
           else    $HOME/$LANG/class
           else    $HOME/class

3
                   RESOURCE_MANAGER property (xrdb)
           else    $HOME/.Xdefaults

4
                   $XENVIRONMENT
           else    $HOME/.Xdefaults-hostname

5
                   Command line options
```

Figure 10-1. Typical resource setting search path on UNIX-based systems

10.2.3 The Language String

In R4, Xt's resource handling was modified to support resource files for different languages. The goal is to have all the language dependencies of an application in files, so that just by selecting a different set of resource files at run time, the application will operate correctly in another language.*

The language to use is selected with a *language string*, which is an application resource defined by Xt: "xnlLanguage" (no symbol `XmNxnlLanguage` is defined for it). The default language string is NULL, which makes Xt behave as it did in R3. But when the

---

*It is important to note that no one has actually done this yet! The mechanism is too new. In fact, the X Consortium is currently reviewing the support for internationalization in Xt and Xlib to determine whether they are sufficient to achieve the above goal. Most likely they will recommend some additional features, but of course since both Xt and Xlib are Consortium standards, all changes must be backwards compatible.

xnlLanguage resource, or the LANG environment variable, is set to a language name such as "spanish," Xt looks first in certain directories for the Spanish app-defaults and user defaults files, before defaulting to the normal app-defaults or user defaults directories.

Note that all app-defaults and user defaults files have the same name (the class name of the application); only the directory in which they are first examined for changes according to the language string. Therefore it is possible to have all the files for all the languages installed on a system at the same time.

The search path for resource files is implementation dependent, but it is always begins with a language string-based directory. Each app-defaults file on UNIX-based systems is normally in a directory */usr/lib/X11/$LANG/app-defaults*. When the user sets LANG to "spanish," for example, Xt looks for an app-defaults file first in */usr/lib/X11/spanish/app-defaults*.

The path searched for user defaults files (which have the same name as the app-defaults file) is more complicated. If the XUSERFILESEARCHPATH environment variable is defined, Xt follows that path. If it is not defined but the XAPPLRESDIR environment variable is defined, Xt will look in $XAPPLRESDIR/LANG first before looking in $XAPPLRESDIR. If XAPPLRESDIR is not defined either, Xt looks in $HOME/LANG and then $HOME.

The remaining resource setting sources are not affected by the language string. As described in the previous section, the next source of resource settings merged is the RESOURCE_MANAGER property set with *xrdb*, or if not set, *.Xdefaults*, followed by the file specified by the XENVIRONMENT environment variable, or if not set, the *.Xdefaults-host* file.

For a summary of the path of resource files searched by Xt, see Figure 10-1.

Most western languages other than English use characters with accents or other marks. These are non-ASCII characters, in the second half of the ISO Latin-1 character set. Most fonts now in the X distribution provide glyphs (bitmaps) for these characters. Therefore, all you have to do is specify these characters in your app-defaults file in the directory named for the desired language. However, most standard English keyboards do not provide a way to type non-ASCII characters (and some computers can't store them). Because of this, the resource file format has been augmented to provide a special syntax for specifying non-ASCII characters. Each character is specified using a backslash followed by a three-character octal number that represents the character. You can use *xfd* to determine the proper octal number to use. Just click on the desired character to have its index displayed. This index is the number you enter in the app-defaults file. For example, Example 10-2 shows a Spanish app-defaults for *xhello*.

Example 10-2. An app-defaults file for the Spanish language

```
*hello.fontList:      *courier-bold*18*iso8859-1
*hello.labelString:   \161Hola, Mundo!
```

The sequence 161 produces the inverted exclamation point that begins the Spanish exclamatory sentence. It is important to know for sure that the font you choose has the desired glyphs. Note that `iso8859-1` means ISO Latin-1, so that if you specify it in your font name, you are guaranteed to have all ISO-Latin-1 characters. Many of the fonts in the *misc* directory (such as the standard terminal fonts) do not include these characters.

10.2.4 Fallback Resources

As you may recall from Chapters 2, 3, and 4, XtAppInitialize has an argument in which you can specify fallback resources, which we didn't use. Many applications won't operate properly without their app-defaults file. *Fallback resources* are a defense in case the user doesn't install the app-defaults file, or if something happens to prevent access to it. They provide minimal application-specific resource settings that either allow the application to run safely or instruct the user to install the app-defaults file properly.

If your app-defaults file is small, you can (and should) put the whole app-defaults file in the fallback resources. However, if your app-defaults is large, it probably makes more sense just to set one or more labels in the application to tell the user that the app-defaults file is not installed properly or cannot be accessed. Remember that the fallback resources are used only if the app-defaults file is not found. Fallback resources are a NULL-terminated list of strings, each containing a resource setting. Example 10-3 shows how they are declared and then passed to XtVaAppInitialize.

Example 10-3. Setting fallback resources in XtAppInitialize

```
main(argc, argv)
int argc;
char **argv;
{
    XtAppContext app_context;
    Widget topLevel, hello;

    static String fallback_resources[] = {
        "*hello.label: App-defaults file not installed or not\
            accessible.",
        "*hello.font: *courier-bold*18*iso8859-1",
        NULL,           /* Must be NULL terminated */
    };
    topLevel = XtVaAppInitialize(
            &app_context,           /* Application context */
            "NoFile",               /* Application class */
            NULL, 0,                /* command-line option list */
            &argc, argv,            /* command line args */
            fallback_resources,     /* for missing app-defaults file */
            NULL);                  /* terminate varargs list */
    .
    .
    .
}
```

Note that there is also a separate function, XtAppSetFallbackResources, that can be used to set the fallback resources separately from the XtAppInitialize call.

10.2.5 Resource Matching Algorithm

When a widget is created, its expanded instance hierarchy and class hierarchy together with its resource names and classes are compared to each entry in the merged resource database. To demonstrate how matches are made, we'll look at a sample widget hierarchy and follow the process of finding the value for one resource of one widget from the merged resource database. Figure 10-2 shows the widget instance hierarchy for the `quit` widget in the *xrowcolumn* application shown in Chapter 3, *More Techniques for Using Widgets*. The figure also shows the corresponding fully specified instance and class names for the `quit` widget. This section describes how this widget's resources are set by the resource manager.*

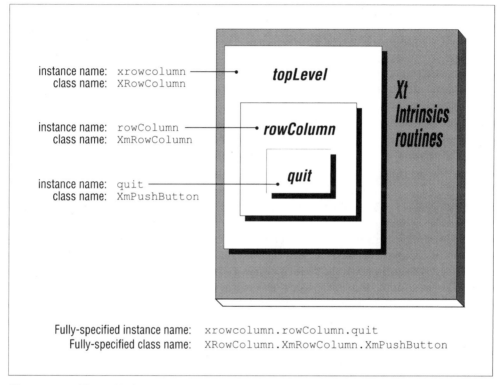

Figure 10-2. The quit widget in a sample widget hierarchy

We know that `quit` is a Command class widget and therefore that Xt will be searching the resource database for each resource in Command's resource list (and the resources in its superclasses' resource lists). It will search for one resource at a time. To demonstrate the conflicts that can occur, we'll use the Core resource `XmNbackground`, which is common to all widgets. It will appear in the resource database as `background`.

---

*The actual algorithm used by Xt differs slightly from that described here, because there are shortcuts that the resource manager takes that are hard to follow even if you have the source code. However, the algorithm described here gives the same result, with more clarity.

The matching process can be thought of as a process of elimination. Let's assume the merged resource database is as shown in Example 10-4.

Example 10-4. A sample merged resource database

```
*rowColumn.background:                    blue      (entry 1)
*background:                              red       (entry 2)
*quit.background:                         green     (entry 3)
*quit.labelString:                        Quit      (entry 4)
*XmPushButton.background:                 yellow    (entry 5)
*XmRowColumn.XmPushButton.background:     violet    (entry 6)
*rowColumn*background:                    pink      (entry 7)
xrowcolumn.background:                    orange    (entry 8)
```

Only resource database entries that specify background as the last element before the colon are possible matches. That eliminates entry 4. The fully specified instance and class hierarchies are then compared with each possible match, beginning with the first component in each hierarchy.

1. Every entry beginning with the asterisk wildcard binding (*) as well as the one beginning with xrowcolumn, matches xrowcolumn, the first component of the fully specified instance name. All those beginning with * also match the first component of the fully specified class name, XRowColumn. Since entry 8 actually contains the string xrowcolumn, the xrowcolumn component is removed for comparison at the next level. Entry 8 now begins with .background.

2. The first component of each resource specification (after removal of previously matched components) is now compared to the second element in the widget's class and instance hierarchies. This should be either rowColumn or XmRowColumn. All the entries that begin with * still match, because * matches any number of levels in the hierarchy. However, there is no second element in entry 8, once the resource name background is removed. Therefore, entry 8 is eliminated. Also, since entries 1, 6, and 7 actually contain the strings rowColumn or XmRowColumn, the leading asterisk and the strings rowColumn and XmRowColumn are removed before comparison of the next level. Example 10-5 shows the resource database as it would appear after the components and entries eliminated so far.

Example 10-5. Sample resource database with eliminated entries and components

```
.background:                    blue      (entry 1)
*background:                     red       (entry 2)
*quit.background:                green     (entry 3)
*XmPushButton.background:        yellow    (entry 5)
.XmPushButton.background:        violet    (entry 6)
*background:                     pink      (entry 7)
```

Note that entries 2 and 7 are now duplicates except for the resource value. The resource manager actually eliminates one of these entries based upon the levels at which each entry matched, whether the instance name or class name matched, whether a tight or loose binding was used, and which had more elements specified. These are the precedence rules to be described in the next section. In order to keep the example clearer, we'll pretend that the resource manager keeps the information necessary to apply all the precedence rules, and keeps all the entries, until the end.

3. Now the contents of the resource database are compared to the third component in the widget's instance and class hierarchies, `quit` and `XmPushButton`. As usual, anything beginning with an asterisk or anything beginning with a period (.) followed by either the expected class or instance name is a match. This matches all but entry 1, which is eliminated.

Before going on to the next comparison, any components that matched specifically (a . or * followed by either string) are removed, which results in the resource database shown in Example 10-6.

Example 10-6. Resource database after final elimination of entries and components

```
*background:      red          (entry 2)
.background:      green        (entry 3)
.background:      yellow       (entry 5)
.background:      violet       (entry 6)
*background:      pink         (entry 7)
```

Now you see that we are left with only the resource names and tight or loose bindings. The matching process is finished, and the precedence analysis begins. The next section describes the precedence rules and then finishes this example to determine the priority of the finalist entries.

10.2.6 Resource Precedence Rules

Because of the way merging works, no two resource specifications in the merged resource database will be alike. (Remember that we are using the term *specification* for the part of the resource setting up to and including the colon.) For example, the merged database could never contain both of the following:

```
XBitmap*rowColumn*background: green
XBitmap*rowColumn*background: red
```

because the merging process would remove the setting that appeared earlier in the list of database sources.

However, the database could contain two or more resource settings that apply to the same resource of the same widget, because of differences in the widget class or instance hierarchy or the bindings. For example, the database could contain:

```
XBitmap*rowColumn*background: green
XBitmap*quit.background: red
```

If the `quit` button is a child of `rowColumn`, both settings apply to the `quit` button's background.

The resource manager provides a set of rules that govern which setting takes precedence in cases where there are two settings for the same resource of the same widget. Here are the four rules:

1. A specification that includes higher components in the instance or class hierarchy takes precedence over one that includes only lower ones.

```
*topLevel*quit.background:          takes precedence over
*rowColumn*quit.background:
```

2. Instance names take precedence over class names at the same level in the hierarchy.

```
*quit.background:                   takes precedence over
*XmPushButton.background:
```

3. Tight bindings take precedence over loose bindings at the same level in the hierarchy.

```
*rowColumn.background:              takes precedence over
*rowColumn*background:
```

4. A name or class that is explicitly stated takes precedence over one that is omitted.

```
*rowColumn*quit.background:         takes precedence over
*rowColumn*background:
```

To understand the application of these rules, let's return to our extended example. In the course of developing that example, we eliminated information about the level at which components occurred. However, the actual process of matching applies the precedence rules at each step. As a result, let's start again with the original appearance of the entries that pass the matching test. The remaining five as they appeared originally are shown in Example 10-7.

Example 10-7. Resource database finalists in original form

```
*background:                            red         (entry 2)
*quit.background:                       green       (entry 3)
*XmPushButton.background:               yellow      (entry 5)
*XmRowColumn.XmPushButton.background:   violet      (entry 6)
*rowColumn*background:                  pink        (entry 7)
```

From here on, we will determine not only which one of these five will take effect, but the actual precedence of the five. In other words, once the one with highest precedence is determined, we'll see which would take effect if that one was commented out, and so on.

The precedence rules are applied in order to determine the order of the finalist entries.

1. Rule 1 specifies that a specification that contains higher components in the instance or class hierarchy takes precedence over one that contains only lower ones. The highest components that appear in our example are `rowColumn` and `XmRowColumn` in entries 6 and 7. Therefore, these two have higher priority than any others.

2. To choose between these two, we continue to Rule 2. Instance names (`rowColumn`) take precedence over class names (`XmRowColumn`). Therefore, entry 7 has the highest precedence, followed by entry 6. Note that the precedence comparison of two finalists proceeds in the same manner as the original matching—from left to right in the entry, one component at a time.

3. To determine the precedence of the remaining three entries, 2, 3, and 5, we begin again with Rule 1. However, Rule 1 does not apply because no two entries here specify different levels in the hierarchy. Entries 3 and 5 contain the quit level and entry 2 nothing (an asterisk does not count for Rule 1 because it is not a *specified* level—it is any level). Rule 2 specifies that the instance name quit takes precedence over the class name Xm-PushButton, and therefore entry 3 has higher priority than entry 5. Rule 3 does not apply, because no two entries are identical except for binding. Because of Rule 4 we know that both entries 3 and 5 are higher priority than entry 2, because 3 and 5 state a name or class that is omitted in 2.

Therefore, the final precedence is as shown here:

```
1.    *rowColumn*background:                    pink     (entry 7)
2.    *XmRowColumn.XmPushButton.background:    violet   (entry 6)
3.    *quit.background:                         green    (entry 3)
4.    *XmPushButton.background:                 yellow   (entry 5)
5.    *background:                              red      (entry 2)
```

Rules 2, 3, and 4 are fairly easy to understand and apply, but many people forget or are confused by Rule 1. People get used to the fact that they can set the resources of all the children of rowColumn with something like entry 7, but then are shocked to find that nothing happens when they attempt to override entry 7 with entry 3—entry 3 seems more specific to them. Even the following entry (using a class name) takes precedence over entry 3 because the rule about being higher in the widget hierarchy carries more weight than the rule that instance names take precedence over class names:

```
*XmRowColumn*background:    pink        (entry 7)
```

The moral of this story is that there is only one way to be sure you are setting a particular resource of a particular widget in such a way as to override all other settings that might apply to that resource: you must specify all the levels in the instance hierarchy, with tight bindings between each component. (But of course, this will not work when another resource file that is merged later also specifies the same resource and all components of the same widget with the instance hierarchy separated by tight bindings.) Since there are no messages telling you which resource specifications are actually being used, you can be tricked into thinking that you have set resources that you actually haven't. Using only tight bindings in the app-defaults file, while more trouble initially, is probably wise in the long run.

Figure 10-3 illustrates the entire process of resource matching.

A useful tool for figuring out the priority of resource files is the *appres* utility. You specify the class name of the application on the command line, and *appres* shows you what resource settings that application will see when run. Note, however, that this does not tell you how these resource settings will actually apply to the widgets in the application, since *appres* has no knowledge of the widget instance hierarchy in your application.

Another tactic in tracing resource settings is to build a routine into your application that gets and prints all the critical resources of a widget. Using XtGetResourceList you can get the list of resources supported by a widget class. Then you can query each of those resources and print most of them out. Remember that certain resources are compiled into internal forms, so you can't print out translation tables, accelerator tables, or callback lists. It may also be difficult to interpret other values, since many of them will have already been convert-

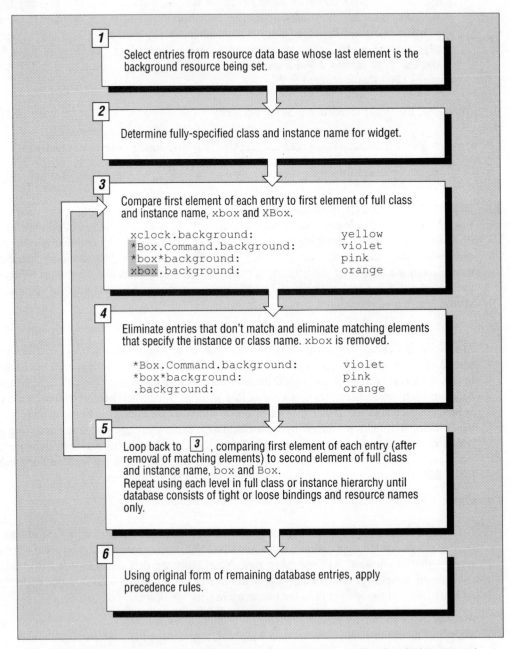

1 Select entries from resource data base whose last element is the background resource being set.

2 Determine fully-specified class and instance name for widget.

3 Compare first element of each entry to first element of full class and instance name, xbox and XBox.

```
xclock.background:          yellow
*Box.Command.background:    violet
*box*background:            pink
xbox.background:            orange
```

4 Eliminate entries that don't match and eliminate matching elements that specify the instance or class name. xbox is removed.

```
*Box.Command.background:    violet
*box*background:            pink
.background:                orange
```

5 Loop back to **3** , comparing first element of each entry (after removal of matching elements) to second element of full class and instance name, box and Box.
Repeat using each level in full class or instance hierarchy until database consists of tight or loose bindings and resource names only.

6 Using original form of remaining database entries, apply precedence rules.

Figure 10-3. Steps in matching resource entries for one resource of widget being created ed from the string form in the resource file into the most convenient internal form. For example, colors will have been changed from strings such as "red" into a pixel value (a number which could change each time the application is run).

10.3 Type Conversion

You already know that Xt is capable of converting resource values from the string representation specified in resource files to the actual type required in code. In fact, Xt does so automatically if the resource list is properly written. This section describes this process in more detail, and tells you how to create converters for converting your own data types.

In R4, a new set of interfaces for type converters was introduced. The new interfaces support display-specific conversions and better control of converted-value caching. This section describes these new interfaces, but does not describe the older ones. Be aware that many existing widgets and applications still use the older interfaces.

10.3.1 Conversions from XmRString

The primary purpose of converters is to allow resource files to contain string values for non-string program variables. (They are also used internally to convert default values that cannot be specified easily in the desired data type.) Secondly, converters confine the details of data conversion to a single routine that is registered with Xt. This is a big benefit because users of the converted types need not know the details of how the conversion takes place, or the internal definition of the target type.

Xt provides converters from XmRString to the representation types listed in Table 10-2. You can use these representation types as target types in resource lists in applications or widgets, without having to register them, if you want the user to be able to specify the resource in a resource file. Note that if you are using standard Xt, the various representation types begin with XtR rather than XmR.

Table 10-2. Built-in Type Converters from XmRString

Target Type	Description of Converter
XmRAcceleratorTable	Compiles a string accelerator table into internal accelerator format (no need to call XtParseAcceleratorTable).
XmRAtom	Converts a string property name into the corresponding Atom.
XmRBoolean	Converts strings "true", "false", "yes", "no", "on", and "off" to corresponding Boolean value (case insensitive).
XmRBool	Same as for XmRBoolean.
XmRCursor	Given a standard X cursor name, returns a cursor ID.
XmRDimension	Converts a width or height value to a Dimension.
XmRDisplay	Given a display name, opens the display and returns a Display structure.

Table 10-2. Built-in Type Converters from XmRString (continued)

Target Type	Description of Converter
XmRFile	Given a filename, opens the file and returns the file descriptor.
XmRFloat	Converts a numeric string to floating point
XmRFont	Given a font name, loads the font (if it is not already loaded), and returns the font ID. See Appendix B, *Specifying Fonts and Colors*, for more information on legal values. The value XtDefaultFont will return the default font for the screen.
XmRFontStruct	Given a font name, loads the font (if it is not already loaded), and returns a pointer to the FontStruct containing font metrics. The value XtDefaultFont will return the default font for the screen.
XmRGeometry	Given a standard geometry string, this converter simply copies a pointer to the string and calls it a new resource type.
XmRInitialState	Converts strings "Normal" or "Iconic" into the symbols NormalState or IconicState.
XmRInt	Converts a numeric string to an integer.
XmRPixel	Converts a color name string (e.g., "red" or "#FF0000") into the pixel value that will produce the closest color possible on the hardware. See Appendix B, *Specifying Fonts and Colors*, for more information on legal values. The two values XtDefaultBackground and XtDefaultForeground are always guaranteed to exist, and to contrast, on any server. However, Motif calculates its own colors to implement its four-color shadow scheme.
XmRPosition	Converts an x or y value to a Position.
XmRShort	Converts a numeric string to a short integer.
XmRTranslationTable	Compiles string translation table into internal translation table format (no need to call XtParseTranslationTable).
XmRUnsignedChar	Converts a string to an unsigned char.
XmRVisual	Converts a string specifying a visual class to a pointer to a supported visual structure of that class.

If there is no converter from XmRString to a particular resource type, it may not be possible to specify that resource type in a resource file. For example, there is no converter for XmRCallback since it would be meaningless to specify a function in a resource file. The only ways to set a callback resource are with XtAddCallback or a static callback list declared in the application.

Most of the Xt converters allow the resources of the base classes Core, Composite, Constraint, and Shell to be set from resource files. Motif provides numerous converters that allow the resources of its widgets to be set from resource files. However, not all Motif widget resources can be set from resource files, because converters are not provided for some. For example, there is currently no widget name to widget ID converter in Motif 1.1. Such a converter would make it possible to specify Form constraint resources such as XmNtopWidget from resource files.

In addition, the Xmu library contains several useful converters. For example, Xmu provides a converter that converts from a filename (string) to a bitmap suitable for use as an icon pixmap. Even though Xmu (like Xaw) is not part of the X Consortium standard, it is part of MIT's core distribution and is available on most systems. However, because the Xmu converters are not built into Xt, you need to register them with a call to XtSetType-Converter or XtAddConverter (from widget code) or XtAppSetType-Converter or XtAppAddConverter (from application code) before using them in an application or widget. (We'll describe the converters and show how to register them in Section 10.3.4.) Xmu also provides a widget name to widget ID converter that could be registered to remedy the lack of one in Motif mentioned above.

10.3.2 Other Built-in Type Conversions

While the conversions from XmRString are the most widely used, since they allow a resource to be specified from a resource file, there are also a number of built-in converters between other data types, for use internally within Toolkit programs.

Most commonly, these converters are used to convert between the resource_type and default_type fields of a resource definition.

Table 10-3 lists those converters automatically recognized by Xt.

Table 10-3. Other Built-in Converters

From	To	Description of Converter
XmRColor	XmRPixel	Converts an XColor structure to a pixel value.
XmRPixel	XmRColor	Converts a pixel value to an XColor structure.
XmRInt	XmRBoolean	Converts an int to a Boolean.
	XmRBool	Converts an int to a Boolean.
	XmRColor	Converts an int to an XColor.
	XmRDimension	Converts an int to a Dimension.
	XmRFloat	Converts an int to a float.
	XmRFont	Converts an int to a Font.
	XmRPixel	Converts an int to a pixel value.
	XmRPixmap	Converts an int to a Pixmap.
	XmRPosition	Converts an int to a Position.
	XmRShort	Converts an int to a short.
	XmRUnsignedChar	Converts an int to an unsigned char.

For example, the default value of the Core resource XmNborderPixmap is set as shown in Example 10-8.

Example 10-8. A resource definition converting an integer to a pixmap

```
static XtResource resources[] = {
   .
   .
   .
    {
   XmNborderPixmap,
   XmCPixmap,
   XmRPixmap,
   sizeof(Pixmap),
   XtOffsetOf(CoreRec, core.border_pixmap),
   XtRImmediate,
   (XtPointer) XtUnspecifiedPixmap
    },
   .
   .
   .

}
```

(Note that the code for the base classes defined by Xt use constants beginning with `Xt`, not `Xm`. However, the value of each of these constants is the same in both versions.)

The specified default value `XtUnspecifiedPixmap` is an integer defined to have a value that does not equal the constant `CopyFromParent` or any valid Pixmap ID. The `initialize` method for the Core widget class checks for this value, and does not set the `background` window attribute unless the application or a resource file has set the `XmNborderPixmap` resource to some value other than the default.

10.3.3 Special Resource Defaults That Do Not Use Conversion

There are two special values, `XmRImmediate` and `XmRCallProc` that can be used only in the `default_type` field of a resource definition. These values require no type conversion. The value provided in the `default_address` field must be of the correct type.

The type `XmRImmediate` means that the value in the `default_address` field is the default value itself, not its address. For a string, this means that the `default_address` field is a pointer to the string, not a pointer to a pointer.

In Example 10-9, the value in the `default_address` field of the `XmNheight` resource definition is the actual default—in this case, zero.

Example 10-9. A resource definition using XmRImmediate

```
static XtResource resources[] = {
   .
   .
   .
    {
   XmNheight,
   XmCHeight,
   XmRDimension,
   sizeof(Dimension),
   XmOffsetOf(RectObjRec, rectangle.height),
```

Example 10-9. A resource definition using XmRImmediate (continued)

```
     XmRImmediate,
     (XtPointer) 0
      },
       .
       .
       .
};
```

The type `XmRCallProc` means that the value in the `default_address` field is a pointer to a function. This function is of type `XtResourceDefaultProc`,* and it is expected to retrieve the desired default value at run time. When the widget instance is created, the function is automatically invoked with these parameters: the widget ID, the resource offset, and a pointer to the `XrmValve` in which to store the result. The function should fill in the `addr` field of the `XrmValue` with a pointer to the default data in its correct type.

In Example 10-10, the value in the `default_address` field of the `XmNscreen` resource definition is the name of a function that retrieves the screen on which the widget is displayed.

Example 10-10. A resource definition using XmRCallProc

```
static XtResource resources[] = {
      .
      .
      {
     XmNscreen,
     XmCScreen,
     XmRPointer,
     sizeof(int),
     XtOffsetOf(CoreRec, core.screen),
     XmRCallProc,
     (XtPointer) XtCopyScreen
      },
      .
      .
};
```

Example 10-11 shows an example of an `XtResourceDefaultProc`.

Example 10-11. An example of an XtResourceDefaultProc

```
/*ARGSUSED*/
void XtCopyScreen(widget, offset, value)
     Widget         widget;
     int            offset;
     XrmValue       *value;
{
     value->addr = (XtPointer)(&widget->core.screen);
}
```

---

*This function type is relevant primarily because the reference page in Volume Five, *X Toolkit Intrinsics Reference Manual*, that describes its calling sequence is listed under this name, `XtResourceDefaultProc`. This reference page is in the Prototype Procedures section in Volume 5.

10.3.4 Registering Type Converters

As noted earlier, not every representation type symbol defined in *Xm.h* is supported by a built-in converter, though Motif and the Xmu library do provide some of the most important converters that are missing in Xt. In addition, you can define your own resource types, and write converter routines to convert from a string representation in a resource file to the appropriate data type. (You can write converters from any type to any other type, but converters from `String` are by far the most useful.)

Table 10-4 lists the converters from `XmRString` provided by the Xmu library.

Table 10-4. Xmu Converters

From	To	Description of Converter
XmRString	XmRBackingStore	The `XmuCvtStringToBackingStore` converter converts the strings "NotUseful", "WhenMapped", and "Always" (in any case) into the corresponding constants (in proper case) for use in setting the `backing_store` window attribute. (See Volume One, *Xlib Programming Manual*, for details on backing store.)
	XmRBitmap	The `XmuCvtStringToBitmap` converter takes the string filename of a file in standard X11 bitmap format and creates a one-plane pixmap containing that bitmap data.
	XmRCursor	The `XmuCvtStringToCursor` converter converts one of the standard cursor names (from *<X11/cursorfont.h>*), a font name and glyph index of the form "FONT fontname index [[font] index]", or a bitmap file name as in `XmRPixmap` below, and converts it to an X `Cursor`.
	XmRJustify	The `XmuCvtStringToJustify` converter converts the strings "right", "left", or "center", in any case, to an enumeration constant suitable for use by a justify resource. This converter is used by the Athena Label widget.
	XmRLong	Converts a string to a long integer.
	XmROrientation	The `XmuCvtStringToOrientation` converter converts the strings "horizontal", or "vertical", in any case, to an enumeration constant suitable for use by an orientation resource. This converter is used by the Athena Scrollbar widget.
	XmRShapeStyle	Converts the strings `ShapeRectangle`, `ShapeOval`, `ShapeEllipse`, and `ShapeRoundedRectangle` in shape style constants, for use in making Xmu calls that access the Shape extension.

Table 10-4. Xmu Converters (continued)

From	To	Description of Converter
	XmRWidget	The XmuCvtStringToWidget converter converts a widget name into the corresponding widget ID. This is commonly done to specify the relative positions of the children of constraint widgets, as in the Athena Form widget resources fromHoriz and from-Vert.
XmRFunction	XmRCallback	Converts a function pointer to a callback list containing that function.

Whether defined in Xmu or in your own program, a converter other than those built into Xt or Motif must be registered with a call to XtAddConverter or XtSetTypeConverter before a resource list is used that references the converted types. Resource lists are used when widgets are created or when the application calls XtGetApplication-Resources. In the application, a converter must be registered after XtAppInitialize but before XtGetApplicationResources.

Within a widget, the class_initialize method is the standard place to register type converters. This method is responsible for doing processing that should be done only once when the first instance of a particular class is created.

Example 10-12 shows the code needed to register the XmuCvtStringToJustify converter in a widget. As noted above, this converter would be used for a resource (such as the Athena Label widget's XtNjustify resource) designed to give the user the option of justifying text (or a graphic object) to the right, left, or center of a widget.*

Example 10-12. Registering a type converter

```
static void
ClassInitialize()
{
        .
        .
        .
    XtSetTypeConverter(XmRString,       /* source type */
            XmRJustify,                 /* target type */
            XmuCvtStringToJustify,      /* converter routine */
            (XtConvertArgList) NULL,
            /* args for converter routine */
            0                           /*# args for converter routine */
            XtCacheAll,                 /*  caching instructions */
            NULL);                      /*  destructor function */

}
```

---

*While it may seem a little backwards to describe how to add a converter before we say how to write one, the availability of the Xmu converters makes it likely that you would in fact want to add converters you haven't written.

Note that `XtSetTypeConverter` was added to Xt in R4. Its predecessor, `XtAdd-`
`TypeConverter`, is still available and can still be used, but has reduced functionality.
`XtAddTypeConverter` cannot be used for conversions that require a server query (such
as those involving colors or fonts), and does not provide the caching control provided by
`XtSetTypeConverter`. Note that the explicit application context version of the call
(`XtAppSetTypeConverter`) is not used in this case, because the `class_initial-`
`ize` method does not pass in a widget from which the application context could be determined.

The first two arguments of `XtSetTypeConverter` are the source and target type, respectively, specified using XmR symbolic constants defined in *<Xm/Xm.h>* (or defined in an application header file or the widget public header file if the type is not standard in Xt).

The third argument is the name of the converter routine, which by convention contains the
string `Cvt`. The Xmu converters all add the prefix `Xmu`.

The fourth and fifth arguments of `XtSetTypeConverter` are an argument list that will
be passed to the converter routine when it is called. Some converter routines require information about the context in which the converter is called. This is usually passed in via an
`XtConvertArgRec` structure, as described in the next section. If no arguments are needed, the fourth and fifth arguments of `XtSetTypeConverter` can be `NULL` and 0 respectively.

The sixth argument specifies whether the results of the conversion should be cached. The basic symbols are `XtCacheNone`, `XtCacheAll`, and `XtCacheByDisplay`. Expensive
conversions should be cached. Xt caches resource values to avoid repetitive conversions of
the same value, which are common in an application made up of many identical widgets. It
is especially important to cache conversions that require round-trips to the server, such as
color, font, and atom conversions. But it is wasteful of memory to cache silly conversions
such as `XtCvtStringToGeometry`, which actually doesn't do any conversion or even
validity checking. (The `XmRGeometry` representation type is a geometry string, as defined
by `XParseGeometry`. It takes no conversion to convert `XtRString` to `Xt-`
`RGeometry`. The converter could at least test the string to make sure it looks like a geometry string.) Another benefit of caching is that Xt remembers unsuccessful conversions and efficiently generates warning messages without attempting any conversion more than once.

The symbol `XtCacheRefCount` can be ORed with any of the above values, in which case
Xt keeps track of how many widgets still exist that used a converted value, and frees the
cached value when the count reaches zero. The application, if it uses the converted value in
a call to `XtGetApplicationResources`, is also counted as one reference. Reference
counting is needed only if an application destroys widgets whose resource values may take
up extensive space. Because reference counting takes up space and requires time, it should
not be done unless necessary. To control reference counting on a widget-by-widget basis, an
application must explicitly set the `XmNinitialResourcesPersistent` resource to
`False` for each widget whose conversions are to be reference counted. These should be
widgets that might be destroyed before the application exits.

The seventh argument of `XtSetTypeConverter` is a pointer to a procedure called a *destructor*. If the reference count for a particular resource reaches zero, Xt calls the destructor
function, and removes the resource value from the conversion cache. The destructor will also
be called when `XtCloseDisplay` is called if the converter was registered with `Xt-`

CachePerDisplay. Before calling XtCallConverter or XtConvertAndStore to convert a value, the client must allocate memory in which to place the result. The job of the destructor is to deallocate this memory. If you are allowing Xt to convert data automatically, by declaring a resource list, Xt allocates the memory, and you don't need a destructor (so specify NULL). If you plan to call XtCallConverter from an application, and you allocate memory statically for the converted value, you don't need a destructor function and can specify NULL for this argument. A destructor is needed only if you allocate memory dynamically for an explicit call to XtCallConverter. (Remember that reference counting happens only if the converter is registered with XtCacheRefCount set and XmNinitialResourcesPersistent set to False for at least one widget. If these conditions are not met, the destructor is only called when XtCloseDisplay is called and if registered with XtCachePerDisplay.)

Xt provides several functions for manipulating reference counts, which are rather obscure and mentioned here only for completeness. XtAppReleaseCacheRefs explicity decrements the reference counts for resource values converted with XtCallConverter. This would be used in the rare occasion where a value has been cached but you don't want it cached. If this is the last reference to the conversion, the registered destructor is called. Xt also defines two built-in callback functions that decrement reference counts, XtCallbackReleaseCacheRef and XtCallbackReleaseCacheRefList.

10.3.4.1 Passing Arguments to a Type Converter

Some type converters need to be registered with additional arguments that provide information needed during the conversion. For example, XmuCvtStringToWidget needs to be passed the parent of the current widget in the application, so that it can compare the name specified in the resource to the names of the children of the parent. Example 10-13 shows the code used by a widget to register the Xmu string-to-widget converter.

Example 10-13. Adding a converter with arguments

```
static void ClassInitialize(w)
Widget w;
{
    static XtConvertArgRec parentCvtArgs[] = {
        {
            XtWidgetBaseOffset,
            (XtPointer)XtOffsetOf(CoreRec, core.parent),
            sizeof(CoreWidget)
        }
    };
    .
    .
    .
    XtSetTypeConverter(XtRString,
            XtRWidget,
            XmuCvtStringToWidget,
            parentCvtArgs,
            XtNumber(parentCvtArgs),
            XtCacheAll,
            NULL);
}
```

The format of the argument list for `XtSetTypeConverter` shown in Example 10-14 looks complicated, but in practice almost all converter argument lists will look very similar to the one in this example. The argument list is specified as an `XtConvertArgRec`:

```
typedef struct {
    XtAddressMode address_mode;
    XtPointer address_id;
    Cardinal size;
} XtConvertArgRec, *XtConvertArgList;
```

The `address_mode` field specifies how the `address_id` field should be interpreted. `address_id` itself is a pointer to the needed data, an offset within the widget instance structure to the data, or a function that provides the needed data. The `size` field specifies the length of the data in bytes.

By specifying the address mode as `XtWidgetBaseOffset` (see below), you can use `XtOffsetOf` to find the offset of appropriate data in the instance structure.* All you have to do is change the name of the instance structure field (in this case `core.parent`), and the structure type that contains that field (in this case `WidgetRec`). Notice that a pointer to this structure type appears in the `sizeof` call (in this case `Widget`).

You have just seen the normal way of specifying the converter arguments. Using different `XtAddressMode` values you can also specify them in other ways. The enumerated type `XtAddressMode` (defined in *<X11/Convert.h>*) specifies the possible values for the `address_mode` field:

```
typedef enum {
        /* address mode parameter representation */
        XtAddress,              /* address */
        XtBaseOffset,           /* offset */
        XtImmediate,            /* constant */
        XtResourceString,       /* resource name string */
        XtResourceQuark,        /* resource name quark */
        XtWidgetBaseOffset,     /* offset */
        XtProcedureArg          /* procedure to call */
} XtAddressMode;
```

- `XtAddress` causes `address_id` to be interpreted as the address of the data.

- `XtBaseOffset` causes `address_id` to be interpreted as the offset from the widget base address. `XtWidgetBaseOffset` (see below) is now slightly preferred, since it works with objects and gadgets as well as widgets.

- `XtImmediate` causes `address_id` to be interpreted as a constant.

---

*You can also use `XtOffset` instead of `XtOffsetOf`, but it is less portable. The usage difference between the two is that `XtOffset` takes a pointer to the structure type, while `XtOffsetOf` takes the structure type itself. If you are converting R3 code to R4 (Motif 1.0 to Motif 1.1), simply change the macro name and add `Rec` to the end of the structure pointer type; this changes it to a structure type, if the widget uses standard naming conventions.

- `XtResourceString` causes `address_id` to be interpreted as the name of a resource that is to be converted into an offset from the widget base address.

- `XtResourceQuark` causes `address_id` to be interpreted as a quark—that is, as an internal compiled form of an `XtResourceString`.

- `XtWidgetBaseOffset` is similar to `XtBaseOffset` except that it searches for the closest windowed ancestor if the object is not a subclass of Core. This must be used in the resource list of objects and gadgets, but can also be used for widgets.

- `XtProcedureArg` specifies that `address_id` is a pointer to a procedure to be invoked to return the conversion argument. `address_id` must contain the address of a function of type `XtConvertArgProc`. This function type takes three arguments: an object (or widget), pointer to size (Cardinal *), and a pointer to an `XrmValue`. The value is returned in the `XrmValue`.

In most cases, you will use `XtWidgetBaseOffset` in widgets, gadgets and objects, as shown in Example 10-13.

When registering a type converter in an application rather than a widget, the structure field specified in the argument list shown in the example would be a field of the `AppData` structure instead of the instance part structure, and `CoreRec` would be replaced by `AppData`.

10.3.5 Explicitly Invoking a Converter

Converters are normally invoked by Xt because the types they convert are specified in a resource list. But this is not the only way in which converters can be invoked. It is possible to manually invoke type converters, the easiest way being `XtConvertAndStore`.* This may be useful in an application, such as for reading an icon pixmap from a file using a converter, or you may need to explicitly invoke a converter from within a converter you want to write. (Converter routines can themselves invoke other converters directly.)

One possible manual use of type converter routines is in the processing of the string parameters passed to action routines. Perhaps in the action routine itself it is more convenient to have some parameters converted to another form. For example, if an action is passed the string "True," the action code might prefer to convert this parameter to a Boolean value. The `CvtStringToBoolean` converter understands many strings that would be interpreted as Boolean, such as "Off," "On," "True," "False," "No," and "Yes," in upper, lower, or mixed case. It saves code to use the converter rather than comparing a string to all these strings in your own code. Example 10-14 shows an action routine of the Athena Text widget (modified for R4) in which a converter is manually invoked.

---

*`XtConvertAndStore` replaced `XtConvert` in R4. Both have the same arguments, but `XtConvertAndStore` returns `Boolean` while `XtConvert` returns `void`. `XtConvertAndStore`'s return value indicates whether the conversion succeeded or failed. `XtConvertAndStore` also implements new display-specific conversion, caching and reference counting features.

Example 10-14. Manually invoking a type converter

```
static void
DisplayCaret(w, event, params, num_params)
Widget w;
XEvent *event;              /* CrossingNotify special-cased */
String *params;             /* Off, False, No, On, True, Yes, etc. */
Cardinal *num_params;       /* 0, 1 or 2 */
{
    .
    .
    .
    if (*num_params > 0) { /* default arg is "True" */
        XrmValue from, to;
        from.size = strlen(from.addr = params[0]);
        if (XtConvertAndStore(w, XtRString, &from, XtRBoolean, &to)
                == False)
            XtAppError(XtWidgetToApplicationContext(w),
                    "DisplayCaret action: String to Boolean\
                    conversion failed");
        else {
            ; /*
             *       (*(Boolean*)to.addr) has boolean value;
             *               do something with it here */
             */
        }
    }
}
```

Note that the *from* and *to* arguments of XtConvertAndStore are pointers to structures containing length/pointer pairs—they are not values. The actual data is passed as a pointer to a pointer. Thus the cast to Boolean (in the comment) must dereference the pointer twice.

The widget argument of XtConvertAndStore is used internally by Xt as the argument for the XtDisplay macro, to get the pointer to the display structure, and for other purposes. In normal applications you can pass any widget here. (For some converters, the widget may need to be realized.)

XtConvertAndStore calls a lower-level routine called XtCallConverter.* If you prefer, you can use this routine. Instead of passing it the widget and the source and destination type, you pass it a display, the name of the conversion routine, any arguments to the routine, and storage in which to place the cache reference count. See Volume Five, *X Toolkit Intrinsics Reference Manual*, for details.

---

*XtCallConverter superceded its rough equivalent R3 routine XtDirectConvert.

10.3.6 Writing a Type Converter

If your application or widget has a data type that you would like the user to be able to set through resource files, and no Xt or Xmu converter exists, you will need to write (and register) a type converter from `XtRString` to your type.

The first step in creating a converter is to decide upon the characteristics of the string you will be converting from, and the C-Language type you will be converting to. Then you can copy an existing similar converter and fill in the code to convert to your desired type. Note that the R4 Athena widgets still use the R3 converter interface. To use the R4 converter functions `XtConvertAndStore` or `XtCallConverter`, or any of the cache reference counting features, you must define your converter using the R4 type `XtTypeConverter`. The difference between R4 and R3 type converters is just that R4 type converters have a display as their first argument, and they must do a display-specific conversion when a server query is involved.

Example 10-15 shows an Xmu converter that shows the essential elements of a converter. It has been modified to be compatible with the R4 resource conversion routines such as `Xt-SetTypeConverter`. (The only difference is the presence of a leading `Display` argument.)

Example 10-15. A simple type converter

```
#define done(address, type) \
        { (*toVal).size = sizeof(type); \
          (*toVal).addr = (caddr_t) address; }
void XmuCvtStringToLong (display, args, num_args, fromVal, toVal)
    Display display;
    XrmValuePtr args;
    Cardinal    *num_args;
    XrmValuePtr fromVal;
    XrmValuePtr toVal;
{
    static long l;

    if (*num_args != 0)
        XtWarningMsg("wrongParameters","cvtStringToLong",
                "XtToolkitError","String to Long\
                conversion needs no extra arguments",
                (String *) NULL, (Cardinal *)NULL);
    if (sscanf((char *)fromVal->addr, "%ld", &l) == 1) {
        done(&l, long);
    } else {
        XtDisplayStringConversionWarning(display, (char *)
                fromVal->addr, XtRLong);
    }
}
```

Note that Xt manages the cache of converted values: converter routines are not responsible for caching their own returned data.

Notice that the `XrmValuePtr` arguments passed into the converter are pointers to structures, not values. The `XrmValue` structure contains an address field and a size field.

`XtDisplayStringConversionWarning` takes as arguments a pointer to the `Display` structure, the string that could not be converted, and the type to which it could not be converted. It issues a warning message with name `conversionError`, type `string`, class `XtToolkitError`, and the default message string "Cannot convert `"src"` to type `dst_type`." (See Chapter 14, *Miscellaneous Toolkit Programming Techniques*, for more information on error and warning messages.)

Many converters need to compare multiple strings in order to convert a value. For example, Motif's string to arrow-direction converter has to determine whether a string matches `Xm-ARROW_UP`, `XmARROW_DOWN`, `XmARROW_LEFT`, or `XmARROW_RIGHT`. Normally this would require up to four time-consuming string comparisons for each conversion. Instead, converters of this type use a shortcut based on quarks. A quark is a unique integer ID for a string, of type `XrmQuark` (defined by Xlib). A call to the Xlib routine `XrmString-ToQuark` returns the quark for a string. A converter determines quarks for each of its reference strings (such as `XmARROW_UP`) only once during run time, and determines a quark for each string to be converted. Then quarks can be compared quickly since they are just integers. (See Volume Two, *Xlib Reference Manual*, for details on quarks.)

When a nonstandard type converter that uses quarks is defined and registered in widget code, the `XrmStringToQuark` calls are normally placed in the `class_initialize` method just before the `XtSetTypeConverter` call.

10.3.6.1 Defining the Default Value

When performing conversions, such as from strings to fonts or colors, for which there is no string representation that all server implementations will necessarily recognize, a type converter should define some set of conversion values that the converter is guaranteed to succeed on, so that these can be used as resource defaults.

For example, Xt's default string-to-pixel converter recognizes the symbols `XtDefault-Foreground` and `XtDefaultBackground`. As part of its conversion, it tests for these values, and establishes the appropriate value based on the string value. The code is shown in Example 10-16.

Example 10-16. Testing for a special-case default value

```
/*
 * CompareISOLatin1 is an undocumented Xt function, allowed
 * since this converter is within Xt.  In your converters,
 * you would use XmuCompareISOLatin1.
 */
if (CompareISOLatin1(str, XtDefaultBackground) == 0) {
    *destructor_data = False;
    if (pd->rv)
        done(Pixel, BlackPixelOfScreen(screen))
    else
        done(Pixel, WhitePixelOfScreen(screen));
}
if (CompareISOLatin1(str, XtDefaultForeground) == 0) {
    *destructor_data = False;
    if (pd->rv)
        done(Pixel, WhitePixelOfScreen(screen))
```

X Toolkit Intrinsics Programming Manual, Motif Edition

Example 10-16. Testing for a special-case default value (continued)

```
            else
                done(Pixel, BlackPixelOfScreen(screen));
        }
```

Although Motif uses Xt's string to pixel value converter when colors are specified in resource files, it uses its own algorithm to calculate the default value depending on the type of screen and on the colors that can be successfully allocated.

10.4 Subparts and Subresources

A subpart is a section of a widget that is replaceable but that cannot operate independently. It is just a further subdivision of the widget into smaller pieces. This section is provided only for completeness; gadgets and objects provide a more elegant way to do this.

Subresources allow subparts of a widget to have separate sets of resources. Since the Athena Text widget was the only example of the use of subresources in MIT's Release 3 Core distribution, we'll describe how Text uses subparts and subresources so you can understand the motivation behind them. You can then compare this concept with the R4 Text widget which is implemented using objects.

The R3 Text widget has three parts: the source, the sink, and the coordinator widget. The source manages the storage of data and the sink manages how it is displayed. The coordinator is the central widget that manages the communication between the source and the sink, and is inoperable without them. Both the source and the sink are replaceable pieces of code. Xaw provides only one source, which edits a string or disk file, and only one sink, which displays text in one color and in one font. The idea of providing the subparts in the first place is that they would allow enhancements to be made without changing the basic editor functionality that is in the coordinator. For example, only the source and sink would need replacing in order to implement a multifont and/or multicolor text widget.

Each subpart has its own resource list so that it truly can be replaced without any modifications to the central widget. These are the subresources.

10.4.1 The Hook Methods

The `initialize_hook`, `set_values_hook`, and `get_values_hook` methods are used by widgets that have subparts. They have the same function as their nonhook counterparts, except that they process only the resources of a subpart, and any subpart instance fields that depend on the subpart resources. These methods are called immediately after their nonhook counterparts.

However, the `initialize_hook` and `set_value_hook` methods have become obsolete in R4 because their arguments have been added to the `initialize` and `set_values` methods. The hook methods are still called for compatibility with existing widgets, but new widgets should move the code that would have been in the hook methods into `initialize` and `set_values`.

The get_values_hook method is passed a single copy of the widget instance structure (the *new* copy already modified in the nonhook methods), and the argument list passed to the Xt routine that triggered the method. The set_values and get_values_hook methods simply take this widget ID and argument list and pass them to XtSetSubvalues or XtGetSubvalues respectively. The initialize method uses the contents of the argument list to validate resource settings for subparts and to set nonresource subpart data.

The get_values_hook method is still used in R4. Example 10-17 shows the get_values_hook for the AsciiSrc subpart of the R3 Text widget (somewhat simplified to show the essential elements).

Example 10-17. Simplified get_values_hook method of the AsciiSrc subpart of the Text widget

```
static void
GetValuesHook(src, args, num_args)
XawTextSource src;
ArgList args;
Cardinal * num_args;
{
        .
        .
        .

    XtGetSubvalues((XtPointer) src,
            sourceResources,
            XtNumber(sourceResources),
            args,
            *num_args);
}
```

10.4.2 Managing Subresources

Managing subresources is very similar to managing application resources. Like the application, the subpart must have a structure containing the fields to set through resources. In the application you call XtGetApplicationResources or XtVaGetApplicationResources to set these fields. In a subpart, the analogous calls are XtGetSubresources or XtVaGetSubresources, which is called from the initialize method.

Like widgets, the resources of subparts can be queried and set manually. XtVaGetSubvalues or XtGetSubvalues queries the values, and XtVaSetSubvalues or XtSetSubvalues sets them. However, because subvalues are not part of any widget, these calls cannot identify what object is being queried or set simply by passing the widget ID. These calls have different arguments than XtSetValues and XtGetValues. Instead of the widget ID, you pass the pointer to the data structure, the resource list, and the number of resources. Therefore, XtSetSubvalues and XtGetSubvalues can be invoked only from within the widget or subpart. Actually, all these routine do is set or get the value in the specified structure.

Any application using the widget will set or get subresources using `XtSetValues` and `XtGetValues` as for normal resources, specifying only the coordinating widget as the first argument. These calls are translated into `XtSetSubvalues` and `XtGetSubvalues` calls by the `set_values` and `get_values_hook` methods. These methods are passed the arguments from the `XtSetValues` or `XtGetValues` calls and translate them into `XtSetSubvalues` or `XtGetSubvalues` calls by adding the data structure and resource list arguments. But in addition, the `set_values` method is responsible for validating the resource settings passed in before it calls `XtSetSubvalues`, and for changing any non-resource subpart structure fields like GCs that depend on resources.

11

Interclient Communications

This chapter discusses communication through the X server between an application and the window manager, and between two applications. The application-window manager communication is performed by code in the Shell widget. The application sets shell resources to control this communication with the window manager. Application-application communication is usually done with a process called selections. This form of communication is already implemented in most widgets that display text, but you may want to implement it in your own custom widgets. Selections can also pass other kinds of data such as graphics. How to use the Motif Clipboard is also described.

In This Chapter:

11

Interclient Communications

Applications share the server with other clients. Server resources, such as screen space and colormaps, must be used in a responsible, consistent manner so that applications can work effectively together. In most window systems, the window system itself embodies a set of rules for application interaction. However, the X Protocol, Xlib, and Xt were all specifically designed to avoid arbitrary conventions, so that they provide "mechanism, not policy."

Instead, the conventions covering interclient communication are described in a separate document, adopted as an X Consortium standard in July, 1989, called the *Inter-Client Communication Conventions Manual* (ICCCM). This chapter will not fully describe the ICCCM, because the job of implementing its rules is given over to a special client called the window manager and a special widget class called Shell and its subclasses.* As a result the details of the ICCCM are, for the most part, irrelevant to the application writer's needs.

In X Toolkit programs, the Shell widget returned by `XtAppInitialize` and used as the top-level window of the application automatically handles most of the required interactions with the window manager. However, the Shell widget needs additional information in certain areas. For example, the application needs to provide an icon pixmap so that the window manager can iconify it properly. The first section in this chapter describes how to set Shell resources to control how an application interacts with the window manager. This portion of the chapter is for application writers, regardless of whether you need to write widgets for your application.

The ICCCM defines the required information that must be sent by the client. The Shell widget class takes care of sending this information. However, *mwm*, the Motif Window Manager, also allows the application to send or be sent optional information. One set of information warns the application when it is about to be killed or when one of its windows is about to be destroyed. A separate set lets the application specify what kind of decorations it wants on its top-level shell widgets. The final set allows *mwm* to notify the application when a certain entry on its system menu has been selected. This entry is normally added to the user's *.mwmrc* as part of the application's installation procedure.

---

*If you do need to look up certain details of the ICCCM, see Appendix L, *Inter-Client Communication Conventions*, in a version of Volume Zero, *X Protocol Reference Manual*, printed on or after June, 1990 (the conventions have changed since the version of the ICCCM printed in earlier editions of Volume One). The ICCCM is also included in *troff* source form in the standard X distribution from MIT.

In X Toolkit applications, widgets can communicate with other widgets using a mechanism called *selections*, which in turn is based on an X mechanism for common storage called *properties*. Whether the widgets involved in transferring selections are part of the same application or different applications is irrelevant. The communication between widgets takes place without input from the application. However, it can be used as a means of communication between applications. The second major section in this chapter will describe these concepts and how to implement selections between your own custom widgets. Only if your application requires a custom widget that must communicate with other widgets should you actually have to write this code. Thus, this part of the chapter is primarily for widget writers.

11.1 Window Manager Interactions

The window manager was introduced in Chapter 1, *Introduction to the X Window System*, but little mention of it has been made since then. You may recall that the window manager is just another client running on a server, except that it is given special authority to manage screen space and other limited server resources like colormaps.* To let the window manager do a better job of mediating competing demands of the various clients, each client gives the window manager information called *window manager hints*. These hints specify what resources each client would like to have, but they are only hints; the window manager is not obligated to honor them, and the client must not depend on them being honored.

Application code has little to do to interact properly with the window manager. The Shell widget returned by `XtAppInitialize` takes care of setting the essential window manager hints. However, there are a number of optional window manager hints that the application may wish to have passed to the window manager. This is done mainly by setting resources of the Shell widget. Also, there are variations in window managers and it takes some effort to make some applications work equally well under all of them.

The next few sections describe the various resources of the Shell widget, including how and when they should be set. Because the Shell widget is part of the Xt standard, these resources are present when writing applications with any widget set.

11.1.1 Shell Subclasses

There are several types of Shell widgets. The Shell widget class itself, specified by the class structure pointer `shellWidgetClass`, is never instantiated directly in applications. Only its subclasses are used. You have seen two subclasses of the Shell widget used earlier in this books: the one used for the application's top-level widget and the one used for popups. The application's top-level widget is created by passing the class structure pointer `applicationShellWidgetClass` as the widget class argument to `XtAppCreate-Shell`; this call is also made internally by `XtAppInitialize`. Popup shells for dialog boxes are created by passing `transientShellWidgetClass` as the widget class argument to `XtCreatePopupShell`. There are two other subclasses of Shell that are

---

*Note that we are using the term *resources* here in a general sense, rather than implying its Xt-specific meaning.

commonly used in applications. One is the `OverrideShellWidgetClass`, passed to `XtCreatePopupShell` when the shell is used for popup menus. The convention is this: the shell should be an OverrideShell when the pointer is grabbed to prevent other windows from getting input while the popup is up, and the shell should be TransientShell for other popups. This is discussed further in Chapter 13, *Menus, Gadgets, and Cascaded Popups.*

The other additional subclass of Shell is `topLevelShellWidgetClass`, which is used to create additional, non-popup, top-level shells. Some applications have multiple permanent top-level windows. One of the top-level shells would be of the `applicationShell-WidgetClass`, and the rest would be of the `topLevelShellWidgetClass`. Each would have a separate icon.

11.1.2 Setting Shell Resources

Shell resources are primarily a way for the user and the application to send in data to be communicated to the window manager. These window manager hints control several major areas of window manager activity: they manage screen space, icons, and keyboard input. We'll discuss these areas one at a time in the following sections. Table 11-1 lists the Shell widget's resources with a brief description of what they control, and whether the application, the user, or Xt normally sets them.

As indicated in Column 3 of the table, some Shell resources are intended to be set only once. These set-once resources can be left to their default values, set in the app-defaults file, or they can be set in the code before the Shell widget is realized; but they should not be set with `XtSetValues` after realization.

Table 11-1. Shell Resources

Resource	Purpose	When Settable
usually set by Xt or Shell itself, depending on the subclass:		
XmNargc	Command-line args count	-
XmNargv	Command-line args	-
XmNoverrideRedirect	Set for popup shells not to be decorated	-
XmNtransient	Set for popup shells	-
XmNwaitForWm	Whether to wait at all	-
XmNwindowGroup	Links popups to main window	-
XmNwmTimeout	Waiting time for slow wm	-
usually set by user:		
XmNiconX	Icon position	Before realization
XmNiconY	Icon position	Before realization
XmNiconic	Sets XmNinitialState to iconic	Before realization
XmNgeometry	Initial size and position	Before realization
XmNtitle	String for title bar	Anytime
usually set by application:		

Table 11-1. Shell Resources (continued)

Resource	Purpose	When Settable
XmNallowShellResize	Does shell ask wm for size change?	Anytime
XmNbaseHeight	Height of fixed components	Anytime
XmNbaseWidth	Width of fixed components	Anytime
XmNheightInc	Desired height increment	Anytime
XmNwidthInc	Desired width increment	Anytime
XmNiconMask	Mask used with icon pixmap	Before realization
XmNiconName	String for icon	Before realization
XmNiconPixmap	Picture for icon	Before realization
XmNiconWindow	Window for icon	Before realization
XmNinitialState	Whether normal or iconic	Before realization
XmNinput	Keyboard input model	Before realization
XmNmaxAspectX	Maximum aspect ratio x/y	Anytime
XmNmaxAspectY	Maximum aspect ratio x/y	Anytime
XmNmaxHeight	Maximum acceptable height	Anytime
XmNmaxWidth	Maximum acceptable width	Anytime
XmNminAspectX	Minimum aspect ratio x/y	Anytime
XmNminAspectY	Minimum aspect ratio x/y	Anytime
XmNminHeight	Minimum acceptable height	Anytime
XmNminWidth	Minimum acceptable width	Anytime
XmNsaveUnder	Should server save under when mapped	Before realization

Several of the Shell resources are set automatically by Xt or the window manager and under normal circumstances should not be modified by an application:

- The XmNargc and XmNargv resources are set by Xt to contain the command-line arguments used to invoke the application. These values may be used by the window manager or a session manager to allow the user to reinvoke the application using the same arguments.

- The XmNwindowGroup resource is used to link popup windows to an application's main window. If not set explicitly, XmNwindowGroup is automatically set to the top-level ancestor of the popup shell, which is usually the application's top-level shell.

- The XmNtransient and XmNoverrideRedirect resources are set automatically by Xt depending on what kind of Shell widget you create. For top-level application shells, both are set to indicate that the window manager should treat this window as a top-level window. For TransientShell popup shells, XmNtransient is set automatically to the shell specified in XmNwindowGroup. When the top-level window is iconified, the TransientShell popup will also be iconified. The TransientShell may also be decorated differently from main application shells.

- XmNoverrideRedirect defaults to True in the OverrideShell class, indicating that the popup can map itself completely without window manager intervention. This type of popup shell is typically used for popup menus, because they should not be decorated or interfered with by the window manager.

- The XmNwaitForWm and XmNwmTimeout resources control the response to delays by the window manager when responding to geometry change requests. By default, Xm-NwaitForWm is True, and XmNwm_timeout is five seconds. When making a geometry request to the window manager, the Shell widget will wait for five seconds for a response. If a response does not arrive within five seconds, the Shell widget will set XmNwaitForWm to False, and assume that the window manager is not functioning. The Shell widget will continue without waiting for the event that would otherwise arrive to report the size of the window, and also without updating Xt's internal cache of window geometries. When this event does arrive later, Xt may set XmNwaitForWm back to True and update its internal cache. These resources should normally be left to their default values.

The XmNgeometry and XmNiconic resources are intended to be specified by the user. Only these two resources use standard command-line options. The XmNgeometry resource is settable using a command-line option of the form:

```
-geometry [width{x}height][{+-}xposition{+-}yposition]
```

(Either the size or position portion of the geometry string may be omitted, as indicated by the square brackets. In specifying the *x* or *y* position, a positive value, indicated by a plus sign, is relative to the top or left side of the reference window, while a negative value, indicated by a minus sign, is relative to the bottom or right side.)

The *–iconic* command-line option, if present, sets the XmNiconic resource, indicating to the window manager that the application should start up as an icon.

The XmNicon_x and XmNicon_y icon position hints are best left specified by the user. Icons' positions are determined by the window manager based on these hints or on an icon-positioning policy. An application with several top-level windows could set the icon position hints in its app-defaults file so that the icons for each top-level window appear side-by-side.

We will discuss the remaining resources in related groups. Section 11.1.3 discusses the ones related to the size of the application's main window and other screen space issues. Section 11.1.4 describes the keyboard input model hint. Section 11.1.5 describes how applications should handle colormaps to cooperate with the window manager. Section 11.1.6 describes the ones that apply to the application's icon.

11.1.3 Screen Space

The Shell widgets of each application have windows that are children of the root window. These are called top-level windows. The window manager directly controls the size and position of the top-level windows of each application. The window manager does not control the geometry of other widgets that are the descendants of the Shells, except indirectly through the geometry management mechanism described in Chapter 12, *Geometry Management*.

The most basic size hint, the one that specifies simply the desired initial height and width, is automatically set by Xt based on the size of the child of the Shell widget. This hint is used by most window managers to display the outline of your application when it first appears on the screen, ready for the user to place and/or size the application. If your application does not have specific size needs, you need not set any additional resources.

The additional size hints specify the application's range of desired sizes, desired increments of sizes, and desired range of aspect ratios. These are set by the `XmNbaseHeight`, `XmNbaseWidth`, `XmNminWidth`, `XmNminHeight`, `XmNmaxWidth`, `XmNmaxHeight`, `XmNwidthInc`, `XmNheightInc`, `XmNminAspectX`, `XmNminAspectY`, `XmNmaxAspectX`, and `XmNmaxAspectY` resources.

Size increment hints are useful for applications that prefer to be in units of a particular number of pixels. Window managers that listen for this hint always resize the window to the base size (for each dimension), plus or minus an integral multiple of the size increment hint for that dimension. If the base size resource has not been set, the minimum size is used as the base. For example, *xterm* uses the font width and font height as width and height increment hints, because it prefers not to have partial characters or dead space around the edges. The bitmap editor application described in Chapter 4, *An Example Application*, should probably set both the width and height increments to the `cell_size_in_pixels`, since the bitmap cells are square.

Most applications that use size increment hints redefine the interpretation of geometry specifications (the `XmNgeometry` resource, settable through the `-geometry` standard command-line option) to reflect the size increments. For example, the width and height in *xterm* geometry specifications are in units of characters, not pixels. The Vt100 widget within *xterm* implements this by having an `XmNgeometry` resource separate from the shell geometry resource with that name. The entry for this resource in the widget resource list specifies the Vt100 instance structure field, not the shell instance structure field. Then the `realize` method for the Vt100 parses the geometry string with `XParseGeometry` (an Xlib routine that returns four separate variables containing the size and position from the geometry string) and sets the width and height fields of the core structure and the various size hints according to the returned variables. (The Vt100 within *xterm* is not a real, self-sufficient widget. For one thing, it has no `set_values` method. For any real widget to implement this approach to interpreting geometry specifications, the `set_values` method would have to multiply the `XmNwidth` and `XmNheight` resource settings by the increment hints.)

An aspect ratio is the ratio of the width to height measurement or vice versa. The `XmNminAspectX` and `XmNminAspectY` resources are used together to determine one extreme of acceptable aspect ratios, and `XmNmaxAspectX` and `XmNmaxAspectY` determine the other extreme. For example, to suggest that the *xmh* application never be more than four times larger in one direction than it is in the other, the following values (as they would appear in the app-defaults file) would suffice:

```
xmh*topLevel.minAspectX:     1
xmh*topLevel.minAspectY:     1
xmh*topLevel.maxAspectX:     4
xmh*topLevel.maxAspectY:     4
```

Remember that every application must be able to do something reasonable given any size for its top-level window, even if the window is too small to be useful or if any of these hints are ignored by the window manager.

11.1.4 Input Model

Window managers also control which window keyboard input will be delivered to by setting the *keyboard focus window* (sometimes called just the *keyboard focus*) to an application's top-level window. The distribution of events according to the current keyboard focus is handled by the server; it is a basic feature of X, not of Xt. Some window managers, like *twm*, use the pointer-following (also called real-estate-driven) model of keyboard input; the window containing the pointer gets the keyboard input. Setting the keyboard focus once to the root window implements the pointer-following model. Other window managers use the click-to-type model, exemplified by the Macintosh™ user interface, requiring that the user click the pointer in the window where keyboard input is to go. The window manager sets the keyboard focus to the window the user clicks on. *mwm* lets the user select between these two focus models by setting a resource.

With some window managers other than *mwm*, how the window manager treats an application window can be modified by the input model hint, which is set by the XmNinput resource. Even though *mwm* doesn't use the value of this hint, Motif applications should set it in case they are used under a window manager that does use the hint.

If XmNinput is set to True, the window manager will set the keyboard focus to this application or not, according to its pointer-following or click-to-type model of keyboard input. However, if it is set to False, the window manager will not set the keyboard focus to this application. If the application sets this resource to False and wants input, it will have to forcefully take the keyboard focus, and then put it back to the original window when finished.

For historical (not logical) reasons, the Intrinsics default for the XmNinput resource is False. However, there is a special internal Shell widget class called VendorShell, which sets appropriate resources for a given widget set. The proper default for a given widget set (which usually has an accompanying window manager) is set by that widget set's Vendor-Shell. The majority of applications need XmNinput set to True unless they don't require keyboard input (and expect never to have accelerators).

There are four models of client input handling defined by the ICCCM:

- No Input. The client never expects keyboard input. *xload* is an example of such an output-only client. This type of client sets XmNinput to False.

- Passive Input. The client expects keyboard input but never explicitly sets the input focus. This describes the vast majority of applications that always accept keyboard input in the window that contains the pointer. This type of client sets XmNinput to True.

- Locally Active Input. The client expects keyboard input, and explicitly sets the keyboard focus, but only does so when one of its windows already has the focus. An example would be a client with subwindows defining various data entry fields that uses Next and Prev keys to move the keyboard focus between the fields, once its top-level window has received the keyboard focus. This type of client sets XmNinput to True.

- Globally Active Input. The client expects keyboard input, and explicitly sets the input focus even when the focus is in windows the client does not own. An example would be a client with a scrollbar that wants to allow users to scroll the window without disturbing the keyboard focus even if it is in some other window. It wants to temporarily set and then reset the keyboard focus when the user clicks in the scrolled region, but not when the user clicks in the scrollbar itself. Thus, it wants to prevent the window manager from setting the keyboard focus to any of its windows. This type of client sets `XmNinput` to `False`.

Note that even if the `XmNinput` resource is not set to `True`, your application will still work under some window managers, including *uwm*, *twm*, and *mwm*. This is because these window managers use the pointer-following keyboard focus model or ignore this hint. However, it is not wise to assume that all window managers will ignore this hint. Therefore, if your application expects keyboard input, and is not of the globally active type described above, you can use the code shown in Example 11-1 to set the `XmNinput` resource.

Example 11-1. Setting the XmNinput resource of a Shell widget

```
main(argc, argv)
int argc;
char *argv[];
{
    .
    .
    .

    /* create the Shell widget, setting resource */
    topLevel = XtVaAppInitialize(&app_context, "Xmh",
            table, XtNumber(table),
            &argc, argv, NULL,
            XmNinput, (XtArgVal)True,
            NULL);
    .
    .
    .

}
```

Note that the `XmNinput` resource should always be hardcoded, since the application may fail if the user is allowed to change the expected style of keyboard focus.

For a further discussion of the keyboard focus, see Section 14.4.

11.1.5 Colormaps

On most color systems, the display uses one or more hardware registers called *colormaps* to store the mapping between pixel values and actual colors, which are specified as relative intensities of red, green, and blue primaries (RGB values).

X allows virtual colormaps to be created by applications. Some high-performance systems even allow all virtual colormaps to be installed in hardware colormaps and used at the same time, even to the level of one colormap per window. Far more commonly, though, there is only one hardware colormap, and virtual colormaps have to be copied into the hardware colormap one at a time as needed. Copying a virtual colormap into the hardware colormap is called *installing* the colormap, and the reverse process where the default colormap is installed is called *uninstalling*. The window manager is responsible for installing and uninstalling colormaps.

If your application has standard color needs (decoration only), then you do not have to worry about the effects of colormaps being installed and uninstalled. Your application should use the standard XmRString to XmRPixel converter to translate color names into pixel values. If the colormap is full, or becomes full at any of the color allocations in the converter, the warning messages place the burden on the user to kill some applications in order to free some colormap cells. (If the converter cannot allocate the desired color, it prints a warning message, and the default for that resource is used. If the default is not XtDefault-Foreground or XtDefaultBackground, it also must be converted and this may also fail. If both allocations fail, the color will default to black. If this is not acceptable, then you will need to write your own type converter.)

If your application absolutely requires accurate colors, a certain number of distinguishable colors, or dynamically changeable colors, you will need to write your own converter to allocate colors. For example, if a color allocation for a known correct color name string fails, it means that all the colormap entries have already been allocated and no entry for that color is available. In this case, your converter might call the Xlib call XCopyColormapAndFree to copy the allocations your application has already made into a new colormap. Then the converter would allocate the color (and all subsequent colors) from the new colormap.

See Chapter 7, *Color*, in Volume One, *Xlib Programming Manual*, for details of various color allocation techniques.

The window manager is responsible for installing and uninstalling colormaps according to its own policy. Typically, the policy is to install the colormap of the application that has the keyboard focus or that contains the pointer. When an application has created a new colormap on a system that supports only one hardware colormap, and that colormap is installed, all applications that were using the other colormap will be displayed using the new colormap. Since the pixel values from the old colormap have not been allocated in the new colormap, all applications that use the old colormap will be displayed with false colors. This is known as "going technicolor."

The window manager may also create standard colormaps to facilitate the sharing of colors between applications. A standard colormap is a colormap allocated with a publicly known arrangement of colors. The Xlib routine XGetStandardColormap allows an application to determine whether the window manager has created a specific standard colormap, and it gets a structure describing the colormap. Xmu provides numerous utilities for creating and using standard colormaps—see Volumes One and Two for a description.

If your application requires more than one colormap, each installed at the same time in a different window, you need to tell the window manager about this so that these colormaps can be properly installed when the application is active. You do this by calling XtSet-WMColormapWindows, specifying the ApplicationShell widget as the first argument, a list of widgets that need certain colormaps as the second argument, and the length of the list as the third argument. This instructs the window manager to read the colormap window attribute of each of the listed widgets, and to install that colormap in each widget (if possible) whenever the application is active. (Of course, any application that depends on the existence of multiple simultaneous colormaps is doomed to run on only a small percentage of existing systems.)

The `colormap` window attribute of a window is an unchangeable characteristic of that window, that is assigned when the window is created (when the widget is realized). The Core `realize` method sets it based on the `XmNcolormap` Core resource of the widget. Therefore, if a widget must have a certain colormap, you must set its `XmNcolormap` resource *while creating the widget*. Attempting to set `XmNcolormap` after a widget is created will have no effect on its colormap window attribute.

11.1.6 Icons

The window manager always manages the icons for each application. Depending on the window manager, these icons may simply contain a text string called the icon name, or they may contain a pattern that identifies the application, called the icon pixmap.

Figure 11-1 shows the icon, under the *uwm* window manager, for an application with a custom icon pixmap (*xcalc*) and for one without (*xterm*).

Figure 11-1. An icon with and without an icon pixmap

An application may supply an icon name by setting the `XmNiconName` resource; if it does not, the window manager will usually use the application name or the value of the `XmNtitle` resource.

The application should supply the pattern for the icon, in the form of a single-plane pixmap, as the `XmNiconPixmap` resource. There are two basic ways to do this: one is by including bitmap data, and the other is by reading it in at run time. The former is easy to do with an Xlib call; the code that needs to be added is shown in Example 11-2. The latter technique, because it involves building a filename and looking in a number of locations for the file, is better done with a converter defined by the Xmu library. This converter technique is more complicated because the converter has to be registered and called with the proper arguments. The example using a converter is provided in the example source code for this book (*xicon2*), but is not shown here. See Chapter 10, *Resource Management and Type Conversion*, for more information on invoking converters.

Example 11-2. Creating an icon pixmap, and setting XmNiconPixmap

```
        .
        .
        .
/*
 * The following needed if not using Motif:
 *   #include <X11/Shell.h>
 */

#include "icon"

main(argc, argv)
int argc;
char **argv;
{
    Pixmap icon_pixmap;
        .
        .
        .
    /* create topLevel here */

    icon_pixmap = XCreateBitmapFromData(XtDisplay(topLevel),
            RootWindowOfScreen(XtScreen(topLevel)),
            icon_bits,
            icon_width, icon_height );

    XtVaSetValues(topLevel, XmNiconPixmap, icon_pixmap, NULL);
        .
        .
        .
    /* realize widgets */
}
```

The included file, *icon*, is in standard X11 bitmap file format. You can create such a file using the *bitmap* application from the standard distribution, or *xbitmap5* from the examples for this book.

The window manager may have a preferred standard size for icons. If so, it will set a property. The application can read this property with the Xlib call XGetIconSizes. To fully support a variety of window managers, an application should be capable of creating icon pixmaps of different sizes, depending on the values returned by XGetIconSizes.

An application has the option of creating its own icon window, and then passing its ID to the window manager for management. This might be done so that the application can draw a multi-colored picture in the icon, instead of the traditional two-color bitmap, or animate the icon. However, as with all hints, the window manager is not guaranteed to honor your desires and may just ignore the icon window you provide. But if you want to try anyway, create the window using Xlib calls, and select input on it so that your application receives Expose events when they occur. Then set the ID of the window using the XmNiconWindow resource, before realizing the application. Then make sure your event loop redraws the icon when it receives Expose events on it. Accomplishing this will require writing your own modified version of XtAppMainLoop to handle the icon events.

11.1.7 Window Manager Decorations

Virtually all current window managers decorate windows on the screen.* These decorations typically include a title bar for the window with gizmos for moving and resizing the window. Current decorating window managers include *twm*, *awm*, *mwm*, *olwm*, and *gwm*.

The way these decorations are implemented can have an impact on Toolkit applications. The window manager places the decorations in a window slightly bigger than the application, and then *reparents* the application's top-level window into the decoration window. Reparenting gives the top-level window a new parent instead of the root window. The window manager actually creates the frame window as a child of the root window, then reparents the application's top-level window into the frame, and then maps the frame window.

Reparenting affects the application mainly when you try to determine a global position (relative to the root window) from the XmNx and XmNy resources of the Shell widget. This is usually done in order to place popups. Under a nonreparenting window manager such as *uwm*, these coordinates are indeed relative to the root window, because the parent of the shell is the root window. However, under a window manager that reparents, the coordinates of the application's main Shell widget are relative to the decoration window, not the root window. Therefore, these coordinates cannot be used for placing popups within the application. Motif's internal code that places a popup uses XtTranslateCoords instead of relying on the position resources.

11.1.8 Interacting With the Motif Window Manager

The application and *mwm* can communicate back and forth through properties stored on the server. The properties are associated with the top-level window of your application, so unlike selections, similar communications can be going on at the same time between different clients and the window manager without interference. The ICCCM, *Inter-Client Communication Conventions Manual*, defines a starting point for what information can be sent back and forth.† *mwm* also defines some other information it is willing to send and receive.

All Shell widgets handle the required communication with the window manager; this section concerns optional communication. Note that applications should not depend on this type of communication. An application may run under a different window manager that doesn't listen to this type of message. Furthermore, an application is not required to use this type of communication, because *mwm* runs fine without it. This type of communication is just icing on the cake. (If you want to know whether *mwm* is running anyway, use the XmIsMotifWMRunning function.)

The next three sections describe the two major groups of protocols and a set of supplementary window manager hints. The first protocol group is defined by the ICCCM, and the second by Motif. You must include the header file *<X11/Protocols.h>* to use any of these features.

---

*The *uwm* window manager doesn't decorate, but it is defunct as of R4 since it doesn't honor the current ICCCM.
†The ICCCM is reprinted as an appendix of Volume Zero, *X Protocol Reference Manual*.

Before you can use these features, you must also prepare the required atoms. The type `Atom` is an ID for the string name for a property. All applications know the name of the property they will use for communication (such as WM_PROTOCOLS), but they don't know the ID for it since it changes each time the server is run. You can get the Atom for a property name by calling `XmInternAtom`. This is called *interning* the atom. All the fully capitalized words used in this section are property names, and must be interned before use.

Both of the following sets of protocols work in the same way. You indicate interest in participating in one or more of them by calling `XmAddProtocols`. Then you register a function, using `XmAddProtocolCallback`, to be called when the window manager sends you a message on a particular protocol. Of course, it is possible to resign from any of the protocols whenever you want.

11.1.8.1 WM_PROTOCOLS

The WM_PROTOCOLS are messages sent to your application from the window manager that notify you of conditions requiring immediate action. There are currently three protocols defined in the ICCCM, but the list may expand.

WM_DELETE_WINDOW indicates that the user has just requested that one of your application's windows be destroyed. Your application should respond by destroying that window if possible without exiting. The idea behind this protocol is that some applications have multiple top-level windows, and if the window manager were simply to delete one without the application's cooperation, the application might not be able to recover. (You should participate in this protocol if you have multiple top-level windows.)

WM_SAVE_YOURSELF indicates that the user has just requested that your application be killed. You should save all data immediately in preparation. This should execute code equivalent to the code you have implemented for your application's quit feature, except that it does everything except exit. (You should participate in this protocol if you have data that could be lost by exiting abnormally.)

WM_TAKE_FOCUS indicates that your application has been given the keyboard focus. You would participate in this protocol if you wanted the keyboard focus to always start in one of your subwindows, instead of your main window.

11.1.8.2 _MOTIF_WM_MESSAGES

The user can configure *mwm*, using an *.mwmrc* file, to add one or more buttons to its system menu and then call your application when any of these buttons are pressed. (If you want this feature in your application, though, you'll have to provide the proper text to be added to the user's *.mwmrc*.)

You indicate interest in this protocol by calling `XmAddProtocols` with the atom for _MOTIF_WM_MESSAGES. The leading underscore is intentional; it indicates a property not defined in the ICCCM. When the user presses one of the system menu buttons, your application receives notification in the form of an `ClientMessage` event. Motif will automatically dispatch this `ClientMessage` event to a function, if you have registered one using `XmAddProtocolCallback`.

The _MOTIF_WM_HINTS property is used in the opposite direction from the protocols described above. It is specified by the application and used by *mwm* if *mwm* is running. The property contains three hints about how the application would like to be treated: `decorations`, `functions`, and `input_mode`.

The value specified in the `decorations` field is combined (using AND) with the setting of the `XmNclientDecoration` shell resource. You can specify whether your application should have a border, resize button, title, window menu button, minimize button, or maximize button.

The `functions` field controls whether functions selected from *mwm* menus (that appear on the root window) should operate on your application. These operations consist of resizing, moving, minimizing, maximizing, and closing (exiting).

The `input_mode` field advises *mwm* to use various obscure focus management conventions when dealing with your application.

Note that *mwm* sets the _MOTIF_WM_INFO property on your application's main top-level shell. This property contains information about whether the *mwm* that is running has been customized (using *.mwmrc*) or if it is standard.

11.2   Selections: Widget-to-Widget Communication

Selections are a general mechanism for communicating information between two clients of the same server. The most familiar example of selections is selecting text from one *xterm* application and pasting it into another. This text can also be pasted into an *xmh* mail composition window, or into an *xedit* application.

In Xt applications, selection is normally implemented within widgets. For example, the Athena Text widget is used by *xmh* and *xedit*, and it is this widget that supports cutting and pasting of text in these applications. The application code of *xmh* and *xedit* does not play a part in the communication of selection data. The fact that selection is implemented in widgets also means that two widgets within the same application can communicate with each other through selections. For example, the Text widget is sometimes used to provide single-line input fields in an application. Since the Text widget supports selections, the user could select the text in one field and paste it into another field. This feature would be present without any code in the application. If the same widget class supports both copying and pasting, selections can be used to move data in a single widget. For example, selections allow you to copy text within an editor in *xterm* and paste the text in a new place (although some editors require keyboard commands to position the insertion point).

Motif provides a high-level interface to the selection mechanism that allows Motif applications or widgets to easily transfer data. See Section 11.3 for a description of this interface. The basic selection mechanism described in this section is valid for all widget sets, not just Motif.

The selection mechanism is not limited to text. It requires only that the sender and recipient have knowledge of the format of the data being transferred. Therefore, selections can be used to transfer graphics between widgets that can understand a common format for communicating graphics. Unfortunately, a standard format for graphics selections has not yet been agreed upon.

The selection mechanism uses properties for transferring data and uses the `Selection-Clear`, `SelectionNotify`, and `SelectionRequest` event types to synchronize the communication. Essentially, a property is common storage. Properties are stored in the server, and are named pieces of data associated with a window on that particular server, that any client of that server can read or write. Because the various clients may not be running on the same host, all communication between applications and between applications and the window manager must take place through the server using properties.*

The basic routines used to implement selections are part of Xlib. Xt provides an interface to the Xlib selection routines that makes selections easier to use in the context of widget code. Since there is a maximum size for the data stored in a single property, communication of large blocks of data using Xlib requires several partial transfers. Xt supplies routines that transparently perform the multiple partial transfers so that they appear to the application program like a single transfer, called an *atomic* transfer.

Xt also supplies a separate set of parallel routines that transfer a large selection one chunk at a time so that it appears as multiple small selections. This is called an *incremental* transfer. Incremental transfer can be preferable on systems with limited memory and more natural when the data is normally stored in small chunks.

The Toolkit selection routines also have built-in timeouts, so that one application won't wait forever for another to provide data.

First we'll give you an overview of how an atomic selection transaction works, and then we'll discuss and demonstrate how to write the code to implement atomic selections in a widget. Following this is a discussion of how incremental selections work, and finally a discussion of the standard selection formats (known as target types).

If you are writing a custom widget that contains data that could be pasted into other instances of the widget or other widgets, you should read on to see how to implement selections. Otherwise, the rest of this chapter is probably only of academic interest to you.

---

*It is not practical to write your own networking routines in an application to communicate with other clients running on different hosts because your client may be communicating with the server using TCP/IP, and the other client may be using DECnet. Both may be the same X application that you wrote, but compiled with a version of Xlib that uses a different protocol layer underneath the X Protocol. When you communicate through the server using properties, the server takes care of the translation.

11.2.1 How Atomic Selection Works

Selections communicate between an *owner* widget and a *requestor* widget.* The owner has the data and the requestor wants it. The owner is the widget in which the user has selected something, and the requestor is the widget in which the user has clicked to paste that something. Many widgets need to act as both owner and requester at different times. The code to handle each of the two roles is separate.

Here is a brief overview of the steps that take place during a single transfer of data from one widget to another. We'll assume we have two instances of the same widget class, which can operate either as the owner or the requestor. Initially, both widgets are in exactly the same state, neither having any text selected, and neither being the owner or requestor. We'll also assume that selections are implemented using actions tied to pointer buttons, as in existing widgets that use selections.

- The user selects an item in Widget *A*, and the widget highlights the item. An action, typically called in response to a `<Btn1Down>` translation, marks the start of a selection. A subsequent `<Btn1Motion>` event (that is, a motion event with button 1 held down) invokes another action to extend the highlighted selection.

- A `<Btn1Up>` event invokes a third action in Widget *A* that actually makes the selection. The action calls `XtOwnSelection` to claim ownership of the PRIMARY selection for Widget *A*. This means that Widget *A* claims the sole right to use the `XA_PRIMARY` property for communication with other widgets, until some other widget claims ownership. (More about `XA_PRIMARY` below.) The call to `XtOwnSelection` also registers three procedures, to be called by Xt in response to selection events. The *lose_ownership_proc* handles the case where Widget *A* loses the selection (because the user has made another selection elsewhere), the *convert_proc* converts the data in the selection to the target property type requested by Widget *B* (see below), and the optional *transfer_done_proc* prepares for the next selection request, if necessary (this function is often `NULL`).

- The user pastes the item into Widget *B*, usually by clicking a pointer button. (By convention, a translation for `<Btn2Down>` invokes the action to do this.)

- The paste action in Widget *B* requests the value of the current selection by calling `XtGetSelectionValue`; this specifies a *target* type, and a *requestor_callback* that will be invoked to actually paste the data when Widget *A* reports that the conversion has been successfully completed.

- The `XtGetSelectionValue` call by Widget *B* also generates a `SelectionRequest` event. In response to this event, Xt invokes the *convert_proc* registered by the call to `XtOwnSelection` in Widget *A*.

- The *convert_proc* in Widget *A* converts the selected item into the appropriate data type for the target property specified by *B*, if possible. The converted data is stored in the `XA_PRIMARY` property.

---

*Note that since selections can be implemented in the application, as they are by non-Xt applications, the words "application" and "widget" are interchangeable in this section.

- Based on the return values from Widget *A*'s conversion procedure, Xt sends a `SelectionNotify` event to inform Widget *B* whether or not the data was successfully converted.

- The `requestor_callback` registered in Widget *B* reads the data from the property and displays it, or if Widget *A* reported that the conversion could not be made, Widget *B* beeps or otherwise indicates that the kind of data selected in Widget *A* cannot be pasted in Widget *B*, or that the kind of data requested by *B* cannot be supplied by *A*.

- Xt notifies Widget *A* that the selection has been transferred, so that the widget's `transfer_done_proc` can disown the selection if the selection is of a kind that can be transferred only once.

Figure 11-2 shows this procedure in graphic form.

The code to implement selections is divided logically into a number of functions within the widget. The next sections show the code necessary to implement both the owner and the requestor roles. The code for each role is separate and cannot share any widget variables with the other role because the transaction may be between two different widget instances.

As an example, we will add support for selections to the BitmapEdit widget described in Chapter 6, *Inside a Widget*, and Chapter 7, *Basic Widget Methods*. Little of the existing code in that widget needs to be changed. The examples show only the code added to implement selections, and describe where to add it.

We will start with the owner role, and then proceed to the requestor role, and then back to the owner role.

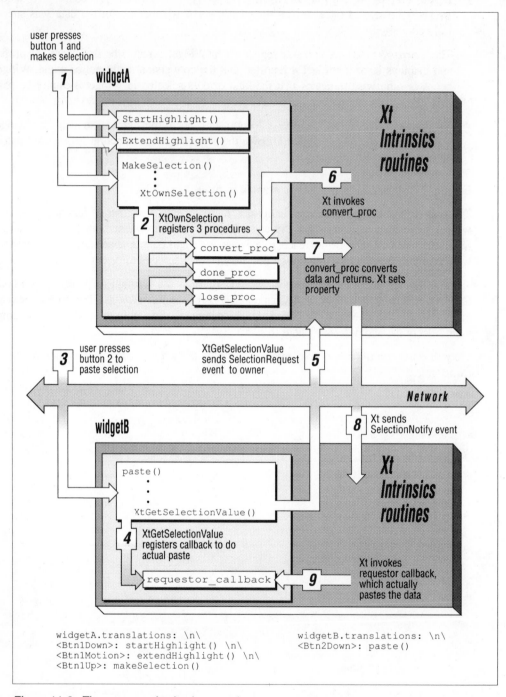

Figure 11-2. The process of selection transfer

11.2.2 Highlighting the Selected Data (Owner)

The selection process begins when the user selects some text in Widget *A*. The widget code for the owner role must contain some code to identify the area or items selected and to highlight the text (or whatever) being selected. This user-interface portion of the owner role is carried out by actions added to the widget. Some event sequences that are not already in use must be mapped to these actions. In existing applications that support selections of text:

- A press of the first pointer button pins a starting point of the selection, dragging the first button extends and highlights the selection, and releasing the first button ends the selection. A subsequent press of the first button starts a new selection, unhighlighting the old one.

- A press of the second button pastes the selection.

- A button press or motion with the third button depressed repositions either end of the selected area.

It is a good idea to stick with existing conventions for the user interface of highlighting a selection, so that your application will operate in a familiar way. But since BitmapEdit already uses all three pointer buttons, unmodified, to set, unset, and toggle bitmap cells, we cannot use unmodified button presses to control selections. But we can (and will) use these same buttons modified by Shift.

A selection in BitmapEdit is any rectangular set of bitmap cells. Accordingly, BitmapEdit will use `Shift<Btn1Down>` to set the top-left corner of a selection rectangle, `Shift<Btn1Motion>` to follow dragging, and `Shift<Btn1Up>` to set the bottom right corner.* Each of these events will invoke a separate action routine, `StartHighlight`, `ExtendHighlight`, and `MakeSelection`, respectively. These translations are added to the widget's default translation table, and the actions are added to the actions table. Example 11-3 shows the action table, the translation table, and the three action routines.

Example 11-3. BitmapEdit: actions that highlight selection

```
static char defaultTranslations[] =
        "Shift<Btn1Down>:     StartHighlight()     \n\
        Shift<Btn1Motion>:   ExtendHighlight()    \n\
        Shift<Btn1Up>:       MakeSelection()      \n\
        Shift<Btn2Down>:     PasteSelection()     \n\
        ˜Shift<Btn1Down>:    DoCell()             \n\
        ˜Shift<Btn2Down>:    UndoCell()           \n\
        ˜Shift<Btn3Down>:    ToggleCell()         \n\
        ˜Shift<Btn1Motion>:  DoCell()             \n\
        ˜Shift<Btn2Motion>:  UndoCell()           \n\
        ˜Shift<Btn3Motion>:  ToggleCell()";
static XtActionsRec actions[] = {
    {"DoCell", DoCell},
    {"UndoCell", UndoCell},
    {"ToggleCell", ToggleCell},
```

---

*For simplicity, we won't copy the third button semantics used in text selections. This could easily be added.

Example 11-3. BitmapEdit: actions that highlight selection (continued)

```
    {"StartHighlight", StartHighlight},
    {"ExtendHighlight", ExtendHighlight},
    {"MakeSelection", MakeSelection},
    {"PasteSelection", PasteSelection},
};
      .
      .
      .
/*
 *  User presses first button (by default), starting highlighting.
 */
static void
StartHighlight(w, event)
Widget w;
XButtonEvent *event;
{
    BitmapEditWidget cw = (BitmapEditWidget) w;
    cw->bitmapEdit.first_box = False;

    cw->bitmapEdit.select_start_x = (cw->bitmapEdit.cur_x + event->x)
            / cw->bitmapEdit.cell_size_in_pixels;
    cw->bitmapEdit.select_start_y = (cw->bitmapEdit.cur_y + event->y)
            / cw->bitmapEdit.cell_size_in_pixels;

    /* clear old selection */
    Redisplay(cw, NULL);
}

/*
 * MakeSelection is call when the first button is released (by
 * default).  This finishes the user's highlighting, and means
 * triggers ownership of the PRIMARY selection.
 */
static void
MakeSelection(w, event)
Widget w;
XButtonEvent *event;
{
    BitmapEditWidget cw = (BitmapEditWidget) w;
    int temp;

    cw->bitmapEdit.select_end_x = (cw->bitmapEdit.cur_x + event->x)
            / cw->bitmapEdit.cell_size_in_pixels;
    cw->bitmapEdit.select_end_y = (cw->bitmapEdit.cur_y + event->y)
            / cw->bitmapEdit.cell_size_in_pixels;

    if ((cw->bitmapEdit.select_end_x == cw->bitmapEdit.select_start_x)
            && (cw->bitmapEdit.select_end_y ==
            cw->bitmapEdit.select_start_y))   {
        Redisplay(cw, NULL);
        return; /* no selection */
    }

    /* swap start and end if end is greater than start */
    if (cw->bitmapEdit.select_end_x < cw->bitmapEdit.select_start_x) {
        temp = cw->bitmapEdit.select_end_x;
        cw->bitmapEdit.select_end_x = cw->bitmapEdit.select_start_x;
        cw->bitmapEdit.select_start_x = temp;
```

Example 11-3. BitmapEdit: actions that highlight selection (continued)

```
        }

        if (cw->bitmapEdit.select_end_y
                < cw->bitmapEdit.select_start_y) {
            temp = cw->bitmapEdit.select_end_y;
            cw->bitmapEdit.select_end_y =
                    cw->bitmapEdit.select_start_y;
            cw->bitmapEdit.select_start_y = temp;
        }

        if (XtOwnSelection(cw, XA_PRIMARY, event->time, convert_proc,
                lose_ownership_proc, transfer_done_proc) ==
                False) {
            XtWarning("bitmapEdit: failed attempting to become
                    selection owner; make a new selection.\n");
            /* Clear old selection, because lose_ownership_proc
             * isn't registered. */
            Redisplay(cw, NULL);
        }
}

/*
 * ExtendHighlight is called when the mouse is being dragged with
 * the first button down (by default).  During this time, the
 * bitmap cells that are selected (by crosses) are dynamically
 * changed as the mouse moves.
 */
static void
ExtendHighlight(w, event)
Widget w;
XMotionEvent *event;
{
    BitmapEditWidget cw = (BitmapEditWidget) w;
    static int last_drawn_x, last_drawn_y;
    int event_cell_x, event_cell_y;

    event_cell_x = cw->bitmapEdit.cur_x + (event->x /
            cw->bitmapEdit.cell_size_in_pixels);
    event_cell_y = cw->bitmapEdit.cur_y + (event->y /
            cw->bitmapEdit.cell_size_in_pixels);

    if ((event_cell_x == last_drawn_x) && (event_cell_y ==
            last_drawn_y))
        return;

    if (cw->bitmapEdit.first_box) {
        DrawBoxOfXs(cw, last_drawn_x, last_drawn_y, False);
        DrawBoxOfXs(cw, event_cell_x, event_cell_y, True);
    }
    else {
        DrawBoxOfXs(cw, event_cell_x, event_cell_y, True);
        cw->bitmapEdit.first_box = True;
    }

    last_drawn_x = event_cell_x;
    last_drawn_y = event_cell_y;
}
/*
```

Example 11-3. BitmapEdit: actions that highlight selection (continued)

```
 *    DrawBoxOfXs fills a rectangular set of bitmap cells with
 *    crosses, or erases them.
 */
static void
DrawBoxOfXs(w, x, y, draw)
Widget w;
Position x, y;
Bool draw;
{
    BitmapEditWidget cw = (BitmapEditWidget) w;
    Position start_pos_x, start_pos_y;
    Dimension width, height;
    GC gc;
    int i, j;

    start_pos_x = cw->bitmapEdit.cur_x +
            cw->bitmapEdit.select_start_x;
    start_pos_y = cw->bitmapEdit.cur_x +
            cw->bitmapEdit.select_start_y;

    /* swap start and end if end is greater than start */
    if (x < start_pos_x) {
        width = start_pos_x - x;
        start_pos_x = x;
    }
    else {
        width = x - start_pos_x;
    }

    if (y < start_pos_y) {
        height = start_pos_y - y;
        start_pos_y = y;
    }
    else {
        height = y - start_pos_y;
    }

    for (i=start_pos_x;i < start_pos_x + width;i++)
        for (j=start_pos_y;j < start_pos_y + height;j++)
            DrawX(cw, i, j, draw);
}
/*
 * DrawX draws an X in a bitmap cell, in white if a black cell, and
 * in black if a white cell.
 */
DrawX(cw, x, y, draw)
BitmapEditWidget cw;
Position x, y;
Bool draw;
{
    GC gc;
    if (cw->bitmapEdit.cell[x + y *
            cw->bitmapEdit.pixmap_width_in_cells] == DRAWN)
        if (draw)
            gc = cw->bitmapEdit.deep_undraw_gc;
        else
            gc = cw->bitmapEdit.deep_draw_gc;
```

Example 11-3. BitmapEdit: actions that highlight selection (continued)

```
    else
       if (draw)
           gc = cw->bitmapEdit.deep_draw_gc;
       else
           gc = cw->bitmapEdit.deep_undraw_gc;
    XDrawLine(XtDisplay(cw), XtWindow(cw), gc,
           x * cw->bitmapEdit.cell_size_in_pixels,
           y * cw->bitmapEdit.cell_size_in_pixels,
           (x + 1) * cw->bitmapEdit.cell_size_in_pixels,
           (y + 1) * cw->bitmapEdit.cell_size_in_pixels);

    XDrawLine(XtDisplay(cw), XtWindow(cw), gc,
           x * cw->bitmapEdit.cell_size_in_pixels,
           (y + 1) * cw->bitmapEdit.cell_size_in_pixels,
           (x + 1) * cw->bitmapEdit.cell_size_in_pixels,
           y * cw->bitmapEdit.cell_size_in_pixels);
}
```

The actions shown in Example 11-3 reference some new instance part fields we have added to *BitmapEditP.h* to store the state of the selection. Four of these variables are the *x* and *y* coordinates in cells of the top-left and bottom-right corners of the highlighted area: `select_start_x`, `select_start_y`, `select_end_x`, and `select_end_y`. These coordinates will be used throughout the owner code. (Because these fields are in units of bitmap cells, not pixels, their type is `int` rather than `Position`.)

The `StartHighlight` action is quite simple. It sets the upper-left corner instance part fields based on the button press position in the triggering event. It also clears the highlighting of the old selection, if one exists, and sets a flag to indicate that this is the beginning of a new selection. The `first_box` flag is added as an instance part field because it will be needed in the `ExtendHighlight` action.

`ExtendHighlight` is responsible for drawing Xs dynamically on the selected cells, much as the window manager draws the outline of a window while it is being moved. Xs are drawn on each cell in a rectangle of bitmap cells beginning from the cell selected in the `Start-Highlight` action and ending at the cell the pointer button was released in. `Extend-Highlight` is triggered by pointer motion events that occur while the first button is held down. It calculates which bitmap cell the pointer is in, and if the cell is not the same as the cell the pointer was in the last time `ExtendHighlight` was called, it erases the previous Xs and draws new ones. This is done using two different GCs—one for drawing in black and the other in white, so the color that contrasts with the current state of each cell can be used. The black GC is also used to copy the main pixmap to the screen, and the latter is just for doing the highlighting.

Code was added to the `initialize` method to create this latter GC. (See the example code distribution for this modified widget instance structure.)

The `MakeSelection` action is triggered when the button is released after dragging, indicating that the selection is complete. This action sets the `select_end_x` and `select_end_y` instance part variables to reflect the bottom-right corner of the selection, and then swaps the top-left and bottom-right coordinates if the end coordinate is to the left or above the start coordinate. If the start and end coordinates are the same, then the action returns, since no selection was made. If a selection was made, `MakeSelection` calls `Xt-OwnSelection`.

11.2.3 Making the Selection with XtOwnSelection (Owner)

Once the area is highlighted, Widget *A* calls `XtOwnSelection` to assert that it wants the right to set the value of a property that will be used to transfer information.

`XtOwnSelection` is called with six arguments:

```
Boolean XtOwnSelection(widget, selection, time, convert_proc,
        lose_ownership_proc, transfer_done_proc)
    Widget widget;
    Atom selection;
    Time time;
    XtConvertSelectionProc convert_proc;
    XtLoseSelectionProc lose_ownership_proc;
    XtSelectionDoneProc transfer_done_proc;
```

The *selection* argument specifies an *Atom*—a number representing a property. Properties are arbitrarily named pieces of data stored on the server. To simplify communication with the server, a property is never referenced by name, but by a unique integer ID called an atom. Standard atoms are defined in *<Xatom.h>* using defined symbols beginning with `XA_`; nonstandard atoms can be obtained from the server by calling the Xlib function `Xt-InternAtom`.

Widgets that support one selection at a time pass the predefined `XA_PRIMARY` atom to `Xt-OwnSelection`. The ICCCM also allows you to use the `XA_SECONDARY` and `XA_CLIP-BOARD` atoms. `XA_SECONDARY` would be used by widgets implementing behavior involving more than one selection (for example, allowing the user to make two selections, and to exchange the data they contain). No current clients implement this behavior. The `XA_CLIP-BOARD` atom should be used by a widget that allows the user to delete a selection. We'll talk more about the properties referenced by the `XA_SECONDARY` and `XA_CLIPBOARD` atoms in Section 11.3.

The purpose of the `XtOwnSelection` call is to make sure that only one widget has the right to set the `XA_PRIMARY` selection property at a time, and to assert that this widget is prepared to honor requests for this data. Notice that when you select text with *xterm*, that text is highlighted only until you select a different area in a different window.

The next three arguments to `XtOwnSelection` specify procedures that will carry out essential parts of the selection operation:

- The *convert_proc* is responsible for converting the selected data into the representation requested by the requestor in its call to `XtGetSelectionValue`; this function is called by Xt when a `SelectionRequest` event arrives, as a result of the requestor calling `XtGetSelectionValue`. The *convert_proc* is of type `XtConvert-SelectionProc`.

- The *lose_ownership_proc* clears the highlighted area when this widget has lost the selection (because some other widget has taken it); this routine is called by Xt when a

SelectionClear event arrives. The *lose_ownership_proc* is of type Xt-LoseSelectionProc.

- The *transfer_done_proc* is called by Xt when the requestor has successfully retrieved the converted value. If this selection is intended to be erased after being transferred once, this function should free any storage allocated in the transfer. If, instead, the owner remains ready for pasting the same selection into other widgets, this function pointer should be NULL. (For example, *xterm* does not clear its selection after pasting once.) The *transfer_done_proc* is of type XtSelectionDoneProc.

The XtOwnSelection call also takes a *time* argument—this should be the time from the event that completed the highlighting, not the constant CurrentTime. If XtOwnSelection returns False, it means that because of network conditions another client has called XtOwnSelection with a more recent time argument.

XtOwnSelection returns True or False to indicate whether Widget *A* has been granted ownership. If True, and if this widget was not already the owner, then the old owner (if any) will receive a SelectionClear event and will clear its highlighted area. The process may end here if the user never pastes the selected data anywhere. If the user selects a different piece of data, the selection owner will receive a SelectionClear itself before ever having converted the data for a requestor.

Otherwise the owner code waits to hear from the requestor that it is ready to paste the selection.

11.2.4 Requesting the Selection (Requestor)

When the user pastes the selection into Widget *B*, Widget *B* becomes the requestor and the second part of the process begins. First of all, Widget *B* needs a translation that maps a certain key or button event to an action that pastes data. This action calls XtGetSelectionValue.

XtGetSelectionValue is called with six arguments:

```
void XtGetSelectionValue (widget, selection, target, callback,
    client_data, time)
Widget widget;
Atom selection;
Atom target;
XtSelectionCallbackProc callback;
XtPointer client_data;
Time time;
```

The *selection* argument is an atom specifying which property is being used to transfer the selection. This will typically be XA_PRIMARY, though in theory two widgets (or two instances of the same widget) could agree to transfer some particular data using other properties.

The *target* argument is another atom, this one specifying a target representation type in which the requestor wants the information. We'll talk more about the possible values for this atom in a moment.

The `callback` argument is a pointer to a callback procedure that actually pastes the data. Xt will call this procedure when the owner has converted the data. The `XtGet-SelectionValue` call registers the callback with Xt, and sends a `Selection-Request` event to the owner.

When the selection owner has successfully converted the data, the owner sends back a `SelectionNotify` event to Xt. Xt then calls the requestor's callback procedure. The callback procedure must handle the pasting of the data into the widget's data structures, and it must handle the case where the data could not be converted into the requested representation. We'll discuss the responsibilities of this procedure in more detail once we've seen the owner's conversion procedure.

The `client_data` argument of `XGetSelectionValue` is normally used to pass the event that triggered the pasting into the requestor callback. The callback will use the coordinates at which the event occurred as the location at which to paste the data.

As in the call to `XtOwnSelection`, the `time` argument should be the time from the event that initiated the pasting, not the constant `CurrentTime`.

11.2.4.1 Possible Target Type Atoms

The `target` argument to `XtGetSelectionValue` is an atom that the requestor uses to tell the owner what kind of information it is looking for from the selection.* This is not necessarily a conversion of the actual selection data. For example, it might be a timestamp on the data, or some characteristic of it, such as its size or font.

To take full advantage of the Xt selection mechanism, you need to understand what atoms can be used as selection targets. However, apart from some standard, predefined atoms, the atom for a property is not known by a client until it queries the server for the atom using an `XInternAtom` call. This call specifies the string name of the property and returns the atom.

Some atoms needed by almost all applications are predefined in the header file *<X11/Xatom.h>*. These atoms are symbolic constants that can be used without an `XInternAtom` call. The constants always start with the prefix `XA_`. See *<X11/Xatom.h>* for the complete list of predefined atoms.

Note that many of the predefined atoms have uses in X other than as target types, and not all are appropriate as selection targets. A few of those that might be useful as targets include:

```
XA_STRING
XA_INTEGER
XA_BITMAP
```

At present, the Athena widgets and the clients in the MIT core X distribution use only `XA_STRING` as a target. However, one can imagine uses for other targets as well. For example, `XA_FONT` might be used as a target to indicate that the requestor doesn't want the text of a selection, but wants only to know its font. `XA_TIMESTAMP` might be used to indicate that the requestor wants a timestamp for the data. Once the

---

*As described earlier, atoms (rather than strings) are always used in network transmissions to identify properties.

XtGetSelectionValue request is made, a SelectionRequest event is generated, which Xt uses to invoke the owner widget's *convert_proc*. The *convert_proc* will need to branch according to the target type passed in by the requestor through Xt, and convert the data accordingly before transferring the selection to the requestor.

For selection of multiple data types to work correctly between any two arbitrarily chosen widgets, there must be conventions about which targets will be supported. As a step in the direction of interwidget selection compatibility, the ICCCM specifies a required target type of XA_TARGETS, to which the owner is supposed to respond by returning a list of the target types into which it is capable of converting data. We'll talk about how to work with this target in Section 11.2.9.

In a custom widget such as BitmapEdit, which has a custom data type not represented by a predefined atom, it is possible to obtain a custom atom using XInternAtom, and use that as the target. Because the XInternAtom call requires a round trip to the server, the best place to do this is in the widget's initialize method.* The returned atom can be stored in a field added to the widget's instance part. BitmapEdit's target type, "CELL_ARRAY," is unique to BitmapEdit. The atom is stored in an instance part field called target so that it is available in *convert_proc* and in the requestor role code. Example 11-4 shows the code added to the initialize method to get an atom for the string "CELL_ARRAY."

Example 11-4. BitmapEdit: getting the atom for a widget-specific target type

```
/* ARGSUSED */
static void
Initialize(request, new)
BitmapEditWidget request, new;
{
        .
        .
        .

    new->bitmapEdit.target_atom = XInternAtom(XtDisplay(new),
            "CELL_ARRAY," False);
```

The target type property name used by BitmapEdit is "CELL_ARRAY."

The third argument to XInternAtom is a Boolean that indicates what to do if the atom doesn't already exist. If this argument is True, XInternAtom will return None if no other client has already initialized this atom. This argument should always be False since your widget might be the first to try to make a selection using this target type atom. In a Motif application, one could use XmInternAtom instead of XInternAtom.

Note that for repeated calls to XInternAtom with the same string as an argument, even from different widgets, the returned atom will be the same. There will be only one atom created for any unique string interned on a given server. (Case is important: "Cell_Array" would return a different atom than "CELL_ARRAY".)

---

*Since Xlib functions causing round-trip requests can impact performance, they should be called only once if possible, and where possible, during the set-up phase of the application as opposed to the event-loop phase. If XInternAtom were called every time the user made a selection, it would slow the application. In addition, since atoms are server resources that are not freed until the server shuts down, it is important to use predefined atoms whenever possible.

This `XInternAtom` call occurs in every instance of the BitmapEdit widget, since all instances need to know the atom to participate in selections using that target type. Both the owner and requestor widgets, in separate applications, will get the same atom in return.

11.2.4.2 The Paste Action from BitmapEdit

To initiate the requestor role, you need to assign an event sequence to trigger the pasting, write an action that calls `XtGetSelectionValue`, and write a callback function that inserts the returned data.

Traditionally, the action to paste data is triggered by a press of the second pointer button. BitmapEdit will use the shifted second button since it uses the unshifted button for other purposes. Example 11-5 shows the action mapped to `Shift<Btn2Down>`.

Example 11-5. BitmapEdit: action to paste a selection

```
static void
PasteSelection(w, event)
Widget w;
XButtonEvent *event;
{
    BitmapEditWidget cw = (BitmapEditWidget) w;
    XtGetSelectionValue(cw, XA_PRIMARY, cw->bitmapEdit.target_atom,
            requestor_callback, event,
            event->time);
}
```

This action can be dropped verbatim into your widget, replacing only the widget name and the name of the instance fields you are using to store the target atom.

11.2.5 Converting the Selection (Owner)

The real challenge in handling selections is writing the *convert_proc*, which converts data to the format specified by the requestor and prepares it for transfer.

As mentioned above, the widget's *convert_proc* is called by Xt when the requestor calls `XtGetSelectionValue`. The procedure is passed the selection atom and the target atom, and is expected to return in its arguments the type, value, size, and format of the converted selection data.

To support the possibility of having to convert the data to any one of several targets, the code branches according to the value of the target passed in, and does its conversions accordingly. In the version of BitmapEdit's *convert_proc* shown here, only one target type is handled. Section 11.2.9.2 describes how to add more target types, including some that are required by the ICCCM such as TARGETS.

Once the conversion is made, the procedure sets the *value_return* argument passed in to a pointer to a block of memory, and *length_return* to the size of the block. This block of memory will be set into a property by Xt and passed to the requestor's callback in the same form—as a pointer to a block of memory and a length. This puts constraints on the formats that can be used for the data.

For text selections, the data is usually a simple character string. The `convert_proc` simply needs to set `*value_return` to a pointer to the string, and `length_return` to the length of the string. For BitmapEdit, however, the required data is a string (of bitmap cell states) *plus* width and height values. Since C provides easy ways to put numeric values into strings and to get them out again at the other end, we've chosen to handle this data by converting the numbers to characters and tacking them on to the beginning of the string.

If your selection is composed of a number of numeric values, you can create a structure containing the values and then pass a pointer to the structure. However, the structure cannot contain pointers, because the data pointed to by these pointers will not be set into the selection property. For example, BitmapEdit cannot pass a pointer to a structure containing a string pointer field and width and height fields because the block of memory pointed to by the string pointer will not be copied.

In this case, the `type_return` can simply be the target atom that was passed in, indicating that the data is of the requested type.

The `format_return` is the size in bits of each element in the array. Since we are passing a compound string, this value is 8. If we were passing a structure, `length_return` would be 1 and `*format_return` would be 8 times the size of the structure in bytes.

Example 11-6 shows BitmapEdit's `convert_proc`.

Example 11-6. BitmapEdit: converting the selection value

```
static Boolean
convert_proc(w, selection, target, type_return, value_return,
        length_return, format_return)
Widget w;
Atom *selection;
Atom *target;
Atom *type_return;
XtPointer *value_return;
unsigned long *length_return;
int *format_return;
{
    BitmapEditWidget cw = (BitmapEditWidget) w;
    int x, y;
    int width, height;

    /* handle all required atoms, and the one that we use */
    /* Xt already handles MULTIPLE, no branch necessary */
    if (*target == XA_TARGETS(XtDisplay(cw))) {
        /* Required atom: see Example 10-10 */
            .
            .
            .
    }
    else if (*target == cw->bitmapEdit.target_atom) {
        char *data;

        width = cw->bitmapEdit.select_end_x -
                cw->bitmapEdit.select_start_x;
        height = cw->bitmapEdit.select_end_y -
                cw->bitmapEdit.select_start_y;

                /* 8 chars is enough for two 3-digit
```

Example 11-6. BitmapEdit: converting the selection value (continued)

```
                    * numbers and two delimiters */
        *length_return = ((width * height) + 8) * sizeof(char);

        data = XtMalloc(*length_return);

        sprintf(data, "%d@%d~", width, height);

        for (x = 0; x < width; x++) {
            for (y = 0; y < height; y++) {
                data[8 + x + (y * width)] = cw->bitmapEdit.cell[(x +
                    cw->bitmapEdit.select_start_x) +
                    ((y + cw->bitmapEdit.select_start_y) *
                    cw->bitmapEdit.pixmap_width_in_cells)];
            }
        }

        *value_return = data;

        *type_return = cw->bitmapEdit.target_atom;

        *format_return = 8;   /* number of bits in char */
        return(True);
    }
    else {
        /* code to handle standard selections: see Example 10-10 */
            .
            .
            .
    }
}
```

This code determines the width and height of the selected rectangle from the instance part fields, and then allocates enough memory to fit a character array big enough to fit the width and height values, delimiters, and a width by height character array. Then it copies the current contents of the selected area into the allocated character array. Finally, it sets `*value_return` to point to the compound string, and sets `*length_return` to the length of this string. `*format_return` is the size in bits of each element in the array, which in this case is 8 bits.

11.2.6 Finally Pasting the Selection (Requestor)

When the owner's *convert_proc* returns, Xt sends a SelectionNotify event to the requestor. The Xt code on the requestor side then invokes the callback routine the requestor registered with the call to XtGetSelectionValue.

The *requestor_callback* function is passed all the same arguments that the owner received in the *convert_proc*, plus the values that the owner returned through the argument of *convert_proc*. In the BitmapEdit widget, it sets instance part fields to paste the data.

Example 11-7 shows the requestor callback function from BitmapEdit.

Example 11-7. BitmapEdit: pasting selection in requestor_callback function

```
/* ARGSUSED */
static void
requestor_callback(w,client_data,selection,type,value,length,format)
Widget w;
XtPointer client_data;  /* cast to XButtonEvent below */
Atom *selection;
Atom *type;
XtPointer value;
unsigned long *length;
int *format;
{
    BitmapEditWidget cw = (BitmapEditWidget) w;
    if ((*value == NULL) && (*length == 0)) {
        XBell(XtDisplay(cw), 100);
        XtWarning("bitmapEdit: no selection or selection timed out:\
                try again\n");
    }
    else {
        XButtonEvent *event = (XButtonEvent *) client_data;
        int width, height;
        int x, y;
        int dst_offset_x, dst_offset_y;
        char *ptr;

        dst_offset_x = (cw->bitmapEdit.cur_x + event->x) /
                cw->bitmapEdit.cell_size_in_pixels;
        dst_offset_y = (cw->bitmapEdit.cur_y + event->y) /
                cw->bitmapEdit.cell_size_in_pixels;

        printf("dst offset is %d, %d\n", dst_offset_x, dst_offset_y);

        ptr = (char *) value;
        width = atoi(ptr);
        ptr = index(ptr, '@');
        ptr++;
        height = atoi(ptr);
        ptr = &value[8];

        for (x = 0; x < width; x++) {
            for (y = 0; y < height; y++) {
                /* range checking */
                if (((dst_offset_x + x) >
                        cw->bitmapEdit.pixmap_width_in_cells)
                        || ((dst_offset_x + x) < 0))
                    break;
                if (((dst_offset_y + y) >
                        cw->bitmapEdit.pixmap_height_in_cells)
                        || ((dst_offset_y + y) < 0))
                    break;
                cw->bitmapEdit.cell[(dst_offset_x + x)
                        + ((dst_offset_y + y) *
                        cw->bitmapEdit.pixmap_width_in_cells)]
                        = ptr[x + (y * width)];
                if (cw->bitmapEdit.cell[(dst_offset_x + x)
                        + ((dst_offset_y + y) *
                        cw->bitmapEdit.pixmap_width_in_cells)]
                        == DRAWN)
```

```
                    DrawCell(cw, dst_offset_x + x,
                             dst_offset_y + y,
                             cw->bitmapEdit.draw_gc);
              else
                    DrawCell(cw, dst_offset_x + x,
                             dst_offset_y + y,
                             cw->bitmapEdit.undraw_gc);
          }
      }
      /* Regardless of the presence of a
       * transfer_done_proc in the owner,
       * the requestor must free the data passed by
       * Xt after using it. */
      XtFree(value);
      Redisplay(cw, NULL);
    }
}
```

The *requestor_callback* first determines whether the conversion was a success by checking the value and data length. If it was not, it beeps and prints a message. This can happen if no selection has been made, or if there is some delay that causes the selection to have timed out before the owner could convert the data.

If the conversion was a success, the *requestor_callback* pastes the data. In Bitmap-Edit's case, the requestor must first convert the data into a more useful form. This means extracting the width and height values, and then setting the widget's cell array based on the data in the character array passed in. Note that the code should check to make sure that the data can be pasted in the desired position. BitmapEdit must make sure that no attempt is made to set a cell array member outside of the bitmap. The routine then updates the screen display of the widget.

The final responsibility of the *requestor_callback* is to free the memory passed in by Xt.

11.2.7 If the Selection is Lost (Owner)

If the owner loses the selection, either because the selection timed out or because the user made a different selection, the *lose_ownership_proc* that was registered with its call to XtOwnSelection will be invoked. Typically, this function simply clears any highlighting or other visual feedback about the selection, and resets to their initial state any internal variables used in handling selections.

Example 11-8 shows the *lose_ownership_proc* from the BitmapEdit widget.

Example 11-8. BitmapEdit: the lose_ownership_proc

```
/* ARGSUSED */
static void
lose_ownership_proc(w, selection)
Widget w;
Atom *selection;
```

Example 11-8. BitmapEdit: the lose_ownership_proc (continued)

```
{
    BitmapEditWidget cw = (BitmapEditWidget) w;

    /* clear old selection */
    cw->bitmapEdit.first_box = False;
    cw->bitmapEdit.select_start_x = 0;
    cw->bitmapEdit.select_start_y = 0;
    cw->bitmapEdit.select_end_x = 0;
    cw->bitmapEdit.select_end_y = 0;
    Redisplay(cw, NULL);
}
```

11.2.8 When the Selection Transfer is Complete (Owner)

The `transfer_done_proc`, registered in the call to `XtOwnSelection`, is called when the transfer is complete. Its job is to do any processing necessary to get ready for the next selection request. In many cases no processing is necessary and this function can be `NULL` in the call to `XtOwnSelection`. However, this function might clear variables or free memory. Some transfers are intended to be made only once to make sure that there is no duplication of information. In these cases, the `transfer_done_proc` would do a lot more, including erasing the visual selection, calling `XtDisownSelection` (and perhaps even erasing the data that was selected).

11.2.9 ICCCM Compliance

For any two widgets to be able to transparently transfer different types of data, there must be agreement about the possible target types and their contents. The ICCCM suggests a list of possible target types, as shown in Table 11-2. If you can, use one of these target types since this will increase the chances that your widget will be able to communicate with widgets written by other people.

Table 11-2. Target Types Suggested in ICCCM

Atom	Type	Meaning
TARGETS	ATOM	List of valid target atoms
MULTIPLE	ATOM_PAIR	Look in the ConvertSelection property
TIMESTAMP	INTEGER	Timestamp used to acquire selection
STRING	STRING	ISO Latin 1 (+TAB+NEWLINE) text
TEXT	TEXT	Text in owner's encoding
LIST_LENGTH	INTEGER	Number of disjoint parts of selection
PIXMAP	DRAWABLE	Pixmap ID
DRAWABLE	DRAWABLE	Drawable ID
BITMAP	BITMAP	Bitmap ID
FOREGROUND	PIXEL	Pixel value
BACKGROUND	PIXEL	Pixel value

Table 11-2. Target Types Suggested in ICCCM (continued)

Atom	Type	Meaning
COLORMAP	COLORMAP	Colormap ID
ODIF	TEXT	ISO Office Document Interchange Format
OWNER_OS	TEXT	Operating system of owner
FILE_NAME	TEXT	Full path name of a file
HOST_NAME	TEXT	See WM_CLIENT_MACHINE
CHARACTER_POSITION	SPAN	Start and end of selection in bytes
LINE_NUMBER	SPAN	Start and end line numbers
COLUMN_NUMBER	SPAN	Start and end column numbers
LENGTH	INTEGER	Number of bytes in selection
USER	TEXT	Name of user running owner
PROCEDURE	TEXT	Name of selected procedure
MODULE	TEXT	Name of selected module
PROCESS	INTEGER, TEXT	Process ID of owner
TASK	INTEGER, TEXT	Task ID of owner
CLASS	TEXT	Class of owner—see WM_CLASS
NAME	TEXT	Name of owner—see WM_NAME
CLIENT_WINDOW	WINDOW	Top-level window of owner
DELETE	NULL	True if owner deleted selection
INSERT_SELECTION	NULL	Insert specified selection
INSERT_PROPERTY	NULL	Insert specified property

Because not every widget will support every possible target type, the ICCCM specifies a target type of XA_TARGETS, to which the owner is required to respond by returning a list of the target types into which it is capable of converting data.

Normally, a requestor would first call XtGetSelectionValue for XA_TARGETS, and then in the callback determine which target it wants to request from the list, and then call XtGetSelectionValue again for the desired target with a separate callback to process the actual data. This is really two separate selection transfers.

XA_TARGETS is not a predefined atom.* To use it, you must use the Xmu atom caching mechanism described in Section 11.2.9.1.

Fortunately, there is existing template code that you can copy to handle XA_TARGETS and some other standard target types that are required by the ICCCM.

This template code uses the Xmu routine XmuConvertStandardSelection. It also uses an Xmu atom-caching facility that eliminates the need for you to make XInternAtom calls for each of the ICCCM standard target atoms.

---

*The X Protocol defines all the predefined atoms. Therefore, even though XA_TARGETS would be convenient to have as a predefined atom, this can't be arranged with changing the protocol (albeit in a minor way). And the protocol is unlikely to be changed in even minor ways when there are workarounds, as in this case.

11.2.9.1 Xmu Atom Caching

In a Motif application, you can use `XmInternAtom` to cache atoms, so that when there are multiple instances of the same widget, only one query of the server will be done. However, Xmu provides an atom caching system that is somewhat more convenient for the atoms it supports.

Xmu's caching facility uses symbols similar to those defined in *<X11/Xatom.h>*, except that in this case they are macros that take an argument and call `XmuInternAtom`. For example, the macro for `XA_TARGETS` is defined as follows in *<X11/Xmu.h>*:

```
#define XA_TARGETS(d)          XmuInternAtom(d, _XA_TARGETS)
```

where d refers to a pointer to a `Display` structure. (This can be returned by the `Xt-Display` macro.) The `XmuInternAtom` function first tries to get the atom for the string "XA_TARGETS" from Xmu's internal cache. If Xmu doesn't yet have a value for the atom, it calls `XInternAtom` to make a server request. Because this facility makes only one query to the server, you can access the atoms in this way every time a selection is made without significant penalty. This allows you to place the `XA_TARGETS()` macro in your selection code instead of adding an instance part variable and setting it in the `initialize` method.

You might use this macro as follows in a *convert_proc* branch dedicated to handling the TARGETS target type:

```
if (*target == XA_TARGETS(XtDisplay(w))) { ...
```

The Xmu atom caching mechanism must be initialized before you can make calls of the form just shown. Example 11-9 shows the code that should be placed in the widget's `initialize` method to initialize this mechanism.

Example 11-9. BitmapEdit: initializing Xmu's atom caching mechanism in the initialize method

```
(void) XmuInternAtom( XtDisplay(new), XmuMakeAtom("NULL") );
```

11.2.9.2 Converting the Standard Selections

The Xmu routine `XmuConvertStandardSelection` can be used to respond to a TARGETS selection request, as well as to other standard targets defined by Xmu.

Example 11-10 shows the portion of the *convert_proc* for BitmapEdit that handles the standard targets.

This code is adapted from the standard client *xclipboard*, and can be copied almost directly into your widget.

Example 11-10. BitmapEdit: converting standard targets in the convert_proc

```
static Boolean
convert_proc(w, selection, target, type_return, value_return,
        length_return, format_return)
Widget w;
Atom *selection;
Atom *target;
Atom *type_return;
```

```
XtPointer *value_return;
unsigned long *length_return;
int *format_return;
{
    BitmapEditWidget cw = (BitmapEditWidget) w;
    int x, y;
    int width, height;
    XSelectionRequestEvent* req = XtGetSelectionRequest(w,
            *selection, (XtRequestId) NULL);

    /* handle all required atoms, and the one that we use */
    if (*target == XA_TARGETS(XtDisplay(cw))) {
        /* TARGETS handling copied from xclipboard.c */
        Atom* targetP;
        Atom* std_targets;
        unsigned long std_length;
        XmuConvertStandardSelection(cw, req->time, selection,
                target, type_return,
                (XtPointer*)&std_targets,
                &std_length, format_return);
        *value_return = XtMalloc(sizeof(Atom)*(std_length + 1));
        targetP = *(Atom**)value_return;
        *length_return = std_length + 1;
        *targetP++ = cw->bitmapEdit.target_atom;
        bcopy((char*)std_targets, (char*)targetP,
                sizeof(Atom)*std_length);
        XtFree((char*)std_targets);
        *type_return = XA_ATOM;
        *format_return = sizeof(Atom) * 8;
        return(True);
    }
    /* Xt already handles MULTIPLE, no branch necessary */
    else if (*target == cw->bitmapEdit.target_atom) {
        /* handle normal selection - code shown in Example 10-6 */
          .
          .
          .
    }
    else {
        if (XmuConvertStandardSelection(cw, CurrentTime, selection,
                target, type_return, value_return,
                length_return, format_return))
            return True;
        else {
            XtWarning("bitmapEdit: requestor is requesting\
                    unsupported selection target type.\n");
            return(False);
        }
    }
}
```

Overall, this code handles the TARGETS atom in the first branch, the normal selection target in the second, and any remaining standard atoms and any unknown atoms as two cases in the third branch. For ICCCM-compliant code, you can copy this entire function into your widget and then write just the second branch. Note that branches that successfully provide the requested data return `True`, and branches that don't return `False`.*

In the first branch you will also need to change the reference to the instance part field that stores the target atom used for selections, `bitmapEdit.target_atom`. If your widget uses a predefined atom or one supported by the Xmu facility, you would reference that atom here instead of the instance part field. If you called `XInternAtom` in `initialize` and stored the result in an instance part field, you specify that here.

Note that `XtGetSelectionRequest` is used to get the time from the `Selection-Request` event that the owner received before Xt called the *convert_proc* function. `XtGetSelectionRequest` was introduced in R4 for this specific reason; it needs to meet the current ICCCM and work around the fact that the *convert_proc* is defined without an event argument. (The *convert_proc* definition could not be changed because of the required backwards compatibility with R3.)

11.2.10 How Incremental Selection Works

An incremental selection is very similar to an atomic transfer, except that you use different set of routines and procedure types, and Xt calls the procedures you register multiple times instead of just once as in atomic transfers. Incremental transfers and atomic transfers are mutually exclusive—an owner can support both, but if the owner doesn't, a requestor cannot use the incremental routines to request a selection owned atomically, or vice versa.

As in an atomic transfer, the owner and the requestor in an incremental transfer only have to make one call each in order to initiate this multiple-section transfer. Here is the procedure:

- The owner calls `XtOwnSelectionIncremental` in response to the user selecting something. `XtOwnSelectionIncremental` returns `True` or `False` to indicate whether ownership was granted. `XtOwnSelectionIncremental` registers four callbacks:

```
XtConvertSelectionIncrProc convert_proc;
XtLoseSelectionIncrProc lose_selection_proc;
XtSelectionDoneIncrProc transfer_done_proc;
XtCancelConvertSelectionProc cancel_conversion_proc;
```

- The user pastes the selection in a widget, which causes that widget to request the selection with `XtGetSelectionValueIncremental`. `XtGetSelectionValueIncremental` registers one callback:

```
XtSelectionCallbackProc requestor_proc;
```

This callback receives the selection data. The *requestor_proc* is called once upon delivery of each segment of the selection value. It is called with type

---

*The ICCCM also specifies that functions implementing selections must be able to respond to a MULTIPLE target value, which is used to handle selections too large to fit into a single property. However, the necessary handling is done by the Intrinsics. Your procedures do not need to worry about responding to the MULTIPLE target value; a selection request with this target type will be transparently transformed into a series of smaller transfers.

`XT_CONVERT_FAIL` when the transfer is aborted—the requestor has the option of keeping or disposing of the partial selection. `XtGetSelectionValues-Incremental` is analogous except that it accepts multiple target/*client_data* pairs which must be received in the *requestor_proc*.

- The request for the selection causes Xt to call the *convert_proc*, which supplies the selection as described for atomic transfers, with the following exceptions. First, *convert_proc* is called repeatedly by Xt to get each segment. Therefore, it must keep track of what segments have been delivered. Second, when the last segment has been delivered, it should store a non-`NULL` value in *value* and zero in *length_return*. Third, the *convert_proc* must be ready to supply an additional requestor while it is still engaged in transferring segments to one requestor. The *convert_proc* is called with a *request_id* argument that identifies the request. You write the *convert_proc* to maintain a record of which segments have been delivered for each `request_id`. One easy way to do this is to use the Xlib context manager.

- When each segment is converted, Xt calls the *requestor_proc* (once for each segment), which extracts the data for the requestor and actually pastes it. This function may paste the data chunk-by-chunk or wait until the entire transfer is complete and then paste the entire selection.

- A zero-length segment terminates the transfer and results in Xt calling the *transfer_done_proc*.

This was the process of a successful transfer. All the remaining callback functions registered are for less common occurrences or unsuccessful transfers. The *cancel_callback* is called by Xt on timeout. This means that the transfer is considered complete even though it failed. In this process the owner frees memory allocated for the transfer.

Calls of the *lose_ownership_proc* do not indicate completion of in-progress transfers—these transfers should continue. It just means that the owner lost ownership of the selection, so that the owner should unhighlight what the user selected.

If *transfer_done_proc* is specified, the owner allocates and frees storage. If *transfer_done_proc* is `NULL`, *convert_proc* must allocate storage using `Xt-Malloc`, `XtCalloc` or `XtRealloc`, but Xt will free that memory. The owner may use `XtDisownSelection` to relinquish ownership. (This is the same routine used to relinquish ownership of an atomic selection.)

11.2.11 Miscellaneous Selection Routines

If the user deletes the information selected, the owner should call `XtDisownSelection`. `XtSetSelectionTimeout` sets the time in which widgets must respond to one another. This is initially set by the `XmNselectionTimeout` resource, and defaults to 5 seconds. The selection timeout prevents hanging when the user pastes but the current owner is slow or hung. `XtGetSelectionTimeout` reads the current selection timeout value. Widgets should not normally require these two calls, since the selection timeout should remain under the user's control.

If the requestor can request more than one target type, such as TARGETS and its normal selection target, it normally does so using separate actions. (Both actions can be invoked by the same triggering event, if desired.) Each action specifies a different target type and a different requestor callback. That way, each requestor callback handles only one type of target.

Beware: there is a danger in this approach. The selection owner might change between the repeated XtGetSelectionValue calls. XtGetSelectionValues (plural) can be used instead if the requestor would like to receive the data in more than one representation. The requestor's single callback function would then be called once for each representation. (The owner's *convert_proc* would also be called once per representation.)

11.3 Motif Cut and Paste Functions and the Clipboard

You've seen that Xt provides an underlying mechanism called *selections* that can transfer data from one widget instance to another, whether or not the instances are in the same application. The communication occurs through the server, using properties. Most widgets that display text already support selections.

You can also use selections in your application code to transfer data to other instances of your application or to or from any other widget or application that understands the format of the data. However, selections are quite cumbersome to implement.

Motif provides some easier-to-use functions that pass data to and from the clipboard. The *clipboard* is actually a property stored in the server, so that any client can read or write it. The clipboard can only hold one piece of data at a time.

Passing a large amount of data can take a few seconds. Therefore, the clipboard is set up so that the application does not actually pass data to the clipboard until the data has been requested by some other application or widget. Your application makes data available by registering a function that supplies the data, and Xt calls that function when the data is requested. Thus if there is any delay in sending the data, it occurs when the data is pasted, not when it is cut.

Motif provides about 15 functions that read and write this data. To copy data to the clipboard, you use the sequence of functions XmClipboardStartCopy, XmClipboardCopy, and XmClipboardEndCopy. To retrieve data from the clipboard, you use XmClipboardInquireLength and XmClipboardRetrieve.

According to the ICCCM, if a widget or application allows the user to delete a selection, the selection owner code should place the deleted data on the CLIPBOARD selection. Since the CLIPBOARD selection is a list of selections, the most recent deletion should be pushed onto the stack of existing selections.

The standard X distribution includes a special client, *xclipboard*, that shows the current value of the CLIPBOARD property, and allows it to be manipulated. Except when a widget asserts ownership of the CLIPBOARD with XtOwnSelection in order to place newly deleted data on it, the *xclipboard* client is the owner of this property. When it starts up, *xclipboard* asserts ownership of the CLIPBOARD selection. If it loses the selection (which will happen whenever a widget or client has newly deleted the contents of a selection), it obtains the contents of the selection from the new owner, then reasserts its own ownership of the selection.

Clients wishing to restore deleted data should request the contents of the CLIPBOARD, using the same techniques as we've shown for the PRIMARY selection. *xclipboard* will respond to these requests, returning the deleted data.

The use of *xclipboard* allows the value of a selection to survive the termination of the original selection owner.

12

Geometry Management

This chapter discusses how composite and constraint widgets manage the layout of widgets, and how to write your own simple composite and constraint widgets.

In This Chapter:

12
Geometry Management

Geometry managing widgets lay out your application's widgets on screen according to certain rules. You cannot hardcode the position of widgets in an application because X applications can be resized and they must reposition their widgets to take advantage of the available space. Because of the window manager, even the initial size of the application may not be the application's preferred size.

Chapter 3, *More Techniques for Using Widgets*, demonstrated how you can use existing composite widgets such as RowColumn and constraint widgets such as Form in the application. You can control widget layout rules with resources. However, you may find that no existing composite or constraint widget can be configured with resources to have the layout rules you need. In this case, you will need to write your own composite or constraint widget or modify an existing one. However, before embarking on writing one of these widgets, you should realize that composite and constraint widgets are complex. First investigate the alternatives! Perhaps you can find a composite or constraint widget from another widget set that has the layout characteristics you need. If you determine that you have no alternative but to write your own composite or constraint widget, you should keep it as simple as possible. It is much easier to write a special-purpose widget that handles a limited layout situation than it is to write a general-purpose composite or constraint widget like RowColumn or Form.

A *composite* widget is defined as any widget that is a subclass of the Xt-defined class Composite. A *constraint* widget is any widget that is a subclass of the Xt-defined class Constraint. Constraint is a subclass of Composite. As you may recall, a composite widget is the simplest kind of geometry-managing widget; it handles all its children equally, or handles each child in a fixed way. For example, the RowColumn widget handles all of its children equally. As an example of a special-purpose composite widget, Section 12.2 describes a composite widget called ScrollBox that manages two scrollbars and a main window. This widget requires that it have exactly three children added in a particular order.

A constraint widget has all the characteristics of composite widgets but maintains configurable data about each child so that it can cater to the needs of each child. By setting the constraint resources of a child of a constraint widget, you configure the constraint widget's layout policy for that child. Constraint widgets are inherently more powerful than composite widgets, but are also more complicated to write. A constraint widget requires all the code of a composite widget, plus code to handle the constraints of each child. Because of this complexity, you should hesitate even further before attempting to write a constraint widget. As an example of the code for a constraint widget, this section describes the Athena Form widget. (The Motif Form widget is too complex to be described here.)

Composite and constraint widgets can be used within widgets as well as within applications. For example, you may recall that the *xbitmap* application was implemented using the BitmapEdit widget that appeared inside a ScrolledWindow or MainWindow widget that in turn added scrollbars. We could rewrite the BitmapEdit widget to provide its own scrollbars, controllable through resources. Although this wouldn't be worth the effort, it could lead to better scrolling performance. This new widget, which might be called ScrolledBitmap, would be a composite widget and have three children: BitmapEdit and two ScrollBar widgets. This kind of *compound* widget is actually made up of several widgets, but to the application writer it should act like a single widget. The advantage of this rewrite would be that the application code would become simpler, and the bitmap editor with scrollbars could be easily used in other applications. The fourth major section of this chapter describes how to write a compound widget.

Chapter 13, *Menus, Gadgets, and Cascaded Popups*, describes how to write a widget capable of being the parent of gadgets, which are windowless widgets.

It is a good idea to define exactly what is meant by the *geometry* of a widget. The geometry of a widget is its position, its size, and its border width. These are the Core fields x, y, width, height, and border_width. Border width is included because window positions are measured from the origin of the parent (the top-left corner inside the border of the parent) to the top-left corner outside the border of the child. Therefore, changing the border width of a widget by 1 pixel moves the origin of that widget 1 pixel along both the *x* and *y* axes relative to its parent. This concept is shown in Figure 12-1.

Geometry management may also control the stacking order of a group of children (that is, which children appear to be on top). However, control of the stacking order requires more programmer effort than control of geometry, because it isn't completely built into Xt.

12.1 How Composite Management Works

Like simple widgets, the characteristics of composite widgets are defined by their methods. The key methods in a composite widget are the Core methods resize and query_ geometry and the Composite methods geometry_manager and change_managed. We will discuss these methods first, and then move on to the other methods defined by Composite, insert_child and delete_child, which are infrequently used.

We'll begin with a summary of what these four most important methods do. In short, they handle interactions with the three generations of widgets involved in direct geometry interactions with a composite widget: the parent of the composite widget, the composite widget itself, and the children of the composite widget.

• The resize method moves and resizes the child widgets as necessary to fit within the composite widget's new size.

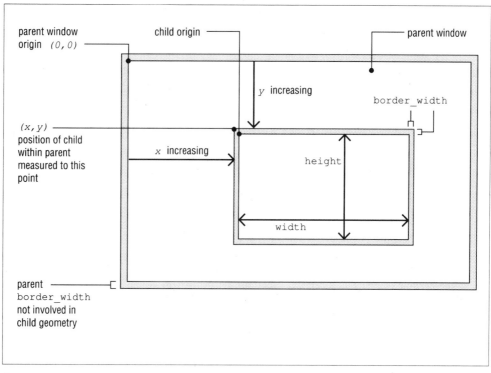

Figure 12-1. Role of border width in widget geometry

- The `query_geometry` method supplies a preferred geometry to a wid's parent when the parent calls `XtQueryGeometry`. The parent makes this call in the process of determining a new layout for its children.

- The `geometry_manager` method handles resize requests from the child widgets. Usually, the only kind of child that will make a resize request to the parent is another composite or constraint widget. However, some simple widgets do request resizing. For example, when a Label widget's string is changed through resources, the Label widget increases its own size (this is allowed only in the `set_values` method). Xt then calls the parent's `geometry_manager` method, which must decide whether this new size is acceptable and then make any changes. When a child widget asks for more space and the composite widget doesn't have enough, the composite widget's `geometry_manager` may ask its own parent for more space by calling `XtMakeGeometryRequest`.

- The `change_managed` method changes the layout of the children when a child is managed or unmanaged. A child is managed initially when `XtRealizeWidget` is called (after children are created with `XtCreateManagedWidget`) or when `XtManageChild` or `XtManageChildren` is called to add an already-realized widget to a composite parent's managed set. (A widget can be unmanaged later to remove it from the screen without destroying it, and then managed again at any time. Each time a child is managed or unmanaged, or destroyed, the `change_managed` method is called.)

The `resize` and `query_geometry` methods were already introduced in Chapter 7, *Basic Widget Methods*, as they are written in simple widgets. In composite widgets, they have the same job, but it is more complicated because they now have children to worry about. We will discuss these methods again in this chapter as they appear in composite widgets.

To write any of these four methods, you need to look at all the ways that geometry changes can occur, so that you know all the situations in which the methods will be called. Here are the four most important situations:

- During the negotiation that takes place to determine the initial size of each widget when an application starts up.

- When the user resizes the entire application.

- When a widget requests a size change from the application.

- When a widget is resized by the application.

As you can see, there are many cases. It helps to be systematic about understanding and programming for these cases. The next four sections describe each of these cases one at a time.

The complexity of the geometry negotiations in the following description may be intimidating. A truly general-purpose composite widget is a large, complex piece of software. You should leave this programming to the widget writers who write commercial widget sets, and concentrate on things that are more important in your application. The purpose of this description is to let you understand how complete composite widgets work, not to suggest that you should try to write one. However, it is possible to write small, special-purpose composite widgets that solve particular layout problems. Composite widgets are simpler when they are more authoritarian—when they don't do as much to try to satisfy the preferences of their children. Section 12.2 describes ScrollBox, a simple composite widget designed solely to manage a main widget and two scrollbars. Writing this kind of widget is manageable because the widget manages a fixed number of children and has simple layout rules.

12.1.1 Initial Geometry Negotiation

At least one geometry negotiation takes place in any application, even if the application is never resized. This geometry negotiation occurs when an application starts up.

Figure 12-2 shows the process of initial geometry negotiation in schematic form.

The call to `XtRealizeWidget` initiates a two-step process. When `XtRealizeWidget` is called on the top-level widget, most or all of the widgets have been created but windows have not been created for them. `XtRealizeWidget` initiates a geometry negotiation that ripples through the widget hierarchy (as is described below). The widgets' `realize` methods (which create windows for the widgets) are not called until this process is complete.

`XtRealizeWidget` first calls the `change_managed` method of every composite widget in the application, beginning with the lowest widgets in the hierarchy (called a *post-order* traversal). Each `change_managed` method determines an initial size for each child and calls `XtMoveWidget` and/or `XtResizeWidget` for the child. All the

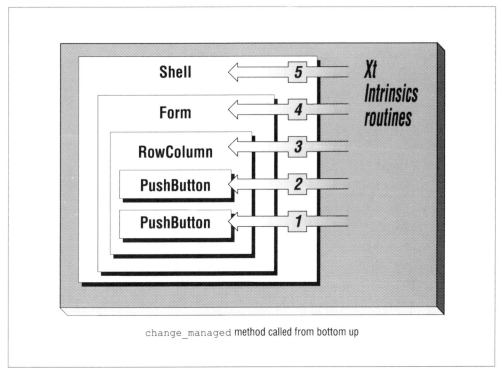

Figure 12-2. Initial geometry negotiation, assuming sufficient shell space

change_managed methods are called until the one in the Shell widget. (Remember that the Shell widget is a composite widget that has only one child.) The child is also a composite widget (except in single-widget applications such as *xhello*). When the Shell widget is reached, the Shell widget size is set to the size of its child and the process stops unless the user has specified an initial geometry for the entire application through the resource database or command line.

A change_managed method can (but is not required to) determine each of its children's preferred geometry by calling XtQueryGeometry for each child. This will result in the query_geometry method of each child being called. Instead of calling XtQuery-Geometry, the change_managed method may use the child's Core width and height fields.

The change_managed method does not determine the composite widget's own size. That job is for the parent of the composite widget, which is another composite widget.

If the user-specified, top-level widget geometry is different from the geometry of the Shell widget's child after all the change_managed methods are called, then the Shell widget resizes its child to the user-specified size. This makes Xt call the resize method of the child composite, and this resize method reconsiders the layout of its children. This process proceeds down the chain of widgets to the bottom. At each stage the resize method can (but need not) call XtQueryGeometry for each child to get each child's opinion of the intended geometry for that child.

Figure 12-3 shows the continued process of initial geometry negotiation if the user has specified the top-level geometry through resources rather than accepting the application's built-in defaults.

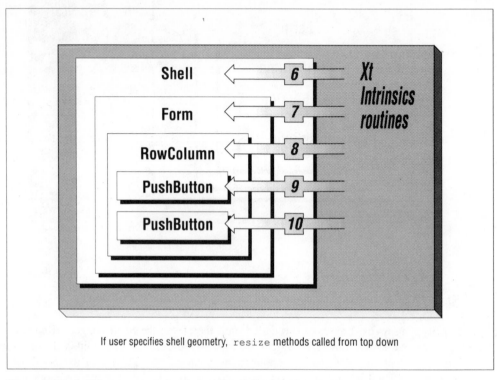

If user specifies shell geometry, resize methods called from top down

Figure 12-3. Initial geometry negotiation, if resizing is necessary

Note that this process and the methods involved are more complicated if the change_managed or resize methods call XtQueryGeometry. XtQuery-Geometry calls a child widget's query_geometry method, as described in Section 12.2.5. When the change_managed or resize methods call XtQueryGeometry, they need to propose a complete geometry for the child by setting fields in the arguments of the XtQueryGeometry call, and then do different things depending upon which of the three different answers it receives from the child. The XtGeometryAlmost answer includes a suggested compromise. The change_managed or resize method will decide on a new size based on the compromise, and may or may not make another Xt-QueryGeometry call to make this suggestion to the child. The code to perform all of this is extensive because the suggestions and answers are in the form of structures with several fields. Only the Frame, MainWindow, and ScrolledWindow classes in the Motif set call Xt-QueryGeometry.

Notice that this process can result in the `resize`, `change_managed`, and possibly the `query_geometry` methods of every widget being called, but the `geometry_manager` method does not play a part.

Once this process is complete, `XtRealizeWidget` calls the `realize` methods of all the widgets and actually creates windows for them. Up to this point, all the methods were simply changing the widget size and position parameters in Xt structures, not the sizes of actual windows. `XtRealizeWidget` also maps all managed widgets.

12.1.2 User Resizes the Application

When `XtRealizeWidget` returns, most applications call `XtAppMainLoop`. Internally, this calls the Xlib call `XNextEvent` which sends the batch of queued window creation and window map requests to the server.* Most window managers can intercept the mapping request for the top-level window and draw a rubber-band outline of the application on the screen, ready for the user to place or resize the application. With certain settings *mwm* can either place windows for you or allow you to place and size them. If the user simply places the application, no new geometry negotiation takes place. But if the user resizes the application, a new round of geometry negotiation takes place, identical to the process described above where the user specified a top-level widget geometry.

In other words, the process that occurs when the user resizes the application with the window manager is the same as when the user specifies top-level widget geometry with resources or the command line. This is also the same as when the user later resizes the existing application. This process was illustrated in Figure 12-2 and Figure 12-3.

This process uses all the methods except `geometry_manager`.

12.1.3 Widget Desires a Size Change

When an application sets a widget resource that affects what is displayed in the widget, it may be logical for the widget to ask its parent for a new size. This would occur in the `set_values` method of the widget. The widget sets its desired geometry into its Core geometry fields (`width`, `height`, `x`, `y`, and `border_width`). Xt finishes calling all the `set_values` methods (because they chain), and then calls `XtMakeGeometry-Request` to ask the parent widget for a geometry change. Note that the `set_values` and `initialize` methods are the only place where widgets are allowed to set their own size directly. (In `set_values` they can do so only because of an `XtVaSetValues` call to change a resource that affects geometry.)

Figure 12-4 shows what happens when a widget requests a size change.

---

*You can find out more about the network optimization done by Xlib in Volume One or Volume Zero.

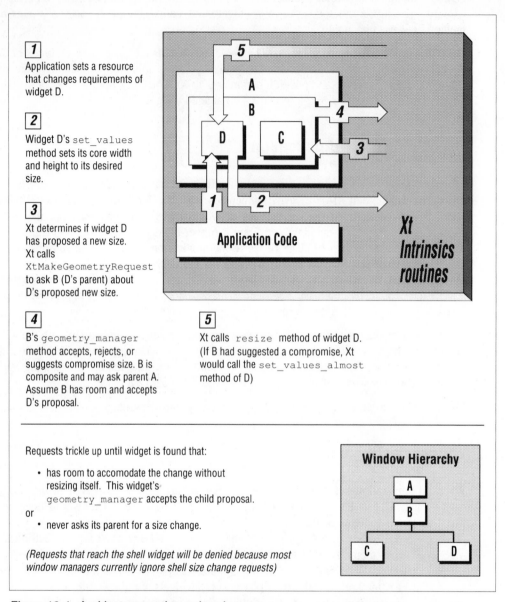

1

Application sets a resource that changes requirements of widget D.

2

Widget D's `set_values` method sets its core width and height to its desired size.

3

Xt determines if widget D has proposed a new size. Xt calls `XtMakeGeometryRequest` to ask B (D's parent) about D's proposed new size.

4

B's `geometry_manager` method accepts, rejects, or suggests compromise size. B is composite and may ask parent A. Assume B has room and accepts D's proposal.

5

Xt calls `resize` method of widget D. (If B had suggested a compromise, Xt would call the `set_values_almost` method of D)

Requests trickle up until widget is found that:

- has room to accomodate the change without resizing itself. This widget's `geometry_manager` accepts the child proposal.

or

- never asks its parent for a size change.

(Requests that reach the shell widget will be denied because most window managers currently ignore shell size change requests)

Window Hierarchy

A
B
C   D

Figure 12-4. A widget requesting a size change

Of course, composite widgets often want a size change because their children have asked to be resized. The composite widget has no knowledge of what caused the child's size change. Therefore, composite widgets call `XtMakeGeometryRequest` themselves to see if their parent will allow them to change size. Composite widgets should request such a change; otherwise their parent may have unused space or have other children that need more space. However, handling the variety of responses to the request is not trivial.

For both simple and composite widgets, Xt calls the `geometry_manager` method of the parent widget when `XtMakeGeometryRequest` is called, and the method is responsible for deciding whether to except, reject, or compromise on the requested geometry. The `geometry_manager` method may have to ask its parent to decide whether it can accept its child's proposal. If so, it makes another `XtMakeGeometryRequest` call. This can go on to arbitrary depth, and the final answer will trickle back down to the parent of the original requestor. The `XtMakeGeometryRequest` call itself will change the child's geometry if the answer is yes. If the answer is no, the child gets this information and may try another geometry. If the answer is a compromise, then the child will get the compromise information returned in its call to `XtMakeGeometryRequest` and make another request to be able to proceed. More on this interaction in Section 12.2.4 and 12.2.6.

This process uses only the `geometry_manager` methods of each widget. However, this method may call `XtQueryGeometry` to determine the needs of each of its children before replying to the `XtMakeGeometryRequest` request. When the process is finished, the `resize` method is called for any widgets that have been resized. However, the `change_managed` method is never involved.

12.1.4 Application Resizes a Widget

An application may change the size of a widget by setting the `XtNx`, `XtNy`, `XtNwidth`, `XtNheight`, or `XtNborderWidth` resources directly (as opposed to setting a resource which indirectly affects the size, as covered in the last section). If that widget has no children, the widget code does nothing, but Xt queries the parent with an `XtMakeGeometryRequest`. The complete negotiation process as described for `XtRealizeWidget` is repeated, except that the current top-level Shell size is used as a user-specified size (because ultimately it is).

Although the widget code did nothing, the `set_values` method sets the new values specified through resources into the Core fields. If the `XtMakeGeometryRequest` request is denied by the parent, Xt sets these Core fields back to their original values. If the parent suggests a compromise, the `set_values_almost` method, which is described below, is called.

If the widget whose size is changed is a widget with children, the negotiation process is the same, except that when it is complete the children of the widget need to be laid out, and if the children have children they need to be laid out too, and so on.

12.2 Writing a Composite Widget

The process of writing a composite widget is the same as writing a simple widget. You copy the three files of some existing composite widget, perhaps Composite itself, make global name changes to make the files a skeleton for a distinct class, and then write new methods.

As mentioned earlier, writing a general-purpose composite widget is not a trivial task and should be done only when other options fail. Because composite widgets have no user interface, you may be able to find a composite widget with the proper characteristics from another widget set. There are several public domain widget sets to look in. Note, however, that commercial widget set vendors may design in a private protocol between their composite widgets and their children, which make the composite widgets unable to correctly manage widgets from other sets. And if you are writing a commercial product, you may have to pay a binary license fee to the commercial widget set vendor for each copy of your product. Especially for large software houses, it is a good idea to have at least one programmer adept at writing composite widgets and the `query_geometry` methods of simple widgets.

Small scale composite widgets that handle a small set of circumstances are not difficult to write, because you can make a number of simplifying assumptions. As an example, this section describes a very simple composite widget called ScrollBox, which is designed to manage a BitmapEdit widget (or any other main widget) and two ScrollBar widgets. It handles only these three widgets, and they must be added in a particular order. Because we know the geometry preferences of these three widgets (the bigger the better, but no size in particular), we can dispense with querying them about their preferred geometry. We also know that none of our children will request to be resized. Therefore, we do not need a `geometry_manager` method.

A ScrollBox widget is shown managing BitmapEdit and two scrollbars in Figure 12-5.*

The Athena Viewport widget does scrollbar management in a more general way than does ScrollBox. It is a subclass of Form that takes any main window as a child and creates scrollbars. It shows only a small portion of the main window and uses the scrollbars to determine which portion of the main window is shown. But Viewport doesn't work well with BitmapEdit because BitmapEdit has a built-in ability to display in a smaller window that conflicts with Viewport's efforts. Besides, Viewport is several times larger and more complicated than ScrollBox, because it includes the scrollbar callback functions and because it honors a child's geometry preferences. ScrollBox is a modest widget that manages the geometry of scrollbars, leaving their connection with the main window up to the application. This demonstrates the essential elements of a composite widget without too much complication.†

The ScrollBox widget code, along with a version of *xbitmap* that uses it, is available in the example source in the *ch09* directory. It lays out its children by adjusting the width and height of the three children so that they fill the ScrollBox widget, while keeping the width of

---

*ScrollBox widens the borders of its children, for an unknown reason. It might as well be admitted that there is probably a bug in it somewhere!

†It is worth noting that the Box widget fails miserably in managing scrollbars, while Form is adequate but has the annoying characteristic that it resizes the width of the scrollbars as well as their length, sometimes resulting in bloated or miniscule scrollbars.

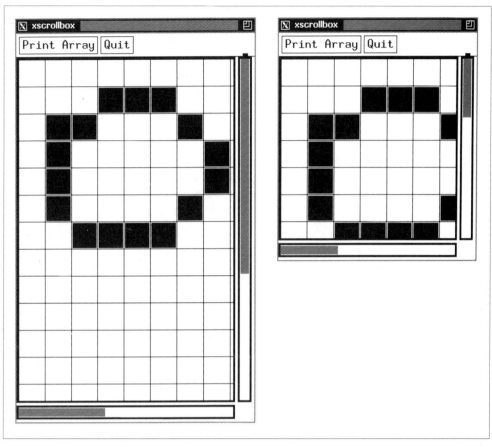

Figure 12-5. A ScrollBox widget at two different sizes

the Scrollbar widgets constant. The width of the Scrollbar widgets is set through their resources and is never modified by ScrollBox.

The first few sections below describe the methods that are used in ScrollBox and that are required in all composite widgets. First, we discuss the Core `initialize`, `realize`, `set_values`, `resize`, and `query_geometry` methods as they are used in composite widgets. Then, we discuss how the ScrollBox widget implements layout calculations in a common routine called by the `set_values`, `resize`, and `change_managed` values. This is followed by further discussion of the `change_managed` and `query_geometry` methods. Then, we go on to discuss the methods not used by ScrollBox, but that would be used in more complicated composite widgets, in particular `geometry_manager`. Finally, we briefly discuss the methods available in composite widgets but rarely needed: `set_values_almost`, `insert_child`, and `delete_child`.

12.2.1 Basic Core Methods in Composite Widgets

Both composite and constraint widgets are subclasses of Core. Therefore, they have all the Core methods described in Chapters 6 and 7. However, since composite and constraint widgets usually have no input and output semantics, the `expose` method is set to `NULL` and the widget has no default translation table or actions. As a result, all the event-oriented fields in the Core class structure become irrelevant to composite and constraint widgets.

But composite and constraint widgets do use the Core `initialize`, `realize`, and `set_values` methods. These methods have the same roles as for simple widgets. The `initialize` method initializes instance part variables and checks initial resource values. The `realize` method sets window attribute values and then creates a window for the widget. The `set_values` method updates any instance part fields that depend on resources. Since composite and constraint widgets don't need GCs, `initialize` and `set_values` don't contain code to create and change GCs as in simple widgets.

These three methods for ScrollBox are absolutely minimal, and call a common routine called `DoLayout` when any actual sizing or positioning of widgets is required. The `initialize` method simply sets the widget's default width and height, the `realize` method is inherited, and the `set_values` method changes the layout of children when either of ScrollBox's two resources is changed. These resources control the vertical and horizontal distance in pixels that will be left between the Scrollbar widgets and the main widget, and between each of these widgets and the borders of ScrollBox. Example 12-1 shows the `set_values` method of ScrollBox.

Example 12-1. ScrollBox: the set_values method

```
/* ARGSUSED */
static Boolean SetValues(current, request, new, args, num_args)
Widget current, request, new;
ArgList args;
Cardinal *num_args;
{
    ScrollBoxWidget sbwcurrent = (ScrollBoxWidget) current;
    ScrollBoxWidget sbwnew = (ScrollBoxWidget) new;

    /* need to relayout if h_space or v_space change */
    if ((sbwnew->scrollBox.h_space != sbwcurrent->scrollBox.h_space) ||
            (sbwnew->scrollBox.v_space !=
            sbwcurrent->scrollBox.v_space))
        DoLayout(sbwnew);

    return False;
}
```

Two more Core methods are used in composite widgets: `resize` and `query_geometry`. The `resize` method changes the layout of its children and is shown in Example 12-2.

Example 12-2. ScrollBox: the resize method

```
static void Resize(w)
Widget w;
{
    ScrollBoxWidget sbw = (ScrollBoxWidget) w;

    DoLayout(sbw);
}
```

The `query_geometry` method answers the parent's inquiry about a size change for this composite widget and is shown in Example 12-3.

Example 12-3. ScrollBox: the query_geometry method

```
/* ARGSUSED */
static XtGeometryResult QueryGeometry(w, request, reply_return)
Widget w;
XtWidgetGeometry *request, *reply_return;
{
    XtGeometryResult result;

    request->request_mode &= CWWidth | CWHeight;

    if (request->request_mode == 0)
    /* parent isn't going to change w or h, so nothing to
     * re-compute */
        return XtGeometryYes;

    /* if proposed size is large enough, accept it.  Otherwise,
     * suggest our arbitrary initial size. */

    if (request->request_mode & CWHeight) {
        if (request->height < INITIAL_HEIGHT) {
            result = XtGeometryAlmost;
            reply_return->height = INITIAL_HEIGHT;
            reply_return->request_mode &= CWHeight;
        }
        else
            result = XtGeometryYes;
    }

    if (request->request_mode & CWWidth) {
        if (request->width < INITIAL_WIDTH) {
            result = XtGeometryAlmost;
            reply_return->width = INITIAL_WIDTH;
            reply_return->request_mode &= CWWidth;
        }
        else
            result = XtGeometryYes;
    }

    return(result);
}
```

Although the `query_geometry` method has the same role in all widgets, composite and simple, a composite widget's size preference depends on its children. Normally this means the `query_geometry` method will query its children and try different layouts until it arrives at the geometry, or some approximation of it, suggested by its parent. This calculation is complicated because the widget may have any kind of child, and their responses to geometry suggestions are unpredictable. ScrollBox ignores this complexity because it knows exactly what kinds of children it will have and what their characteristics are. Therefore, its `query_geometry` method is basically the same as the `query_geometry` method of a simple widget.

To be more precise, what this `query_geometry` method does is accept any size suggested by the parent which is larger than the minimum useful size of the application. When the suggested size is too small, the `query_geometry` method uses the minimum useful size as a compromise. Note, however, that this is really hardcoding the characteristics of the child into our composite widget. It would be better to add resources to control the minimum useful size.

12.2.2 Laying Out Child Widgets

Composite widgets need to calculate a layout and manipulate their child widgets from `set_values`, from `resize`, and from `change_managed`. Therefore, in most composite widgets this common code is placed in a single routine called `DoLayout`. Example 12-4 shows the `DoLayout` routine from ScrollBox.

Example 12-4. ScrollBox: private routine to lay out child widgets

```
/* ARGSUSED */
static DoLayout(w)
Widget w;
{
    ScrollBoxWidget sbw = (ScrollBoxWidget) w;
    Widget main, vscroll, hscroll;
    Widget child;
    Dimension mw, mh; /* main window */
    Dimension vh;      /* vertical scrollbar length (height) */
    Dimension hw;      /* horizontal scrollbar length (width) */
    Position vx;
    Position hy;
    int i;

    if (sbw->composite.num_children != 3)
        XtAppError(XtWidgetToApplicationContext(sbw),
                "ScrollBox: must manage exactly three widgets.");

    for (i = 0; i < sbw->composite.num_children; i++) {
        child = sbw->composite.children[i];
        if (!XtIsManaged(child)) {
            XtAppError(XtWidgetToApplicationContext(sbw),
                "ScrollBox: all three widgets must be managed.");
        }
    }

    /* Child one is the main window, two is the vertical scrollbar,
     * and three is the horizontal scrollbar. */

    main = sbw->composite.children[0];
    vscroll = sbw->composite.children[1];
    hscroll = sbw->composite.children[2];

    /* Size all three widgets so that space is fully utilized. */
```

```
mw = sbw->core.width - (2 * sbw->scrollBox.h_space) -
        vscroll->core.width - (2 * vscroll->core.border_width)
        - (2 * main->core.border_width);

mh = sbw->core.height - (2 * sbw->scrollBox.v_space) -
        hscroll->core.height - (2 * hscroll->core.border_width)
        - (2 * main->core.border_width);

vx = main->core.x + mw + sbw->scrollBox.h_space +
        main->core.border_width + vscroll->core.border_width;
hy = main->core.y + mh + sbw->scrollBox.v_space +
        main->core.border_width + hscroll->core.border_width;

vh = mh; /* scrollbars are always same length as main window */
hw = mw;

XtResizeWidget(main, mw, mh);

XtResizeWidget(vscroll, vscroll->core.width, vh);
XtMoveWidget(vscroll, vx, vscroll->core.y);

XtResizeWidget(hscroll, hw, hscroll->core.height);
XtMoveWidget(hscroll, hscroll->core.x, hy);
}
```

In general, DoLayout moves and resizes the child widgets according to its layout policy. This routine may query the children with XtQueryGeometry before making decisions, but it is not required to. In this case, there is no need to because ScrollBox handles only two types of widgets with no size preferences.

DoLayout is passed only one argument, ScrollBox's own widget ID (a pointer to its widget instance structure). But the composite children field in ScrollBox's instance structure is an array of the IDs of all the children, and num_children is the number of children.*

When each child is added to a composite widget, its ID is added to the children field of the composite part of the instance structure, and the num_children field is incremented. Therefore, the code to lay out the children is usually a loop that treats each child one at a time. This often takes two passes, since the routine needs to know which children are managed before it can determine their final geometries. All children, even unmanaged ones, are listed in the children and num_children fields.

This particular DoLayout procedure makes sure that there are exactly three children and that they are all managed. Then, it calculates the positions and sizes for all the children so that they will fill all the available space in ScrollBox's own window. Finally, it calls Xt-ResizeWidget and XtMoveWidget, which check to see if there was any change before making Xlib calls to move and resize the windows.

Geometry Management

---

*Incidentally, the children and num_children fields are resources. However, they are read-only from outside the widget code; the application should never set them with XtSetValues.

12.2.3 The change_managed Method

In every composite widget, the `change_managed` method is called once (and only once, even when there are multiple children) during the `XtRealizeWidget` process to determine an application's initial layout. `change_managed` is also called when an application later unmanages a managed widget or manages an unmanaged widget (as long as the `Xt-NmappedWhenManaged` resource has its default value). Therefore, `change_managed` also calls `DoLayout`.

An application unmanages a widget to remove the widget from visibility without destroying it, and at the same time to tell the composite widget to change the layout of the remaining widgets to fill the gap. This is done by calling `XtUnmanageChild` or `XtUnmanage-Children`. The application can then make the composite widget redisplay the widget by calling `XtManageChild` or `XtManageChildren`. This response depends on the Core `XtNmappedWhenManaged` resource having its default value, `True`. When set to `False`, the management state has no effect on mapping, and the application must call `Xt-MapWidget` and `XtUnmapWidget` instead. Usually an application does this so that a widget will become invisible *without* triggering a re-layout to fill in the space it has vacated. Therefore, `change_managed` need not check the `XtNmapWhenManaged` resource of each child. Example 12-5 shows the `change_managed` method of ScrollBox.

Example 12-5. A basic change_managed method

```
static void ChangeManaged(w)
ScrollBoxWidget w;
{
    ScrollBoxWidget sbw = (ScrollBoxWidget) w;
    DoLayout(sbw);
}
```

12.2.4 The geometry_manager Method

The `geometry_manager` method responds to requests by the children to be resized. ScrollBox does not manage widgets that request to be resized, so theoretically it should not need a `geometry_manager`, but as of R4, Xt requires that all composite widgets have one. ScrollBox's geometry manager method is very simple, and is shown in Example 12-6.

Example 12-6. A simple geometry_manager method

```
static XtGeometryResult
GeometryManager(w, request, reply)
Widget w;
XtWidgetGeometry *request;
XtWidgetGeometry *reply;
{
    return XtGeometryYes;
}
```

Section 12.2.6 describes what would take place in a more complex `geometry_manager`, and Section 12.4.6 provides an example.

You have now seen all the code in ScrollBox! To summarize, a very basic composite widget such as ScrollBox has a standard `initialize` method, `resize` and `change_managed` methods that just call `DoLayout`, and a `set_values` method that calls `DoLayout` when any resource that affects layout is changed. The `DoLayout` routine actually lays out the children. The widget's `query_geometry` method is basically just like a simple widget's `query_geometry`. Now we'll move on to describe what may be added to this skeleton to make more fully-featured composite widgets.

12.2.5 XtQueryGeometry and the query_geometry Method

We have mentioned that `XtQueryGeometry` calls a child's `query_geometry` method, but not the details of how this works. The `query_geometry` method for simple widgets is described in Chapter 7, *Basic Widget Methods*. The role of this method in composite widgets is the same, but the details of its job are different. You may recall that this method is passed pointers to two `XtWidgetGeometry` structures, one which specifies the parent's proposed geometry, and the other which is used by the child to return a compromise geometry. These two structures are allocated by the method that calls `XtQueryGeometry` and passed as pointers to that call. The `XtGeometryResult` enum returned by the `query_geometry` method is passed right through as the returned value of `XtQueryGeometry`.

Composite and constraint widgets play the role of both parent and child. When you write a composite widget, you may call `XtQueryGeometry` in several places to get the child's response to your proposed size. You will also need to write a `query_geometry` method so that your composite can respond to its parent's `XtQueryGeometry` request.

A `query_geometry` method in a composite widget should base its response on the size preferences of its children. It should calculate a new layout based on the proposed geometry passed in, and then query its children to get their opinions of their new geometry. If any of the children is a composite widget, they may query their children, and so on. Therefore, these requests tend to trickle down to the lowest widget in the hierarchy. ScrollBox took the biggest shortcuts in its `query_geometry` method. Not only didn't it query its children, but it hardcoded its response based on the characteristics of the kind of main window it expected. This would be the first place to begin improving ScrollBox.

Note, however, that a composite widget is allowed to be authoritarian and not ask its children whether they like the sizes they are about to be given. However, this kind of composite widget will not be suitable as a parent of a widget that really needs certain size preferences.

In R4 and later, a parent must specify a complete proposed geometry when calling `Xt-QueryGeometry`, not just the changes it intends to make as was specified in R3.

12.2.6 XtMakeGeometryRequest and the geometry_manager Method

`XtMakeGeometryRequest` calls are made for two reasons. First, when a composite widget honors its children's size preferences, it may find that its current size is inadequate to lay out its children. In this case, it should ask its parent to be resized by calling `XtMakeGeometryRequest`. Second, Xt calls `XtMakeGeometryRequest` for a widget when the application has changed a resource that affects geometry.

As mentioned above, `XtMakeGeometryRequest` calls the parent's `geometry_manager` method. The parent's `geometry_manager` has the job of deciding whether the size proposed by the child is acceptable. A subclass of Composite must either define a `geometry_manager` method, or set this field in the class structure to NULL, because there is no default method to inherit. The `XtInheritGeometryManager` symbol can be used only in subclasses of a class that defines a `geometry_manager` method. Any composite widget allowing its children to suggest resizing will require a `geometry_manager` method of its own.

The way the arguments and returned values are passed between `XtMakeGeometry-Request` and the parent's `geometry_manager` method is almost exactly parallel to the way `XtQueryGeometry` calls the child's `query_geometry` method. Both calls take pointers to two structures of the same types where one is used for a returned compromise. Both take no more arguments other than the widget ID. Both return an enum value of type `XtGeometryResult`. The returned value of the `geometry_manager` method is, generally speaking, passed through as the returned value of `XtMakeGeometryRequest`. Review Section 7.6 so that these structures, their fields and values, and the returned values are fresh in your mind.

One difference between the way the `query_geometry` and `geometry_manager` methods are invoked is that the `geometry_manager` method can return a fourth enum value, `XtGeometryDone` (in addition to `XtGeometryYes`, `XtGeometryNo`, and `Xt-GeometryAlmost`). The return codes of the `geometry_manager` method are summarized in Table 12-1. `set_values_almost` is to accept the compromise geometry proposed by the parent or to propose a different geometry to the parent. Once a new geometry is proposed by the `set_values_almost` method, Xt calls the parent's `geometry_manager` method again, and the cycle repeats until the `geometry_manager` returns `XtGeometryYes` or `XtGeometryDone`, or until the child gives up trying to change size. Figure 12-6 illustrates this process.

Most widgets inherit this method from the Core widget by specifying `XtInheritSet-ValuesAlmost` in the Core class part initialization. This inherited method always approves the suggestion made by the parent `geometry_manager` method. If your widget really depends on being certain sizes, however, you will need to write a `set_values_almost` method. You should never specify a NULL `set_values_almost` method because Xt will print a warning message when `set_values_almost` would have been called, and continue as if it had been called and had returned `XtGeometryYes`.

The `set_values_almost` method is passed pointers to two `XtWidgetGeometry` structures: `request` and `reply`. The `request` structure contains the child's original request and `reply` includes the `geometry_manager` method's compromise geometry if `geometry_manager` returned `XtGeometryAlmost`. To accept the compromise, the

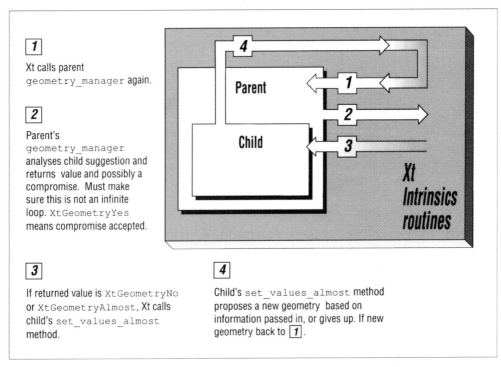

1

Xt calls parent `geometry_manager` again.

2

Parent's `geometry_manager` analyses child suggestion and returns value and possibly a compromise. Must make sure this is not an infinite loop. `XtGeometryYes` means compromise accepted.

3

If returned value is `XtGeometryNo` or `XtGeometryAlmost`, Xt calls child's `set_values_almost` method.

4

Child's `set_values_almost` method proposes a new geometry based on information passed in, or gives up. If new geometry back to **1**.

Figure 12-6. Geometry negotiation by the set_values_almost method

procedure must copy the contents of the reply geometry into the request geometry; to attempt an alternate geometry, the procedure may modify any part of the request argument; to terminate the geometry negotiation and retain the original geometry, the procedure must set `request->request_mode` to zero.

If `geometry_manager` returned `XtGeometryNo`, it will not have generated a compromise. In this case, the `set_values_almost` method may suggest a new geometry, but it is probably not worth it since the method has no information upon which to base its changes to its previous suggestion. The `set_values_almost` method at this point should usually just set `request->request_mode` to zero to terminate the geometry negotiation.

12.2.7 The insert_child and delete_child Methods

The Composite class has an instance part structure that contains an array of all the widget's children (even those not currently managed), the current number of children, and the total number of child slots available. The `insert_child` method inserts the ID of a child into this array. It is called when the child is created by a call to `XtCreateWidget` or `Xt-CreateManagedWidget`. Most widgets inherit the `insert_child` method from the Composite class by specifying the symbolic constant `XtInheritInsertChild` in the class structure initialization. A class would replace the default `insert_child` method to control the position of each child added, or to limit the number or classes of widgets that can be added.

A composite widget can control the position of each child added by calling a function whose pointer is stored in the instance part field `insert_position`. The function should return the number of widgets before the widget. The `XtNinsertPosition` resource sets this function pointer. The default `insert_position` function returns the current number of children. Of course, because this resource's value is a function pointer, it can be specified in the application only at run time, never through the resource files or command line.

The `delete_child` method removes the ID of a child from the child array and is called when the application calls `XtDestroyWidget`. This method is almost always inherited from Composite by specifying the symbolic constant `XtInheritDeleteChild` in the class structure initialization.

12.3 How Constraint Management Works

The first thing to realize about constraint widgets is that everything said about composite widgets is still true. Because Constraint is a subclass of Composite, all the methods described above are still present and have the same tasks. However, constraint widgets also maintain a structure full of data attached to each child, set through resources. Every time it lays out the children, the constraint widget reads this data to determine how to handle that child. Of course, it still may query each children to get its opinion of a new size. The constraint information adds another level of complexity to the situation.

Like composite widgets, constraint widgets can be drastically simplified by reducing flexibility and features. The Athena Form widget, for example, never queries its children for their geometry input and never asks its parent for a size change. Furthermore, its constraints for each child are quite limited. This makes Form quite short and simple, but also means that it doesn't always do the right thing.

12.4 Writing a Constraint Widget

The following sections describe the portions of the Athena Form widget that relate to geometry management. We have chosen the Athena Form widget instead of the Motif Form widget because the Athena Form widget is less than one quarter the size and is much simpler to understand. The principles at work are similar, and an understanding of the Athena implementation should give you a good start towards understanding geometry management under Motif.

However, before we start, an introduction to the constraints of the Athena Form widget is in order. As you should remember, constraints appear to the user to be resources of the child widgets managed by the Form. Looking at these resources gives you a good idea of the kinds of things that can be done with Athena Form constraints.

- The resources `XtNhorizDistance` and `XtNfromHoriz` specify the widget position in terms of a specified number of pixels horizontally away from another widget in the form. As an example, `XtNhorizDistance` could equal 10 and `XtNfromHoriz` could be the widget ID of another widget in the Form. (When specified in a resource file, `XtNfromHoriz` is set using the instance name of another widget in the form.) The new widget will always be placed 10 pixels to the right of the widget defined in `XtNfromHoriz`, regardless of the size of the Form. If `XtNfromHoriz` equals NULL, then `XtNhorizDistance` is measured from the left edge of the Form.

- Similarly, the resources `XtNvertDistance` and `XtNfromVert` specify the widget position in terms of a specified number of pixels vertically away from another widget in the Form. If `XtNfromVert` equals NULL, then `XtNvertDistance` is measured from the top of the Form.

  When set in the application, the values for `XtNfromHoriz` and `XtNFromVert` must be widget IDs. But in the resource database, widget names are used instead, since the actual widget ID changes each time the application is run. Athena uses an Xmu converter from widget name to widget ID, which is useful when setting constraints from resource files. However, Motif does not provide such a converter.

- The `XtNtop`, `XtNbottom`, `XtNleft`, and `XtNright` resources tell the Form where to position the child when the Form is resized. The values of these resources are specified by the enum `XtEdgeType`, which is defined in *<X11/Xaw/Form.h>*.

- The values `XtChainTop`, `XtChainBottom`, `XtChainLeft`, and `XtChainRight` specify that a constant distance is to be maintained from an edge of the child to, respectively, the top, bottom, left, and right edges of the Form.

- The value `XtRubber` specifies that a proportional distance from the edge of the child to the left or top edge of the Form is to be maintained when the Form is resized. The proportion is determined from the initial position of the child and the initial size of the Form. Form provides a `StringToEdgeType` conversion to allow the resize constraints to be easily specified in a resource file.

12.4.1 The Core Resource List

The Form widget has only one resource of its own, `XtNdefaultDistance`, as shown in Example 12-7. This resource is used only as the default for two of the Constraint resources, `XtNhorizDistance` and `XtNvertDistance`. `XtNdefaultDistance` is used to set the instance field `default_spacing`, which is used in only one place in the widget, in the Constraint `initialize` method described in Section 12.4.4.

Example 12-7. Form: the Core resource list

```
#define Offset(field) XtOffsetOf(FormRec, form.field)
static XtResource resources[] = {
    {
        XtNdefaultDistance,
        XtCThickness,
```

Example 12-7. Form: the Core resource list (continued)

```
        XtRInt,
        sizeof(int),
        Offset(default_spacing),
        XtRImmediate,
        (XtPointer)4
    }
};
#undef Offset
```

12.4.2 The Constraint Resource List

The Form widget has three groups of constraint resources. `XtNhorizDistance`, `Xt-NfromHoriz`, `XtNvertDistance`, and `XtNfromVert` together control the initial position of a child. `XtNtop`, `XtNleft`, `XtNbottom`, and `XtNright` govern repositioning of the child when Form is resized. The `XtNresizable` resource controls whether the `geometry_manager` of this widget will honor requests to change the geometry of this child. Note that `XtNresizable` does not control whether this constraint widget can resize a child—only whether or not it will do so because of a request from the child.*

For more details about how these constraint resources work, read about them on the reference page for the Form widget in Volume Five, *X Toolkit Intrinsics Reference Manual*.

Constraint resources are also called simply *constraints*, particularly because they are stored in a Core instance field called `constraints`. Example 12-8 shows Form's constraint resource list.

Example 12-8. Form: constraint resource list

```
static XtEdgeType defEdge = XtRubber;

#define Offset(field) XtOffsetOf(FormConstraintsRec, form.field)
static XtResource formConstraintResources[] = {
    {
    XtNhorizDistance,
    XtCThickness,
    XtRInt,
    sizeof(int),
    Offset(dx),
    XtRImmediate,
    (XtPointer)DEFAULTVALUE
    },
    {XtNfromHoriz, XtCWidget, XtRWidget, sizeof(Widget),
        Offset(horiz_base), XtRWidget, (XtPointer)NULL},
    {XtNvertDistance, XtCThickness, XtRInt, sizeof(int),
        Offset(dy), XtRImmediate, (XtPointer)DEFAULTVALUE},
    {XtNfromVert, XtCWidget, XtRWidget, sizeof(Widget),
        Offset(vert_base), XtRWidget, (XtPointer)NULL},

    {XtNtop, XtCEdge, XtREdgeType, sizeof(XtEdgeType),
```

---

*The fact that Form does not provide individual control over the resizability of each child is a major weakness.

Example 12-8. Form: constraint resource list (continued)

```
            Offset(top), XtREdgeType, (XtPointer)&defEdge},
        {XtNbottom, XtCEdge, XtREdgeType, sizeof(XtEdgeType),
            Offset(bottom), XtREdgeType, (XtPointer)&defEdge},
        {XtNleft, XtCEdge, XtREdgeType, sizeof(XtEdgeType),
            Offset(left), XtREdgeType, (XtPointer)&defEdge},
        {XtNright, XtCEdge, XtREdgeType, sizeof(XtEdgeType),
            Offset(right), XtREdgeType, (XtPointer)&defEdge},

        {XtNresizable, XtCBoolean, XtRBoolean, sizeof(Boolean),
            Offset(allow_resize), XtRImmediate, (XtPointer)False},
};
#undef Offset
```

The corresponding data structure that this resource list references, FormConstraints, is defined in the private include file for the widget. Its definition is shown in Example 12-9.

Example 12-9. Form: constraint data structure

```
typedef struct _FormConstraintsPart {
/*
 * Constraint Resources.
 */
    XtEdgeType  top, bottom,    /* where to drag edge on resize    */
                left, right;
    int         dx;             /* desired horiz offset            */
    int         dy;             /* desired vertical offset         */
    Widget      horiz_base;     /* measure dx from here if non-null */
    Widget      vert_base;      /* measure dy from here if non-null */
    Boolean     allow_resize;   /* True if child may request resize */
/*
 * Private constraint variables.
 * These store the dimensions of the child prior to layout.
 */
    int         virtual_width, virtual_height;
/*
 * Size of this child as it would be if we did not impose the
 * constraint that its width and height must be greater than zero (0).
 */
    LayoutState layout_state;    /* temporary layout state    */
} FormConstraintsPart;

typedef struct _FormConstraintsRec {
    FormConstraintsPart form;
} FormConstraintsRec, *FormConstraints;
```

The constraints part structure should be considered an instance part structure. This structure has public fields set through resources and private fields that hold state data, just like an instance part structure. Note also that the FormConstraints structure is built the same way as instance structures, by combining part structures for each class into a complete constraint structure. This allows subclasses of Form to create their own constraint part structure and add it after the Form constraint part.

When a widget is created as a child of a constraint widget, the constraint instance structure (`FormConstraintsRec`, in this case) is placed in the `constraints` field of the Core instance structure. Xt makes the constraint resources stored there settable, like resources defined by the child even though they are actually defined and used by the parent.

Note that the constraint resource list of a widget can be queried with `XtGet-ConstraintResourceList`, although this is rarely needed in widget or application code.

12.4.3 Class Structure Initialization

The Form class is a subclass of Constraint. Therefore, its class structure contains class parts for Core, Composite, Constraint, and Form. Example 12-10 shows the class structure initialization of Form. Several methods referenced here have not been discussed so far in this book. They are the Core methods `class_initialize` and `class_part_init`, and the Constraint methods `initialize` and `set_values`. These and all the geometry management-related methods of Form are discussed in Section 12.4.6.

Example 12-10. Form: class structure initialization

```
FormClassRec formClassRec = {
  { /* Core class fields    */
    /* superclass           */    (WidgetClass) &constraintClassRec,
    /* class_name           */    "Form",
    /* widget_size          */    sizeof(FormRec),
    /* class_initialize     */    ClassInitialize,
    /* class_part_init      */    ClassPartInitialize,
    /* class_inited         */    False,
    /* initialize           */    Initialize,
    /* initialize_hook      */    NULL,
    /* realize              */    XtInheritRealize,
    /* actions              */    NULL,
    /* num_actions          */    0,
    /* resources            */    resources,
    /* num_resources        */    XtNumber(resources),
    /* xrm_class            */    NULLQUARK,
    /* compress_motion      */    True,
    /* compress_exposure    */    True,
    /* compress_enterleave  */    True,
    /* visible_interest     */    False,
    /* destroy              */    NULL,
    /* resize               */    Resize,
    /* expose               */    XtInheritExpose,
    /* set_values           */    SetValues,
    /* set_values_hook      */    NULL,
    /* set_values_almost    */    XtInheritSetValuesAlmost,
    /* get_values_hook      */    NULL,
    /* accept_focus         */    NULL,
    /* version              */    XtVersion,
    /* callback_private     */    NULL,
    /* tm_table             */    NULL,
    /* query_geometry       */    PreferredGeometry,
    /* display_accelerator  */    XtInheritDisplayAccelerator,
```

Example 12-10. Form: class structure initialization (continued)

```
      /* extension            */    NULL
   },
   { /* Composite class fields */
      /* geometry_manager      */    GeometryManager,
      /* change_managed        */    ChangeManaged,
      /* insert_child          */    XtInheritInsertChild,
      /* delete_child          */    XtInheritDeleteChild,
      /* extension             */    NULL
   },
   { /* Constraint class fields */
      /* subresourses          */    formConstraintResources,
      /* subresource_count     */    XtNumber(formConstraintResources),
      /* constraint_size       */    sizeof(FormConstraintsRec),
      /* initialize            */    ConstraintInitialize,
      /* destroy               */    NULL,
      /* set_values            */    ConstraintSetValues,
      /* extension             */    NULL
   },
   { /* Form class fields   */
      /* layout                */    Layout
   }
};
WidgetClass formWidgetClass = (WidgetClass)&formClassRec;
```

Note that the Form class is the first widget we have shown that defines a class part field—a method of its own, called `layout`. Since this method is not known to Xt, Xt will never call it. The widget must invoke this method itself at the appropriate times (you will see this invocation in the methods below). This code is made into a method instead of just a private function only to make it possible for subclasses of this widget to inherit or replace the method. Having such a method requires that the widget have a `class_part_init` method to handle the inheritance if a subclass specifies the `layout` method with the symbolic constant `XtInheritLayout` (also defined in this class's private header file).

Section 12.2.1 described which Core and Composite methods are required for composite widgets, and how to initialize the other Core and Composite fields for a composite widget. The same is true for constraint widgets.

However, the Constraint part is probably new to you. The `ConstraintClassPart` structure contains seven fields. The first three fields are where the constraint resource list, the number of resources, and the size of the constraint instance structure are entered. This resource list and instance structure were described in the last section. These fields are analogous to the `resources`, `num_resources`, and `widget_size` fields in the Core class part.

The three next fields, `initialize`, `destroy`, and `set_values` are methods defined by the Constraint class. These methods have the same field names as methods of Core, but are fields of a different structure, and contain pointers to different functions that you may need to write. To differentiate Constraint methods from the Core methods, we will precede the names of Constraint fields with the word "Constraint" and the names of Core fields with the word "Core" throughout this chapter.

Two of the three Constraint methods will be described where they fit in below. We'll describe one of them, Constraint `destroy`, now, because it is not used in Form and is less likely to be needed in the constraint widgets you may write. The Constraint `destroy` method is called when a child is destroyed, just before the Core `destroy` method of the child. It is responsible for freeing any memory allocated by the constraint widget that was used to manage that child. However, like the Core `destroy` method, it does not need to free memory allocated by Xt, such as the constraint data structure for the child.

12.4.4 The Constraint initialize Method

The Constraint `initialize` method is called when a widget is created, soon after the Core `initialize` method. It has the same two responsibilities as the Core initialize method, and one additional responsibility. It must:

- Validate the ranges of resource settings, since they may be user-supplied.

- Compute the value of any private constraint instance part fields that depend on constraint resource values (public constraint instance part fields).

- Set child Core geometry fields to match the constraint resources. For example, if a constraint for the maximum height of a widget is set and the initial value set by the child is larger, the Constraint `initialize` method resets the height field in the Core instance structure.

However, like the Core `initialize` method, the Constraint `initialize` method is responsible only for constraint resources and for Core geometry resources. It need not handle any resources of superclasses (other than the Core geometry resources).

The Form widget performs only one of the tasks listed above, initializing constraint resources. In Form's case, the Constraint `initialize` method (shown in Example 12-11) simply sets the initial values of the `XtNvertDistance` and `XtNhorizDistance` constraint resources to the current value of the `XtNdefaultDistance` Form resource, unless the user has specified a value for either constraint resource. This is done only so that the application can set the Form resource once and have it apply to every child that does not override the value.

Form doesn't validate the values of any user-supplied resource values as it should. For example, the user may supply a negative value for the `XtNhorizDistance` or `XtNvertDistance` resources. This would certainly make the layout look bad, but it could also cause the Form widget to go into an infinite loop on geometry negotiations. In general, all `initialize` methods in Core and Constraint should check for ranges of reasonable values of resources where this makes sense. Range checking eliminates a potential source of bugs. Range checking in `set_values` is also a good idea to give the programmer good warning messages).

Example 12-11. Form: the Constraint initialize method

```
#define DEFAULTVALUE -9999

/* ARGSUSED */
static void ConstraintInitialize(request, new)
    Widget request, new;
{
    FormConstraints form = (FormConstraints)new->core.constraints;
    FormWidget fw = (FormWidget)new->core.parent;

    form->form.virtual_width = (int) new->core.width;
    form->form.virtual_height = (int) new->core.height;

    if (form->form.dx == DEFAULTVALUE)
        form->form.dx = fw->form.default_spacing;

    if (form->form.dy == DEFAULTVALUE)
        form->form.dy = fw->form.default_spacing;
}
```

Note that the Constraint instance part structure (`FormConstraints`) and the Form widget instance structure (`FormWidget`) are accessed by casting two different fields of the child's instance structure passed in.

The Constraint `initialize` method and the child's Core `initialize` are passed the same two copies of the child's instance structure: `request`, and `new`. The `request` widget is the widget as originally requested. The `new` widget starts with the values in the request, but it has already been updated by calling all superclass `initialize` methods.

12.4.5 The class_part_init Method

The `class_part_init` method should be present in a class that defines new methods in its class part structure. These new methods will never be called by Xt since Xt has no knowledge of when to call them. They can only be invoked directly from the widget code. The purpose of making them methods instead of just functions is to allow subclasses to inherit or replace the functions. The `class_part_init` method actually resolves this inheritance by setting each method field to the pointer provided by this class (the subclass is inheriting the method) or to the pointer provided by the subclass (the subclass is replacing the method). Example 12-12 shows a `class_part_init` method for a class that defines only one new method in its class part structure. This method is the Form widget's layout code.

Example 12-12. Form: the class_part_init method

```
static void ClassPartInitialize(class)
    WidgetClass class;
{
    register FormWidgetClass c = (FormWidgetClass) class;

    if (c->form_class.layout == XtInheritLayout)
        c->form_class.layout = Layout;
}
```

The `XtInheritLayout` symbol is defined in the private include file for any class that defines new class part methods (one for each new method). Its value is always `_XtInherit`.

Form itself sets the `layout` field to a pointer to its `Layout` function. When its `class_part_init` method is called when the first instance of Form is created, it does nothing because the `layout` field is not `XtInheritLayout`. When a subclass is defined that sets the `layout` field to a function, the same thing happens: Form's `class_part_init` method is called because it is chained downward (the `class_part_init` methods of all superclasses are called), and it still does nothing because the `layout` field is not `XtInheritLayout`. Thus, the subclass has replaced Form's method. But if the subclass sets the `layout` field to XtInheritLayout, Form's `class_part_init` method sets the field to its own `Layout` function. The subclass has inherited Form's method.

Usually, only the class that defines a particular new method resolves the inheritance by checking for the value of that field in its `class_part_init` method. There is no point in a subclass also checking for an `XtInherit` value, since the downward chaining means that the superclass will have already processed and replaced the `XtInherit` value before the subclass `class_part_init` method is called.

12.4.6 The geometry_manager Method

`geometry_manager` methods handle requests from the children to be resized. Therefore, they typically use the proposed geometry passed in from the child to calculate a new experimental layout, and actually move and resize the children if the new layout is acceptable. However, when the request is just a query, the method should be able to return the same values without actually moving or resizing anything.

The Form `geometry_manager` method is shown in Example 12-13. Note that Form uses the `allow_resize` field (the `XtNresizable` resource) to determine whether to even consider the resize request. Then, if the request specifies a width and height, Form will accept the change by returning `XtGeometryYes`. The `XtMakeGeometryRequest` call that invoked the `geometry_manager` will actually make the geometry change before returning to the child's code. If the request specifies any other geometry change (border width, position, or stacking order), Form will deny the request. Finally, if the request was not a query, Form actually does the new layout. Note that Form never returns `XtGeometry-Done` since it never makes the geometry changes itself. Instead it returns `XtGeometry-Yes` when it agrees with the changes, and lets Xt make the changes.

Note that the `allowed` structure in this routine could be replaced by individual *width* and *height* variables. Also note that the `reply` structure is never filled; it is used only when the `geometry_manager` method wants to suggest a compromise.

Example 12-13. Form: the geometry_manager method

```
/* ARGSUSED */
static XtGeometryResult GeometryManager(w, request, reply)
    Widget w;
    XtWidgetGeometry *request;
    XtWidgetGeometry *reply;    /* RETURN */
{
    FormConstraints form = (FormConstraints)w->core.constraints;
    XtWidgetGeometry allowed;
```

Example 12-13. Form: the geometry_manager method (continued)

```
    if ((request->request_mode & ~(XtCWQueryOnly |
            CWWidth | CWHeight)) ||
            !form->form.allow_resize)
        return XtGeometryNo;
    if (request->request_mode & CWWidth)
        allowed.width = request->width;
    else
        allowed.width = w->core.width;

    if (request->request_mode & CWHeight)
        allowed.height = request->height;
    else
        allowed.height = w->core.height;

    if (allowed.width == w->core.width && allowed.height ==
            w->core.height)
        return XtGeometryNo;

    if (!(request->request_mode & XtCWQueryOnly)) {
        /* reset virtual width and height. */
        form->form.virtual_width = w->core.width = allowed.width;
        form->form.virtual_height = w->core.height = allowed.height;
        RefigureLocations( (FormWidget)w->core.parent );
    }
    return XtGeometryYes;
}
```

The RefigureLocations called from the geometry_manager method is a private function analogous to the DoLayout routine used in ScrollBox, except that Refigure-Locations calls Form's layout method that contains the actual layout code so that the method can be inherited or replaced by subclasses. The layout method calculates a layout and moves and resizes the children. RefigureLocations is also called from the change_managed method, as described in Section 12.4.9. Example 12-14 shows the RefigureLocations function and Form's layout method, which it calls. (The if statement that branches depending on the value of the no_refigure field allows an application to turn relayout on and off, as described in Section 12.4.11.)

Example 12-14. Form: private functions: RefigureLocations and the layout method

```
static void RefigureLocations(w)
    FormWidget w;
{
    /* no_refigure supports the relayout recalculation
      delay described later in this chapter */
    if (w->form.no_refigure) {
        w->form.needs_relayout = True;
    }
    else {
        (*((FormWidgetClass)w->core.widget_class)->form_class.layout)
                ( w, w->core.width, w->core.height );
        w->form.needs_relayout = False;
    }
}
/* ARGSUSED */
```

Example 12-14. Form: private functions: RefigureLocations and the layout method (continued)

```
static Boolean Layout(fw, width, height)
    FormWidget fw;
    Dimension width, height;
{
    int num_children = fw->composite.num_children;
    WidgetList children = fw->composite.children;
    Widget *childP;
    Position maxx, maxy;
    static void LayoutChild();
    Boolean ret_val;

    for (childP = children; childP - children < num_children;
            childP++) {
        FormConstraints form = (FormConstraints)
                (*childP)->core.constraints;
        form->form.layout_state = LayoutPending;
    }

    maxx = maxy = 1;
    /*
     * Layout children one at a time, and determine
     * necessary size for self
     */
    for (childP = children; childP - children
            < num_children; childP++) {
        /*
         * Layout child then find position of bottom right
         * outside corner of child
         */
        if (XtIsManaged(*childP)) {
            Position x, y;
            LayoutChild(*childP);
            x = (*childP)->core.x + (*childP)->core.width
                    + ((*childP)->core.border_width << 1);
            y = (*childP)->core.y + (*childP)->core.height
                    + ((*childP)->core.border_width << 1);
            if (maxx < x) maxx = x;
            if (maxy < y) maxy = y;
        }
    }

    fw->form.preferred_width = (maxx += fw->form.default_spacing);
    fw->form.preferred_height = (maxy += fw->form.default_spacing);

    /* Now ask parent to resize us.  If it says Almost, accept the
     * compromise.  If Almost and parent chose smaller size, or No
     * and we were smaller than necessary, children will be clipped,
     * not laid out again.
     */
    if (fw->form.resize_in_layout
            && (maxx != fw->core.width || maxy != fw->core.height)) {
        XtGeometryResult result;
        result = XtMakeResizeRequest( fw, (Dimension)maxx,
                (Dimension)maxy, (Dimension*)&maxx,
                (Dimension*)&maxy );
        if (result == XtGeometryAlmost)
```

```
        result = XtMakeResizeRequest( fw, (Dimension)maxx,
                (Dimension)maxy, NULL, NULL );
    fw->form.old_width  = fw->core.width;
    fw->form.old_height = fw->core.height;
    ret_val = (result == XtGeometryYes);
} else ret_val = False;

return ret_val;
}
```

The `layout` method treats one child at a time, first initializing the `layout_state` private constraint instance field of each child to `LayoutPending`. The `LayoutChild` routine will start from this value. Next, it calls `LayoutChild` for each child, and at the same time keeps a running total of the sizes of the children so that when the loop is finished it knows how big to be to fit all the children. Finally, it requests of its parent that it be just big enough to fit its children. If the parent denies the request, the code makes no attempt to make another request. If the parent offers a compromise, it is accepted. The Form widget, in either case, may be too big or too small to fit its children. If it is too small, some of its children will be clipped.

The `LayoutChild` routine is shown in Example 12-15. What it does is simple, although it is a little hard to follow because it is called recursively. It moves the child according to the `XtNfromHoriz` and `XtNfromVert` constraint resources.* These resources specify that a child be placed to the right of or below another particular child.

Example 12-15. Form: the LayoutChild private function

```
static void LayoutChild(w)
    Widget w;
{
    FormConstraints form = (FormConstraints)w->core.constraints;
    Position x, y;
    Widget ref;

    switch (form->form.layout_state) {

        case LayoutPending:
                form->form.layout_state = LayoutInProgress;
                break;

        case LayoutDone:
                return;

        case LayoutInProgress:
                String subs[2];
                Cardinal num_subs = 2;
                subs[0] = w->core.name;
                subs[1] = w->core.parent->core.name;
                XtAppWarningMsg(XtWidgetToApplicationContext(w),
                        "constraintLoop","xawFormLayout",
                        "XawToolkitError", "constraint loop\
```

---

*Form resizes children only when it is resized—never during normal layout.

Example 12-15. Form: the LayoutChild private function (continued)

```
                                detected while laying out child\
                                '%s' in FormWidget '%s'",
                                subs, &num_subs);

                return;
        }

    x = form->form.dx;
    y = form->form.dy;

    if ((ref = form->form.horiz_base) != (Widget)NULL) {
        LayoutChild(ref);
        x += ref->core.x + ref->core.width +
                (ref->core.border_width
                << 1);
    }
    if ((ref = form->form.vert_base) != (Widget)NULL) {
        LayoutChild(ref);
        y += ref->core.y + ref->core.height +
                (ref->core.border_width
                << 1);
    }
    XtMoveWidget( w, x, y );
    form->form.layout_state = LayoutDone;
}
```

If neither `XtNfromHoriz` nor `XtNfromVert` are set for the child, it is simply placed the default distance from the top-left corner of the Form. When one child is set, the next child must be placed relative to that child. However, the other child may be later in the list and not properly positioned yet. Therefore, the code calls `LayoutChild` to lay out the child that this child is positioned relative to.

The `layout_state` field catches circular settings for the `XtNfromHoriz` and `Xt-NfromVert` resources. For example, if widget *A* is specified to the right of widget *B*, and widget *B* is specified to the right of widget *A*, there is no solution. `LayoutChild` would be caught in an infinite loop of calling itself. When first called from the `layout` method, the `layout_state` is `LayoutPending`. This is changed to `LayoutInProgress` in the `switch` statement. If the function is called again for the same child, this state will cause the warning message to be printed and the function to exit. The Form widget does not exit—it just gives up processing the invalid constraint resource setting and prints a warning message.

12.4.7 The resize Method

The `resize` method calculates a layout to fit in the new dimensions of Form and moves and resizes the children accordingly. Form's `resize` method is shown in Example 12-16. It consists of a loop that treats each managed child one at a time. The position and dimensions of each child are calculated with the help of the private function `TransformCoord` (also shown in Example 12-16) and the child is moved and resized. `TransformCoord` handles one parameter at a time, and uses a position, the size before resizing, the size after resizing, and the constraints settings to arrive at the appropriate value for the parameter. The old width and height of the Form widget are initialized in the Core `initialize` method and updated at the end of the `resize` method.

Example 12-16. Form: the resize method

```
static void Resize(w)
    Widget w;
{
    FormWidget fw = (FormWidget)w;
    WidgetList children = fw->composite.children;
    int num_children = fw->composite.num_children;
    Widget *childP;
    Position x, y;
    Dimension width, height;

    for (childP = children; childP - children < num_children;
            childP++) {
        FormConstraints form = (FormConstraints)
                (*childP)->core.constraints;
        if (!XtIsManaged(*childP)) continue;
        x = TransformCoord( (*childP)->core.x, fw->form.old_width,
                fw->core.width, form->form.left );
        y = TransformCoord( (*childP)->core.y, fw->form.old_height,
                fw->core.height, form->form.top );

        form->form.virtual_width =
                TransformCoord((Position)((*childP)->core.x
                + form->form.virtual_width
                + 2 * (*childP)->core.border_width),
                fw->form.old_width, fw->core.width,
                form->form.right )
                - (x + 2 * (*childP)->core.border_width);

        form->form.virtual_height =
                TransformCoord((Position)((*childP)->core.y
                + form->form.virtual_height
                + 2 * (*childP)->core.border_width),
                fw->form.old_height, fw->core.height,
                form->form.bottom )
                - ( y + 2 * (*childP)->core.border_width);

        width = (Dimension)
                (form->form.virtual_width < 1) ? 1 :
                form->form.virtual_width;
        height = (Dimension)
                (form->form.virtual_height < 1) ? 1 :
                form->form.virtual_height;

        XtConfigureWidget( *childP, x, y, (Dimension)width,
                (Dimension)height, (*childP)->core.border_width);

    }

    fw->form.old_width = fw->core.width;
    fw->form.old_height = fw->core.height;
}

static Position TransformCoord(loc, old, new, type)
    register Position loc;
    Dimension old, new;
    XtEdgeType type;
```

Example 12-16. Form: the resize method (continued)

```
{
    if (type == XtRubber) {
        if ( ((int) old) > 0)
            loc = (loc * new) / old;
    }
    else if (type == XtChainBottom || type == XtChainRight)
        loc += (Position)new - (Position)old;

    return (loc);
}
```

This `resize` method stores the new size of the children in the `virtual_width` and `virtual_height` constraint part fields, and uses their previous values to arrive at the new size. This is done because Form's `XtNtop`, `XtNbottom`, `XtNleft`, and `XtNright` constraints specify the geometry of the child based on its previous geometry.

Notice that the `for` loop in this particular `resize` method loops through the children directly, using pointer arithmetic. This is equivalent to using a loop that increments an integer and then uses the integer to index the `children` array. For example, the first five lines of the loop could also be expressed as:

```
int i;

for (i = 0; i < num_children; i++) {
    FormConstraints form = (FormConstraints)
            (children[i])->core.constraints;
    if (!XtIsManaged(children[i])) continue;
    x = TransformCoord( (children[i])->core.x,
            fw->form.old_width, fw->core.width, form->form.left );
        .
        .
        .
}
```

12.4.8 The Core and Constraint set_values Methods

When the application calls `XtSetValues` to set the resources of a child of a constraint widget, Xt calls the child's Core `set_values` method and then the parent's Constraint `set_values` method. Both methods are passed the same arguments. Constraint `set_values` validates the ranges of constraint resource settings and computes the value of any private constraint instance part fields that depend on constraint resource values. It should also set child Core geometry fields to match the changes in constraint resources. For example, if a constraint for the maximum height of a widget is changed to a value smaller than the widget's current height, then the Constraint `set_values` procedure should reset the height field in the widget.

Both Core and Constraint `set_values` must return `True` or `False` to indicate whether redisplay of the widget is necessary. For composite and constraint widgets, this value is usually meaningless because there is nothing to redisplay. But these might be useful if, for some reason, you write a composite widget that does have display semantics.

Form defines both the Core and Constraint `set_values` methods as empty functions that return `False`. An easier way to do this is to specify `NULL` for them in the class structure initialization.

12.4.9 The change_managed Method

The `change_managed` method is responsible for making the initial layout of an application and changing the layout when any child changes management state. Form's `change_managed` method (shown in Example 12-17) calls `RefigureLocations` to actually do a layout. (`RefigureLocations` is a private routine equivalent to `DoLayout` in ScrollBox, described in Section sgeoman.) Form's `change_managed` method also stores the previous size of the children in the `virtual_width` and `virtual_height` constraint part fields for use in the `resize` method as described in Section 12.4.7.

Example 12-17. Form: the change_managed method

```
static void ChangeManaged(w)
    Widget w;
{
    FormWidget fw = (FormWidget)w;
    FormConstraints form;
    WidgetList children, childP;
    int num_children = fw->composite.num_children;
    Widget child;

    /*
     * Reset virtual width and height for all children.
     */

    for (children = childP = fw->composite.children;
            childP - children < num_children; childP++) {
        child = *childP;
        if (XtIsManaged(child)) {
            form = (FormConstraints)child->core.constraints;

            if ( child->core.width != 1)
                form->form.virtual_width = (int) child->core.width;
            if ( child->core.height != 1)
                form->form.virtual_height = (int) child->core.height;
        }
    }
    RefigureLocations( (FormWidget)w );
}
```

12.4.10 The query_geometry Method

Form's `query_geometry` method (shown in Example 12-18) is the minimal version, almost identical to the one described for simple widgets in Chapter 7, *Basic Widget Methods*. The `preferred_width` and `preferred_height` instance variables are set in the Form class `Layout` method to the size that just fits the current layout.

Example 12-18. Form: the query_geometry method

```
static XtGeometryResult PreferredGeometry( widget, request, reply  )
    Widget widget;
    XtWidgetGeometry *request, *reply;
{
    FormWidget w = (FormWidget)widget;

    reply->width = w->form.preferred_width;
    reply->height = w->form.preferred_height;
    reply->request_mode = CWWidth | CWHeight;
    if (  request->request_mode & (CWWidth | CWHeight) ==
            reply->request_mode & CWWidth | CWHeight
            && request->width == reply->width
            && request->height == reply->height)
        return XtGeometryYes;
    else if (reply->width == w->core.width && reply->height ==
            w->core.height)
        return XtGeometryNo;
    else
        return XtGeometryAlmost;
}
```

12.4.11 Delaying Geometry Recalculation

During an application's initial layout, the `change_managed` method of a composite widget is called only once even though many children may have been managed. However, after that, `change_managed` is called once for every child that changes management state. Many composite or constraint widgets, especially ones that have complicated layout code, provide a public function (such as the one shown in Example 12-19) that the application can call to turn off layout recalculation until a group of windows is managed or unmanaged, and then call again to trigger recalculation once the whole group of children has been managed or unmanaged.

To implement this delay, you need an instance variable to hold a Boolean value indicating whether to delay or not (`no_refigure`, in this case). You set and unset this variable in this public routine and you test it in `change_managed`.

Example 12-19. Form: the public function for delaying calls to change_managed

```
void XawFormDoLayout(w, doit)
Widget w;
Boolean doit;    /* False, don't recalculate; True, do */
{
    register FormWidget fw = (FormWidget)w;

    fw->form.no_refigure = !doit;

    if ( XtIsRealized(w) && fw->form.needs_relayout )
        RefigureLocations( fw );
}
```

12.5 Compound Widgets

A compound widget is a combination of widgets put together to make a higher-level, user-interface object. For example, a ScrolledWindow widget is itself a composite widget, but it automatically creates its own ScrollBar children. Similarly, the code for MessageBox can create its own Shell parent, and it creates PushButtonGadget children that read OK, Cancel, and Help.

Compound widgets create their children in their `initialize` method, and set resources to position them. Often they also provide resources of functions that make it easy for the application to configure some characteristics of their children. The application can manipulate the children only through these resources, because it cannot access the widget IDs of the compound widget's subwidgets without breaking the rules of data hiding. Thus, compound widgets are convenient for programming, but they make it more difficult to take advantage of all the configurable aspects of the subwidgets.

The main widget of the compound widget may be a subclass of Core, Composite, or Constraint. If it is a subclass of Core, the widget manages the positions and sizes of its children manually whenever it is resized. The success of this strategy is dependent on the children never trying to resize themselves and on the application never trying to resize the children directly.* The latter will not be a problem unless the application breaks the data-hiding rules by manipulating the child directly. The Text widget is an example of this kind of widget. It creates and manages its own scrollbar.

Compound widgets normally define only a few methods and inherit the rest. Compound widgets based on Core will move and resize their children manually in their `resize` method. If the widget is a subclass of Composite or Constraint, the normal geometry management facilities manage the position and size of the children. If it is a subclass of Constraint, the main widget sets the constraints of the children to control the geometry management process by providing a Constraint `initialize` method.

---

*When a child of a simple widget calls XtMakeGeometryRequest because it wants to change its size, XtMakeGeometryRequest always makes the requested changes and returns XtGeometryYes. Therefore, a simple widget parent really has no control over its child if the child wants to resize itself. A simple widget cannot even tell that the child has resized itself.

A compound widget always needs a `destroy` method that destroys the children it created. Compound widgets also need a `set_values` method to manage their resources.

12.6 Stacking Order

We promised earlier to say a bit more about how composite or constraint widgets can control the stacking order of their children. We noted that this must be done manually, because Xt doesn't provide much support for it. This is because most applications do not stack widgets—the whole concept of geometry management is based on each widget trying to lay out its children *without* stacking them. However, there are applications where it makes sense to stack widgets. For example, an application that provides note cards, where each card is a widget, would want to stack them showing only the corner of hidden cards.

There is no Core resource for stacking order, and therefore it can't be set with `XtSetValues` unless you define the resources in your own widget class. Xt provides no call to restack windows; you must use the Xlib functions `XConfigureWindow`, `XRestackWindows`, `XRaiseWindow`, or `XLowerWindow`. When a widget suggests a stacking order for itself through its `query_geometry` method, Xt takes care of making the required Xlib call if the parent agrees with the change. However, stacking requests of unrealized widgets have no effect (so stacking order won't be set this way in the initial geometry negotiation). Therefore, the most robust method to handle stacking order is for your composite widget to make the appropriate Xlib calls directly to change the stacking order of its children. `XRestackWindows` is probably the best call to use. Since restacking the windows doesn't change their requirements for screen space, it shouldn't affect either the parent or the children adversely. The appropriate place to call `XRestackWindows` depends on when you want to change the stacking order. (Note that the stacking change won't become visible until the next time Xt is waiting for an event.)

You can control the initial stacking order of a group of children by creating them in the desired order. The most recently created widget appears on the bottom. (This is the opposite of what you might expect if you know that newly created X windows appears on top of their siblings. The difference is due to the way a composite widget maintains its list of children.)

13

Menus, Gadgets, and Cascaded Popups

This chapter begins by describing how to use Motif popup and cascaded menus. Then it describes how menus actually work, and several ways to create menu widgets. One of these ways involves the use of windowless widgets, or gadgets. This chapter also describes how to use more advanced features of the Xt pop up mechanism, including modal cascades, to implement cascading pop up menus and dialog boxes.

In This Chapter:

Gadgets and Popups

13

Menus, Gadgets,
and Cascaded Popups

In Chapter 3, *More Techniques for Using Widgets*, we show a simple example that pops up a menu and a dialog box. We used Motif's widget creation functions to create these widgets and we let Motif handle their placement when they were popped up. We popped them up by creating a callback that called `XtManageChild`. This chapter continues where Chapter 2 left off by describing how to create other types of menus, and how to create cascaded menus and dialog boxes with Motif.

Motif, however, is atypical since it hides the actual Xt mechanisms that support popup widgets. After describing how Motif handles popups, this chapter continues by exploring these underlying mechanisms. The examples in the second part of the chapter use the R4 Athena widgets, since they expose Xt's underlying mechanisms effectively. Even though Motif hides these details, it is helpful to understand exactly what is happening underneath.

This chapter also discusses cascaded popups—popups that call other popups—and the event management necessary for them to shut out other input elsewhere in the application and system.

Finally, this chapter discusses windowless widgets called *gadgets*, which have been designed to reduce window system overhead. Their most important use is to implement the panes in menu widgets. Gadgets were originally developed by Digital as a part of DECWindows, and were carried over into the version of Xt shipped with Motif 1.0. The MIT X Consortium Intrinsics support a somewhat different implementation of gadgets beginning in Release 4. As mentioned earlier, Motif 1.1 is based on the R4 Xt Intrinsics. As an example of a widget that manages gadgets, we will show the R4 Athena SimpleMenu widget and its gadget children.

Also introduced in R4 is the *object*, which is another kind of windowless widget even simpler than a gadget. Objects are not usually used in menus, so we will reserve discussion of them until Chapter 14, *Miscellaneous Toolkit Programming Techniques*.

In this chapter, we use the term *menu* broadly to refer to any user-interface element that lists many options and allows the user to select one or more. A menu might consist of a list of commands, only one of which can be selected at a time, or a list of nonexclusive Boolean settings that can be turned on or off, or a list of exclusive choices (such as the colors or patterns for a paint palette). A menu that invokes commands will start in the same state each time, while the other two types may have different contents in any particular invocation, showing the settings invoked the previous time or all previous times, or a modified list of choices.

Menus are one of the most important user-interface elements in window-based applications. They offer the same feature as push buttons—a way for the user to invoke application functions or set parameters—but in a more organized and more easily accessible fashion when there are more than a few buttons.

Figure 13-1 compares a menu to a box full of buttons.

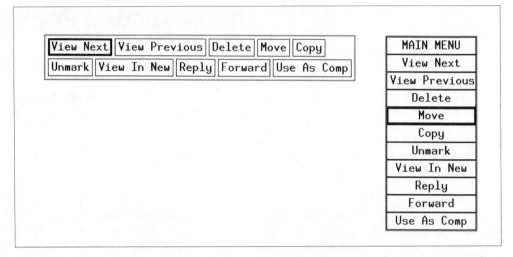

Figure 13-1. Athena Command widgets in an Athena Box widget, and the same commands as a Motif menu

The menu takes up less space because only its title is visible until it is called up.* As a result, you can have more menus than you could have permanent button boxes. Commands can be presented in smaller, more closely related groups. The user will spend less time searching for the desired command.

The commands in the menu are also easier to read because they are arranged one per row. The commands in the menu may even be easier to invoke because it is more natural to drag the mouse up and down than from side to side. And last but not least, menus avoid the worst problem with button boxes: when the application is resized, button boxes may place each command widget in a different position, making it more difficult for the user to find commands.†

---

*Some menus don't even display a title—they simply pop up at the pointer position in response to a particular pointer button/keypress combination. This is the behavior of the menus provided by *xterm* and the system menu of *mwm*. However, this is not very desirable behavior from a user-interface point of view, since it gives the user no visual feedback that a menu is available or how to invoke it. The user needs the manual—something graphical user interfaces are designed to avoid.

†To be fair, there is something to be said for the fact that all the available commands are always visible in an application that uses button boxes. You can invoke a button in a box with just a button click, while in a menu it requires a press, a drag, and a release. When there are only a small number of commands, putting the command widgets in a box is probably better than using a menu.

Some of the applications in the core distribution from MIT use button boxes instead of menus because there was no menu widget in the Athena widget set until Release 4. And some of the applications that do use menus have implemented them directly with Xlib.

13.1 Menu Styles and Implementation

The conventions for the appearance and user interface of menus (look and feel) in widget sets probably varies more than any other aspect of the user interface.

There are several different styles of menus. As we've pointed out earlier, a button box is itself a style of menu. However, in this chapter we will be focusing on popup menus—menus that are not visible until the user presses a pointer button or a key-button combination.

There are several different styles of popup menu. Probably the most familiar is the pulldown menu popularized by the Apple Macintosh. A *pulldown menu* has a label permanently visible in the application, usually on a menu bar at the top. When the pointer is clicked on the label, and then dragged downwards, the menu is pulled down like a window shade, and remains displayed as long as the pointer button is depressed. The currently selected item (as indicated by the pointer position within the menu) is highlighted, and is executed when the pointer button is released.

The variation adopted by Motif and OPEN LOOK (possibly to avoid legal entanglements with Apple) is a menu in which the pointer need not be dragged down to display the menu. Instead, it appears below the menu title as soon as the button is depressed in the menu title. The distinction between pulldown and drop-down menus is a subtle one.

In some cases, selecting an item on the menu or moving off the right side of certain menu panes causes a second menu to appear next to the first (usually to the right). This is referred to as a *cascading menu*. (Another type of cascading popup is a dialog box that pops up another dialog box.)

Finally, there is the pure *spring-loaded popup menu* used by many of the standard X clients, which displays no menu label, and simply pops up at the pointer position, given the appropriate key or button press. For example, the menus in *xterm* pop up when you hold the Control key and press the first or second button while the pointer is anywhere in the *xterm* window. Motif calls this type of menu simply a *popup* menu (as opposed to pulldown or option menus). We will refer to these menus using the term spring-loaded since the term popup is too generic.

One can also imagine many other possible menu styles. For example, an effective user interface could be constructed using only horizontal menus, emulating the single-line menu popularized by Lotus for its character-based 123 spreadsheet. Any given button might either execute an action, or pop up a lower-level menu, which would overlay (and thus appear to replace) the first menu.

In this chapter, though, we will focus on the two styles of menu you are most likely to encounter in X applications: the pulldown menu and the pure spring-loaded popup menu.

In code, the difference between spring-loaded and pulldown menus is primarily the method by which the user invokes the menu and where the menu is placed; one menu widget class can usually work in either way. In Motif, both the pulldown and popup menu styles are actually RowColumn widgets inside Shell widgets, but they are popped up in slightly different ways.

All the differences described so far concern user-interface conventions. The Xt specification, however, classifies popups using a different criteria—while the menu is popped up, how is input dispatched to other parts of the application and to other applications? Also, is the menu subject to window management? The three styles are called modeless popups, modal popups, and spring-loaded popups.

Modeless popups are windows that, once popped up, are subject to window manager control, and for all intents and purposes act like regular applications in themselves. A help window that stayed up, and could be moved and resized like a regular window once popped up, is an example of this type of popup. It is referred to as "modeless" because it doesn't put the application into a special mode, in which only input to the popup is allowed.

A modal popup may or may not be visible to the window manager, but it always disables user-event processing by the application, except in the popup itself. A dialog box that requires the user to enter data or click on a button is an example of a modal popup. Input may still be possible to other applications.

As defined by Xt, a spring-loaded popup is invisible to the window manager and disables user input to all windows in all applications, except to the popup itself. The most important thing about spring-loaded popups is that they are invoked with a key or pointer button press, whereas another type of popup might be invoked as a routine part of application processing, or just because the pointer entered a particular window. Note that even though the term spring-loaded has been used in two different contexts above, both actually refer to the same kinds of widgets. The first use referred to a characteristic user-interface style, and the second to a characteristic absence of window management and disabling of input to other applications. Throughout this chapter, though, we use the term "spring-loaded popup" to refer to menus that pop up at the pointer position when a mouse button is pressed, such as that used by *xterm*, as opposed to popup or pulldown menus.

13.2 Using Motif Menus

Chapter 3, *More Techniques for Using Widgets*, showed how to create and use a Motif pulldown menu. This section demonstrates how to use a Motif popup menu, and then shows how to implement cascaded menus—menus that pop up other menus.

The forthcoming Volume Six, *X Motif Programming Manual*, will describe more thoroughly how to use menus, such as how to add mnemonics and accelerators.

13.2.1 Popup Menus

Using a Motif popup menu is really not much different from using a Motif pulldown menu. The first difference, obviously, is that you use `XmCreatePopupMenu` instead of `Xm-CreatePulldownMenu`. The most significant difference, however, is that you are responsible for placing the popup. As you may recall, a pulldown menu is automatically positioned just below the button whose callback invoked the menu. A popup menu, on the other hand, is usually invoked by a button press in the custom window or main window of the application. The menu usually pops up at the pointer position.

A popup menu can be popped up in response to a button press in a particular widget only if the button press does not already have another meaning in that widget. For example, a Label widget can be used as the widget that will detect a button press and pop up a popup menu, because it doesn't otherwise use button presses for anything. Although a PushButton button widget could pop up a popup menu in its `XmNactivateCallback`, this would confuse the user because this callback is normally associated with executing a command.

Widgets that don't already use button presses usually don't have a callback triggered by them. Therefore, actions or event handlers are often used to place and to pop up menus. Example 13-1 shows the code to create, place, and pop up a popup menu using an event handler.

Example 13-1. Creating, placing, and popping up a popup menu

```
#include <Xm/Xm.h>
/*
 * Public include files for widgets used in this file.
 */
#include <Xm/RowColumn.h>
#include <Xm/PushB.h>
#include <Xm/PushBG.h>
#include <Xm/Label.h>

/*
 * menu pane button callback function
 */
/*ARGSUSED*/
void PaneChosen(w, client_data, call_data)
Widget w;
XtPointer client_data;    /* cast to pane_number */
XtPointer call_data;
{
    int pane_number = (int) client_data;
    printf("Pane %d chosen.\n", pane_number);
}

static void
PostMenu (w, client_data, event)
Widget          w;
XtPointer       client_data;
XEvent          *event;
{
    Widget popup = (Widget) client_data;

    XmMenuPosition(popup, event);
```

Example 13-1. Creating, placing, and popping up a popup menu (continued)

```
        XtManageChild (popup);
}

main(argc, argv)
int argc;
char **argv;
{
        .
        .
        .

    Widget menu, label, entry[10];
        .
        .
        .

    label = XtCreateManagedWidget(
        "label",      /* widget name */
        xmLabelWidgetClass,      /* widget class */
        box,      /* parent widget*/
        NULL,      /* argument list*/
        0    /* arglist size */
        );

    menu = XmCreatePopupMenu(label, "menu", NULL, 0);

    XtAddEventHandler(label, ButtonPressMask, False, PostMenu, menu);

    for (i = 0; i < 10; i++) {
        sprintf(buf, "menupane%d", i);
            menupane[i] = XtCreateManagedWidget(buf, /* widget name */
                    xmPushButtonGadgetClass, menu, NULL, 0);

        XtAddCallback(menupane[i], XmNactivateCallback,
                PaneChosen, i);
    }

    XtRealizeWidget(topLevel);

    XtAppMainLoop(app_context);
}
```

The standard way to place a popup menu is to call XmMenuPosition just before calling
XtManageChild in the function that pops up the widget. This places the popup with the
center of its top edge at the pointer position, but forces the entire menu on the screen (if part
would otherwise extend off the screen).

Note that by default Motif will only pop up a popup menu in response to mouse button 3.
This can be changed by setting the XmNmenuPost resource of the popup menu.

13.2.2 Cascaded Menus

Cascaded menus in Motif are always pulldown menus, regardless of whether the parent menu
is popup or pulldown. The first step in implementing a submenu is to create it with Xm-
CreatePulldownMenu. Next, you create a CascadeButtonGadget as a child of the main
menu, and set its XmNsubMenuId resource to the ID of the submenu. Then populate the

submenu with gadget entries and register their callback functions. Example 13-2 shows the code needed to add a submenu to Example 13-1.

Example 13-2. Adding a cascading submenu

```
#include <Xm/CascadeBG.h>

main(argc, argv)
int argc;
char **argv;
{
    .
    .
    .
    Widget menu, cascade, submenu, subentry[10];
    .
    .
    /* create main menu */
    .
    .
    submenu = XmCreatePulldownMenu(menu, "submenu", NULL, 0);

    cascade = XtVaCreateManagedWidget("cascade",
            xmCascadeButtonGadgetClass, menu,
            XmNsubMenuId, submenu,
            NULL);
    for (i = 0; i < 10; i++) {
        sprintf(buf, "subentry%d", i);
            subentry[i] = XtCreateManagedWidget(buf, /* widget name */
                    xmPushButtonGadgetClass, submenu, NULL, 0);
        XtAddCallback(subentry[i], XmNactivateCallback,
                PaneChosen, i);
    }
    .
    .
    .
}
```

Note that the submenu is created before the CascadeButtonGadget that will invoke the submenu. This makes it possible to set XmNsubMenuId while creating the CascadeButton-Gadget.

13.3 Basic Xt Popup Support

As mentioned above, Motif hides Xt's mechanisms that support popups. This section exposes these mechanisms by describing how to create and use a menu using the Athena widgets in two different menu styles: spring-loaded and pulldown. The purpose of this exercise is to expose some of the issues involved in event management of popups. Seeing how to do the event management explicitly should help you to use popups more effectively.

The challenge of creating a popup with Box and Command buttons is to make it pop up and down at the right times, and to control its event handling to fit the menu style. We will also experiment with creating a cascaded menu, in which one menu pane in a main menu invokes a submenu.

Finally, this section describes how to create a menu using the R4 Athena SimpleMenu widget and its gadget children.

13.3.1 A Spring-loaded Menu: Pointer Grabbing

A spring-loaded menu should pop up when a button press occurs in a particular widget; usually the application's main window. The menu should stay visible as long as the user holds down that button, and disappear when the button is released. If the button is released in a menu pane, the function registered for that pane should be invoked. If the button is released outside the menu, no function should be invoked but the menu should still be popped down.

The only tricky part of implementing a spring-loaded menu is getting the menu to pop down when the button is released outside the menu. Since this occurs outside the menu and possibly outside the application, the X server will not send the button release event to the application unless a *grab* is in effect. Normally, user events are sent to the window that contains the pointer. But after an application makes a grab, the X server sends all events of particular types to the window that made the grab, even if the pointer is no longer in the window.

The X server defines several types of grab: keyboard grabs, pointer grabs, and server grabs. Keyboard and pointer grabs control only input from the indicated device, while server grabs make the server act on requests from one application exclusively. (Server grabs are mainly used by window managers.) Pointer grabs are used for controlling events in popups when a pointer button pops up the popup, and keyboard grabs are used when a key press pops up the popup. We will discuss pointer grabs since keyboard grabs are analogous (and keyboard-triggered popups are less common).

There are two types of pointer grabs: passive grabs and active grabs. An *active grab* is invoked directly with the Xt function `XtGrabPointer`. This function tells the server that you want the grab to begin right away and to continue until specifically released with `XtUngrabPointer`. Active grabs are not normally used for popups.*

A *passive grab* tells the server that you want a grab to begin when a certain key or button combination is pressed in a certain window (the combination that is to pop up the popup). The grab continues until the button in the combination is released. This is perfect for menus because we need the grab only until the button is released. (Also, as you'll see in the section on pulldown menus, you can register several passive grabs for the same key-button combination as long as each grab is initiated by a press in a different window. This technique lets you have as many pulldown menus as you want. Since spring-loaded popups are generally invoked by a press in the same window—the main window of the application—you will need to use a different key-button combination for each different menu.)

---

*One reason that `XtGrabPointer` is rarely used for popups is that it requires that the window that will receive the grabbed events be visible. This is often not the case. In a menu, for example, the window that you want to grab the events may be hidden by the menu panes even when the menu is popped up. Another reason is that you need to call `XtUngrabPointer` to release the grab when finished. Passive grabs match the task better.

Passive grabs of a key or button and active grabs of the pointer or the keyboard we will call *global grabs*, since they affect not only this application but prevent distribution of the grabbed events to other applications running on the same server. This terminology is to distinguish the global grab from the effects of Xt's local *grab mode*, which simulates a global grab but requires no call to the server and affects only the distribution of events within the application. The Xt grab mode cannot commandeer events that occur outside the application like a global grab can. When an Xt grab is in effect, Xt redirects user events to the popups even if they occur somewhere else in the application. (Non-user events continue to be dispatched to widgets so that they can redraw themselves).

The Xt grab mode can be either exclusive or nonexclusive. Exclusive and nonexclusive Xt grabs differ only when a popup has popped up another popup—a so-called cascaded popup. An *exclusive* Xt grab redirects all user events that occur within the application to the latest popup in the cascade. A nonexclusive Xt grab redirects events to whichever popup the pointer is in, or the latest popup if the pointer is outside all the popups (but still in the application).

Here are examples of the two kinds of Xt grab modes. Consider an application that pops up a dialog box to get a filename from the user. The application wants to read the file. If the file can't be opened, the application pops up another dialog telling this to the user. This error popup takes no input, so input is still desired in the filename entry popup. This situation calls for a nonexclusive grab. By contrast, consider an application that uses the same filename entry popup to save a file. If the file exists, it would pop up a dialog that would ask whether the existing file should be overwritten. This popup must be answered before a new filename is chosen. This situation would call for an exclusive grab. In brief, an exclusive grab constrains input to the the latest widget in the cascade, while a nonexclusive grab allows input to any widget in the cascade. We'll talk more about the Xt grab mode in Section 13.3.3, when we talk about popup cascades.

Xt provides three ways of popping widgets up and down:

- There are three built-in callback functions: `XtCallbackNone`, `XtCallback-Exclusive`, and `XtCallbackNonexclusive`. Each of these functions pops up a widget with a different type of Xt grab mode, as indicated by its name. `XtCallback-None` makes no grab at all. `XtCallbackExclusive` makes an exclusive Xt grab, while `XtCallbackNonexclusive` makes a nonexclusive grab.

  `XtCallbackPopdown` is the corresponding built-in callback function to pop down a widget.

- There are two built-in actions, `XtMenuPopup` and `XtMenuPopdown`, that pop up or pop down a widget. You can use these actions in translation tables in the app-defaults file or application code. `XtMenuPopup` always asserts an exclusive Xt grab and a passive global grab if the pointer or keyboard invoked it.

- There are three functions, `XtPopup`, `XtPopupSpringLoaded`, and `XtPopdown`, that you can call directly in your application code to pop up or pop down a widget. `Xt-Popup` has a *grab_kind* argument that lets you specify whether to assert an exclusive or nonexclusive grab mode, or no grab. `XtPopupSpringLoaded` always asserts an exclusive Xt grab and makes an global pointer grab so that a button release outside a menu can be used to trigger the popping down of the menu.

Each of these ways is appropriate for different situations, and they are often used in combination. Each is described in the sections below.

Passive global grabs can be invoked directly using the Xt functions `XtGrabButton` and `XtGrabKey`. However, Xt takes care of making the appropriate passive global grab if you use `XtPopupSpringLoaded` or the `XtMenuPopup` action to pop up your shell widget. As we will see, the other ways to pop up a widget do not make any global grab, which makes them inappropriate for popping up main menus.* However, they are still useful for some types of dialog boxes and for cascading submenus, if the main menu has used `XtMenu-Popup` to assert an exclusive grab. We'll return to this subject in Section 13.3.3.

A popup menu globally grabs the pointer to force the user to make a menu choice before leaving the menu, or to pop down the menu if no choice is made. However, this global grab is necessary for another reason as well. The X server automatically grabs the pointer beginning at a button press and ending at the release of the same button. Since the initial button press pops up the menu, the next button release would also arrive at the same widget—the application main window or the menu title—even if the pointer were already in the menu. Furthermore, the application main window would get all `EnterNotify` and `Leave-Notify` events, so the Command widgets in the menu wouldn't get any of them. When the menu is popped up with `XtMenuPopup` action, the passive global grab it makes cancels the automatic global grab. (Again, pointer grabs redirect only the events caused directly by the pointer; `ButtonPress`, `ButtonRelease`, `EnterNotify`, `LeaveNotify`, and `MotionNotify`. All other events (most notably `Expose` events) occur and are delivered normally.)

With that background, let's take a look at an application that provides a spring-loaded menu. The *xmenu1* application's permanent appearance is a variation of *xbox*; it displays a large Label widget that we are using to simulate an application's main window and a Command widget for quitting. Pressing any button in the Label widget calls up the menu, which operates as described at the beginning of this section. *xmenu1* is shown in Figure 13-2. As usual, we suggest you compile and run this example now.

The relevant code in *xmenu1* consists of an action routine to place the popup, code to add the action, a callback routine to handle when a menu item has been chosen, and code to create the Box populated with Command widgets that will act as the menu. Example 13-3 shows the complete code.

Example 13-3. xmenu1: complete code

```
/*
 *   xmenu1.c - simple spring-loaded menu
 */

#include <stdio.h>

/*
 * Standard Toolkit include files:
```

---

*With `XtPopupSpringLoaded` you can write callback functions that are the equivalent of `XtCallback*`, except that they will pop up a menu with the necessary passive global grab. You can also write your own version of the `XtMenuPopup` action if it doesn't do what you want. You will need `XtRegisterGrabAction` to do this. This function tells Xt to automatically start a passive global grab whenever a certain action is invoked.

Figure 13-2. xmenu1: application with spring-loaded popup menu

Example 13-3. xmenu1: complete code (continued)

```
 */
#include <X11/Intrinsic.h>
#include <X11/StringDefs.h>

#include <X11/Shell.h>

/*
 * Public include files for widgets used in this file.
 */
#include <X11/Xaw/Command.h>
#include <X11/Xaw/Box.h>
#include <X11/Xaw/Label.h>

/*
 * The popup shell ID is global because both dialog and pshell
 * are needed in the dialogDone callback, and both can't be
 * passed in without creating a structure.
 */
Widget pshell;

/*ARGSUSED*/
void PlaceMenu(w, event)
Widget w;
XButtonEvent *event;
{
    /* should make sure coordinates allow menu to fit on screen */

    /* move submenu shell to slightly left and above button
     * press position */
    XtVaSetValues(pshell,
            XtNx, event->x_root - 10,
            XtNy, event->y_root - 10,
            NULL);
```

Example 13-3. xmenu1: complete code (continued)

```
}
/*
 * quit button callback function
 */
/*ARGSUSED*/
void Quit(w, client_data, call_data)
Widget w;
XtPointer client_data, call_data;
{
    exit(0);
}

/*
 * menu pane button callback function
 */
/*ARGSUSED*/
void PaneChosen(w, client_data, call_data)
Widget w;
XtPointer client_data;    /* cast to pane_number */
XtPointer call_data;
{
    int pane_number = (int) client_data;
    printf("Pane %d chosen.\n", pane_number);
    XtPopdown(pshell);
}

main(argc, argv)
int argc;
char **argv;
{
    XtAppContext app_context;
    Widget topLevel, box, quit, label, menulabel, menubox,
            menupane[10];
    int i;
    String buf[50];

    static XtActionsRec trial_actions[] = {
        {"placeMenu", PlaceMenu},
    };

    topLevel = XtVaAppInitialize(
        &app_context,          /* Application context */
        "XMenu1",              /* application class name */
        NULL, 0,               /* command line option list */
        &argc, argv,           /* command line args */
        NULL,                  /* for missing app-defaults file */
        NULL);                 /* terminate varargs list */

    box = XtCreateManagedWidget(
        "box",                 /* widget name */
        boxWidgetClass,        /* widget class */
        topLevel,              /* parent widget*/
        NULL,                  /* argument list*/
        0                      /* arglist size */
        );

    label = XtCreateManagedWidget(
        "label",               /* widget name */
```

Example 13-3. xmenu1: complete code (continued)

```
            labelWidgetClass,      /* widget class */
            box,                   /* parent widget*/
            NULL,                  /* argument list*/
            0                      /* arglist size */
            );
    quit = XtCreateManagedWidget(
            "quit",                /* widget name */
            commandWidgetClass,    /* widget class */
            box,                   /* parent widget*/
            NULL,                  /* argument list*/
            0                      /* arglist size */
            );
    pshell = XtCreatePopupShell(
            "pshell",
            transientShellWidgetClass,
            topLevel,
            NULL,
            0
            );
    menubox = XtCreateManagedWidget(
            "menubox",             /* widget name */
            boxWidgetClass,        /* widget class */
            pshell,                /* parent widget*/
            NULL,                  /* argument list*/
            0                      /* arglist size */
            );
    menulabel = XtCreateManagedWidget(
            "menulabel",           /* widget name */
            labelWidgetClass,      /* widget class */
            menubox,               /* parent widget*/
            NULL,                  /* argument list*/
            0                      /* arglist size */
            );
    for (i = 0; i < 10; i++) {
        sprintf(buf, "menupane%d", i);
        menupane[i] = XtCreateManagedWidget(buf, /* widget name */
                commandWidgetClass, menubox, NULL, 0);

        XtAddCallback(menupane[i], XtNcallback, PaneChosen, i);
    }

    XtAppAddActions(app_context, trial_actions,
            XtNumber(trial_actions));

    XtAddCallback(quit, XtNcallback, Quit, 0);

    XtRealizeWidget(topLevel);

    XtAppMainLoop(app_context);
}
```

The PlacePopup action just places the popup slightly to the left and above the position where the pointer button that popped it up was clicked, using the coordinates reported in the button event. The offset of ten pixels from the pointer position simply helps to make sure

Gadgets and Popups

that the pointer is inside the menu.* Remember that the window created by a popup shell widget is a child of the root window and therefore is placed relative to the root window. The ButtonPress event pointer coordinates relative to the root window are used.

The PaneChosen callback function is a stub function used in this example as the notify callback for all the menu panes. In this example, it simply prints the name of the chosen pane to *stdout* and then pops down the menu using XtPopdown. In a real application, a different callback function would probably be registered for each pane.

Instead of calling XtPopdown in each of these separate callback functions, you could write a single additional callback function that calls XtPopdown, and then add it to the callback list for the Command widget that makes up each menu pane.

As usual, the popup is created by first creating a popup shell, then a Box widget as its child, and then a series of Label and Command widgets as children of Box. The popup shell and the box are invisible. As with all menus, what you actually see is the array of children.

Note that this program does not include any code that would pop up the menu. We've done that from the app-defaults file shown in Example 13-4. The translations we have defined for the Label widget invoke Xt's built-in XtMenuPopup action.

Example 13-4. XMenu1: the app-defaults file

```
!
! Appearance Resources
!
*quit.label:      Quit
*label.label:      This is a Pretend Main Window; Press in here.
*menulabel.label:    MAIN MENU
!
! make all entries in menu same width
! (needs adjusting for longest entry)
!
*menulabel.width:    135
*menubox.Command.width:  135
!
! Pane Strings
!
*menupane0.label:  View Next
*menupane1.label:  View Previous
*menupane2.label:  Delete
*menupane3.label:  Move
*menupane4.label:  Copy
*menupane5.label:  Unmark
*menupane6.label:  View In New
*menupane7.label:  Reply
*menupane8.label:  Forward
*menupane9.label:  Use As Comp
!
! make Box leave no space around Command widgets in menu
```

---

*It is important to provide a consistent user interface, so you should use the same offset in all menus. Menus in commercial widget sets such as the OPEN LOOK widgets have carefully designed and documented policies about popup window placement. This allows the user's "pointer reflexes" to be trained, so that using menus becomes as automatic and easy as possible.

Example 13-4. XMenu1: the app-defaults file (continued)

```
!
*pshell.Box.hSpace: 0
*pshell.Box.vSpace: 0
!
! Functional Resources
!
*menubox.Command.translations:\
    <EnterWindow>:      highlight()                 \n\
    <LeaveWindow>:      reset()                     \n\
    <BtnUp>:            set() notify() unset()
*label.translations:\
    <BtnDown>: placeMenu() XtMenuPopup(pshell)
*pshell.translations:\
    <BtnUp>: XtMenuPopdown(pshell)
```

There are a number of settings designed to give the Box widget a characteristic menu appearance: all of the Command widgets are forced to have the same size (rather than the size of their label), and the Box widget is forced to leave no space between the command widgets.

However, it is the new translations that are the critical part of this app-defaults file. The Label widget must be given translations so that a button press will pop up the widget. The supplied translation maps a button press into a call to the application action PlacePopup and then to Xt's predefined XtMenuPopup action. The argument to XtMenuPopup in the translation is the instance name of the popup shell. Xt converts this string name into the widget ID of the popup shell before it can pop up the widget.

We are replacing rather than overriding this widget's translations because it is a Label widget and has no default translations.

The menu panes are Command widgets, but we need to adjust their event response so that they will be triggered on a button release with no corresponding press (since the press that popped up the menu occurred in the application main window). We are replacing their translations to get rid of the translation for ButtonPress (which would still be present if we used the #augment directive, and we would have to create an action that did nothing in order to replace it with #override). The translation for ButtonRelease (abbreviated BtnUp in the translation table) calls all the actions that usually occur in Command widgets with both press and release.

Perhaps least obvious is the translation we have added to pop down the menu when the pointer button is released outside the menu. As mentioned earlier, Xt makes a passive global pointer grab on the popup shell (pshell) in the XtMenuPopup action. When the pointer is inside the menu, the Command widgets intercept these grabbed events, because they are descendants of pshell and they have a translation for ButtonRelease events. This invokes the actions in the selected Command widget. But when the pointer is outside the menu, the grabbed events are sent directly to the widget that was specified in the grab call, namely pshell. Therefore, the translation to pop down the menu on button release must be added to pshell. (Again, this translation table is simply replaced because the popup shell normally has no translations.)

13.3.2 A Pulldown Menu

What are the desired characteristics of a pulldown menu? There is a Command widget or the like permanently visible in the application, with a label indicating some common characteristic of the items in the menu. When a button is pressed in this widget, the menu should pop up on or just below the button. Dragging the pointer down through the menu with the button still held should highlight the entry that is pointed to. Releasing the button in an entry should invoke or set that entry and pop down the menu. Moving out of the menu should not change this behavior, except that if the button is released anywhere outside of a menu pane, the menu should pop down without executing any entry.

If you compile and run *xmenu2* you can try out this style of menu. The appearance of this application is shown in Figure 13-3.

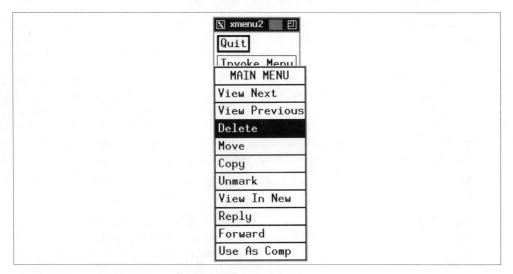

Figure 13-3. xmenu2: a pulldown menu

Invoking a menu as a pulldown is a simple enhancement of the spring-loaded invocation method just shown. We can do everything exactly the same as in the spring-loaded example, except that a pulldown menu should appear just below the pressme widget, not at the position of the pointer. Therefore, all we need to change is the placement code. However, since the coordinates in the event are not necessary for placing the popups, we can use a callback function instead of an action to place the popup. (In general, it is better to use an existing callback than to add an action to do the same thing.)

Popup shell widgets have XtNpopupCallback and XtNpopdownCallback callback resources; the functions on these callback lists are called whenever the popup is popped up or down using any of the Xt mechanisms.

In the last example we created an action called PlaceMenu, that moves the popup shell before it was actually popped up. We included it in a translation along with the standard action XtMenuPopup, which was actually used to pop up the widget. *xmenu2* also uses the standard action XtMenuPopup to pop up the widget, but it uses the

`XtNpopupCallback` resource to provide the code to place the widget. Using the callback saves having to reference the placement action in the translation table. This is preferable, since the placement code should almost always be hardcoded rather than user-configurable. Another advantage of the popup and popdown callbacks is that you may arrange for a popup to be popped up or down in more than one way, and it may be convenient to have certain code called automatically in all cases.

(You can also use the `XtNpopupCallback` resource to specify a callback function to create a popup widget the first time it is popped up, instead of at application startup. The one problem is that the functions on the callback list are invoked every time the widget is popped up. To make sure that your function callback creates the popup only once (the first time), the callback function should remove itself from the callback list by calling `XtRemove-Callback`.)

There is not enough difference between *xmenu1* and *xmenu2* to merit showing the complete code. All we have done is changed the `PlaceMenu` function from an action into a callback and changed its placement logic to place the popup relative to the invoking Command widget. We have then modified the app-defaults file accordingly.

Example 13-5 shows the `PlaceMenu` routine (now a callback, not an action) and the code to register it as a callback.

Example 13-5. xmenu2: code to place pulldown menu

```
/*ARGSUSED*/
void PlaceMenu(w, client_data, call_data)
Widget w;
XtPointer client_data;
XtPointer call_data;
{
    Position x, y;
    Dimension height;

    /*
     * translate coordinates in application top-level window
     * into coordinates from root window origin.
     */
    XtTranslateCoords(pressme,      /* Widget */
            (Position) 0,           /* x */
            (Position) 0,           /* y */
            &x, &y);                /* coords on root window */

    /* get height of pressme so that menu is positioned below */
    XtVaGetValues(pressme,
            XtNheight, &height,
            NULL);

    /* move popup shell one pixel above and left of this position
     * (it's not visible yet) */
    XtVaSetValues(pshell,
            XtNx, x - 1,
            XtNy, y + height,
            NULL);
}

main(argc, argv)
int argc;
```

Example 13-5. xmenu2: code to place pulldown menu (continued)

```
char **argv;
{
    .
    .
    .
    XtAddCallback(pshell, XtNpopupCallback, PlaceMenu, NULL);
    .
    .
    .
}
```

Xt calls the functions on the XtNpopupCallback list before it pops up the widget. This means that PlaceMenu is called before the XtMenuPopup action, placing the widget before it is popped up.

Note that the XtTranslateCoords routine determines the root window coordinates at the origin of the pressme widget. Because of the reparenting done by most window managers, this information cannot be obtained by using XtGetValues to read the XtNx and XtNy resources.*

Example 13-6 shows the translation portion of the app-defaults file.

Example 13-6. XMenu2: translation portion of the app-defaults file

```
!
! Translation resources
!
*pressme.translations:\
    <EnterWindow>:      highlight()                 \n\
    <LeaveWindow>:      reset()                     \n\
    <BtnDown>:          set() XtMenuPopup(pshell) reset()
!
*pshell.translations:\
    <BtnUp>:            XtMenuPopdown(pshell)
!
*menubox.Command.translations:\
    <EnterWindow>:      set()                       \n\
    <LeaveWindow>:      unset()                     \n\
    <BtnUp>:            notify() unset()
```

These translations are different from those for *xmenu1* only in that pressme is a Command widget, which already has its own translation table, rather than a widget without existing translations such as Label (which we used as a fake main window). We have modified the translations of pressme to be suitable for this use. Note that the translation no longer calls PlaceMenu as an action because it is now a callback.

---

*Incidentally, XTranslateCoordinates, the Xlib equivalent of XtTranslateCoords, gets the same information and a little more by querying the server. XtTranslatCoords does not have to make a server request because Xt stores this data locally. Each time a window in this application is moved, Xt receives this information as an event and updates its knowledge of the position of each window. This is an important optimization, because server queries are subject to network delays and tend to slow applications.

The translations for the menu pane Command widgets are also somewhat different from *xmenu1*, but only for cosmetic reasons. This iteration of the *xmenu* example uses the `set` and `unset` actions instead of `highlight` and `reset` or `unhighlight` to make the Command widgets highlight their entire box instead of just an area near the border. (Although this modification makes the menu look more like a typical menu, it also seems to make it slower.)

To create several menus you simply need to replicate the code shown here, changing the variable names for each menu. The passive global grabs invoked by Xt for each menu do not interfere with each other even if they specify the same key/button combination, because they specify different windows in which the key/button combination will begin the grab.

It is sometimes useful to be able to get a list of children in a menu, especially if you add and subtract menu entries. You can do this by querying the *XtNchildren* and *XtNnumChildren* resources of the parent. The value of *XtNchildren* is a list of the widget ID's of the children. This technique allows you to eliminate maintaining global variables for every pane of every menu.

13.3.3 Cascaded Menus

A cascaded menu is a menu in which one or more panes do not invoke functions but instead bring up additional menus.

The techniques used to bring up cascaded menus can also be used to have dialog boxes bring up other dialog boxes. However, cascaded menus are more challenging because they rely on the passive global pointer grab to receive the `ButtonRelease` event that occurs outside the menu and application.

You can implement a cascaded menu the same way for both spring-loaded and pulldown menus simply by adding to the code we've already written to implement a single menu. We'll show you *xmenu5*, the spring-loaded version, since it is slightly shorter. (*xmenu4* is the equivalent pulldown version.) Both are included in the example source code. In this example, only one menu pane will be used to invoke a submenu. However, this technique can be generalized to have additional panes bring up additional submenus.

First, let's describe exactly how we expect the cascaded menu to work. Figure 13-4 shows both menus popped up. (Compile the program and try it.)

The main menu works as described above. However, one of the panes—the one that brings up the submenu—has an arrow pointing to the right after its label. This pane does not highlight itself when the pointer moves inside (telling the user that this pane is different). Instead, when the user moves the pointer out through the right edge of the pane, the submenu pops up. The submenu operates just like the main menu. When the button is released inside either menu, the callback function associated with the chosen pane will be invoked. When the button is released outside of either menu, both menus pop down. If the pointer is moved back out of the submenu into the main menu, only the submenu pops down.

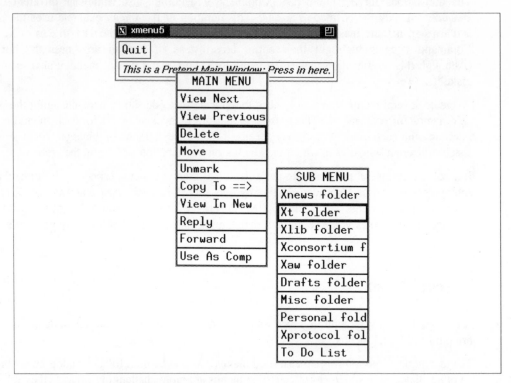

Figure 13-4. xmenu5: cascaded spring-loaded menus

To create the submenu, we create a new popup shell, Box widget, and a set of Command widgets, and add callbacks for each function the submenu panes will invoke (in this example, one common callback). Then we write three actions: `PlaceMenu` (which you have already seen), `CheckRightAndPopupSubmenu` (which places and pops up the submenu if the pointer leaves the main menu pane through its right side), and `PopdownSubmenu` (which pops down the submenu if the pointer leaves the submenu). These actions are shown in Example 13-7.

Example 13-7. xmenu5: actions that place, pop up, and pop down main menus and submenus

```
/*ARGSUSED*/
void PlaceMenu(w, event, params, num_params)
Widget w;
XEvent *event;
String *params;
Cardinal *num_params;
{
    XButtonEvent *bevent = (XButtonEvent *) event;

    /* should make sure coordinates allow menu to fit on screen */

    /* move submenu shell to slightly left and above button
     * press position */
    XtVaSetValues(pshell,
```

```
                    XtNx, bevent->x_root - 10,
                    XtNy, bevent->y_root - 10,
                    NULL);
}

/*ARGSUSED*/
void CheckRightAndPopupSubmenu(w, event, params, num_params)
Widget w;
XEvent *event;
String *params;
Cardinal *num_params;
{
    XLeaveWindowEvent *leave_event = (XLeaveWindowEvent *) event;
    Dimension height, width;

    XtVaGetValues(w,
        XtNheight, &height,
        XtNwidth, &width,
        NULL);

    if ((leave_event->x > width) && (leave_event->y > 0)
            && (leave_event->y < height)) {
        /* move submenu shell to start just right of pane,
         * using an arbitrary offset to place pointer in
         * first item. */
        XtVaSetValues(subshell,
                XtNx, leave_event->x_root,
                XtNy, leave_event->y_root - 12,
                NULL);
        XtPopup(subshell, XtGrabNonexclusive);
    }
}

/*ARGSUSED*/
void PopdownSubmenu(w, event, params, num_params)
Widget w;
XEvent *event;
String *params;
Cardinal *num_params;
{
    XtPopdown(subshell);
}
```

As usual, the app-defaults file specifies which events trigger these actions. We'll show this file in a moment, but for now you need to know just that CheckRightAndPopup-Submenu and PopdownSubmenu are triggered by LeaveNotify events. We want the submenu to pop up and down only when the pointer leaves through certain parts of certain sides of the widget—the entire right side of a pane for popping it up, and the part of the sub-menu touching the main menu on the left side for popping it down. These two actions are called in response to all LeaveNotify events, and they check if the pointer left through the correct parts before popping up and down the submenu.

As you may recall, we mentioned earlier that no matter what the arguments, XtPopup and all other Xt facilities for grabbing, except XtMenuPopup and XtPopupSpring-Loaded, make no passive global grab, and therefore can't be used for spring-loaded or

Gadgets and Popups

pulldown main menus. It turns out that for submenus the opposite is true—XtPopup and XtCallback* work fine, but XtMenuPopup is inappropriate because no new passive grab is needed. The original grab directs events normally to all widgets in the application, including the submenu, and directs all events that occur outside the application to pshell.

The CheckRightAndPopupSubmenu action calls XtPopup with a grab mode of Xt-GrabNonexclusive. This grab mode controls Xt's event dispatching within the application—it has nothing to do with the passive global grab that Xt makes from the XtMenu-Popup action. XtGrabNonexclusive means that widgets in the cascade but outside of the submenu will continue to get events normally. The grab mode specified in the call to XtPopup, or specified by the standard popup callback function selected (XtCallback-Exclusive or XtCallbackNonexclusive) merely control the event dispatching within the application.

As an exercise, you may want to modify the example so that CheckRightAndPopup-Submenu calls XtPopup with a grab mode of XtGrabExclusive, and see how the menus work as a result. The XtGrabExclusive mode means that only the most recent popup popped up will get events, while XtGrabNonexclusive means that all popups in a popped-up cascade will get events. In this case, when the submenu is popped up, it alone will get pointer events if you use grab mode XtGrabExclusive, while both it and the main menu will get pointer events if you use grab mode XtGrabNonexclusive. Because of the logic that pops down the submenu when the pointer leaves it through the portion adjoining the main menu, you can see this difference only if you move out through another part of the submenu and then around into the main menu again. (In the example code distribution, *xmenu5.c* uses XtGrabNonexclusive and *xmenu4.c* uses XtGrab-Exclusive, so that you can compare the results of these two flags.)

The user-interface conventions for a particular widget set usually specify which kinds of popups should have exclusive grabs and which nonexclusive. Note that the effect of these two grab modes is the same unless there is more than one popup widget in a cascade visible.

CheckRightAndPopupSubmenu places the submenu itself (instead of using a separate action) because the menu should be placed only when it is first popped up. If the placement code were a separate action, it would be called every time a LeaveWindow event arrived, even if not through the correct border of the widget. (Remember that this code is in an action rather than a callback because it uses the contents of the event.)

The translation portion of the app-defaults file for *xmenu5* is shown in Example 13-8.

Example 13-8. XMenu5: translation portion of app-defaults file

```
!
! Appearance resources
!
*menupane5.label:   Copy To ==>
    .
    .     (other appearance resources not shown)
    .
!
! Translation resources
!
!  popping down both menus
*pshell.translations:\
```

```
        <BtnUp>: XtMenuPopdown(subshell) XtMenuPopdown(pshell)
!
!  popping up main menu
*label.translations:\
        <BtnDown>: placeMenu() XtMenuPopup(pshell)
!
!  popping down submenu
*menubox.menupane5.translations:\
        <LeaveWindow>:      checkRightAndPopupSubmenu()
!
! Main Menu translations
*menubox.Command.translations:\
        <EnterWindow>:      highlight()                    \n\
        <LeaveWindow>:      reset()                        \n\
        <BtnUp>:            set() notify() unset()
!
! Sub Menu translations
*subbox.translations:\
        <LeaveWindow>:      popdownSubmenu(subbox)
*subbox.Command.translations:\
        <EnterWindow>:      highlight()                    \n\
        <LeaveWindow>:      reset()                        \n\
        <BtnUp>:            set() notify() unset()
```

The first three translation tables handle popping up the main menu and making the menu Command widgets work as expected. We've seen these in previous examples.

The translation table for pshell pops down one or both menus; no error or warning is caused if only the main menu is up. This translation table works because the button release is sent to pshell if it occurs outside a menu regardless of whether just the main menu or both menus are up.

In this case, menu pane 5 is the pane that will pop up the submenu. The label for this pane is shown at the top of Example 13-8. The translation for this pane replaces all the normal translations for highlighting and notifying with a single translation for LeaveWindow events. These events in this widget trigger the CheckRightAndPopupSubmenu action which has already been described.

The translations for the subbox widget invoke PopdownSubmenu action to check whether the pointer left the submenu. In this case, the submenu is popped down, but the original popup remains visible.

The pane that will pop up the submenu and its event handling characteristics is controlled from the app-defaults file. Therefore, it may seem like you can change which menu pane invokes the submenu simply by changing the app-defaults file. This is true here, because the menu actions are nonfunctional and simply call a common callback. But it would not be possible if each pane invoked its own callback. To give the user the freedom to rearrange the menu, you would have to use actions instead of callbacks.

Note that you can define accelerators for any of the menus shown up to this point simply by placing settings for the XtNaccelerators resource in the app-defaults file. You would set this resource for every Command widget in the menus. This provides keyboard shortcuts

Gadgets and Popups

for popping up the menu and choosing a pane. However, remember to make sure that each key combination is unique.

13.3.4 Using the R4 SimpleMenu Widget

Once you have R4, you can use a real menu widget: the R4 SimpleMenu widget. The internals of this widget and its children, which are gadgets, are described later. This section describes a simple application that uses the SimpleMenu widget.*

R4 supplies three types of panes to be used with the SimpleMenu widget: SmeBSB (an entry composed of a bitmap, a string, and another bitmap), SmeLine (a horizontal line between entries), and Sme (a blank entry). The SimpleMenu widget is itself a subclass of the popup shell widget, and therefore no separate popup shell needs to be created.

R4 also provides a MenuButton widget, which is a subclass of Command with built-in placement and popup code. Using a MenuButton to invoke a menu makes it even simpler to implement a pulldown menu, since the popup and placement code can be eliminated from the application.

The *xmenu7* application shown in Example 13-9 creates a SimpleMenu widget with panes of all three types. The menu is invoked in pulldown style using the R4 MenuButton widget.†

As an additional enhancement, the menu marks or unmarks each item when it is selected in addition to calling a callback function. This iteration marks entries with the X logo, which is available as a standard bitmap in */usr/include/X11/bitmaps* (on UNIX systems).

Figure 13-5 shows the appearance of the program.

Example 13-9. xmenu7: using the SimpleMenu widget and its children

```
/* xmenu7.c */

#include <stdio.h>

#include <X11/Intrinsic.h>
#include <X11/StringDefs.h>
#include <X11/bitmaps/xlogo16>

#include <X11/Xaw/MenuButton.h>
#include <X11/Xaw/SimpleMenu.h>
#include <X11/Xaw/SmeBSB.h>
#include <X11/Xaw/SmeLine.h>

#define NUM_MENU_ITEMS 12

static String menu_entry_names[] = {
   "quit",
   "item1",
   "item2",
   "item3",
```

---

*Note that if you have an R3 version of the Xt Intrinsics library, you cannot use the SimpleMenu widget even if you can get its code. The widget depends on changes to Xt introduced in R4.

†This example was written by Chris Peterson of MIT Project Athena and modified only slightly by the authors.

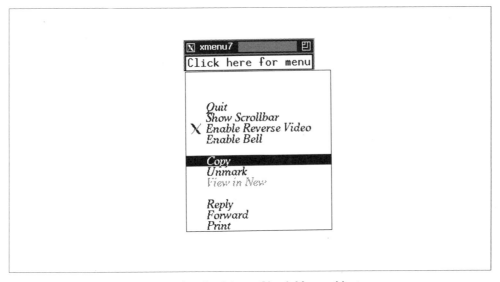

Figure 13-5. xmenu7: a menu using the Athena SimpleMenu widget

Example 13-9. xmenu7: using the SimpleMenu widget and its children (continued)

```
    "line",
    "item5",
    "item6",
    "item7",
    "blank",
    "menu1",
    "menu2",
    "menu3",
};
static Boolean status[NUM_MENU_ITEMS];
static Pixmap mark;

/* ARGSUSED */
static void
MenuSelect(w, client_data, garbage)
Widget w;
XtPointer client_data;
XtPointer garbage;               /* call_data */
{
    int pane_num = (int) client_data;

    printf("Menu item %s has been selected.\n", XtName(w));

    if (pane_num == 0)           /* quit selected. */
        exit(0);

    if (status[pane_num])
        XtVaSetValues(w,
                XtNleftBitmap, None,
                NULL);
    else
        XtVaSetValues(w,
```

```
                    XtNleftBitmap, mark,
                    NULL);

    status[pane_num] = !status[pane_num];
}

void
main(argc, argv)
char **argv;
int argc;
{
    XtAppContext app_context;
    Widget topLevel, menu, button, entry;
    int i;
    Arg arglist[1];

    topLevel = XtVaAppInitialize(
        &app_context,          /* Application context */
        "XMenu7",              /* Application class */
        NULL, 0,               /* command line option list */
        &argc, argv,           /* command line args */
        NULL,                  /* for missing app-defaults file */
        NULL);                 /* terminate varargs list */

    button = XtCreateManagedWidget("menuButton",
            menuButtonWidgetClass, topLevel,
            arglist, (Cardinal) 0);

    menu = XtCreatePopupShell("menu", simpleMenuWidgetClass,
            button, NULL, 0);

    for (i = 0; i < NUM_MENU_ITEMS ; i++) {
        String item = menu_entry_names[i];

        if (i == 4)   /* use a line pane */
            entry = XtCreateManagedWidget(item,
                    smeLineObjectClass, menu,
                    NULL, 0);
        else if (i == 8) /* blank entry */
            entry = XtCreateManagedWidget(item, smeObjectClass, menu,
                    NULL, 0);
        else {
            entry = XtCreateManagedWidget(item, smeBSBObjectClass,
                    menu, NULL, 0);

            XtAddCallback(entry, XtNcallback, MenuSelect,
                    (XtPointer) i);
        }
    }

    mark = XCreateBitmapFromData(XtDisplay(topLevel),
            RootWindowOfScreen(XtScreen(topLevel)),
            xlogo16_bits, xlogo16_width, xlogo16_height);

    XtRealizeWidget(topLevel);
    XtAppMainLoop(app_context);
}
```

You will notice that each pane has an `XtNleftBitmap` resource, which is alternately set to the X logo or to nothing each time that item is selected.

The app-defaults file for *xmenu7* is shown in Example 13-10.

Example 13-10. XMenu7: app-defaults file

```
!
! For Color workstations only.
!
XMenu7*SimpleMenu*foreground:            SteelBlue
XMenu7*SimpleMenu*menuLabel.foreground:   Gold
XMenu7*SimpleMenu*line.foreground:        Grey

XMenu7*MenuButton.label:          Click here for menu

XMenu7*SimpleMenu*menuLabel.vertSpace:     100
XMenu7*SimpleMenu*menuLabel.leftMargin:     70
XMenu7*SimpleMenu.label: Main Menu
XMenu7*SimpleMenu*item1*label: Show Scrollbar
XMenu7*SimpleMenu*item2*label: Enable Reverse Video
XMenu7*SimpleMenu*item3*label: Enable Bell
XMenu7*SimpleMenu*item4*label: Disable Auto-Repeat
XMenu7*SimpleMenu*item5*label: Copy
XMenu7*SimpleMenu*item6*label: Unmark
XMenu7*SimpleMenu*item7*label: View in New
XMenu7*SimpleMenu*menu1*label: Reply
XMenu7*SimpleMenu*menu2*label: Forward
XMenu7*SimpleMenu*menu3*label: Print
XMenu7*SimpleMenu*quit*label:             Quit
XMenu7*SimpleMenu*RowHeight:         16
XMenu7*SimpleMenu*item7*sensitive:      off
XMenu7*SimpleMenu*HorizontalMargins:    30
! Just for fun:
XMenu7*font: *times*medium*18*iso8859-1
!XMenu7*item7*font: *helv*medium*24*iso8859-1
!XMenu7*item8*font: *helv*bold*24*iso8859-1

*quit*accelerators:\
    <Key>q: notify()
*item1*accelerators:\
    <Key>1: notify()
*item2*accelerators:\
    <Key>2: notify()
*item3*accelerators:\
    <Key>3: notify()
*item5*accelerators:\
    <Key>5: notify()
*item6*accelerators:\
    <Key>6: notify()
*item7*accelerators:\
    <Key>7: notify()
*menu1*accelerators:\
    <Key>m: notify()
```

This file simply sets various cosmetic features of the menu. (See Appendix C, *Naming Conventions*, for information on font-naming conventions.) Naturally, you could easily set the strings for each menu entry in this file. Note that there are no translation tables in this file because MenuButton and SimpleMenu are doing exactly what they were designed to do.

Accelerators can be defined for menus with gadget children, but not in the usual sense. They cannot be defined to invoke the actions of the gadget children, but they can invoke global application actions, which for menus is usually good enough. For example, in the R4 *xmh*, one item on one of the menus incorporates new mail. From the widget, the `notify` action of the menu pane gadget calls the `DoIncorporateNewMail` callback function. The `XtNaccelerators` resource for the SimpleMenu widget itself (not the gadgets) maps a Meta-I key event into a call to the `XmhIncorporateNewMail` global action. `XmhIncorporateNewMail` then calls `DoIncorporateNewMail`. This use of accelerators depends on having both a callback and an action form of each function.

13.3.5 Delayed Popup Creation

As we've seen, a popup may consist of a single widget, or it may be a shell widget which contains a composite widget which contains a number of children. In the latter case, creating all those widgets (or gadgets) takes time. It may be beneficial to create those widgets using idle time in the application instead of delaying startup. In either case, it may make sense to create the popup only when it is needed, to minimize wasted resources.

If your goal is to speed startup, and you want all menus created even if some are never used, you can register a work procedure to create each popup, as described in Section 8.5. As you may recall, a work procedure uses idle time in the application to call a function, which must return swiftly. If you use this technique, you add one work procedure for each popup you need to create, and you need to add code to make sure that the popup has been created before the user is allowed to use it.

If your goal is to create only the required popups, you can create the popup in a callback function or action routine that you have registered to place or pop up the popup. In this case, you would have a static variable in the callback or action to make sure that the popup widgets are only created the first time the popup is popped up. You need to have created the popup shell before this can work.

There is also another way to create only the required popups. Shell widgets have an `XtNcreatePopupChildProc` resource which you can set to a function that creates the Shell's children. See `XtCreatePopupChildProc(2)` in Volume Five, *X Toolkit Intrinsics Reference Manual*, for the calling sequence of this function type. The Xt specification does not say whether an `XtCreatePopupChildProc` is called just once when the shell is first popped up or every time it is popped up. But the MIT implementation of Xt calls it every time the shell is popped up, so you will again need a static variable to make sure the children are only created once.

13.4 About Dialog Boxes

Although we have been talking so far exclusively about menus, much that has been said is also true of dialog boxes. Both menus and dialog boxes that get user input usually need to get that input before other application functions can be invoked. Of course, one way to disable all other application functions is to make all other widgets insensitive with XtSet-Sensitive (passing it False). Setting the sensitivity of one common ancestor does this efficiently, but even this is too slow because all the widgets redraw themselves dimmed or grayed. It is much faster to use a global grab. Unlike menus, which require the global grab in order to get button release events outside the application so they can pop down properly, dialog boxes do not, strictly speaking, need a grab. But they sometimes make the grab anyway to disable other application functions.

Dialog boxes can also invoke other dialog boxes. For example, a dialog box that gets input might check the validity of the input before popping down the dialog, and if incorrect, pop up a message telling the user the problem with the input. Cascaded dialog boxes are implemented the same way as cascaded menus. Note that, as a general rule, sub-dialog boxes are popped up with grab mode XtGrabExclusive, which means that the user must satisfy the most deeply nested dialog first. However, it is often desirable to leave a Help dialog on the screen until after the dialog it provides help for has been removed.

Some popups do not need to disable other application functions. For example, imagine a dialog box that informed the user of some fact without requiring confirmation. This kind of popup would be popped up with grab mode XtGrabNone, allowing the user to continue with other application functions.

We pointed out earlier that the built-in callback functions for popping up a widget are not useful for menus because they make no passive global pointer grab. However, they come in handy for dialog boxes. The functions XtCallbackNone, XtCallbackExclusive, and XtCallbackNonexclusive can be used to pop up dialog boxes, as long as the position of the dialog box need not depend on information in an event.

We haven't shown how to use Xt's standard callback for popping down a widget: Xt-CallbackPopdown. Instead of calling XtPopdown in the callback functions for each menu entry, we can add XtCallbackPopdown to the callback list after the existing callback function. XtCallbackPopdown requires an XtPopdownId structure to be passed as the *client_data* argument. This structure must contain the popup shell and the widget that invoked the popup (the MenuButton or Command widget).

All three of the standard popup callbacks set the invoking widget to insensitive mode before popping up the widget. XtCallbackPopdown resets the invoking widget to sensitive mode. Therefore, if you use XtCallbackNone, XtCallbackNonexclusive, or XtCallbackExclusive without also using XtCallbackPopdown, remember to set the widget to sensitive mode yourself. This feature is useless but also harmless when the popup is spring-loaded, because the invoking widget is often the main application window and that widget rarely responds to sensitivity.

In certain rare cases, you may want to use XtAddGrab and XtRemoveGrab directly to append a widget to or remove a widget from the current popup cascade. These functions are called internally by the Xt facilities that pop widgets up and down, and should not be necessary on their own. Note that these functions never make a request to the server to start or release a passive global pointer grab—they affect only Xt's internal event dispatching. (However, the functions `XtGrabKey`, `XtGrabKeyboard`, `XtGrabButton`, and `Xt-GrabPointer` do initiate global grabs. These functions are described in Chapter 14, *Miscellaneous Toolkit Programming Techniques*.)

13.5 Gadgets

When an application includes many different menus with many fields each, the overhead of having separate widgets for every menu pane becomes significant. Because each widget requires structures on the client side and windows on the server side, every widget increases the executable size and server memory usage and increases the traffic over the network. It is always a good idea to minimize the number of widgets used in your application.

Writing a single widget that implements an entire menu, including all its panes, solves this problem. The widget could define subresources for configuring each pane. (The callback list would be one of these subresources. `XtCallCallbacks` could not be used to invoke these callbacks because it cannot distinguish between subparts. However, the callbacks can be called directly by looping through the callback list. This is awkward, but not too difficult.) This widget would not lack flexibility if the subparts are implemented as completely separate code so that the types of menu panes are extensible. However, gadgets turn out to be an easier and more elegant solution to the problem.

As of Release 4, Xt provides gadgets, which are simplified widgets that do not create windows.* Gadgets require less memory than widgets on the client side (and less disk space for the executable file) and consume none at all on the server side. Gadgets can be used for the panes of a menu, solving all of the problems just discussed. A gadget is fully configurable using the resource database just like a widget, and can have its own callback list.

However, the reduced consumption of gadgets does have a price. Gadgets have to draw on their parent's window, and they share this space with the parent and with all other gadget children. The gadgets and the parent must agree to draw in certain areas only. For this reason, gadgets must be used with a special composite widget parent that is prepared to manage them properly.

The Release 4 SimpleMenu widget is such a parent. It is a composite widget designed to manage gadget children. The gadgets provided by Release 4 are Sme, SmeBSB, and Sme-Line (where Sme stands for Simple Menu Entry). These provide a blank entry (and generic menu entry superclass), an entry which can contain a bitmap, a string, and another bitmap (thus BSB), and an entry that draws a horizontal line. We will use and describe this widget and these gadgets both to show how menu widgets are built and to demonstrate how the parent and the gadgets work together.

---

*The OSF Motif 1.0 Intrinsics support a different implementation of gadgets than those described here. Motif 1.1, however, uses the R4 standard Intrinsics, which includes the gadget implementation described here.

Gadgets do not handle events automatically as widgets do, and because they have no windows, the server does not handle overlapping between them. This places certain demands on the parent. All the gadgets that are children of a particular parent share that parent's window. The parent is responsible for coordinating the gadget children, telling them about events by calling their functions. Therefore, the composite widget that manages a group of gadgets must be specially designed for that purpose, not a general-purpose composite or constraint widget such as Box or Form. It is possible for a composite widget to manage both gadget and widget children, but its code has to be more involved to do this.

Like normal widgets, gadgets provide their own code to redraw themselves in their `expose` method. However, since gadgets do not receive events, they depend on the parent to directly call their `expose` method. The parent keeps track of the geometry of each child, and when the parent's `expose` method is called, this method calculates whether the area exposed overlaps any of the gadget children. If the area exposed does overlap a gadget, the parent's `expose` method calls that gadget's `expose` method, which redraws the area.

A gadget's actions also have to work differently from widget actions because of the fact that gadgets don't get events. A gadget defines its actions as methods—as fields in its class part structure—instead of in an action list and translation table. It initializes these fields directly to pointers to functions during class initialization. The parent widget has corresponding actions that are defined and operate like normal actions, except that they determine which gadget the event that invoked the action occurred in and call the gadget method corresponding to that action. In other words, the parent has actions that operate the gadget children.

One weakness of a menu composed of gadget panes is that gadgets cannot have an accelerator table. Therefore, accelerators cannot be used to provide a keyboard equivalent that would invoke each menu pane.

The parent of gadgets has to position the gadget children so that they do not overlap, or take care of the consequences if they do overlap. Since the gadgets draw on the parent's window, if they did overlap they would draw over each other's graphics, with unpredictable results. The parent would have to calculate the area of overlap between two gadgets, and clear this area before letting one of the gadgets draw itself. (A gadget could clear its own area before drawing, but this would be unnecessary in many cases, and would cause flashing.)

Gadgets are subclasses of RectObj, one of the invisible superclasses of Core that we have so far ignored because for widgets it is safe to assume that Core is the top of the widget class hierarchy.* The actual class hierarchy leading up to Core is shown in Figure 13-6.

The "unnamed class" actually has a name (WindowObj) but this class is intentionally undocumented in the Xt specification so that its characteristics can be changed in later releases without compatibility problems. You should never create subclasses directly from the unnamed class.

The superclasses of Core are not real classes in the sense that they do not play by all the rules we have described in Chapter 6, *Inside a Widget*. For one thing, each shares what we call the Core class structure instead of adding its own part structure. Applications are never

---

*In R3, the header files for these invisible classes are not so invisible. They were all present in */usr/include/X11* with all the other Xt header files. In R4, only the header files for RectObj are public, so that you can write and compile gadgets.

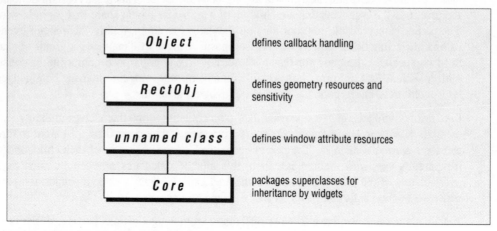

Figure 13-6. Class hierarchy derivation of Core

intended to create instances of these superclasses—they are really just part of the implementation of Xt. Instead of developing all the characteristics of widgets in one large base class Core, it made more sense to implement Xt in object-oriented fashion by dividing the implementation into separate pseudo-classes. It is important to know what each early class defines simply so that you know what characteristics are available in gadgets and which are available only in widgets. Each class defines the following features:

- Object defines only the `XtNdestroyCallback` resource and the underlying support for callbacks in general.

- RectObj defines the geometry resources (`XtNx`, `XtNy`, `XtNwidth`, `XtNheight`, and `XtNborder_width`) and the resources that control sensitivity: `XtNancestor-Sensitive` and `XtNsensitive`. RectObj itself doesn't use the sensitivity resources. They are provided at this level in the hierarchy so that sensitivity can be set for gadgets. Gadgets draw themselves according to these resources (gray if insensitive), and check these resources in their action routines (stored in their class part methods), invoking their callback function only if sensitive.

- The unnamed class (WindowObj) adds many window-oriented resources: ones that control window attributes such as the background pixmap, permanent window features such as the window depth, and event resources such as translations and accelerators. It also includes the `XtNmappedWhenManaged` resource. This class is known as the unnamed class because it never appears in widget, gadget, or application code. Widgets are subclassed from Core, while gadgets are subclassed from RectObj. The exact features of unnamed class are subject to change and should not be relied upon.

The Core class structure actually is inherited all the way from RectObj. Therefore, the class structure in gadgets is the Core class structure you are already familiar with. All the event-related fields in the Core class part structure of gadgets are unused. The only exception is the `expose` method, which is present, but draws on the parent's window and is not called in the usual way by Xt because the gadget receives no events. The remaining non-event-related fields have the same purpose as for widgets, including all the remaining methods.

Without further ado, let's take a look at a gadget, and then at a gadget parent.

13.5.1 Inside a Gadget

Many portions of a gadget's code are exactly the same as those of a widget, as described in Chapter 6, *Inside a Widget*. This section summarizes the parts that are identical so that you know that nothing is left out, and describes the differences in detail.

The code for gadgets and widgets includes the same three implementation files with the same naming conventions. As in Chapter 6, we'll take the three implementation files one at a time, beginning with the private header file, then the code file, and then the public header file.

As in widget code, many of the conventions described here are automatically taken care of for you when you are writing a new gadget if you copy all three files of an existing gadget and then globally change the gadget class name.

The Athena menu pane gadgets are implemented in two class levels:

- Sme (Simple Menu Entry) defines the callback for an entry, the actions to highlight, unhighlight, and notify, and the code that allows subclasses to inherit or replace these actions (because they are defined as methods). The actual functions for highlight and unhighlight are empty, while the notify action calls the callback. The expose method of this gadget is also empty. This gadget can be used by itself to create a blank entry.

- SmeBSB and SmeLine are each subclasses of Sme. SmeLine replaces only the expose method of its superclass. SmeBSB replaces both the expose method and the highlight and unhighlight actions of the superclass. (Sme can be subclassed to create new types of menu entries.)

The following sections describe both Sme and SmeBSB.

13.5.2 Private Header File

The private header file for a gadget is identical in format to the private header file for a widget. It defines a class part structure for this class of gadget and then a complete class structure including the class parts of superclasses and this class. The only difference is that a gadget inherits its features from Object and RectObj, whereas a widget inherits from Core. Example 13-11 shows the complete class structure of the R4 Athena Sme gadget.

Example 13-11. Sme gadget: class part and complete class structure declaration

```
typedef struct _SmeClassPart {
    void (*highlight)();
    void (*unhighlight)();
    void (*notify)();
    XtPointer extension;
} SmeClassPart;
```

```
/* Full class record declaration */
typedef struct _SmeClassRec {
    RectObjClassPart    rect_class;
    SmeClassPart    sme_class;
} SmeClassRec;

#define XtInheritHighlight      ((_XawEntryVoidFunc) _XtInherit)
#define XtInheritUnhighlight    XtInheritHighlight
#define XtInheritNotify         XtInheritHighlight
```

Notice that the complete class structure declaration does not include the class part for the Object class, even though it is a superclass. This is because all the superclasses of Core share the same class part structure.

The class part structure for Sme defines three methods—these are essentially the gadget's actions, but they will be invoked by the gadget parent's actions, not directly by Xt. The extension field allows fields to be added to this structure in a future version while retaining binary compatibility. In a future version this field could be changed to point to an extension structure.*

Any class that defines methods must provide code to allow them to be inherited or replaced by subclasses. The Sme class therefore must define the XtInherit constants that allow the methods to be inherited. The *.c* code file provides the class_part_init method that allows them to be replaced. (See Section 12.4.5.)

In the private header file for SmeBSB, the class part structure would contain only the extension field, because SmeBSB will be using the highlight, unhighlight, and notify fields defined by Sme. However, the *.c* file will initialize these fields to point to its own functions.

The instance part structure and complete instance structure of Sme are shown in Example 13-12.

Example 13-12. Sme gadget: instance part and complete instance structure declaration

```
typedef struct {
    /* resources */
    XtCallbackList callbacks;    /* The callback list */
} SmePart;

typedef struct _SmeRec {
    ObjectPart      object;
    RectObjPart     rectangle;
    SmePart     sme;
} SmeRec;
```

The SmePart adds a callbacks resource. The complete SmeRec includes the prior elements in the widget hierarchy: ObjectPart and RectObjPart. Note that unlike the

---

*Note that the extension field is defined as type XtPointer. In R4, all occurrences of caddr_t have been replaced with XtPointer. On most systems, XtPointer will be defined to be caddr_t. But for some architectures, caddr_t is too small to hold a pointer to a function. On such systems, XtPointer will be defined to be larger. The caddr_t type will continue to work on most systems, but you are advised to use XtPointer instead for maximum portability.

class structure, the Object class does appear in the complete instance structure, because the superclasses of Core do not share instance structures.

The instance part structure for SmeBSB includes the usual fields to maintain the graphics state of the entry, including the label, colors, font, GCs, and positioning information. The complete instance structure for SmeBSB is the same as the one for Sme but with the Sme-BSBPart structure added at the end.

13.5.3 The Gadget Source File

The source file for a gadget is identical in form to a widget source file. The only differences are that the superclass of a gadget in the class structure initialization is `rectObjClass-Rec`, and the complete instance structure type is called `SmeObject` for a gadget where it would have been `SmeWidget` if the entry was a true widget. Therefore, `SmeObject` is the type into which you cast the pointer to the instance structure before accessing the structure's fields in all the widget methods.

In addition, several of the Core class structure fields that might be used in a widget are never used in gadgets. The following is the complete list of fields that are always initialized to a certain value in a gadget:

- `realize` set to `NULL`

- `actions` set to `NULL`

- `num_actions` set to 0 (zero)

- `compress_motion` set to `False`

- `compress_exposure` set to `False`

- `compress_enterleave` set to `False`

- `visible_interest` set to `False`

- `resize` set to `NULL`

- `display_accelerators` set to `NULL`

Setting these fields otherwise (of the right type) probably won't cause the gadget to crash, but won't accomplish anything useful either.

Gadgets, like widgets, should always define the `query_geometry` method, and either define `set_values_almost` or initialize it to `XtInheritSetValuesAlmost`. The remainder of the fields and methods have the same purpose and are used in the same way as for widgets.

There are, however, slight differences in the code for certain gadget methods. The `expose` method checks not only its own sensitivity but also its parent's sensitivity before deciding whether to draw the entry in normal colors or grayed. When creating GCs using `XCreate-GC` or creating any other server resources from the `initialize` method using an Xlib call, you must remember to use the parent's window, since the gadget has no window. (`Xt-Window` is not smart enough to give you the parent's window ID in the case of gadgets.)

Also, the parent's resource values, such as `background_pixel`, may be used to provide data in common among all instances of a subclass like SmeBSB.

13.5.4 The Public Header File

The only difference in the public header file between widgets and gadgets is that what would have been `Widget` for a widget is `Object` for a gadget. As mentioned previously, if you are writing a gadget you should start by copying the files for an existing gadget and then globally change names. Then you will start with the proper conventions already in place.

13.5.5 The Gadget Parent

A gadget parent is a composite widget designed to manage gadget children. Gadget parents perform all the geometry management tasks that all composite widgets perform, which are described in Chapter 12, *Geometry Management*. Gadgets also follow all the rules of normal widget children. However, gadget parents also have the added responsibility of managing the overlap of gadgets or making sure they don't overlap, and of handling events for the gadgets and calling gadget code. This section describes the gadget-managing role of the gadget parent.

The Athena SimpleMenu widget is designed to manage the gadget children already described, Sme, SmeLine, and SmeBSB (and any other subclass of Sme that is written later). It forms a vertical menu with horizontal panes. It is quite a large widget because it contains all the geometry management code in addition to code for managing events for the gadgets. We'll concentrate just on the code that manages events for the gadgets, since the geometry management code is described in Chapter 12, *Geometry Management*.

Let's begin with the `expose` method. SimpleMenu's `expose` method does no drawing of its own. It simply calls the `expose` methods of the gadget children. However, it compares the region passed into its `expose` method to determine which gadgets need redrawing. Example 13-13 shows SimpleMenu's `expose` method.

Example 13-13. SimpleMenu: expose method calling gadget children's expose methods

```
#define ForAllChildren(smw, childP) \
    for ( (childP) = (SmeObject *) (smw)->composite.children ; \
        (childP) < (SmeObject *) ( (smw)->composite.children + \
        (smw)->composite.num_children );   (childP)++ )

/* ARGSUSED */
static void
Redisplay(w, event, region)
Widget w;
XEvent * event;
Region region;
{
    SimpleMenuWidget smw = (SimpleMenuWidget) w;
    SmeObject * entry;
    SmeObjectClass class;
```

```
    if (region == NULL)
        XClearWindow(XtDisplay(w), XtWindow(w));

    /*
     * Check and Paint each of the entries - including the label.
     */

    ForAllChildren(smw, entry) {
        if (!XtIsManaged ( (Widget) *entry))
            continue;

        if (region != NULL)
            switch(XRectInRegion(region, (int) (*entry)->rectangle.x,
                    (int) (*entry)->rectangle.y,
                    (unsigned int) (*entry)->rectangle.width,
                    (unsigned int) (*entry)->rectangle.height)) {
                case RectangleIn:
                case RectanglePart:
                    break;
                default:
                    continue;
                }
        class = (SmeObjectClass) (*entry)->object.widget_class;

        if (class->rect_class.expose != NULL)
            (class->rect_class.expose)((Widget) *entry, NULL, NULL);
    }
}
```

Note that this `expose` method is also called from elsewhere in the widget code (specifically, from the `resize` and `geometry_manager` methods) to redraw the gadgets. In these cases, the region passed in is set to `NULL`, and the method clears its window and redraws all the gadgets.

Also note how this `expose` method invokes the `expose` methods of its children. All `expose` methods (and in fact all methods) are stored in the class structure, not the instance structure. Composite widgets keep only a list of the instance structures of their children. However, one field in each instance structure points to the class structure for that child. This is the `widget_class` field of the Object instance part.* In this example, the *entry* counter variable is a pointer to the gadget ID (opaque pointer to the instance structure) of one of the children. Another variable, *class*, declared as a pointer to the `SmeObjectClass` class structure (the expected class of the children), is set to the `widget_class` field in the instance structure of one of the children. Then the `expose` field of this class structure is checked to see if it is `NULL`, and if not it is invoked.

Note that the class of the children is hardcoded in this method. This widget can manage only Sme widgets and its subclasses.

---

*The Core instance part structure (not complete) is the concatenation of the instance parts of the three superclasses Object, RectObj, and the unnamed class. Therefore, it also includes a `widget_class` field. Since composite widgets do not normally need to invoke the methods of their children, you shouldn't need to access this field.

The `resize` method of SimpleMenu must resize the children when it is resized itself. (Actually, this is unlikely, since the SimpleMenu widget itself is a subclass of Shell and is therefore not managed by any parent.) This method is invoked only when the user resizes the menu using the window manager. Since this widget has the authority to determine the geometry of its children, it can simply resize them. This particular resize method (shown in Example 13-14) simply sets their width to be the same as its own.

Example 13-14. SimpleMenu: resize method

```
static void
Resize(w)
Widget w;
{
    SimpleMenuWidget smw = (SimpleMenuWidget) w;
    SmeObject * entry;

    if ( !XtIsRealized(w) ) return;

    ForAllChildren(smw, entry)  /* reset width of all entries. */
        if (XtIsManaged( (Widget) *entry))
            (*entry)->rectangle.width = smw->core.width;

    Redisplay(w, (XEvent *) NULL, (Region) NULL);
}
```

Notice that this `resize` method invokes the `expose` method (`Redisplay`) because the gadgets don't have `resize` methods, and will not redraw themselves in response to their size change.*

Now let's look at SimpleMenu's actions. Their only purpose is to call the gadgets' actions when the appropriate events arrive. These actions are added in the usual way: they are declared at the top of the *.c* file, then registered with an action list that is entered into the class structure initialization, and then defined. One of the three actions is shown in Example 13-15.

Example 13-15. SimpleMenu: the Notify action routine

```
/* ARGSUSED */
static void
Notify(w, event, params, num_params)
Widget w;
XEvent * event;
String * params;
Cardinal * num_params;
{
    SimpleMenuWidget smw = (SimpleMenuWidget) w;
    SmeObject entry = smw->simple_menu.entry_set;
    SmeObjectClass class;

    if ( (entry == NULL) || !XtIsSensitive((Widget) entry) )
        return;
```

---

*The gadget children could have `resize` methods, and this resize method could call the children's `resize` methods. The gadget's `resize` methods would simply call their `expose` method. However, this does exactly the same thing as the code shown while being more complicated.

Example 13-15. SimpleMenu: the Notify action routine (continued)

```
        class = (SmeObjectClass) entry->object.widget_class;
        (class->sme_class.notify)( (Widget) entry );
}
```

This action determines whether the chosen entry is sensitive and, if so, calls the `notify` method of that gadget. As described above in the section on the gadget children, gadgets define their actions as methods so that they can conveniently be called by their parent. Since these methods are stored in the class structure not the instance structure, this is done using the technique described above for the `expose` method.

Although not critical to its handling of gadgets, SimpleMenu does one more interesting thing. It registers the `PositionMenuAction` action in the global application action list (as opposed to the internal widget action list) so that the application or app-defaults file can refer to this action in translation tables without needing to register the action. This action can be triggered by any type of event in the widget and positions the menu according to data in the event type. (SimpleMenu has a resource that controls whether this placement process makes sure that the menu is not off the screen.)

A widget can add an action to the global action list by calling `XtAddAction` just like an application would, but from its `class_initialize` method.

Any composite widget that is capable of managing gadgets must declare a Composite extension structure in the *.c* file and set the `accepts_objects` field of that structure to `True`. It must then set the pointer to the extension structure into the Composite class part structure in the `class_part_initialize` method. Extension structures were introduced in Chapter 6, *Inside a Widget*, and are discussed further in Chapter 14, *Miscellaneous Toolkit Programming Techniques*. Example 13-16 shows this code from *SimpleMenu.c*.

Example 13-16. SimpleMenu.c: Setting accepts_objects in the Composite extension structure

```
CompositeClassExtensionRec extension_rec = {
    /* next_extension */   NULL,
    /* record_type */      NULLQUARK,
    /* version */          XtCompositeExtensionVersion,
    /* record_size */      sizeof(CompositeClassExtensionRec),
    /* accepts_objects */  True,
};
static void
ClassPartInitialize(wc)
WidgetClass wc;
{
    SimpleMenuWidgetClass smwc = (SimpleMenuWidgetClass) wc;
/*
 * Make sure that our subclass gets the extension rec too.
 */
    extension_rec.next_extension = smwc->composite_class.extension;
    smwc->composite_class.extension = (XtPointer) &extension_rec;
}
```

This code, with names changed, will appear in all gadget parents.

14

Miscellaneous Toolkit
Programming Techniques

*This chapter describes various Xt functions that have not been treated else-
where in the book.*

In This Chapter:

14
Miscellaneous Toolkit Programming Techniques

This chapter discusses various Xt facilities that didn't fit neatly into any other chapter. Many of them are functions provided mostly because Xt uses them internally, and they are unlikely to be useful in application or widget code. Some of them are quite important for accomplishing certain tasks. You should scan the contents of this chapter to familiarize yourself with these facilities so that you will be aware of them.

The topics covered are errors and warning messages, objects, a description of all of Xt's macros and functions for getting information, the Core `accept_focus` method, how to interpret key events, Xt's facilities for memory management, making global grabs, file finding and internationalization, multiple application contexts, multiple top-level shells, and connecting to multiple servers.

14.1 Errors and Warnings

There are several broad categories of errors that may occur in Xt applications. One is the X server error, which is a form of event that tells the client that some parameter in an earlier request was illegal, or that no more server memory is available. A second is the connection failure error generated by Xlib when the connection with the server fails (usually due to a system crash or network interruption). Xlib provides the `XSetErrorHandler` and `XSetIOErrorHandler` functions to allow the application to provide a routine to handle these two types of errors. Xt provides no interface to these routines—Toolkit applications must use the Xlib routines to customize these error handlers (Xlib uses default error handlers when the application does not use these routines to specify them). For a description of these error handlers and the routines for changing them, see Volume One, *Xlib Programming Manual*.

A third category is made up of error and warning messages that Xt reports when function parameters are specified improperly, when a translation is incorrectly specified, and for many other reasons. For a complete listing of all errors and warnings that can be generated by Xt, see Volume Five, *X Toolkit Intrinsics Reference Manual*, Appendix D, *Standard Errors and Warnings*. Xt provides separate parallel routines for errors and for warnings. The difference between Xt errors and Xt warnings is that errors are fatal and the application exits after printing the error, while warnings are nonfatal and the application continues. The main purpose of these facilities is to generate consistent messages.

Two levels of interface are provided:

- A high-level interface that takes an error name and class and looks the error up in an error resource database. The high-level fatal error handler is invoked by a call to `XtApp-ErrorMsg`; the high-level nonfatal error handler is invoked by a call to `XtApp-WarningMsg`. The high-level functions construct a string and pass it to the lower-level interface.

- A low-level interface that takes a simple string, which is printed out as the error message. The low-level fatal error handler is invoked by a call to `XtAppError`; the low-level nonfatal error handler is invoked by a call to `XtAppWarning`.

These error-reporting interfaces are used internally by Xt, but widget or application code can also use them. For example, when a resource is given an illegal value in a resource file, the widget or application can report the error or warning to the user (which depends on whether the widget or application can continue after the error—most widgets issue only warnings and then fall back on their default value).

The low-level handlers are much easier to use, but they do not support internationalization (alternate languages) at all since the messages are hardcoded in the application. The high-level handlers can potentially support internationalization, but not as elegantly as the normal resource database since Xt searches for the error database file in a fixed location, not using the language string. If you want your application or widget to run in more than one language, you should use the high-level handlers, but only one database for one language can be installed on a system at a time. This is likely to be improved in later releases of Xt.

To use the low-level handlers, you specify the string message as the sole argument to `Xt-AppError` or `XtAppWarning`.

Contrary to what you might expect, the high-level handlers `XtAppErrorMsg` and `Xt-AppWarningMsg` are actually harder to use than the low-level handlers. You must pass six arguments to the calls that generate the errors or warnings, and then to take advantage of their benefits you must set up an error resource database. The first three arguments are the name, type, and class of the error. The use of these three arguments is not yet standardized since they are not widely used. However, in Xt itself, the name identifies the error message, and the type identifies the task that was in progress when the error occurred (or the section of code). The class, within Xt, is always `XtToolkitError`. The three remaining arguments of `XtAppErrorMsg` and `XtAppWarningMsg` are a default message, a parameter list, and the number of parameters. The default message will be printed only if no matching message is found in the database. Because Xt does not define or install any error database, it uses these default messages only, and ignores the name, type, and class information. (Xt uses the high-level handlers so that an error resource file can be installed to print all the errors in a foreign language.) The parameter list is used together with the message in the database. The message may be in standard *printf* format, and the parameters are used to fill in any variable fields.

Example 14-1 shows one of the rare cases where `XtAppErrorMsg` is invoked in the Athena widgets.

Example 14-1. How to invoke XtAppErrorMsg (from AsciiSrc.c)

```
if (src->ascii_src.string == NULL)
    XtAppErrorMsg(XtWidgetToApplicationContext(src),
            "NoFile", "asciiSourceCreate", "XawError",
            "Creating a read only disk widget and no file \
            specified.", NULL, 0);
```

The error resource database is stored in a file, */usr/lib/X11/XtErrorDB*, under most UNIX-based operating systems. Since this database is made up of one file, you must append the resource settings you need to this file rather than replacing it. The resource name searched for in the database is the concatenation of the *name* and *type* arguments specified in the calls to `XtAppErrorMsg` or `XtAppWarningMsg`.

You can redefine the routine that prints the message in order to change the fixed part of the message or to add features like logging of errors and warnings. Use `XtAppSetError-MsgHandler` and `XtAppSetWarningMsgHandler` (if you are using the high-level handlers) or `XtAppSetErrorHandler` and `XtAppSetWarningHandler` (if you are using the low-level handlers). See the reference pages for `XtErrorMsgHandler`(2) and `XtErrorHandler`(2) in Volume Five, *X Toolkit Intrinsics Reference Manual*, for a description of how to define a new error or warning handler. The default error and warning messages printed are:

```
X Toolkit Error:   message.        (for errors)
X Toolkit Warning: message.        (for warnings)
```

Remember that Xt itself uses these messages (not just your widget code), so that they must remain appropriate when called from anywhere in the Xt, widget, or application code. If you want the message to identify the name of the widget set or widget, you must include this information in the part of the message filled in from the string you pass or from the resource database.

Table 14-1 summarizes Xt's calls for issuing errors and warnings and for modifying the messages issued.

Table 14-1. Xt Error and Warning Message Utilities

Message	Low Level	High Level
Issue Error	XtAppError	XtAppErrorMsg
Issue Warning	XtAppWarning	XtAppWarningMsg
Set Error Handler	XtAppSetErrorHandler	XtAppSetErrorMsgHandler
Set Warning Handler	XtAppSetWarningHandler	XtAppSetWarningMsgHandler

Miscellaneous

Note, however, that for the high-level routines that use the error and warning resource database, there is only one database common to all application contexts, at least in the sample implementation of Xt provided by MIT under R3 and R4.

When writing a high-level error or warning handler you will need to call `XtGetError-Database` to get a pointer to the error resource database and `XtGetErrorDatabase-Text` to get the message for a particular set of arguments passed to `XtAppErrorMsg` or `XtAppWarningMsg`. For details on how to use these functions, see the reference pages in Volume Five, *X Toolkit Intrinsics Reference Manual*.

`XtDisplayStringConversionWarning` is a convenience routine to be used in resource type converters that convert from `XmRString` to any representation type. It calls `XtAppWarningMsg` with the appropriate arguments to issue a suitable warning. Note however, that the class used is `XtToolkitError`. It may be better to use a class that describes the widget or widget set that defines the converter.

14.2 Objects

Most of this book describes how to use widgets, which are subclasses of the Core widget class. Chapter 13, *Menus, Gadgets, and Cascaded Popups*, also discusses using gadgets, which are subclasses of the RectObj widget class. As described there, gadgets are windowless widgets that are especially useful for menu panes, because they cut back on the overhead that would be required to implement the same thing using a widget for each pane.

The third and final Xt class you can subclass is the Object widget class. Objects are windowless widgets like gadgets, but they lack geometry resources, sensitivity resources, and the `expose` method. They provide support for resources and callbacks, and that is all.

The primary use of objects is to create replaceable subparts of a widget. For example, the R4 Athena Text widget uses objects to implement its source and sink, which control the storage and the display of the data respectively. By replacing the source and sink, you could develop a multi-color or multi-font editor without having to rewrite the central widget which implements all the editing commands.

An object has the following methods: `class_initialize`, `class_part_initialize`, `set_values`, and `get_values_hook`. All these methods have the same purposes as in widgets.

While a gadget uses part of its parent's window, an object shares its parent's entire window, and is not managed at all by its parent since it has no geometry. The parent of an object is normally a widget that is a subclass of Core but not Composite or Constraint (unlike gadget parents).

But like gadgets, objects depend on cooperation by their parent, and require a specially designed parent. The object parent's methods make calls to functions defined by the object child instead of doing the work themselves. The object child's functions can be either semi-public functions or they can be class methods defined by the object. The latter is done so that subclasses of the object can replace the functions.

As an example, let's look at how the Athena Text widget handles drawing. The drawing is done by the TextSink object, and its subclass AsciiSink. Although an object has no `expose` method, it provides an equivalent function that draws on the parent. This function is either a semi-public function (public to its parent but not to the application writer), or it is a class method. The Text widget uses both techniques. TextSink provides a semi-public function `XawTextSinkDisplayText`, which is called by Text whenever drawing is needed.

A object `XawTextSinkDisplayText`, this function calls one of TextSink's class methods called DisplayText. DisplayText is a class method so that subclasses of TextSink can replace it or inherit it. AsciiSink does replace this method with code that draws the text in a single constant-width font, in the foreground and background colors. So in order to write a Text widget that draws in more than two colors, you would just have to write an object that is a new subclass of TextSink.

When Text calls `XawTextSinkDisplayText`, this function calls one of TextSink's class methods called DisplayText. DisplayText is a class method so that subclasses of TextSink can replace it or inherit it. AsciiSink does replace this method with code that draws the text in a single constant-width font, in the foreground and background colors. So in order to write a Text widget that draws in more than two colors, you would just have to write an object that is a new subclass of TextSink.

An object may assume that it should draw on its parent, but this is not necessarily the case, since an object could have an object as its parent. An object also has no idea of its own size, since it has no geometry data in its instance structure, and therefore doesn't by itself know what size window it is drawing into. To solve both these problems, `XawTextSink-DisplayText` passes the parent's widget ID and the parent's size into the objects drawing code.

14.3 Macros For Getting Information

Xt provides several macros and functions for getting information about widgets. Some of these, such as `XtIsRealized` and `XtIsManaged`, you have seen before in the context of widget methods.

Some of these are macros and some are functions, and some are macros when used in widget code and functions when used in application code. This does not affect how they can be used, so we won't bother to specify which can be both functions and macros. We will use the term "macro" for all of these informational routines. In Volume Five, *X Toolkit Intrinsics Reference Manual*, they are listed alphabetically, together with all of the Intrinsics functions.

Xt provides two basic macros for determining the class of a widget: `XtIsComposite` and `XtIsSubclass`. These are primarily used internally by Xt to implement geometry management, but you may find a use for them. For example, you might write a composite widget that uses `XtIsComposite` to treat composite children differently than simple children, or uses `XtIsSubclass` to treat constraint children or one of your own classes uniquely. There are lots of convenience functions for `XtIsSubclass` that determine if a widget is a subclass of a particular class. These are `XtIsObject`, `XtIsRectObj`, `XtIsWidget`, `XtIsComposite`, `XtIsConstraint`, `XtIsShell`, `XtIsOverrideShell`, `Xt-`

`IsWMShell`, `XtIsVendorShell`, `XtIsTransientShell`, `XtIsTopLevel-Shell`, and `XtIsApplicationShell`.

You have already seen `XtIsManaged` used in composite widgets. See Chapter 12, *Geometry Management*.

You have also already seen `XtIsRealized` used in various methods to make sure a widget has a window before operations are attempted on the window. For example, the `expose` method calls `XtIsRealized` before drawing into the window.

`XtIsSensitive` checks the value of the `XmNsensitive` resource for a widget and its ancestors. If any of them is `False`, it returns `False`. Remember that sensitivity controls whether a widget responds to user events.

`XtHasCallbacks` lets you tell whether a widget class has a callback of a certain resource name, and whether any callback functions have actually been added to it. It returns the enum value `XtCallbackNoList` if there is no callback list, `XtCallbackHasNone` if there is a callback list with no functions on it, and `XtCallbackHasSome` if there is a callback list containing functions pointers.

`XtNameToWidget` searches a hierarchy for the widget ID of the specified widget instance name. Its primary use from the application is to get the IDs of the child widgets of a compound widget such as Dialog, so that their resources can be set directly. This is a violation of the rules of data hiding, however, and is not recommended. In widget code, `XtNameToWidget` is used to provide a layer of abstraction so that widgets can be identified using string names. For example, it is used by the converter defined by Form that allows widget names to be specified in resource files. The opposite function, which returns a widget instance name given the widget ID, is `XtName` (which perhaps should have been called "XtWidgetToName").

`XtWindowToWidget` gives you the `Widget` which corresponds to the specified X window ID. This is used mainly by Xt, but you may find a use for it.

`XtDisplayOfObject`, `XtScreenOfObject`, and `XtWindowOfObject` search the parental hierarchy of an object to discover the closest windowed ancestor and then return a pointer to a `Display` structure, a pointer to a `Screen` structure, or a `Window` ID. These macros are useful for making Xlib calls from within code that implements a subclass of Object.

`XtGetApplicationNameAndClass` returns the name and class strings of an application. The name is usually `argv[0]` stripped of any directories, while the class is the string passed as the second argument of `XtAppInitialize`. These are the name and class used by Xt to look up resources for the application and its widgets. You are not likely to need this function.

14.4 The accept_focus Method and the Keyboard Focus

The keyboard focus is the window to which the server sends keyboard events. The window manager controls which top-level window gets the keyboard focus (using either a click-to-type or pointer-following model). Once an application's top-level window gets the focus, it can set the focus to one of its children; that's the way Motif's keyboard traversal code works. As described in Chapter 5, *More About Motif*, within a Motif application, you can have either a click-to-type or pointer-following model, although keyboard operation is only possible if the click-to-type model is used.

The Core class part structure includes a field for the `accept_focus` method. Theoretically, this method lets a widget set the keyboard focus to one of its children when it gets the keyboard focus. A typical example is an application that wants to set the keyboard focus to the text entry child of a dialog box whenever the dialog box is given the keyboard focus by the window manager. This would be done so that the user can type with the pointer anywhere in the dialog widget instead of just with the pointer in the text entry widget.

To implement this example, the text entry child would need an `accept_focus` method that would set the keyboard focus to itself using the Xlib call `XSetInputFocus`. The dialog box would need an `accept_focus` method that called `XtCallAcceptFocus` on the text entry widget child. The application can call `XtCallAcceptFocus` on the dialog widget in response to `FocusIn` events to start this process, and set the focus back to `PointerRoot` on `FocusOut` events. For details on these events, see Volume Two, *Xlib Reference Manual*. This procedure for giving the child of a dialog the keyboard focus is necessary because the application can't find out the name of the child that should have the focus without breaking widget encapsulation rules.

In reality, none of the Motif widgets (and none of the Athena widgets, for that matter) use the `accept_focus` method. The keyboard traversal code is implemented separately.

An `accept_focus` method should return a Boolean value to report whether it succeeded in setting the keyboard focus, and `XtCallAcceptFocus` returns this same value.

The `XtSetKeyboardFocus` function redirects keyboard events that occur within an application to any widget within that application. This is different from `XSetInputFocus` in that no request to the server is made, and the redirection of keyboard events is handled entirely by Xt's event dispatching mechanism. However, `XtSetKeyboardFocus` should not be used in Motif applications, since it interferes with the keyboard traversal code.

14.5 Keyboard Interpretation

Keyboard handling in X is designed so that you can write a program that will operate on systems with widely different physical keyboards. To accomplish this, there are several layers of mappings:

- The first mapping is between physical keys and keycodes (a number for each key), and varies between servers. A `KeyPress` event includes only the keycode and information about what other keys and buttons were being held at the time of the keypress. Programs that interpret keycodes directly will operate on only one type of system.

- The next mapping is between keycodes and keysyms, which are symbolic constants beginning with `XK_` that represent the meaning of a key press. This mapping takes into account whether Shift or other modifier keys were being held during the press. Xlib provides the routine `XLookupString` that converts the keycode in a key event to the appropriate keysym. Portable programs use keysyms to interpret key events. The keycode to keysym mapping is server-wide. It can be changed, but this is normally done only to accomplish radical changes in the placement of keys such as changing a QWERTY style keyboard to DVORAK.

- The final mapping is between keysyms and strings. For printing characters, `XLookupString` also returns a string representation of the interpretation of the key pressed. For example, if the key marked *A* was pressed with no other keys held down, the string returned would be *a*. A text entry widget, for example, would append this string to the string being displayed, but modify the string in other ways to handle keysyms that do not have a string representation such as `XK_Backspace`. The values of keysyms are arranged logically so that all printing characters have a particular range.

Motif adds virtual key bindings to this model, as described in Section 5.9.

When you write an action that accepts key events, you will usually need to interpret the meaning of the key pressed. Xt provides its own interface to `XLookupString`: `XtTranslateKeycode`. You pass several fields of the key event to `XtTranslateKeycode`, and it returns the keysym. However, `XtTranslateKeycode` does not return the string interpretation of the key event that would be returned by `XLookupString`. If you need that string, you will have to call `XLookupString`.

Xt provides `XtTranslateKeycode` because Xt also provides routines for changing the way the translation returned by `XtTranslateKeycode` is done. `XtSetKeyTranslator` allows you to specify your own procedure to convert from the key event information to a keysym. The default key event translation procedure is `XtTranslateKey`, and so you can restore the default translator if necessary, and so that you can call it from your own translator to get default translations (you need to add only the code that makes the translations not done by the default translator). See `XtKeyProc` in Volume Five, *X Toolkit Intrinsics Reference Manual*, for details on providing a key event translation procedure.

Among these routines for modifying the interpretation of key events is a facility for changing the handling of capitalization. For example, most keyboards have the question mark (*?*) symbol over the slash (*/*) symbol on one key. The standard case converter converts a press of this key with the Shift key held down to the `XK_question` keysym. In rare cases a keyboard may have a different symbol over / and put *?* somewhere else. Also, some keyboards have two or more symbols on a single key, some of which are not represented at all by standard keysyms. The case converter handles these situations. The case converter is usually called from the key translator described above. To call the case converter, use `XtConvertCase`, and to change the case converter, call `XtRegisterCaseConverter`. See `XtCaseProc` in Volume Five, *X Toolkit Intrinsics Reference Manual*, for details on writing a case converter procedure.

Note that the translation manager uses these same key translation and case converter routines to interpret translation tables. Therefore, make sure that you add features only to them, keeping existing features.

Xt also provides two routines that may help in interpreting key events: `XtGetKeysymTable` and `XtKeysymToKeycodeList`. The former returns the entire mapping of keycodes to keysyms for the server, while the latter tells you what keycodes are listed for the specified keysym. Neither function is necessary for routine keyboard handling.

From within an action routine, you can call `XtGetActionKeysym` to get the keysym that resulted in the action being called. This can be very useful, since the event passed to the action contains only the keycode of the key that was pressed. However, there is another way to acheive a similar result. You can use string parameters of actions to pass in the keysym that you specified in the translation table. For example, if you provide the translation `:<Key>q : Quit(q)`, the Quit action will be passed the string "q" in its *params* argument. However, `XtGetActionKeysym` is very useful if you translate a wide range of key events to one action, and then want to distinguish between them in the action.

14.6 Memory Allocation

Xt provides routines for performing routine memory allocation and deallocation. The routines `XtMalloc`, `XtCalloc`, `XtRealloc`, and `XtFree` are equivalents of the standard C routines `malloc`, `calloc`, `realloc`, and `free` but they add error checking and reporting. The allocation routines make sure the allocation succeeded, and if it did not, they print a (fatal) error message. `XtFree` makes sure the passed pointer is not NULL before calling `free`.

`XtNew` is a macro which allocates storage for one instance of the passed type and returns a pointer. For example, `XtNew(XtCallbackList)` allocates storage for one callback list structure. `XtNewString` is a macro that allocates storage for a string, copies the string into the new storage, and returns the pointer. For example, a string can be copied into new storage using the following:

```
static String buf[] = "How do you do?";
String p;

p = XtNewString(buf);
```

After this sequence, p points to a separate string that contains "How do you do?" Then `buf` can be changed without affecting p.

14.7 Action Hooks and Calling Actions Directly

Xt allows you to register any number of functions to be called whenever any action in an application context is invoked. This is done with `XtAppAddActionHook`. Note that there is just one "action hook" in the application context, so that all the action hook functions registered for that application context are called whenever *any* of the actions in that application context are invoked. The registration does not specify any particular action or any particular widget.

The main reason for registering an action hook is to record all the actions that were invoked in an application, so that they can be played back later using `XtCallActionProc`. An action hook function is called with all the same arguments that are passed to an action, plus the string name of the action. The action hook function would store this information as a unit each time it was called. When it comes time to play back the recorded actions, it would pass all the information in each unit to `XtCallActionProc`.

An action hook can be removed with `XtRemoveActionHook`.

14.8 Xt Grabbing Functions

Grabs are used mostly for popup menus and dialog boxes. As described in Chapter 13, *Menus, Gadgets, and Cascaded Popups*, Xt has its own *grab mode* that controls the distribution of events within one application, which can be used to restrict events to one popup in a cascade or allow events to go to any popup in a cascade. As also described there, popup menus in particular need a passive global grab of the pointer in order to detect button releases that occur completely outside the application so that menus can be popped down properly. A passive global grab actually instructs the server to redirect events to a certain window. All the grabbing needs of popups are satisfied by the built-in action `XtMenu-Popup`, or by the function `XtPopupSpringLoaded`, which can be used in a callback function. If necessary, you can write your own version of `XtMenuPopup` and register it with `XtRegisterGrabAction` so that the appropriate passive global grab is in effect.

The above facilities should be quite sufficient for your needs in the area of popups. However, it is possible that you may need an global grab for some other purpose. Perhaps you need all keyboard events in one window for a short time and don't want to change existing translations or accelerators for keyboard events in other widgets. This is only one plausible scenario.

The Xlib functions for grabbing are `XGrabKey`, `XGrabButton`, `XGrabKeyboard`, and `XGrabPointer`. Each of these functions has an analogue for ungrabbing. But Xt provides its own version of all eight of these functions. You should use the Xt versions because they are integrated into Xt and take care of things like making sure the widget that is to get the grab has been realized. In other words, if you do need the server to redirect events for you using a grab, use the following functions: `XtGrabKey`, `XtGrabButton`, `XtGrab-Keyboard`, `XtUngrabKeyboard`, and `XtUngrabPointer`. For more on global grabs, see Chapter 8 in Volume One, *Xlib Programming Manual*.

14.9 File Finding and Internationalization

Xt's facilities for allowing an application to run in different languages are mostly built into the resource database mechanism. Where Xt searches for resource files depends on a language string, which can be set within resources at run time or with an environment variable to affect one user's environment. This is described in Chapter 10, *Resource Management and Type Conversion*.

The functions that Xt uses to implement its search for resource files are also available to you for searching for application files. This allows you to provide separate data files for each language for a help system, for example. The primary function you would use to do this is Xt-ResolvePathname, since it searches directories in a standard order based on X/Open Portability Guide conventions.

If you want to find a file but are not interested in internationalization, you can use XtFind-File. This function can simplify code that reads files, since it helps handle differences in file systems.

14.10 Application Contexts

The introduction to application contexts in Section 3.9 described their use in 99 percent of applications. As you may recall, their purpose is chiefly to attain portability to certain systems that do not provide a separate address space for each process.

Xt provides parallel versions of many routines—one set that uses the default application context, and one set that has an explicit application context argument. The routines that use the default application context are remnants of an earlier release when application contexts did not work properly. To acheive the desired portability, you must now use the versions with the explicit argument. We have done this throughout this book. In Volume Five, *X Toolkit Intrinsics Reference Manual*, the reference pages for all the functions that use the default application context note the fact that they should no longer be used.

Table 14-2 shows the complete list of routines that have two versions.

Table 14-2. Xt Routines That Use Default and Explicit Application Contexts

Default	Explicit
(registering functions)	
XtAddActions	XtAppAddActions
XtAddConverter	XtAppAddConverter
XtAddInput	XtAppAddInput
XtTimeOut	XtAppTimeOut
XtWorkProc	XtAppWorkProc
(creating shells)	
XtCreateApplicationShell	XtAppCreateShell
(event dispatching)	

Default	Explicit
XtMainLoop	XtAppMainLoop
XtNextEvent	XtAppNextEvent
XtPeekEvent	XtAppPeekEvent
XtPending	XtAppPending
XtProcessEvent	XtAppProcessEvent
(error and warning messages)	
XtError	XtAppError
XtErrorMsg	XtAppErrorMsg
XtGetErrorDatabase	XtAppGetErrorDatabase
XtGetErrorDatabaseText	XtAppGetErrorDatabaseText
XtSetErrorHandler	XtAppSetErrorHandler
XtSetErrorMsgHandler	XtAppSetErrorMsgHandler
XtSetWarningHandler	XtAppSetWarningHandler
XtSetWarningMsgHandler	XtAppSetWarningMsgHandler
XtWarning	XtAppWarning
XtWarningMsg	XtAppWarningMsg
(selection timeouts)	
XtGetSelectionTimeout	XtAppGetSelectionTimeout
XtSetSelectionTimeout	XtAppSetSelectionTimeout
(action hooks)	
(no equiv)	XtAppAddActionHook
(toolkit initialization)	
(no equiv)	XtAppInitialize
(resources)	
(no equiv)	XtAppSetFallbackResources
XtSetTypeConverter	XtAppSetTypeConverter
(no equiv)	XtAppReleaseCacheRefs

Note that `XtCreateApplicationShell` and `XtAppCreateShell` have names that don't follow the example set by all the rest.

14.10.1 Multiple Application Contexts

The use of more than one application context in a single program presents possibilities that you might wish to explore. Having more than one application context in the same program allows you to have one program that when run looks like two or more independent programs. This approach saves disk space and memory on systems that don't provide shared libraries, since the grouped programs can share a single copy of the libraries.*

---

*In SunView, many of the basic applications were grouped in a single binary probably for this reason. The Xlib and Xt libraries are quite large. For example, on a Sony NWS-841 workstation, the executable image of a "hello, world" application written with Xt uses 300K of disk space. One of the most complicated existing X applications, *xterm*,

Having two application contexts makes each sub-application more separate than if they were just under different top-level Shell widgets. Each widget class has an action list, and each application context has a separate context-wide action list. When the translation manager looks for an action, it looks in the widget class action list first, and then the application context action list. Therefore, each sub-application could add an action to its application context without conflict with another sub-application adding a different action of the same name.

On parallel processing machines, each separate application context could run in parallel. However, it is difficult to write portable code to take advantage of this, since each architecture has different conventions for indicating parallelisms in C code.

14.10.2 Rewriting XtAppMainLoop for Multiple Application Contexts

To use multiple application contexts, you need to write your own equivalent of XtApp-MainLoop to dispatch events to your multiple application contexts. This is necessary because XtAppMainLoop dispatches events only from one application context, and it never returns so you can't call it again for the other.

The available tools are XtAppNextEvent, XtAppPeekEvent, XtAppPending, Xt-AppProcessEvent, and the Xlib functions XFlush and XSync. Rewriting XtApp-MainLoop for two or more application contexts is tricky, because you don't want to let the dispatching of any one application context get behind. It is not as simple as dispatching events from each application context alternately, since the events might not occur alternately. It is easy to get stuck waiting for events in one application context while events queue up at the other. There is little experience in how this should be done properly, and no examples in the distribution from MIT. However, hypothetically, the following describes how it could work.

To do this properly, you have to understand how Xlib's network optimization works. Xlib buffers up many types of requests and sends (flushes) them to the server as a group.* A flush is most commonly caused by a routine such as XtAppNextEvent that waits for an event if none are available. It is because XtAppNextEvent waits forever for an event that the routine could get locked waiting for events in one application context while the user types frantically in the other.

The answer is to use XtAppPending to determine whether an event is available on a particular application context, and then call XtAppProcessEvent if there is an event to process. Then continue to do the same on each other application context. However, this alone is not enough. Neither XtAppPending nor XtAppProcessEvent called in this manner cause Xlib's buffer of requests to be sent to the server. Therefore, periodic calls to XSync or XFlush are necessary to flush the output buffer. The difficult part is to call these enough to flush the buffer when necessary, but not so much as to eliminate the advantages of the buffering. There is no ideal solution to this problem.

---

uses 450K of disk space on this system. Therefore, the various libraries account for about two-thirds of the disk space used, even for a large program.

*For a detailed discussion of Xlib's network optimization and its effects, see the introduction to Volume Zero, *X Protocol Reference Manual*.

Miscellaneous

On multi-tasking systems it is perhaps possible to `fork` so that each application context runs in a separate process.

14.10.3 Functions Used with Multiple Application Contexts

`XtWidgetToApplicationContext` and `XtDisplayToApplicationContext` could be useful if you use more than one application context in an application. `XtWidget-ToApplicationContext` is also useful in widget code, to call error-issuing routines that require an application context argument, such as `XtAppWarning` and `XtApp-WarningMsg`.

14.11 Multiple Top-level Shells

A single application can have more than one top-level window. In other words, you are not restricted to containing your application's entire user interface in a single rectangle. If you have one section of the application that is most appropriate as a long, thin vertical window that looks like a long, permanent menu, and another section that is a long, horizontal bar such as a ruler, each of these could be a separate top-level window. That way, not only is less screen space wasted than if these two windows were placed within a single rectangle, but the user can move the two windows around separately using the window manager. The user can also iconify them separately when not needed.

To create additional top-level application shell widgets, you call `XtAppCreateShell` or `XtVaAppCreateShell`. (`XtCreateApplicationShell` is now superceded.) The class specified in the call should be `topLevelShellWidgetClass`.

As you may know, a single server may have several screens attached. At present, all shells created will appear on the default screen. There is no way for the application to specify that a shell be created on a particular screen, but then again, doing this is usually unwise anyway because not many users actually have more than one screen. The user can specify which screen is considered the default screen using the *–display* command-line option.

14.12 Connecting to Multiple Servers

One of the great features of the server-client model is that a single program can connect to several servers to display on the screens of several users. For example, this would allow you to create an X-based version of the UNIX utility *wall* in which one user can make a message appear on all user's screens throughout a network. You could also create a conferencing program in which each user has a window on their screen in which they can type and view typing by others in real time, and their typing will appear on all the other user's screens.

The Xt application opens a connection with a server using `XtOpenDisplay` (this routine requires an explicit application context argument). Once you have opened the connection, you will want to create a shell widget on the server's default screen using `XtCreate-`

`ApplicationShell` or `XtAppCreateShell`. Then, you create widgets for each server simply by using the appropriate Shell widget as parent. Thereafter, `XtAppMain-Loop` dispatches events from all the connections to the appropriate widget.

14.13 Class Extension Structures

X Consortium standards, once adopted, can only be changed in ways that are binary and source compatible with the original standard specification. Xt became an X consortium standard in Release 3. Therefore, Release 4 and later releases are required to be source and binary compatible with Release 3. *Source compatibility* means that properly coded applications and widgets written to the R3 specification should compile and work under R4 and later releases. Source compatibility is maintained by keeping all programming interfaces intact while adding features with new interfaces. *Binary compatibility* means that widgets written and compiled with R3 must be able to be linked with R4 Xt and Xlib libraries and still run. Source compatibility is necessary but not sufficient for binary compatibility. The major addition requirement of binary compatibility is that fields added to structures must be added to the end of the structure.

In Chapter 6, *Inside a Widget*, you saw how a class structure for a widget class is built by nesting the class part structures of all its superclasses into one big structure, the class record. The X consortium could not simply add fields to the class part structures of the basic Xt classes without breaking binary compatibility with existing subclasses because the class parts of basic Xt classes appear in the middle of the class record of subclasses. Therefore, they used extension structures to add these fields.

Class extension structures allowed the X consortium to add to the class structures of basic Xt classes. The last field of each basic Xt class is called `extension`. This field can be set to a pointer to the class's extension structure, which contains its added fields. New features that required additional class structure fields were added to the Composite and Constraint classes in R4. Therefore, these two classes now have extension structures.

Some classes, such as Core, do not have an extension structure because no additional class fields have yet been necessary. They still have the `extension` field, but it is not used.

A class extension structure is defined in the private header file of a widget class. The extension structure for Composite is called `CompositeClassExtensionRec` as shown in Example 14-2.

Example 14-2. Common fields in a class extension record

```
typedef struct {
    XtPointer next_extension;/* 1st 4 mandated for all ext rec */
    XrmQuark record_type;    /* NULLQUARK; on CompositeClassPart */
    long version;            /* must be XtCompositeExtensionVersion */
    Cardinal record_size;    /* sizeof(CompositeClassExtensionRec) */
    Boolean accepts_objects;
} CompositeClassExtensionRec, *CompositeClassExtension;
```

All extension structures start with the same four fields. The only field in this structure actually used by Composite is `accepts_objects`, the use of which is described in Section

12.4.5. The `accepts_objects` field is only used by Composite widgets that have the code necessary to accept gadget children. When a widget class needs an extension feature, the widget class initializes the extension structure in its *.c* file, and then in the `class_initialize` method sets the `extension` field to point to the extension structure.

When a widget class does not need an extension feature—for example, a Composite widget that does not accept gadget children—the widget class does not provide code in the `class_initialize` method to set the `extension` field.

The *.c* file of all widget classes should initially set all `extension` fields to NULL. The difference between classes that use extension features and those that don't is only the presence or absence of code in `class_initialize` to set the `extension` fields.

The four required fields in an extension structure are:

next_extension   Specifies the next record in the list, or NULL.

record_type   Specifies the particular structure declaration to which each extension record instance conforms.

version   Specifies a symbolic constant supplied by the definer of the structure.

record_size   Specifies the total number of bytes allocated for the extension record.

When you initialize an extension structure of a given class in the *.c* file, you always set these four fields to the same values. Example 14-3 shows how to initialize the Composite extension structure. The first two fields are usually NULL and NULLQUARK. The reference page for each class that has an extension structure will document how to initialize the third and fourth fields.

```
CompositeClassExtensionRec extension_rec = {
    /* next_extension */    NULL,
    /* record_type */       NULLQUARK,
    /* version */           XtCompositeExtensionVersion,
    /* record_size */       sizeof(CompositeClassExtensionRec),
    /* accepts_objects */ True,   /* only new field */
};
```

The `next_extension` field implies correctly that you can nest extension structures. Perhaps a later release of Xt will require the addition of more Composite class fields. These could be added to the end of the existing extension structure, or a new extension structure could be defined and a pointer to it placed in `next_extension`. This allows additions to be made to a class structure without breaking binary compatibility.

You may be wondering whether you should use extension structures when extending your own widgets. Probably not. Because you are likely to release your set of widgets as a package, you have no need for binary compatibility with previous releases (of your own). Binary compatibility would only be an advantage if you wanted to replace a few widgets from a former release and save users who may have subclassed the widgets you have replaced from recompiling their widgets. For the trouble involved, the benefit is very small.

A

Athena, OPEN LOOK, and Motif

This appendix gives an overview of the widgets available in the AT&T widget set (also known as Xt+) and OSF Motif widget set. It gives a sense of the look and feel of applications developed with each set, and provides the inheritance hierarchy and overview of the available widgets.

In This Appendix:

A
Athena, OPEN LOOK, and Motif

This section provides an overview and comparison of the widgets in MIT's Athena widget set, AT&T's OPEN LOOK widget set (also known as Xt+), and the Open Software Foundation's Motif.*

As we've already discussed, the Athena widgets were developed to test and demonstrate the Xt Intrinsics. They are used as the basis for some of the standard MIT clients and many public domain applications, but are not expected to be used for most commercial applications because Xaw is not a complete environment.

A number of vendors have developed proprietary widget sets. For example, Sony Microsystems offers S-windows, a widget set for its News workstations. However, given that one of the purposes of widgets is to provide a common look and feel for X applications, it is natural there should be a shakeout as vendors align themselves with one or two major contenders.

As it has turned out, the two major contenders for a graphical user-interface standard, OPEN LOOK and Motif, are put forth by the two major contenders for an underlying UNIX operating system standard, AT&T and the Open Software Foundation.

It is theoretically possible to write an application that will run under either of these widget sets, using one set of source code interspersed with #ifdef symbols for conditional compilation. This becomes difficult when you use any of the Xt-level features Motif alone provides, however.

OPEN LOOK is somewhat unusual in that it started out not as a set of widgets, but as a user-interface specification. The specification, originally developed by Sun Microsystems with AT&T backing, was widely circulated for comment before any implementations were begun. The objective was to develop a graphical user-interface standard for UNIX workstations—one that would be implementation-independent, and, it was hoped, implemented separately by many different vendors.

At present, the two major implementations of OPEN LOOK are Sun's XView toolkit (which is not based on Xt, but instead provides an application-programmer's interface similar to Sun's proprietary SunView windowing system), and AT&T's OPEN LOOK Xt-based widget set. XView is on the R4 distribution from MIT. Both of these toolkits will be available to all

---

*OPEN LOOK is a registered trademark of AT&T and Motif is a registered trademark of Open Software Foundation, Inc.

AT&T UNIX System V Release 4 licensees. In our discussions, we are referring specifically to AT&T's OPEN LOOK toolkit, which does not necessarily include every OPEN LOOK feature. Nor should its implementation be considered the only way to provide features called for by OPEN LOOK.

The Open Software Foundation's Motif toolkit is based on a combination of widget sets originally developed by two OSF sponsors, Digital and Hewlett Packard. The look and feel of the widget set was proposed by HP/Microsoft. It is designed to emulate the look and feel of the IBM/Microsoft Presentation Manager standard widely expected to be adopted in the microcomputer world. Motif 1.1, released in August 1990, is described here.

Table A-1 compares the widgets available in Athena, AT&T OPEN LOOK set, and Motif.

Table A-1. Comparison of Athena, OPEN LOOK, and Motif Widgets

Simple widgets (mostly controls):

Athena	OPEN LOOK	Motif	Description
Command	OblongButton	PushButton	Invokes a command
—	—	DrawnButton	Invokes a command
Toggle	RectButton	ToggleButton	Chooses a setting
—	CheckBox*	CheckBox, RadioBox	Alternate way of choosing a setting
MenuButton	ButtonStack	CascadeButton	Invokes a menu, displays label
—	AbbrevStack	OptionMenu	Invokes a menu, displays default
—	—	ArrowButton	Reverses direction of movement
—	ScrollingList*	List	Displays a list of selectable strings
Scrollbar	Scrollbar	ScrollBar	Scrolls through an associated window
—	Slider	Scale*	Sets (or displays) an analog value
Grip	—	—	Resize point for panes in VPaned
Label	StaticText	Label	Displays a fixed string
Text	Text	Text	Displays editable text
—	TextField	TextField	Displays a single line of editable text
—	—	Separator	Displays a line or other separator

*CheckBox, ScrollingList, and Scale are technically composite widgets.

Popups (subclasses of shell):

Athena	OPEN LOOK	Motif	Description
SimpleMenu	Menu	MenuShell	Parents a popup menu
—	Notice	DialogShell	Displays a dialog requiring input
—	PopupWindow	MessageBox	Displays a more complex dialog
—	Help	MessageBox	Displays a help window

Composite and Constraint Widgets:

Athena	OPEN LOOK	Motif	Description
—	BulletinBoard	BulletinBoard	Free-form placement area
—	—	DrawingArea	Free-form drawing area
Box	—	—	Displays children in order added
—	ControlArea	RowColumn	Arranges children in rows or columns
Form	Form	Form	Manages children relative to each other
—	Exclusives	—	Makes RectButton children exclusive
—	Nonexclusives	—	Makes RectButton children nonexclusive
—	FooterPanel	—	Provides a consistently-sized message area
—	—	Frame	Gives consistent border to enclosed widgets
—	ScrollingList*	SelectionBox	Provides a selectable list of strings, plus a text area for entering a new value
—	—	Command	Provides a selectable list of commands
—	—	FileSelectionBox	Provides a selectable list of filenames
—	Caption	—	Displays a label and one child widget
Viewport	ScrollingWindow	ScrolledWindow	Displays a scrollable child window
—	—	MainWindow	ScrolledWindow with special appearance
VPaned	—	PanedWindow	Displays panes resizable in one direction

*Checkbox, ScrollingList, and Scale are technically composite widgets.

Comparable widgets share a line in the table. Widgets for which no equivalent occurs in a given set are indicated by a hyphen in the appropriate column. Note that comparisons are approximate only, since widgets have complex behavior that may distinguish them significantly from another widget with an ostensibly similar purpose.

The following sections provide an overview of the widgets available in the OPEN LOOK and Motif widget sets. Throughout, we contrast them with the Athena widgets, which have been used as examples in this book, to give you an idea of the additional features provided by the commercial widget sets.

Keep in mind that the look and feel of an application is controlled by the window manager as well as by the widget set. Both AT&T and OSF supply window managers to complement their widgets.

Note that both widget sets make additions to the basic X Toolkit API. In the AT&T OPEN LOOK widget set, these API additions are rather minor. There is one essential function, `Ol-Initialize`, which sets initial values needed by other routines and by certain widgets. `OlInitialize` creates a base window, which from the programmer's point of view is identical to the Intrinsics-supplied TopLevelShell widget class, but which automatically handles certain features of the OPEN LOOK interface. There are also several convenience functions, mostly having to do with conversions between pixel sizes and various standard units. More importantly, there is a facility for registering help screens for each element in an application.

Motif 1.0 made more extensive API additions and even changes, modifying all of the base widget classes, and other Intrinsics features. Therefore, the Motif 1.0 Intrinsics are not compatible with the MIT R3 or R4 Intrinsics. Motif 1.0 support for windowless widgets, or "gadgets," is part of OSF's proprietary version of the Intrinsics, which is not completely compatible with the version of gadgets support in the MIT R4 release. However, Motif 1.1 is to be fully compatible with the MIT Release 4 Intrinsics.

In addition, Motif makes heavy use of convenience functions. Rather than using `Xt-CreateManagedWidget` to create each widget, there is a separate creation routine for each widget. In some cases, a convenience routine creates more than one widget. Rather than using separate calls to `XtCreatePopupShell` and `XtCreateManagedWidget` to create a popup shell and the dialog box it displays, you might call a function such as `Xm-CreateMessageDialog` to create both widgets at once. Some convenience routines create special configurations of a single, complex widget (e.g., a composite widget with specific children.)

In Motif, all resources are referred to by names beginning with `XmN` or `XmC` rather than the familiar `XtN` and `XtC`.

Motif also uses the `call_data` argument of callback functions extensively. Almost every widget has a structure defined as `widgetclassCallbackStruct` (e.g., `XmToggle-ButtonCallbackStruct`). This struct contains different fields for each widget, but each contains a field called `reason`. The `reason` field defines which callback has been called. So using this feature allows you to have a single piece of code to handle all callbacks for a widget.

In the Motif 1.0 Intrinsics, the search path for resources has been expanded to support language-specific resource defaults (to support internationalization of applications).

Both Motif and OPEN LOOK offer clear advantages over Xaw. Unfortunately, however, the choice of which one to use may depend on company marketing goals and politics rather than on clear technical merit. We encourage independent developers to try both and to base your opinions on the ease of programming and the preferences of your users, rather than on marketing hype by one side or the other. Both Motif and OPEN LOOK come with their own window manager and have defined their own protocols for communication between their Shell widgets and their window manager. By setting resources of Shell widgets you can control some aspects of how these window managers will handle your application.

A.1 The AT&T OPEN LOOK Widgets

Figure A-1 shows the overall look and feel of an OPEN LOOK application.

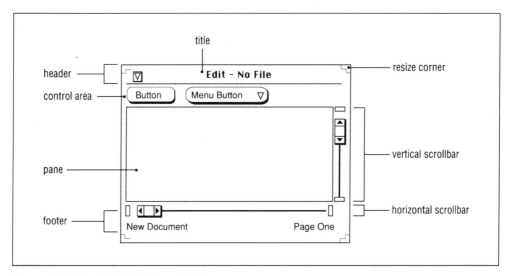

Figure A-1. An OPEN LOOK application

The base window of an application always has these elements:

* A title bar, or header, with a title supplied by the application centered in the bar. The title might be the application name, or the name of a file being edited. If the application doesn't provide a title, the title bar displays the string "Untitled."

* A "window mark" on the left side of the title bar. If the user clicks on this mark with the first (leftmost) pointer button, the window closes.

* A window menu that comes up automatically when you click on the title bar with the third (rightmost) pointer button.

* One or more panes for input and display of application data.

- One or more control areas, containing buttons that invoke application actions or menus containing additional actions. Control areas can be horizontal, vertical, or both.

Optional elements include resize corners (which allow the user to resize the application by dragging them with the first pointer button), horizontal and/or vertical scrollbars, and a footer area for displaying messages.

Some of these elements do not correspond to widgets, but are produced by the OPEN LOOK window manager, *olwm*, as window decoration. For example, the header, including title bar, window mark and window menu, are provided by the window manager, as are the optional resize corners. However, control areas, panes, scrollbars, and the footer area do correspond to particular widgets.

In addition to base windows, applications may have several kinds of popup. Both pull-down and pure popup menus are supported, as well as several standard kinds of notices and dialogs. Probably OPEN LOOK's best-known feature is the "pushpin" metaphor that allows frequently-accessed popup menus to be kept on the screen rather than hidden again after they have been used.

The following sections discuss some of the widgets AT&T has provided to support the OPEN LOOK user interface. Figure A-2 shows the overall widget inheritance hierarchy.

Note that there are a number of widgets that are never instantiated by the application programmer, but are used by other widgets. For example, the checkbox is actually a composite widget that manages a check widget as its child! The Pushpin used in popups and the Magnifier used in Help windows (and the Help window itself) are examples of other widgets that are not instantiated directly.

A.1.1 Application Controls

Most applications will have at least one control area, with pointer-selectable buttons that invoke commands or menus, or choose settings.

One of the areas where OPEN LOOK clearly stands out over the Athena widgets is in the rich set of controls it provides. Athena has one kind of Command widget; OPEN LOOK has six.

A.1.1.1 Command Buttons

The Athena Command widget implements one of the most basic user-interface idioms—a button that invokes an action when you click on it with the pointer. The Athena widgets include a subclass of Command, the MenuButton widget, which includes code for placing a popup menu.

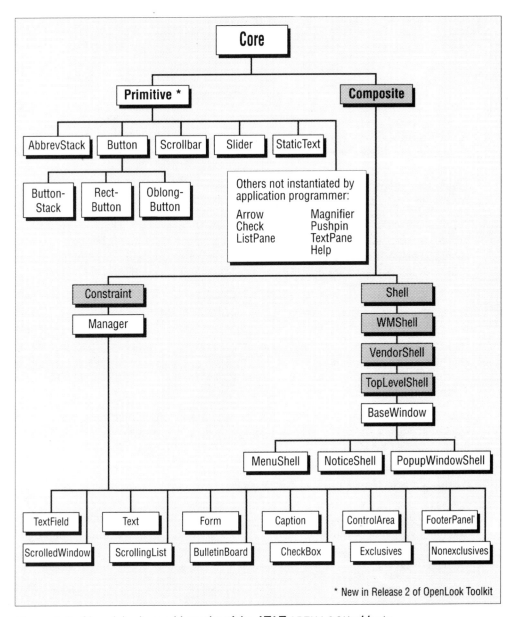

Figure A-2. Class inheritance hierarchy of the AT&T OPEN LOOK widgets

The OPEN LOOK widget set implements similar functions using the OblongButton and ButtonStack widgets. Figure A-3 shows a Control Area containing OblongButton and ButtonStack widgets.

The OblongButton widget provides many niceties lacking from the Athena Command widget. One of the most important is that OblongButton has a resource that allows one button among several to be designated as the default, in which case the button is bordered by a

Figure A-3. An OPEN LOOK ControlArea with OblongButton and ButtonStack widgets

double line, to give the user immediate visual feedback about which button to choose when several are available.

The OblongButton also has the notion of a "busy" state in which it cannot perform the action because it is already doing it. (This is different from a widget that is insensitive (meaning its function is unavailable), though in practice the effect is quite similar.) The label and border of an insensitive button are dimmed; the background of a busy button is filled with a stippled pattern.

The ButtonStack widget is similar to the OblongButton but invokes a menu rather than a single command. Clicking on it with one mouse button (usually Button 3) pops up a menu (which may in turn include other ButtonStack widgets, for cascading popups.) Clicking on the ButtonStack with another mouse button (usually Button 1) activates the default item for the menu. Visually, a ButtonStack is differentiated from an OblongButton by the presence of an arrowhead that points in the direction that the menu will pop up.*

In addition, there is an AbbrevStack widget, which performs similar functions as the Button-Stack widget, but shows up only as a small unlabelled box with the default choice for the menu displayed beside it.

A.1.1.2 Exclusive and Nonexclusive Settings

The Athena Toggle widget provides the concept of a button that establishes a setting (for example, sets an application resource) instead of performing an action. It highlights itself when selected, but remains highlighted until selected again. However, in the Athena Widget set, there is no visual distinction between a Command widget and a Toggle widget.

OPEN LOOK provides such a distinction. In contrast to OblongButton, which always indicates that an action will be performed, a RectButton indicates that an option setting will be chosen. This setting may be exclusive or nonexclusive, as determined by the RectButton widget itself, depending on whether the widget is managed by an Exclusives, or Nonexclusives composite widget. The RectButton widget class will not work correctly unless managed by one of these two composite widgets. The Exclusives and Nonexclusives widgets are themselves usually children of a Menu or ControlArea widget.

---

*In an earlier implementation of the toolkit, a ButtonStack widget had a double border on its bottom half, giving it the appearance of a stack of regular buttons. Hence its name, which is now merely historical.

In an Exclusives widget, RectButton widgets are laid out side by side in one or more columns. One or none of the RectButton widgets is chosen as the default, which is indicated by a double border. Once a RectButton is selected, it is shown with a dark border. The Exclusives widget makes sure that no more than one RectButton is selected at a time.

In a Nonexclusives widget, RectButtons are displayed with separation between each button. As when used in an Exclusives widget, a dark border indicates that the option has been chosen. However, more than one button may be chosen at a time.

Figure A-4 shows examples of exclusive and nonexclusive settings on menus. Note that, like the OblongButton, a RectButton may display a pixmap instead of a label. This makes the RectButton useful for a palette in a paint program.

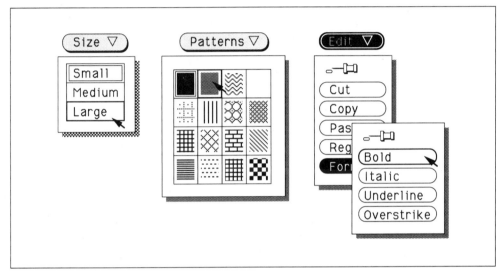

Figure A-4. OPEN LOOK RectButtons controlled by Exclusives and Nonexclusives widgets

The CheckBox widget provides an alternate way to display nonexclusive settings to the user. It displays a small box next to the label and displays a checkmark in the box when the option is selected. Checkboxes appear in ControlAreas rather than on menus. Figure A-5 shows examples of CheckBox widgets.

Figure A-5. An OPEN LOOK CheckBox widget

A.1.1.3 Analog Controls

In addition to the various kinds of buttons outlined above, OPEN LOOK provides an analog control called a Slider. A Slider widget is used analogously to a Scrollbar but is used for setting a numeric value. Figure A-6 shows a Slider widget.

Figure A-6. An OPEN LOOK Slider widget

A.1.2 Composite Widgets

Composite widgets are in many ways the most important widgets in any widget set. They define the way that widgets work together, and they give consistency to an application.

A.1.2.1 Menus and Control Areas

As we've already discussed, command buttons of any kind are usually displayed as part of a menu or control area.

Menus can either pop up below a ButtonStack or an AbbrevStack, or if the button is itself displayed on a menu, to the right, in a menu cascade. Figure A-4 showed examples of menus.

The Menu widget is a popup widget created with `XtCreatePopupShell`. It has a single child, which is a ControlArea widget.

The ControlArea widget places its children in rows or columns. Resources allow the application to specify a fixed width and/or height, or a fixed number of rows or columns. ControlArea widgets are usually used as the parent of OblongButton, ButtonStack, Exclusives, or Nonexclusives widgets (which in turn manage RectButton widgets, as described in the next section).

A.1.2.2 General Purpose Composite Widgets

We've already discussed the Composite widgets relating to control areas and menus. However, there are several general-purpose composite widgets in the OPEN LOOK set as well.

The BulletinBoard widget provides a free-form area for placing subwindows. Widgets can be placed on a BulletinBoard at arbitrary x and y coordinates; if no coordinates are specified, they appear in the upper left corner. The BulletinBoard provides no management of its children, and is often used to estabish the base frame for an application, since it allows the application programmer to place the major components of the application, rather than having to go by some Composite widget's arbitrary placement decisions.

A BulletinBoard is often used as the main window of an application.

The Form widget is a constraint widget similar to the Athena Form widget. It allows the placement of widgets to be specified relative to each other, and with rules governing their separation or relative position.

The Caption widget is like an Athena Label widget turned inside out. Like the Label widget, it prints a string. However, while the label widget's string is printed inside a visible widget border, a Caption string appears outside a bordered area. Caption is a composite widget class, and its label typically refers to a child widget of any size, which the Caption widget manages. The label can be aligned on either the right, left, top or bottom of the child widget.

The FooterPanel widget provides a consistent method for placing a footer along the bottom of another window. The footer panel takes two children. The top child is typically the main composite widget of the application; the bottom widget may contain a control or message area. The basic feature of the FooterPanel widget is that when the widget is resized, it applies all the change in the vertical direction to the top child, maintaining the bottom child at a constant height.

A.1.2.3 Scrollbars and Scrollable Windows

OPEN LOOK scrollbars use the visual metaphor of an elevator on a cable, but functionally they are similar to the Athena Scrollbar widget. The drag area (the thumb in an Athena Scrollbar widget) doesn't change size; instead, as shown in Figure A-7, there is a separate area that indicates the proportion of the data that is currently being displayed.

Scrollbars may be oriented either horizontally or vertically.

Scrollbars are used as a component of a ScrolledWindow widget, which, like the Athena Viewport widget, provides a scrollable view of a data area in a child widget. The child widget is typically larger than the view area, but only the area in the parent's view area can be seen at any one time. Figure A-1 showed a ScrolledWindow widget as the main application pane. The ScrollingList widget displays a scrollable list of editable text fields, and provides facilities for choosing and displaying one of the fields as "currently selected." Items can be selected from the list, changed, copied, and so on. This widget is useful for providing an interface to select a file for reading or writing.

Figure A-7. An OPEN LOOK Scrollbar

Figure A-8 shows a ScrollingList widget.

Figure A-8. An OPEN LOOK ScrollingList widget

A.1.3 Popups

In addition to Menu widgets, the OPEN LOOK widget set contains three other special types of popup widgets: Notices, PopupWindows, and Help windows. A Notice is used to request confirmation or other information from the user. The widget contains a text area, where the message to the user is displayed, and a control area containing one or more buttons, one of which must be the default button.

Figure A-9 shows an OPEN LOOK Notice widget.

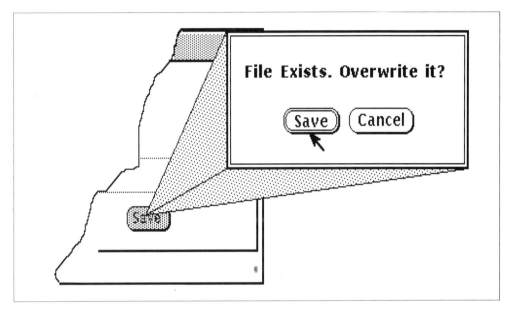

Figure A-9. An OPEN LOOK Notice

A Notice grabs the pointer. The only input allowed is to the Notice. Once the user has clicked a button, the Notice disappears.

The second special popup type is a PopupWindow, which can be used for more complex pop-ups. Unlike a Notice, which is a subclass of OverrideShell, a PopupWindowShell is a sub-class of WMShell, and so is decorated by the window manager. It has all the visual attributes of a top-level window, including resize corners, etc. In addition, it displays a pushpin in the upper left corner. If the user clicks on the pushpin with the pointer, the menu doesn't go away when its action has been performed, but stays on the screen. This allows the user to keep menus (and other frequently-referenced popups, such as help screens) "pinned" on the display, where they can be moved like regular windows. (Menus can also display a pushpin; its presence or absence is controlled by a widget resource.)

A PopupWindow typically contains an upper control area that may include menus, and a lower control area that may be used for buttons invoking widget actions. Resources allow for automatic creation of several buttons, including a "reset to factory" button, a "set defaults" button, and several other ways of setting standard properties for an application.

Figure A-10 shows a PopupWindow.

Figure A-10. *An OPEN LOOK PopupWindow*

A Help window is not instantiated in the usual way. Instead, an application uses the Ol-RegisterHelp function to register help text with the toolkit. Text can be associated with a widget class, a widget instance, or a window. When the user clicks the second pointer button on an object, the Help widget is automatically displayed by the toolkit. The Help widget includes a Magnifier subwidget, which displays a magnifying glass containing an image of the part of the screen on which the user clicked the pointer. Figure A-11 shows a Help window.

Figure A-11. *An OPEN LOOK Help window*

A.1.4 Text Widgets

OPEN LOOK offers three separate text widgets. The StaticText widget is similar to the Athena Label widget in that it displays a fixed text string. However, it can handle longer strings by using wordwrapping to break the string onto multiple lines.

The OPEN LOOK Text widget is very similar to the Athena Text widget. It provides a general-purpose editable text widget, with editing commands customizable via a translation table.

One of the annoying weaknesses of the Athena Text widget is that it is difficult and inefficient to use as a single-line editable field. (A program can add translations for the Return key to limit the text to a single line.) OPEN LOOK addresses this need with the TextField widget, useful for developing form-driven applications. TextField widgets were shown in Figure A-11.

The TextField widget provides simple editing commands, and scrolling if the string is too long to be displayed. When the keyboard focus leaves the widget, or when the Tab or Return key is pressed, it passes the data in the field to the application for validation.

A.1.5 Drawing Areas

Like the Athena widget set, the AT&T OPEN LOOK widgets provide no widget explicitly labeled as a drawing area. As described in this book, one is expected either to create a custom widget for an application's main window, or to use a very basic widget class, and add actions for drawing.

The AT&T OPEN LOOK widget set does include a Stub widget class (which is not documented in the manual, but is included in the source), which is useful for providing a window for drawing.

A.2 The OSF/Motif Widgets

Figure A-12 shows the general look of a Motif application, the Motif Reference Editor, *mre*. *mre*, developed by Mitch Trachtenberg, is OSF demo software, which is available as part of the Motif distribution.

As with the AT&T OPEN LOOK widget set, some of the features of a main application window are actually decoration provided by the window manager, *mwm*. As shown in Figure A-11, these include the title bar, which displays:

- The title provided by the application.

Figure A-12. Look and feel of a Motif application

- A Menu button, which drops down a menu containing basic window manipulation commands.

- A "Minimize" button, which iconifies the application.

- A "Maximize" button, which causes the application window to fill the entire screen.

You will also recognize Motif's version of many of the common controls discussed in the section on the AT&T OPEN LOOK widget set.

Figure A-13 shows the inheritance hierarchy of the Motif widgets. The Intrinsics-supplied widget classes are shaded grey.

The Primitive and Manager widgets are not generally instantiated and exist only to provide resources and other features inherited by other widgets.

In addition, Motif supports a Gadget class, which, as described in Chapter 13, *Menus, Gadgets, and Cascaded Popups*, is subclassed from RectObj rather than Core. Gadget equivalents exist for the Label widget, some classes of Button widgets, and the Separator widget. Gadgets are not shown in Figure A-13.

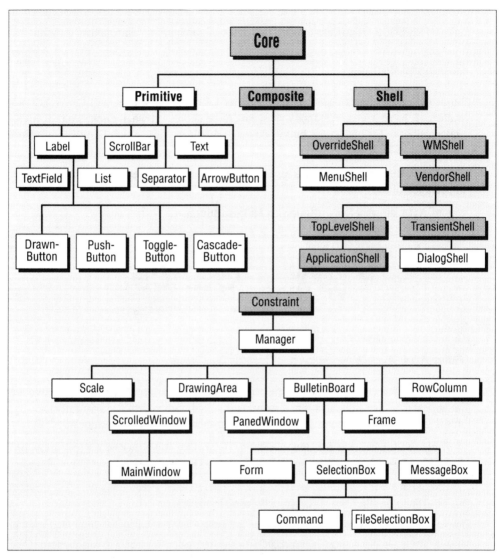

Figure A-13. Class inheritance hierarchy of the Motif widget set

A.2.1 Application Controls

Like OPEN LOOK, Motif has a much richer set of application controls than Athena.

A.2.1.1 Command Buttons

Motif's PushButton is equivalent to Athena's Command widget and OPEN LOOK's Rect-Button. It has a 3-D appearance and seems to be depressed when clicked on. It invokes separate callbacks for button up, button down, and button click, much like the equivalent widgets in other sets.

The DrawnButton works similarly, but allows the programmer to provide a pixmap for the appearance of the button.

Figure A-14 shows a DrawnButton and a PushButton.

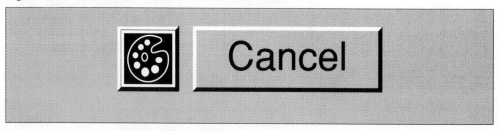

Figure A-14. Motif DrawnButton and PushButton widgets

The CascadeButton is similar in effect to OPEN LOOK's ButtonStack—it can have a particular appearance that indicates that a menu is invoked, rather than a single callback. Typically, this is simply an arrow pointing in the direction where the menu will appear.

A ToggleButton is used for option setting, much like OPEN LOOK's RectButton or Check-Box. Figure A-16 shows a box containing a set of ToggleButtons.

The Separator widget can be used to draw a line or other separator between a group of widgets in a menu or other box. It is typically used in menus.

The List widget displays a list of strings set by the application and allows the user to select one or more of the strings. The selected data is passed to a callback function. (We'll talk more about this widget in the section on scrolling.)

A.2.1.2 Analog Controls

Motif's Scale widget is similar to OPEN LOOK's Slider but is more powerful since it can be used to display as well as to control analog values.

A.2.2 Composite Widgets

As with OPEN LOOK, we've divided the discussion of Composite widgets into three areas: Menus and Control Areas, General-Purpose Composite Widgets, and Scrollable Windows. These distinctions are somewhat arbitrary and with menus the sections overlap with the one on popups, which appears later.

A.2.2.1 Menus and Control Areas

Motif provides a special Shell widget class called MenuShell for managing popup menus. However, most actual menu displays are managed by the RowColumn composite widget, which, like OPEN LOOK's ControlArea, displays buttons in rows or columns.

Through resources, the RowColumn widget can be configured to create such specialized, predefined elements as a MenuBar (which can only accept CascadeButton widgets as children), several different styles of pulldown or popup menu panes, and several preconfigured control areas, such as a "Radio Box" containing multiple exclusive ToggleButton gadgets.

Here you can begin to see the wide divergence in programming style made possible by the Xt Intrinsics. It is possible to create a hierarchy of relatively simple widgets to perform separate parts of a task, or a single, very complex widget which is highly configurable. In one of its incarnations, the RowColumn widget is equivalent to an OPEN LOOK ControlArea plus an Exclusives widget; in another, a ControlArea plus a Nonexclusives.

In general, Motif widgets are more complex and have many more resources than widgets provided in other widget sets. To simplify their use, though, Motif provides numerous convenience functions. For example, `XmCreateRadioBox` will create a RowColumn widget with one specialized set of resources, while `XmCreateMenuBar` will create one that is entirely different in appearance and function.

Figure A-15 shows a RowColumn widget configured as a MenuBar and Figure A-16 shows one configured as a RadioBox (each with appropriate children).

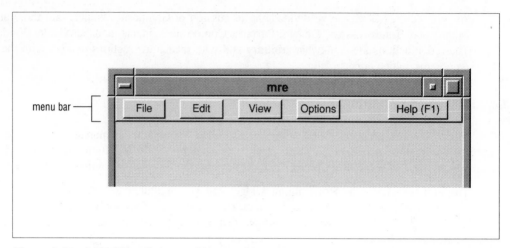

menu bar ⎤

Figure A-15. A Motif RowColumn widget configured as a MenuBar

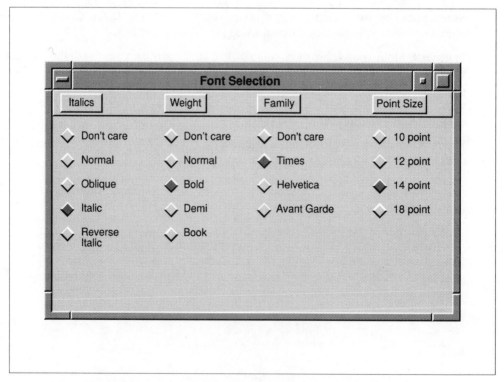

Figure A-16. A Motif RowColumn widget configured with four RadioBoxes

Figure A-17 shows a RowColumn widget implementing a pulldown menu.

Items on Motif menus can be selected by dragging the pointer down the menu and releasing it when the chosen item is highlighted. Alternately, the pointer can simply be clicked on the menu title to drop down the menu. Clicking on an item in the menu selects it; clicking anywhere other than in the menu pops the menu down without executing any item.

Note also that as a general feature, Motif menus support accelerators. That is, there are keyboard equivalents for every menu item. These keyboard accelerators are listed after the menu label, as shown above. In addition, typing the underlined letter in any menu item label when the pointer is in the menu will select that menu item. These underlined letters are called "mnemonics."

The items on a menubar or menu pane simply appear as labels but when selected take on the 3-D appearance of a PushButton.

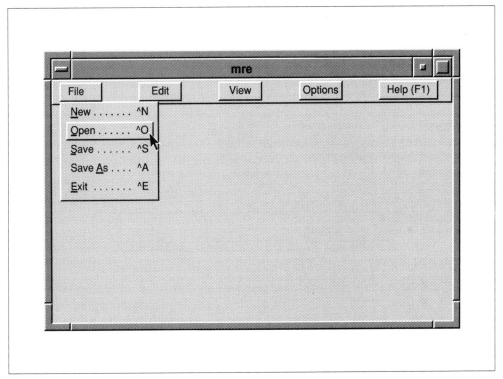

Figure A-17. A Motif RowColumn widget configured as a pulldown menu

A.2.2.2 General Purpose Composite Widgets

The BulletinBoard widget provides simple composite management, allowing widgets to be placed arbitrarily anywhere within its confines. The only constraint is that they are not allowed to overlap.

The Form widget is a subclass of BulletinBoard that, like the widgets of the same name in other sets, allows children to be laid out relative to each other or to one or another of the sides of the Form. The children will thus always maintain their proper relative position when the application is resized.

Figure A-18 shows a fully configured Form.

Figure A-18. A Motif Form widget and children

The Frame widget is used simply to provide a consistent border for widgets that might not otherwise have one. One use is to give a RowColumn widget a border with a 3-D appearance.

A.2.2.3 Scrollable Windows

A Motif ScrollBar is illustrated in Figure A-19.

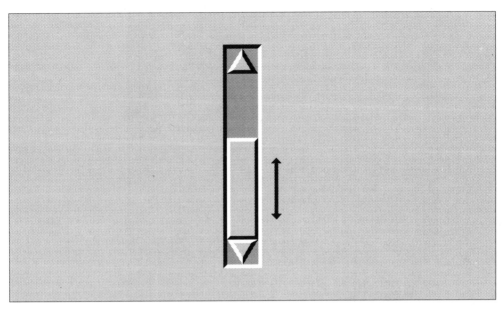

Figure A-19. A Motif ScrollBar

Like the Athena Scrollbar widget, the scrollbar has a "thumb" or slider that can be dragged up and down to scroll the associated window. You can also click above or below the thumb to move it a screenful at a time. Unlike the Athena widget, it also displays arrows at either end that can be used to scroll line by line. The associated window scrolls in the indicated direction as long as the pointer button is held down in one of the arrows.

There are several different types of scrolling windows. The ScrolledWindow widget, like Athena's Viewport, provides a general mechanism for attaching scrollbars to some other window.

The MainWindow widget is a subclass of ScrolledWindow with a special appearance reserved for application main windows. Figure A-14 showed a MainWindow widget.

Using the XmCreateScrolledList function, a List widget can be created as a child of a ScrolledWindow, giving the effect of a simple scrolled list. In addition, there are several flavors of more complex scrolling lists. These include the SelectionBox widget, and its two subclasses, Command and FileSelectionBox.

A general-purpose SelectionBox is akin to a ScrolledWindow/List combination, but adds a Text widget for entering additional data not on the list. The SelectionBox also adds at least three buttons labeled by default *OK*, *Cancel*, and *Help*.

Figure A-20 shows a SelectionBox.

Items

*Foreground . . . . black

*activeForeground . . . . black

*activeBackground . . . . gray

*topShadowColor . . . . white

*bottomShadowColor . . . . black   ————— list box

————— scroll bars

Selection

————— selection box

Edit   Add   Delete   Help   ————— push button

Figure A-20. A Motif SelectionBox

A FileSelectionBox is a SelectionBox specially designed to present a list of filenames for selections. A Command widget is a special kind of SelectionBox whose list consists of the history of commands entered in the Text widget. Each time a new command is entered, it is added to the history list.

A.2.3 Popups

Motif defines two classes of Shell widgets: DialogShell, which is used for parenting Dialog boxes, and MenuShell, which is used for menus. These classes are rarely instantiated directly, but are instead created by convenience functions that also create their composite children.

For example, functions exist to create a DialogShell with a variety of pre-configured MessageBox widgets as the visible child.

As we've already discussed, a specially configured RowColumn widget is used to create a menu pane as the visible child of a MenuShell widget.

A.2.4 Text Widgets

Like Athena and the AT&T OPEN LOOK widgets, Motif provides a Text widget that supports a complete editing command set. Like Athena, and unlike AT&T's OPEN LOOK widget set, both single- and multiline editing is supported by a single widget. But arranging for single-line editing is easier with Motif than with Athena.

A.2.5 Drawing Areas

As you may recall, to do drawing in the Athena widgets we either created a custom widget or instantiated a Core widget in order to obtain a window for drawing. The Motif DrawingArea widget class answers this need in Motif. It provides a window for drawing and provides very simple, bulletin-board like composite management of children.

Though the name of this widget class sounds promising, you should be aware that Motif really provides no more sophisticated drawing capabilities than Athena or the AT&T OPEN LOOK widget set. In each case, once you have selected the widget to draw on, you simply draw in its window using Xlib calls.

B

Specifying Fonts and Colors

This appendix describes the possible values for color, font, and geometry resource specifications.

In This Appendix:

B
Specifying Fonts and Colors

This appendix describes the possible values for color, font, and geometry resource specifications.

B.1 Color Specification

Many clients have resources and command-line options that allow you to specify the color of the window background, foreground (the color that text or graphic elements will be drawn in), or window border. For example, the following resources might be set for a Label widget:

```
*background:    orange    set the background color to orange
*foreground:    black     set the foreground color to black
*borderColor:   black     This must be Halloween!
```

The corresponding command-line options have the form:

–bg color   sets the background color

–fg color   sets the foreground color

–bd color   sets the border color

Some clients allow additional options to specify color for other elements, such as the cursor, highlighting, and so on.

By default, the background is usually white and the foreground black, even on color workstations. You can specify a new color using either the names in the X Window System's color name database or hexadecimal values.

B.1.1 Color Names

The *rgb.txt* file, usually located in */usr/lib/X11* on UNIX systems, is supplied with X and consists of predefined colors assigned to specific (but not necessarily intuitive) names.*

---

*A corresponding compiled file called *rgb.pag* contains the definitions used by the server; the *rgb.txt* file is the human-readable equivalent.

The following are some of the default color names that come with the X Window System. (See Appendix A, *System Management*, in Volume Three, *X Window System User's Guide, Motif Edition*, for information on customizing color name definitions.) This file is not part of the X standard, so vendors are free to modify it. However, most will just add to it, or redefine the values associated with each color name for better effects on their display hardware.

aquamarine	mediumaquamarine	black	blue
cadetblue	cornflowerblue	darkslateblue	lightblue
lightsteelblue	mediumblue	mediumslateblue	midnightblue
navyblue	navy	skyblue	slateblue
steelblue	coral	cyan	firebrick
gold	goldenrod	mediumgoldenrod	green
darkgreen	darkolivegreen	forestgreen	limegreen
mediumforestgreen	mediumseagreen	mediumspringgreen	palegreen
seagreen	springgreen	yellowgreen	darkslategray
darkslategray	dimgray	dimgray	lightgray
lightgray	khaki	magenta	maroon
orange	orchid	darkorchid	mediumorchid
pink	plum	red	indianred
mediumvioletred	orangered	violetred	salmon
sienna	tan	thistle	turquoise
darkturquoise	mediumturquoise	violet	blueviolet
wheat	white	yellow	greenyellow

As of R4, a number zero through three can be appended to each of these names in order to get various intensities of each color. In addition, a complete range of grays are provided by using the name *gray* or *gray* followed by a number from zero through 100. There are also a few colors not provided in the R3 database, such as *snow* and *misty rose*. These names can be used directly when the specific color is wanted.

For example, the command line:

```
% xterm -bg lightblue -fg darkslategray -bd plum &
```

creates an *xterm* window with a background of light blue, foreground of dark slate gray, and border of plum. Note that the RGB values in the color database provided by MIT are correct for only one type of display; you may find that the color you get is not exactly what you expect given the name. To combat this, vendors may have corrected the RGB values to give colors closer to what the name implies.

At the command line, a color name should be typed as a single word (for example, `darkslategray`). However, you can type the words comprising a color name separately if you enclose them in quotes, as in the following command line:

```
% xterm -bg "light blue" -fg "dark slate gray" -bd plum &
```

B.1.2 Hexadecimal Color Specification

You can also specify colors more exactly using a hexadecimal color string. You probably won't use this method unless you require a color not available by using a color name. Moreover, you shouldn't use this method unless necessary because it tends to discourage the sharing of colors between applications. In order to understand how this works, you may need a little background on how color is implemented on most workstations.

B.1.2.1 The RGB Color Model

Most color displays on the market today are based on the RGB color model. Each pixel on the screen is actually made up of three phosphors: one red, one green, and one blue. Each of these three phosphors is excited by a separate electron beam. When all three phosphors are fully illuminated, the pixel appears white to the human eye. When all three are dark, the pixel appears black. When the illumination of each primary color varies, the three phosphors generate a subtractive color. For example, equal portions of red and green, with no admixture of blue, makes yellow.

As you might guess, the intensity of each primary color is controlled by a three-part digital value—and it is the exact makeup of this value that the hexadecimal specification allows you to set.

Depending on the underlying hardware, different servers may use a larger or smaller number of bits (from 4 to 16 bits) to describe the intensity of each primary. To insulate you from this variation, clients are designed to take color values containing anywhere from 4 to 16 bits (1 to 4 hex digits), and the server then scales them to the hardware. As a result, you can specify hexadecimal values in any one of the following formats:

```
#RGB
#RRGGBB
#RRRGGGBBB
#RRRRGGGGBBBB
```

where R, G, and B represent single hexadecimal digits and determine the intensity of the red, green, and blue primaries that make up each color.

When fewer than four digits are used, they represent the most significant bits of the value. For example, #3a6 is the same as #3000a0006000.

What this means concretely is perhaps best illustrated by looking at the values that correspond to some colors in the color name database. We'll use 8-bit values (two hexadecimal digits for each primary) because that is the way they are defined in the *rgb.txt* file:

```
#000000      black
#FCFCFC      white
#FF0000      red
#00FF00      green
#0000FF      blue
#FFFF00      yellow
#00FFFF      cyan
#FF00FF      magenta
#5F9F9F      cadet blue
#42426F      cornflower blue
#BFD8D8      light blue
#8F8FBC      light steel blue
#3232CC      medium blue
#23238E      navy blue
#3299CC      sky blue
```

```
#007FFF        slate blue
#236B8E        steel blue
```

As you can see from the colors given above, pure red, green, and blue result from the corresponding bits being turned full on. All primaries off yields black, while all nearly full on gives white. Yellow, cyan, and magenta can be created by pairing two of the other primaries at full intensity. The various shades of blue shown above are created by varying the intensity of each primary—sometimes in unexpected ways.

The bottom line here is that if you don't intimately know the physics of color, the best you can do is to look up existing colors from the color name database and experiment with them by varying one or more of the primaries till you find a color you like. Unless you need precise colors, you are probably better off using color names.

If you do specify a color using a hexadecimal value, try to use the same value for several applications so that they will share a color call.

In any event, using hexadecimal values for colors is not generally recommended, since it discourages sharing of color cells.

B.1.2.2 How Many Colors are Available?

The number of distinct colors available on the screen at any one time depends on the amount of memory available for color specification.

A color display uses multiple bits per pixel (also referred to as multiple planes or the *depth* of the display) to select colors. Programs that draw in color use the value of these bits as a pointer to a lookup table called a *colormap*, in which each entry (or *colorcell*) contains the RGB values for a particular color.* As shown in Figure B-1, any given pixel value is used as an index into this table—for example, a pixel value of 16 will select the sixteenth colorcell.

This implementation explains several issues that you might encounter in working with color displays.

First, the range of colors possible on the display is a function of the number of bits available in the colormap for RGB specification. If 8 bits are available for each primary, then the range of possible colors is 256^3 (somewhere over 16 million colors). This means that you can create incredibly precise differences between colors.

However, the number of different colors that can be displayed on the screen at any one time is a function of the number of planes. A four-plane system can index 2^4 colorcells (16 distinct colors); an eight-plane system can index 2^8 colorcells (256 distinct colors); and a 24-plane system can index 2^{24} colorcells (over 16 million distinct colors).

If you are using a four-plane workstation, the fact that you can precisely define hundreds of different shades of blue is far less significant than the fact that you can't use them all at the same time. There isn't space for all of them to be stored in the colormap at one time.

---

*There is a type of high-performance display in which pixel values are used directly to control the illumination of the red, green, and blue phosphors, but far more commonly, the bits per pixel are used indirectly, with the actual color values specified independently, as described here.

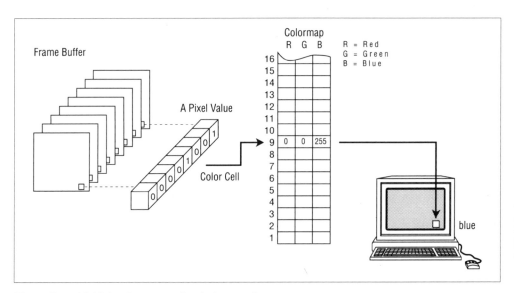

Figure B-1. Multiple planes used to index a colormap

This limitation is made more significant by the fact that X is a multiclient environment. When X starts up, usually no colors are loaded into the colormap. As clients are invoked, certain of these cells are allocated. But when all of the free colorcells are used up, it is no longer possible to request new colors. When this happens, you will usually be given the closest possible color from those that have already been allocated. However, you may instead be given an error message and told that there are no free colorcells.

In order to minimize the chance of running out of colorcells, many programs use "shared" colorcells. Shared colorcells can be used by any number of applications, but they can't be changed by any of them. They can be deallocated only by each application that uses them, and when all applications have deallocated the cell, it is available for setting again. Shared cells are most often used for background, border, and cursor colors.

Alternately, some clients have to be able to change the color of graphics they have already drawn. This requires another kind of cell, called private, which can't be shared. A typical use of a private cell would be for the palette of a color mixing application. Such a program might have three bars of each primary color, and a box which shows the mixed color. The primary bars would use shared cells, while the mixed color box would use a private cell.

In summary, some programs define colorcells to be read-only and shareable, while others define colorcells to be read/write and private.

To top it off, there are even clients that may temporarily swap in a whole private colormap of their own. Because of the way color is implemented, if this happens, all other applications will be displayed in unexpected colors.

In order to minimize such conflicts, you should request precise colors only when necessary. By preference, use color names or hexadecimal specifications that you specified for other applications.

For more information on color, see Chapter 7, *Color*, in Volume One, *Xlib Programming Manual*.

B.2 Font Specification

Most widgets that display text allow you to specify the font to be used in displaying text in the widget, via either the `XtNfont` resource, or the *–fn* and *–font* command-line options.

The X Window System supports many different display fonts, with different sizes and type styles. (These are *screen* fonts and are not to be confused with *printer* fonts.)

For Release 3 and subsequent releases, Adobe Systems, Inc., and Digital Equipment Corporation jointly contributed five families of screen fonts (Courier, Helvetica, New Century Schoolbook, Symbol and Times) in a variety of sizes, styles, and weights for 75 dots per inch monitors. Bitstream, Inc. contributed its Charter font family in the same sizes, styles, and weights for both 75 and 100 dots per inch monitors.

Most Release 2 fonts have been moved to the user-contributed distribution (*/usr/X11r3/contrib/fonts*).

In Release 3 and later, fonts are stored in three directories:

Directory	Contents
/usr/lib/X11/fonts/misc	Six fixed-width fonts (also available in Release 2), the cursor font.
/usr/lib/X11/fonts/75dpi	Fixed- and variable-width fonts, 75 dots per inch.
/usr/lib/X11/fonts/100dpi	Fixed- and variable-width fonts, 100 dots per inch.

These three directories (in this order) comprise X's default font path. The font path can be changed with the *fp* option to the *xset* client, as described in Volume Three, *X Window System User's Guide, Motif Edition*. (The font path, together with a great deal of other information about the server defaults, can be listed with *xset query*.) All fonts in the font path can be listed with *xlsfonts*, and the characters in a font can be displayed on the screen with *xfd*.

The names of each font file in the font directories has a filename extension of *.snf*, which stands for *server natural format*. Fonts are distributed in *binary distribution format* (*bdf*), and may need to be adapted for a given server.

B.2.1 Font Naming Conventions

In Release 2, font names were determined by the names of the files in which they are stored, without the *.snf* extension. For example, the file *fg-16.snf* contains the font named fg-16.

If you do a listing of any of the current font directories, you'll notice that the filenames also have *.snf* extensions. However, font names are not determined by the names of the files in which they are stored.

Now, a font's name is determined by the contents of the font property named FONT* rather than the name of the file in which the font is stored.

If you run *xlsfonts*, you'll get an intimidating list of names similar to the one shown in Figure B-2, which upon closer examination contains a great deal of useful information:

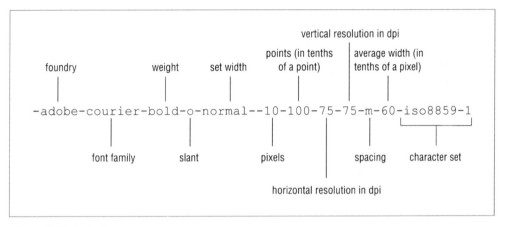

Figure B-2. A font name

This rather verbose line is actually the name of the font stored in the file *courBO10* (in the *75dpi* directory). This font name specifies the foundry (Adobe), the font family (Courier), weight (bold), slant (Oblique), set width (normal), size of the font in pixels (10), size of the font in tenths of a point (100—measured in tenths of a point, thus equals 10 points), horizontal resolution (75dpi), vertical resolution (75dpi), spacing (m, for monospace), average width in tenths of a pixel (60—measured in tenths of a pixel, thus equals 6 pixels) and character set (iso8859-1).

The meaning of many of these statistics is obvious. Some of the less obvious information is explained below.

Foundry   The type foundry (in this case, Adobe) that digitized and supplied the font.

---

*A property is a piece of information associated with a window or a font. See Volume One, *Xlib Programming Manual*, for more information about properties.

Set width	A value describing a font's proportionate width, according to the foundry. Typical set widths include: normal, condensed, narrow, double width. All of the newer fonts have the set width *normal*.
Pixels and points	Type is normally measured in points, a printer's unit equal to 1/72 of an inch. The size of a font in pixels depends on the resolution of the display font in pixels. For example, if the display font has 100 dots per inch (dpi) resolution, a 12 point font will have a pixel size of 17, while with 75 dpi resolution, a 12 point font will have a pixel size of 12.
Spacing	Either m (monospace, i.e., fixed-width) or p (proportional, i.e., variable-width).

Horizontal and vertical resolution

> The resolution in dots per inch that a font is designed for. Horizontal and vertical figures are required because a screen may have different capacities for horizontal and vertical resolution.

Average width	Mean width of all characters in the font, measured in tenths of a pixel, in this case 6 pixels.
Character set	ISO, the International Standards Organization, has defined character set standards for various languages. The iso8859-1 in Figure B-2 represents the ISO Latin 1 character set, which is used by all of the fonts in the *75dpi* and *100dpi* directories. The ISO Latin 1 character set is a superset of the standard ASCII character set, which includes various special characters used in European languages other than English. See Appendix H of Volume Two, *Xlib Reference Manual*, for a complete listing of the characters in the ISO Latin 1 character set.

This font-naming convention is intended to allow for the unique naming of fonts of any style, resolution and size. It is powerful, but unwieldy.

To create a label widget that displays text in the font stored in the file *courBO10*, you could use the resource setting:

```
*label:  -adobe-courier-bold-o-normal--10-100-75-75-m-60-iso8859-1
```

Since typing a font name of this length is neither desirable nor practical, the X Window System developers have provided two alternatives: wildcarding and aliasing.

B.2.2 Font Name Wildcarding

Any unnecessary part of a font name can be "wildcarded" by specifying a question mark (?) for any single character and an asterisk (*) for any group of characters.

For example, using a wildcarded font name, the resource specification above could be written:

```
*label:  *courier-bold-o-*-100*
```

(Note that when using wildcards with the *-fn* command line option, you must take care to quote the font names, since the UNIX shell has special meanings for the wildcard characters * and ?. This can be done by enclosing the entire font name in quotes, or by escaping each wildcard character by typing a backslash before it.)

If more than one font in a given directory matches a wildcarded font name, the server chooses the font to use. If fonts from *more than one directory* match the wildcarded name, the server will always choose a font from the directory that is earlier in the font path. Thus, if a wildcarded font name matches a font from both the *75dpi* and *100dpi* directories, and the *75dpi* directory comes first in the font path, the server chooses the font from that directory.

In creating a wildcarded font name, you need to decide which parts of the standard font name must be explicit and which parts can be replaced with wildcards. As the previous example illustrates, you can use a single wildcard character for multiple parts of the font name. For instance, the final asterisk in the example stands for the sequence:

```
-75-75-m-60-iso8859-1
```

in the explicit font name. The idea is to specify enough parts of the font name explicitly so that the server gives you the font you have in mind.

It's helpful to familiarize yourself with the available font families, weights, slants, and point sizes. The following list gives these statistics for the fonts in the directories *75dpi* and *100dpi* in the standard X distribution from MIT.* (The fonts in the *misc* directory are holdovers from Release 2 and have short, manageable names that should not require wildcarding.)

Font families	Charter, Courier, Helvetica, New Century Schoolbook, Symbol, Times
Weights	Medium, bold
Slants	Roman (r), an upright design
	Italic (i), an italic design slanted clockwise from vertical
	Oblique (o), an obliqued upright design, slanted clockwise from vertical
Point sizes	8, 10, 12, 14, 18, 24

If you're unfamiliar with the general appearance of a particular font family, try displaying one of the fonts with *xfd*, as described in Volume Three, *X Window System User's Guide, Motif Edition*.

As a general rule, we suggest you type the following parts of a font name explicitly:

- Font family
- Weight
- Slant
- Point size

Note that it's better to match the point size field, which is measured in tenths of a point (the 100 in the previous example, equal to 10 points), than the pixel field (the 10). This allows your wildcarded font name to work properly with monitors of different resolutions. For

---

*For fonts other than those shipped by MIT, other families, weights, slants, point sizes, etc., may apply.

example, say you use the following name to specify a 24 point (size), medium (weight), Italic (slant) Charter (family) font:

```
*charter-medium-i-*-240-*
```

This will match either of the following two font names (the first for 75 dpi monitors and the second for 100 dpi monitors):

```
-bitstream-charter-medium-i-normal--25-240-75-75-p-136-iso8859-1
-bitstream-charter-medium-i-normal--33-240-100-100-p-136-iso8859-1
```

depending on which directory comes first in your font path. Specifying font size explicitly in pixels (25 for the first or 33 for the second) rather than in points would limit you to matching only one of these fonts.

Given the complexity of font names and the rules of precedence used by the server, you should use wildcards carefully.

B.2.3 Font Name Aliasing

Another way to abbreviate font names is by aliasing—that is, by associating them with alternative names. You can create a file (or files) called *fonts.alias*, in any directory in the font search path, to set aliases for the fonts in that directory. The X server uses both *fonts.dir* files (see Section B.2.5) and *fonts.alias* files to locate fonts in the font path.

Be aware that when you create or edit a *fonts.alias* file, the server does not *automatically* recognize the aliases in question. You must make the server aware of newly created or edited alias files by resetting the font path with *xset* as described in Section B.2.4.

The *fonts.alias* file has a two-column format similar to the *fonts.dir* file (described in a moment): the first column contains aliases, the second contains the actual font names. If you want to specify an alias that contains spaces, enclose the alias in double quotes. If you want to include double quotes or other special characters as part of an alias, precede each special symbol with a backslash.

When you use an alias to specify a font in a command line, the server searches for the font associated with that alias in every directory in the font path. Therefore, a *fonts.alias* file in one directory can set aliases for fonts in other directories as well. You might choose to create a single alias file in one directory of the font path to set aliases for the most commonly used fonts in all the directories. Example B-1 shows a sample *fonts.alias* file.

Example B-1. Sample fonts.alias file

```
xterm12    -adobe-courier-medium-r-normal--12-120-75-75-m-70-iso8859-1
xterm14    -adobe-courier-medium-r-normal--14-140-75-75-m-90-iso8859-1
xterm18    -adobe-courier-medium-r-normal--18-180-75-75-m-110-iso8859-1
```

As the names of the aliases suggest, this sample file contains aliases for three fonts (of different point sizes) that are easily readable in *xterm* windows.

You can also use wildcards within the font names in the right hand column of an alias file. For instance, the alias file above might also be written:

```
xterm12      *courier-medium-r-*-120*
xterm14      *courier-medium-r-*-140*
xterm18      *courier-medium-r-*-180*
```

Once the server is made aware of aliases, you can specify an alias in resource specifications or on the command line:

```
xterm.font: xterm12
```

or:

```
% xterm -fn xterm12
```

If you are accustomed to the Release 2 font naming convention (each font name being equivalent to the name of the file in which it is stored, without the *.snf* extension), there is a way to emulate this convention using alias files. In each directory in the font path, create a *fonts.alias* file containing only the following line:

```
FILE_NAMES_ALIASES
```

Each filename (without the *.snf* extension) will then serve as an alias for the font the file contains. Note that an alias file containing this line applies only to the directory in which it is found. To make every font name equivalent to the name of the file in which it is stored, you need to create a *fonts.alias* file such as this in every font directory.

If you've specified FILE_NAMES_ALIASES in an alias file, you can choose the fonts in that directory by means of their filenames, as we did in the resource example at the end of Chapter 2, *Introduction to the X Toolkit and Motif.*

B.2.4 Making the Server Aware of Aliases

After you create (or update) an alias file, the server does not automatically recognize the aliases in question. You must make the server aware of newly created or edited alias files by "rehashing" the font path with *xset.* Enter:

```
% xset fp rehash
```

on the command line. The *xset* option *fp* (font path) with the `rehash` argument causes the server to reread the *fonts.dir* and *fonts.alias* files in the current font path. You need to do this every time you edit an alias file. (You also need to use *xset* if you add or remove fonts. See Volume Three, *X Window System User's Guide, Motif Edition,* for details.)

B.2.5 The fonts.dir Files

In addition to font files, each font directory contains a file called *fonts.dir.* The *fonts.dir* files serve, in effect, as databases for the X server. When the X server searches the directories in the default font path, it uses the *fonts.dir* files to locate the font(s) it needs.

Each *fonts.dir* file contains a list of all the font files in the directory with their associated font names, in two-column form. (The first column lists the font file and the second column lists the actual font name associated with the file.) The first line in *fonts.dir* lists the number of entries in the file (i.e., the number of fonts in the directory).

Example B-2 shows the *fonts.dir* file from the directory */usr/lib/X11/fonts/100dpi*. As the first line indicates, the directory contains 24 fonts.

Example B-2. fonts.dir file in /usr/lib/X11/fonts/100dpi

```
24
charBI08.snf  -bitstream-charter-bold-i-normal--11-80-100-100-p-68-iso8859-1
charBI10.snf  -bitstream-charter-bold-i-normal--14-100-100-100-p-86-iso8859-1
charBI12.snf  -bitstream-charter-bold-i-normal--17-120-100-100-p-105-iso8859-1
charBI14.snf  -bitstream-charter-bold-i-normal--19-140-100-100-p-117-iso8859-1
charBI18.snf  -bitstream-charter-bold-i-normal--25-180-100-100-p-154-iso8859-1
charBI24.snf  -bitstream-charter-bold-i-normal--33-240-100-100-p-203-iso8859-1
charB08.snf   -bitstream-charter-bold-r-normal--11-80-100-100-p-69-iso8859-1
charB10.snf   -bitstream-charter-bold-r-normal--14-100-100-100-p-88-iso8859-1
charB12.snf   -bitstream-charter-bold-r-normal--17-120-100-100-p-107-iso8859-1
charB14.snf   -bitstream-charter-bold-r-normal--19-140-100-100-p-119-iso8859-1
charB18.snf   -bitstream-charter-bold-r-normal--25-180-100-100-p-157-iso8859-1
charB24.snf   -bitstream-charter-bold-r-normal--33-240-100-100-p-206-iso8859-1
charI08.snf   -bitstream-charter-medium-i-normal--11-80-100-100-p-60-iso8859-1
charI10.snf   -bitstream-charter-medium-i-normal--14-100-100-100-p-76-iso8859-1
charI12.snf   -bitstream-charter-medium-i-normal--17-120-100-100-p-92-iso8859-1
charI14.snf   -bitstream-charter-medium-i-normal--19-140-100-100-p-103-iso8859-1
charI18.snf   -bitstream-charter-medium-i-normal--25-180-100-100-p-136-iso8859-1
charI24.snf   -bitstream-charter-medium-i-normal--33-240-100-100-p-179-iso8859-1
charR08.snf   -bitstream-charter-medium-r-normal--11-80-100-100-p-61-iso8859-1
charR10.snf   -bitstream-charter-medium-r-normal--14-100-100-100-p-78-iso8859-1
charR12.snf   -bitstream-charter-medium-r-normal--17-120-100-100-p-95-iso8859-1
charR14.snf   -bitstream-charter-medium-r-normal--19-140-100-100-p-106-iso8859-1
charR18.snf   -bitstream-charter-medium-r-normal--25-180-100-100-p-139-iso8859-1
charR24.snf   -bitstream-charter-medium-r-normal--33-240-100-100-p-183-iso8859-1
```

The *fonts.dir* files are created by the *mkfontdir* client when X is installed. *mkfontdir* reads the font files in directories in the font path, extracts the font names, and creates a *fonts.dir* file in each directory. If *fonts.dir* files are present on your system, you probably won't have to deal with them, or with *mkfontdir*, at all. If the files are not present, or if you have to load new fonts or remove existing ones, you will have to create files with *mkfontdir*. Refer to Volume Three, *X Window System User's Guide, Motif Edition*, for details.

B.3 Window Geometry

All clients that display in a window take a geometry option that specifies the size and location of the client window.* The syntax of the geometry option is:

```
-geometry geometry
```

The *–geometry* option can be (and often is) abbreviated to *–g*, unless there is a conflicting option that begins with *g*.

---

*The Release 2 syntax:

```
=geometry
```

is no longer supported.

The corresponding resource is `XtNGeometry`, which can be set in a resource file as follows:

```
*mywidget.geometry:    geometry_string
```

The argument to the geometry option (`geometry`), referred to as a "standard geometry string," has the form:

```
widthxheight±xoff±yoff
```

The variables `width` and `height`, are values in pixels for many clients. However, application developers are encouraged to use units that are meaningful to the application. For example, *xterm* uses columns and rows of text as width and height values in the *xterm* window. `xoff` (x offset), and `yoff` (y offset) are always in pixels.

You can specify any or all elements of the geometry string. Incomplete geometry specifications are compared to the resource manager defaults and missing elements are supplied by the values specified there. If no default is specified there, and *uwm* is running, the window manager will require you to place the window interactively.

The values for the *x* and *y* offsets have the following effects:

Table B-1. Geometry Specification: x and y Offsets

Offset Variables	Description
+xoff	A positive *x* offset specifies the distance that the left edge of the window is offset from the left side of the display.
+yoff	A positive *y* offset specifies the distance that the top edge of the window is offset from the top of the display.
−xoff	A negative *x* offset specifies the distance that the right edge of the window is offset from the right side of the display.
−yoff	A negative *y* offset specifies the distance that the bottom edge of the window is offset from the bottom of the display.

For example, the command line:

```
% xclock -geometry 125x125-10+10 &
```

places a clock 125x125 pixels in the upper-right corner of the display, 10 pixels from both the top and the right edge of the screen.

For *xterm*, the size of the window is measured in characters and lines. (80 characters wide by 24 lines long is the default terminal size.) If you wanted to use the vt100 window in 132-column mode, with 40 lines displayed at a time, you could use the following geometry options:

```
% xterm -geometry 132x40-10+350 &
```

This will place an *xterm* window 132 characters wide by 40 lines long in the lower-right corner, 10 pixels from the right edge of the screen and 350 pixels from the top of the screen.

Some clients may allow you to specify geometry strings for the size and position of the icon or an alternate window, usually through resources (in an *Xdefaults* or other resource file). See the appropriate client reference pages in Part Three of Volume Three, *X Window System User's Guide, Motif Edition*, for a complete list of available resources.

You should be aware that, as with all user preferences, you may not always get exactly what you ask for. Clients are designed to work with a window manager, which may have its own rules for window or icon size and placement. However, priority is always given to specific user requests, so you won't often be surprised.

C

Naming Conventions

This appendix describes a suggested set of conventions for naming widgets, and elements within widget code.

C
Naming Conventions

This appendix proposes a set of conventions for naming certain elements of widget code.* If the naming conventions used in all widget sets are consistent, there will be several benefits:

- It will be much easier for programmers to move from toolkit to toolkit without needing to constantly refer to manuals to figure out how to properly name various items.

- It will be easier to mix widgets from different widgets sets in one application.

- It will make it possible for automatic code generators to work with lots of widgets without making special modifications for any toolkit.

These conventions are common between the OPEN LOOK and Motif widget sets with a few minor differences. However, the Athena widget set currently does not follow the conventions described.

It is important to note that these suggestions are in no way blessed (or damned) by the X Consortium—they are simply a guideline that we suggest you follow in the interests of promoting the benefits listed above. We will use Motif as an example.

A toolkit uses a special prefix with all its widgets. In the case of Motif, this prefix is *m*. Using that prefix and a hypothetical Label widget as an example, the conventions are as follows:

Toolkit library name	*libXm.a*
Widget class name	`XmLabel`
Include directives	`<Xm/Label.h>`
`class_name` field in the core structure	`Label`
Enumerated resource values	`XmCAPITALIZED_WORDS`
Public function names	`XmLabelFunctionName()`

_____

*This appendix is based on a *comp.windows.x* network news posting by Gene Dykes of Cornell University.

Truncated include file names	Strip the lowercase letters a word at a time until the basename is nine characters or fewer (but strip as few letters as possible from the initial word). Thus:

```
<Xm/VeryLongWidgetName.h>
```

becomes:

```
<Xm/VeryLWN.h>
```

but:

```
<Xm/Verylongwidgetname.h>
```

becomes:

```
<Xm/Verylongw.h>
```

(Note difference in `VeryLong` (two words) and `Very-long` (one word).)

Macro names for preprocessor in include files	`#ifndef XM_LABEL_H`

This is to prevent header files from being included more than once.

If a widget has a corresponding gadget, then `Gadget` is appended to the widget name, so `XmLabelGadget` is the gadget class name.

Widget class pointer	`xmLabelWidgetClass`
Gadget class pointer	`xmLabelGadgetClass`
Create function for widgets or gadgets	`Widget XmCreateLabel (parent, name, arglist, argcount)`

This is a shortcut to using `XtCreateWidget`. However, in the case of top-level widgets (menus, dialogs, MainWindow), it also creates the shell widget and creates the requested widget within it.

The special Create functions can also be used as convenience routines for specialized widget instances. For example, `XmCreateWorkingDialog` and `XmCreateWarningDialog` actually create a Message-Box whose `XmDialogType` resources are respectively `XmDIALOG_WARNING` and `XmDIALOG_WORKING`.

OPEN LOOK uses conventions similar to Motif, but leaves the prefixes off the widget class name. We recommend that you supply a prefix for any widgets you write, especially if there is any chance that some other widget set may use the same class name. In other words, if we wrote a new Label widget, we might call it OraLabel, not just Label, so that we could still use the Athena Label widget in the same application.

D

Release Notes

This appendix summarizes changes between Release 3 and Release 4 of the X Toolkit, as it applies to writing or converting widgets and applications.

In This Appendix:

☞

D
Release Notes

The Xt specification is the definition of the X Consortium standard for Xt. This appendix describes the changes to the Xt Intrinsics specification between Release 3 and Release 4. This appendix separates them according to whether they affect just application writers, just widget writers, or both, so that you can read the sections appropriate to your needs.

In the majority of cases, Xt applications correctly written for Release 3 will be source compatible with Release 4. However, there have been many additions to Xt that you may wish to use when converting an application or widget to R4 or writing one from scratch. This is a fairly complete summary of the additions and changes that have been made to the Intrinsics since Release 3.

Some of the information provided below describes behavior that is not new but that is newly documented in R4—behavior that was in the R3 implementation of Xt (and still present in R4) but was not in the R3 Xt specification. These places are noted.

D.1 Summary of New Functions and Procedure Types

`XtAppInitialize` is the new function to be used for initializing Xt applications.

`XtAppSetFallbackResources` allows you to provide a set of backup resources that will be used in case the app-defaults file is not installed. An argument in `XtAppInitialize` is provided for this purpose, so `XtAppSetFallbackResources` is rarely needed.

The following functions are the new varargs versions of existing functions: `XtVaSetValues`, `XtVaGetValues`, `XtVaCreateWidget`, `XtVaCreateManagedWidget`, `XtVaAppCreateShell`, `XtVaGetSubresources`, `XtVaGetApplicationResources`, `XtVaCreatePopupShell`, `XtVaSetSubvalues`, `XtVaGetSubvalues`, and `XtVaAppInitialize`.

`XtInitializeWidgetClass` initializes a widget or object class without creating any widget or object. This is normally done in order to make available the type converters registered by that class before the first instance of that class is created, so that resources for the first instance can be set while creating it using `XtVaTypedArg`, a new feature of `XtVaSetValues` and `XtVaCreateWidget`.

`XtVaCreateArgsList` is for copying an argument list before using the `XtVaNested-List` symbol in one of the varargs interfaces.

`XtPopupSpringLoaded` pops up a widget and creates a global passive grab of the button being held.

The following functions are new Xt interfaces for making global passive and active grabs: `XtGrabKey`, `XtUngrabKey`, `XtGrabKeyboard`, `XtUngrabKeyboard`, `XtGrabButton`, `XtUngrabButton`, `XtGrabPointer`, and `XtUngrabPointer`. These are rarely needed since the grabbing needed to implement popups is built in to existing functions such as `XtMenuPopup` and the new function `XtPopupSpringLoaded`.

`XtInsertEventHandler` and `XtInsertRawEventHandler` are new functions that allow you to position an event handler at the beginning or end of the current list of event handlers for a certain event. They are also capable of moving an already registered event handler in the list.

`XtCallCallbackList` is similar to `XtCallCallbacks` but is slightly more efficient because it avoids the lookup of the callback resource in the widget.

`XtGetConstraintResourceList` is the new analogue to the existing `XtGetResourceList`. Both functions give you access to a widget's resource list.

`XtDisplayStringConversionWarning` supercedes `XtStringConversionWarning` for use in type converters that convert from `XtRString`.

R4 provides a completely new interface for type converters, which provides more controllable caching and display-specific conversions. The new function for registering a type converter is `XtAppSetTypeConverter`. There is a new type converter calling sequence, described in `XtConverter(2)` in Volume Five, *X Toolkit Intrinsics Reference Manual*. The new functions for calling a converter directly are `XtConvertAndStore`, `XtCallConverter`, though these are less necessary now that the new `XtVaTypedArg` symbol in the varargs interfaces is available.

`XtOffsetOf` is a new, more portable version of `XtOffset` (used in defining a resource list). Also in the resource list, the symbol `XtProcedureArg`, when used in the field normally specified as `XtBaseOffset`, instructs Xt to get the default value by calling the function of type `XtConvertArgProc` that is specified in the default value field.

The new functions for controlling the caching of type converters are `XtCallbackReleaseCacheRef`, `XtCallbackReleaseCacheRefList`, and `XtAppReleaseCacheRefs`.

Xt now provides an action hook, which allows you to record the actions being invoked in an application for later playback (this is one way to implement keyboard macros). `XtAppAddActionHook` registers a function that will be called whenever any action in the application is invoked. The action hook function is passed all the information passed to the action, plus the string action name. `XtRemoveActionHook` lets you unregister an action hook function. `XtCallActionProc` lets you call an action function directly to play back recorded actions. The function prototype of an action hook is `XtActionHookProc`.

`XtGetActionKeysym` is used within an action routine to get the keysym that invoked the action. This is useful because the event passed to the action contains only the keycode.

`XtGetKeysymTable` and `XtKeysymToKeycodeList` are two more functions for controlling the mapping of keycodes to keysyms. These functions are rarely needed.

`XtRegisterGrabAction` allows you to write an action that when invoked will automatically result in a global grab of the pointer or key that invoked the action. Internally in Xt this is used to register `XtMenuPopup`, so it is rarely needed.

`XtLastTimestampProcessed` is useful in selection processing, since some events that trigger selections do not include a timestamp. `XtGetSelectionRequest` is used in the *convert_proc* in selections to get the time from the selection request event.

`XtDisplayOfObject`, `XtScreenOfObject`, and `XtWindowOfObject` are the equivalents of `XtDisplay`, `XtScreen`, and `XtWindow` that work for objects, which are the windowless and sometimes geometryless forms of widgets. `XtIsObject` is a macro that lets you distinguish an object from a widget.

`XtDisplayToApplicationContext` is sometimes useful in applications that open connections to more than one display.

`XtName` converts a widget ID to a widget name, the opposite of `XtNameToWidget`.

`XtSetWMColormapWindows` sets the value of the WM_COLORMAP_WINDOWS property on a widget's window. This is done in order to tell the window manager that windows in this application other than the top-level window need special colormaps installed.

Release 4 introduces a set of new selection interfaces which allow the owner and requestor to handle the selection in arbitrary chunks. This is called an *incremental* transfer, to differentiate it from the existing interfaces that implement an *atomic* transfer. The protocols for both are very similar, but the procedures written by the owner and requestor to convert and receive data may be called multiple times in an incremental transfer, instead of just once as in the atomic transfer. The new functions and procedure types are: `XtCancelConvertSelectionProc`, `XtCancelSelectionCallbackProc`, `XtConvertSelectionIncrProc`, `XtLoseSelectionIncrProc`, `XtSelectionDoneIncrProc`, `XtSelectionIncrCallbackProc`, `XtGetSelectionValueIncremental`, `XtGetSelectionValuesIncremental`, and `XtOwnSelectionIncremental`. See Chapter 11, *Interclient Communications*, for a description of how these functions and procedure types are used.

`XtGetApplicationNameAndClass` allows an application to get its own resource name and class. This function is rarely needed.

Xt implements its handling of the language string using `XtResolvePathname`, which calls `XtFindFile`. These two functions are provided for applications that need to search the file system for files. `XtResolvePathname` searches using X/Open language localization conventions, while `XtFindFile` searches arbitrary paths.

D.2 Application Writing

The major changes from an application writer's point of view include windowless objects, varargs-style interfaces, fallback resources, and locale-driven finding of data files.

D.2.1 New Function for Initializing an Application

Instead of XtInitialize, applications should now use XtAppInitialize or XtVaAppInitialize to initialize the X Toolkit internals, create an application context, open and initialize a display and create the initial application shell instance. Its arguments are somewhat different from XtInitialize. See Chapter 3, *More Techniques for Using Widgets*, or Volume Five, *X Toolkit Intrinsics Reference Manual*, for details. XtAppInitialize calls XtToolkitInitialize, XtCreateApplicationContext, XtAppSetFallbackResources, XtOpenDisplay, and XtAppCreateShell.

One argument of XtAppInitialize is a string containing resources that will be the backup in case the application's app-defaults file is not present. These are called fallback resources, and the argument is *fallback_resources*.

D.2.2 Varargs Interfaces

All Xt interfaces that require ArgList arguments now have analogs which conform to the ANSI C variable-length argument list ("varargs") calling convention. The name of the analog is formed by prefixing "Va" to the name of the corresponding ArgList procedure. For example, the varargs version of XtCreateWidget is XtVaCreateWidget. Each procedure whose name starts with XtVa takes as its last arguments, in place of the corresponding ArgList/Cardinal parameters, a variable-length parameter list of resource name and value pairs where each name is of type String and each value is of type XtArgVal. The end of the list is identified by a name entry containing NULL. The ArgList and varargs interfaces may be used interchangeably within the same application. Table D-1 shows the ArgList functions and the analogous varargs functions:

Table D-1. ArgList Functions and Varargs Counterparts

ArgList	Varargs
XtAppCreateShell	XtVaAppCreateShell
XtAppInitialize	XtVaAppInitialize
XtCreatePopupShell	XtVaCreatePopupShell
XtCreateManagedWidget	XtVaCreateManagedWidget
XtCreateWidget	XtVaCreateWidget
XtGetApplicationResources	XtVaGetApplicationResources
XtGetSubresources	XtVaGetSubresources.
XtGetSubvalues	XtVaGetSubvalues
XtGetValues	XtVaGetValues

ArgList	Varargs
XtSetSubvalues	XtVaSetSubvalues
XtSetValues	XtVaSetValues

D.2.2.1 Special Types for Varargs List Members

Two special symbols are defined for use only in varargs lists: XtVaTypedArg and Xt-VaNestedList. Each can be used in place of a resource name to indicate that the following fields should be treated differently than a normal resource value. XtVaTypedArg allows you to use the subsequent four arguments to instruct Xt how to invoke the proper type converter to convert the given value into the type required by the widget. To use Xt-VaTypedArg while creating the first instance of a widget class, however, you must call XtInitializeWidgetClass first.

XtVaNestedList lets you include an ArgList in a varargs list. This is normally done to include the same list of resource settings in several calls to create widgets. Xt-VaCreateArgsList dynamically allocates a varargs list, for use with XtVaNested-List in multiple calls.

For more information on XtVaTypedArg and XtVaNestedList, see Chapter 3, *More Techniques for Using Widgets*.

D.2.3 Loading the Resource Database

There have been several extensions in the way the resource database is loaded.

D.2.3.1 The Language String

In R4, a mechanism for making applications portable between languages is introduced. It allows the application writer to create separate app-defaults files for each language. Each of these files will have the same name, but they will have different paths. A *language string* determines the path.* In other words, Xt will look for the app-defaults file in */usr/lib/X11/LANG/app-defaults* before it looks in */usr/lib/X11/app-defaults*. This is done for both the application's app-defaults file and the user's XAPPLRESDIR file. For details on the exact order of searching and merging for resource files, see Chapter 10, *Resource Management and Type Conversion*.

---

*This mechanism conforms to the *X/Open Portability Guide* language localization conventions.

The language string is a user-specified value. The language string can be set by setting the LANG environment variable, by setting the –xnlLanguage command-line option, or by setting the "xnlLanguage" resource in a resource file. If no language string is found, the empty string is used, and Xt defaults to its R3 behavior.

The environment variable XUSERFILESEARCHPATH can be set to define a path that will be searched before the directory defined by XAPPLRESDIR.

D.2.3.2 New Built-In Application Resources

There are three new built-in application resources that affect the global operation of Xt.

`XtNxnlLanguage`, class `XtCXnlLanguage` sets the language string to be used when reading application and user resource files.

`XtNDefaultFont`, class `XtCDefaultFont` allows the application to supply a font name to use if the font supplied for any other resource cannot be loaded.

`XtNmultiClickTime`, class `XtCMultiClickTime` sets the time used by Xt to detect double and triple clicks in the translation manager. This resource may also be modified dynamically by the application, which is useful since the multi-click time is unique for each Display. If no value is specified, the initial value is 200 milliseconds.

`XtSetMultiClickTime` is a convenience routine to set the multi-click time dynamically, and `XtGetMultiClickTime` reads the multi-click time.

D.2.3.3 Fallback Resources

One argument of `XtAppInitialize`, *fallback_resources*, allows you to specify backup resource settings in case the app-defaults file is not installed properly. You can set a complete copy of the app-defaults file here, or a minimal set of resources that makes the application tell the user that the real app-defaults file in not installed. For an example of setting fallback resources, see Chapter 10, *Resource Management and Type Conversion*.

The fallback resources can also be set with `XtAppSetFallbackResources`, although this is rarely needed since an argument is provided in `XtAppInitialize`.

D.2.4 Parsing the Command Line

There are two new option styles that you can specify in an option list so that Xt will parse them. They are `XrmoptionResArg`, which instructs Xt to use the next argument as input to `XrmPutLineResource`, and `XrmoptionSkipNArgs`, which instructs Xt to ignore this option and the next `OptionDescRec.value` arguments. These option styles are not usually needed. For more on defining option styles, see Chapter 3, *More Techniques for Using Widgets*.

The RESOURCE_NAME environment variable is now used. If no –*name* option is specified on the command line when the user invokes the application, `XtAppInitialize` (or `Xt-OpenDisplay` if called directly) reads the RESOURCE_NAME environment variable to get an application name to be used in extracting applicable resource specifications from the resource database. If RESOURCE_NAME is not set, the final component of `argv[0]` is used. If `argv[0]` does not exist or is the empty string, the application name is "main".

D.3 Changes Affecting Both Application and Widget Writing

D.3.1 Actions

Several new functions associated with actions have been defined.

D.3.1.1 Directly Invoking Actions

Normally, action procedures are invoked by the Intrinsics when an event or event sequence arrives for a widget. Occasionally it may be desirable to invoke an action procedure directly, without generating (or synthesizing) an event. One such circumstance is an application or subclass action routine which envelopes an existing (superclass) action routine. `XtCall-ActionProc` can be used to do this. `XtCallActionProc` is also useful for playing back actions recorded with `XtAppAddActionHook`.

D.3.1.2 Action Hook Registration

An application can use `XtAppAddActionHook` to specify a procedure that will be called just before every action routine is dispatched by the translation manager.

Action hooks should not modify any of the data pointed to by the arguments other than the `client_data` argument.

`XtRemoveActionHook` removes an action hook procedure. (Notice that the `XtApp-AddActionHook` takes an application context argument, which `XtRemoveAction-Hook` doesn't, thus the asymmetry in their names.)

D.3.1.3 Obtaining Event Information in an Action Procedure

When an action procedure is invoked on a `KeyPress` or `KeyRelease` event, it often needs the keysym and modifiers corresponding to the event which caused it to be invoked, since the event passed in the action procedure contains only the keycode. In order to avoid repeating the processing that was just performed by the Intrinsics to match the translation entry, the keysym and modifiers are stored for the duration of the action procedure and are made available to the client with `XtGetActionKeysym`. `XtGetActionKeysym` retrieves the keysym and modifiers that matched the final event specification in the translation table entry.

D.3.1.4 Registering Button and Key Grabs For Actions

`XtRegisterGrabAction` registers a grab that will be initiated when the given action is invoked in response to `KeyPress` or `ButtonPress` events. This function is used internally by Xt to register the grab for the `XtMenuPopup` action.

D.3.1.5 Action Functions and Unrealized Widgets

Action procedures may not assume that the widget in which they are invoked is realized; an accelerator specification can cause an action procedure to be called for a widget which does not yet have a window. Widget writers should note which of a widget's callback lists are invoked from action procedures and warn clients not to assume the widget is realized in those callbacks. (This is newly documented but also true of R3.)

D.3.2 Reserved Names for Resources and Actions

Resource names beginning with the two-character sequence "xt" and resource classes beginning with the two-character sequence "Xt" are reserved to the Intrinsics for implementation-dependent uses. Consequently, all symbols beginning with `XtNxt` and `XtCXt` are reserved.

The Intrinsics reserve all action names and parameters starting with the characters "Xt" for future standard enhancements. Users, application and widgets should not declare action names or pass parameters starting with these characters except to invoke specified built-in functions.

In general, applications should not declare or define anything beginning with Xt in any case, since these are generally associated with the Xt standard and could conflict or be confusing.

D.3.3 Resource String Identifier Convention

Definitions of `XtN`, `XtC`, and `XtR` constants should have just a single space between the symbol and the value, and no comment. This prevents preprocessor warnings from multiple, slightly different definitions for the same symbol.

D.3.4 Resource File Format

As of R4, the resource file format is defined in the Xlib specification instead of by Xt, and the following was added: To include arbitrary octets in a string, use the 4-character sequence "\nnn" where nnn is the numeric value of the octet specified as an octal constant. For example, a value containing a `NULL` byte may be stored by including "\000" in the string. This is one way to specify ISO-Latin1 strings that are above the 128 ASCII characters—these strings are needed for Western languages other than English.

D.3.5 Modifier Names

If both an exclamation point (!) and a colon (:) are specified at the beginning of the modifier list, it means that the listed modifiers must be in the correct state and that no other modifiers except the standard modifiers can be asserted. Any standard modifiers in the event are applied as for colon (:) above.

D.3.6 Determining Specification Revision Level

Widget and application developers who wish to maintain a common source pool which will build properly with implementations of the Intrinsics at different revision levels of the Xt specification may use the symbolic macro XtSpecificationRelease.

Since XtSpecificationRelease is new to Release 4, widgets and applications desiring to build against earlier implementations should test for the presence of this symbol and assume only Release 3 interfaces if the definition is not present.

D.3.7 Implementation-specific Datatype Definitions

To increase the portability of widget and application source code between different system environments, Xt defines several datatypes whose precise representation is explicitly dependent upon, and chosen by, each individual implementation. For best portability, applications must only depend on the data type characteristics listed here. These characteristics were not documented until Release 4.

These implementation-defined datatypes are:

Boolean
: A datum that contains a zero or non-zero value. Unless explicitly stated, clients should not assume that the non-zero value is equal to the symbolic value True.

Cardinal
: An unsigned datum with a minimum range of $[0 \ldots 2^{16} -1]$.

Dimension
: An unsigned datum with a minimum range of $[0 \ldots 2^{16} -1]$.

Position
: A signed datum with a minimum range of $[-2^{15} \ldots 2^{15} -1]$.

XtPointer
: A datum large enough to contain a char*, int*, function pointer, structure pointer, or long value. A pointer to any type or function, or a long value, may be converted to an XtPointer and back again and the result will compare equally to the original value. In ANSI C environments it is expected that XtPointer will be defined as void*.

XtArgVal
: A datum large enough to contain an XtPointer, Cardinal, Dimension, or Position value.

XtEnum
: A datum large enough to encode at least 128 distinct values, two of which are the symbolic values True and False. The symbolic values True

Release Notes

and `False` are also defined to be equal to `True` and `False`, respectively.

D.3.8 Event Handlers

Event handlers now have an additional final argument, *continue_to_dispatch*. This argument specifies whether or not the remaining event handlers registered for the current event should be called. This feature should be used with care.

`XtInsertEventHandler` registers an event handler procedure before or after all previously registered event handlers.

`XtInsertRawEventHandler` registers an event handler procedure that receives events before or after all previously registered event handlers without selecting for the events.

D.3.9 Error and Warning Handlers

The routines that install error and warning handlers now return the previous handlers.

D.4 Changes Affecting Widget Writing

The Xt specification has undergone several sets of revisions in the course of adoption as an X Consortium standard specification. The Release 3 specification was the first X Consortium standard for Xt. Release 4 and future releases will have complete source compatibility with widgets and applications written to previous Consortium standard revisions.

The Intrinsics do not place any special requirement on widget programmers to retain source or binary compatibility for their widgets as they evolve, but several conventions have been established to assist those developers who want to provide such compatibility. In particular, widget programmers may wish to define class extension records, as described in Section 14.13.

D.4.1 New Name for Core Class

Prior to R4, the official name of the Core class was `WidgetClass`. An alias has been added to allow the Core widget to be referenced using the name `CoreWidgetClass`, which makes its naming parallel with all other classes. Similarly, all other symbols that reference Core class structures also have analogous aliases, as shown in Table D-2.

Table D-2. New Naming for Core Class Symbols and Variables

Existing Symbol	Added Symbol
Core Class Structure	
WidgetClassRec	CoreClassRec
*WidgetClass	*CoreWidgetClass
widgetClassRec	coreClassRec
widgetClass	coreWidgetClass
Core Instance Structure	
WidgetRec	CoreRec
*Widget	*CoreWidget

D.4.2 File Content Changes

D.4.2.1 Changes to Private .h Files

This file will contain the complete widget class extension structure for this widget, if any, and the symbolic constant identifying the class extension version, if any. These extensions are necessary only if the widget writer wants to maintain binary compatibility with previous versions of the widget. This binary compatibility matters most for Xt's own built-in classes. You are unlikely to need to define an extension structure. However, you will need to initialize the extension structures defined by Composite and Constraint when writing subclasses of those classes. See Section 14.13.

D.4.2.2 Changes to .c Files

The XtVersion symbol has now been defined as meaning the *implementation* version, as opposed to the specification version. Therefore, code that sets the version field of the class structure initialization to XtVersion may be rejected at run time if linked with other implementations. If a widget binary is compatible with other implementations of Xt, the special value XtVersionDontCheck should be used in the version field to disable version checking. If a widget needs to compile alternative code for different revisions of the Intrinsics interface definition, it may use the symbol XtSpecificationRelease.

D.4.3 Class Extension Structures

When a widget class is rewritten, it may be necessary to add new fields to the existing widget class structure. To allow this to be done without requiring recompilation of all subclasses, the last field in a class part record can be an extension pointer. If no extension fields for a class have yet been defined, implementations should set the value of the extension pointer to NULL.

If extension fields exist, as is the case with the Composite, Constraint, and Shell classes, subclasses can provide values for these fields by setting the extension pointer in their class structure to point to a statically declared extension record containing the values. Setting the extension field is never mandatory; code that uses fields in the extension record must always check the extension field and do some appropriate default action if it is NULL.

In order to permit multiple subclasses and libraries to chain extension records from a single extension field, extension records should be declared as a linked list and each extension record definition should contain the following four fields at the beginning of the structure declaration:

```
struct {
    XtPointer next_extension;
    XrmQuark record_type;
    long version;
    Cardinal record_size;
    ...
};
```

next_extension	Specifies the next record in the list, or NULL.
record_type	Specifies the particular structure declaration to which each extension record instance conforms. The record_type field identifies the contents of the extension record and is used by the allocator of the record to locate its particular extension record in the list. record_type is normally assigned the result of XrmStringToQuark for a registered string constant. The Intrinsics reserve all record type string names beginning with the two characters "XT" for future uses. The value NULLQUARK may also be used by the class part owner in extension records attached to the class part extension field to identify the extension record unique to that particular class.
version	Specifies a symbolic constant supplied by the person who defined the structure. The version field is an owner-assigned constant which may be used to identify binary files which have been compiled with alternate definitions of the extension record data structure. The private header file for a widget class should provide a symbolic constant for subclasses to use to initialize this field.
record_size	Specifies the total number of bytes allocated for the extension record. The record_size field includes the four common header fields and should normally be initialized with sizeof().

D.4.3.1 Composite Class Extension Structure

A Composite class extension record has been defined. The first four fields in this structure are described above.

```
typedef struct {
    XtPointer next_extension;
    XrmQuark record_type;
    long version;
    Cardinal record_size;
    Boolean     accepts_objects;
} CompositeClassExtensionRec, *CompositeClassExtension;
```

The `version` field can be initialized using the `XtCompositeExtensionVersion` symbolic constant.

The `accepts_objects` field allows Xt to check to make sure that the composite parent is capable of managing the type of child being created. If not, a fatal error occurs. Note that a fatal error also occurs if no composite extension record is defined.

D.4.3.2 Constraint Class Extension Structure

The extension record defined for Constraint is as follows:

```
typedef struct {
    XtPointer next_extension;
    XrmQuark record_type;
    long version;
    Cardinal record_size;
    XtArgsProc get_values_hook;
} ConstraintClassExtensionRec, *ConstraintClassExtension;
```

The `record_type` should be initialized to `NULLQUARK`. The `version` field should be initialized to `XtConstraintExtensionVersion`.

D.4.3.3 New Constraint get_values_hook method

If the Constraint widget or any of its superclasses have declared a `ConstraintClassExtension` record in the constraint class part extension fields with a record type of `NULLQUARK` and the `get_values_hook` field in the extension record is non-`NULL`, `XtGetValues` calls this `get_values_hook` method to allow the parent to return derived constraint fields. The Constraint `get_values_hook` method is for processing the resources of subparts.

The Constraint extension `get_values_hook` method is called after the Core `get_values_` hook methods are called.

D.4.3.4 Shell Class Extension Structure

The extension record defined for Constraint is as follows:

```
typedef struct {
    XtPointer next_extension;
    XrmQuark record_type;
    long version;
    Cardinal record_size;
    XtGeometryHandler root_geometry_manager;
} ShellClassExtensionRec, *ShellClassExtension;
```

The symbolic constant for the `ShellClassExtension` version id is `XtShell-ExtensionVersion`.

The `root_geometry_manager` field specifies a procedure which acts as the parent geometry manager for geometry requests made by shell widgets. When a shell widget calls `XtMakeGeometryRequest` or `XtMakeResizeRequest`, the `root_geometry_manager` procedure is invoked to negotiate the new geometry with the window manager. If the window manager permits the new geometry, the `root_geometry_manager` should return `XtGeometryYes`; if the window manager denies the geometry request or does not change the window geometry within some timeout interval (equal to `wm_timeout` in the case of WMShells), the `root_geometry_manager` should return `XtGeometryNo`. If the window manager makes some alternate geometry change, the `root_geometry_manager` may either return `XtGeometryNo` and handle the new geometry as a resize, or may return `XtGeometryAlmost` in anticipation that the shell will accept the compromise. If the compromise is not accepted, the new size must then be handled as a resize. Subclasses of Shell which wish to provide their own `root_geometry_manager` are strongly encouraged to use enveloping to invoke their superclass' `root_geometry_manager` under most situations, as the window manager interaction may be very complex.

If no ShellClassPart extension record is declared with `record_type` equal to `NULLQUARK`, then `XtInheritRootGeometryManager` is assumed.

D.4.4 New XtNvisual Resource

Shell widgets now have a resource for the visual they will use. This is normally inherited by all their child widgets. If a visual other than the default is chosen, usually the `Xt-Ncolormap` resource also must be set. See Chapter 8, *Events*, Volume One, *Xlib Programming Manual*, for a discussion of visuals and how to choose one.

D.4.5 Methods

Arguments were added to the procedure definitions for the `initialize` and `set_values` methods, to pass in the argument list specified in the function that resulted in the method invocation. The added arguments are unlikely to be used in a widget that has no subpart. The added arguments make the `initialize_hook` and `set_values_hook` functions obsolete, but they have been retained for those widgets which used them.

The Core `realize` method now uses `CopyFromParent` as the default colormap, not the default colormap of the screen.

The chaining of Composite and Constraint methods was not specified in R3, but is now. The self-contained fields in Composite widget classes are:

- `geometry_manager`
- `change_managed`
- `insert_child`
- `delete_child`
- `accepts_objects`

The self-contained field in Constraint widget classes is:

- `constraint_size`

The self-contained field in Shell widget classes are:

- `root_geometry_manager`

In addition, for subclasses of Constraint, the following fields of the `ConstraintClassPart` and `ConstraintClassExtensionRec` structures are downward chained (beginning at Constraint):

- `resources`
- `initialize`
- `set_values`
- `get_values_hook`

For subclasses of Constraint, the following field of `ConstraintClassPart` is upward chained (ending at Constraint):

- `destroy`

Release Notes

D.4.6 Mapping Order of Realized Child Widgets

Newly specified in R4 is the following: when calling the realize procedures for children of a composite widget, XtRealizeWidget calls the procedures in reverse order of appearance in the composite.children list. By default, this will result in the stacking order of any newly created subwindows being top-to-bottom in the order of appearance on the list and the most recently created widget will be at the bottom.

D.4.7 Callback Lists

D.4.7.1 XtNunrealizeCallback

If a widget class defines a resource XtNunrealizeCallback as a callback list, Xt will call any callback function registered when unrealizing a widget of that class.

D.4.7.2 Internal Format of Callback Lists

Newly documented in R4 is the fact that the internal representation of a callback list, the value of the XtRCallback resource, is implementation-dependent; clients may not make assumptions about the value stored in this resource. To determine whether a widget is capable of supporting a callback list, or whether callbacks have been registered, XtHasCallbacks can be used (not new to R4)—it returns XtCallbackNoList, XtCallbackHasNone or XtCallbackHasSome.

D.4.7.3 New Routine to Call Callback List

XtCallCallbackList executes the procedures in a callback list, specifying the callback list by address. In other words, the function calls all the procedures on the callback list without reference to the widget those callback functions are registered for. This function avoids the callback list lookup overhead.

D.4.8 Resource Lists

XtOffsetOf determines the byte offset of a field within a structure type. It performs the same function as XtOffset, but is more portable.

D.4.8.1 Base Offsets in Resource List

XtWidgetBaseOffset has been added as an address mode which can be used in resource lists. XtWidgetBaseOffset is similar to XtBaseOffset except that it searches for the closest windowed ancestor if the object is not a subclass of Core.

D.4.8.2 XtProcedureArg

In the field usually specified as XtBaseOffset, you can specify XtProcedureArg instead. This instructs Xt to call a procedure of type XtConvertArgProc to get the resource value.

D.4.8.3 Default Resource Values

The default_address field in each resource list element specifies the address of the default resource value. As a special case, if the default_type is XtRString, then the value in the default_addr field is the pointer to the string rather than a pointer to the pointer.

D.4.8.4 Getting a Constraint Resource List

XtGetConstraintResourceList gets the constraint resource list structure for a widget class.

D.4.9 Converters

D.4.9.1 New Xt Resource Representations

The following resource representation types are now defined by the Intrinsics.

Table D-3. New Representation Types

Resource Type	Structure or Field Type
XtRBitmap	Pixmap, depth=1
XtRGeometry	char*, format as defined by XParseGeometry
XtRInitialState	int
XtRLongBoolean	long
XtRObject	Object
XtRStringTable	char**
XtRVisual	Visual*

<X11/StringDefs.h> now defines the following resource types as a convenience for widgets, although they do not have any corresponding datatype assigned: XtREditMode, XtRJustify and XtROrientation.

D.4.9.2 New Xt Resource Converters

Xt now defines converters from `XtRString` to `XtRInitialState`, from `XtRString` to `XtRVisual`, and from `XtRString` to `XtRAtom`.

The `XtRString` to `XtRInitialState` conversion accepts the values `NormalState` or `IconicState` as defined by the Inter-Client Communications Conventions.

The `XtRString` to `XtRVisual` conversion calls `XMatchVisualInfo` using the `Xt-Nscreen` and `XtNdepth` resources and returns the first matching `Visual` on the list. The widget resource list must be certain to specify any resource of type `XtRVisual` after the depth resource. The allowed string values are the Protocol visual class names: `StaticGray`, `StaticColor`, `TrueColor`, `GrayScale`, `PseudoColor`, and `DirectColor`.

The string to font and font structure converters no longer evaluate the constant `Xt-DefaultFont` to the font in the screen's default graphics context. Instead, they do the following:

1. Query the resource database for the resource whose full name is "xtDefaultFont", class "XtDefaultFont" (that is, no widget name/class prefixes) and use a type `XtRString` value returned as the font name, or a type `XtRFont` or `XtRFontStruct` value directly as the resource value.

2. If the resource database does not contain a value for xtDefaultFont, class XtDefaultFont, or if the returned font name cannot be successfully opened, an implementation-defined font in ISO8859-1 character set encoding is opened. (One possible algorithm is to perform an `XListFonts` using a wildcard font name and use the first font in the list. This wildcard font name should be as broad as possible to maximize the probability of locating a usable font; for example, "-*-*-*-R-*-*-*-120-*-*-*-*-ISO8859-1".)

3. If no suitable ISO8859-1 font can be found, issue an error message.

D.4.9.3 New Fn for Issuing Conversion Warnings

`XtDisplayStringConversionWarning` supercedes `XtStringConversion-Warning` as the convenience routine for resource converters that convert from string values.

D.4.9.4 New Resource Converters Interface

A new interface declaration for resource type converters was defined to provide more information to converters, to support conversion cache cleanup with reference counting, and to allow additional procedures to be declared to free resource values. The old interfaces remain (for backwards compatibility) and a new set of procedures was defined which work only with the new type converter interface.

D.4.9.4.1 **Registering a Resource Converter.** To register a new converter for all application contexts in a process, use XtSetTypeConverter. To register a new converter in a single application context, use XtAppSetTypeConverter. XtAddConverter and XtAppAddConverter are superceded by these new routines. The new routines provide a cache_type argument that specifies when and how conversions made with this converter should be cached. Another argument specifies a procedure, called a *destructor*, that will be called to free resource values when the reference count reaches zero.

D.4.9.4.2 **XtDestructor Functions.** To allow the Intrinsics to free cached resource values produced by type converters when widgets are destroyed or displays are closed, you may provide a resource destructor procedure. You register one in the call that registers the new-style type converter.

D.4.9.4.3 **New Resource Converter Procedure Type.** A resource converter procedure pointer is now of type XtTypeConverter. In R3 it was XtConverter. XtTypeConvert has two new arguments, *display*, and *converter_data*. The converter_data field specifies a location into which the converter may store converter-specific data that is associated with this conversion.

Any converter that queries the server to get the conversion should use the *display* argument to specify which server to query. For example, the XtRString to XtRPixel convert uses its *display* argument in the XAllocColor Xlib call it makes. The display argument can also be used when generating error messages, to identify the application context (with the function XtDisplayToApplicationContext).

The new style converter now must return True if the conversion was successful and False otherwise. If the conversion cannot be performed due to an improper source value, a warning message should also be issued with XtAppWarningMsg or XtDisplayStringConversionWarning.

D.4.9.4.4 **Invoking a Resource Converter.** XtConvertAndStore and XtCallConverter supercede XtConvert and XtDirectConvert respectively. The new routines include caching for converted values and caching for whether the previous conversion for the given value succeeded, and better support for application contexts.

D.4.9.4.5 **Caching and Reference Counting.** XtAppReleaseCacheRefs explicitly decrements the reference counts for resources obtained from XtCallConverter.

As a convenience to clients needing to explicitly decrement reference counts via a callback function, the Intrinsics define two callback procedures; XtCallbackReleaseCacheRef and XtCallbackReleaseCacheRefList.

`XtConvertAndStore` looks up and calls a resource converter, copying the resulting value, and freeing a cached resource when a widget is destroyed. `XtConvertAndStore` adds `XtCallbackReleaseCacheRef` to the `XtNdestroyCallback` list of the specified widget if the conversion returns an `XtCacheRef` value.

By default, `XtCreateWidget` performs processing equivalent to `XtConvertAndStore` when initializing a widget instance. Because there is extra memory overhead required to implement reference counting, clients may distinguish those widgets which are never destroyed before the application exits from those which may be destroyed and whose resources should be deallocated. To specify whether or not reference counting is to be enabled for the resources of a particular widget when the widget is created, the client can specify a value for the Boolean resource `XtNinitialResourcesPersistent`, class `XtCInitialResourcesPersistent`.

When `XtCreateWidget` is called, `XtNinitialResourcesPersistent` must be set to `False` in either the arg list or the resource database for the resources referenced by this widget to be reference counted, regardless of how the type converter may have been registered. The effective default value is `True`. Only clients which expect to destroy one or more widgets and want resources deallocated should specify `False` for `XtNinitialResourcesPersistent`.

Even if `XtNinitialResourcesPersistent` is `True`, resources are still freed and destructors called when `XtCloseDisplay` is called if the conversion was registered as `XtCacheByDisplay`.

D.4.10   Keyboard Handling

D.4.10.1   KeyCode-to-KeySym Conversions

The Intrinsics maintain tables internally to map keycodes to keysyms for each open display. Translator procedures and any other client may share a single copy of this table to perform the same mapping.

`XtGetKeysymTable` returns a pointer to the keycode to keysym mapping table for a particular display.

D.4.10.2   KeySym-to-KeyCode Conversions

`XtKeysymToKeycodeList` returns the list of keycodes that map to a particular keysym in the keyboard mapping table maintained by the Intrinsics.

D.4.11 Selections

Selection requests for the TIMESTAMP target are now answered automatically by Xt.

Also, XtGetSelectionRequest has been added. XtGetSelectionRequest retrieves the SelectionRequest event which triggered the convert_selection procedure. This is necessary for some ICCCM target types. XtGetSelectionRequest may only be called from within a convert_selection procedure.

A whole set of routines for incremental transfers have been added. An incremental transfer is just like an atomic transfer, except that the functions you write to convert and get the data must expect to be called multiple times for the same selection. The basic three functions that parallel the functions provided for atomic transfers are XtOwnSelection-Incremental, XtGetSelectionValueIncremental, and XtGetSelection-ValuesIncremental. The function types registered with these three basic functions are XtConvertSelectionIncrProc, XtLoseSelectionIncrProc, Xt-SelectionDoneIncrProc, XtCancelConvertSelectionProc, Xt-SelectionIncrCallbackProc, and XtCancelSelectionCallbackProc.

XtLastTimestampProcessed retrieves the timestamp from the most recent call to XtDispatchEvent which contained a timestamp. (XtDispatchEvent records the last timestamp in any event which contains a timestamp.)

D.4.12 Objects

Although widget writers are free to treat Core as the base class of the widget hierarchy, there are actually three classes above it. These classes are Object, RectObj (Rectangle Object), and the unnamed class. All of these classes, their subclasses and all widgets are referred to generically as *objects*. By convention, the term *widget* refers only to a direct subclass of Core and the term *gadget* refers to a direct subclass of RectObj. A direct subclass of Object is an object. Note that the term object is also used generically to encompass all objects, gadgets, and widgets.

The basic difference between a widget and a gadget is that a widget has a window on the server side, but a gadget doesn't. Therefore, gadgets share their parent's window. Chapter 13, *Menus, Gadgets, and Cascaded Popups*, describes how gadgets work and how to use the gadgets provided with the R4 Athena Widget set. An object is also a sort of windowless widget, but it has no geometry resources, expose method, or sensitivity. The Object class exists to enable programmers to use the Intrinsics' classing and resource handling mechanisms for things besides widgets. Objects make obsolete many common uses of subparts and subresources.

Formal support for objects is new to Release 4. Motif 1.0 was based on a modified version of the R3 Intrinsics which included gadgets, but this version is not compatible with the R4 Consortium standard Intrinsics described here. Motif 1.1, however, is based on the R4 standard Intrinsics described here.

Composite widget classes that wish to accept gadget children must set the `accepts_objects` field in the `CompositeClassExtension` structure to `True`. `XtCreateWidget` will generate an error message otherwise.

D.4.12.1 The Gadget Parent

The Intrinsics will clear areas of a parent window obscured by RectObj children, causing `Expose` events, under these circumstances:

- A RectObj child is managed or unmanaged, and the parent is a Composite widget.

- In a call to `XtSetValues` on a RectObj child, one or more `set_values` procedures returns True in a call to `XtSetValues`, indicating that the child needs to be redisplayed.

- In a call to `XtSetValues` on a RectObj child, a change in geometry is made; areas will be cleared corresponding to both the old and the new child geometries.

When a gadget is playing the role of a widget, developers must be reminded to avoid making assumptions about the object passed in the *Widget* argument to a callback procedure.

The Intrinsics define an unnamed class between RectObj and Core for possible future use. The content of the class record for this class and the result of an attempt to subclass or to create a widget of this unnamed class are undefined.

D.4.12.2 Xt Functions That Take Any Object

In R3, all functions which had an argument of type `Widget` or `WidgetClass` could accept any class of widget. Now that objects have been implemented, this is no longer true. The following lists describe what classes are valid in all Xt functions that accept widget or widget class arguments or that return such values.

The `WidgetClass` arguments to the following procedures may be `objectClass` or any subclass:

XtCheckSubclass	XtInitializeWidgetClass
XtCreateWidget	XtIsSubclass
XtGetConstraintResourceList	XtVaCreateWidget
XtGetResourceList	

The Widget arguments to the following procedures can be of class Object or any subclass:

XtAddCallback	XtIsShell
XtAddCallbacks	XtIsSubclass
XtCallCallbacks	XtIsToplevelShell
XtCheckSubclass	XtIsTransientShell
XtClass	XtIsVendorShell
XtConvert	XtIsWidget

```
XtConvertAndStore            XtIsWMShell
XtCreateWidget               XtName
XtDestroyWidget              XtNameToWidget
XtDisplayOfObject            XtReleaseGC
XtGetApplicationResources    XtRemoveAllCallbacks
XtGetGC                      XtRemoveCallback
XtGetSubresources            XtRemoveCallbacks
XtGetSubvalues               XtScreenOfObject
XtGetValues                  XtSetKeyboardFocus  (descendant)
XtHasCallbacks               XtSetValues
XtIsApplicationShell         XtSuperclass
XtIsComposite                XtVaCreateWidget
XtIsConstraint,              XtVaGetApplicationResources
XtIsManaged (returns False if XtVaGetSubresources
   not RectObj or subclass)
XtIsObject                   XtVaGetSubvalues
XtIsOverrideShell            XtVaGetValues
XtIsRealized (returns the state of XtVaSetValues
   the nearest windowed ancestor)
XtIsRectObj                  XtWidgetToApplicationContext
XtIsSensitive (returns False  XtWindowOfObject
   if not RectObj or subclass)
```

The return value of these procedures will be of class Object or a subclass:

```
XtCreateWidget
XtVaCreateWidget
XtParent
XtNameToWidget
```

The return value of these procedures will be objectClass or a subclass: `XtClass`, `XtSuperclass`.

D.4.12.3   Xt Functions That Take Any RectObj

The WidgetClass arguments to the following procedures may be `rectObjClass` or any subclass: `XtCreateManagedWidget`, `XtVaCreateManagedWidget`.

The Widget arguments to the following procedures can be of class `RectObj` or any subclass:

```
XtConfigureWidget            XtQueryGeometry
XtMakeGeometryRequest        XtResizeWidget
XtMakeResizeRequest          XtSetSensitive
XtManageChild                XtTranslateCoords
XtManageChildren             XtUnmanageChild
XtMoveWidget                 XtUnmanageChildren
```

The return value of the following procedures will be of class RectObj or a subclass: `XtCreateManagedWidget`, `XtVaCreateManagedWidget`.

Release Notes

D.4.12.4 Xt Functions That Take Any Core

The Widget arguments to the following procedures must be of class Core or any subclass:

XtAddEventHandler	XtInstallAccelerators
XtAddGrab	XtInstallAllAccelerators (both
	destination and source)
XtAddRawEventHandler	XtMapWidget
XtAugmentTranslations	XtOverrideTranslations
XtBuildEventMask	XtOwnSelection
XtCallAcceptFocus	XtRealizeWidget
XtCallActionProc	XtRemoveEventHandler
XtCreatePopupShell	XtRemoveGrab
XtCreateWindow	XtRemoveRawEventHandler
XtDisownSelection	XtResizeWindow
XtDisplay	XtScreen
XtGetSelectionRequest	XtSetKeyboardFocus (subtree)
XtGetSelectionValue	XtSetMappedWhenManaged
XtGetSelectionValueIncremental	XtSetWMColormapWindows
XtGetSelectionValues	XtUngrabButton
XtGetSelectionValuesIncremental	XtUngrabKey
XtGrabButton	XtUngrabKeyboard
XtGrabKey	XtUngrabPointer
XtGrabKeyboard	XtUninstallTranslations
XtGrabPointer	XtUnmapWidget
XtInsertEventHandler	XtUnrealizeWidget
XtInsertRawEventHandler	XtVaCreatePopupShell
XtWindow	

The return value of the following procedure will be of class Core or a subclass: Xt-WindowToWidget.

D.4.12.5 Xt Functions That Take Any Composite

The Widget arguments to the following procedures must be of class Composite or any subclass: XtCreateManagedWidget, XtVaCreateManagedWidget.

D.4.12.6 Xt Functions That Take Any Shell or a Subclass

The WidgetClass arguments to the following procedures must be of class Shell or a subclass: XtCreatePopupShell, XtVaCreatePopupShell, XtAppCreateShell.

The Widget arguments to the following procedures must be of a subclass of Shell:

XtCallbackExclusiv	XtPopdown
XtllbackNone	XtPopup
XCallbackNonexclusive	XtPopupSpringLoaded
XtCallbackPopdown	

The return value of the following procedures will be of a subclass of Shell:

```
XtAppCreateShell
XtAppInitialize
XtCreatePopupShell
XtVaCreatePopupShell
```

D.4.12.7 Macros for Getting Object Information

The display pointer, screen pointer and window of a widget or of the closest widget ancestor of a gadget are available by calling `XtDisplayOfObject`, `XtScreenOfObject`, and `XtWindowOfObject`. `XtIsObject` tells you whether a class is a subclass of Object but not of RectObj.

`XtName` returns a pointer to the instance name of the specified object. The name does not include the names of any of the object's ancestors.

D.4.13 Miscellaneous

D.4.13.1 XtNameToWidget

`XtNameToWidget` now allows an asterisk (*) to separate widget names, to match any number of intermediate widgets. The method whereby `XtNameToWidget` searches the hierarchy for a matching widget has been more carefully spelled out: see `XtNameToWidget` in Volume Five, *X Toolkit Intrinsics Reference Manual*.

D.4.13.2 New Exposure Compression Controls

The `compress_exposure` field of the Core structure can now be set to additional values to tailor the exposure compression for a particular widget. The four basic values are shown in Table D-4.

Table D-4. Flags for compress_exposure Field of Core Class Structure

Symbol	Description
XtExposeCompressMaximal	All expose series currently in the queue are coalesced into a single event without regard to intervening nonexposure events. If a partial series is in the end of the queue, the Intrinsics will block until the end of the series is received. This setting is not advised, since `ConfigureNotify` events may be between Expose event series.

Symbol	Description
XtExposeCompressMultiple	Consecutive series of exposure events are coalesced into a single event when an exposure event with count==0 is reached and either the event queue is empty or the next event is not an exposure event.
XtExposeCompressSeries	Each series of exposure events is coalesced into a single event when an exposure event with count==0 is reached.
XtExposeNoCompress	No exposure compression is performed; every selected event is individually dispatched to the expose procedure, with a region argument of NULL.

Note that the first two values are different names for the settings available under R3, False and True respectively. The most useful value is XtExposeCompressMultiple. Any of the above values can be optionally ORed with any combination of the following flags (all implementation-defined):

Table D-5. Optional OR Flags for compress_exposure Field of Core Class Structure

Symbol	Description
XtExposeGraphicsExpose	Specifies that GraphicsExpose events are also to be dispatched to the expose method. GraphicsExpose events will be compressed, if specified, in the same manner as Expose events.
XtExposeGraphicsExposeMerged	Specifies in the case of XtExposeCompressMultiple and XtExposeCompressMaximal that series of GraphicsExpose and Expose events are to be compressed together, with the final event type determining the type of the event passed to the expose procedure. If this flag is not set, then only series of the same event type as the event at the head of the queue are coalesced. This flag also implies XtExposeGraphicsExpose.
XtExposeNoExpose	Specifies that NoExpose events are also to be dispatched to the expose procedure. NoExpose events are never coalesced with other exposure events, nor with each other.

D.4.13.3   Requesting Key and Button Grabs

Xt now provides a set of key and button grab interfaces that are parallel to those provided by Xlib. Toolkit applications and widgets that need to passively grab keys or buttons should use the following Intrinsics routines rather than the corresponding Xlib routines.

The new Xt routines are: `XtGrabKey`, `XtUngrabKey`, `XtGrabKeyboard`, `XtUngrabKeyboard`, `XtGrabButton`, `XtUngrabButton`, `XtGrabPointer`, and `XtUngrabPointer`.

Remember that these routines are interfaces to Xlib grab routines: they are not the same as the Xt grab mode which affects only the dispatching of events within your application.

To affect dispatching of events outside of your application, in R3 you needed to make a Xlib call to grab the pointer, or use MenuPopup, the standard action that made the grab for you (which is now also called `XtMenuPopup`). Given the new R4 grab routines, you can pop up a menu using any of the popup mechanisms (`XtPopup`, `XtPopupSpringLoaded`, `XtCallbackExclusive`, `XtCallbackNonexclusive`, or `XtCallbackNone`) and still get the desired grab by calling `XtGrabButton`, or by using `XtRegisterGrabAction`.

D.4.13.4   New Macros for Widget Superclass Determination

To test if a given widget is a subclass of an Intrinsics-defined class, the Intrinsics define macros or functions equivalent to `XtIsSubclass` (which existed in R3) for each of the built-in classes. These procedures are: `XtIsObject`, `XtIsRectObj`, `XtIsWidget`, `XtIsComposite`, `XtIsConstraint`, `XtIsShell`, `XtIsOverrideShell`, `XtIsWMShell`, `XtIsVendorShell`, `XtIsTransientShell`, `XtIsTopLevelShell`, and `XtIsApplicationShell`.

All of these macros and functions have just one argument, the object. These procedures may be faster than calling `XtIsSubclass` directly for the built-in classes.

D.4.13.5   Macros and Procedure Equivalents

Any Xt function may be implemented as both a macro and a procedure. Any such macro will expand to code that evaluates each of its arguments exactly once, fully protected by parentheses, so that arbitrary expressions may be used as arguments. Applications may use `#undef` to remove a macro definition and ensure that the actual function is referenced.

`XtNew`, `XtNumber`, `XtOffsetOf`, `XtOffset`, and `XtSetArg` are macros which do not have function equivalents, and may expand their arguments in a manner other than that described above. Therefore, their arguments cannot contain arbitrary expressions. Arguments for these macros should not include expressions that increment a variable, because an argument might be referenced twice.

D.4.13.6 Finding File Names

The Intrinsics provide procedures to look for a file by name using string substitutions in a list of file specifications. There are two routines provided; `XtFindFile` and `XtResolve-Pathname`. `XtFindFile` uses an arbitrary set of client-specified substitutions and `Xt-ResolvePathname` uses a set of standard substitutions corresponding to the *X/Open Portability Guide* language localization conventions, and is used by Xt's language localization support.

D.4.13.7 Improved Multi-display Support in Xmu

Multi-display programs should now be able to use the Xmu type converters. Xmu also provides utilities for managing the multiple display data structures.

E

The xbitmap Application

This appendix shows the complete code for the BitmapEdit widget and a relatively complex version of xbitmap, which is described in Chapter 4, An Example Application.

In This Appendix:

E

The xbitmap Application

This appendix shows the complete code for the BitmapEdit widget (without selections), and for an advanced version of the *xbitmap* application (*xbitmap5* in the example distribution) which is similar to those *xbitmap3* described in Chapter 4 except that it both reads and writes X11 bitmap files (*xbitmap3* was capable of writing them only).

All source code from this book is available free from numerous sources, as described in the Preface.

E.1 The BitmapEdit Widget

Example E-1. BitmapEdit: complete widget code

```
/*
 * BitmapEdit.c - bitmap editor widget.
 */

#include <Xm/XmP.h>
#include <X11/StringDefs.h>

#include <stdio.h>

#include "BitmapEdiP.h"

#define INTERNAL_WIDTH    2
#define INTERNAL_HEIGHT 4

#define DEFAULT_PIXMAP_WIDTH    32  /* in cells */
#define DEFAULT_PIXMAP_HEIGHT   32  /* in cells */

#define DEFAULT_CELL_SIZE   30  /* in pixels */

/* values for instance variable is_drawn */
#define DRAWN 1
#define UNDRAWN 0

/* modes for drawing */
#define DRAW 1
#define UNDRAW 0

#define MAXLINES 1000    /* max of horiz or vertical cells */
#define SCROLLBARWIDTH 15

#define DEFAULTWIDTH 300  /* widget size when show_all is False */
```
define DEFAULTHEIGHT 300

```
#define offset(field) XtOffsetOf(BitmapEditRec, field)
static XtResource resources[] = {
/* not needed in Motif - already defined by Primitive.
 *      {
 *    XtNforeground,
 *    XtCForeground,
 *    XtRPixel,
 *    sizeof(Pixel),
 *    offset(bitmapEdit.foreground),
 *    XtRString,
 *    XtDefaultForeground
 *      },
 */
     {
   XtNtoggleCallback,
   XtCToggleCallback,
   XtRCallback,
   sizeof(XtPointer),
   offset(bitmapEdit.callback),
   XtRCallback,
   NULL
     },
     {
   XtNcellSizeInPixels,
   XtCCellSizeInPixels,
   XtRInt, sizeof(int),
   offset(bitmapEdit.cell_size_in_pixels),
   XtRImmediate,
   (XtPointer)DEFAULT_CELL_SIZE
     },
     {
   XtNpixmapWidthInCells,
   XtCPixmapWidthInCells,
   XtRDimension,
   sizeof(Dimension),
   offset(bitmapEdit.pixmap_width_in_cells),
   XtRImmediate,
   (XtPointer)DEFAULT_PIXMAP_WIDTH
     },
     {
   XtNpixmapHeightInCells,
   XtCPixmapHeightInCells,
   XtRDimension,
   sizeof(Dimension),
   offset(bitmapEdit.pixmap_height_in_cells),
   XtRImmediate,
   (XtPointer)DEFAULT_PIXMAP_HEIGHT
     },
     {
   XtNcurX,
   XtCCurX,
   XtRInt,
   sizeof(int),
   offset(bitmapEdit.cur_x),
   XtRImmediate,
```

```
       (XtPointer) 0
        },
        {
       XtNcurY,
       XtCCurY,
       XtRInt,
       sizeof(int),
       offset(bitmapEdit.cur_y),
       XtRString,
       (XtPointer) NULL
        },
        {
       XtNcellArray,
       XtCCellArray,
       XtRString,
       sizeof(String),
       offset(bitmapEdit.cell),
       XtRImmediate,
       (XtPointer) 0
        },
        {
       XtNshowEntireBitmap,
       XtCShowEntireBitmap,
       XtRBoolean,
       sizeof(Boolean),
       offset(bitmapEdit.show_all),
       XtRImmediate,
       (XtPointer) True
        },
};

/* Declaration of methods */

static void Initialize();
static void Redisplay();
static void Destroy();
static void Resize();
static Boolean SetValues();
static XtGeometryResult QueryGeometry();

/* these Core methods not needed by BitmapEdit:
 *
 * static void ClassInitialize();
 * static void Realize();
 */

/* the following are private functions unique to BitmapEdit */
static void DrawPixmaps(), DoCell(), ChangeCellSize();

/* the following are actions of BitmapEdit */
static void DrawCell(), UndrawCell(), ToggleCell();

/* The following are public functions of BitmapEdit, declared extern
 * in the public include file: */
char *BitmapEditGetArray();

static char defaultTranslations[] =
    "<Btn1Down>:     DrawCell()                \n\
    <Btn2Down>:     UndrawCell()               \n\
```

```
    <Btn3Down>:      ToggleCell()              \n\
    <Btn1Motion>:    DrawCell()                \n\
    <Btn2Motion>:    UndrawCell()              \n\
    <Btn3Motion>:    ToggleCell()";

static XtActionsRec actions[] = {
      {"DrawCell", DrawCell},
      {"UndrawCell", UndrawCell},
      {"ToggleCell", ToggleCell},
};

/* definition in BitmapEdit.h */
static BitmapEditPointInfo info;

BitmapEditClassRec bitmapEditClassRec = {
    {
    /* core_class fields */
    /* superclass          */ (WidgetClass) &xmPrimitiveClassRec,
    /* class_name           */ "BitmapEdit",
    /* widget_size          */ sizeof(BitmapEditRec),
    /* class_initialize     */ NULL,
    /* class_part_initialize   */ NULL,
    /* class_inited         */ False,
    /* initialize           */ Initialize,
    /* initialize_hook      */ NULL,
    /* realize              */ XtInheritRealize,
    /* actions              */ actions,
    /* num_actions          */ XtNumber(actions),
    /* resources            */ resources,
    /* num_resources        */ XtNumber(resources),
    /* xrm_class            */ NULLQUARK,
    /* compress_motion      */ True,
    /* compress_exposure    */ XtExposeCompressMultiple,
    /* compress_enterleave  */ True,
    /* visible_interest     */ False,
    /* destroy              */ Destroy,
    /* resize               */ Resize,
    /* expose               */ Redisplay,
    /* set_values           */ SetValues,
    /* set_values_hook      */ NULL,
    /* set_values_almost    */ XtInheritSetValuesAlmost,
    /* get_values_hook      */ NULL,
    /* accept_focus         */ NULL,
    /* version              */ XtVersion,
    /* callback_private     */ NULL,
    /* tm_table             */ defaultTranslations,
    /* query_geometry       */ QueryGeometry,
    /* display_accelerator  */ XtInheritDisplayAccelerator,
    /* extension            */ NULL
    },
    { /* Primitive class fields */
    /* border_highlight     */      _XtInherit,
    /* border_unhighlight   */      _XtInherit,
    /* translations         */      XtInheritTranslations,
    /* arm_and_activate     */      NULL,
    /* syn_resources        */      NULL,
    /* num_syn_resources    */      0,
```

```
    /* extension            */          NULL,
    },
    {
    /* extension            */          0,
    },
};

WidgetClass bitmapEditWidgetClass = (WidgetClass) & bitmapEditClassRec;

static void
GetDrawGC(w)
Widget w;
{
    BitmapEditWidget cw = (BitmapEditWidget) w;
    XGCValues values;
    XtGCMask mask = GCForeground | GCBackground | GCDashOffset |
            GCDashList | GCLineStyle;

    /*
     * Setting foreground and background to 1 and 0 looks like a
     * kludge but isn't.  This GC is used for drawing
     * into a pixmap of depth one.  Real colors are applied with a
     * separate GC when the pixmap is copied into the window.
     */
    values.foreground = 1;
    values.background = 0;
    values.dashes = 1;
    values.dash_offset = 0;
    values.line_style = LineOnOffDash;

    cw->bitmapEdit.draw_gc = XCreateGC(XtDisplay(cw),
            cw->bitmapEdit.big_picture, mask, &values);
}

static void
GetUndrawGC(w)
Widget w;
{
    BitmapEditWidget cw = (BitmapEditWidget) w;
    XGCValues values;
    XtGCMask mask = GCForeground | GCBackground;

    /* this looks like a kludge but isn't.  This GC is used for drawing
     * into a pixmap of depth one.  Real colors are applied as the
     * pixmap is copied into the window.
     */
    values.foreground = 0;
    values.background = 1;

    cw->bitmapEdit.undraw_gc = XCreateGC(XtDisplay(cw),
            cw->bitmapEdit.big_picture, mask, &values);
}

static void
GetCopyGC(w)
Widget w;
{
    BitmapEditWidget cw = (BitmapEditWidget) w;
    XGCValues values;
```

xbitmap Application

```
    XtGCMask mask = GCForeground | GCBackground;

    values.foreground = cw->primitive.foreground;
    values.background = cw->core.background_pixel;

    cw->bitmapEdit.copy_gc = XtGetGC(cw, mask, &values);
}

/* ARGSUSED */
static void
Initialize(treq, tnew, args, num_args)
Widget treq, tnew;
ArgList args;
Cardinal *num_args;
{
    BitmapEditWidget new = (BitmapEditWidget) tnew;
    new->bitmapEdit.cur_x = 0;
    new->bitmapEdit.cur_y = 0;

    /*
     * Check instance values set by resources that may be invalid.
     */

    if ((new->bitmapEdit.pixmap_width_in_cells < 1) ||
            (new->bitmapEdit.pixmap_height_in_cells < 1))   {
        XtWarning("BitmapEdit: pixmapWidth and/or pixmapHeight is too\
                small (using 10 x 10).");
        new->bitmapEdit.pixmap_width_in_cells = 10;
        new->bitmapEdit.pixmap_height_in_cells = 10;
    }

    if (new->bitmapEdit.cell_size_in_pixels < 5) {
        XtWarning("BitmapEdit: cellSize is too small (using 5).");
        new->bitmapEdit.cell_size_in_pixels = 5;
    }

    if ((new->bitmapEdit.cur_x < 0) ||  (new->bitmapEdit.cur_y < 0)) {
        XtWarning("BitmapEdit: cur_x and cur_y must be non-negative\
                (using 0, 0).");
        new->bitmapEdit.cur_x = 0;
        new->bitmapEdit.cur_y = 0;
    }

    if (new->bitmapEdit.cell == NULL)
        new->bitmapEdit.cell = XtCalloc(
                new->bitmapEdit.pixmap_width_in_cells *
                new->bitmapEdit.pixmap_height_in_cells, sizeof(char));
    else
        new->bitmapEdit.user_allocated = True;/* user supplied cell array */

    new->bitmapEdit.pixmap_width_in_pixels =
            new->bitmapEdit.pixmap_width_in_cells *
            new->bitmapEdit.cell_size_in_pixels;

    new->bitmapEdit.pixmap_height_in_pixels =
            new->bitmapEdit.pixmap_height_in_cells *
            new->bitmapEdit.cell_size_in_pixels;

    /*
     * Motif Primitive sets width and height to provide enough room for
```

```
       * the highlight and shadow around a widget.  BitmapEdit
       * doesn't use these features.  A widget that did use these
       * features would *add* its desired dimensions to those set
       * by Primitive.  To use this widget with another widget set, remove
       * the following two lines.
       */
      new->core.width = 0;
      new->core.height = 0;

      if (new->core.width == 0) {
          if (new->bitmapEdit.show_all == False)
              new->core.width = (new->bitmapEdit.pixmap_width_in_pixels
                      > DEFAULTWIDTH) ? DEFAULTWIDTH :
                      (new->bitmapEdit.pixmap_width_in_pixels);
          else
              new->core.width = new->bitmapEdit.pixmap_width_in_pixels;
      }

      if (new->core.height == 0) {
          if (new->bitmapEdit.show_all == False)
              new->core.height =
                      (new->bitmapEdit.pixmap_height_in_pixels >
                      DEFAULTWIDTH) ? DEFAULTWIDTH :
                      (new->bitmapEdit.pixmap_height_in_pixels);
          else
              new->core.height = new->bitmapEdit.pixmap_height_in_pixels;
      }

      /* tell Primitive not to allow tabbing to this widget */
      XtVaSetValues(new,
              XmNtraversalOn, False,
              NULL);

      CreateBigPixmap(new);
      GetDrawGC(new);                    (widget)
      GetUndrawGC(new);
      GetCopyGC(new);

      DrawIntoBigPixmap(new);
}
/* ARGSUSED */
static void
Redisplay(w, event)
Widget w;
XExposeEvent *event;
{
      BitmapEditWidget cw = (BitmapEditWidget) w;
      register int x, y;
      unsigned int width, height;
      if (!XtIsRealized(cw))
          return;

      if (event) {   /* called from btn-event or expose */
          x = event->x;
          y = event->y;
          width = event->width;
          height =  event->height;
```

```
    }
    else {            /* called because complete redraw */
        x = 0;
        y = 0;
        width = cw->bitmapEdit.pixmap_width_in_pixels;
        height = cw->bitmapEdit.pixmap_height_in_pixels;
    }

    if (DefaultDepthOfScreen(XtScreen(cw)) == 1)
        XCopyArea(XtDisplay(cw), cw->bitmapEdit.big_picture,
                XtWindow(cw), cw->bitmapEdit.copy_gc, x +
                cw->bitmapEdit.cur_x, y + cw->bitmapEdit.cur_y,
                width, height, x, y);
    else
        XCopyPlane(XtDisplay(cw), cw->bitmapEdit.big_picture,
                XtWindow(cw), cw->bitmapEdit.copy_gc, x +
                cw->bitmapEdit.cur_x, y + cw->bitmapEdit.cur_y,
                width, height, x, y, 1);
}

/* ARGSUSED */
static Boolean
SetValues(current, request, new, args, num_args)
Widget current, request, new;
ArgList args;
Cardinal *num_args;
{
    BitmapEditWidget curcw = (BitmapEditWidget) current;
    BitmapEditWidget newcw = (BitmapEditWidget) new;
    Boolean do_redisplay = False;

    if (curcw->primitive.foreground != newcw->primitive.foreground) {
        XtReleaseGC(curcw, curcw->bitmapEdit.copy_gc);
        GetCopyGC(newcw);
        do_redisplay = True;
    }

    if ((curcw->bitmapEdit.cur_x != newcw->bitmapEdit.cur_x) ||
            (curcw->bitmapEdit.cur_y != newcw->bitmapEdit.cur_y))
        do_redisplay = True;

    if (curcw->bitmapEdit.cell_size_in_pixels !=
            newcw->bitmapEdit.cell_size_in_pixels) {
        ChangeCellSize(curcw, newcw->bitmapEdit.cell_size_in_pixels);
        do_redisplay = True;
    }

    if (curcw->bitmapEdit.pixmap_width_in_cells !=
            newcw->bitmapEdit.pixmap_width_in_cells)  {
        newcw->bitmapEdit.pixmap_width_in_cells =
                curcw->bitmapEdit.pixmap_width_in_cells;
        XtWarning("BitmapEdit: pixmap_width_in_cells cannot be set\
                by XtSetValues.\n");
    }

    if (curcw->bitmapEdit.pixmap_height_in_cells !=
            newcw->bitmapEdit.pixmap_height_in_cells) {
        newcw->bitmapEdit.pixmap_height_in_cells =
                curcw->bitmapEdit.pixmap_height_in_cells;
```

(widget)

```
            XtWarning("BitmapEdit: pixmap_height_in_cells cannot be set\
                    by XtSet.Values.\n");
    }

    return do_redisplay;
}

static void
Destroy(w)
Widget w;
{
    BitmapEditWidget cw = (BitmapEditWidget) w;
    if (cw->bitmapEdit.big_picture)
        XFreePixmap(XtDisplay(cw), cw->bitmapEdit.big_picture);

    if (cw->bitmapEdit.draw_gc)
        XFreeGC(XtDisplay(cw), cw->bitmapEdit.draw_gc);

    if (cw->bitmapEdit.undraw_gc)
        XFreeGC(XtDisplay(cw), cw->bitmapEdit.undraw_gc);

    if (cw->bitmapEdit.copy_gc)
        XFreeGC(XtDisplay(cw), cw->bitmapEdit.copy_gc);

    /* Free memory allocated with Calloc.  This was done
     * only if application didn't supply cell array.
     */
    if (!cw->bitmapEdit.user_allocated)
        XtFree(cw->bitmapEdit.cell);
}
static void
DrawCell(w, event)
Widget w;
XEvent *event;
{
    BitmapEditWidget cw = (BitmapEditWidget) w;
    DrawPixmaps(cw->bitmapEdit.draw_gc, DRAW, cw, event);
}
static void
UndrawCell(w, event)
Widget w;
XEvent *event;
{
    BitmapEditWidget cw = (BitmapEditWidget) w;
    DrawPixmaps(cw->bitmapEdit.undraw_gc, UNDRAW, cw, event);
}
static void
ToggleCell(w, event)
Widget w;
XEvent *event;
{
    BitmapEditWidget cw = (BitmapEditWidget) w;
    static int oldx = -1, oldy = -1;
    GC gc;
    int mode;
    int newx, newy;
```

(handwritten annotations: "(widget)" and "(XButtonEvent)")

xbitmap Application

```
    /* This is strictly correct, but doesn't
     * seem to be necessary */
    if (event->type == ButtonPress) {
        newx = (cw->bitmapEdit.cur_x + ((XButtonEvent *)event)->x) /
        cw->bitmapEdit.cell_size_in_pixels;
        newy = (cw->bitmapEdit.cur_y + ((XButtonEvent *)event)->y) /
        cw->bitmapEdit.cell_size_in_pixels;
    }
    else {
        newx = (cw->bitmapEdit.cur_x + ((XMotionEvent *)event)->x) /
        cw->bitmapEdit.cell_size_in_pixels;
        newy = (cw->bitmapEdit.cur_y + ((XMotionEvent *)event)->y) /
        cw->bitmapEdit.cell_size_in_pixels;
    }

    if ((mode = cw->bitmapEdit.cell[newx + newy *
            cw->bitmapEdit.pixmap_width_in_cells]) == DRAWN) {
        gc = cw->bitmapEdit.undraw_gc;
        mode = UNDRAW;
    }
    else {
        gc = cw->bitmapEdit.draw_gc;
        mode = DRAW;
    }

    if (oldx != newx || oldy != newy) {
        oldx = newx;
        oldy = newy;
        DrawPixmaps(gc, mode, cw, event);
    }
}
static void
DrawPixmaps(gc, mode, w, event)
GC gc;
int mode;
Widget w;
XButtonEvent *event;
{
    BitmapEditWidget cw = (BitmapEditWidget) w;
    int newx = (cw->bitmapEdit.cur_x + event->x) /
            cw->bitmapEdit.cell_size_in_pixels;
    int newy = (cw->bitmapEdit.cur_y + event->y) /
            cw->bitmapEdit.cell_size_in_pixels;
    XExposeEvent fake_event;

    /* if already done, return */
    if (cw->bitmapEdit.cell[newx + newy *
            cw->bitmapEdit.pixmap_width_in_cells] == mode)
        return;

    /* otherwise, draw or undraw */
    XFillRectangle(XtDisplay(cw), cw->bitmapEdit.big_picture, gc,
            cw->bitmapEdit.cell_size_in_pixels*newx + 2,
            cw->bitmapEdit.cell_size_in_pixels*newy + 2,
            (unsigned int)cw->bitmapEdit.cell_size_in_pixels - 3,
            (unsigned int)cw->bitmapEdit.cell_size_in_pixels - 3);
```

```
    cw->bitmapEdit.cell[newx + newy *
            cw->bitmapEdit.pixmap_width_in_cells] = mode;
    info.mode = mode;
    info.newx = newx;
    info.newy = newy;

    fake_event.x = cw->bitmapEdit.cell_size_in_pixels * newx -
            cw->bitmapEdit.cur_x;
    fake_event.y = cw->bitmapEdit.cell_size_in_pixels * newy -
            cw->bitmapEdit.cur_y;
    fake_event.width = cw->bitmapEdit.cell_size_in_pixels;
    fake_event.height = cw->bitmapEdit.cell_size_in_pixels;

    Redisplay(cw, &fake_event);
    XtCallCallbacks(cw, XtNtoggleCallback, &info);
}

CreateBigPixmap(w)
Widget w;
{
    BitmapEditWidget cw = (BitmapEditWidget) w;
    /* always a 1 bit deep pixmap, regardless of screen depth */
    cw->bitmapEdit.big_picture = XCreatePixmap(XtDisplay(cw),
            RootWindow(XtDisplay(cw), DefaultScreen(XtDisplay(cw))),
            cw->bitmapEdit.pixmap_width_in_pixels + 2,
            cw->bitmapEdit.pixmap_height_in_pixels + 2, 1);
}

DrawIntoBigPixmap(w)
Widget w;
{
    BitmapEditWidget cw = (BitmapEditWidget) w;
    int n_horiz_segments, n_vert_segments;
    XSegment segment[MAXLINES];
    register int x, y;

    XFillRectangle(XtDisplay(cw), cw->bitmapEdit.big_picture,
            cw->bitmapEdit.undraw_gc, 0, 0,
            cw->bitmapEdit.pixmap_width_in_pixels
            + 2, cw->bitmapEdit.pixmap_height_in_pixels + 2);

    n_horiz_segments = cw->bitmapEdit.pixmap_height_in_cells + 1;
    n_vert_segments = cw->bitmapEdit.pixmap_width_in_cells + 1;

    for (x = 0; x < n_horiz_segments; x++) {
        segment[x].x1 = 0;
        segment[x].x2 = (short) cw->bitmapEdit.pixmap_width_in_pixels;
        segment[x].y1 = (short) cw->bitmapEdit.cell_size_in_pixels * x;
        segment[x].y2 = (short) cw->bitmapEdit.cell_size_in_pixels * x;
    }

    XDrawSegments(XtDisplay(cw), cw->bitmapEdit.big_picture,
            cw->bitmapEdit.draw_gc, segment, n_horiz_segments);

    for (y = 0; y < n_vert_segments; y++) {
        segment[y].x1 = (short) y * cw->bitmapEdit.cell_size_in_pixels;
        segment[y].x2 = (short) y * cw->bitmapEdit.cell_size_in_pixels;
        segment[y].y1 = 0;
        segment[y].y2 = (short) cw->bitmapEdit.pixmap_height_in_pixels;
```

xbitmap Application

```
        }

        XDrawSegments(XtDisplay(cw), cw->bitmapEdit.big_picture,
                cw->bitmapEdit.draw_gc, segment, n_vert_segments);

        /* draw current cell array into pixmap */
        for (x = 0; x < cw->bitmapEdit.pixmap_width_in_cells; x++) {
            for (y = 0; y < cw->bitmapEdit.pixmap_height_in_cells; y++) {
                if (cw->bitmapEdit.cell[x + (y *
                        cw->bitmapEdit.pixmap_width_in_cells)] == DRAWN)
                    DoCell(cw, x, y, cw->bitmapEdit.draw_gc);
                else
                    DoCell(cw, x, y, cw->bitmapEdit.undraw_gc);
            }
        }
}

/* A Public function, not static */
char *
BitmapEditGetArray(w, width_in_cells, height_in_cells)
Widget w;
int *width_in_cells, *height_in_cells;
{
    BitmapEditWidget cw = (BitmapEditWidget) w;

    *width_in_cells = cw->bitmapEdit.pixmap_width_in_cells;
    *height_in_cells = cw->bitmapEdit.pixmap_height_in_cells;
    return (cw->bitmapEdit.cell);
}

/* ARGSUSED */
static void
Resize(w)
Widget w;
{
    BitmapEditWidget cw = (BitmapEditWidget) w;
    /* resize does nothing unless new size is bigger than entire pixmap */
    if ((cw->core.width > cw->bitmapEdit.pixmap_width_in_pixels) &&
            (cw->core.height > cw->bitmapEdit.pixmap_height_in_pixels)) {
        /*
         * Calculate the maximum cell size that will allow the
         * entire bitmap to be displayed.
         */
        Dimension w_temp_cell_size_in_pixels, h_temp_cell_size_in_pixels;
        Dimension new_cell_size_in_pixels;

        w_temp_cell_size_in_pixels =
                cw->core.width / cw->bitmapEdit.pixmap_width_in_cells;
        h_temp_cell_size_in_pixels =
                cw->core.height / cw->bitmapEdit.pixmap_height_in_cells;

        if (w_temp_cell_size_in_pixels < h_temp_cell_size_in_pixels)
            new_cell_size_in_pixels = w_temp_cell_size_in_pixels;
        else
            new_cell_size_in_pixels = h_temp_cell_size_in_pixels;

        /* if size change mandates a new pixmap, make one */
        if (new_cell_size_in_pixels != cw->bitmapEdit.cell_size_in_pixels)
```

```
                ChangeCellSize(cw, new_cell_size_in_pixels);
    }
}
static void
ChangeCellSize(w, new_cell_size)
Widget w;
int new_cell_size;
{
    BitmapEditWidget cw = (BitmapEditWidget) w;
    int x, y;

    cw->bitmapEdit.cell_size_in_pixels = new_cell_size;

    /* recalculate variables based on cell size */
    cw->bitmapEdit.pixmap_width_in_pixels =
            cw->bitmapEdit.pixmap_width_in_cells *
            cw->bitmapEdit.cell_size_in_pixels;

    cw->bitmapEdit.pixmap_height_in_pixels =
            cw->bitmapEdit.pixmap_height_in_cells *
            cw->bitmapEdit.cell_size_in_pixels;

    /* destroy old and create new pixmap of correct size */
    XFreePixmap(XtDisplay(cw), cw->bitmapEdit.big_picture);
    CreateBigPixmap(cw);

    /* draw lines into new pixmap */
    DrawIntoBigPixmap(cw);

    /* draw current cell array into pixmap */
    for (x = 0; x < cw->bitmapEdit.pixmap_width_in_cells; x++) {
        for (y = 0; y < cw->bitmapEdit.pixmap_height_in_cells; y++) {
            if (cw->bitmapEdit.cell[x + (y *
                    ppcw->bitmapEdit.pixmap_width_in_cells)] == DRAWN)
                DoCell(cw, x, y, cw->bitmapEdit.draw_gc);
            else
                DoCell(cw, x, y, cw->bitmapEdit.undraw_gc);
        }
    }
}

static void
DoCell(w, x, y, gc)
Widget w;
int x, y;
GC gc;
{
    BitmapEditWidget cw = (BitmapEditWidget) w;
        /* otherwise, draw or undraw */
    XFillRectangle(XtDisplay(cw), cw->bitmapEdit.big_picture, gc,
            cw->bitmapEdit.cell_size_in_pixels * x + 2,
            cw->bitmapEdit.cell_size_in_pixels * y + 2,
            (unsigned int)cw->bitmapEdit.cell_size_in_pixels - 3,
            (unsigned int)cw->bitmapEdit.cell_size_in_pixels - 3);

}
static XtGeometryResult QueryGeometry(w, proposed, answer)
```

xbitmap Application

```
Widget w;
XtWidgetGeometry *proposed, *answer;
{
    BitmapEditWidget cw = (BitmapEditWidget) w;

    /* set fields we care about */
    answer->request_mode = CWWidth | CWHeight;

    /* initial width and height */
    if (cw->bitmapEdit.show_all == True)
        answer->width = cw->bitmapEdit.pixmap_width_in_pixels;
    else
        answer->width = (cw->bitmapEdit.pixmap_width_in_pixels >
                DEFAULTWIDTH) ? DEFAULTWIDTH :
                cw->bitmapEdit.pixmap_width_in_pixels;

    if (cw->bitmapEdit.show_all == True)
        answer->height = cw->bitmapEdit.pixmap_height_in_pixels;
    else
        answer->height = (cw->bitmapEdit.pixmap_height_in_pixels >
                DEFAULTWIDTH) ? DEFAULTWIDTH :
                cw->bitmapEdit.pixmap_height_in_pixels;

        if ( ((proposed->request_mode & (CWWidth | CWHeight))
                == (CWWidth | CWHeight)) &&
                proposed->width == answer->width &&
                proposed->height == answer->height)
            return XtGeometryYes;
        else if (answer->width == cw->core.width &&
                answer->height == cw->core.height)
            return XtGeometryNo;
        else
            return XtGeometryAlmost;
    }
```

E.2 The BitmapEdiP.h Private Header File

Example E-2. BitmapEdiP.h: complete private header file

```
/*
 * BitmapEditP.h - Private definitions for BitmapEdit widget
 */

#ifndef _ORABitmapEditP_h
#define _ORABitmapEditP_h

/*
 * Include private header file of superclass.
 * In this case, however, Primitive's header file is
 * thrown into XmP.h.
```

```
 */
#include <Xm/XmP.h>

/*
 * Include public header file for this widget.
 */
#include "BitmapEdit.h"

/* New fields for the BitmapEdit widget class record */

typedef struct {
    int make_compiler_happy;    /* keep compiler happy */
} BitmapEditClassPart;

/* Full class record declaration */
typedef struct _BitmapEditClassRec {
    CoreClassPart        core_class;
    XmPrimitiveClassPart    primitive_class;
    BitmapEditClassPart    bitmapEdit_class;
} BitmapEditClassRec;

extern BitmapEditClassRec bitmapEditClassRec;

/* New fields for the BitmapEdit widget record */
typedef struct {
    /* resources */
    Pixel    foreground;
    XtCallbackList callback;/* application installed callback function(s) */
    Dimension    pixmap_width_in_cells;
    Dimension     pixmap_height_in_cells;
    int cell_size_in_pixels;
    int cur_x, cur_y;        /* position of visible corner in big pixmap */
    char *cell;              /* array for keeping track of array of bits */
    Boolean show_all;        /* whether bitmap should display entire bitmap */

    /* private state */
    Dimension    pixmap_width_in_pixels;
    Dimension    pixmap_height_in_pixels;
    Pixmap big_picture;
    GC        draw_gc;       /* one plane, for drawing into pixmap */
    GC        undraw_gc;     /* one plane, for drawing into pixmap */
    GC        copy_gc; /* defaultdepthofscreen, for copy'g pixmap into window */
    Boolean user_allocated; /* whether user allocated cell array */
} BitmapEditPart;

/*
 * Full instance record declaration
 */
typedef struct _BitmapEditRec {
    CorePart            core;
    XmPrimitivePart        primitive;
    BitmapEditPart        bitmapEdit;
} BitmapEditRec;

#endif /* _ORABitmapEditP_h */
```

E.3 The BitmapEdit.h Public Header File

Example E-3. BitmapEdit.h: complete public header file

```
#ifndef _ORABitmapEdit_h
#define _ORABitmapEdit_h

/* BitmapEdit Widget public include file */

/*
 * The public header file for the immediate superclass normally
 * must be included.  However, not in this case because the public
 * header file for Primitive is in Xm.h, which is already included
 * in all Motif applications.
 */

/* #include <Xm/Superclass.h>  */

/*
 * This public structure is used as call_data to the callback.
 * It passes the x, y position of the cell toggled (in units of
 * cells, not pixels) and a mode flag that indicates whether the
 * cell was turned on (1) or off (0).
 */
typedef struct {
    int mode;
    int newx;
    int newy;
} BitmapEditPointInfo;

#define XtNtoggleCallback "toggleCallback"
#define XtNcellSizeInPixels "cellSizeInPixels"
#define XtNpixmapWidthInCells "pixmapWidthInCells"
#define XtNpixmapHeightInCells "pixmapHeightInCells"
#define XtNcurX "curX"
#define XtNcurY "curY"
#define XtNcellArray "cellArray"
#define XtNshowEntireBitmap "showEntireBitmap"


#define XtCToggleCallback "ToggleCallback"
#define XtCCellSizeInPixels "CellSizeInPixels"
#define XtCPixmapWidthInCells "PixmapWidthInCells"
#define XtCPixmapHeightInCells "PixmapHeightInCells"
#define XtCCurX "CurX"
#define XtCCurY "CurY"
#define XtCCellArray "CellArray"
#define XtCShowEntireBitmap "ShowEntireBitmap"

extern char *BitmapEditGetArray(); /* w */
    /* Widget w; */

/* Class record constants */
extern WidgetClass bitmapEditWidgetClass;

typedef struct _BitmapEditClassRec *BitmapEditWidgetClass;
typedef struct _BitmapEditRec       *BitmapEditWidget;

#endif /* _ORABitmapEdit_h */
/* DON'T ADD STUFF AFTER THIS #endif */
```

E.4 xbitmap5

Example E-4. xbitmap5: complete application code

```
/*
 * xbitmap5.c
 */
#include <Xm/Xm.h>

#include <Xm/PanedW.h>
#include <Xm/RowColumn.h>
#include <Xm/PushB.h>
#include <Xm/DrawingA.h>
#include <Xm/ScrolledW.h>

#include "BitmapEdit.h"

#include <stdio.h>

#define DRAWN 1
#define UNDRAWN 0

/*
 * Data structure for private data.
 * (This avoids lots of global variables.)
 */
typedef struct {
    GC draw_gc, undraw_gc, invert_gc;
    Pixmap normal_bitmap;
    Widget showNormalBitmap, showReverseBitmap;
    Dimension pixmap_width_in_cells, pixmap_height_in_cells;
} PrivateAppData;

static void CellToggled(), SetUpThings();

PrivateAppData private_data;
String filename;      /* filename to read and write */
static Boolean file_contained_good_data = False;

/* ARGSUSED */
static void
PrintOut(widget, client_data, call_data)
Widget widget;
XtPointer client_data, call_data;    /* unused */
{
    XWriteBitmapFile(XtDisplay(widget), filename,
            private_data.normal_bitmap,
            private_data.pixmap_width_in_cells,
            private_data.pixmap_height_in_cells, 0, 0);
}

/*ARGSUSED*/
static void
RedrawSmallPicture(w, event, params, num_params)
Widget w;
XEvent *event;
String *params;
Cardinal *num_params;
{
    GC gc;
```

```
    if (w == private_data.showNormalBitmap)
        gc = DefaultGCOfScreen(XtScreen(w));
    else
        gc = private_data.invert_gc;

    if (DefaultDepthOfScreen(XtScreen(w)) == 1)
        XCopyArea(XtDisplay(w), private_data.normal_bitmap, XtWindow(w),
                gc, 0, 0, private_data.pixmap_width_in_cells,
                private_data.pixmap_height_in_cells, 0, 0);
    else
        XCopyPlane(XtDisplay(w), private_data.normal_bitmap, XtWindow(w),
                gc, 0, 0, private_data.pixmap_width_in_cells,
                private_data.pixmap_height_in_cells, 0, 0, 1);
}

String
FillCell(w)
Widget w;
{
    String cell;
    int x, y;
    XImage *image;
    cell = XtCalloc(private_data.pixmap_width_in_cells *
            private_data.pixmap_height_in_cells, sizeof(char));
    /* Convert pixmap into image, so that we can
     * read individual pixels */
    image = XGetImage(XtDisplay(w), private_data.normal_bitmap, 0, 0,
        private_data.pixmap_width_in_cells, private_data.pixmap_height_in_cells,
        AllPlanes, XYPixmap);

    for (x = 0; x < private_data.pixmap_width_in_cells; x++) {
        for (y = 0; y < private_data.pixmap_height_in_cells; y++) {
            cell[x + (y * private_data.pixmap_width_in_cells)] =
            XGetPixel(image, x, y);
        }
    }
    return(cell);
}

main(argc, argv)
int argc;
char *argv[];
{
    XtAppContext app_context;
    Widget topLevel, form, scrolledW, bigBitmap, buttonbox, quit, output;
    Arg args[5];
    int i;
    extern exit();
    unsigned int width, height; /* NOT Dimension: used in Xlib calls */
    int junk;
    String cell;

    static XrmOptionDescRec table[] =
    {
        {"-pw",            "*pixmapWidthInCells",   XrmoptionSepArg, NULL},
        {"-pixmapwidth",   "*pixmapWidthInCells",   XrmoptionSepArg, NULL},
        {"-ph",            "*pixmapHeightInCells",  XrmoptionSepArg, NULL},
        {"-pixmapheight",  "*pixmapHeightInCells",  XrmoptionSepArg, NULL},
```

```
        {"-cellsize",        "*cellSizeInPixels",        XrmoptionSepArg, NULL},
    };

    topLevel = XtVaAppInitialize(
            &app_context,        /* Application context */
            "XBitmap5",          /* Application class */
            table, XtNumber(table),  /* command line option list */
            &argc, argv,         /* command line args */
            NULL,                /* for missing app-defaults file */
            NULL);               /* terminate varargs list */

    if (argv[1] != NULL)
        filename = argv[1];
    else {
        fprintf(stderr, "xbitmap: must specify filename on command line.\n");
        exit(1);
    }

    form = XtCreateManagedWidget("form", xmPanedWindowWidgetClass, topLevel,
            NULL, 0);

    buttonbox = XtCreateManagedWidget("buttonbox", xmRowColumnWidgetClass,
            form, NULL, 0);

    output = XtCreateManagedWidget("output", xmPushButtonWidgetClass,
            buttonbox, NULL, 0);

    XtAddCallback(output, XmNactivateCallback, PrintOut, NULL);

    quit = XtCreateManagedWidget("quit", xmPushButtonWidgetClass,
            buttonbox, NULL, 0);

    XtAddCallback(quit, XmNactivateCallback, exit, NULL);

    switch (XReadBitmapFile(XtDisplay(quit),
            RootWindowOfScreen(XtScreen(quit)), filename,
            &width, &height, &private_data.normal_bitmap, &junk, &junk)) {
        case BitmapSuccess:
            file_contained_good_data = True;
            if ((private_data.pixmap_width_in_cells != width) ||
                    (private_data.pixmap_height_in_cells != height)) {
                i = 0;
                XtSetArg(args[i], XtNpixmapWidthInCells, width);    i++;
                XtSetArg(args[i], XtNpixmapHeightInCells, height);   i++;
                private_data.pixmap_width_in_cells = width;
                private_data.pixmap_height_in_cells = height;
                cell = FillCell(quit);
                XtSetArg(args[i], XtNcellArray, cell);    i++;
            }
            break;
        case BitmapOpenFailed:
            fprintf(stderr, "xbitmap: could not open bitmap\
                    file, using fresh bitmap.\n");
            break;
        case BitmapFileInvalid:
            fprintf(stderr, "xbitmap: bitmap file invalid.\n");
            exit(1);
        case BitmapNoMemory:
            fprintf(stderr, "xbitmap: insufficient server memory\
```

```
                          to create bitmap.\n");
                exit(1);
        default:
            fprintf(stderr, "xbitmap: programming error.\n");
            exit(1);
    }


    scrolledW = XtVaCreateManagedWidget("scrolledW",
            xmScrolledWindowWidgetClass, form, NULL, 0);

    /* args are set above if file was read */
    bigBitmap = XtCreateManagedWidget("bigBitmap",
            bitmapEditWidgetClass, scrolledW, args, i);

    XtAddCallback(bigBitmap, XtNtoggleCallback, CellToggled, NULL);

    if (!file_contained_good_data) {
        XtVaGetValues(bigBitmap,
                XtNpixmapHeightInCells, &private_data.pixmap_height_in_cells,
                XtNpixmapWidthInCells, &private_data.pixmap_width_in_cells,
                NULL);

        private_data.normal_bitmap = XCreatePixmap(XtDisplay(quit),
                RootWindowOfScreen(XtScreen(quit)),
                private_data.pixmap_width_in_cells,
                private_data.pixmap_height_in_cells, 1);
    }

    SetUpThings(topLevel);

    private_data.showNormalBitmap = XtVaCreateManagedWidget(
            "showNormalBitmap", xmDrawingAreaWidgetClass,
            buttonbox, XmNwidth, private_data.pixmap_width_in_cells,
            XmNheight, private_data.pixmap_height_in_cells,
            NULL);

    private_data.showReverseBitmap = XtVaCreateManagedWidget(
            "showReverseBitmap", xmDrawingAreaWidgetClass,
            buttonbox, XmNwidth, private_data.pixmap_width_in_cells,
            XmNheight, private_data.pixmap_height_in_cells,
            NULL);

    XtAddCallback(private_data.showReverseBitmap,
            XmNexposeCallback, CellToggled, NULL);
    XtAddCallback(private_data.showNormalBitmap,
            XmNexposeCallback, CellToggled, NULL);
    XtRealizeWidget(topLevel);
    XtAppMainLoop(app_context);
}

static void
SetUpThings(w)
Widget w;
{
    XGCValues values;

    values.foreground = 1;
    values.background = 0;

    /* note that normal_bitmap is used as the drawable because it
```

```
         * is one bit deep.  The root window may not be one bit deep. */
        private_data.draw_gc = XCreateGC(XtDisplay(w),
                private_data.normal_bitmap,
                GCForeground | GCBackground, &values);

        values.foreground = 0;
        values.background = 1;
        private_data.undraw_gc = XCreateGC(XtDisplay(w),
                private_data.normal_bitmap,
                GCForeground | GCBackground, &values);

        /* this GC is for copying from the bitmap
         * to the small reverse widget */
        values.foreground = WhitePixelOfScreen(XtScreen(w));
        values.background = BlackPixelOfScreen(XtScreen(w));
        private_data.invert_gc = XtGetGC(w,
                GCForeground | GCBackground, &values);
}
/* ARGSUSED */
static void
CellToggled(w, client_data, info)
Widget w;
XtPointer client_data;   /* unused */
XtPointer info; /* call_data (from widget) */
{
        BitmapEditPointInfo *cur_info = (BitmapEditPointInfo *) info;
        /*
         * Note: BitmapEditPointInfo is defined in BitmapEdit.h
         */

        XDrawPoint(XtDisplay(w), private_data.normal_bitmap,
                ((cur_info->mode == DRAWN) ? private_data.draw_gc :
                private_data.undraw_gc), cur_info->newx, cur_info->newy);

        RedrawSmallPicture(private_data.showNormalBitmap);
        RedrawSmallPicture(private_data.showReverseBitmap);

}
```

xbitmap Application

F

Sources of Additional Information

This appendix describes where you can get more information about the X Toolkit and about X in general, including other books on the subject and the various ways to get the source code for X.

In This Appendix:

Sources of Additional Information

This appendix lists a few of the official and unofficial sources for information about the X Window System and associated software.

Note that some of this detailed information may become dated rather quickly. The best source of current information is the *comp.windows.x* network news group, described later in this appendix.

This book documents Release 4, the current public release level of the X software as of June 1990. Even so, many people continue to use R3 since there is a considerable delay between the date that MIT distributes a new release and the date by which vendors integrate that release into their own products and issue updates. An R3 version of this manual is available while demand is sufficient to continue reprinting. (All changes to Xt in R4 are backwards compatible so that any software that runs under R3 will also run under R4. But the converse is not true.)

F.1 Getting the X Software

You can get the X software directly from MIT on three 9-track 1600 BPI magtapes written in UNIX *tar* format or on one 9-track 6250 BPI magtape, along with printed copies of MIT's manuals, by sending a check in U.S. currency for U.S. $400 to:

> MIT Software Distribution Center
> Technology Licensing Office
> MIT E32-300
> 77 Massachusetts Avenue
> Cambridge, MA 02139

Their telephone number is (617) 253-6966, and the "X Ordering Hotline" is (617) 258-8330. If you want the tapes and manuals shipped overseas, the price is $500. The manual set alone is $125 including U.S. shipping or $175 including overseas shipping.

Other distribution media or formats are not available from the MIT Software Distribution Center, but are from other independent vendors such as ICS, mentioned later. The Release tape comes with source code for sample servers for Sun, HP, IBM, Apollo, Sony, DEC and several other workstations, source code for clients written by MIT, sources for the toolkits

Xt, XView (in R4), Interviews, and Andrew, contributed software written outside MIT (including the examples in this book), and sources and postscript files for all MIT's documentation. Note that the servers supplied are sample servers only; commercial vendors typically release optimized (faster) servers for the same machines.

Sites that have access to the Internet can retrieve the distribution from the following machines using anonymous *ftp*. Here are the current sites:

Location	Hostname	Address	Directory
Western USA	*gatekeeper.dec.com*	16.1.0.2	*pub/X11/R4 or R3*
Central USA	*mordred.cs.purdue.edu*	128.10.2.2	*pub/X11/R4 or R3*
Central USA	*giza.cis.ohio-state.edu*	128.146.8.61	*pub/X11/R4 or R3*
Southeast USA	*uunet.uu.net*	192.48.96.2	*X/R4*
Northeast USA	*crl.dec.com*	192.58.206.2	*pub/X11/R4*
UK Janet	*src.doc.ic.ac.uk*	129.31.81.36	*X.V11R4*
UK niftp	*uk.ac.ic.doc.src*		*<XV11R4>**
Australia	*munnari.oz.au*	128.250.1.21	*X.V11R4*

DO NOT do anonymous *ftp* during normal business hours, and please use the machine nearest you.

The distribution is also available by UUCP from UUNET, for sites without Internet access. The files are split up to be small enough for UUCP distribution. See the preface for instructions on getting files from UUNET if you are not a UUNET subscriber.

F.1.1 Bug Fixes

Critical bug fixes as well as a limited number of important new features are available from the archive server *xstuff@expo.lcs.mit.edu*. Electronic mail sent to this address is forwarded to a program which responds with the requested information. The rest of this section and the two that follow it (entitled Notes and Fairness) explain how to use *xstuff*.

The *xstuff* server is a mail-response program. This means that you mail it a request, and it mails back the response.

The *xstuff* server is a very dumb program. It does not have much error checking. If you don't send it commands that it understands, it will just answer "I don't understand you."

The *xstuff* server reads your entire message before it does anything, so you can have several different commands in a single message. It treats the "Subject:" header line just like any other line of the message. You can use any combination of upper and lower case letters in the commands.

The archives are organized into a series of directories and subdirectories. Each directory has an index, and each subdirectory has an index. The top-level index gives you an overview of what is in the subdirectories, and the index for each subdirectory tells you what it contains.

If you are bored with reading documentation and just want to try something, then send the server a message containing the line:

```
send index fixes
```

When you get the index back, it will contain the numbers of all of the fixes and batches of fixes in the archive. Then you can send the server another message asking it to send you the fixes that you want:

```
send fixes 1 5 9 11-20
```

If you are using a mailer that understands "@" notation, send to *xstuff@expo.lcs.mit.edu*. If your mailer deals in "!" notation, try sending to *{someplace}!mit-eddie!expo.lcs.mit.edu!xstuff*. For other mailers, you're on your own.

The server has four commands. Each command must be the first word on a line.

help   The command *help* or *send help* causes the server to send you the help file. No other commands are honored in a message that asks for help (the server figures that you had better read the help message before you do anything else).

index   If your message contains a line whose first word is *index*, then the server will send you the top-level index of the contents of the archive. If there are other words on that line that match the name of subdirectories, then the indexes for those subdirectories are sent instead of the top-level index. For example, you can say:

```
index
```

or:

```
index fixes
```

You can then send back another message to the *xstuff* server, using a *send* command (see below) to ask it to send you the files whose name you learned from that list.

index fixes and *send index fixes* mean the same thing: you can use *send* instead of *index* for getting an index.

If your message has an *index* or a *send index* command, then all other *send* commands will be ignored. This means that you cannot get an index and data in the same request. This is so that index requests can be given high priority.

send   If your message contains a line whose first word is *send*, then the *xstuff* server will send you the item(s) named on the rest of the line. To name an item, you give its directory and its name. For example:

```
send fixes 1-10
```

Once you have named a category, you can put as many names as you like on the rest of the line. They will all be taken from that category. For example:

```
send fixes 1-10 11-20 21-30
```

Each *send* command can reference only one directory. If you would like to get one fix and one of something else, you must use two *send* commands.

You may put as many *send* commands as you like into one message to the server, but the more you ask for, the longer it will take to receive. See the Fairness Section below, for an explanation. Actually, it's not strictly true that you can put as many *send* commands as you want into one message. If the server must use UUCP mail to send your files, then it cannot send more than 100K bytes in one message. If you ask for more than it can send, then it will send as much as it can and ignore the rest.

path   The *path* command exists to help in case you do not get responses from the server when you mail to it.

Sometimes the server is unable to return mail over the incoming path. There are dozens of reasons why this might happen, and if you are a true wizard, you already know what those reasons are. If you are an apprentice wizard, you might not know all the reasons, but you might know a way to circumvent them.

If you put in a *path* command, then everything that the server mails to you will be mailed to that address, rather than to the return address on your mail. The server host *expo.lcs.mit.edu* does not have a direct UUCP connection to anywhere; you must go through *mit-eddie* (the UUCP name of *eddie.mit.edu*) or somewhere else.

F.1.1.1 Notes

The *xstuff* server acknowledges every request by return mail. If you don't get a message back in a day or two you should assume that something is going wrong, and perhaps try a *path* command.

The *xstuff* server does not respond to requests from users named *root*, *system*, *daemon*, or *mailer*. This is to prevent mail loops. If your name is "Bruce Root" or "Jane Daemon", and you can document this, I will happily rewrite the server to remove this restriction. Yes, I know about Norman Mailer and Waverley Root. Norman doesn't use netmail and Waverley is dead.

F.1.1.2 Fairness

The *xstuff* server contains many safeguards to ensure that it is not monopolized by people asking for large amounts of data. The mailer is set up so that it will send no more than a fixed amount of data each day. If the work queue contains more requests than the day's quota, then the unsent files will not be processed until the next day. Whenever the mailer is run to send its day's quota, it sends the requests out shortest-first.

If you have a request waiting in the work queue and you send in another request, the new request is added to the old one (thereby increasing its size) rather than being filed anew. This prevents you from being able to send in a large number of small requests as a way of beating the system.

The reason for all of these quotas and limitations is that the delivery resources are finite, and there are many people who would like to make use of the archive.

F.2 Netnews

The Usenet network newsgroups and mailing lists are probably the most valuable source of information about X. The current list of public mailing lists that discuss X is as follows:

News Group	Description
motif@alphalpha.com	People interested in the OSF's Motif X toolkit. This mailing list is also gatewayed to the Usenet newsgroup *comp.windows.x.motif*. If you receive that newsgroup, you don't need to get this mailing list.
x11-3D@expo.lcs.mit.edu	People interested in X and 3-D graphics.
x-ada@expo.lcs.mit.edu	X and ada.
ximage@expo.lcs.mit.edu	People interested in image processing and X.
xpert@expo.lcs.mit.edu	General discussion of X. This mailing list is also gatewayed to the Usenet newsgroup *comp.windows.x*. If you receive that newsgroup, you don't need to get this mailing list.
xvideo@expo.lcs.mit.edu	Discussion of video extensions for X.

The developers of X post notices of fixes to the software to the newsgroup *comp.window.x*, and this is where users and developers around the world ask and answer questions.

F.3 Training and Consulting

Numerous independent vendors provide courses on X programming. Several sources that we are aware of include:

- *Integrated Computer Solutions* (ICS), 163 Harvard Street, Cambridge, MA 02139; (617) 547-0510. Courses on Xlib, Motif, strategic overviews of X. Also provides consulting services and manages an X user's group.

- *Hands-On Learning*, 27 Cambridge Street, Burlington, MA 01803; (617) 272-0088. Courses on Xlib and Xt.

- X tutorials are now a regular feature of UNIX conventions such as the UNIX EXPO, Usenix, Uniforum, the annual X conference at MIT, and Xhibition, the conference organized by ICS. Also contact commercial server vendors for information on courses they offer.

Certain staff members at O'Reilly and Associates have developed training materials and can give training lectures or consult when time permits.

Training companies wishing to be listed here should send us information on the courses they offer.

F.3.1 Phone Support

X programming is a very new field, and since everyone who knows enough to help you is overworked, you are likely to hear "you're on your own" if you try to call for help. There are no support lines from the developers of X, because X was developed by a university, not a system manufacturer or software house. When X becomes widely supported as a commercial product, the situation should change as vendors offer support.

ICS provides phone support for a fee. See Section F.3 for their telephone number.

F.4 The X Consortium

The X Consortium can be reached at:

> MIT X Consortium
> 545 Technology Square Rm. 217
> Cambridge, MA 02139

The consortium's phone number is (617) 253-8861; its current members are shown below.

ACER Counterpoint, Inc.	Matrox International
AT&T	Megatek Corp.
Adobe Systems	Mitsubishi Electric Corporation
Advanced Graphics Engineering	NCR Corporation
Apollo Computer, Inc.	NEC Corporation
Apple Computer, Inc.	NTT Corporation
Ardent Computer	Network Computing Devices, Inc.
BULL MTS	Nova Graphics International
CETIA	O'Reilly & Associates, Inc.
CalComp	OMRON Tateisi Electronics
Canterbury University, England	Open Software Foundation
Carnegie Mellon University	PCS Computer Systeme GmbH
Codonics, Inc.	Prime Computer, Inc.
Control Data Corporation	Reuters
Cray Research, Inc.	Samsung Software America
Data General	Sequent Computer Systems Inc.
Digital Equipment Corp.	Siemens AG
Eastman Kodak Company	Silicon Graphics Computer Systems
Evans & Sutherland	Societe de Gestion et d'Informatique Publicis
Fujitsu America, Inc.	Software Productivity Consortium
GfxBase	Solbourne Computer Inc.
Hewlett Packard Company	Sony Corporation
IBM Corporation	Stanford University
INESC*	Stellar Computer Inc.
Integrated Computer Solutions, Inc.	Sun Microsystems, Inc.
Integrated Solutions, Inc.	Tatung Science and Technology

---

*Instituto de Engenharia de Sistemas e Computadores

Interactive Development Environments
Interactive Systems Corp.
Jupiter Systems
Key Systems Engineering Corp.
Landmark Graphics Corp.
Locus Computing Corp.
MIPS Computer Systems
MITRE Corp.

Tektronix, Inc.
Texas Instruments
UNICAD, Inc.
Unisys Corp.
University of Lowell
Visual Technology, Inc.
Wang Laboratories
X/Open Company Ltd.

Most of these companies are preparing products based on X.

F.5 Finding Out for Yourself

If, heaven forbid, you don't find an answer to your problem in one of the books in our X Window System Series, and you can't get anyone to help you, what do you try next?

X is unusual in that the source code is freely available. It should be possible for most X programmers to get a copy of the X source code from the sources listed above. There you can look at some examples of how others have used X to write applications. In "Star Wars," the saying was "Use the Force, Luke." In X, it is "Use the Source, Luke." However, you may find that many of the applications on the release tape use out-of-date techniques, because they were written *before* the release.

Whenever looking at the code for the server or any of the programming libraries such as Xlib or Xt, however, remember that the X standards are defined by documents, not by code. In other words, don't depend on any of the undocumented details of the code you happen to have access to, since some other vendor may not implement the standard in the same way.

Nevertheless, it can sometimes be useful to see how things are actually being done. Once you understand how the code is organized, you can look up certain details about how X works as long as you have a good knowledge of C and a little persistence.

Xlib and the server are two distinct chunks of code. Each contains code for sending and receiving information to and from the other over the network using protocol requests, replies, events, and errors. The source tree as supplied on the X distribution tape places the Xlib source in the directory *base/lib/X*, where *base* is the top of the entire source tree. Their server source is placed in *base/server*.

The procedure for finding out something about an Xlib routine is normally to search for the routine in the Xlib code, and then figure out what it does. Sometimes the answer can be found there. Many of the routines, however, simply place their arguments in a protocol request and send it to the server. Then you will have to look in the server code for the answer. To find the correct place in the server code, you will need the symbol for the protocol request, which is the first argument in the `GetReq` call.

The server code is much more involved than Xlib itself. The device-dependent portions are in *base/server/ddx* and the device-independent portions are in *base/server/dix*. The device-independent code should be your first stop, because it is here that protocol requests from Xlib arrive and are dispatched to the appropriate code. Search for the protocol request symbol you found in Xlib. It will appear in several source files. Start with the occurrence in *dispatch.c*, and try to figure out what the code does. This will require following leads to other routines.

If you don't find a routine in *base/server/dix*, then it must be in the device-dependent code. *base/server/ddx* has one directory in it for each brand of hardware to which a sample server has been ported. It also contains the directories */mi*, */cfb*, */mfb*, and */snf*, which contain routines used in writing the sample server device-dependent code. Note that servers may include code ostensibly for other machines.

Glossary

X uses many common terms in unique ways. A good example is "children." While most, if not all, of these terms are defined where they are first used in this manual, you will undoubtedly find it easier to refresh your memory by looking for them here.

Glossary

This glossary is an expanded version of the glossary from Volume One, *Xlib Programming Manual* (which in turn is based on the glossary in the *Xlib–C Language X Interface*, by Jim Gettys, Ron Newman, and Bob Scheifler). As such, it contains definitions of many Xlib terms not actually used in this book, but which you might come across in other reading, or in comments in code. In some cases, these Xlib terms may be used in the definitions of the Xt terms given in this glossary. Any term used in a definition, for which another entry exists in the glossary, is generally shown in italics.

accelerator

> An *accelerator* is a *translation* that maps events in one widget to actions in another. The name is based on the most frequent use for this feature, namely to provide keyboard shortcuts to invoke application or widget functions that would otherwise have only a pointer-driven interface.

accept_focus method

> The *accept_focus method* of a child is invoked when a parent offers the *keyboard focus* to a child by calling XtCallAcceptFocus. This method is part of the Core widget class.

access control list

> X maintains lists of hosts that are allowed access to each server controlling a display. By default, only the local host may use the display, plus any hosts specified in the *access control list* for that display. This access control list can be changed by clients on the local host. Some server implementations may implement other authorization mechanisms in addition to or instead of this one. The list can currently be found in */etc/X#.hosts* where # is the number of the display, usually 0 (zero). The access control list is also known as the host access list.

action　An *action* is a function bound by a *translation*, to be invoked in response to a user event.

actions table

> An *actions table* is an array of function pointers and corresponding strings by which *actions* can be referenced in a *translation table*. The use of actions requires a widget to define both an actions table and a translation table.

active grab

A grab is *active* when the pointer or keyboard is actually owned by a single grabbing client. See also *grab*.

ancestor

If window *W* is an *inferior* of window *A*, then *A* is an *ancestor* of *W*. The *parent* window, the parent's parent window, and so on are all ancestors of the given window. The *root window* is the ancestor of all windows on a given screen.

application context

An *application context* specifies a connection to a server. When an application program has connections to multiple servers, the application context coordinates events and their dispatching, so all connections get processed.

argument list

An *argument list* is used in a call to create a widget in order to "hardcode" the value of widget resources, and also in calls to XtSetValues or XtGetValues. It consists of an array of Arg structures, each consisting of a resource name and the value to which it should be set.

Athena widget

MIT distributes a set of widgets developed by MIT's Project Athena in the *Athena Widget* library, Xaw. The include files for Athena widgets reside in */usr/include/X11* under Release 3 and *usr/include/X11/Xaw* under Release 4.

atom

An *atom* is a unique numeric ID corresponding to a string name. Atoms are used to identify properties, types, and selections in order to avoid the overhead of passing arbitrary-length strings over the network. See also *property*.

background

Windows may have a *background*, consisting of either a solid color or a tile pattern. If a window has a background, it will be repainted automatically by the server whenever there is an Expose event on the window. If a window does not have a background, it will be transparent. By default, a window has a background. See also *foreground*.

backing store

When a server maintains the contents of a window, the off-screen saved pixels are known as a *backing store*. This feature is not available on all servers. Even when available, the server will not maintain a backing store, unless told to do so with a window attribute. Use the DoesBackingStores Xlib macro to determine if this feature is supported.

bit gravity
When a window is resized, the contents of the window are not necessarily discarded. It is possible to request the server (though no guarantees are made) to relocate the previous contents to some region of the resized window. This attraction of window contents for some location of a window is known as *bit gravity*. For example, an application that draws a graph might request that the contents be moved into the lower-left corner, so that the origin of the graph will still appear in the lower-left corner. See also *window gravity*.

bit plane
On a color or gray scale display, each pixel has more than one bit defined. Data in display memory can be thought of either as pixels (multiple bits per pixel) or as bit planes (one bit plane for each usable bit in the pixel). The *bit plane* is an array of bits the size of the screen.

bitmap A *bitmap* is a pixmap with a depth of one bit. There is no bitmap type in X11. Instead, use a pixmap of depth 1. See also *pixmap*.

border A window can have a border that is zero or more pixels wide. If a window has a border, the border can have a solid color or a tile pattern, and it will be repainted automatically by the server whenever its color or pattern is changed or an `Expose` event occurs on the window.

button grabbing
A pointer grab that becomes active only when a specified set of keys and/or buttons are held down in a particular window is referred to as a *button grab*.

byte order
The order in which bytes of data are stored in memory is hardware-dependent. For pixmaps and bitmaps, *byte order* is defined by the server, and clients with different native byte ordering must swap bytes as necessary. For all other parts of the protocol, the byte order is defined by the client, and the server swaps bytes as necessary.

callback A *callback* is an application function registered with a widget by the application using either of the calls `XtAddCallback` or `XtAddCallbacks` or through an argument list. A widget declares one or more *callback lists* as resources; applications add functions to these lists in order to link widgets to applications code.

change_managed method
When a parent should change its managed widgets, the *change_managed method* is invoked, at which time a parent reorganizes its children. The `change_managed` method is part of the Composite widget class.

child, children
1) A widget created by `XtCreateWidget` is a *child* of the widget specified as its *parent*. The parent controls the layout of its children.
2) The *children* of a window are its first-level subwindows. All of these windows were created with the same window as parent. A client creates its top-level window as a child of the root window.

class   1) (X Toolkit) A widget's *class* determines what methods will be called for it and what instance variables it has. For widget users, a widget's class is declared in the *.h* file for the widget.

2) (Xlib) There are two uses of the term *class* in X: window class and visual class. The window class specifies whether a window is `InputOnly` or `Input-Output`. The visual class specifies the color model that is used by a window. See the classes `DirectColor`, `GrayScale`, `PseudoColor`, `StaticColor`, `StaticGray`, and `TrueColor`. Both window class and visual class are set permanently when a window is created.

class_initialize method
This method—part of the Core widget—is invoked when a widget class is initialized. That is, it is called when the first instance of a particular class is created.

client   An application program connects to the window system server by an interprocess communication (IPC) path, such as a TCP connection or a shared memory buffer. This program is referred to as a *client* of the window system server. More precisely, the client is the IPC path itself; a program with multiple paths open to one or more servers is viewed by the protocol as multiple clients. X Resources are available only as long as the connection remains intact, not as long as a program remains running. Normally the connection and the program terminate concurrently, but the client's resources may live on if `XChangeCloseDownMode` has been called.

clipping region
In many graphics routines, a bitmap or list of rectangles can be specified to restrict output to a particular region of the window. The image defined by the bitmap or rectangles is called a *clipping region*, or clip mask. Output to child windows is automatically clipped to the borders of the parent unless `subwindow_mode` of the GC is `IncludeInferiors`. Therefore the borders of the parent can be thought of as a clipping region.

colorcell   An entry in a colormap is known as a *colorcell*. An entry contains three values specifying red, green, and blue intensities. These values are always 16-bit unsigned numbers, with zero being minimum intensity. The values are truncated or scaled by the server to match the display hardware. See also *colormap*.

colormap
A *colormap* consists of a set of colorcells. A pixel value indexes into the colormap to produce intensities of Red, Green, and Blue to be displayed. Depending on hardware limitations, one or more colormaps may be installed at one time, such that windows associated with those maps display with true colors. Regardless of the number of installable colormaps, any number of virtual colormaps can be created. When needed, a virtual colormap can be installed and the existing installed colormap might have to be uninstalled. The colormap on most systems is a limited resource that should be conserved by allocating read-only colorcells whenever possible, and by selecting RGB values from the predefined color database. Read-only cells may be shared between clients. See also *colorcell*, *DirectColor*, *GrayScale*, *PseudoColor*, *StaticColor*, *StaticGray*, and *TrueColor*.

Composite widget

A *Composite widget* is designed to manage the geometry of children; that is, a Composite widget instance can be passed in the parent argument to XtCreate-Widget.

connection

The communication path between the server and the client is known as a *connection*. A client usually (but not necessarily) has only one connection to the server over which requests and events are sent.

Constraint widget

The *Constraint widget* is a subclass of Composite. A Constraint widget has more information about each child than a Composite widget.

constraints

A Constraint widget provides a list of resources, or *constraints*, for its children. The constraints give the Constraint widget information about how each child should be layed out.

containment

A window *contains* the pointer if the window is viewable and if the hotspot of the cursor is within a visible region of the window or a visible region of one of its inferiors. The border of the window is included as part of the window for containment. The pointer is in a window if the window contains the pointer but no inferior contains the pointer.

coordinate system

The *coordinate system* has x horizontal and y vertical, with the origin (0, 0) at the upper-left. Coordinates are discrete, and in terms of pixels. Each window and pixmap has its own coordinate system. For a window, the origin is inside the border, if there is one. The position of a child window is measured from the origin of the parent to the outside corner of the child (not the child's origin).

Core widget

The *Core widget* is the basic class in the Toolkit. All widgets that can be displayed are subclasses of Core.

cursor A *cursor* is the visible shape of the pointer on a screen. It consists of a hotspot, a shape bitmap, a mask bitmap, and a pair of pixel values. The cursor defined for a window controls the visible appearance of the pointer when the pointer is in that window.

delete_child method

The *delete_child method* is invoked on a parent after its child is deleted. This method is part of the Composite widget and is usually inherited.

depth The *depth* of a window or pixmap is the number of bits per pixel.

dereference

To access the contents of a pointer, you must *dereference* it.

descendants
> See *inferiors*.

destroy method
> The *destroy method* is invoked when a widget has been destroyed. This method is part of the Core widget and is used to deallocate memory and GCs.

device
Keyboards, mice, tablets, track-balls, button boxes, etc. are all collectively known as input *devices*.

DirectColor
> *DirectColor* is a visual class in which a pixel value is decomposed into three separate subfields for colormap indexing. One subfield indexes an array to produce red intensity values; the second subfield indexes a second array to produce blue intensity values; and the third subfield indexes a third array to produce green intensity values. The RGB (red, green, and blue) values in the colormap entry can be changed dynamically. This visual class is normally found on high-performance color workstations.

display
A *display* is a set of one or more *screens* that are driven by a single X server. The Xlib `Display` structure contains all information about the particular display and its screens as well as the state that Xlib needs to communicate with the display over a particular connection. In Xlib, a pointer to a `Display` Structure is returned by `XOpenDisplay`. In most Xt applications, the `Display` is part of the *application context*, and need not be referenced directly. If necessary, a display can be opened directly with a call to `XtOpenDisplay`, and a pointer to the currently open display can be returned by the `XtDisplay` macro.

drawable
> Both windows and pixmaps may be used as destinations in graphics operations. These are collectively known as *drawables*.

encapsulation
> *Encapsulation* is a key concept in object-oriented programming. Objects are defined in such a way that their internals are hidden from the programs that use them; the only way to access an object should be through its published interfaces.

event
An X *event* is a data structure sent by the server that describes something that just happened that may be of interest to the application. There are two major categories of events: user input and window system side effects. For example, the user pressing a keyboard key or clicking a mouse button generates an event; a window being moved on the screen also generates events—possibly in other applications as well if the movement changes the visible portions of their windows. It is the server's job to distribute events to the various windows on the screen.

event compression
> *Event compression* is an Xt feature that allows some events to be ignored or repackaged before they are given to a widget. This happens on the client side, rather than in the server.

event handler

An *event handler* is a function that is called by Xt when a particular event is received. Event handlers have the same purpose as translations and actions—to call a function in response to an event—but event handlers have lower overhead and are not user-configurable.

event mask

Events are requested relative to a window or widget. The set of event types a client requests relative to a window is described using an *event mask*, a bitwise OR of defined symbols specifying which events are desired.

The `event_mask` is a window attribute, which can be set in Xlib with `XSelectInput`, and is also specified in calls that grab the pointer or keyboard. The `do_not_propagate_mask` attribute is also an event mask, and it specifies which events should not be propagated to ancestor windows. In Xt, you never need to set a window's `event_mask` or `do_not_propogate_mask` directly. The translation manager automatically selects the required events.

event propagation

Device-related events *propagate* from the source window to ancestor windows until a window that has selected that type of event is reached, or until the event is discarded explicitly in a `do_not_propagate_mask` attribute.

event source

The smallest window containing the pointer is the *source* of a device-related event.

expose method

When `Expose` events are received, the Intrinsics invoke the *expose method*. A widget should perform its redisplay activities in this method. The `expose` method is part of the Core widget class.

exposure

Window *exposure* occurs when a window is first mapped, or when another window that obscures it is unmapped, resized, or moved. Servers do not guarantee to preserve the contents of windows when windows are obscured or reconfigured. `Expose` events are sent to clients to inform them when contents of regions of windows have been lost and need to be regenerated.

extension

Named *extensions* to the core protocol can be defined to extend the system. Extension to output requests, resources, and event types are all possible, and expected. Extensions can perform at the same level as the core Xlib.

font

A *font* is an array of characters or other bitmap shapes such as cursors. The protocol does no translation or interpretation of character sets. The client simply indicates values used to index the font array. A font contains additional metric information to determine intercharacter and interline spacing.

foreground

The pixel value that will actually be used for drawing pictures or text is referred to as the *foreground*. The foreground is specified as a member of a graphics context. See also *background*.

frozen events

Clients can *freeze* event processing while they change the screen, by grabbing the keyboard or pointer with a certain mode. These events are queued in the server (not in Xlib) until an `XAllowEvents` call with a counteracting mode is given.

GC   The term *GC* is used as a shorthand for graphics context. See *graphics context*.

geometry management

A Composite parent controls its children through *geometry management*, thereby manipulating the size and placement of widgets within a window on the display.

get_values_hook method

The *get_values_hook method* is invoked by the Intrinsics when someone calls `Xt-GetValues`. This method is part of the Core widget class. Its role is to get the resource values of a subpart using `XtGetSubvalues`.

glyph   A *glyph* is an image, usually of a character in a font, but also possibly of a cursor shape or some other shape.

grab   Keyboard keys, the keyboard, pointer buttons, the pointer, and the server can be *grabbed* for exclusive use by a client, usually for a short time period. In general, these facilities help implement various styles of user interface. Popup widgets generally make a *passive grab*. Server grabs are generally used only by window managers.

graphics context

Various information for interpreting graphics primitives is stored in a *graphics context* (GC), such as foreground pixel, background pixel, line width, clipping region, etc. Everything drawn to a window or pixmap is modified by the GC used in the drawing request.

graphics primitive

A *graphics primitive* is an Xlib call that sends a protocol request to the server, instructing the server to draw a particular shape at a particular position. The graphics context specified with the primitive specifies how the server interprets the primitive.

gravity   See *bit gravity* and *window gravity*.

GrayScale

GrayScale is a visual class in which the red, green, and blue values in any given colormap entry are equal, thus producing shades of gray. The gray values can be changed dynamically. `GrayScale` can be viewed as a degenerate case of `PseudoColor`.

hint   Certain properties, such as the preferred size of a window, are referred to as *hints*, since the window manager makes no guarantee that it will honor them.

host access list

See *access control list*.

hotspot   A cursor has an associated *hotspot* that defines the point in the cursor which corresponds to the coordinates reported for the pointer.

identifier

Each server resource has an *identifier* or *ID*, a unique value that clients use to name the resource. Any client can use a resource if it knows the resource ID.

inferiors

The *inferiors* of a window are all of the subwindows nested below it: the children, the children's children, etc. The term *descendants* is a synonym.

inheritance (single vs. multiple)

Inheritance is the ability to obtain methods from a *superclass*. Multiple inheritance, which is not supported by Xt, would allow a class to obtain methods from multiple unrelated superclasses.

initialize method

The *initialize method* is invoked when a widget is created. It initializes instance variables and checks resource values. This method is part of the Core widget class.

initialize_hook method

The *initialize_hook method* is called just after the initialize method, and is responsible for initializing subpart instance variables and checking subpart resource values. This method is part of the Core widget class.

input focus

See *keyboard focus*.

InputOnly window

A window that cannot be used for graphics requests is called an *InputOnly* window. `InputOnly` windows are invisible and can be used to control such things as cursors, input event distribution, and grabbing. `InputOnly` windows cannot have `InputOutput` windows as inferiors.

InputOutput window

The normal kind of window that is used for both input and output is called an *InputOutput* window. It usually has a background. `InputOutput` windows can have both `InputOutput` and `InputOnly` windows as inferiors.

input manager

Control over keyboard input may be provided by an *input manager* client. This job is more often done by the window manager.

insert child method

A widget's *insert child method* is invoked when someone specifies it as a parent in an `XtCreateWidget` call. This method is part of the Composite widget class. This method is usually inherited.

instance An *instance* is a particular widget that has a class. An instance ID is returned by `XtCreateWidget`.

instantiate

When you *instantiate* a class, you create an instance of it.

Intrinsics

The X Toolkit defines functions and datatypes called *Intrinsics*.

key grabbing

A keyboard grab that occurs only when a certain key or key combination is pressed is called a *key grab*. This is analogous to button grabbing. Both are forms of passive grabs.

keyboard focus

The *keyboard focus* is the window that receives main keyboard input. By default the focus is the root window, which has the effect of sending input to the window that is being pointed to by the mouse. It is possible to attach the keyboard input to a specific window with `XSetInputFocus`. Events are then sent to the window independent of the pointer position.

keyboard grabbing

All keyboard input is sent to a specific window (or client, depending on `owner_events`) when the *keyboard* is *grab*bed. This is analogous to mouse grabbing. This is very much like a temporary keyboard focus window.

keycode A *keycode* is a code in the range 8-255 inclusive that represents a physical or logical key on the keyboard. The mapping between keys and keycodes cannot be changed, and varies between servers. A list of keysyms is associated with each keycode. Programs should use keysyms instead of keycodes to interpret key events.

keysym A *keysym* is a `#define`'d symbol which is a portable representation of the symbol on the cap of a key. Each key may have several keysyms, corresponding to the key when various modifier keys are pressed. You should interpret key events according to the keysym returned by `XLookupString` or `XLookupKeysym`, since this translates server-dependent keycodes into portable keysyms.

listener A *listener* style window manager sets the keyboard focus to a particular window when that window is clicked on with a pointer button. This is the window manager style used with the Apple Macintosh. This style is also referred to as click-to-type.

loose binding

A *loose binding* refers to the use of an asterisk (*) wildcard in a *resource specification* to indicate that the specification applies to zero or more hierarchy levels of widget instances or classes.

mapping

A window is said to be *mapped* if an `XMapWindow` or `XMapRaised` call has been performed on it. Unmapped windows are never viewable. Mapping makes a window eligible for display. The window will actually be displayed if the following conditions are also met:

1) All its ancestors are mapped.
2) It is not obscured by siblings.
3) The window manager has processed the request, if for a top-level window.

message In object-oriented programming, a *message* is used to invoke an object's methods. In Xt, you can think of the Intrinsics functions used to create, destroy, and set resource values as sending messages to widget classes.

method A *method* is a function internal to widget class that the Intrinsics invoke under specified conditions. Methods are provided as pointers to functions in widget class records.

modal popup

A *modal popup* is a popup widget that grabs the pointer when a mouse button is pressed in a particular window.

modeless popup

A *modeless popup* is a popup widget that doesn't grab the pointer on a mouse button.

modifier keys

Shift, Control, Meta, Super, Hyper, Alt, Compose, Apple, Caps Lock, Shift Lock, and similar keys are called *modifier keys*.

monochrome

A *monochrome* screen has only two colors: black and white. Monochrome is a special case of the `StaticGray` visual class, in which there are only two colormap entries.

non-maskable event

A *non-maskable event* is an event that is not selected by the application or widget via an event mask, but is instead sent automatically by the X server. The non-maskable events are `MappingNotify`, `ClientMessage`, `Selection-Clear`, `SelectionNotify`, and `SelectionRequest`.

object In object-oriented programming, an *object* is a self-contained program unit containing both data and procedures.

object-oriented programming

Object-oriented programming is a way of defining classes and creating instances so that objects respond to messages with methods. One of its major benefits is the encapsulation of code.

obscure Window *A obscures* window *B* if *A* is higher in the global stacking order, and the rectangle defined by the outside edges of *A* intersects the rectangle defined by the outside edges of *B*. See *occlude*.

occlude Window *A occludes* window *B* if both are mapped, if *A* is higher in the global stacking order, and if the rectangle defined by the outside edges of *A* intersects the rectangle defined by the outside edges of *B*. The (fine) distinction between the terms *obscures* and *occludes* is that for *obscures*, the windows have to be mapped, while for *occludes* they don't. Also note that window borders are included in the calculation. Note that InputOnly windows never obscure other windows but can occlude other windows.

padding Some bytes are inserted in the data stream to maintain alignment of the protocol requests on natural boundaries. This *padding* increases ease of portability to some machine architectures.

parent A *parent* is a Composite widget instance specified as the parent argument in Xt-CreateWidget. Parents control a child's layout.

parent window

Each new window is created with reference to another previously-created window. The new window is referred to as the *child*, and the reference window as the *parent*. If *C* is a child of *P*, then *P* is the parent of *C*. Only the portion of the child that overlaps the parent is viewable.

passive grab

A *passive grab* is a grab that will become active only when a specific key or button is actually pressed in a particular window.

pixel value

A *pixel value* is an N-bit value, where *N* is the number of bit planes used in a particular window or pixmap. For a window, a pixel value indexes a colormap to derive an actual color to be displayed. For a pixmap, a pixel value will be interpreted as a color in the same way when it has been copied into a window.

pixmap A *pixmap* is a three-dimensional array of bits. A pixmap is normally thought of as a two-dimensional array of pixels, where each pixel can be a value from 0 to (2^N-1), where *N* is the depth (z-axis) of the pixmap. A pixmap can also be thought of as a stack of *N* bitmaps. A pixmap may have only one plane. Such a pixmap is often referred to as a bitmap, even though there is no bitmap type in X11.

plane When a pixmap or window is thought of as a stack of bitmaps, each bitmap is called a *plane*.

plane mask

Graphics operations can be restricted to affect only a subset of bit planes in a drawable. A *plane mask* is a bit mask describing which planes are to be modified.

pointer The *pointer* is the pointing device currently attached to the cursor, and tracked on the screens. This may be a mouse, tablet, track-ball, or joystick.

pointer grabbing

A client can actively *grab* control of the pointer, causing button and motion events to be sent to that client rather than to the client the pointer indicates.

pointing device

A *pointing device* is typically a mouse or tablet, or some other device with effective two-dimensional motion, that usually has buttons. There is only one visible cursor defined by the core protocol, and it tracks whatever pointing device is currently attached as the pointer.

popup   A *popup* is a widget outside the normal parental hierarchy of geometry management. It is a child window of the root window that is popped up temporarily to give the user a piece of information, or to get some information from the user.

post-order traversal

When a tree structure is subject to *post-order traversal*, its root is visited last; for example, a function might process the left descendant, the right descendant, and then the root.

pre-order traversal

When a tree structure is subject to *pre-order traversal*, its root is visited first; for example, a function might process the root, and then the left and right descendant.

private header file

A *private header file* contains the internal class definitions of a widget. For example, the Label widget's internal class definitions are contained in the private header file *LabelP.h*. This file is included only in the widget *.c* file of this class and any subclasses, never in the application.

property

Windows may have associated *properties*, each consisting of a name, a type, a data format, and some data. The protocol places no interpretation on properties; they are intended as a general-purpose data storage and intercommunication mechanism for clients. There is, however, a list of predefined properties and property types so that clients might share information such as resize hints, program names, and icon formats with a window manager via properties. In order to avoid passing arbitrary-length property-name strings, each property name is associated with a corresponding integer value known as an atom. See also *atom*.

PseudoColor

PseudoColor is a visual class in which a pixel value indexes the colormap entry to produce independent red, green, and blue values. That is, the colormap is viewed as an array of triples (*RGB values*). The RGB values can be changed dynamically.

public header file

A *public header file* contains the declarations (e.g., class widget pointer) necessary to use a widget. For example, `labelWidgetClass` declarations are contained in the public header file *label.h*. This header file is included in the widget *.c* file and in the application source file.

quark A *quark* is an integer ID that identifies a string. In the context of Xt, this string is usually a name, class, or type string for the resource manager. Like atoms and resource IDs, quarks eliminate the need to pass strings of arbitrary length over the network. The quark type is `XrmQuark`, and the types `XrmName`, `XrmClass`, and `XrmRepresentation` are also defined to be `XrmQuark`.

query geometry method
Parents call `XtQueryGeometry` to invoke the child's *query geometry method* to find out a child's preferred geometry. This method is part of the Core widget class.

raise Changing the stacking order of a window so as to occlude all sibling windows is to *raise* that window.

real estate
The window management style characterized by the input being sent to whichever window the pointer is in is called *real-estate-driven*. This is the most common style of input management used in X.

realize method
The *realize method* creates a window on the display and is part of the Core widget class.

rectangle
A *rectangle* specified by [x,y,w,h] has an (infinitely thin) outline path with corners at [x,y], [x+w,y], [x+w,y+h], and [x,y+h]. When a rectangle is filled, the lower-right edges are not drawn. For example, if w=h=0, nothing would be drawn when drawing the rectangle, but a single pixel when filling it. For w=h=1, a single pixel would be drawn when drawing the rectangle, four pixels when filling it.

redirect Window managers (or other clients) may wish to enforce window layout policy in various ways. When a client attempts to change the size or position of a window, or to map one, the operation may be *redirected* to the window manager, rather than actually being performed. Then the window manager (or other client that redirected the input) is expected to decide whether to allow, modify, or deny the requested operation before making the call itself. See also *window manager*.

reparenting
The window manager often *reparents* the top-level windows of each application in order to add a title bar and perhaps resize boxes. In other words, a window with a title bar is inserted between the root window and each top-level window. See also *save-set*.

reply   Information requested from the server by a client is sent back to the client in a *reply*. Both events and replies are multiplexed on the same connection with the requests. Requests that require replies are known as round-trip requests, and, if possible, should be avoided since they introduce network delays. Most requests do not generate replies. Some requests generate multiple replies. Xt caches frequently-used data on the client side of the connection in order to minimize the need for round-trip requests. See Volume Zero, *X Protocol Reference Manual*, for a detailed discussion of the X Protocol.

representation type

A symbolic constant beginning with *XtR*, which is defined in *<X11/StringDefs.h>* or an application or widget header file, and which is used to define the data type of a resource. Xt automatically converts between resource settings, which are strings, and various representation types.

request   A command to the server is called a *request*. It is a single block of data sent over the connection to the server. See Volume Zero, *X Protocol Reference Manual*, for a detailed discussion of the X Protocol.

resize method

The *resize method* of a widget is called when the widget's parent has changed its size. This method is part of the Core widget class. In composite widgets, this method calculates a new layout for the children. In simple widgets, this method recalculates instance variables so that the `expose` method can redraw the widget properly.

resource

1) A widget or application variable whose value can be set by the user or application programmer via the *Resource Manager*.
2) In the X Protocol and server documentation, windows, pixmaps, cursors, fonts, graphics contexts, and colormaps are known as *resources*. They all have unique identifiers (IDs) associated with them for naming purposes.

resource database

The *resource database* is the collection of possible places where resource specifications can be made. The most important of these are the *app-defaults file*, where the programmer specifies resource defaults, the RESOURCE_MANAGER server *property*, which the user can set with *xrdb*, and the *.Xdefaults* file in the user's home directory, where he or she specifies local resource preferences.

Resource Manager

The *Resource Manager* is a part of Xlib that merges a database consisting of several ASCII files, a server property, and values hardcoded by the application, and determines a unique value for each resource of each widget. It resolves conflicts between multiple settings for the same resource according to its internal precedence rules, and provides the widget or application with the resulting value.

resource setting

A *resource setting* is the actual value of a resource variable.

resource specification

A *resource specification* describes a "pathname" to a widget resource, using widget class and/or instance names, resource class or instance names, and optional wildcards. For example, the resource specification:

```
xbox.box.quit.label: Quit
```

specifies that the label resource of the quit widget, which is contained in the box widget in the *xbox* application, should be set to "Quit." The specification:

```
*Command.background: blue
```

which uses wildcards and widget classes, specifies that the background (color) resource of all Command widgets in any application should be set to "blue." It is up to the Resource Manager to resolve differences between resource specifications, which may have varying levels of specificity in the various locations that make up the resource database.

RGB values

See *colorcell*.

root

The *root* of a window, pixmap, or graphics context (GC) is the same as the root window of whatever drawable was specified in the call to create the window, pixmap, or GC. These resources can be used only on the screen indicated by this window. See *root window*.

root window

Each screen has a *root window* covering it. It cannot be reconfigured or unmapped, but otherwise acts as a full-fledged window. A root window has no parent.

round-trip request

A request to the server that generates a reply is known as a *round-trip request*. See *reply*.

save-set

The *save-set* of a client is a list of other clients' windows which, if they are inferiors of one of the client's windows at connection close, should not be destroyed, and which should be reparented and remapped if the client is unmapped. Save-sets are typically used by window managers to avoid lost windows if the manager should terminate abnormally. See *reparenting* for more background information.

scan line

A *scan line* is a list of pixel or bit values viewed as a horizontal row (all values having the same y coordinate) of an image, with the values ordered by increasing x coordinate values.

scan line order

An image represented in *scan line order* contains scan lines ordered by increasing y coordinate values.

screen A *screen* may not have physically independent monitors. For instance, it is possible to treat a color monitor as if it were two screens, one color and the other black and white or to have two separate color and monochrome screens controlled by one server. There is only a single keyboard and pointer shared among the screens. A `Screen` structure contains the information about each screen and the list is a member of the `Display` structure.

scrollbar
A *scrollbar* is an area on a window that allows a user to view different portions of a window's information by scrolling, or moving.

selection
Selections are a means of communication between clients using properties and events. From the user's perspective, a selection is an item of data which can be highlighted in one instance of an application and pasted into another instance of the same or a different application. The client that highlights the data is the owner, and the client into which the data is pasted is the requestor. Properties are used to store the selection data and the type of the data, while events are used to synchronize the transaction and to allow the requestor to indicate the type it prefers for the data and to allow the owner to convert the data to the indicated type if possible.

server The *server* provides the basic windowing mechanism. It handles IPC connections from clients, demultiplexes graphics requests onto the screens, and multiplexes input back to the appropriate clients. It controls a single keyboard and pointer and one or more screens that make up a single display.

server grabbing
The *server* can be *grabbed* by a single client for exclusive use. This prevents processing of any requests from other client connections until the grab is complete. This is typically a transient state for such tasks as rubber-banding, or to execute requests indivisibly.

set_values method
The Intrinsics invoke a widget's *set_values method* when one of the widget's resource values is changed. This method should return TRUE or FALSE to indicate whether the widget's `expose` method should be invoked.

set_values_almost method
The *set_values_almost method* is invoked when a parent rejects a widget's geometry request, but the parent sends back a compromise. This method is part of the Core widget class.

set_values_hook method
A widget can provide a *set_values_hook method* to allow the application to set resources of subparts.

sibling Children of the same parent window are known as *sibling* windows.

spring-loaded popup
When a button press triggers a popup, the popup is called a *spring-loaded popup*.

stacking order

Sibling windows may stack on top of each other, obscuring lower windows. This is similar to papers on a desk. The relationship between sibling windows is known as the *stacking order*. The first window in the stacking order is the window on top.

StaticColor

The *StaticColor* visual class represents a multiplane color screen with a predefined and read-only hardware colormap. It can be viewed as a degenerate case of `PseudoColor`. See *PseudoColor*.

StaticGray

The *StaticGray* visual class represents a multiplane monochrome screen with a predefined and read-only hardware colormap. It can be viewed as a degenerate case of `GrayScale`, in which the gray values are predefined and read-only. Typically, the values are linearly increasing ramps. See *GrayScale*.

stipple

A *stipple* is a single plane pixmap that is used to tile a region. Bits set to 1 in the stipple are drawn with a foreground pixel value; bits set to 0, with a background pixel value. The stipple and both pixel values are members of the GC.

status

Many Xlib functions return a *status* of TRUE or FALSE. If the function does not succeed, its return arguments are not disturbed.

subclass

A widget *subclass* has its own features plus many of the features of its superclasses. For example, since Composite is a subclass of Core, Composite has all the fields in Core plus its own unique fields. A subclass can inherit or replace most superclass features.

superclass

One widget is a *superclass* of a second widget when the second widget includes the first, or the Core widget is a *superclass* of the Composite widget because the Composite widget's definition depends on, or includes, the Core widget.

tight binding

A *tight binding* refers to the use of a dot (.) in a *resource specification* to indicate that the widget class or instance on the right side of the dot is a child of the widget whose class or instance name is on the left side of it.

tile

A pixmap can be replicated in two dimensions to *tile* a region. The pixmap itself is also known as a *tile*.

time

A *time* value in X is expressed in milliseconds, typically since the last server reset. Time values wrap around (after about 49.7 days). One time value, represented by the constant `CurrentTime`, is used by clients to represent the current server time.

top-level window

A child of the root window is referred to as a *top-level window*.

translation

A *translation* maps an event or event sequence into an action name. Once a translation is installed in a widget, the named action function will be invoked when the specified event sequence occurs in the widget. Translations are specified as ASCII strings.

translation table

A *translation table* lists one or more translations.

TrueColor

The *TrueColor* visual class represents a high-performance multiplane display with predefined and read-only RGB values in its hardware colormap. It can be viewed as a degenerate case of DirectColor, in which the subfields in the pixel value directly encode the corresponding RGB values. Typically, the values are linearly increasing ramps. See *DirectColor*.

type property

A *type property* is used to identify the interpretation of property data. Types are completely uninterpreted by the server; they are solely for the benefit of clients.

viewable

A window is *viewable* if it and all of its ancestors are mapped. This does not imply that any portion of the window is actually visible, since it may be obscured by other windows.

visible   A region of a window is *visible* if someone looking at the screen can actually see it; that is, the window is viewable and the region is not obscured by any other window.

visual   The specifications for color handling for a window, including visual class, depth, RGB/pixel, etc., are collectively referred to as a *visual*, and are stored in a structure of type Visual.

visual class

Visual class refers to DirectColor, GrayScale, PseudoColor, StaticColor, StaticGray, or TrueColor. It is a definition of the colormap type but not its depth.

widget   The basic object in a toolkit, a *widget* includes both code and data, and can therefore serve as an input or output object.

window gravity

When windows are resized, subwindows may be repositioned automatically by the server, relative to an edge, corner, or center of the window. This attraction of a subwindow to some part of its parent is known as *window gravity*. Window gravity is a window attribute. See also *bit gravity*.

window manager

The user manipulates windows on the screen using a *window manager* client. The window manager has authority over the arrangement of windows on the screen, and the user interface for selecting which window receives input. See also *redirect*.

XYPixmap

> The data for an image is said to be in *XYPixmap* format if it is organized as a set of bitmaps representing individual bit planes. This applies only to the server's internal data format for images. It does not affect normal programming with pixmaps.

ZPixmap

> The data for an image is said to be in *ZPixmap* format if it is organized as a set of pixel values in scan line order. This applies only to the server's internal data format for images. It does not affect normal programming with pixmaps.

zoomed window

> Some applications have not only a normal size for their top-level window and an icon, but also a *zoomed window* size. This could be used in a painting program (similar to the MacPaint fat bits). The zoomed window size preferences can be specified in the window manager hints.

Master Index

The master index provides a thorough, combined index to Volume Four (Motif Edition) and Volume Five, making it easy to look up all appropriate references to a topic in either volume. Note, however, that Volume Five's master index is based on the Athena version of Volume Four (the generic edition) instead of the Motif edition of Volume Four (this book). As a result, you should use the master index in this volume when you want to look up Motif-specific information.

You will find main entries in boldface type. Page numbers are marked with a volume number to indicate which book the pages refer to. Page numbers preceded by a "IV" refer to Volume Four, X Toolkit Intrinsics Programming Manual, Motif Edition. Those that are preceded by a "V" refer to Volume Five, X Toolkit Intrinsics Reference Manual.

Master Index

Master Index

C

caching, old size, IV:230
  resource, IV:318
  standard atoms, IV:365
  Xmu; initializing, IV:365
  XtCacheAll constant, V:638
  XtCacheByDisplay constant, V:638
  XtCacheNone constant, V:638
  XtCacheRefCount constant, V:638
callbacks, V:376-377, 413
  about, IV:30, 34, 44-45, 587; V:638
  adding, IV:46-48;
    more than one, IV:91;
    to callback list, V:67-68;
    to callback resource, V:65-66
  arguments to, IV:48, 89
  as resources, IV:44
  callback list, IV:90;
    deleting method, V:296-297;
    determining status, V:213;
    executive methods, V:133;
    popping down widget, V:128-129;
    popping up widget, V:124-127;
    XtCallbackExclusive, V:124-125;
    XtCallbackNone, V:126;
    XtCallbackNonexclusive, V:127;
    XtCallbackPopdown, V:128-129;
    XtCallCallbacks, V:133;
    XtHasCallbacks, V:213;
    XtRemoveCallback, V:296;
    XtRemoveCallbacks, V:297
  contrasted with actions, IV:133
  format, IV:48
  naming conventions, IV:48
  passing data, IV:87-89
  procedure, V:376-377
  reasons, IV:30-31
  structure, IV:89
  XtAddCallback, V:65-66
  (see also XtCallbackProc; XtTimerCallback-
    Proc.)
Caption widget, IV:483
cascading popups, about, IV:413, 415, 431-436
  example, IV:432-433
case converter, IV:251
  XtRegisterCaseConverter, V:290
chained methods, (see inheritance)
change_managed method, IV:374-376,
    388-389
  in constraint widgets, IV:407

CheckBox widget, IV:155
CirculateNotify event, V:654
CirculateRequest event, V:655
class, about, IV:22, 587
  class_initialize method, IV:203, 317, 396, 451,
    470
  class_part_initialize method, IV:203, 396, 399,
    451
  extension stucture, IV:469
  hierarchy, IV:185;
    Athena widgets, IV:203;
    gadgets, IV:443-445;
    (see also widgets.)
  name; defined in Core class part, IV:199;
    matching widgets, IV:66
  part, IV:186;
    combining into class record, IV:186
  record, IV:185;
    allocating storage, IV:189;
    BitmapEdit widget, IV:186-187;
    contents, IV:185
  structure, IV:185-211;
    adding resource list to, IV:194
client, about, IV:7, 588
  client-server model, IV:7
ClientMessage event, V:656-657
clipboard functions, IV:369-370
clipping region, IV:588
color, IV:56, 125, 206-207, 312-313, 338
  determining available, IV:504
  displaying, IV:504
  false, IV:339
  hexadecimal specification, IV:502
  names, IV:501
  RGB model, IV:503
  specifying, IV:501
colorcell, IV:504
  about, IV:588
  read-only, IV:505
  read/write, IV:505
  shared, IV:505
  (see also colormap.)
colormap, about, IV:55, 504, 588
  installing, IV:339
  virtual, IV:338
  window attribute, IV:206, 340
ColormapNotify event, V:658
command, command buttons, IV:478, 480, 490;
    V:524-527
  command line; compiling, IV:39;
    options (see options)

Master Index

widget_size, IV:199;
xrm_class, IV:199;
  (see also methods, set_values_hook.)
hidden superclasses, IV:205
in Template widget, V:579
instance record; height field, IV:377;
  width field, IV:377
methods, V:442
resources, IV:54
superclasses, IV:443
(see also methods.)
counter incrementing, inside XtSetArg, IV:53
CreateNotify event, V:663-664
Ctrl key, IV:248
(see also modifiers.)
cursor, about, IV:206, 311, 589
hotspot, IV:593
window attribute, IV:206
cut and paste, (see selections)

D

data, data transfer completion method, V:412
data types, V:631;
  implementation-specific, IV:529
database; obtaining for display, V:159
(see also XtDatabase.)
DECnet, IV:345
decoration, IV:35, 342
default, character set, IV:164
multiple click timing, IV:253
size, IV:230
delete_child method, IV:374
depth, IV:55, 219, 589
descendants, IV:589
destroy method, IV:204, 215, 233-234
about, IV:233
Constraint, IV:398
example from BitmapEdit, IV:234
DestroyNotify event, V:665
destructors, IV:318
details in translations, (see translations)
device, IV:590
dialog boxes, IV:441
creating, IV:81
Dialog widget, IV:410; V:528-530
different kinds of, IV:159
DirectColor, IV:590
directories, font, IV:506
display, about, IV:7, 590

adding; XtOpenDisplay, V:266-267
closing, V:139
connecting to multiple displays, IV:468
depth, IV:504
display_accelerator method, IV:264
initializing, V:168-169
lists, IV:221
option (–display), IV:99
pointer; returning for widget, V:167
XtCloseDisplay, V:139
(see also XtDisplayInitialize.)
DISPLAY environment variable, IV:55
distributed processing, IV:8
DoesBackingStore Xlib macro, IV:206
DoesSaveUnders Xlib macro, IV:206
double clicks, IV:252-253
downward chaining, IV:201
drawing, about, IV:124-125, 188, 199-202, 215,
  221-224
after Expose event, IV:203
bitmap cells, IV:209
coordinate system, IV:5
due to set_values method changes, IV:226
in expose method, IV:216
into Core widget, IV:121
into DrawingArea widget, IV:123
window attributes, IV:205-206
DrawingArea widget, IV:120, 129, 497
drawing from application, IV:123
updating, IV:124
DrawnButton widget, IV:156

E

encapsulation, IV:33, 590
enter/leave compression, IV:289
EnterNotify event, IV:246-247, 289, 422;
  V:666-671
EnterWindow event, IV:269
environment variables, DISPLAY, IV:55
XAPPLRESDIR, IV:300
XENVIRONMENT, IV:300
error database, V:96-98, 185-186
error handling, IV:107, 455-458
and application contexts, IV:458
calling fatal error handler, V:93-94, 173-175
error resource database, IV:457;
  obtaining, V:95;
  XtAppGetErrorDatabase, V:95;
  XtAppGetErrorDatabaseText, V:96-98;

Master Index

X Toolkit Intrinsics Programming Manual, Motif Edition

in gadgets, IV:443

input events; XtRemoveInput, V:301

KeymapNotify, V:683

KeyPress, IV:247, 462; V:684-686

KeyRelease, IV:244, 247; V:684-686

LeaveNotify, IV:246-247, 289, 422; V:666-671

list of types and structure names, IV:276-277

MapNotify, V:687-688

MappingNotify, V:689-690

MapRequest, V:691

mocking up from action, IV:222

MotionNotify, IV:247, 253, 269, 289, 422; V:692-694

NoExpose, IV:243; V:680-681

nonmaskable, IV:241, 259, 271-273, 595; example of handlers, IV:241, 259, 271

processing, V:243

processing one event; XtProcessEvent, V:283

propagation, IV:259

PropertyNotify, V:695

ReparentNotify, V:696

ResizeRequest, V:697

returning next event, V:103, 262

selecting, IV:259

SelectionClear, IV:345, 355; V:698

SelectionNotify, IV:345, 356, 360; V:699

SelectionRequest, IV:345-346, 356; V:700

structures, V:650

translation table abbreviations, IV:242-243

UnmapNotify, V:687-688

using inside actions or event handlers, IV:274-275; V:375

VisibilityNotify, IV:200, 243; V:701-702

XEvent; example, IV:275; V:375; union, V:649

XtAppNextEvent, V:103

XtAppPending, V:106, 278

(see also expose.)

expo.lcs.mit.edu, IV:39

expose, Expose events, IV:27, 215, 223, 422; V:72, 672-673

exposure, IV:12; compression, IV:223, 289; XtAddExposureToRegion, V:72; (see also events, Expose.)

method, IV:201, 215, 221-224, 273; example from BitmapEdit, IV:222; in gadgets, IV:443, 447, 449

extensions, about, IV:13, 591

structures, IV:451, 469

F

fallback resources, IV:304, 526

File menu, creating, IV:78-79

example, IV:80

files, character limit in filenames, IV:184

file events; (see event handlers)

file input, IV:278-280; registering file, V:75, 86-87; source masks, IV:278; XtAddInput, V:75; XtAppAddInput, V:86-87

using names in resources, IV:311

FileSelectionBox widget, IV:152

floating point numbers, IV:312

FocusIn event, IV:246, 269; V:674-679

FocusOut event, IV:246, 269; V:674-679

fonts, about, IV:591

aliasing, IV:510

creating databases (mkfontdir), IV:512

directories, IV:506

display (xfd), IV:506

families, IV:506, 509

font conventions, IV:xxx; V:x;

font lists, IV:164

font option (–font), IV:98-99

fonts.dir files, IV:511

foreign language, IV:162-169

naming convention, IV:507

printer, IV:506

represented by compound strings, IV:162-169

screen, IV:506

specifying, IV:312, 501

using filename as alias, IV:511

wildcarding, IV:508

foreground, about, IV:591

option (–foreground, –fg), IV:99

Form widget, IV:158, 392-409, 494; V:531-534

about, IV:71-73, 483, 494

adding children, V:533

child resources, V:532

creating, V:533

deleting children, V:533

destroying, V:533

example, IV:494

layout method, IV:397

resources, V:531-532

Frame widget, IV:74, 158, 378

ftp, IV:39

GraphicsExpose event, IV:273; V:72, 680-681
gravity, IV:592
GravityNotify event, V:682
GrayScale, IV:592
Grip widget, V:535-537

H

hardcoding, resources, IV:43, 103, 106
  translations, IV:136
header files, IV:34, 51, 56, 184, 279, 443, 518
  not included twice, IV:187
  private, IV:597
  public, IV:597
height, IV:377
  checking in initialize method, IV:216
help, Help button; creating, IV:79-85
  Help dialogue box; creating, IV:79-85
  help text, IV:85
hexadecimal color specification, IV:502
hints, about, IV:332-344, 592
  icon position, IV:335
  position, IV:59
  size, IV:335-336
  size increment, IV:336
hooks, IV:464; V:205, 329
host access list, IV:592
Hyper key, IV:248
  (see also modifiers.)

I

ICCCM, IV:12, 331, 354, 357, 363-367
icon, creating pixmap, IV:340-341
  iconic option, (–iconic), IV:99
  popups, IV:334
  setting; name, IV:340;
    pixmap, IV:331, 340
  size and position, IV:514
  starting application as, IV:335
identifier, IV:593
ifndef statement, IV:187
image caching, IV:169-171
implementation file, (see widget)
include files, IV:34, 51, 56, 184, 187
  in widget implementation, IV:190
incremental selections, IV:367
inferiors, IV:593
inheritance, about, IV:23, 49, 57, 197-207, 593

adding features to superclass, IV:207
  among Motif widgets, IV:23, 473
  among OPEN LOOK widgets, IV:473, 479
  in widget class and instance record,
    IV:185-186
  of chained methods, IV:201
  of conflicting methods, IV:207
  of Core resources, IV:54, 56
  of self-contained methods, IV:201
  of superclass method, IV:204
  resources, IV:191, 193-194
  styles, IV:200-202
  using XtInherit constants, IV:201
  widget not using resource value, IV:59
initial size, IV:377
initialize method, IV:215-221, 357, 384, 535
  about, IV:216
  Constraint, IV:398
  creating GCs in, IV:219
  example from BitmapEdit, IV:218
initialize_hook method, IV:325
input, focus, IV:593
  from file, IV:278-280
  from pipe, IV:280-281
  input events method, V:397-398
  InputOnly window, IV:593
  InputOutput window, IV:202, 593
  manager, IV:593
  queue; determining events, V:106, 278;
    examining head, V:104-105, 277;
    XtAppNextEvent, V:103;
    XtAppPeekEvent, V:104-105;
    XtAppPending, V:106, 278;
    XtPeekEvent, V:277
  source masks, IV:278
insert_child method, IV:374
insert_position, V:407
instance, about, IV:22, 593
  record, IV:185;
    adding variables to, IV:188;
    allocating storage, IV:189;
    BitmapEdit widget, IV:187-188;
    contents, IV:185
  structures, IV:185-211, 216;
    constraints in, IV:395
Inter-Client Communication Conventions
    Manual, (see ICCCM)
Intrinsics, IV:190
  about, IV:10, 594
  Intrinsic.h header file, IV:34
  IntrinsicP.h header file, IV:190

introduction to classes, V:423-428
selection timeout, V:112

J

JumpProc, V:560

K

key events, (see events or translations)
key translation, registering, V:319
  XtKeyProc, V:402-404
  XtSetKeyTranslator, V:319
keyboard, keyboard focus, IV:337;
  about, IV:337, 461;
  accept/reject method, IV:387;
  in Motif widgets, IV:173-174;
  redirecting input, V:317-318;
  setting, IV:337;
  styles, IV:337, 594;
  (see also accept_focus; XmNinput resource;
    XtSetKeyboardFocus.)
  keyboard grabbing; (see grabs)
  keyboard shortcuts; (see accelerators)
keycodes, about, IV:244, 462, 594
  translating; keycode-to-keysym, V:339-342;
    XtTranslateKey, V:339-340;
    XtTranslateKeycode, V:341-342
KeymapNotify event, V:683
KeyPress event, IV:247; V:684-686
KeyRelease event, IV:247; V:684-686
keysyms, about, IV:244, 462, 594
  converting case, IV:251; V:379-380
  determining case, V:147
  key generated, IV:249
  keysymdef.h header file, IV:245, 248
  naming conventions, IV:245
  XtCaseProc, V:379-380
  XtConvertCase, V:147

L

Label widget, IV:25, 32, 119, 228, 375, 422,
  518
  about, V:538-540
  creating, V:540
  destroying, V:540
  Label.h file, IV:34

resources, V:538-540
labels, setting, IV:50
LANG environment variable, IV:303
language, portability, IV:49
  string, IV:525
layout Form method, IV:397
LeaveNotify event, IV:246-247, 289, 422;
  V:666-671
LeaveWindow event, IV:269, 430, 434
libraries, Xext, IV:13
  Xlib, IV:39
  Xm, IV:39
  Xt, IV:39
lint, IV:48, 105
List widget, IV:158, 269, 490
  about, V:541-545
  creating, V:543
  destroying, V:543
  resources, V:541-543
loose bindings, IV:299, 594

M

macros, IV:459-460
main loop, IV:34, 38
  customizing example, IV:288
  internals, IV:288
  XtAppMainLoop, V:102
  XtMainLoop, V:243
MainWindow widget, IV:74-85, 158, 378
  creation example, IV:77
Manager widget, IV:25
MapNotify event, V:687-688
mapping, IV:243
MappingNotify event, V:689-690
MapRequest event, V:691
  about, IV:56, 594
  XtMapWidget, V:252
  XtPopdown, V:279
  XtPopup, V:280-281
  (see also MappingNotify event; widgets, map-
    ping.)
mechanism without policy, IV:11, 331
memory allocation, IV:463
  for widget instance record, IV:199
MenuButton widget, V:546-549
  creating, V:549
  destroying, V:549
  resources, V:546-547
menus, about, IV:38, 413-451, 482

accelerators in, IV:435, 440
cascaded, IV:415, 431-436
menu items, IV:80
menu pane, IV:80
menubar, IV:74
panes, IV:66
pointer grabbing, IV:420, 422
popping down, IV:420, 427, 435
popping up, IV:426
popping up with callbacks, IV:428
pulldown, IV:415, 428-430;
  example, IV:429-430
SimpleMenu widget, example, IV:436, 438
spring-loaded, IV:415, 420
XtMenuPopdown, IV:421; V:253
XtMenuPopup, IV:421; V:254-255
messages, about, IV:33, 595
OOP vs. Xt, IV:33
Meta key, IV:248
methods, about, IV:202-204, 595
accept_focus, IV:203, 461;
  about, IV:585
and instance structure, IV:185
change_managed, IV:374-376, 388, 407;
  about, IV:587;
  in constraint widgets, IV:407
class_initialize, IV:203, 317, 451;
  about, IV:588
class_part_initialize, IV:203
Constraint; destroy, IV:398; V:437;
  initialize, IV:398-399;
  resizing, IV:404
declarations in widget implementation file,
  IV:196-197
delete_child, IV:374, 391-392;
  about, IV:589
destroy, IV:204, 215, 233-234, 398;
  about, IV:590;
  example, IV:233-234
display_accelerator, IV:264
drawing; due to changes in set_values, IV:226;
  in expose, IV:216
expose, IV:33, 203, 215-216, 221-224, 273,
  443, 447-449, 591;
  XtExposeProc, V:438
Form layout, IV:397
gadget; expose, IV:447;
  query_geometry, IV:447;
  set_values_almost, IV:447
geometry_manager, IV:374-375, 381, 400
get_values_hook, IV:204, 325, 533;

about, IV:592;
  example, IV:326
in OOP, IV:33
inheritance; adding to superclass, IV:207;
  of superclass, IV:204
initialize, IV:202, 215-221, 216, 398;
  about, IV:593;
  calling XInternAtom, IV:215-221, 384;
  example, IV:216, 218;
  in constraint widget, IV:398
initialize_hook, IV:202, 325;
  about, IV:593
insert_child, IV:374;
  about, IV:593
insert_position, IV:391-392
not known to Xt, IV:397
query_geometry, IV:204, 215, 230-233, 375;
  about, IV:215, 230-233, 374, 598;
  in constraint widget, IV:385, 408;
  in gadgets, IV:408, 447
realize, IV:203, 336, 379, 384;
  about, IV:598
reconciliation, IV:207
resize, IV:203, 215, 227-230, 374, 378, 404;
  about, IV:599;
  in composite widget, IV:384-385;
  in constraint widget, IV:405-406;
  in gadget parent, IV:450
resources and set_values, IV:225-227
set_values, IV:203, 215-216, 225-227, 379,
  381, 384, 406;
  about, IV:601;
  redrawing, V:434
set_values_almost, IV:203, 381, 390-391;
  about, IV:601;
  in gadgets, IV:447
set_values_hook, IV:203, 325, 327;
  about, IV:601
vs. actions, IV:33
minimal useful size, IV:386
mkfontdir, IV:512
mnemonics, IV:263
Mod keys, IV:248
(see also modifiers.)
modal cascade, IV:416
modal popups, IV:416
modifiers, !, IV:251
adding, IV:249
and event sequences, IV:253
case-specifics, IV:251
colon, IV:251-252

displaying list, IV:249
for button events, IV:254
keys, IV:247-252, 595; V:712-719
matching exactly, IV:251
negating, IV:250
None, IV:251
monochrome, IV:595
Motif, application's look and feel, IV:488
popup widgets, IV:496
version 1.0 vs. 1.1, IV:413
Motif widgets, IV:39, 68-69, 71, 487-497
about, IV:21
command, IV:490
DrawingArea, IV:497
inheritance among, IV:23
Text, IV:497
(see also Form widget; Label widget;
PanedWindow widget; PushButton widget;
RowColumn widget; Scrollbar widget.)
_MOTIF_WM_HINTS, IV:344
_MOTIF_WM_INFO, IV:344
_MOTIF_WM_MESSAGES, IV:343
motion compression, IV:289
MotionNotify event, IV:247, 269, 289, 422;
V:692-694
multiple, click timing, IV:253
toplevel shells, IV:468
mwm, interclient communication, IV:342
keyboard focus in, IV:338
.mwmrc file, IV:331, 343
use of input hint, IV:337

N

name option (–name), IV:99
naming conventions, for widgets, IV:517
newlines, in translations, IV:240
NoExpose event, V:680-681
nonfatal error, IV:243
registering method, V:115
registering procedure, V:331, 333
(see also error handling; errors.)
nonmaskable events, (see events)
non-widget objects, V:423
notify method, IV:451
notify modes, (see translations)

O

objects, V:443-446
about, IV:32, 595
in R4, IV:541-545
Object class, IV:444; V:423
objectClass, V:444
ObjectClassPart, V:443
ObjectClassRec, V:444
object-oriented programming, IV:xxvi, 32-33,
273, 595
ObjectPart, V:444
ObjectRec, V:445
(see also gadgets.)
obscure, IV:595
occlude, IV:595
OOP, (see objects, object-oriented programming)
OPEN LOOK, application's look and feel,
IV:477
popup widgets, IV:485
OPEN LOOK widgets, IV:477-487
command, IV:478-480
text, IV:487
optimization, IV:138, 230, 466
options, abbreviating, IV:98
argument styles, IV:101
–background, IV:98-99, 501
–border, IV:99, 501
–bordercolor, IV:99
–borderwidth, IV:99
command line, IV:97;
styles, IV:101
custom, IV:301
defining your own, IV:99
–display, IV:99
–font, IV:99
–foreground, IV:99, 501
–geometry, IV:336, 512-514
handling errors in, IV:103
–iconic, IV:99, 335
options table example, IV:101
overriding standard, IV:102
–rv/+rv, IV:99
–selectionTimeout, IV:99
standard, IV:98
–synchronous, IV:99
–title, IV:99
–xrm, IV:98, 301
OR operator, V:71, 120, 298, 302
OverrideShell widget, IV:78, 334; V:447,
452-460

overriding, redirect, IV:334;
  window attribute, IV:206
  standard options, IV:102
  translations, IV:135-136

P

padding, IV:596
Paned widget, about, IV:70; V:550-556
  adding pane, V:554
  child resources, V:552
  deleting pane, V:554
  destroying, V:556
  functions, V:555
PanedWindow widget, IV:69, 158
parent, about, IV:596
  window, IV:596
parsing, command-line arguments, IV:99-103
  translations, IV:136
part (vs. record), IV:186
passive grab, IV:420
path resources, IV:301
pipe input, IV:280-281
pixel values, about, IV:125, 596
pixmap, about, IV:56, 222, 596
  built-in, IV:170
  freeing, IV:233
  icon, IV:340
  XYPixmap format, IV:603
  ZPixmap format, IV:604
plane, IV:596
  (see also bit, bit plane.)
plane mask, IV:596
pointer, IV:420
  about, IV:4, 596
  dereferencing, IV:589
  device, IV:596
  events (see events or translations)
  grabbing, IV:596
  (see also grabs.)
popup menus, example, IV:422, 425-426
popup widgets, IV:475
  Motif, IV:496
  OPEN LOOK, IV:485
popups, about, IV:19, 78, 597
  cascading, IV:413
  creating, IV:79, 81; V:151-153;
    before popping up, IV:85;
    in work procedure, IV:287; V:420
  example, IV:84

  from callback function, IV:85
  linking group, IV:334
  mapping, V:280-281
  menus, IV:413
  menus, spring-loaded using Box widget,
    IV:422, 425-427
  modal, IV:416;
    about, IV:595
  modeless, IV:416;
    about, IV:595
  OverrideShell, IV:334
  sensitivity, IV:441
  spring-loaded, IV:416, 601
  unmapping, V:279
  when application is iconified, IV:334
  (see also XtCreatePopupShell.)
portability, IV:106, 278, 446, 462, 465-466
position, about, IV:59, 312
  hints, IV:335
  relative to root window, IV:342
  setting with resources, IV:58
PRIMARY selection, IV:346
Primitive widget, IV:25, 120
  PrimitiveClassPart, IV:187
  PrimitivePart, IV:187
printer fonts, (see fonts)
private header file, BitmapEdiP.h, IV:185-189
private instance variables, IV:188
process input, XtAppMainLoop, V:102
program structure, IV:34
properties, about, IV:345, 597
  and atoms, IV:354
PropertyNotify event, V:695
protocol, _MOTIF_WM_MESSAGES atom,
  IV:343
  network, IV:6
  WM_DELETE_WINDOW atom, IV:343
  WM_PROTOCOLS atom, IV:343
  WM_SAVE_YOURSELF atom, IV:343
  WM_TAKE_FOCUS atom, IV:343
Protocols.h header file, IV:342
PseudoColor, IV:597
public, functions, IV:114, 118, 208
  header file, IV:34, 448;
    BitmapEdit.h, IV:184, 207-209
  instance variables (see resources)
  routines, IV:408
pulldown menu, IV:415, 428
  creating, IV:79
  example, IV:430
  vs. spring-loaded, IV:416

Master Index

push buttons, IV:17
PushButton widget, IV:17, 25, 44-48, 66, 68, 134
PushButtonGadget, IV:66
  example using, IV:118

Q

quarks, IV:324, 597
query_geometry method, IV:204, 230-233, 447
  about, IV:230
  example from BitmapEdit, IV:233
  gadgets, IV:408, 447

R

RadioBox widget, IV:155
raise, IV:598
raw event handlers, IV:274; V:76-77
  (see also events.)
realization, IV:38, 222, 226
realize method, IV:201, 204, 206, 336, 384, 535
RealizeProc, V:438
reason, in callbacks, IV:30
rectangle, IV:598
RectObj, IV:205, 443-447, 541-543; V:423, 448-451
redrawing windows, IV:27, 221
regions, IV:223, 449; V:72
registering, actions (see actions)
  callbacks, V:65-68
  converters, IV:316-321; V:69, 83-85, 290
  event handlers, IV:271-273; V:70-71
  fatal error handlers, IV:203, 455-458; V:109-110, 314
  file, V:75, 86-87
  nonfatal error handlers, IV:455-458; V:114-115, 316, 331, 333
  raw event handler, V:76-77
  work procedure, V:79, 89
Release 4 (R4), IV:246, 413, 415, 442, 469
  compared to R3, IV:521-548
removing, callbacks, V:295-297
  grabs, V:300
  input, V:301
  raw event handlers, V:302-303
  timeouts, V:304
reparenting, IV:342, 430, 598
  (see also window manager.)

ReparentNotify event, V:696
reply, IV:598
representation types, IV:92, 94
  about, IV:293, 296, 599
  new in R4, IV:537
ResizeRequest event, V:697
resizing, IV:374
  about, IV:67, 215, 227-230, 373, 379
  caching old size, IV:230
  resize method, IV:215, 227-230, 227, 374;
    example from BitmapEdit, IV:229;
    in gadgets, IV:450
  (see also methods, resize.)
Resource Manager, IV:599
  RESOURCE_MANAGER property, IV:300
  (see actions)
resources, about, IV:25, 37, 39, 49, 54, 56, 294-297, 599; V:431-432
  and set_values method, IV:225-227
  application, IV:91
  caching, IV:318
  callbacks, IV:44
  checking validity, IV:216
  classes and instances, IV:94
  comment character in files, IV:299
  constraint, IV:71, 392; V:434-437
  copying; XtGetValues, V:205-206;
    XtSetValues, V:329-330
  database; about, IV:599;
    obtaining, V:159;
    sources, IV:300
  default address; interpreting, IV:297
  default value; converting, IV:314;
    retrieving, IV:315; V:191-192;
    setting, IV:95, 314
  defined; by Core, IV:54;
    characteristics, IV:94-95;
    in widget, IV:191, 193-194
  fallback, IV:304
  file format, V:709
  Form widget, IV:71, 392, 394
  format of definitions, IV:298-299
  freeing compound strings, IV:53
  hardcoding; advantages, IV:43, 103, 105;
    disadvantages, IV:104
  in instance record, IV:188
  inheritance of, IV:49, 191, 193-194
  interactions between, IV:57-59;
    example, IV:58
  loading; from .Xdefaults file, IV:58;
    with xrdb, IV:58

ShellClassPart, V:454-456
ShellPart, V:457-459
types, V:453;
    XtIsShell, V:234
sibling, IV:601
Simple widgets, IV:474
SimpleMenu widget, IV:436-440, 448-451;
    V:563-568
single-line input field, IV:344
sink, in Athena Text widget, IV:325
size, IV:373
    hints, IV:335-336
    preferences, IV:389
    sizeof, IV:199
Sme, IV:436-448; V:569-570
SmeBSB, V:571-573
SmeLine, V:575
software architecture, IV:9
source, compatibility, IV:469
    files for widget, IV:184
    in Athena Text widget, IV:325
    obtaining source code, IV:39
spring-loaded menu, IV:420-427, 601
    vs. pulldown, IV:416
    (see also popups.)
stacking order, IV:374, 410, 601
standard colormaps, Xmu utilities, IV:339
StaticColor, IV:602
StaticGray, IV:602
status, IV:602
stdio.h file, IV:190
stipple, IV:602
storage, allocating; XtMalloc, V:248;
    XtNew, V:260
    freeing (XtFree), V:178
    resizing (XtRealloc), V:289
strings, copying (XtNewString), V:261
    error message (XtStringConversionWarning),
      V:335
    setting, IV:50
    string to bitmap converter, IV:316
    StringDefs.h header file, IV:34, 51, 94, 190,
      316; V:721
    StringToWidget resource converter, IV:393
StripChart widget, V:576-578
structure, determining field's byte offset, V:264
    of Motif applications, IV:34
    (see also XtOffset.)
subclass, IV:25
    about, IV:602
submenus, IV:434

cascading, IV:435
creating, IV:432
popping up, IV:431
(see also XtPopup.)
subparts, IV:199, 204, 325-327
subresources, IV:199, 204, 325-327
    managing, IV:326-327
Super key, IV:248
    (see also modifiers.)
superclass, IV:198, 226
    about, IV:23, 602
    class structure, IV:186
    gadget, IV:447
    inheritance, IV:57
    of Core, IV:443
synchronous option, IV:99
syntax functions, IV:103

T

TCP/IP, IV:345
Template widget, V:579-586
Text widget, IV:154, 199, 344; V:587-604
    creating, V:599
    default bindings, V:597-598
    edit modes, V:587
    Motif, IV:497
    OPEN LOOK text widgets, IV:487
    resources, V:588-591
TextField widget, IV:154
tight bindings, IV:299, 602
tilde, IV:250
tiling, IV:56
    about, IV:602
time, IV:602
timeouts, about, IV:281
    adding, IV:281
    and visibility interest, IV:284
    callback method, V:413
    example, IV:283
    invoking procedure after timeout, V:88
    removing, IV:283-284
    selection timeout value, V:99, 112
    XtAddTimeout, V:78
    XtAppAddTimeOut, V:88
    XtAppGetSelectionTimeout, V:99
    XtAppSetSelectionTimeout, V:112
    XtGetSelectionTimeout, V:194
    XtRemoveTimeOut, V:304
    XtSetSelectionTimeout, V:322

Master Index

XtTimerCallbackProc, V:413
timing, multiple clicks, IV:253
title option (–title), IV:99
Toggle widget, V:605-610
ToggleButton widget, IV:155
toolkits, XtInitialize, V:214-218
XtToolkitInitialize, V:337
top-level, TopLevelShell, V:461-462
topLevelShellWidgetClass, IV:333; V:452-460
widget, IV:37;
  (see also Shell widget.)
window, IV:602
training, IV:579
TransientShell, V:463-464
transientShellWidgetClass, IV:78, 332;
  V:452-460
translations, IV:133-137, 259
  # augment directive, IV:135
  ! modifier symbol, IV:251
  # override directive, IV:135
  # replace directive, IV:135
  about, IV:31, 44, 56, 131, 134, 602
  augmenting, IV:135-136
  compiling; table, V:275-276;
    when widget class initialized, IV:196;
    XtParseTranslationTable, V:275-276
  defining; default in Core class part, IV:199;
    in source, IV:137
  details in, IV:244-247
  differences between directives, IV:241
  double-clicks, IV:252
  event abbreviations, IV:242-243
  event sequences, IV:252-254
  hardcoding, IV:136
  in widget implementation file, IV:194-196
  inheritance, IV:195
  interactions between, IV:254-259
  keyboard events, IV:244-245
  merging, IV:255; V:268;
    widget translations, V:119
  modifiers, IV:247-252, 249;
    and event sequences, IV:253
  Motion events, IV:253
  newlines in, IV:240
  *Notify details, IV:246
  order, IV:255
  overriding, IV:135-136; V:268
  parsing, IV:136
  removing, V:347
  replacing, IV:135, 137
  resource converters, IV:312

syntax, IV:240
tilde modifier symbol, IV:250
Translation Manager (see actions)
translation table, IV:603; V:711;
  example, IV:134
XtAugmentTranslations, V:119
XtUninstallTranslations, V:347
(see also accelerators; actions.)
translations, , modifier symbol, IV:251-252
traversal, post-order, IV:597
pre-order, IV:597
TrueColor, IV:603
type converters, IV:42
  about, IV:107
  explicitly invoking, IV:321-322;
    example, IV:322
  format, IV:323-325
  passing arguments to, IV:319;
    example, IV:319
  registering, IV:316-321
  (see also resources.)
type property, IV:603
typedefs, IV:189

U

UIL, IV:175-179
units of measurement, setting, IV:172
unmanaging widget, IV:388
UnmapNotify event, V:687-688
upward chaining, IV:201
user interface language, (see UIL)
uunet, IV:39
uwm, IV:414

V

varargs interfaces, advantages and disadvantages, IV:109
  compared to ArgList functions, IV:524
VendorShell widget, IV:337; V:465
Viewport widget, IV:382; V:611-613
virtual colormaps, IV:206, 338
visibility interest, IV:199, 284-285
VisibilityNotify event, V:701-702
visual class, IV:603

W

warning handler, calling high-level, V:117-118,
 364-365
  (see also XtAppWarningMsg; XtWarning;
   XtWarningMsg.)
warnings, IV:455
  listing, V:703
  (see also error handling.)
WCL toolkit aid, IV:179
widgets, IV:63
  about, IV:10, 17, 21, 603
  accept_focus method, V:122
  actions example, IV:234, 236
  adding to parent list, IV:18; V:249-251
  as data types, IV:37
  callback list; (see callbacks)
  child widget; creating/managing, IV:63, 375;
   V:150;
   layout of, IV:386-387
  class; determining subclass (XtIsSubclass),
   V:235;
   obtaining (XtClass), V:138;
   verifying (XtCheckSubclass), V:137;
   XtIsComposite, V:226;
   XtIsConstraint, V:227;
   XtIsShell, V:234;
   XtIsSubclass, V:235
  converting (R3 to R4), IV:521
  Core, V:438-442
  creating, IV:34, 91; V:154-156;
   additional top-level, V:90-91, 149;
   custom widget, V:579-586, 580;
   Motif vs. Xt, IV:75;
   working window, V:157-158;
   (see also XtAppCreateShell; XtCreateAppli-
    cationShell; XtCreateMgdWidget;
    XtCreateWidget.)
  declaring class record pointer, IV:204
  default size, IV:230
  defining conventions, IV:184, 299;
   summary, IV:211
  destroying, IV:30, 233-234; V:162-163
  display pointer, V:167
  displaying; non-editable string, V:538-540;
   real-time graphic chart, V:576-578
  dragging attachment point, V:535-537
  Exclusives and Nonexclusives, IV:480
  framework of code, IV:183-211
  geometry (see geometry management)
  hierarchy, IV:85;

  creating, IV:65
  implementation files, IV:184, 189-207
  include files, IV:184
  inheritance among (Motif), IV:23
  installing accelerators (see accelerators)
  instance structure, IV:216
  internals, IV:183-211
  macros for, IV:459
  management, IV:63, 230-233; V:228;
   child, IV:216-221;
   row-column geometry, V:541-545;
   XtIsManaged, V:228;
   (see also XtManageChild; XtManageChil-
    dren.)
  mapping, IV:56;
   changing map_when_managed field, V:320;
   to display, V:252;
   windows, IV:38;
   XtSetMappedWhenManaged, V:320
  merging translations, V:119
  modal widget; XtAddGrab, V:73-74;
   XtRemoveGrab, V:300
  moving (XtMoveWidget), V:257
  moving/resizing, IV:55; V:140-141;
   XtConfigureWidget, V:140-141
  name defined, IV:199
  naming conventions, IV:517
  parent widget (XtParent), V:273
  popping down (XtMenupopdown), V:253
  popping up, IV:80-85; V:254-255
  private header file, IV:184-189
  public functions, IV:115, 118
  public header file, IV:184, 207-209
  realizing, IV:226;
   XtIsRealized, V:231;
   XtRealizeWidget, V:287-288
  record size, IV:199
  removing, IV:18; V:348-349
  resizing, IV:68, 227-230, 374-383;
   by application, IV:381;
   by parent, IV:379;
   per core dimensions, V:307;
   XtMakeResizeRequest, V:247;
   XtResizeWidget, V:306;
   XtResizeWindow, V:307
  retrieving event mask, V:120-121
  returning screen pointer (XtScreen), V:310
  routines for creating, IV:160-162
  scrolling viewing area in another widget,
   V:557-562
  sensitivity (see sensitivity)

sets; about, IV:10, 20;
  compared, IV:474;
  Motif, IV:20, 487-497;
  OPEN LOOK, IV:20, 477-487;
  special defaults, IV:337
source file, IV:184; V:583
subclass, V:235
superclass; inheritance, IV:57;
  XtSuperclass, V:336
techniques for writing, IV:209
text-editing widget, V:587-604
translating; XtNameToWidget, V:259;
  XtTranslateCoords, V:338;
  XtWindowToWidget, V:369
unmapping, V:350
WidgetProc, V:438
Window widget, V:581
windowless (see gadgets)
windows; destroying (XtUnrealizeWidget),
  V:351;
  returning (XtWindow), V:367
XtWidgetToApplicationContext, V:366
(see also individual widgets alphabetically.)
width, IV:377
  checking in initialize method, IV:216
wildcards, in font names, IV:508
  in resource specifications, IV:42, 298
window, creating, V:157-158
  geometry, IV:512
  gravity, IV:603
  hierarchy, IV:85
  unnamed class, IV:444
  WindowObj class, IV:205
  zoomed, IV:604
window attributes, IV:207
  about, IV:205
  background, IV:205
  backing_store, IV:206, 316
  bit_gravity, IV:205
  border, IV:205
  colormap, IV:206, 340
  cursor, IV:206
  event_mask, IV:206
  override_redirect, IV:206
  save_under, IV:206
  setting in realize method, IV:206-207
window manager, IV:67-68, 331-344, 373
  about, IV:12, 35, 603
  and decoration, IV:342
  and icons, IV:340-341
  click-to-type, IV:337

colormaps, IV:338-339
focusing styles, IV:246
hints, IV:12, 332-344
input models, IV:337
interacting with, IV:332-344
keyboard focus, IV:337-338
listener, IV:594
pointer focus, IV:337
real estate driven, IV:337, 598
redirect, IV:598
reparenting, IV:342, 430, 598
save-set, IV:600
screen layout, IV:335-336
WM_DELETE_WINDOW, IV:343
WM_PROTOCOLS, IV:343
WM_SAVE_YOURSELF, IV:343
WMShell widget, V:466-469
WM_TAKE_FOCUS, IV:343
wm_timeout, V:455
work procedures, about, V:79
  creating pop up in, V:420
  registering, IV:286-287; V:89
  removing, IV:286; V:305
  XtAddWorkProc, V:79
  XtAppAddWorkProc, V:89
  XtAppRemoveWorkProc, V:305

X

X, about, IV:3
  extensions to, IV:13
  X Consortium address, IV:580
  X Protocol, IV:6, 345
  X source software, IV:575
  X Toolkit; (see toolkits)
  XView, IV:11
XA_CLIPBOARD atom, IV:354
  (see also selections.)
XA_MULTIPLE property, IV:367
XAPPLRESDIR environment variable,
  IV:300
XA_PRIMARY atom, IV:346, 354
  (see also selections.)
XA_SECONDARY atom, IV:354
  (see also selections.)
XA_TARGETS atom, IV:357
  (see also selections.)
Xatom.h file, IV:354, 356
XawPanedAllowResize, V:554
XawPanedGetMinMax, V:555

Master Index

Books That Help People Get More Out of Computers

If you want more information about our books, or want to know where to buy them, we're happy to send it.

❑ Send me a free catalog of titles.

❑ What bookstores in my area carry your books (U.S. and Canada only)?

❑ Where can I buy your books outside the U.S. and Canada?

❑ Send me information about consulting services for documentation or programming.

Name _____

Address _____

_____

City _____

State, ZIP _____

Country _____

Books That Help People Get More Out of Computers

If you want more information about our books, or want to know where to buy them, we're happy to send it.

❑ Send me a free catalog of titles.

❑ What bookstores in my area carry your books (U.S. and Canada only)?

❑ Where can I buy your books outside the U.S. and Canada?

❑ Send me information about consulting services for documentation or programming.

Name _____

Address _____

_____

City _____

State, ZIP _____

Country _____

NAME _____
COMPANY _____
ADDRESS _____
CITY _____ STATE _____ ZIP _____

NO POSTAGE
NECESSARY IF
MAILED IN THE
UNITED STATES

BUSINESS REPLY MAIL

FIRST CLASS MAIL PERMIT NO. 80 SEBASTOPOL, CA

POSTAGE WILL BE PAID BY ADDRESSEE

O'Reilly & Associates, Inc.

632 Petaluma Avenue
Sebastopol, CA 95472-9902

NAME _____
COMPANY _____
ADDRESS _____
CITY _____ STATE _____ ZIP _____

NO POSTAGE
NECESSARY IF
MAILED IN THE
UNITED STATES

BUSINESS REPLY MAIL

FIRST CLASS MAIL PERMIT NO. 80 SEBASTOPOL, CA

POSTAGE WILL BE PAID BY ADDRESSEE

O'Reilly & Associates, Inc.

632 Petaluma Avenue
Sebastopol, CA 95472-9902